Dictionary of Literary Biography

Dictionary of Literary Biography Documentary Series

Dictionary of Literary Biography Yearbooks

1980 edited by Karen L. Rood, Jean W. Ross, and Richard Ziegfeld (1981)

1981 edited by Karen L. Rood, Jean W. Ross, and Richard Ziegfeld (1982)

1982 edited by Richard Ziegfeld; associate editors: Jean W. Ross and Lynne C. Zeigler (1983)

1983 edited by Mary Bruccoli and Jean W. Ross; associate editor Richard Ziegfeld (1984)

1984 edited by Jean W. Ross (1985)

1985 edited by Jean W. Ross (1986)

1986 edited by J. M. Brook (1987)

1987 edited by J. M. Brook (1988)

1988 edited by J. M. Brook (1989)

1989 edited by J. M. Brook (1990)

1990 edited by James W. Hipp (1991)

1991 edited by James W. Hipp (1992)

1992 edited by James W. Hipp (1993)

1993 edited by James W. Hipp, contributing editor George Garrett (1994)

1994 edited by James W. Hipp, contributing editor George Garrett (1995)

1995 edited by James W. Hipp, contributing editor George Garrett (1996)

1996 edited by Samuel W. Bruce and L. Kay Webster, contributing editor George Garrett (1997)

1997 edited by Matthew J. Bruccoli and George Garrett, with the assistance of L. Kay Webster (1998)

1998 edited by Matthew J. Bruccoli, contributing editor George Garrett, with the assistance of D. W. Thomas (1999)

1999 edited by Matthew J. Bruccoli, contributing editor George Garrett, with the assistance of D. W. Thomas (2000)

2000 edited by Matthew J. Bruccoli, contributing editor George Garrett, with the assistance of George Parker Anderson (2001)

2001 edited by Matthew J. Bruccoli, contributing editor George Garrett, with the assistance of George Parker Anderson (2002)

Concise Series

Concise Dictionary of American Literary Biography, 7 volumes (1988–1999): *The New Consciousness, 1941–1968; Colonization to the American Renaissance, 1640–1865; Realism, Naturalism, and Local Color, 1865–1917; The Twenties, 1917–1929; The Age of Maturity, 1929–1941; Broadening Views, 1968–1988; Supplement: Modern Writers, 1900–1998.*

Concise Dictionary of British Literary Biography, 8 volumes (1991–1992): *Writers of the Middle Ages and Renaissance Before 1660; Writers of the Restoration and Eighteenth Century, 1660–1789; Writers of the Romantic Period, 1789–1832; Victorian Writers, 1832–1890; Late-Victorian and Edwardian Writers, 1890–1914; Modern Writers, 1914–1945; Writers After World War II, 1945–1960; Contemporary Writers, 1960 to Present.*

Concise Dictionary of World Literary Biography, 10 volumes projected (1999–): *Ancient Greek and Roman Writers; German Writers; African, Caribbean, and Latin American Writers; South Slavic and Eastern European Writers.*

Dictionary of Literary Biography® • Volume Two Hundred Seventy

American Philosophers
Before 1950

American Philosophers
Before 1950

Edited by
Philip B. Dematteis
Saint Leo University

and

Leemon B. McHenry
California State University, Northridge

A Bruccoli Clark Layman Book

THOMSON

GALE™

Detroit • New York • San Diego • San Francisco • Cleveland • New Haven, Conn. • Waterville, Maine • London • Munich

THOMSON
GALE

Dictionary of Literary Biography
Volume 270: American Philosophers
Before 1950
Philip B. Dematteis and Leemon B. McHenry

Advisory Board
John Baker
William Cagle
Patrick O'Connor
George Garrett
Trudier Harris
Alvin Kernan
Kenny J. Williams

Editorial Directors
Matthew J. Bruccoli and Richard Layman

Senior Editor
Karen L. Rood

LIBRARY OF CONGRESS CATALOGING-IN-PUBLICATION DATA

American philosophers before 1950 / edited by Philip B. Dematteis and Leemon McHenry.
      p. cm. — (Dictionary of literary biography ; v. 270)
"A Bruccoli Clark Layman book."
Includes bibliographical references and index.
      ISBN 0-7876-6014-0
      1. Philosophy, American—Bio-bibliography—Dictionaries.
      I. Dematteis, Philip Breed. II. McHenry, Leemon B., 1950– .
      III. Series.
B851.A43 2002
191—dc21   2002015632

To Beverley Jones Dunlap Spong

Contents

Plan of the Series

. . . Almost the most prodigious asset of a country, and perhaps its most precious possession, is its native literary product—when that product is fine and noble and enduring.

Mark Twain*

The advisory board, the editors, and the publisher of the *Dictionary of Literary Biography* are joined in endorsing Mark Twain's declaration. The literature of a nation provides an inexhaustible resource of permanent worth. Our purpose is to make literature and its creators better understood and more accessible to students and the reading public, while satisfying the needs of teachers and researchers.

To meet these requirements, *literary biography* has been construed in terms of the author's achievement. The most important thing about a writer is his writing. Accordingly, the entries in *DLB* are career biographies, tracing the development of the author's canon and the evolution of his reputation.

The purpose of *DLB* is not only to provide reliable information in a usable format but also to place the figures in the larger perspective of literary history and to offer appraisals of their accomplishments by qualified scholars.

The publication plan for *DLB* resulted from two years of preparation. The project was proposed to Bruccoli Clark by Frederick G. Ruffner, president of the Gale Research Company, in November 1975. After specimen entries were prepared and typeset, an advisory board was formed to refine the entry format and develop the series rationale. In meetings held during 1976, the publisher, series editors, and advisory board approved the scheme for a comprehensive biographical dictionary of persons who contributed to literature. Editorial work on the first volume began in January 1977, and it was published in 1978. In order to make *DLB* more than a dictionary and to compile volumes that individually have claim to status as literary history, it was decided to organize volumes by topic, period, or

*From an unpublished section of Mark Twain's autobiography, copyright by the Mark Twain Company

genre. Each of these freestanding volumes provides a biographical-bibliographical guide and overview for a particular area of literature. We are convinced that this organization—as opposed to a single alphabet method—constitutes a valuable innovation in the presentation of reference material. The volume plan necessarily requires many decisions for the placement and treatment of authors. Certain figures will be included in separate volumes, but with different entries emphasizing the aspect of his career appropriate to each volume. Ernest Hemingway, for example, is represented in *American Writers in Paris, 1920–1939* by an entry focusing on his expatriate apprenticeship; he is also in *American Novelists, 1910–1945* with an entry surveying his entire career, as well as in *American Short-Story Writers, 1910–1945, Second Series* with an entry concentrating on his short fiction. Each volume includes a cumulative index of the subject authors and articles.

Since 1981 the series has been further augmented by the *DLB Yearbooks*, which update published entries, add new entries to keep the *DLB* current with contemporary activity, and provide articles on literary history. There have also been nineteen *DLB Documentary Series* volumes, which provide illustrations, facsimiles, and biographical and critical source materials for figures, works, or groups judged to have particular interest for students. In 1999 the *Documentary Series* was incorporated into the *DLB* volume numbering system beginning with *DLB 210: Ernest Hemingway*.

We define literature as the *intellectual commerce of a nation:* not merely as belles lettres but as that ample and complex process by which ideas are generated, shaped, and transmitted. *DLB* entries are not limited to "creative writers" but extend to other figures who in their time and in their way influenced the mind of a people. Thus the series encompasses historians, journalists, publishers, book collectors, and screenwriters. By this means readers of *DLB* may be aided to perceive literature not as cult scripture in the keeping of intellectual high priests but firmly positioned at the center of a nation's life.

DLB includes the major writers appropriate to each volume and those standing in the ranks behind them. Scholarly and critical counsel has been sought in deciding which minor figures to include and how full their entries should be. Wherever possible, useful references are made to figures who do not warrant separate entries.

Each *DLB* volume has an expert volume editor responsible for planning the volume, selecting the figures for inclusion, and assigning the entries. Volume editors are also responsible for preparing, where appropriate, appendices surveying the major periodicals and literary and intellectual movements for their volumes, as well as lists of further readings. Work on the series as a whole is coordinated at the Bruccoli Clark Layman editorial center in Columbia, South Carolina, where the editorial staff is responsible for accuracy and utility of the published volumes.

One feature that distinguishes *DLB* is the illustration policy–its concern with the iconography of literature. Just as an author is influenced by his surroundings, so is the reader's understanding of the author enhanced by a knowledge of his environment. Therefore *DLB* volumes include not only drawings, paintings, and photographs of authors, often depicting them at various stages in their careers, but also illustrations of their families and places where they lived. Title pages are regularly reproduced in facsimile along with dust jackets for modern authors. The dust jackets are a special feature of *DLB* because they often document better than anything else the way in which an author's work was perceived in its own time. Specimens of the writers' manuscripts and letters are included when feasible.

Samuel Johnson rightly decreed that "The chief glory of every people arises from its authors." The purpose of the *Dictionary of Literary Biography* is to compile literary history in the surest way available to us–by accurate and comprehensive treatment of the lives and work of those who contributed to it.

The *DLB* Advisory Board

Introduction

Within the 2,500 years of philosophy in Western civilization one can discern distinct periods of unity, such as the classical age of Greek philosophy that began in the fifth century B.C. with Democritus and Socrates and ended in the fourth century B.C. with Aristotle; the epoch of Roman philosophy that extended from the first century B.C. to the second century A.D. and included Cicero, Lucretius, Epictetus, Marcus Aurelius, and Sextus Empiricus; the medieval Christian period from St. Augustine in the late fourth and early fifth centuries to St. Thomas Aquinas in the thirteenth century; the British empiricists from Francis Bacon in the late sixteenth and early seventeenth centuries to David Hume in the eighteenth century; and the Continental rationalists from René Descartes in the early seventeenth century to Gottfried Wilhelm Leibniz in the late seventeenth and early eighteenth centuries. American philosophy from the colonial period to the twenty-first century is a relatively recent addition to this history, but since its classical period at the end of the nineteenth and beginning of the twentieth centuries it has continued to exert a major influence on the philosophical world.

Several important figures in American philosophy who are represented in this volume began or ended their philosophical careers elsewhere. George Santayana was born in Spain, never relinquished his Spanish citizenship, and did not set foot in the United States between the time he left it in 1912 and his death in Rome in 1952; nevertheless, the philosophical milieu at Harvard University, where he studied and then taught for twenty-one years, undeniably shaped his thought. As he himself said near the end of his life, "my intellectual relations and labours still unite me closely to America; and it is as an American writer that I must be counted if I am counted at all." Rudolf Carnap was a German who became a prominent member of the Vienna Circle and a leading exponent of logical positivism in the 1930s. He ended his career at the University of California, Los Angeles, with other logical positivists who sought refuge from Nazism in Europe. The English mathematician and philosopher Alfred North Whitehead could justifiably have been included among the classical American philosophers in this volume: the "process philosophy" he developed after he moved to Harvard in the 1920s produced many disciples and a school of thought that flourished in the United States; Whitehead is,

however, placed with his earlier philosophical influences in *DLB 262: British Philosophers, 1800–2000*.

Most of the philosophers represented in this volume were influenced by, and reacted against, the mainstream of thought in Great Britain and continental Europe. This characterization is particularly true of the eighteenth- and nineteenth-century American philosophers—Puritans such as Jonathan Edwards and the major figures of the classical period such as Santayana, Charles Sanders Peirce, William James, Josiah Royce, and John Dewey—but it also holds for the philosophers who represent the two dominant approaches to philosophy at the end of the twentieth and beginning of the twentieth-first centuries: analytic philosophy, represented by C. I. Lewis, W. V. Quine, Saul Kripke, and Donald Davidson; and postmodern philosophy, represented by Richard Rorty. (Since this volume is devoted to philosophers who rose to prominence before 1950, only Lewis is included here; Quine, Kripke, Davidson, and Rorty will be treated in a later *DLB* volume, *American Philosophers, 1950–2000*.)

By comparison with some other periods in the history of philosophy, American philosophy can be seen as disparate and fragmented. In the first half of the twentieth century, for example, there were absolute idealists at Harvard and in St. Louis, where the Hegelian William Torrey Harris was superintendent of schools; Thomists at Catholic universities such as Georgetown, Loyola, and Fordham; personalists such as Borden Parker Bowne and Edgar Sheffield Brightman at Boston University; followers of the Scottish realists at Harvard and Princeton; Kantians at Chicago; and pragmatists at Harvard, Michigan, and Chicago. From one point of view, pluralism is the dominant theme. As the British philosopher and scholar of American philosophy T. L. S. Sprigge says in his essay "The Distinctiveness of American Philosophy" in Peter Caws's *Two Centuries of Philosophy in America* (1980), the pluralism expressed in James's philosophy is a guiding ideal in American philosophy generally. There are, however, distinctive ideas that originated with American thinkers and common threads among them. A vast frontier and a new nation created the opportunity to think afresh.

As the stern religious orthodoxy of Edwards and his Puritan followers lost its stranglehold, new paths formed. The New England Transcendentalists Ralph Waldo Emerson and Henry David Thoreau propounded an individualist philosophy with an emphasis on the relationship of human beings to the rest of nature. Emerson is best known for his espousal of self-reliance, which grew out of his own attempt to forge an identity for himself. As the United States struggled to identify itself as a nation separate from Britain after the colonial period, Emerson became the preeminent American philosopher of his time; he shaped the developing American culture on the lecture circuit from Boston to St. Louis that was known as "the lyceum." The poet Oliver Wendell Holmes Sr. declared "The American Scholar," Emerson's best-known lecture, "our intellectual Declaration of Independence."

According to the Transcendentalist creed, humanity is a god in ruins needing only to recapture its relationship to nature to realize its divinity. Whereas Emerson preached this vision, Thoreau tried to put it to practice by living for two years in a cabin on land owned by Emerson at Walden Pond, outside the town of Concord, Massachusetts. Explaining the purpose of his experiment at Walden, Thoreau wrote: "I went to the woods because I wished to live deliberately, to front only the essential facts of life, and see if I could not learn what it had to teach, and not, when I came to die, discover that I had not lived." Whether or not Emerson and Thoreau were successful in their attempts to live according to their ideals, they expressed in ministerial tones the virtues of the simple life and spiritual freedom that struck a chord in the popular American mind and continues in various manifestations to this day.

The classical period of American philosophy, also known as "the golden age," began after the Civil War and ended at the beginning of World War II—roughly, 1865 to 1940. In this period American philosophy achieved a fullness of expression and originality that parallels other great periods of philosophy in Britain and Europe. This flowering can be traced directly to the growth of the American university system and the conscious aim on the part of philosophy departments to develop the profession of philosophy; the story is well told in Bruce Kuklick's *The Rise of American Philosophy* (1977). In the first wave Peirce, James, Royce, and Dewey were all associated with the newly formed graduate school in philosophy at Johns Hopkins University: Peirce and James as lecturers, Royce and Dewey pursuing their Ph.D.s. But the wellspring shifted quickly to Harvard under the leadership of President Charles William Eliot, who encouraged avant-garde speculation free from the hold of Christian orthodoxy. To remedy the deficiency in the philosophy department that he recognized in 1860, Eliot hired James and Royce. Santayana, who studied under James and Royce, joined the department as a faculty member on the completion of his Ph.D. Peirce lectured there on occasion, and if not for Eliot's personal dislike of him, he would have been a Harvard philosopher.

The second wave included Lewis, William Ernest Hocking, and Whitehead, who filled the gaps left when James and Royce died and Santayana resigned. Many of the other American philosophers represented in the *DLB* volumes on American philosophers were students or professors in Harvard's great department, including Quine, Kripke, Davidson, George Herbert Mead, Susanne K. Langer, Mary Whiton Calkins, Charles Hartshorne, Arthur O. Lovejoy, Stephen C. Pepper, Paul Weiss, Hilary Putnam, Robert Nozick, John Rawls, and David Lewis. (Weiss, Putnam, Nozick, Rawls, and Lewis will be treated in *American Philosophers, 1950–2000*.) It became the flagship for philosophy in the United States.

The intellectual culture of Boston also contributed to the flourishing of American philosophy in the late nineteenth century. The Metaphysical Club was founded in 1871 by James, Peirce, Chauncey Wright, and the jurist Oliver Wendell Holmes Jr. to discuss "the very tallest and broadest questions." This venue provided the setting for the origin of pragmatism—perhaps the most distinctive doctrine of American philosophy but sometimes misrepresented by European critics as practical Yankee know-how or the glorification of American Big Business. Peirce is recognized as the founder of pragmatism, but James reformulated Peirce's original idea and became a sort of ambassador of this new American philosophy abroad. Pragmatism focuses on ideas that make a practical difference. James formulated the notion as a theory of truth: an idea is true if it works or has practical value. Peirce's version was more limited in scope: he intended it to be a method of resolving disagreements, following the model of scientific investigation. James, by contrast, understood pragmatism to apply to all of experience, including religious beliefs. In an attempt to disown the view that James attributed to him, Peirce changed the name of his doctrine to "pragmaticism," which, he said, was "ugly enough to be safe from kidnappers."

Peirce said that the Metaphysical Club was named "half-ironically, half-defiantly," since "agnosticism was then riding its high horse, and was frowning superbly upon all metaphysics." He was impressed by the contrast between the intellectual progress made by empirical science and the lack of agreement even on fundamental characteristics by metaphysicians. Metaphysics, he argued, is in a deplorable condition because philosophers adopt some a priori stance and then, in the fashion of what he called "the method of tenacity," argue with one another to no fruitful end. He conceived pragmatism as a way of rescuing metaphysics by bringing it into a condition like that of the natural sciences. But as developed by James and Dewey, pragmatism became a method aimed at practical results and opposed to metaphysical claims to certitude and finality. As other antimetaphysical currents of thought developed in the twentieth century, including logical positivism, phenomenology, deconstruction, instrumentalism, conventionalism, and postmodernism, the pragmatic point of view gained a large following. In addition to Peirce, James, and Dewey, pragmatism was advanced in one form or another by Mead, C. I. Lewis, Quine, Putnam, and Rorty. James once remarked that the evolution of an idea goes through three stages: first, it is attacked as absurd; next, it gains slow acceptance within the current modes of thought; and finally, its original attackers claim that the idea is so obviously true that they discovered it themselves. So it was, James said, with the pragmatic theory.

Pragmatism can be traced to a distinction Peirce found in the work of the eighteenth-century German philosopher Immanuel Kant between the "pragmatic," which focuses on rules of art and technique that are based on experience, and the "practical," which applies to moral laws that Kant regards as a priori. But the original pragmatists were rejecting Cartesian metaphysics, on the one hand, and absorbing the central ideas of Charles Darwin's *On the Origin of Species by Means of Natural Selection* (1859), on the other hand. Descartes's metaphysics had exercised a strong hold since the seventeenth century by postulating two distinct types of substance, a cogitating mind and an inert physical matter, but this theory led to the notorious "mind/body problem" (the difficulty of explaining how two utterly different substances could interact with one another) and a morass of epistemological problems stemming from the representational view of perception. In the nineteenth century philosophy became a battleground between the two Cartesian substances. The materialists attempted to absorb the mental into the physical, while the idealists attempted the reverse process. Early pragmatists such as Peirce, James, and Dewey rejected Cartesian foundationalism (the attempt to place knowledge on a foundation of indubitable beliefs) as grandiose and beyond the limits that human knowledge could attain. In an effort to overcome the materialist and idealist strategies, they found in Darwin's theory a new direction. Instead of two substances, mind and matter, the pragmatists followed a new path cut by evolutionary theory. Max H. Fisch in *Classic American Philosophers* (1951) identifies this strategy as an attempt to "naturalize mind" and "mentalize nature" via the fundamental role experience played in their system of nature. Moreover, in reformulating the role of knowledge in the evolutionary picture, true ideas become useful instruments in the human adaptive process. That is, their pragmatic value is survival. Much of the groundbreaking work for this philosophy took place in James's *The Principles of Psychology* (1891). Although the teleological conception of mind James advanced was in many respects un-Dar-

winian, Darwin's theory nonetheless provided the "fertile opening" into which he struck. James attempted to render biology and psychology continuous by focusing on the purposeful evolution of the organism and the function of mentality in nature. Consciousness grows more complex and intense the higher one rises in the animal kingdom. And for James, consciousness is not merely an epiphenomenon of the nervous system lacking causal efficacy but counts for something in the evolutionary process: it is primarily a selective agency that is closely aligned with the interests of the organism.

One of the greatest innovations of *The Principles of Psychology* was the concept of the "specious present" developed in the chapter "The Stream of Thought." It played an all-important role in James's theory of consciousness as a continuous stream made up of individual durations. In his study of the mind from within, James finds that one's experience of the present is never a moving knife-edge or instantaneous slice but, rather, a unit of experience that includes the immediate past, the present, and anticipation of the future. James argues that the discrete pulses of experience are compatible with the continuity of consciousness, as drops of water are to the flow of a stream. The watery metaphor stuck when James sought a broader base for philosophizing in his radical empiricism and metaphysical pluralism. Reflections on the content of the specious present and the stream of consciousness provided clues for understanding all forms of existence as streams of experience. Royce, Santayana, Whitehead, and Hartshorne developed metaphysical systems with some affinity to James's method of generalizing from psychological phenomena. In Royce's system, for example, the Absolute is conceived as one grand specious present in which the whole of cosmic history is eternally present.

As opposed to the pluralism advocated by James, monistic philosophies developed by Royce, Hocking, Calkins, Brand Blanshard, and Errol E. Harris (Blanshard and Harris will be treated in *American Philosophers, 1950–2000*) followed the nineteenth-century German idealist philosopher Georg Wilhelm Friedrich Hegel in focusing on the unity of the entire universe conceived as Absolute Mind or Consciousness. Royce was James's most astute sparring partner. He was by far the most influential and articulate proponent of absolute idealism in the United States. His system emerged in opposition to the realists and pragmatists by arguing that statements can be true or false only if an Absolute Knower exists to provide the ultimate standard by which such statements can be declared meaningful. Reality, for absolute idealists such as Royce, is a divine, timeless unity and the source of all being and perfection.

One other thread of speculative philosophy in the United States is process philosophy. Like absolute idealism, it focuses on system building in the grand tradition, but it gives primacy to the idea of process as the basis of reality. Whitehead's *Process and Reality* (1929) is the classic expression of this line of thought. Whitehead argues that the dominant "substance philosophies" of Western thought are inadequate to express the dynamic nature of reality depicted by the advancing sciences. His simultaneous attack on Aristotelianism and Cartesianism led to a metaphysics of process in which events are the fundamentally real entities. Whitehead advanced his theory by showing its affinity with James's view: events are "drops of experience." James emphasized the selective character of consciousness; Whitehead generalized this notion to apply to all of nature as a creative process of becoming. The selectivity of consciousness is merely an instance of what occurs in more basic forms in nature. Among the many who studied with Whitehead at Harvard were Hartshorne, Langer, and Weiss; they became the major interpreters of his thought and developed their own versions of process metaphysics. But as mainstream philosophy became more and more antimetaphysical and antitheistic, process philosophy was largely taken up by theologians, who saw in the ideas of Whitehead and Hartshorne a new avenue for developing a nontraditional theism. Philosophically minded physicists have also turned to Whitehead's views as an ontological basis from which to work out unified theories in physics and solutions to the puzzling developments of quantum mechanics.

In the early twentieth century philosophy took a "linguistic turn" with the rise of logical positivism and various forms of linguistic and conceptual analysis. Coolheaded analysis was in, and grand speculation was out. Analytic philosophy began with the realist reaction against what was seen as the grandiose systems of the absolute idealists. Philosophers who count themselves as analytic typically trace their influences to the pioneering work of the British philosophers Bertrand Russell, G. E. Moore, Gilbert Ryle, J. L. Austin, P. F. Strawson, and the Austrian-born Ludwig Wittgenstein, all of whom are treated in *DLB 262: British Philosophers, 1800–2000*. Logical positivists such as Carnap, Otto Neurath, Moritz Schlick, Herbert Feigl, and the Englishman A. J. Ayer (who is included in *DLB 262*) also contributed currents of thought that became essential to mainstream philosophy and created a renewed suspicion of any attempt to revive metaphysics. Carnap is best known for his rigorous use of the logic of Russell and Whitehead's *Principia Mathematica* (1910–1913) to formalize the terms of a scientific theory and separate those that report observations from those that are metaphysical in character. Legitimate theoretical terms such as *force, mass,* and *energy* admit of explicit observational definition, whereas terms that have no such definition will be rejected as metaphysical.

The linguistic and conceptual analysis that began in England and the United States in the 1920s and 1930s was interrupted by the outbreak of World War II. What was to become the mainstream of Anglo-American philosophy flourished in the second half of the century. It and other movements will be the subject of *American Philosophers, 1950–2000*.

–Leemon B. McHenry

Acknowledgments

This book was produced by Bruccoli Clark Layman, Inc. Karen L. Rood is senior editor. Philip B. Dematteis was the in-house editor.

Production manager is Philip B. Dematteis.

Administrative support was provided by Ann M. Cheschi and Carol A. Cheschi.

Accountant is Ann-Marie Holland.

Copyediting supervisor is Sally R. Evans. The copyediting staff includes Phyllis A. Avant, Caryl Brown, Melissa D. Hinton, Philip I. Jones, Rebecca Mayo, Nancy E. Smith, and Elizabeth Jo Ann Sumner. Freelance copyeditors are Brenda Cabra and Alice Poyner.

Editorial associates are Amelia B. Lacey, Michael S. Martin, Catherine M. Polit, and William Mathes Straney.

In-house prevetting by Nicole A. La Rocque.

Permissions editor and database manager is Amber L. Coker.

Layout and graphics supervisor is Janet E. Hill. The graphics staff includes Zoe R. Cook and Sydney E. Hammock.

Office manager is Kathy Lawler Merlette.

Photography supervisor is Paul Talbot. Photography editor is Scott Nemzek.

Digital photographic copy work was performed by Joseph M. Bruccoli.

Systems manager is Marie L. Parker.

Typesetting supervisor is Kathleen M. Flanagan. The typesetting staff includes Patricia Marie Flanagan, Mark J. McEwan, and Pamela D. Norton. Freelance typesetters are Wanda Adams and Rebecca Mayo.

Walter W. Ross did library research. He was assisted by Jo Cottingham and the following other librarians at the Thomas Cooper Library of the University of South Carolina: circulation department head Tucker Taylor; reference department head Virginia W. Weathers; reference department staff Brette Barron, Marilee Birchfield, Paul Cammarata, Gary Geer, Michael Macan, Tom Marcil, Rose Marshall, and Sharon Verba; interlibrary loan department head John Brunswick; and interlibrary loan staff Robert Arndt, Hayden Battle, Alex Byrne, Bill Fetty, Marna Hostetler, and Nelson Rivera.

Dictionary of Literary Biography® • Volume Two Hundred Seventy

American Philosophers
Before 1950

Borden Parker Bowne

(14 January 1847 – 1 April 1919)

John Howie
Southern Illinois University at Carbondale

BOOKS: *The Philosophy of Herbert Spencer: Being an Examination of the First Principles of His System* (New York: Nelson & Phillips / Cincinnati: Hitchcock & Walden, 1874);

Studies in Theism (New York: Phillips & Hunt / Cincinnati: Hitchcock & Walden, 1879; London: Sampson Low, Marston, Searle & Rivington, 1882);

Metaphysics: A Study in First Principles (New York: Harper, 1882; revised, 1898);

Introduction to Psychological Theory (New York: Harper, 1886);

Philosophy of Theism (New York: Harper, 1887); revised and enlarged as *Theism: Comprising the Deems Lectures for 1902* (New York & Cincinnati: American Book Co., 1902);

The Principles of Ethics (New York, Cincinnati & Chicago: American Book Co., 1892);

Theory of Thought and Knowledge (New York: Harper, 1897);

The Christian Revelation (Cincinnati: Curts & Jennings / New York: Eaton & Mains, 1898);

The Christian Life: A Study (Cincinnati: Curts & Jennings / New York: Eaton & Mains, 1899);

The Atonement (Cincinnati: Curts & Jennings / New York: Eaton & Mains, 1900);

The Immanence of God (Boston & New York: Houghton, Mifflin / Cambridge, Mass.: Riverside Press, 1904; London: Constable, 1905);

Personalism (Boston & New York: Houghton Mifflin, 1908; London: Constable, 1908);

Studies in Christianity (Boston & New York: Houghton Mifflin, 1909; London: Constable, 1909);

A Man's View of Woman Suffrage (Boston, 1910);

The Essence of Religion (Boston & New York: Houghton Mifflin, 1910; London: Constable, 1911);

Kant and Spencer: A Critical Exposition (Boston & New York: Houghton Mifflin, 1912; London, 1912);

Representative Essays of Borden Parker Bowne, edited by Warren E. Steinkraus (Utica, N.Y.: Meridian, 1981).

Edition: *Philosophy of Theism,* introduction by Sydney E. Ahlstrom (Hicksville, N.Y.: Regina Press, 1975).

OTHER: "The Philosophical Outlook," in *Congress of Arts and Science,* volume 1, edited by Howard Rogers (Boston: Houghton, Mifflin, 1905), pp. 171–172.

SELECTED PERIODICAL PUBLICATIONS–
UNCOLLECTED: "Philosophy in Germany," *Independent,* 26 (22 January 1874): 4–5;

"'The Old Faith and the New' by D. F. Strauss, a Review," *Methodist Review,* 56 (April 1874): 268–296;

"Ulrici's Logic," *New Englander,* 33 (July 1874): 458–492;

"The Materialistic Gust," *Independent,* 26 (30 July 1874): 2–3;

"Prof. Ulrici's *Gott und die Natur,*" *New Englander,* 33 (October 1874): 623–654;

"Immortality or Pessimism," anonymous, *Independent,* 27 (7 January 1875): 10–11;

"Draper's Religion and Science," anonymous, *Independent,* 27 (4 February 1875): 10–11;

"Of Materialism," anonymous, *Independent,* 27 (6 May 1875): 14–15;

"The Religion of Childhood," *Independent,* 27 (10 June 1875): 5;

"Professor Tyndall on Materialism," anonymous, *Independent,* 27 (23 December 1875): 14–15;

"*The Cosmic Philosophy,* by John Fiske, a Review," *Methodist Review,* 58 (October 1876): 655–678;

"The Anti-Design Argument Stated," *Independent,* 29 (22 March 1877): 1–2;

"The Assumption of the Anti-Design Argument," *Independent,* 29 (29 March 1877): 1–2;

"The Design Argument," *Independent,* 29 (5 July 1877): 2–3;

"The Foundations," *Chautauqua Assembly Daily Herald,* 2 (23 August 1877): 1;

"Postulates of Scientific Knowledge," *Chautauqua Assembly Daily Herald,* 2 (24 August 1877): 2;

"The Conservation of Energy," *Zion's Herald,* 54 (11 October 1877): 321;

"The New Logic," *Zion's Herald,* 54 (5 November 1877): 361;

"The 'Prayer Test' Improved," *Zion's Herald,* 54 (20 December 1877): 401; (27 December 1877): 409;

"The New Gospel," *Zion's Herald,* 55 (31 January 1878): 33;

"Shall We Kill Our Advanced Scientists?" *Zion's Herald,* 55 (21 February 1878): 57;

"Relation of Ethics to Theism; or Is There Morality without God?" *Chautauqua Assembly Herald,* 3 (20 August 1878): 3, 7;

"Reasons for Believing That Man Has a Soul," *Chautauqua Assembly Herald,* 3 (October 1878): 4;

"Scientific Conversazione," *Chautauqua Assembly Herald,* 3 (March 1879): 1, 4–5;

"The Divine Foreknowledge," *Zion's Herald,* 56 (6 March 1879): 73;

"Some Objections to Theism," *Methodist Review,* 31 (April 1879): 224–226;

"The 'As Ifs' of Atheism," *Chautauqua Assembly Herald,* 4 (September 1879): 4;

"The Beliefs of Unbelievers," *Chautauqua Assembly Herald,* 4 (January 1880): 1–3;

"A Difficulty in the Materialistic Theory of Life," *Independent,* 32 (20 May 1880): 2–3;

"A New Aspect of Natural Selection," *Independent,* 32 (22 July 1880): 2–3;

"Ethics of Evolution," *Methodist Review,* 62 (July 1880): 430–455;

"First Lecture Lesson in Philosophy," *Chautauqua Assembly Herald,* 5 (6 August 1880): 2;

"Second Lecture Lesson in Philosophy," *Chautauqua Assembly Herald,* 5 (7 August 1880): 4;

"Third Lecture Lesson in Philosophy," *Chautauqua Assembly Herald,* 5 (9 August 1880): 2;

"Fourth Lecture Lesson in Philosophy," *Chautauqua Assembly Herald,* 5 (16 August 1880): 2–3;

"The Doctrine of Perception," *Chautauqua Assembly Herald,* 7 (4 August 1882): 4; (7 August 1882): 2;

"The Doctrine of Error," *Chautauqua Assembly Herald,* 7 (8 August 1882): 4;

"Postulates of Scientific Knowledge," *Chautauqua Assembly Herald,* 7 (9 August 1882): 2;

"Knowledge and Sentiment," *Chautauqua Assembly Herald,* 7 (10 August 1882): 6;

"The Unity of the World-Ground," *Chautauqua Assembly Herald,* 7 (11 August 1882): 3, 6;

"The World-Ground as Intelligent," *Chautauqua Assembly Herald,* 7 (12 August 1882): 4–5;

"The Argument from Design," *Chautauqua Assembly Herald,* 7 (15 August 1882): 5;

"Closing Lecture," *Chautauqua Assembly Herald,* 7 (16 August 1882): 3, 6; (18 August 1882): 6;

"Evolution in Psychology," *Independent,* 35 (27 December 1883): 1641;

"Science Must Go," *Independent,* 36 (24 January 1884): 98;

"Manicheism in Advanced Thought," *Zion's Herald,* 61 (23 April 1884): 129;

"What Is Truth?" *Independent,* 36 (18 September 1884): 1185;

"Concerning the 'Christian Consciousness,'" *Independent,* 37 (8 January 1885): 35–36;

"'Paradise Found,'" *Zion's Herald,* 62 (1 April 1885): 97;

"A Word about the New Education," *Independent,* 37 (9 April 1885): 449;

"New Departures in Education," *Christian Advocate, New York,* 50 (28 May 1885): 343;

"The College Must Go," *Zion's Herald,* 62 (3 June 1885): 169;

"Nerves as Scientists," *Independent,* 37 (13 August 1885): 1029–1030;

"Review: Lotze's *Microcosmus* (Trans. Hamilton and Jones)," *Andover Review,* 4 (October 1885): 391–392;

"Concerning Liberality," *Zion's Herald,* 63 (27 January 1886): 25;

"An American Philosophy," *Independent,* 38 (4 February 1886): 134;

"Religion in Education," *Zion's Herald,* 63 (31 March 1886): 97;

"Conn on Evolution," *Zion's Herald,* 63 (2 June 1886): 169;

"Religion in the Schools," *Zion's Herald,* 63 (14 July 1886): 217;

"The Mind Cure," *Independent,* 38 (15 July 1886): 875–876;

"About Tips," *Independent,* 38 (2 September 1886): 1105;

"Second Probation," *Zion's Herald,* 63 (10 November 1886): 353;

"Some Shortcomings of the Labor Debate," *Independent,* 38 (16 December 1886): 1619–1620;

"Realistic Philosophy," *Zion's Herald,* 64 (20 April 1887): 121;

"Logic and Life," *Christian Thought,* 4 (May–June 1887): 401–419; republished in *British and Foreign Evangelical Review,* 36 (October 1887): 723–740;

"What Is Rationalism?" *Independent,* 40 (26 January 1888): 99–100;

"If It Were So, What of It?" *Independent,* 40 (24 May 1888): 641–642;

"The Natural History of Atheism," *Andover Review,* 10 (July–December 1888): 169–182;

"Physiological Psychology," *Independent,* 40 (23 August 1888): 1062;

"On Evolving Something from Nothing," *Independent,* 40 (18 October 1888): 1332;

"Theology and Reason," *Zion's Herald,* 66 (19 December 1888): 401;

"A = A," *Independent,* 41 (20 June 1889): 788;

"Notes on Philosophy–I: The Question," *Independent,* 42 (15 May 1890): 651;

"Notes on Philosophy–II: Idealism–What Is It?" *Independent,* 42 (22 May 1890): 687;

"Notes on Philosophy–III: Problem of Knowledge," *Independent,* 42 (5 June 1890): 772;

"Notes on Philosophy–IV: Problem of Knowledge," *Independent,* 42 (12 June 1890): 806–807;

"Notes on Philosophy–V: Space and Time as Ideal," *Independent,* 42 (26 June 1890): 871–872;

"Notes on Philosophy–VI: Skepticism," *Independent,* 42 (10 July 1890): 952–953;

"Notes on Philosophy–VII: Pantheism," *Independent,* 42 (24 July 1890): 1018–1019;

"Notes on Philosophy–VIII: Natural and Supernatural," *Independent,* 42 (31 July 1890): 1050–1051;

"Notes on Philosophy–IX: The Fallacy of the Universal," *Independent,* 42 (21 August 1890): 1155;

"The Press Exclusion Law," *Christian Advocate, New York,* 57 (28 January 1892): 50;

"Science, Ignorance and Religion," *Independent,* 45 (2 February 1893): 137–138;

"Evolution *and* Evolution," *Methodist Review,* 75 (September–October 1893): 681–696;

"Some Popular Mistakes Respecting Evolution," *Methodist Review,* 75 (November–December 1893): 849–866;

"The Value of Logic–I: The Logical Habit," *Christian Advocate, New York,* 59 (13 December 1894): 811;

"The Value of Logic–II: Facts and Theories," *Christian Advocate, New York,* 59 (20 December 1894): 827;

"The Value of Logic–III: The Deceit of Words," *Christian Advocate, New York,* 60 (13 January 1895): 3–4;

"Balfour's *The Foundations of Belief,*" *Zion's Herald,* 73 (1 May 1895): 274;

"Faith in Our Immortality," *Independent,* 48 (2 April 1896): 439;

"Ethical Legislation by the Church," *Methodist Review,* 80 (May 1896): 370–386;

"Divine Immanence," *Independent,* 50 (30 June 1898): 841;

"Distinguo," *Independent,* 50 (8 September 1898): 695–697;

"Secularism and Christianity," *Methodist Review, South,* 48 (1899): 203–217;

"Comments on Dr. Steele's Paper," *Zion's Herald,* 77 (4 October 1899): 1265;

"Aberrant Moralizers," *Methodist Review,* 82 (March 1900): 247–261;

"Thoughts for the Present Distress in Matters Biblical," *Zion's Herald,* 78 (7 March 1900): 298–300; (14 March 1900): 331–333;

"What Is Faith Respecting the Scriptures?" *Independent*, 52 (19 August 1900): 919–921;

"What Is 'Special Creation'?" *Independent*, 52 (8 November 1900): 2684–2686;

"Queries Respecting the New Psychology," *Independent*, 54 (10 July 1902): 1633–1634;

"One of the World's Heroes," anonymous, *Youth's Companion*, 81 (3 January 1903): 8;

"Supernatural in Religion," *Zion's Herald*, 81 (14 January 1903): 42–43;

"As to Miracles," *Independent*, 55 (15 January 1903): 150–152;

"Religious Experience," *Zion's Herald*, 81 (21 January 1903): 74–75;

"The Recession of Mechanism," *Independent*, 55 (22 January 1903): 245–248;

"Spencer's Nescience," *Independent*, 56 (14 January 1904): 67–81;

"Mr. Spencer's Philosophy," *Methodist Review*, 86 (July 1904): 513–531;

"Herbert Spencer and Religion," *Homiletic Review*, 48 (July 1904): 513–531;

"Address on Behalf of the University Faculties," *Zion's Herald*, 82 (2 November 1904): 1392–1393;

"A Remarkable Book," *Zion's Herald*, 82 (20 November 1904): 1518–1519;

"The Value of Philosophy in Education," *Christian Advocate, New York*, 80 (3 August 1905): 1216–1217;

"Progress of the Last Twenty-Five Years in Religious Thought," *Homiletic Review*, 48 (December 1905): 408–413;

"The Passing of Mechanical Naturalism," *Homiletic Review*, 51 (January 1906): 16–20;

"Philosophy of Christian Science," *Christian Advocate, New York*, 83 (19 March 1908): 450–451;

"Darwin and Darwinism," *Hibbert Journal*, 8 (1909–1910): 122–138;

"Present Status of the Argument for Life after Death," *North American Review*, 191 (January 1910): 96–104;

"Address to the Methodist Social Union," *Zion's Herald*, 88 (2 March 1910): 267–270;

"Jesus or Christ?" *Methodist Review*, 92 (March–April 1910): 177–193;

"Concerning Miracles," *Harvard Theological Review*, 3 (April 1910): 143–166;

"Woman and Democracy," *North American Review*, 191 (April 1910): 527–536;

"This Mortal Shall Put on Immortality," *Zion's Herald*, 89 (13 April 1910): 449;

"Present Status of the Conflict of Faith," *Methodist Review*, 105 (May 1922): 358–369;

"The Passing of Educational Fiatism," *Personalist*, 4 (April 1923): 77–89.

The Boston University philosopher Borden Parker Bowne developed a system that he called "Kantianized Berkelianism," "transcendental empiricism," and, finally, in 1905, "Personalism." Regarded as "the father of Personalism," he trained many teachers of theology and philosophy and continues to exert considerable influence through the journals *The Personalist* and *Idealistic Studies*. A proponent of theistic idealism, Bowne challenged Thomas Henry Huxley and other natural scientists who dabbled in metaphysics, criticized the English evolutionary philosopher Herbert Spencer and the radical German theologian David Friedrich Strauss, debated with the Scottish common-sense realist philosopher James McCosh, and defended John Henry Newman's change of loyalty from High Anglicanism to Roman Catholicism. He was relentless in attacking uncritical Darwinianism, easygoing utilitarianism, all forms of materialism, and religious fundamentalism and literalism. In a 17 August 1908 letter William James called Bowne's *Personalism* (1908) "a splendid addition to American philosophy." According to Warren E. Steinkraus, "America's foremost civil rights leader and Nobel Prize winner, Martin Luther King, Jr., acknowledged that Bowne's Personalism was his 'basic philosophical position' and gave him a 'metaphysical basis for the dignity and worth of all human personality.'"

Bowne was born in Leonardville (today Atlantic Highlands), New Jersey, on 14 January 1847, one of the six children of Joseph and Margaret Parker Bowne. Joseph Bowne, a farmer and justice of the peace, was an abolitionist who preached in the local Methodist church. Margaret Bowne was of Quaker stock and despised sham and vanity. Traits of both parents ran deep in Bowne.

Bowne attended the local elementary school until he was sixteen, after which, as was then the custom, he spent a winter teaching in the same school. According to his biographer Francis John McConnell,

There was in the school a notable rowdy who had driven out teacher after teacher, making it difficult for the school board to get anyone even to attempt to teach. The bully's mirth when he learned that Borden Bowne was to be the new teacher was at high pitch, and all the youngsters were on tiptoe with expectancy, waiting for the first encounter. Sure enough, as young Bowne stood just in front of the rowdy's desk one morning, the rowdy rose behind the desk and leaned toward Bowne with an insulting remark. Bowne seized the rebel by the back of the neck as he leaned forward, bent the body down till the posterior made a most excellent presentation for punishment, and then plied a rod so mightily that the bully fainted. It was a rough pedagogy, to be sure, but it brought quiet and made possible keeping open the school.

When he was seventeen, Bowne went to live with friends in Brooklyn, New York, where he worked as a delivery-truck driver for a grocer. Deciding that he wanted to attend New York University, he prepared for the entrance examinations by taking courses at Pennington Seminary and through independent study. He passed the examinations with distinction and enrolled at the university on 17 September 1867. He paid his expenses by working in his brother William's feed and grain store in Jersey City. At a quarterly conference of the Methodist Church on 19 October he received a license to preach, and he delivered his first sermon on 29 December.

After graduating as valedictorian from New York University in June 1871, Bowne joined the New York East Conference of the Methodist Episcopal Church. He served less than a year as pastor of the church at Whitestone, Long Island, before leaving to study in Paris, Halle, and Göttingen. His first book, *The Philosophy of Herbert Spencer: Being an Examination of the First Principles of His System* (1874), appeared while he was still a student at Halle; it was a collection of articles he had written for the journal *New Englander* in 1872. The work is a scathing attack on Spencer's materialistic metaphysics: Bowne says that Spencer's "gospel of agnosticism may do for well-fed and prosperous pachyderms, but the weary and heavy-laden must turn to Moses and the prophets, and the Man of Nazareth." He charges that even Spencer, with blatant inconsistency, admits that his "Unknown Cause" worked through the prophets and Jesus. "In his present position," Bowne concludes, "this modern Samson parallels the ancient by pulling the temple on his own head."

Bowne returned from Europe in 1874 and accepted a position on the editorial staff of a New York journal, *The Independent;* he also taught modern languages at New York University. In a review of Strauss's *Der alte und der neue Glaube* (1872; translated as *The Old Faith and the New,* 1873) in the *Methodist Review* for April 1874 Bowne notes that "the amount of talent necessary to construct" Strauss's argument "is not remarkably great, but the amount required to believe it borders on the supernatural." As for Strauss's attempted reconstruction of religion, "the new faith turns out to be an old bankrupt who has failed a thousand times and who now seeks to cover his lack of capital by extensive advertising and insolent pretense." He calls Strauss's proposal to worship the cosmos instead of a supernatural deity an "atavism in religion" that will prove hollow and vacuous in any crucial testings.

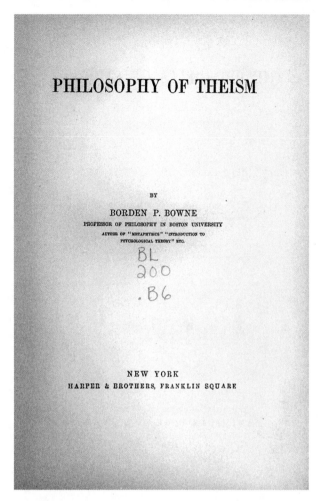

PHILOSOPHY OF THEISM

BY

BORDEN P. BOWNE

PROFESSOR OF PHILOSOPHY IN BOSTON UNIVERSITY

AUTHOR OF "METAPHYSICS" "INTRODUCTION TO PSYCHOLOGICAL THEORY" ETC.

BL
200
.B6

NEW YORK
HARPER & BROTHERS, FRANKLIN SQUARE

Title page for the 1887 work in which Bowne discusses the nature of God. Some of his comments were used against him when he was tried for heresy by the Methodist Church in 1904 (Thomas Cooper Library, University of South Carolina).

In 1876 Bowne received his master of arts degree from New York University and became professor of philosophy at Boston University, which had been founded by the Methodists seven years previously. For eight summers, beginning in 1877, he delivered parts of books and articles on which he was working as lectures on the Chautauqua circuit in western New York State. After he became well known he received attractive offers from Presidents Noah Porter of Yale University and William Rainey Harper of the University of Chicago, but he remained at Boston University. He served as the first dean of the graduate school from 1888 until his death.

Bowne was a thoughtful and kind teacher, but he was impatient with students who were lazy or indifferent and merciless toward the pompous and ignorant. He is said to have quipped about a shallow-minded but verbose student, "he should be arrested for intellectual indecent exposure."

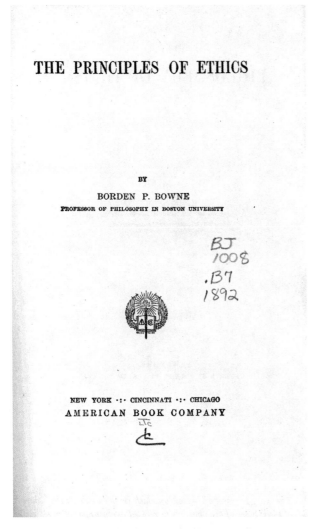

THE PRINCIPLES OF ETHICS

BY

BORDEN P. BOWNE
PROFESSOR OF PHILOSOPHY IN BOSTON UNIVERSITY

BJ
1008
.B7
1892

NEW YORK ·:· CINCINNATI ·:· CHICAGO
AMERICAN BOOK COMPANY

Title page for Bowne's 1892 exposition of his views on morality, in which he advocates women's suffrage (Thomas Cooper Library, University of South Carolina)

When a poorly prepared student stammered and finally admitted, "I know it, Professor, but I can't express it," Bowne retorted, "Then send it by slow freight." To another student struggling toward an answer in a circuitous and long-winded fashion Bowne observed, "If you proceed in that way, you will wear out a great deal of philosophic shoe leather." Of a critic who had not read the book he was criticizing Bowne commented, "He's bald on the inside of his head."

Although he was acquainted with the writings of the German idealist philosopher Georg Wilhelm Friedrich Hegel and the American Hegelian William Torrey Harris, Bowne drew his primary inspiration from his direct contact with such German philosophers as Rudolf Hermann Lotze, Hermann Ulrici, and J. E. Erdmann during his two years of study in Germany. Writing at a time when the impact of science and the

higher biblical criticism on religious thought in the United States was at its strongest, Bowne attempted to bring science and religion together in a comprehensive metaphysical perspective. He was concerned with two interrelated questions: how can one account for knowledge, and what is the nature of reality?

For Bowne, knowing involves forming concepts of the things known. An object exists only as it is conceived or as it stands in relation to thought; things cannot be known as they are in themselves. The question "What is reality?" thus reduces to the question "How must reality be conceived?" The latter question, in turn, requires one to understand the nature of thought and its function in the knowing relationship.

In *Theory of Thought and Knowledge* (1897) Bowne elaborates a theory of knowledge that he calls "transcendental empiricism." Thought apprehends universally valid truths. Even that which is subjective, such as psychological facts peculiar to an individual, can grasp something that is valid for all. Unless thought can transcend its subjective origin, its universality and objectivity of thought cannot be affirmed, and judgment becomes indistinguishable from mere association of ideas. Truth and error arise only at the level of judgment. Whatever comprises the basic conditions for executing a judgment will at the same time serve as the indispensable conditions of all knowledge. These conditions are: first, the unity and identity of the thinking self, which is indispensable for the existence of any rational consciousness whatever; second, the logical laws of identity and contradiction, which are required for thought to have any enduring and consistent meaning; and third, the reality of the connection among the objects of thought. According to Bowne, the self is what comprehends and acts on both the subject and the predicate terms in a judgment. As such, it is the enduring basis and presupposition of all judgments.

As to how the self attains knowledge, Bowne rejects both naive realism and the idealism of the eighteenth-century British philosopher George Berkeley. Naive realism holds that the mind passively receives the imprints of objects through the senses. For Bowne, by contrast, although reception is passive to a degree, states of sensibility become material for thought only when they are acted on by intelligence. Logical activity is implicit in even the most rudimentary sensation. By relating and interpreting sense experiences, thought is able to reach "a world of reality and of rational system." For Bowne, then, the activity of mind is basic to all knowledge.

Berkeley had held in works such as *A Treatise Concerning the Principles of Human Knowledge* (1710) and *Three Dialogues between Hylas and Philonous* (1713) that human experience of the "external world" results from ideas in the mind of God being somehow implanted in the human mind. This Berkelian idealism, according to Bowne, creates an unbridgeable dualism between divine thought and human thought that makes knowledge impossible.

Bowne follows, but modifies, the German philosopher Immanuel Kant's *Kritik der reinen Vernunft* (1781; revised, 1787; translated as *Critique of Pure Reason,* 1855) in holding that the self acquires knowledge through the use of categories that make meaningful experience possible. The categories fix, define, and relate the objects with which the mind deals. The most indispensable category is that of time, under which events are related: antecedence and consequence are imposed on experience by the mind. The category of space is a mode of mental synthesis whereby the mind perceives coexistent objects as mutually external. The categories of space, time, identity, motion, quality, quantity, being, and causality are basic to "mechanical sciences" such as physics and chemistry. The category of identity refers to "sameness of meaning" in logic and to "continuity of existence" in metaphysics. As continuity, identity keeps experience from being chaotic. Since space is a phenomenon or appearance, motion, which requires space, is also a phenomenon. The knowledge that the mechanical sciences can give is, therefore, not knowledge of reality as it is in itself but only as it appears to the mind.

The inadequacy of mechanical science to provide knowledge of reality suggests that the category of being is needed. By this primary metaphysical category Bowne means "substantive existence," or abiding reality. This sort of being is to be distinguished from "being" as applied to events and "being" as objective appearance that exists only in perception. Metaphysical being provides the fixed and defined point of reference for intelligence and enables one to articulate experience. Qualities are qualities *of* this something. To deny validity to this category of being is to abandon even solipsism, which claims that only the individual mind exists, as a possible view.

According to Bowne, things are groups or associations of qualities viewed under the category of being. Such associations bring order out of the chaotic manifold of sense perceptions and provide "independent objectivity." Sense qualities become enduring objects of experience through the application of the category of being. Closely related to the category of being is that of causality. Causality is found in three forms: the self-determination of a free agent, an antecedent determining a consequent in logic, and things mutually interacting with each other.

The categories of being, space, time, and causation must be supplemented by the higher category of purpose, which Bowne defines as intelligent and voli-

Painting of Bowne by an unknown artist (Boston University)

tional causality. To understand experience completely is to integrate it into an all-inclusive system of meaning. The system needed is one that is directed internally "in self-determining, self-conscious causality, guiding itself according to plan and purpose." This sort of causality is manifest only in a self-active person. The category of the person, or personhood, then, is the basis of all understanding and explanation.

The unmistakable trait of being is the power to act; thus, causality is essential to being. In *Metaphysics: A Study in First Principles* (1882; revised, 1898) Bowne says that "Being and action are inseparable" and that "To be is to act; the inactive is nonexistent." The core of any being is its activities. This position is not Berkelian idealism: Bowne does not say, like Berkeley, that "to be is to be perceived." To capture the "true essence" or "nature" of a thing is to find a rule or law according to which it acts or changes. The being of anything is its activity, not its passivity in relation to some other activity. But an entity must continue as "identical with itself" through its activities and changes. The only adequate conception of reality must fuse diversity and identity, change and continuity. One finds this combination within oneself; this conception is that of "personhood."

Bowne argues that to bridge the dualism of thought and thing one must consider things as "products of creative thought" and, therefore, as essentially knowable by intelligence. Human minds and things have "a common source" in the metaphysical person, God. This common source makes experience understandable.

In *Philosophy of Theism* (1887) Bowne calls God "the Ultimate One," "the independent," "the absolute," and "the infinite." God is self-active intelligence, the personal "Perfect Being." The source of the system of things and of all of its laws and principles, God is an agent who manifests causality in the freedom of self-determination. This "dynamic determination" is purposive and volitional; it can explain mechanism in a way that mechanism cannot explain itself, can account for evidence of "design" in nature, and can distinguish error from truth. Mechanism also cannot provide an account of rationality; on the mechanistic view, strictly speaking, no knowledge is possible.

If one assumes that a self-active intelligence is the source of the universe, one finds that the facts confirm the assumption. Although knowledge is piecemeal, no contradictions are encountered between the various pieces. Theism, then, is implicit in all knowledge. While it cannot be proved, to deny it is to court absurdity: if one denies that the "world-ground" is a personal, self-active intelligence, then one is implicitly claiming that an irrational power is doing rational work, that an unconscious entity is producing consciousness, that nonintelligence is bringing about intelligence, that necessity is creating freedom, and that the purposeless is manifesting itself through purpose. The hypothesis of a self-active person accounts more adequately for the universe than does the rival mechanistic perspective.

God is "the founder and conductor of the world-process." In relation to himself God is unchangeable and nontemporal, but in relation to his creation God's activity is "essentially temporal." As the Perfect Being, God has the intellectual, aesthetic, and moral traits in perfection. Human "moral nature," "the structure of society," and "the course of history" all testify to the moral character of the world-ground. History and nature disclose "a power not ourselves" producing righteousness and inculcating the virtues of industry, prudence, foresight, and self-control. In *The Immanence of God* (1904) Bowne says that God is omnipresent, active equally in the fall of the leaf and in the purposiveness manifest in the vast cosmic movement.

Philosophy seeks to know what experience means and what underlies the cosmic process. In its search it is goaded by the necessities of thought and finds that immediate experience is interpreted as a continuous and abiding world by a permanent self with its categories or "rational principles." As "forms of mental arrangement," the categories prescribe the ordering of experience; they do not create the content of experi-

ence. Volitional causality, or "causality as dynamic or productive efficiency," alone brings a terminus to what otherwise might be an unending regress. Only volitional causality, grounded in the activity of a self, can provide a true beginning for any sequence; no mechanistic view can ever offer such an absolute beginning.

In the article "Cardinal Newman and Science," published in *The Independent* on 9 October 1890 and republished in *Representative Essays of Borden Parker Bowne* (1981), Bowne defends Newman's change from High Anglicanism to Catholicism by insisting that Newman's critics have ignored the complexity of the situation and have supposed science to have a special potency for undermining intelligent Catholicism. For Bowne, basic interests and sympathies, rather than formal logical procedures, govern what an individual believes; a shift in these underlying concerns will bring about changes in belief. Reasoning always rests on some such foundation, and without agreement concerning these assumptions and postulates, all argument is useless. Newman's change in belief was based on a conception of the infallible church and monastic piety and cannot be undermined by arguments based on other assumptions and postulates. Nor, contends Bowne, can science dissolve these "wordy wars" between philosophers and theologians. Science can claim no "metaphysical constructions," and its "facts" must be carefully distinguished from its conjectures or theories about the facts. The church may properly insist on its own set of facts as significant lodestars in its quest for truth. Although Bowne does not endorse Newman's change, he holds that it has an integrity and inner consistency that Newman's critics are too dull-witted to grasp.

In 1900 Bowne came to the defense of a colleague in the Boston University School of Theology, Hinckley G. Mitchell, who was threatened with the loss of his professorship because he was suspected of holding unorthodox views about the authorship of the books of the Old Testament. A few years later Bowne himself was tried for heresy by the Methodist Church in a trial that lasted from 6 to 12 April 1904. The charges, supported by passages from his books, were that

He denies the Trinitarian conception of the Deity and also the moral attributes of the Deity. . . . His teaching on miracles is such as to weaken if not destroy faith in large portions of the Old and New Testaments. His views on the inspiration of Scripture are contrary to the teachings of the Scriptures themselves . . . and tend to destroy faith in the authority of the Bible in matters of faith and practice. . . . He denies the Doctrine of the Atonement. . . . He teaches such views of the divine government and of the future of souls as to destroy the force of Christ's teaching about future punishment of the wicked and the future reward of the righteous. . . .

He teaches views on the subject of Sin and Salvation, on Repentance, Justification, Regeneration, and Assurance of Salvation through the Witness of the Spirit that do not represent the views of the Methodist Episcopal Church as expressed in our standard works of theology.

At the trial Bowne listened to the passages from *Metaphysics* and *Philosophy of Theism* that were read in support of the first charge and replied,

I am astonished with a great astonishment to find these things brought forward as proofs of a Unitarian view. They really have no more connection with the specific doctrine of the Trinity than they have with the binomial theorem, or the Roosevelt administrative policy of the Panama Canal. Those propositions would prove me guilty of stealing horses just as quickly as they prove me guilty of Unitarianism.

Bowne chided those who believed in errorless and infallible Scriptures for staying in a "closet" and urged them to come into the open and consult reality. He pointed out that the condition of biblical manuscripts, along with the diversity of versions, was enough to assure any reasonable person that inerrancy was a fiction and suggested that those who claimed historical accuracy withdraw their claim until they made Chronicles and Kings tell the same story. According to a person who was present at the trial, Bowne's accuser revealed a total incapacity to comprehend the ideas of the man he had branded as a heretic. Bowne was acquitted of all charges.

Bowne had not returned to Europe since his student days, except for a trip in 1883 with his wife, Kate Morrison Bowne. In the fall of 1905 he embarked on an eleven-month lecture tour around the world. Traveling westward, he, his wife, and his wife's sister visited Japan, China, India, and Europe. His lectures in Japan were so successful that seven of his books were translated into Japanese.

A champion of women's rights, Bowne defended women's suffrage in his *The Principles of Ethics* (1892); in a pamphlet, *A Man's View of Woman Suffrage* (1910); and in articles such as "Woman and Democracy" (1910) in the *North American Review,* in which he satirizes the arguments against giving the vote to women by applying them to men:

Let us, then, list to some fine old dowager, less acerb and more philosophic as she argues the matter:

My sisters, let us not be too hard on the men. Of course, they are not women and cannot be, but we must beware of arousing sex antagonism. Let us, rather, inquire if there be not plain indication in the nature of things of what man's sphere is. And if we

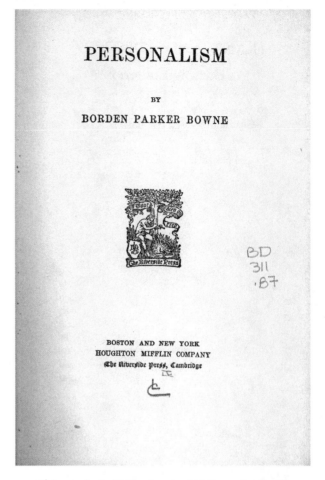

Title page for the 1908 volume in which Bowne describes the philosophy he is considered to have founded (Thomas Cooper Library, University of South Carolina)

look about, we see at once that this sphere is very definitely marked out. Men are manifestly intended to be the breadwinners of the race. And the sphere thus indicated is certainly great enough to consume all masculine energy and satisfy all masculine ambition. Let us, then, be careful of adding to the labors of men the additional burden of thinking on political problems.

And when we rise to the higher thought of fatherhood, what a sacredness this bestows on man, and certainly he can ask for nothing higher. He should, therefore, prepare himself for all his duties in this august relation, and not trouble himself about these other relatively unimportant matters of managing the political world. . . . Some of the heavier work in housecleaning would very properly fall to his lot. A course in scrubbing and tending the furnace and many similar things would be of far higher utility than much of the vaunted education.

Of course this does not mean that men are without intelligence. Some of them are very bright and might properly be trusted with the suffrage. And, further-

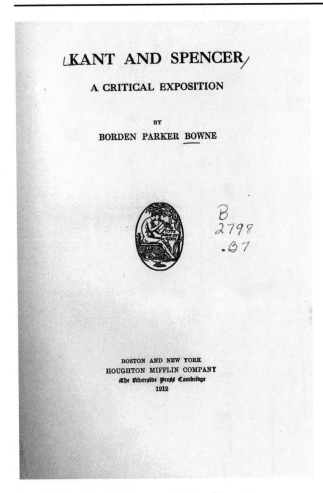

KANT AND SPENCER

A CRITICAL EXPOSITION

BY

BORDEN PARKER BOWNE

B
2798
.07

BOSTON AND NEW YORK
HOUGHTON MIFFLIN COMPANY
The Riverside Press Cambridge
1912

*Title page for the posthumous collection of Bowne's lectures on
Immanuel Kant and Herbert Spencer (Thomas Cooper
Library, University of South Carolina)*

more, it is not from any enmity or hostility on our part
that we are opposed to men voting; it is, rather, from
our love for them and our unwillingness unduly to burden them that we protest against their enfranchisement.
And they are safe in that love. We will guard their
interests. If they wish anything, let them apply to us
and we will see to it that the right is done, but let them
abide in that sphere in which it has pleased Providence
to call them.

In early 1910 Bowne was preparing for a lecture
series on Berkeley to be given in England; he was also
planning a trip to Constantinople (today Istanbul), Turkey, where he had been appointed a director of the
American School for Girls. On 1 April, however, he
had a heart attack while teaching a class. He died at his
home that afternoon. Later that year his wife published
a collection of his sermons as *The Essence of Religion*. A
collection of his lectures appeared in 1912 as *Kant and
Spencer: A Critical Exposition*.

Shortly after Bowne's death his friend at Harvard, William Ernest Hocking, remarked that Bowne's
metaphysics was the fruit of "a mind of distinction and
power" and that its effect and interest were both "permanent." Steinkraus refers to "the vigor and timeless-
ness" of Bowne's thought. In *American Philosophies of
Religion* (1936) Henry Nelson Wieman and Bernard
Eugene Meland contend that Bowne's "thinking has
probably reached the minds of more professing Christian people than any other philosopher of religion in the
United States." Frederick Mayer lists among Bowne's
contributions his conception of God as good and merci-
ful, in contrast to the views of John Calvin; his under-
cutting of the naturalistic tradition; and his arguments
for personalism as a unifying philosophy that acknowledges the harmony of reason and faith and the interdependence of science and religion. L. Harold DeWolf
cites as Bowne's abiding legacy his emphasis on God as
a person who has close relations with individuals, his
refutations of skeptics and agnostics, his emphasis on
righteousness as central to religious living, his checking
of excessive emotionalism, and his stress on religious
education. Bowne's immediate philosophical heirs at
Boston University, where a professorship in philosophy
was named for him in 1925, were Albert C. Knudson
and Edgar Sheffield Brightman, the first holder of the
Borden Parker Bowne Professorship. In later years his
ideas were developed by Ralph Tyler Flewelling, DeW-
olf, and Peter A. Bertocci.

Letters:
"Borden Parker Bowne's Letters to William Torrey
Harris," edited by Daniel S. Robinson, *Philosophi-
cal Forum*, 13 (1955): 89–95.

Biographies:
Kate Morrison Bowne, "An Intimate Portrait of
Bowne," *Personalist*, 2 (1921): 5–15;
Francis John McConnell, *Borden Parker Bowne: His Life
and Philosophy* (New York & Cincinnati: Abingdon
Press, 1929).

References:
Theodore Appel, "First Principles or The Science of
Things," *Reformed Quarterly Review*, 5 (October
1883): 413–449;
Rannie Belle Baker, "The Metaphysics of True Personalism," in her *The Concept of a Limited God: A Study
in the Philosophy of Personalism* (Washington, D.C.:
Shenandoah, 1934), pp. 101–122;
Peter A. Bertocci, "Borden Parker Bowne: Philosophical Theologian and Personalist," *Religion in Life*,
29 (Autumn 1960): 587–597;

Edgar Sheffield Brightman, "Bowne: Eternalist or Temporalist?" *Personalist,* 28 (Summer 1947): 257–265;

Brightman, "Personalism and the Influence of Bowne," in *Proceedings of the 6th International Congress of Philosophy* (New York: Longmans, Green, 1927), pp. 161–164;

Rufus Burrow, "Borden Parker Bowne's Doctrine of God," *Encounter,* 53 (Autumn 1992): 381–400;

George A. Coe, "Borden Parker Bowne," *Journal of Philosophy, Psychology, and Scientific Methods,* 7 (26 May 1910): 281–282;

Coe, "The Empirical Factor in Bowne's Thinking," in *Studies in Philosophy and Theology,* edited by Emil Carl Wilm (New York: Abingdon Press, 1922), pp. 17–21;

G. Watts Cunningham, "Borden Parker Bowne (1847–1910)," in his *The Idealistic Argument in Recent British and American Philosophy* (New York: Century, 1933), pp. 315–333;

Mary H. Dearing, "Reminiscences of Borden Parker Bowne," *Philosophical Forum,* 15 (1957–1958): 51–55;

L. Harold DeWolf, "Bowne: He Restored Belief in God as a Person," *Together,* 7 (June 1963): 25–27;

Ralph Tyler Flewelling and Rudolf Eucken, *Personalism and the Problems of Philosophy: An Appreciation of the Work of Borden Parker Bowne* (New York & Cincinnati: Methodist Book Concern, 1915);

Jose A. Franquiz Ventura, *Borden Parker Bowne's Treatment of the Problem of Change and Identity* (Rio Piedras: University of Puerto Rico, 1942);

J. P. Gordy, "The Metaphysics of Borden Parker Bowne," *New Englander,* 41 (November 1882): 809–836;

Carroll D. W. Hildebrand, "Bowne's Doctrine of Freedom," *Personalist,* 13 (April 1932): 103–110;

William Ernest Hocking, "The Metaphysics of Borden Parker Bowne," *Methodist Review,* 105 (May 1922): 371–374;

Gilbert H. Jones, *Lotze und Bowne: Eine Vergleichung ihrer philosophischen Arbeit* (Weida, Germany: Thomas, 1909);

Albert C. Knudson, "Bowne as Teacher and Author," *Personalist,* 1 (July 1920): 5–14;

Knudson, "Bowne in American Theological Education," *Personalist,* 28 (1947): 247–256;

Knudson, *The Philosophy of Personalism* (New York: Abingdon Press, 1927);

Frederick Lazarus, *The Metaphysics of Ramanuja and Bowne* (Bombay: Chetana, 1962);

Wilbur Long, "The Religious Philosophy of Bowne and James," *Personalist,* 5 (1924): 250–263;

Daniel L. March, "Borden Parker Bowne," *Bostonia,* 10 (April 1937): 3–13;

Frederick Mayer, "Bowne," in his *A History of American Thought* (Dubuque, Iowa: W. C. Brown, 1951), pp. 235–245;

Francis John McConnell, "Bowne and Personalism," in *Personalism and Theology,* edited by Brightman (Boston: Boston University Press, 1943), pp. 21–39;

McConnell, "Bowne and Social Questions," in *Studies in Philosophy and Theology,* pp. 128–143;

McConnell, "Bowne in American Ethical Progress," *Personalist,* 28 (Summer 1947): 237–246;

McConnell, "Memorial Address–Borden Parker Bowne," *Zion's Herald,* 88 (20 April 1910); 491–494;

Charles Bertram Pyle, *The Philosophy of Borden Parker Bowne and Its Application to the Religious Problem* (Columbus, Ohio: S. F. Harriman, 1910);

Edward T. Ramsdell, "Pragmatism and Rationalism in the Philosophy of Borden Parker Bowne," *Personalist,* 16 (Winter 1935): 23–35;

Ramsdell, "The Religious Pragmatism of Borden Parker Bowne," *Personalist,* 15 (1934): 305–314;

Ramsdell, "The Sources of Bowne's Pragmatism," *Personalist,* 16 (1935): 132–141;

Floyd Hiatt Ross, *Personalism and the Problem of Evil, Etc. (A Study in the Personalism of Bowne, Knudson, and Brightman),* Yale Studies in Religion, no. 11 (New Haven: Yale University Press, 1940);

Harmon L. Smith, "Borden Parker Bowne: Heresy at Boston," in *American Religious Heretics, Formal and Informal Trials,* edited by George H. Shriver (New York: Abingdon Press, 1966), pp. 148–187;

Warren E. Steinkraus, "Borden Parker Bowne and Albert Schweitzer," *Personalist,* 50 (Winter 1969): 75–84;

Steinkraus, "Bowne's Correspondence," *Idealistic Studies,* 2 (May 1972): 182–189;

Steinkraus, "The Eucken-Bowne Friendship," *Personalist,* 51 (Summer 1970): 401–406;

F. Thomas Trotter, "Borden Parker Bowne 1847–1910: An Estimate of His Contribution and Continuing Influence" *Philosophical Forum,* 18 (1960–1961): 51–84;

Trotter, "Methodism's Last Heresy Trial," *Christian Advocate* (New York), 4 (1960): 9–10;

William H. Werkmeister, "The Personalism of Bowne," in his *A History of Philosophical Ideas in America* (New York: Ronald Press, 1949), pp. 103–121;

Henry Nelson Wieman and Bernard Eugene Meland, *American Philosophies of Religion* (Chicago & New York: Willett, Clark, 1936).

Papers:

Borden Parker Bowne's papers are at Boston University.

Edgar Sheffield Brightman

(20 September 1884 – 25 February 1953)

Randall E. Auxier
Southern Illinois University at Carbondale

BOOKS: *The Sources of the Hexateuch, J, E and P, in the Text of the American Standard Edition, According to the Consensus of Scholarship,* edited by Brightman (New York, Cincinnati & Chicago: Abingdon Press, 1918);

Religious Values (New York, Cincinnati & Chicago: Abingdon Press, 1925);

An Introduction to Philosophy (New York: Holt, 1925; London: Cape, 1925; revised edition, New York: Holt, 1951; London: Pitman, 1951);

Immortality in Post-Kantian Idealism (Cambridge, Mass.: Harvard University Press, 1925);

A Philosophy of Ideals (New York: Holt, 1928);

The Problem of God (New York, Cincinnati & Chicago: Abingdon Press, 1930);

The Finding of God (New York, Cincinnati & Chicago: Abingdon Press, 1931);

Is God a Person? (New York: Association Press, 1932);

Moral Laws (New York, Cincinnati & Chicago: Abingdon Press, 1933);

Personality and Religion (New York, Cincinnati & Chicago: Abingdon Press, 1934);

Historical Outline of the Bible, by Brightman and Walter G. Muelder (Berea, Ky.: Berea College Press, 1936);

The Future of Christianity (New York, Cincinnati & Chicago: Abingdon Press, 1937);

A Philosophy of Religion (New York: Prentice-Hall, 1940; London & New York: Skeffington, 1947);

The Spiritual Life (New York & Nashville: Abingdon-Cokesbury Press, 1942);

Nature and Values (New York & Nashville: Abingdon-Cokesbury Press, 1945);

Our Faith in God, anonymous (Nashville: Abingdon-Cokesbury Press, 1949);

Persons and Values (Boston: Boston University Press, 1952);

Person and Reality: An Introduction to Metaphysics, edited by Peter A. Bertocci, Jannette Elthina Newhall, and Robert S. Brightman (New York: Ronald Press, 1958);

Edgar Sheffield Brightman

Studies in Personalism: Selected Writings of Edgar Sheffield Brightman, Borden Parker Bowne Professor of Philosophy, Boston University, 1924–1953, edited by W. E. Steinkraus and Robert N. Beck, introductory essay by Brand Blanshard (Utica, N.Y.: Meridian, 1984).

OTHER: *Proceedings of the Sixth International Congress of Philosophy, Harvard University, Cambridge, Massachusetts, United States of America, September 14, 15,*

16, 17, 1926, edited by Brightman (New York & London: Longmans, Green, 1927);

"The Finite Self," in *Contemporary Idealism in America,* edited by Clifford Barrett (New York: Macmillan, 1932), pp. 169–195;

"Religion as Truth," in *Contemporary American Theology,* edited by Vergilius Ferm (New York: Round Table Press, 1932), pp. 53–81;

"The World of Ideas," in *Religion and Public Affairs,* edited by Harris F. Rall (New York: Macmillan, 1937), pp. 161–196;

Personalism in Theology: A Symposium in Honor of Albert Cornelius Knudson, by Associates and Former Students, edited by Brightman (Boston: Boston University Press, 1943);

"Russell's Philosophy of Religion," in *The Philosophy of Bertrand Russell,* edited by Paul Arthur Schilpp, The Library of Living Philosophers, volume 5 (Evanston, Ill.: Northwestern University Press, 1944), pp. 537–556;

"The Philosophy of World Community," in *World Order,* edited by F. E. Johnson (New York: Macmillan, 1945), pp. 14–30;

"Radhakrishnan and Mysticism," in *The Philosophy of Sarvepalli Radhakrishnan,* edited by Schilpp, The Library of Living Philosophers, volume 8 (New York: Tudor, 1952), pp. 391–415.

SELECTED PERIODICAL PUBLICATIONS–
UNCOLLECTED: "The More than Human Values of Religion," *Journal of Religion,* 1 (1921): 326–377;

"Personalism as a Philosophy of Religion," *Crozer Quarterly,* 5 (1928): 381–395;

"The Dialectic of Religious Experience," *Philosophical Review,* 38 (1929): 557–573;

"A Temporalist View of God," *Journal of Religion,* 12 (1932): 545–555;

"Immediacy?" *Idealismus,* 1 (1934): 87–101;

"An Empirical Approach to God," *Philosophical Review,* 46 (1937): 147–169;

"What Is Personality?" *Personalist,* 20 (1939): 129–138;

"Is Christianity Reasonable?" *Religion in the Making,* 1 (1941): 393–414.

Edgar Sheffield Brightman was a philosopher of religion whose influence was greatest from 1930 until about 1960, when shifting social and academic trends led to a decline in interest in the sort of philosophy and theology he espoused. His concepts of the finite/infinite God and of the relationships among consciousness, person, and value, however, remain per-

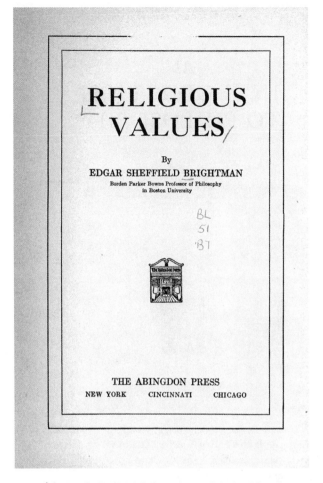

Title page for Brightman's first major work in the philosophy of religion, published in 1925 (Thomas Cooper Library, University of South Carolina)

manent contributions to American philosophy of the twentieth century.

Brightman was born in Holbrook, Massachusetts, on 20 September 1884, the only child of George Edgar and Mary Sheffield Brightman, both of whom were descended from old and distinguished New England families. His father was a Methodist minister; as a result of the required itinerancy of that denomination, Brightman spent his childhood in several places in New England, including the islands of Nantucket and Martha's Vineyard. He graduated from high school in Whitman, Massachusetts, in 1901. Considered too young to begin college, he worked in a Provincetown grocery and meat market for a year before entering Brown University in 1902.

At Brown, Brightman studied classics and philosophy and gained facility in Greek, Latin, French, and German; later in life he learned Spanish, Hebrew, and Sanskrit. In spite of some difficult cir-

AN
INTRODUCTION
TO PHILOSOPHY

BY
EDGAR SHEFFIELD BRIGHTMAN
BORDEN PARKER BOWNE PROFESSOR OF PHILOSOPHY
IN BOSTON UNIVERSITY

BD
21
.B7

NEW YORK
HENRY HOLT AND COMPANY

*Title page for Brightman's 1925 work that became a
widely used textbook (Thomas Cooper Library,
University of South Carolina)*

cumstances, including the death of his father and
being badly burned in an accident, he graduated in
June 1906. From 1906 to 1908 he assisted in the
teaching of Greek and philosophy at Brown and also
taught at Pembroke College in Cambridge while
working on his master of arts degree, which was
awarded by Brown in 1908. He entered the School of
Theology at Boston University in 1908, receiving a
bachelor of theology degree (S.T.B.) in 1910 and,
with it, ordination in the Methodist Episcopal
Church. While completing the preliminary requirements for a Ph.D., he served as a student pastor in
several churches in Rhode Island and Massachusetts.

Brightman received a fellowship to study at the
University of Berlin in 1910–1911 and at the University of Marburg in 1911–1912 while writing his dissertation on truth in the theology of Albrecht Ritschl.
He returned to the United States in the winter term of
1912 to take a position at Nebraska Wesleyan University in Lincoln, teaching courses in philosophy,

experimental and general psychology, religion, and
the Bible. He received his Ph.D. from Boston University in June 1912. A month later he married Charlotte
Hülsen, whom he had met in Germany. In June 1914
a son, Howard Hülsen Brightman, was born. Charlotte Brightman died of facial cancer less than a year
later. Scholars have speculated that her early death
might have caused Brightman to question his view of
God in a way that eventually led to his assertion that
God is finite.

Brightman joined the faculty of Wesleyan University in Middletown, Connecticut, in the fall of 1915
as an associate professor. There he met Irma B. Fall,
whom he married on 8 June 1918. They had two children: Miriam in 1921 and Robert Sheffield in 1928.
Brightman's first book, *The Sources of the Hexateuch, J, E
and P, in the Text of the American Standard Edition, According to the Consensus of Scholarship* (1918), is a summation
of all of the German scholarship proceeding from the
then highly controversial documentary hypothesis of
biblical authorship. The documentary hypothesis asserts
that the early books of the Hebrew Bible were written
by different persons over a long period of centuries
and edited into a single document sometime after the
end of the Babylonian exile in 538 B.C. Professing the
same sorts of ideas had resulted in the heresy trial of
Brightman's Boston University teacher and philosophical role model, Borden Parker Bowne, fourteen years
earlier, but the book established Brightman's reputation in the field of Old Testament scholarship. He was
promoted to full professor at Wesleyan in 1919, but in
the fall of that year he moved to the Graduate School
of Boston University.

In 1920 Brightman began publishing articles in
a variety of scholarly and popular periodicals that
identified him as a follower of "Boston personalism,"
the philosophical and religious school of thought
established by Bowne. Boston personalism was an
American Protestant version of a generalized movement in late-nineteenth-century intellectual life—one
that included Pope Leo XIII and Charles Renouvier
in Europe—that holds the personal form of experiencing to be metaphysically ultimate. In the Protestant
version this idea took on a Kantian coloring, with the
ideas of "personal" and "experience" understood in
terms of the active contribution of subjectivity to the
content and form of experience. Rather than seeing
the world as passively received by the physical
senses, personalists saw the world as actively formed
and informed by the structures, habits, values, and
principles of personality, both human and divine, and
they believed that no experience could be explained
except by reference to the person. Other thinkers in
the Boston personalist tradition have included Ralph

Tyler Flewelling, Albert C. Knudson, Francis J. McConnell, L. Harold DeWolf, Peter A. Bertocci, Walter G. Muelder, Martin Luther King Jr., and Erazim V. Kohák. Like Brightman, all of these men regarded themselves as followers of Bowne.

Brightman developed his own version of personalism by incorporating influences from many sources that laid particular stress on conceiving both God and the human person as finite and temporal beings whose modes of relation are limited by the conditions under which they can experience one another. God is conceived as a personal being, vast and powerful but not omniscient or omnipotent. Even God has to deal with what Brightman calls "the Given," which means that God is conscious of the universe only under the conditions that make the experience of anything at all possible for a personal being. Brightman's God is aware of things that cause him to suffer, and he cannot immediately share in the inner lives of creatures. Human persons, in turn, cannot know God immediately or participate directly in the divine inner life but must imagine and infer God's nature from the interaction of their own purposes with the wider universe, which includes God's purposes—whatever those may be. From the experiences of the human person, a conception of God as a changing, temporal personal being is the most defensible view, according to Brightman. Indeed, Brightman goes so far as to claim that if one thinks of God properly, one cannot avoid the conclusion that God is not entirely at peace with himself, since the existence of the created universe is evidence of some unsatisfied need or unaccomplished plan. Brightman is not inclined to see the human species as a final or even an especially important part of the realization of divine purposes; but he acknowledges that theology and philosophy, as human activities, are obliged to exaggerate the human form of knowing.

Brightman was made the first Borden Parker Bowne Professor of Philosophy at Boston University in 1925. That year he published his first major effort in the philosophy of religion, *Religious Values,* as well as *An Introduction to Philosophy,* which became one of the most widely used textbooks of its kind. In 1928 his *A Philosophy of Ideals* appeared. These early works contain the seeds of his empirical epistemology and his stance on value in relation to consciousness, which he worked out in greater detail as the years wore on.

Brightman spent the academic year 1930–1931 on sabbatical with his family in Germany. This respite from teaching and administrative duties resulted in two of his most important books, *The Problem of God* (1930) and *The Finding of God* (1931). The

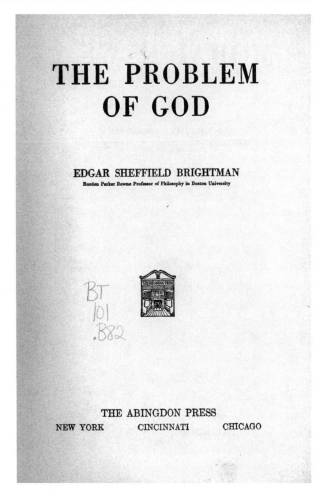

THE PROBLEM
OF GOD

EDGAR SHEFFIELD BRIGHTMAN
Borden Parker Bowne Professor of Philosophy in Boston University

THE ABINGDON PRESS
NEW YORK   CINCINNATI   CHICAGO

Title page for Brightman's 1930 book, in which he discusses the various conceptions of God that have succeeded one another through the course of Western history (Thomas Cooper Library, University of South Carolina)

first marks a breakthrough in Brightman's thinking, for in these pages he synthesizes the lessons learned from historical study of the Bible with his own philosophical personalism. The conceptions of God that have replaced one another in the course of Western history, he says, are evidence for and within human consciousness itself of something greater than history. The changes in the way God is conceived not only record the development of human consciousness but also point to the realization of divine purposes as they relate to human life and development.

In Germany, Brightman had the opportunity to examine at first hand the emerging phenomenological school of philosophy, particularly the thought of Edmund Husserl and Martin Heidegger. Phenomenologists, like personalists, hold that conscious experience reflects deeper structures that can be understood by the right methods, namely those

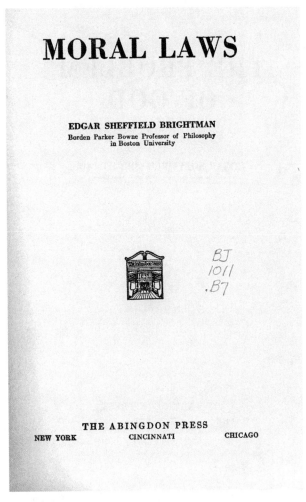

MORAL LAWS

EDGAR SHEFFIELD BRIGHTMAN
Borden Parker Bowne Professor of Philosophy
in Boston University

BJ
1011
.B7

THE ABINGDON PRESS
NEW YORK   CINCINNATI   CHICAGO

*Title page for Brightman's 1933 work, in which he argues
that universal and fundamental moral principles are
presupposed in the very act of being conscious of
the world around one (Thomas Cooper
Library, University of South Carolina)*

that attend carefully to the ways in which experience takes on its varying forms and moods. Phenomenology played an increasingly significant role in his conception of the self in the books he wrote after 1931. At the same time, he was digesting the "process" metaphysics of Alfred North Whitehead, the English mathematician and logician who had moved to the United States to pursue speculative philosophy at Harvard University in 1924. Process philosophers believe that relations are the fundamental reality and that temporal relations are the most pervasive and revealing relations human beings can study. Whitehead and the younger process thinker Charles Hartshorne exercised a great influence on Brightman's thought from the early 1930s until his death.

During this period Brightman was also developing a critique of American pragmatism and pragmatic naturalism. He appreciated much of what the pragmatists and naturalists had to say, but he believed that in their enthusiasm for science they had overlooked something basic about how human beings know what they know: that all forms of knowing are inferential and require the givenness of the world to the self; and that the self, whatever it may do with what is given, can argue only from its own meager resources.

The most important of Brightman's works, in terms of its impact, was *Moral Laws* (1933). Here Brightman argues that a personalistic stance in epistemology and metaphysics derives from a priori knowledge of universal and fundamental moral principles of the universe, which are presupposed in the very act of being personally conscious in and of the world. Like the pragmatists and the process philosophers, Brightman did not believe that values and facts were separate aspects of reality; he held, rather, that consciousness itself is an act of valuation, both of the self and of its objects, and that all other values derive from this act. Without the category of the personal, no principle of order or value has any meaning. This notion became important practically through its influence on the thought and life of Brightman's student King, who synthesized Brightman's moral vision with other sources within and outside the tradition of Boston personalism. Brightman was a thoroughgoing pacifist, even in the midst of World War II, and believed that social justice was achievable on a thoroughly rational and empirical basis, if only the ideal of personality could be grasped and applied in practice. Violence and war never can make any progress toward this goal, he maintained.

In 1934 Brightman published *Personality and Religion,* based on his Lowell Lectures at King's Chapel in Boston. Widely reviewed and well received, the book represents Brightman at the height of his powers. Little in it is new to Brightman's thought, but the arrangement and exposition of the ideas of the personhood of humans and God, God's finite/infinite character, and the social consequences of such a view are presented forcefully, compactly, and persuasively. It is also stylistically the best of Brightman's books, perhaps because it was written to be delivered as lectures to the public. Brightman's prose is crisp and clear; his arguments are easily followed; and while the writing is nearly emotionless and the form of appeal almost wholly rational, it can produce a deeply affective experience in the reader. For example, in *Personality and Religion* Brightman gives voice to an ideal of community called "organic pluralism," which is in many ways a personalistic application of Whitehead's "philosophy of organism" to the practical situation of human communities. He attempts to solve

Brightman lecturing to one of his classes at Boston University in the mid 1940s

the problem of the individual in the community by balancing absolute organicism, in which the individual is wholly subservient to the collective, against absolute pluralism, in which the community is subordinate to the individual. The ideal of "personal religion" as a kind of existential freedom before God and others that grounds political freedom connects the sort of personhood the community has with the personhood of the individuals who make it up. One finds echoes here of Whitehead's phrase "religion is what a man does with his solitariness." Brightman espouses a democratic ideal and sees both national socialism and anarchism as antithetical to his proposed balance. He does, however, allow that some forms of communism may be consistent with the ideal of personal religion, as they are "religious" in the relevant sense without realizing it.

Brightman applied his basic ideas in such books as *The Future of Christianity* (1937), *The Spiritual Life* (1942), and *Nature and Values* (1945). In 1940 he systematized and catalogued all of the historical and current philos-ophies of religion and criticized them from a personalist viewpoint in *A Philosophy of Religion* (1940), a popular book that was republished many times. As he aged, Brightman became more interested in Asian and Latin American thought, mystical experience, meditation, and process philosophy. His final work was a systematic metaphysics that he left unfinished at his death on 25 February 1953. It was pieced together by his son Robert, his longtime secretary and later professor of theology Jannette Elthina Newhall, and his student and successor as Bowne Professor, Bertocci, as *Person and Reality: An Introduction to Metaphysics* (1958). In spite of its half-finished condition, the work should have been Brightman's crowning achievement. The world had changed in the intervening years, however, and Brightman's influence was quickly overshadowed by newer trends.

During his lifetime Edgar Sheffield Brightman enjoyed a high reputation among philosophers and theologians. His books were widely reviewed in both the scholarly and popular press, and he served as

NATURE AND VALUES

by

EDGAR SHEFFIELD BRIGHTMAN

THE FONDREN LECTURES FOR
1945
SOUTHERN METHODIST UNIVERSITY

B
828.5
.B7

ABINGDON-COKESBURY PRESS
New York   •   Nashville

Title page for one of the books in which Brightman applies his personalistic principles to specific issues (Thomas Cooper Library, University of South Carolina)

president of three national organizations: the American Theological Society in 1933–1934; the American Philosophical Association, Eastern Division, in 1936–1937; and the National Association of Biblical Instructors from 1941 to 1943. His textbooks in philosophy of religion and introductory philosophy remained popular well into the 1970s, and a sizable body of interpretive literature on his thought exists and increases every year. His reputation, however, is not now what it was during his lifetime. As interest in theism has declined as a scholarly topic, so have personalism and Brightman. Brightman's lasting historical importance is assured, however, as one of the dominant influences in Martin Luther King Jr.'s moral and philosophical thought.

Letters:

Hartshorne and Brightman on God, Process, and Persons: The Correspondence, 1922–1945, edited by Randall E. Auxier and Mark Y. A. Davies (Nashville: Vanderbilt University Press, 2001).

Bibliography:

Bogumił Gacka, *Bibliography of American Personalism* (Lublin, Poland: Oficyna Wydawnicza "Czas," 1994), pp. 41–57.

Biography:

Walter G. Muelder, "Edgar S. Brightman: Person and Moral Philosopher," in *The Boston Personalist Tradition in Philosophy, Social Ethics, and Theology,* edited by Paul Deats and Carol Robb (Macon, Ga.: Mercer University Press, 1986), pp. 105–120.

References:

Rufus Burrow Jr., *Personalism: A Critical Introduction* (St. Louis: Chalice Press, 1999);

Peter V. Corea, ed., *The Philosophical Forum, Volume XII: Memorial Volume Dedicated to Edgar Sheffield Brightman* (Boston: Boston University Press, 1954);

Paul Deats and Carol Robb, eds., *The Boston Personalist Tradition in Philosophy, Social Ethics, and Theology* (Macon, Ga.: Mercer University Press, 1986);

Bogumił Gacka, *American Personalism* (Lublin, Poland: Oficyna Wydawnicza "Czas," 1995), pp. 73–93;

James Alfred Martin Jr., *Empirical Philosophies of Religion* (Morningside Heights, N.Y.: King's Crown Press, 1945), pp. 28–50;

James John McLarney, *The Theism of Edgar Sheffield Brightman* (Washington, D.C.: Catholic University of America, 1936);

Andrew Reck, *Recent American Philosophy: Studies of Ten Representative Thinkers* (New York: Random House, 1964), pp. 311–336;

Floyd Hiatt Ross, *Personalism and the Problem of Evil,* Yale Studies in Religion, no. 11 (New Haven: Yale University Press / London: H. Milford, Oxford University Press, 1940).

Papers:

The Edgar Sheffield Brightman Papers are in the Special Collections Division of the Mugar Memorial Library at Boston University.

Mary Whiton Calkins

(30 March 1863 – 26 February 1930)

Sharon Scherwitz
University of Wisconsin—La Crosse

BOOKS: *Sharing the Profits* (Boston: Ginn, 1888);

Association: An Essay Analytic and Experimental, Psychological Review, monograph supplement, no. 2 (New York & London: Macmillan, 1896);

An Introduction to Psychology (New York: Macmillan / London: Macmillan, 1901);

Der Doppelte Standpunkt in der Psychologie (Leipzig: Veit, 1905);

The Persistent Problems of Philosophy: An Introduction to Metaphysics through the Study of Modern Systems (New York: Macmillan / London: Macmillan, 1907; revised edition, New York: Macmillan, 1912; revised again, 1917; revised and enlarged, 1925);

A First Book in Psychology (New York: Macmillan, 1910; revised, 1911; revised again, 1912; revised again, 1914);

The Good Man and the Good: An Introduction to Ethics (New York: Macmillan, 1918).

OTHER: Thomas Hobbes, *The Metaphysical System of Hobbes as Contained in Twelve Chapters from His "Elements of Philosophy Concerning Body," and in Briefer Extracts from His "Human Nature" and "Leviathan,"* edited by Calkins (La Salle, Ill.: Open Court, 1905);

"The Limits of Genetic and Comparative Psychology," in *Congress of Arts and Science, Universal Exposition, St. Louis, 1904,* volume 5: *Biology; Anthropology; Psychology; Sociology,* edited by Howard J. Rogers (Boston & New York: Houghton, Mifflin, 1906), pp. 712–734;

"Biographical Introduction," in *The Poems of Sophie Jewett,* Memorial Edition (New York: Crowell, 1910), pp. v–xix;

Julian Offray de La Mettrie, *Man a Machine: Including Fredrick The Great's "Eulogy" on La Mettrie's "The Natural History of the Soul,"* edited and translated by Calkins, philosophical and historical notes by Gertude Carmen Bussey (Chicago: Open Court, 1912);

Mary Whiton Calkins

"Arthur Schopenhauer and His Philosophy," in *German Classics of the Nineteenth and Twentieth Centuries: Masterpieces of German Literature, Translated into English,* volume 15, edited by Kuno Francke and William Guild Howard (New York: German Publication Society, 1914), pp. 1–16;

"The Foundation in Royce's Philosophy for Christian Theism," in *Papers in Honor of Josiah Royce on His*

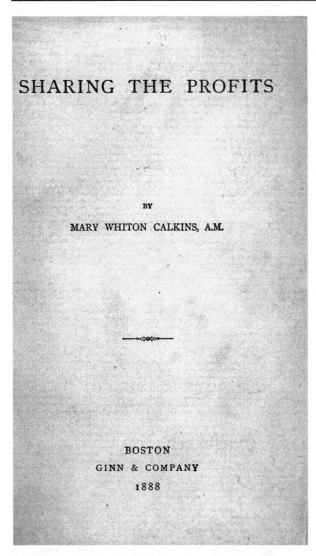

SHARING THE PROFITS

BY

MARY WHITON CALKINS, A.M.

BOSTON
GINN & COMPANY
1888

*Title page for Calkins's first book, in which she expresses
her socialist views (Howard-Tilton Memorial
Library, Tulane University)*

Sixtieth Birthday (New York: Longmans, Green, 1916), pp. 54–68;

"Knowledge," in *Immanuel Kant,* edited by Emil C. Wilm (New Haven: Yale University Press, 1925), pp. 17–22;

John Locke, *Locke's Essay Concerning Human Understanding, Books II and IV (with Omissions),* edited by Calkins (Chicago: Open Court, 1927);

George Berkeley, *Essay, Principles, Dialogue, with Selections from Other Writings,* edited by Calkins (New York: Scribners, 1929);

"The Philosophical *Credo* of an Absolutistic Personalist," in *Contemporary American Philosophy,* volume 1, edited by George Adams Montague and William P. Pepperell (New York: Macmillan, 1930), pp. 197–218;

"Mary Whiton Calkins," in *A History of Psychology in Autobiography,* volume 1, edited by Carl Murchison (Worcester, Mass.: Clark University Press, 1930), pp. 31–62.

SELECTED PERIODICAL PUBLICATIONS–
UNCOLLECTED: "Psychology as Science of Selves," *Philosophical Review,* 9 (1900): 490–501;

"The Order of the Hegelian Categories in the Hegelian Argument," *Mind,* 12 (1903): 317–340;

"A Reconciliation between Structural and Functional Psychology: Presidential Address," *Psychological Review,* 13 (1906): 61–80;

"Psychology: What Is It About?" *Journal of Philosophy, Psychology, and Scientific Methods,* 4, no. 25 (1907): 673–683; 5, nos. 1, 3, and 5 (1908);

"Psychology as Science of Self: I. Is Self Body or Has it Body? II. The Nature of the Self III. The Description of Consciousness," *Journal of Psychology and Philosophy,* 5 (1908): 12–19, 64–68, 113–121;

"The Idealist to the Realist," *Journal of Philosophy,* 8 (1911): 449–458;

"H. W. Bergson: Personalist," *Philosophical Review,* 21 (1912): 666–675;

"Discussion: Bertrand Russell on NeoRealism," *Philosophical Review,* 24 (1915): 533–537;

"The Self in Scientific Psychology," *American Journal of Psychology,* 26 (October 1915): 495–524;

"The Case of Self against Soul," *Psychological Review,* 24 (1917): 278–300;

"Militant Pacifism," *International Journal of Ethics,* 28 (1918): 70–79;

"The New Rationalism and Objective Idealism," *Philosophical Review,* 28, no. 1 (1919): 598–605;

"Personalistic Conception of Nature," *Philosophical Review,* 28, no. 2 (1919): 115–146;

"The Metaphysical Monist as a Sociological Pluralist," *Journal of Philosophy,* 17 (1920): 681–685;

"The Truly Psychological Behaviorism," *Psychological Review,* 28 (1921): 1–18;

"The Foundations of Psychology," *Journal of Philosophy,* 20 (1923): 5–15;

"The 'Personal Idealist's' Concern for Psychology," *Personalist,* 5 (1924): 5–11;

"Converging Lines in Contemporary Psychology," *British Journal of Psychology,* 16 (1926): 135–158;

"Critical Comments on the *Gestalt-Theorie,*" *Psychological Review,* 33 (March 1926): 135–158;

"That Ambiguous Concept of Meaning," *American Journal of Psychology,* 39 (1927): 7–22;

"Self Awareness and Meaning," *American Journal of Psychology,* 38 (1927): 441–448;

"Value–Primarily a Psychological Conception," *Journal of Psychological Studies,* 3 (1928): 413–426;

"The Self Psychology of the Psychoanalysts," by Calkins and Eleanor A. Gamble, *Psychological Review,* 37 (1930): 277–304.

Both a philosopher and a psychologist, Mary Whiton Calkins merged speculative metaphysics with rigorous scientific research. She held the concept of the person to be the meeting point of these approaches, and she spent a lifetime fusing a "psychology of selves" paradigm in psychology with a personal-idealist philosophical account of reality. As her friend and colleague Eleanor A. Gamble said in the volume *In Memoriam: Mary Whiton Calkins 1863–1930* (1931), "that personalism should prevail both in psychology and philosophy was her most passionate interest as a scholar and as a teacher." An able historian of philosophy and one of the most prominent students of the American idealist philosopher Josiah Royce, Calkins developed a position that she described as "absolutistic personalistic idealism."

Calkins was born in Hartford, Connecticut, on 30 March 1863 to Wolcott Calkins, a Presbyterian minister, and Charlotte Whiton Calkins. The family moved to Philadelphia when she was two and to Buffalo, New York, when she was four. In Buffalo she attended public school and took private lessons in German. One of her best friends at that time was Sophie Jewett, who later became a poet and professor at Wellesley College. In 1880 the Calkinses moved to Newton, Massachusetts, where Mary Calkins attended high school. Her graduation essay, "The Apology Plato Should Have Written," on Socrates' wife, Xanthippe, exhibited the gentle intellectual wit that distinguished her writing throughout her life.

In 1882 Calkins entered Smith College, where she majored in classics and philosophy and often challenged her professors with her tough questions. She was particularly influenced by Professor Garman in psychology and Professor Harry Norman Gardiner in philosophy. She later credited Garman with sparking her interest in philosophy. She spent the year 1883–1884 in England studying Greek at the University of Cambridge. She received her B.A. in 1885. In the winter of 1886 she studied German philosophers at Leipzig University. She earned her M.A. from Smith in 1888.

In 1890, while tutoring Greek at Wellesley, Calkins was offered an instructorship in the college's new department of philosophy. She began graduate work at Clark and Harvard Universities to qualify herself for the position. At Clark she studied experimental psychology under Edmund Stanford, working closely with him on dream studies; she woke herself up every

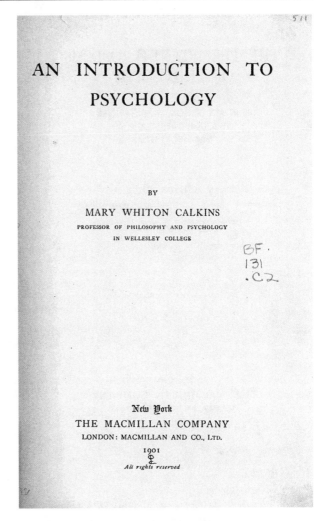

Title page for Calkins's first psychology textbook, which, along with her *A First Book in Psychology (1910)*, influenced a generation of students (Thomas Cooper Library, University of South Carolina)

night to record her dreams. That same year she was the only student in a seminar with William James at Harvard. In her contribution to *A History of Psychology in Autobiography* (1930) she recalled, "I began the serious study of psychology with William James. Most unhappily for them and most fortunately for me the other members of his seminar in psychology dropped away in the early weeks of the fall of 1890; and James and I were left not, as in Garfield's vision of Mark Hopkins and himself, at either end of a log but quite literally at either side of a library fire." For the next six years she took graduate courses in psychology and philosophy at Harvard; she was the only woman among the students and teachers. Of all of her professors, she was particularly influenced by Royce.

Calkins fulfilled the requirements for the Ph.D. with the highest praise from her teachers; even psychology professor Hugo Munsterberg, who was not noted

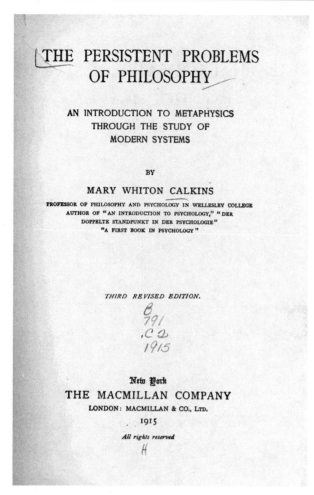

THE PERSISTENT PROBLEMS
OF PHILOSOPHY

AN INTRODUCTION TO METAPHYSICS
THROUGH THE STUDY OF
MODERN SYSTEMS

BY

MARY WHITON CALKINS

PROFESSOR OF PHILOSOPHY AND PSYCHOLOGY IN WELLESLEY COLLEGE
AUTHOR OF "AN INTRODUCTION TO PSYCHOLOGY," "DER
DOPPELTE STANDPUNKT IN DER PSYCHOLOGIE"
"A FIRST BOOK IN PSYCHOLOGY"

THIRD REVISED EDITION.

B
791
.C2
1915

New York
THE MACMILLAN COMPANY
LONDON: MACMILLAN & CO., LTD.
1915

All rights reserved

H

*Title page for the third revised edition of Calkins's classic
introductory philosophy text, first published
in 1907 (Thomas Cooper Library,
University of South Carolina)*

for his enlightened views toward women undergraduates, praised her as his best student. A glowing description of her performance on her unofficial oral examinations was signed by Royce, James, Munsterberg, George Santayana, G. H. Palmer, and Paul H. Harris; James claimed that it was the best examination he had ever witnessed. Despite the praise, and despite Munsterberg's pleading, Harvard Corporation remained firm in its male-only policy and denied Calkins a degree. She published what was to have been her doctoral dissertation, a study of the association of ideas written under James's direction, as a monograph in 1896. In the volume *In Memoriam: Mary Whiton Calkins 1863–1930* the Boston University personalist philosopher Edgar Sheffield Brightman recalled that

> when, years later, she was offered the Radcliffe degree in lieu of the Harvard degree which she had so fully earned, she deemed it fairer to decline the honor and thus continue her protest against the earlier injustice.

The degree was not essential to her, but the cause of justice to women was.

Calkins taught philosophy, psychology, and Greek and served as chairperson of the Department of Philosophy and Psychology at Wellesley until her retirement in 1929. She founded the first psychological laboratory at a women's college and one of the first such laboratories in the country. There she performed and supervised studies on association, memory, sensation, aesthetics, and synaesthesia. She wrote six books (including the monograph of her dissertation) and at least sixty-eight articles in psychology and thirty-seven in philosophy and religion. Her psychology textbooks, *An Introduction to Psychology* (1901) and *A First Book in Psychology* (1910), shaped the development of a generation of students of the subject. In philosophy she wrote the classic *The Persistent Problems of Philosophy: An Introduction to Metaphysics through the Study of Modern Systems* (1907) and *The Good Man and the Good: An Introduction to Ethics* (1918) and edited or translated books of selections from the works of John Locke, Thomas Hobbes, George Berkeley, and Julian Offray de La Mettrie. Brightman remarked in *In Memoriam: Mary Whiton Calkins 1863–1930:* "One would have to search far to find any recent philosopher whose attainments in the combined fields of psychology, ethics, history, and constructive metaphysics surpass those of Miss Calkins."

In her original philosophical work Calkins merged the idealisms of Berkeley, Royce, and the nineteenth-century German philosopher Georg Wilhelm Friedrich Hegel to create her absolutistic personal idealism. Whereas other personalists, such as Brightman, Border Parker Bowne, John Herman Randall Jr., George H. Howison, and the British philosopher J. M. E. McTaggart, had finite conceptions of the self, Calkins extended the idea of the person into a complete metaphysics. In her view, reality is composed of selves, all of which are included in the Absolute; and the Absolute is a person. She tried to reconcile this concept of the Absolute Person with the Christian perspective in which she was brought up and to which she held throughout her life. She also attempted to show that the insights of philosophers such as Henri Bergson, Bertrand Russell, and Alfred North Whitehead are best expressed in a personalistic framework. She pursued a similar project in psychology, trying to bring together functionalism, structuralism, Gestalt, behaviorism, and Freudianism under the paradigm "psychology of selves." Her personalistic psychology gained prominence from 1900 to 1930 and provided a starting point for the later person-focused work of psychologists such as Gordon Allport.

In 1905 Calkins became the first woman president of the American Psychological Association. In *A History of Psychology in Autobiography* she recalled that

I was a member in 1905 of the Executive Committee of the American Psychological Association. Dr. Munsterberg had planned a lunch-meeting of the Committee at the Harvard Union, but the burly head-waiter stoutly protested our entrance. No woman, he correctly insisted, might set foot in the main hall; nor was it possible to admit so many men, balanced on one woman only, to the ladies dining-room. It was almost by main force that Professor Munsterberg gained his point and the Committee its lunch.

In 1909 Calkins was the first woman to be given an honorary Litt.D. by Columbia University; Smith, her alma mater, conferred an LL.D. on her in 1910. In 1918 she was the first woman elected president of the American Philosophical Association; she was one of the few persons to hold the presidencies of both the American Psychological Association and the American Philosophical Association and the only woman ever to do so. In 1927 she lectured on conceptions of meaning and value at Bedford College of the University of London. In 1928 she was made an honorary member of the British Psychological Association, the only woman of her time to receive such an honor.

To Calkins, philosophy was not a set of abstractions but a guide to living. Her philosophical ideas motivated her to be socially and politically active: she was particularly interested in the issues of women's suffrage, labor unions, and industrial problems. Her socialist beliefs had been expressed in her first book, *Sharing the Profits* (1888). An officer of the Consumer League and a member of the Social Science Club of Newton, the Civil Liberties Union, and the Fellowship of Reconciliation, she was a friend and supporter of the social worker Jane Addams and the Socialist politician Norman Thomas. She advocated pacifism during World War I and protested the 1921 trial of the Italian anarchists Nicola Sacco and Bartolomeo Vanzetti for a robbery and murder in South Braintree, Massachusetts (they were executed in 1927). In *In Memoriam: Mary Whiton Calkins 1863–1930* Brightman noted that Calkins had

a keen sense of social justice . . . such causes as world peace and the Sacco-Vanzetti case elicited public utterances and whole-hearted loyalty from her. . . . She firmly believed that practical consequences followed from philosophy and she was deeply impressed by Royce's doctrine of the "Beloved Community," from which she inferred the

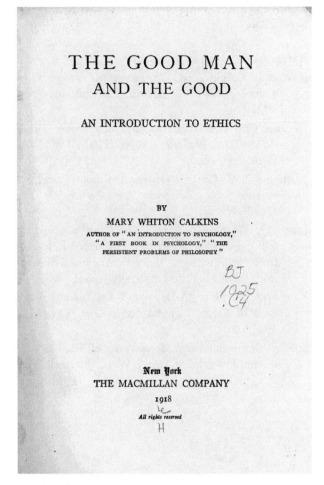

THE GOOD MAN
AND THE GOOD

AN INTRODUCTION TO ETHICS

BY

MARY WHITON CALKINS

AUTHOR OF " AN INTRODUCTION TO PSYCHOLOGY,"
"A FIRST BOOK IN PSYCHOLOGY," "THE
PERSISTENT PROBLEMS OF PHILOSOPHY "

New York
THE MACMILLAN COMPANY
1918
All rights reserved

Title page for Calkins's textbook on moral theory (Thomas Cooper Library, University of South Carolina)

solidarity of the human race and the duty of international cooperation. . . . The sense of social justice which led her to be devoted to the cause of the Great Society was extended in her thinking to the Cosmic Society, which she conceived as unified in the Absolute Self.

Mary Whiton Calkins was working on a book on religion at her death on 26 February 1930. Several of her students paid tribute to her in *In Memoriam: Mary Whiton Calkins 1863–1930:* "Best of all the people I have known, Miss Calkins lived her own beautiful philosophy," "I know of no one who lived more completely what she taught," and "She has been to me one of the most inspiring personalities I have known, not only to scholarly work, but to vigorous and enthusiastic living." The most apt tribute was from Brightman: "She believed that the aim of philosophy was 'to provide a sound theoretical foundation for noble living' and she fulfilled that aim in her life."

References:

Raymond Calkins, ed., *In Memoriam: Mary Whiton Calkins 1863–1930* (Boston: Merrymount Press, 1931);

Florence Converse, *Wellesley College: A Chronicle of Years 1875–1938* (Wellesley, Mass.: Hathaway House Bookshop, 1939);

Josephine Nash Curtis, "On the Psychology and Science of Selves," *American Journal of Psychology,* 26 (1915): 69–97;

Diana De Kryger-Monsman, "The Conception of the Self in Absolute Idealism with Special Reference to the Philosophy of Mary W. Calkins," dissertation, Johns Hopkins University, 1934;

Eleanor A. Gamble, "A Defense of Psychology as Science of Selves," *Psychological Bulletin,* 12 (1915): 194–202;

Stanley Grannum, "The Metaphysics of Self Involved in the Thought of James Ward, Fredrick Tennant, and Mary Whiton Calkins," dissertation, Boston University, 1949;

Edna Heidbreder, "Mary Whiton Calkins: A Discussion," *Journal of the History of the Behavioral Sciences,* 8 (1972): 56–68;

Albert C. Knudson, *The Philosophy of Personalism* (New York: Abingdon Press, 1927);

Bruce Kuklick, *The Rise of American Philosophy: Cambridge, Massachusetts 1860–1930* (New Haven: Yale University Press, 1977);

Josiah Royce, "Comment by Professor Royce: Extracts from a Letter to Miss Calkins," in John McDermott, ed., *Papers in Honor of Josiah Royce* (New York: Longmans, Green, 1916);

Sharon Scherwitz, "Mary Whiton Calkins on Self and Person," M.A. thesis, Southern Illinois University at Carbondale, 1980;

Gummaraju Srinivasan, *Personalism: An Evaluation of Hindu and Western Types* (Dehli: Research Publications in Social Sciences, 1972);

Orlo Strunk, "The Self-Psychology of Mary Whiton Calkins," *Journal of the History of the Behavioral Sciences,* 8 (1972): 196–203.

Rudolf Carnap

(18 May 1891 – 14 September 1970)

Alan Richardson
University of British Columbia

BOOKS: *Der Raum: Ein Beitrag zur Wissenschaftslehre,* Kant-Studien, Ergänzungshefte, no. 56 (Berlin: Reuther & Reichard, 1922);

Physikalische Begriffsbildung, Wissen und Wirken, volume 39 (Karlsruhe: Braun, 1926);

Der logische Aufbau der Welt (Berlin-Schlachtensee: Welt-kreis, 1928; enlarged edition, Hamburg: Meiner, 1961); translated by Rolf A. George as "The Logical Structure of the World," in *The Logical Structure of the World; Pseudoproblems in Philosophy* (Berkeley & Los Angeles: University of California Press, 1967; London: Routledge & Kegan Paul, 1967), pp. 5–300;

Scheinprobleme in der Philosophie: Das Fremdpsychische und der Realismusstreit (Berlin-Schlachtensee: Weltkreis, 1928); translated by George as "Pseudoproblems in Philosophy," in *The Logical Structure of the World; Pseudoproblems in Philosophy,* pp. 305–343;

Abriss der Logistik mit besonderer Berücksichtigung der Relationstheorie und ihrer Anwendungen, Schriften zur wissenschaftlichen Weltauffassung, volume 2 (Vienna: Springer, 1929);

Wissenschaftliche Weltauffassung: Der Wiener Kreis, by Carnap, Hans Hahn, and Otto Neurath (Vienna: Wolf, 1929); translated by Robert S. Cohen and Maria Neurath as *Scientific World-Conception: The Vienna Circle* (Dordrecht, Netherlands: Reidel, 1983);

The Unity of Science, revised and translated by Max Black, Psyche Miniatures, General Series, no. 63 (London: Kegan Paul, Trench, Trübner, 1934);

Logische Syntax der Sprache, Schriften zur wissenschaftlichen Weltauffassung, volume 8 (Vienna: Springer, 1934); translated by Amethe Smeaton, Countess von Zeppelin, as *The Logical Syntax of Language* (London: Kegan Paul, Trench, Trübner, 1937; New York: Harcourt, Brace, 1937);

Die Aufgabe der Wissenschaftslogik, Einheitswissenschaft, no. 3 (Vienna: Gerold, 1934); translated by Hans Kaal as "The Task of the Logic of Science," in *Unified Science: The Vienna Circle Monograph Series*

Originally Edited by Otto Neurath, edited by Brian McGuinness (Dordrecht, the Netherlands & Boston: Reidel, 1987), pp. 46–66;

Philosophy and Logical Syntax, Psyche Miniatures, General Series, no. 70 (London: Kegan Paul, Trench, Trübner, 1935; Cleveland: Bell & Howell, 1963);

Studies in Semantics, 2 volumes (Cambridge, Mass.: Harvard University Press, 1942, 1943; London: Geoffrey Cumberlege, Oxford University Press, 1942, 1943)—comprises volume 1, *Introduction to Semantics;* volume 2, *Formalization of Logic;*

Meaning and Necessity: A Study in Semantics and Modal Logic (Chicago: University of Chicago Press, 1947; enlarged, 1956);

Logical Foundations of Probability (Chicago: University of Chicago Press, 1950; London: Routledge & Kegan Paul, 1951; revised and enlarged, 1962);

The Continuum of Inductive Methods (Chicago: University of Chicago Press, 1952);

An Outline of a Theory of Semantic Information, by Carnap and Yehoshua Bar-Hillel (Cambridge, Mass.: Research Laboratory of Electronics, Massachusetts Institute of Technology, 1952);

Einführung in die symbolische Logik, mit besonderer Berücksichtigung ihrer Anwendungen (Vienna: Springer, 1954); translated by William H. Meyer and John Wilkinson as *Introduction to Symbolic Logic and its Applications* (New York: Dover, 1958); German version revised and enlarged (Vienna: Springer, 1960);

Induktive Logik und Wahrscheinlichkeit, edited by Wolfgang Stegmüller (Vienna: Springer, 1959);

Philosophical Foundations of Physics: An Introduction to the Philosophy of Science, edited by Martin Gardner (New York: Basic Books, 1966); republished as *An Introduction to Philosophy of Science* (New York & London: Basic Books, 1974);

Two Essays on Entropy, edited by Abner Shimony (Berkeley & London: University of California Press, 1977).

OTHER: Walter Dubislav, *Die Definition,* edited by Carnap and Hans Reichenbach (Leipzig: Meiner, 1931);

International Encyclopedia of Unified Science, 19 parts in 2 volumes, edited, with contributions, by Carnap, Otto Neurath, and Charles Morris (Chicago & London: University of Chicago Press, 1938–1970); republished as *Foundations of the Unity of Science: Toward an International Encyclopedia of Unified Science,* 2 volumes (Chicago: University of Chicago Press, 1955, 1970);

"Truth and Confirmation," in *Readings in Philosophical Analysis,* edited by Herbert Feigl and Wilfrid Sellars (New York: Appleton-Century-Crofts, 1949), pp. 119–127;

"The Methodological Character of Theoretical Concepts," in *The Foundations of Science and the Concepts of Psychology and Psychoanalysis,* edited by Feigl and Michael Scriven (Minneapolis: University of Minnesota Press, 1956), pp. 38–76;

Hans Reichenbach, *The Philosophy of Space and Time,* translated by Maria Reichenbach and John Freund, introduction by Carnap (New York: Dover, 1958);

Reichenbach, *Modern Philosophy of Science: Selected Essays,* translated and edited by Maria Reichenbach, foreword by Carnap (London: Routledge & Kegan Paul, 1959);

"The Elimination of Metaphysics through Logical Analysis of Language," translated by Arthur Pap, in *Logical Positivism,* edited by A. J. Ayer (New York: Free Press, 1959), pp. 60–81;

"Intellectual Autobiography" and "Replies and Systematic Expositions," in *The Philosophy of Rudolf Carnap,* edited by Paul Arthur Schilpp, The Library of Living Philosophers, volume 11 (La Salle, Ill.: Open Court / London: Cambridge University Press, 1963), pp. 3–84, 859–1018;

Studies in Inductive Logic and Probability, 2 volumes, edited, with contributions, by Carnap and Richard Jeffrey (Berkeley, Los Angeles & London: University of California Press, 1971, 1980).

SELECTED PERIODICAL PUBLICATIONS–UNCOLLECTED: "Über Protokollsätze," *Erkenntnis,* 3 (December 1932): 215–228; translated by Richard Creath and Richard Nollan as "On Protocol Sentences," *Noûs,* 21 (December 1987): 457–470;

"On the Character of Philosophic Problems," translated by Alexander Malisoff, *Philosophy of Science,* 1 (January 1934): 5–19;

"Testability and Meaning," *Philosophy of Science,* 3 (October 1936): 419–471; 4 (January 1937): 1–40.

Rudolf Carnap was a leading member of the Vienna Circle and a major exponent of logical empiricism. The Vienna Circle was a group of scientists and philosophers who met in Vienna from the early 1920s to the late 1930s. Led by Moritz Schlick, Professor of the Philosophy of the Inductive Sciences at the University of Vienna, the Vienna Circle included the economist and sociologist Otto Neurath; the mathematicians Hans Hahn, Karl Menger, and Kurt Gödel; the physicist Philipp Frank; the historian and sociologist Edgar Zilsel; and the philosophers Friedrich Waissman, Felix Kaufmann, and Herbert Feigl. Inspired by the techniques of modern science and the development of mathematical logic, the Vienna Circle promoted a philosophical approach, known at first as logical positivism and later as logical empiricism, that aimed not at the establishment of truths about a realm of objects thought to be peculiar to philosophy but at the clarification of the meanings of words and statements and at the promotion of strict scientific standards in philosophy. The Vienna Circle self-consciously built on similar efforts in earlier positivism, in phenomenology, in neo-Kantianism, and in the early writings of Ludwig Wittgenstein.

Carnap's work in Vienna and, later, in the United States was influential in setting the agenda of analytic philosophy in the twentieth century. Carnap was perhaps the major advocate within the logical empiricist movement of the new mathematical logic, and his writings on the logic of scientific confirmation, formal semantics, probability theory, and the theory of information showed both the strengths and the limitations of formal logic as a tool for conceptual clarification. Pioneering the semantics of modal logic, the development of alternative logical systems, Bayesian confirmation theory, and the logic of decision, he pointed the way to many of the central areas of technical philosophy today. Perhaps most significantly, his debates with W. V. Quine on the distinction between analytic and synthetic statements were a key moment in the development of a new understanding of the nature of analytic philosophy.

Carnap was born on 18 May 1891 in Ronsdorf in the Wuppertal region of Germany to Johannes S. Carnap, a ribbon manufacturer, and Anna Carnap, née Dörpfeld, a schoolteacher. Carnap's mother taught him at home, imbuing him with a spirit of tolerance. Carnap was inspired by watching her write a book on the life and ideas of her father, the teacher and pastor Friedrich Wilhelm Dörpfeld, that was published in 1897; in his "Intellectual Autobiography" in *The Philosophy of Rudolf Carnap* (1963) Carnap says, "I was fascinated by the magical activity of putting words on paper, and I have loved it ever since." After Carnap's father died in 1898, the family moved to the nearby town of Barmen, where Carnap attended the gymnasium.

From 1910 to 1914 Carnap studied mathematics, physics, and philosophy at the University of Jena and the University of Freiburg in Breisgau. He received his first major philosophical inspiration at the University of Jena in 1910 when he took the logic course taught by Gottlob Frege; he later took two more courses with Frege on logic and mathematics and began to see the philosophical importance of the new mathematical logic that was being developed by Frege and by Bertrand Russell in England.

Carnap began studying physics at the graduate level in 1913 with the intention of taking a doctorate in the subject, but with the outbreak of World War I in 1914 Carnap, despite his pacificist and internationalist leanings, enlisted in the German army and was sent to the front. In 1917 he was transferred to an electronics laboratory in Berlin that was developing a wireless telegraph and wireless telephone. During this period he became more actively engaged in socialist and internationalist causes.

After the war ended in 1918, Carnap returned to the University of Jena. His interest in logic and the

Entrance to the Mathematical Seminar of the University of Vienna, where the Vienna Circle met from 1922 to 1939

methodology of relativistic physics led him to decide to write a thesis in which he would try to find an axiom system for physical kinematics. Unable to find anyone in the physics or philosophy departments capable of supervising such a thesis, he switched to a more general discussion of the philosophical foundations of geometry. Bruno Bauch, a neo-Kantian at Jena, supervised the thesis, which was completed in 1921 and published in 1922 as a supplementary volume of the journal *Kant-Studien* under the title *Der Raum: Ein Beitrag zur Wissenschaftslehre* (Space: A Contribution to the Theory of Knowledge).

Der Raum is an attempt to clarify what is at issue in debates over the nature and source of knowledge of space. Carnap distinguishes three kinds of space: formal space, which is dealt with in geometry; intuitive space, which the philosophical discipline known as phenomenology takes as its object of study; and physical space, which is the province of physics. Following the mathematician David Hilbert and, especially, Russell, he argues that formal space is a pure relational structure defined by axioms; the study of it is thus a branch of logic. He agrees with the mathematician Henri Poincaré that the metrical structure of physical space is a convention: that is, mathematical physics requires quantitative concepts such as distance, velocity, and acceleration, which are derived from the coordination of a purely logical structure of formal geometry with experience, which does not intrinsically have a metrical structure. The choice of metric geometry is thus a convention that is not based on experience but that makes mathematical physics possible. Intuitive space performs two roles for Carnap. First, he argues that what is available in the intuition of spatial objects is not a full metric geometry but only a local topological geometry stitched together in such a fashion as to allow a metric structure to be imposed on it. Second, appeal to a sort of intuition that he associates with the phenomenologist Edmund Husserl—a so-called eidetic intuition or *Wesensschau* (intuition of essences)—allows Carnap a way of explaining the peculiarly spatial features of space. That is, the formal structures of mathematical space have potentially infinitely many models, including models that are not "spatial"—for example, the space of colors has a structure that can be modeled as a formal axiom system. Intuition allows physical geometry to be about space and not about colors, tones, or any other structure of experientially available objects.

Der Raum illustrates a key characteristic of Carnap's philosophy from the beginning to the end of his career: by clarifying the subject matters appropriate to mathematics, philosophy, and physics, he is trying to persuade mathematicians, philosophers, and physicists that they are talking about different things, thereby putting an end to fruitless battles among the practitioners of those disciplines. Clarifying concepts always had a pacifying function for Carnap, who saw philosophical disputes as arising largely from a lack of clarity in regard to the notions that are allegedly at issue.

Carnap lived in Buchenbach, near Freiburg, from 1921 until 1926. Although he claims in his "Intellectual Autobiography" to have spent this time in "relative isolation," Herbert Spiegelberg maintains that Carnap took part in Husserl's advanced seminars in phenomenology at Freiburg in 1924 and 1925. He also continued to work on the methodology of physics. His interest in this topic was motivated by the development of relativity theory, which seemed to provide a reason to believe that non-Euclidean geometry had a physical significance and also to support his idea that metrical structures, and quantitative concepts generally, are not derived from but imposed on experience. Carnap radicalized his understanding of conventionalism in his monograph *Physikalische Begriffsbildung* (Physical Concept Formation, 1926), where he makes two key claims. First, quantitative concepts and mathematically

expressed laws are the hallmark of the objectivity of science, because they abstract from the particular qualitative "feel" of individual experience and allow each person to find, via mathematical transformations, the objects spoken of by others. Second, quantitative concepts are not derived from experience but coordinated with it. Thus, all objective scientific knowledge has a conventional element.

During his years in Buchenbach, Carnap began to think about the project of a general epistemology, or theory of knowledge, that he gave the Husserlian title "constitution theory." This epistemology would show how an objective conceptual understanding of the world can be achieved despite the fact that knowledge begins in the flux of experience; it would show how one can go, as he wrote in the title of an unpublished manuscript of 1922, "from chaos to reality."

In 1926 Carnap was hired as a *Privatdozent* (unsalaried lecturer) at the University of Vienna. His mandatory *Habilitationsschrift* (inaugural dissertation) was an elaboration of his epistemological project and a draft for what became his first major contribution to philosophy, *Der logische Aufbau der Welt* (translated as "The Logical Structure of the World," 1967). Carnap's main preoccupation from 1922 until its publication in 1928, *Der logische Aufbau der Welt* is a philosophical tour de force that operates on several levels. At the most general level Carnap seeks to inform his readers of the philosophical usefulness of modern logic. The "constitution theory" at the heart of *Der logische Aufbau der Welt* is, in essence, a general theory of concept definition using the symbolic language of the second edition (1925–1927) of Russell and Alfred North Whitehead's *Principia Mathematica* (1910–1913); the theory, because it is part of logic, could be employed anywhere in philosophy or science. At a more specific level the bulk of the book is an extended example of the power of constitution theory to transform epistemology: Carnap seeks to show how knowledge of an objective world is possible in science, despite the subjective origins of knowledge in individual sensation.

Two major interpretations of *Der logische Aufbau der Welt* exist. According to the first, the work is a high-water mark of reductionist empiricism in that it sketches a procedure by which all concepts of science are ultimately definable in terms of sensation. Quine states this empiricist interpretation succinctly in his "Epistemology Naturalized" (1969): "To account for the external world as a logical construct of sense data—such, in Russell's term, was the program. It was Carnap, in his *Der logische Aufbau der Welt* of 1928, who came nearest to executing it." With this work Carnap seems to have become truly a logical empiricist: logic serves as the language and the tool with which to show that all legitimate discourse is ultimately about experience. The final main section of the book, accordingly, is given over to showing how the concepts of metaphysics are not definable in terms of experience and, thus, are not scientifically legitimate. Logic and empiricism join to form a positivism dedicated to the elimination of metaphysics.

The strict empiricist interpretation of *Der logische Aufbau der Welt* has, however, come under attack. Quine admits that although, on his interpretation, the whole point of *Der logische Aufbau der Welt* is to define all legitimate scientific concepts in terms of experience, Carnap's actual procedure changes at the crucial moment. Just at the point, beginning in section 126, when the sensory qualities are moved from inside the individual mind and projected onto a physical space-time manifold, Carnap drops strict definition in favor of methodological rules of assignment. Thus, Carnap's own procedure seems to indicate that the concepts of science cannot be defined in terms of experience. Moreover, this result is not surprising: the impossibility of defining physical concepts in terms of experience was the whole point of the conventionalism that Carnap was advocating at the same time he was writing *Der logische Aufbau der Welt*. If conventionalism is correct, then the project of explicit definition should break down right where it does; and indeed, Carnap speaks in conventionalist terms in precisely those sections. The incompatibility of strict definition and conventionalism has led to a robust literature of interpretation of *Der logische Aufbau der Welt* that has paid greater attention to the phenomenological, neo-Kantian, and conventionalist contexts in which the work was written.

Despite these complications, the general direction of Carnap's project is clear enough: he was endeavoring to reform philosophy by adopting modern logic as a general language for conceptual understanding with a view to demarcating legitimate and meaningful concepts from the pseudoconcepts that had traditionally infected the discipline. He pursues this theme with gusto in his 1928 pamphlet, *Scheinprobleme in der Philosophie: Das Fremdpsychische und der Realismusstreit* (translated as "Pseudoproblems in Philosophy," 1967). His general point of view is illustrated in his discussions of the controversy in regard to realism in metaphysics. In Carnap's view a scientifically acceptable distinction between the real and the unreal is easy to draw: for example, horses are real, and unicorns are not real, because horses have existed in space and time and unicorns have not. This clear and useful distinction is not, however, what seems to be at stake in disputes among metaphysicians over, for example, the reality of material objects. Realists and idealists agree that mountains, for example, are real in a sense that unicorns or trolls are

Moritz Schlick, the leader of the Vienna Circle

not, but they want to say something more: realists claim that mountains are wholly independent of minds, and idealists disagree. Always the pacifist, Carnap worries that this dispute is not resolvable, since no bit of evidence tells in favor of one hypothesis and against the other; the "dependence on the mind" at issue here is not the same as when one says that optical illusions or auditory hallucinations are dependent on the mind. According to Carnap, this situation provides a criterion for detecting nonsense: if two seemingly opposed theses cannot be distinguished by any evidence, they are pseudotheses; and either at least one concept in them is a pseudoconcept, or they are both logically ill formed. In the realism dispute the pseudoconcept is that of reality, since neither the empirical concept of reality nor any other concept that allows sense to be made of the dispute is at stake.

Carnap had joined the Vienna Circle, then still a private discussion group organized by Schlick and meeting in the Mathematical Seminar of the University of Vienna, on his arrival at the university in 1926. Among the works the group read was Wittgenstein's *Tractatus Logico-Philosophicus* (1921), and several of the members met occasionally with Wittgenstein. Carnap's relations with Wittgenstein were tense, and Wittgenstein soon requested that Carnap not come to any more face-to-face meetings with him.

In 1929, in celebration of Schlick's decision to remain in Vienna rather than accept a position at the University of Bonn, the Vienna Circle entered its public phase with the publication of a pamphlet, *Wissenschaftliche Weltauffassung: Der Wiener Kreis* (translated as *Scientific World-Conception: The Vienna Circle,* 1983), by Carnap, Neurath, and Hahn, which sought to give a general introduction to the spirit of the philosophy pursued by the group. Expressing the technoscientific and social-democratic political vision of the Vienna Circle, the pamphlet argues that science and a scientific philosophy are the means to a more rational way of life and a more just social order. At the same time, a wider group, the Verein Ernst Mach (Ernst Mach Society), was promoting the scientific world-conception in public lectures throughout the city. The activities of the Vienna Circle began to take on an international scope with a conference on scientific philosophy held in Prague in 1929; it was organized in conjunction with the Berlin Society for Empirical/Scientific Philosophy, which included Hans Reichenbach and Richard von Mises among its members.

In 1929 Carnap published a short introduction to modern logic, *Abriss der Logistik mit besonderer Berücksichtigung der Relationstheorie und ihrer Anwendungen* (Outline of Logistics with Particular Attention to the Theory of Relations and Its Applications), as part of a series of monographs, "Schriften zur wissenschaftlichen Weltauffassung" (Writings on the Scientific World-Conception), edited by Schlick and Frank. The first half of the book is a fairly standard introduction to the logical system of *Principia Mathematica;* the second half, which is more indicative of Carnap's own interests, is given over to applications of the system. Here Carnap sketches the constitution theory of *Der logische Aufbau der Welt* and gives the bare bones of his abandoned thesis project, the axiomatization of physical kinematics. The book leaves no doubt that in Carnap's eyes the significance of the new logic is as a tool for conceptual clarification, not as a source of substantive knowledge.

In 1930 Carnap and Reichenbach became the editors of a new journal, *Erkenntnis* (Knowledge), that promoted scientific philosophy—especially the sort of scientific philosophy that was dubbed logical positivism by Schlick's former student, Feigl, in 1931. *Erkenntnis* became the main organ of the Vienna Circle and published many influential statements of logical positivist philosophy, including Carnap's 1932 article, "Überwendung der Metaphysik durch logische Analyse der Sprache," which became famous in the English-speaking world with its 1959 translation as "Elimina-

tion of Metaphysics through Logical Analysis of Language." In this paper Carnap uses arguments familiar from *Der logische Aufbau der Welt* and *Scheinprobleme in der Philosophie* to target what he considers the obscurantism of Martin Heidegger's existentialist philosophy. Taking Heidegger's pronouncement in *Was ist Metaphysik?* (1929; translated as "What Is Metaphysics?" 1977) that "Das Nichts selbst nichtet" (The Nothing itself nothings [or nihilates]) as his central case, Carnap shows that Heidegger's language violates logical constraints on meaningfulness and is therefore, quite literally, nonsense.

Erkenntnis also published many disputes among the members of the Vienna Circle; the best known is the at times acrimonious "protocol sentence dispute" over the experiential foundations of knowledge. In a review of *Der logische Aufbau der Welt* in 1928 Neurath had argued that in Carnap's account experience is private and subjective and thus indescribable in the language of science. Neurath favored the view that the foundations of empirical knowledge are neither private experiences nor reports of such experiences but so-called protocol sentences that are couched in the language of physical science and report intersubjectively available events—sentences such as "Otto reports that he saw the pointer read '2' at 3:15 P.M." Neurath's view led away from the idealism or subjectivism he saw in *Der logische Aufbau der Welt* to physicalism, the doctrine that all of reality is material. Responding to Neurath in 1932 in his *Erkenntnis* article "Über Protokollsätze" (translated as "On Protocol Sentences," 1987), Carnap argues that the question as to the foundations of knowledge is not itself a factual one: it is a matter of expediency and convention. For logical reasons, the foundations of empirical knowledge have to be sentences, not experiences, but which sentences are protocol sentences is determined by convention. Carnap prefers protocol sentences taken from within the language of science—thus far he agrees with Neurath—but this preference is, for him, not an expression of a fact about the structure of empirical knowledge but a choice of a framework for reconstructing or rationalizing such knowledge.

In 1931 Carnap had become Professor of the Philosophy of the Natural Sciences at the University of Prague, but he maintained close personal and professional relationships with the other members of the Vienna Circle. His work in the early 1930s centered around three main concerns: the foundations of empirical knowledge, the status of logic, and the nature of the philosophical enterprise. The three came together in a 1932 *Erkenntnis* essay that was translated, revised, and augmented by Max Black and published in 1934 as *The Unity of Science.* Carnap's first major piece to appear in

English, *The Unity of Science* introduces a key element of his mature point of view: the distinction between the formal and the material modes of speech. His continuing effort to distinguish genuine philosophical problems from pseudoproblems leads Carnap to conclude that philosophy deals with logical structures and that logic inheres in language; the confusions of earlier philosophers stemmed from the mistaken belief that philosophy is about things rather than about linguistic structures. For example, philosophers concerned with the foundations of mathematics tried to make sense of the metaphysical status of abstract objects such as numbers, mathematical points, and the continuum. Carnap thinks that the way out of such fruitless pursuits is to see the questions as being not about numbers but about proposals for the use of languages that include numerals as basic terms. In *The Unity of Science* he proposes to translate all "material mode" philosophical claims into a more proper "formal mode"; thus, a "philosophical" sentence such as "Five is a number" would become "'5' is a numeral." Sentences that resist translation into the formal mode–for example, "Numbers subsist in a realm of abstract entities"–are pseudosentences that have no meaning. Among the key uses of the formal mode of speech would be the elimination of talk of "experience" and "the structure of experience" in discussions of empirical knowledge in favor of "protocol sentences" and "the logical structure of the protocol language." With this move the philosopher is excused from having to provide an account of the nature of subjective experience and can see himself or herself as engaged in constructing languages for empirical science.

On 8 February 1933 Carnap married Elizabeth Ina von Stöger; they had four children. During this period Carnap's reputation spread to the English-speaking world, where a few of his Vienna Circle colleagues had immigrated to escape the rise of fascism in Austria. The new American journal *Philosophy of Science* published Carnap's "On the Character of Philosophic Problems" in a translation by the editor, Alexander Malisoff, as the lead article in the first issue in January 1934. In the early and mid 1930s several leading philosophers from the United States and Great Britain, including Quine, A. J. Ayer, Ernest Nagel, and Charles Morris, visited Carnap and attended meetings of the Vienna Circle, taking home with them the spirit of logical positivism.

Carnap's own work was becoming increasingly technical as he dealt with the foundations of logic and mathematics. In his next book, *Logische Syntax der Sprache* (1934; translated as *The Logical Syntax of Language,* 1937), which is often considered his masterpiece, Carnap, building on the work in metalogic (the study of the components of systems of logic) by Hilbert, Gödel, and Alfred Tarski, attempts to erect a

VERÖFFENTLICHUNGEN DES
VEREINES ERNST MACH

WISSENSCHAFTLICHE WELTAUFFASSUNG

DER WIENER KREIS

HERAUSGEGEBEN VOM VEREIN ERNST MACH
1929   PREIS S 2.— (RM 1.20)
ARTUR WOLF VERLAG / WIEN

Title page for the manifesto of the Vienna Circle, in which Carnap, Otto Neurath, and Hans Hahn state the group's logical positivist philosophy (from Friedrich Stadler, The Vienna Circle: Studies in the Origins, Development, and Influence of Logical Empiricism, *2001)*

general framework for discussing logical systems and for distinguishing the logical and empirical portions of any given language. Philosophy, he says, can only be the investigation of the logical systems of scientific knowledge if the language of science can be divided into logical and empirical parts–the logical parts providing the meanings of the terms of the language and the empirical parts expressing potential facts about the objects referred to by those terms.

In *Logische Syntax der Sprache* Carnap for the first time includes logic in the scope of tolerance, arguing that alternative logical systems are possible and that the proper business of metalogic is the investigation of a potentially infinite number of properly constructed logical languages. "Logical syntax" is Carnap's term for a metalogical discipline designed to provide precise descriptions of the formation and transformation rules that constitute a proper logical framework. The task of the philosopher is to propose languages to be used for certain purposes; "logical syntax" is the name of the philosophical language within which such proposals are made. This attitude toward logic is encapsulated in Carnap's gloss on his "Principle of Tolerance" in *The Logical Syntax of Language:*

> *In logic, there are no morals.* Everyone is at liberty to build up his own logic, i.e. his own form of language, as he wishes. All that is required of him is that, if he wishes to discuss it, he must state his methods clearly and give syntactical rules rather than philosophical arguments.

Carnap's thoughts on these matters were influenced by the recent publication of Gödel's two "incompleteness theorems." Gödel had shown that the logical system of *Principia Mathematica* is incomplete, in the sense that a true arithmetical sentence exists that can be formulated in the language of *Principia Mathematica* but cannot be proved in the logical system of the work, provided that the system is consistent (if it were inconsistent, everything could be proved in it). The sentence that is not provable in *Principia Mathematica*–called "the Gödel sentence"–is a sentence that "says" of itself that it is not provable in *Principia Mathematica*. Gödel had, moreover, shown in his second incompleteness theorem that the sentence "If *Principia Mathematica* is consistent, then the Gödel sentence is not provable and, thus, true" is itself provable in the system of *Principia Mathematica*. Two important points follow from Gödel's results. First, arithmetical truth is not the same as provability in the language of Russell and Whitehead's logic; after all, Gödel has constructed a sentence that is true but not provable in that logic. Second, the second incompleteness theorem rules out the possibility that the consistency of *Principia Mathematica* is provable in the logic of *Principia Mathematica*: if the logic of *Principia Mathematica* could prove its own consistency, then one could prove the Gödel sentence in it; but if one could prove the Gödel sentence in it, one could prove that *Principia Mathematica* was not consistent. Thus, any proof of its own consistency in *Principia Mathematica* would show that *Principia Mathematica* was inconsistent. This paradox seemed to rule out the so-called Hilbert Program in the foundations of mathematics once and for all: Hilbert had tried to show, using only the resources of finitary mathematics–a foundationally unproblematic fragment of classical mathematics that refers only to finite numbers and does not quantify over infinite sets–that all of classical mathematics was consistent, but Gödel showed that any proof of the consistency of classical mathematics has to use resources that are beyond the scope of classical mathematics.

Gödel's work interacted with Carnap's in several ways. First, Gödel's theorems were examples of the important results that can be achieved only in metalogic. In *Principia Mathematica* Russell and Whitehead had simply employed their logical system without inquiring into its adequacy to the job of logically securing all mathematical truths; Gödel's theorems were proofs about *Principia Mathematica* rather than proofs within it. By taking logical systems as his topic, Gödel was able to move the debates about the foundations of mathematics forward. Carnap's general project was to provide a precise rendering of the resources needed for the sort of metalogical work Gödel had done.

Second, Gödel's results suggested to Carnap a crucial distinction between logical proof or deduction, on the one hand, and logical consequence, on the other. Saying that the Gödel sentence is true means that it is a consequence of the axioms of *Principia Mathematica*. Gödel's theorems, however, show that the Gödel sentence cannot be deduced from the axioms. The theorems thus require a distinction between consequence and proof; and Carnap, in *Logische Syntax der Sprache,* attempts to define this distinction rigorously.

Third, and perhaps most important, Gödel's results placed severe restrictions on what could be done in Carnap's program. Carnap was interested in analyzing scientific languages, such as that of the General Theory of Relativity, to investigate questions such as whether claims made in them (for example, the curvature of space-time in the language of the General Theory of Relativity) were logico-mathematical or physical and empirical ones in those languages. His key problem was how to divide a language into logico-mathematical or analytic sentences, on the one hand, and empirical or synthetic sentences, on the other hand. Gödel's theorems entail that for any language of scientific interest– that is, any language that includes classical mathematics–the division between the analytic and synthetic sentences has to be given in a syntax language of greater mathematical strength than the original language. But since the distinction was supposed to use only the analytic resources of the syntax language–philosophy is an a priori, not an empirical, discipline–a regress problem arises: to show that the syntactic definition of analyticity for the object language is legitimate, one must give a definition of analyticity for the syntax language, but that is only possible by ascending into a "metalanguage" stronger than the syntax language, which itself has to be investigated in turn, and so on. This regress raises questions about whether the division between the analytic and synthetic sentences of a language can be drawn in any informative and precise fashion.

Carnap's fame spread in the wake of *Logische Syntax der Sprache*. In 1934 he was invited to give a series of lectures on logical syntax at the University of London. During this trip he met Russell and had discussions with his host, the logician L. Susan Stebbing, and C. K. Ogden, who had translated Wittgenstein's *Tractatus Logico-*

Philosophicus and shared Carnap's interest in international languages (Carnap spoke Esperanto; Ogden was a leader of the "Basic English" movement). Revised versions of Carnap's London lectures were published in 1935 as *Philosophy and Logical Syntax*. Also, Quine had been in Prague when Carnap's wife was preparing the typescript for *Logische Syntax der Sprache* and had been able to read the work before its publication; he gave a series of lectures on Carnap's philosophy when he returned to Harvard University in 1935.

By the mid 1930s the rise of fascism in Germany and Austria had crushed the hopeful internationalist and progressivist politics that the Vienna Circle had confidently endorsed in 1929, and many of the members were trying to emigrate from Europe. The Carnaps left Prague for the United States in December 1935; Carnap never again resided in Europe. Amid the general political horror of European fascism, a more personal tragedy struck the Vienna Circle on 22 June 1936, when a deranged former student, Hans Nelböck, shot and killed Schlick on the steps of the main building of the University of Vienna. Perhaps even more shocking than the event itself was the reaction to the murder in the Austrian popular press, which claimed that Schlick's scientific philosophy had created the conditions for spiritual crisis in his students and that Nelböck had simply acted as one might expect of someone who had been deprived of his values. Johann Sauter, a lecturer in philosophy of law at the University of Vienna writing under the pseudonym "Doktor Austriacus," made the inevitable connection with the Jews, who, according to Sauter, celebrated Schlick as their foremost thinker. (In fact, Schlick was not Jewish.)

Carnap was awarded an honorary doctorate at the Harvard University tercentenary celebrations in September 1936. A one-term visiting position at the University of Chicago in the winter quarter of 1936 led to a continuing appointment as professor of philosophy the following fall. His reception at Harvard and Chicago had been arranged by Quine and Morris, respectively.

During this period Carnap came to understand and accept Tarski's work in the semantics of formal languages. It was a moment of great illumination for Carnap, since traditional semantic terms such as "true" had been problematic for logical empiricism. The traditional correspondence theory of truth holds that a sentence such as "Snow is white" is true because the sentence refers to a state of affairs that does, in fact, exist. The logical empiricists regarded the correspondence theory as a metaphysical pseudothesis, because it requires a sentence to speak both of language and of the world simultaneously. Tarski's accomplishment, in Carnap's eyes, was to make talk of truth scientifically

Carnap in 1935, the year he immigrated to the United States (photograph by Francis Schmidt)

acceptable by showing how to remove the metaphysics from the intuition behind the correspondence theory. The correspondence theory gets its plausibility from the fact that claims such as "'Snow is white' is true if and only if snow is, in fact, white" are accepted as a matter of course. Such claims are read by correspondence theorists as indicating that truth is a correspondence between sentences or propositions, on the one hand, and facts, states of affairs, or aspects of reality, on the other hand. Tarski's key idea was to convert the claim to one about language. He thought that one had an adequate definition of truth for a language if that definition allowed one to derive in the metalanguage all of the "T-sentences" (sentences such as "'Snow is white' is true if and only if snow is white") for the language. He then showed how to construct such a definition of truth for formal languages. Talk of truth thus becomes, in essence, not a matching of sentences and reality but a translation procedure from the object language, for which the truth definition is given, to the metalanguage, within which the truth definition for the object language is given.

Tarski's ideas helped Carnap on two fronts. In philosophy of science and epistemology they allowed him, finally, to separate clearly the concepts of truth and confirmation. Distinguishing these concepts allowed him to give up any lingering ideas that he had to build a theory of meaningfulness on the basis of a prior account of confirmation. Truth and meaning were semantic notions that could be wholly absorbed into metalogic in a Tarskian manner, while verification and confirmation were technical concepts distinct from meaning and truth and for which an inductive logic could be pursued as a future task. Carnap's first important technical paper on the confirmation and empirical meaningfulness of theoretical terms in science, and one of the first articles he wrote in English, was "Testability and Meaning" (1936). It provided mature logical empiricism with a model of how to do philosophy of science. In logic, Tarski's work on truth allowed Carnap to simplify his distinction between analytic and synthetic sentences in a given language: analytic sentences were those of which truth was a consequence, in the metalanguage, of the truth definition for the language; all other sentences were synthetic. Carnap worked on his general semantic program through the late 1930s and early 1940s.

In the mid 1930s Carnap became co-editor, with Neurath and Morris, of the *International Encyclopedia of Unified Science.* The encyclopedia project was most vocally promoted by Neurath, who saw it as the crowning achievement of logical empiricism and a work that would rival the encyclopedia of the French Enlightenment philosophes. In an era of fascism and nationalism, Neurath wanted to stress the international and cooperative character of scientific research and to present an account of the "mosaic of the sciences" that showed how the various disciplines could fit together to provide the knowledge needed for social planning and political action. He was particularly concerned to argue that the social sciences do not differ in kind from the natural sciences. The editors persuaded the University of Chicago Press to publish the encyclopedia, and the first of what became the nineteen parts of the work, an introduction to the project, appeared in 1938. It included essays by each of the three editors and shorter contributions by Russell, the American pragmatist philosopher John Dewey, and the Danish physicist Niels Bohr. Carnap's contribution, "The Logical Foundations of the Unity of Science," is a characteristically precise investigation of the various possible meanings of the phrase "unity of science" and a proposal that one of those meanings be accepted as the appropriate one. Carnap argues that although the question as to whether the laws of, say, biology or psychology could be derived from the laws of physics is still an open one, a single language capable of expressing the claims of all the sciences must nevertheless be possible; otherwise, "it would not be possible to connect singular statements and laws of different fields in such a way as to derive predictions from

them." This consequence seemed to Carnap to be antithetical both to the actual practice of science and to the very notion of the systematic knowledge of the world that science is meant to be.

Carnap's main contribution to the encyclopedia was his 1938 monograph, *Foundations of Logic and Mathematics,* which constitutes part 3 of volume one. His main order of business is to show that in any given language, logic and mathematics are analytic; and his procedure shows the full influence of Tarski's work for the first time. He again clearly expresses the idea that logic provides a set of tools rather than a fixed body of doctrine: "The task is not to decide which of the different systems is 'the right logic' but to examine their formal properties and the possibilities for their interpretation and application in science. It might be that a system deviating from the ordinary form will turn out to be useful as a basis for the language of science."

Carnap extended and generalized the ideas of the 1938 monograph in his *Studies in Semantics,* published in two volumes: *Introduction to Semantics* (1942) and *Formalization of Logic* (1943). This work was given an important impetus by Carnap's experiences in the academic year 1940–1941, when he, Tarski, and Russell were visiting professors at Harvard University. In addition to the greater elaboration and precision he brings to the semantic point of view in these volumes, Carnap begins to take his own principle of logical tolerance more seriously in them: although he had been arguing against "logical correctness" and the hegemony of traditional logical systems since 1934, his own work had both employed and concerned itself with the logic of *Principia Mathematica* or fragments of that system. In *Formalization of Logic* he suggests that his semantic methods could be extended to modal logic—"the theory of such concepts as logical necessity, possibility, impossibility, etc."—and announces another book that will deal with this branch of logic:

It seems that as yet the modalities have not been introduced into the more important logic of functions [that is, predicate logic]. The construction of this more interesting but also more complex system, both in semantical and in syntactical form, will be the chief task of the next volume. Then, in addition to logical modalities, other kinds of modalities will be studied, among them the concepts of causal necessity, possibility, etc. Further, the question will be discussed whether modal concepts . . . are useful or even necessary in certain special fields, e.g. in the metalanguage used for semantics and perhaps in psychology, in statements concerning believing, knowing, and similar propositional attitudes.

The volume, which appeared in 1947 as *Meaning and Necessity: A Study in Semantics and Modal Logic,* is a key contribution to logic, philosophy of language, and semantics. Carnap develops what he calls "the method of extension and intension" as the tool for semantic analysis of logical systems, including quantified modal logic and the logic of belief. "Extension" and "intension" are terms in logic and metaphysics similar in meaning to the perhaps more familiar "denotation" and "connotation," respectively. The extension of the word "horse" is the set of all horses that have ever existed or will ever exist, while the intension is the meaning of the word–the concept or idea of horse. Many philosophers would say that the intension determines the extension: the extension is the set of things that the word picks out because of what it means. The distinction has seemed necessary to account for the logical peculiarities of ascriptions of belief: for example, one may not validly deduce from the premises "George IV wonders whether Scott is the author of Waverly" and "Scott is the author of Waverly" the conclusion "George IV wonders whether Scott is Scott." While acknowledging the traditional use of the terms "extension" and "intension," Carnap engages in his characteristic activity of clarifying their meanings before using them. Rather than taking "intension" as a primitive semantic term, he defines it in terms of logical truth or analyticity. For example, "human" and "rational animal" have the same intension if and only if it is logically true that whatever is human is a rational animal and whatever is a rational animal is human.

Carnap makes the first real strides toward a semantics for quantified modal logic in *Meaning and Necessity*. Necessity is an old concept in philosophy: the idea that necessary truths such as "All bachelors are unmarried men" or "2 + 2 = 4" can be explicated in terms of their being true in all "possible worlds" goes back at least to the German rationalist philosopher Gottfried Wilhelm Leibniz, who died in 1716. Carnap asks what precise logical sense can be made of the notion of "possible worlds"; his answer, roughly, is that necessary truth is truth that obtains regardless of the way the world in fact is or that obtains however the world might be. A "way the world might be," in turn, is a sentence that says of every sentence in the language that has no logical operators in it whether that sentence or its negation is true. Thus, if the language has one predicate letter, F, and two individual names, a and b, there are four "ways the world might be" expressible in this language: *Fa* and *Fb; Fa* and not *Fb;* not *Fa* and *Fb;* and not *Fa* and not *Fb*. Carnap calls each of the sentences that expresses a way the world might be a "state description." The necessary truths of a language are those sentences of the language that are true on all state descriptions. In the example, "*Fa*" is not a logical truth

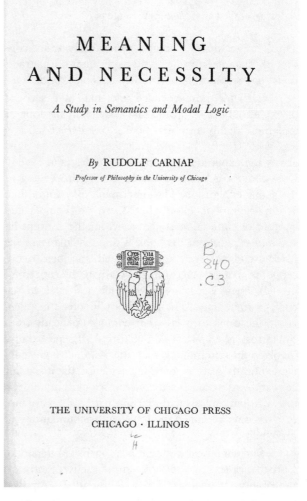

MEANING
AND NECESSITY

A Study in Semantics and Modal Logic

By RUDOLF CARNAP
Professor of Philosophy in the University of Chicago

THE UNIVERSITY OF CHICAGO PRESS
CHICAGO · ILLINOIS

Title page for the 1947 volume in which Carnap first formulates his philosophical method of "explication" (Thomas Cooper Library, University of South Carolina)

(since it is false on the last two state descriptions), while "*Fa* or not *Fa*" is a necessary truth.

Like most of Carnap's works, *Meaning and Necessity* operates on two levels. At the level of theoretical knowledge it deals with meaning, necessary truth, intension, and "intensional isomorphism," a highly complicated solution to the problem of the logic of belief sentences. At the level of method it shows how he believes philosophy should be done. Carnap's first formulation of his philosophical method of "explication" is given early in *Meaning and Necessity*:

The task of making more exact a vague or not quite exact concept used in everyday life or in an earlier stage of scientific or logical development, or rather of replacing it by a newly constructed, more exact concept, belongs among the most important tasks of logical analysis and logical construction. We call this the task of explicating, or of giving an *explication* for, the earlier concept; this earlier concept, or sometimes the term for it, is called the *explicandum,* and the new concept, or its term, is called an *explicatum* of the old one.

Thus, for example, Carnap's syntactically exact concept of "state description" is an explication of the traditional philosophical notion of the "possible world."

Carnap's most extended and influential account of explication takes up the first chapter of his longest and most highly technical book, *Logical Foundations of Probability* (1950). He says that the philosopher must clarify the explicandum, in order to understand exactly what concept is being explicated, before proceeding to the actual explication. This description may sound like a duplication of effort; but Carnap's complicated account of explication is necessary, for the concept he seeks to explicate in the book is one that many of his readers had not even known existed: the logical concept of probability. According to Carnap, the concept of probability, as used in everyday life and even in science, is ambiguous. The probability involved in calculating the odds of a fair coin coming up heads on a single toss is empirical and statistical; the probability involved in determining that the sentence "the coin landed heads" is true, given the evidence that it is a fair coin and was tossed exactly once, is a logical or analytic one. Carnap draws the distinction partly in an attempt to overcome certain disputes over the foundations of probability.

The empirical concept is properly understood, Carnap argues, in the "frequentist" sense: statistical probability statements are well-grounded empirical statements based on long experience with things such as coins. The logical concept, on the other hand, is a quantitative one having to do with degree of confirmation. As Carnap puts the point in his "Intellectual Autobiography," statistical probability statements occur within a science, while logical probability statements are statements about statements in science. Thus, an epidemiologist might seek the empirical probability that a member of a population will become ill in a given epidemic, whereas the philosophy of science is interested in the probability that certain claims in epidemiology, such as "Jones will get ill with influenza," are true, given the other claims accepted in that science at the time. The concepts of logical probability and degree of confirmation come together in *Logical Foundations of Probability* with that of induction: the key philosophical claim in the book is that a logic of induction is simply a logic of probability, and that the concept that must bear the weight of the attempt to formulate a logic of induction is "degree of confirmation" of a scientific hypothesis in light of the evidence.

By the time *Logical Foundations of Probability* appeared, Carnap and his fellow logical empiricists in North America, including Feigl, Hempel, and Reichenbach, had become a significant force in American philosophy, especially in logic, philosophy of science, and philosophy of language. They had acquired home-grown allies in Nagel, Morris, and Quine and had begun training graduate students such as Richard Jeffrey, Hilary Putnam, and Wesley Salmon. Carnap, however, felt somewhat alienated at Chicago, where the philosophy department was moving in a more historically minded and humanistic direction under the leadership of Richard McKeon and Mortimer Adler. In 1950, at Reichenbach's behest, Carnap was offered a Flint Visiting Professorship at Reichenbach's school, UCLA. But he refused to sign the loyalty oath that the University of California system required and instead spent 1950 at the University of Illinois in Urbana-Champaign.

By 1950 all the pieces of Carnap's mature philosophy were in place. Using the tools of modern logic and metalogic, Carnap took his task to be the explication of scientific and metascientific concepts—the latter including explanation, confirmation, reduction, and theory—and the elaboration and proposal of formal languages adequate to the clear and precise formulation of scientific theories. All of this effort was aimed at clarifying the conceptual resources of philosophy and science and promoting the scientific world-conception through detailed, technical work. His interest in semantics and the logic of belief and decision moved him in the direction of modal and intensional logics as the logics necessary for sciences such as psychology and for philosophy itself.

In 1950, however, Carnap's friend Quine, in a talk at a colloquium of the University of Chicago philosophy department, attempted to undermine the foundations of Carnap's philosophy by denying the distinction between analytic and synthetic sentences and the account of ontological questions that Carnap built on that distinction. Part of the talk was published the next year as "On Carnap's Views on Ontology"; the main argument against the analytic/synthetic distinction occurred in Quine's other key 1951 essay, "Two Dogmas of Empiricism." If Quine's argument is correct, then the distinction between the logical and the empirical that Carnap's philosophy requires is ill founded. Indeed, almost nothing in Carnap's mature philosophy is not put under pressure by Quine—for example, Quine also argues that modal and intensional logics are ill founded. The Chicago colloquium set off a dispute between Carnap and Quine that was carried out in several important papers, including what is probably Carnap's best-known article, "Empiricism, Semantics, and Ontology" (1950). It was republished, together with other papers Carnap wrote in the course of the dispute with Quine, in the appendix to the second edition of *Meaning and Necessity* in 1956.

Quine's rejection of the analytic/synthetic distinction collapses all of the crucial distinctions in Carnap's philosophy, especially that between an analytic logic of scientific language and an empirical psychological account of how scientific claims come to be believed. According to Quine, philosophy is not a formal logical discipline, as Carnap thought, but a descriptive cognitive psychology of human beings. The split between a formalist and a naturalist understanding of analytic philosophy began in earnest in the Carnap-Quine dispute and continues today. The dispute between the two men themselves, while significant and heartfelt, was not rancorous. They remained friends to the end of Carnap's life, and Quine dedicated his magnum opus, *Word and Object* (1960)—which continued and deepened his critique of Carnap's ideas—to Carnap.

Carnap went on with his technical work while the dispute was in progress. *The Continuum of Inductive Methods* (1952) continues *Logical Foundations of Probability,* offering a general theory of inductive methods that can be characterized via the values of a single parameter and a "metamethod" for finding an optimal inductive method, given a description of the sort of world one lives in. Also in 1952 he co-authored with Yehoshua Bar-Hillel *An Outline of a Theory of Semantic Information,* an exploration of a cybernetic conception of the information content of messages that gives Carnap a place in the history of electronic and computer engineering.

In 1952 Carnap began two years of work at the Institute for Advanced Study at Princeton. In 1954 he assumed the chair in philosophy at UCLA left vacant by Reichenbach's death the previous year. At UCLA Carnap found himself in a much friendlier philosophical environment than at Chicago: he had students and colleagues, including Richard Montague, Keith Donellen, and David Kaplan, who were doing work similar to his own. UCLA was a major center for formal logic and philosophy of language in the 1950s and 1960s.

Also in 1954, in an effort to reintroduce formal logic and the spirit of scientific philosophy into German-language philosophy, Carnap published *Einführung in die symbolische Logik, mit besonderer Berücksichtigung ihrer Anwendungen* (Introduction to Symbolic Logic, with Particular Attention to Its Applications). The work follows his first logic book, the 1929 *Abriss der Logistik,* in its organization and concentration on applications of logic in the sciences; some of the examples he uses are, despite the twenty-five intervening years, exactly the same. On the other hand, the entire first half of the book, in which the technical details of formal logic are given, is completely different. Although Carnap's

Title page for a collection of Carnap's articles on inductive logic and probability (Thomas Cooper Library, University of South Carolina)

vocabulary for describing the tools of modern logic has altered almost beyond recognition, his sense of the role of logic in the clarification of scientific and philosophical claims is virtually unchanged from his writings of the 1920s.

Throughout the 1940s and 1950s Carnap and his fellow logical empiricists clearly and precisely articulated the canonical conception of the appropriate methods, problems, and tasks of philosophy of science at midcentury. The deductive-nomological and inductive-statistical accounts of scientific explanation, the formulation of the hypothetico-deductive method in science, frequentist models of statistical probability, and logical systems of induction and confirmation were all fruits of the logical-empiricist project. Carnap's 1956 essay, "The Methodological Character of Theoretical Concepts," helped establish the view of theories as partially interpreted axiom systems as the standard one.

Through *Einführung in die symbolische Logik, mit besonderer Berücksichtigung ihrer Anwendungen* Carnap

Carnap in 1962 (photograph by Adya)

dynamics of scientific theory change. He claims that the methods employed by the logical empiricists could not explain revolutionary changes in scientific theorizing such as the move from Ptolemaic to Copernican astronomy or from Newtonian to Einsteinian dynamics. According to Kuhn, such revolutionary changes in science can only be explained by attending to actual details of the practice and social contexts of the scientific work, not through a rational reconstruction of it using the tools of modern logic. After the work of Kuhn and the others, many philosophers of science have not simply tried to construct a logically precise notion of confirmation, for example, but have looked in some detail at how the notion of confirmation has actually been used in the relevant scientific communities.

Carnap's importance was acknowledged when *The Philosophy of Rudolf Carnap,* the eleventh volume in the Library of Living Philosophers series, appeared in 1963 after almost a decade in preparation. Carnap's contributions to the volume give a sense of his meticulous mind and dutiful approach to philosophical friends and foes alike: the book includes more than 250 pages of his responses to the essays of the other contributors, treating each of them at some length, in addition to his "Intellectual Autobiography" of more than 80 pages. Also in 1963 Carnap received an honorary LL.D. from the University of California.

Carnap's wife died in 1964. The following year he received a doctorate of humane letters from the University of Michigan. In 1966 appeared the last of his books that Carnap lived to see published: *Philosophical Foundations of Physics: An Introduction to the Philosophy of Science.* It was based on tapes of Carnap's 1958 UCLA graduate seminar in the philosophy of science and edited by his erstwhile student, the science journalist Martin Gardner. This book is one of the few places where one may find a comprehensive and relatively informal account of the entire range of logical-empiricist concerns in philosophy of science, such as explanation, confirmation, theories of causality, and the relations of observational and theoretical terms. In addition to these canonical topics, the book returns to some issues that had animated Carnap from the beginning of his career: conventionalism, physical geometry, and the relation of qualitative and quantitative concepts.

Rudolf Carnap received an honorary Ph.D. from the University of Oslo in 1969. He continued to be active philosophically up to his death on 14 September 1970. His last book, *Studies in Inductive Logic and Probability* (1971, 1980), written and edited with Jeffrey, includes his final thoughts on inductive logic and probability. Shortly after his death the Philosophy of Science Association biennial conference in Boston was dedicated to him, and distinguished philosophers such as Feigl,

acquired a champion in the German academic world, Wolfgang Stegmüller, who in 1959 translated and edited *Induktive Logik und Wahrscheinlichkeit* (Inductive Logic and Probability), a collection of some previously published and unpublished writings of Carnap's. Carnap's place in German philosophy was also enhanced by the publication in 1961 of the second edition of *Der logische Aufbau der Welt,* which was unchanged from the first except for an additional preface that connected his concerns of 1928 with his current ones.

Carnap officially retired in 1961 but remained at UCLA as professor emeritus for the rest of his life. By 1962 he was the leading exponent of logical empiricism. That year perhaps the strongest attack on the logical empiricist philosophy of science occurred within the pages of the *International Encyclopedia of Unified Science,* of which he was still a co-editor. Monograph number 8 of volume two was Thomas S. Kuhn's *The Structure of Scientific Revolutions.* Kuhn's monograph was the turning point in a struggle by philosophers such as Paul Feyerabend, Russell Hanson, and Michael Scriven to broaden the scope of the tools available in philosophy of science and to reconnect the canonical issues of the discipline with the historical practice of science. Kuhn argues that an account of science must explain the actual historical

Hempel, and Quine offered homages that were published in the proceedings of the conference, *PSA 1970: In Memory of Rudolf Carnap* (1971). The homages depict a man of almost unparalleled kindness and intellectual honesty and mention his tolerant attitude in philosophy, his opposition to the Vietnam War, his support of nonviolent civil-rights protests, and his trip in early 1970 to visit two Mexican philosophers held as political prisoners. Maria Reichenbach, the widow of his friend and fellow logical empiricist, provided perhaps the most moving tribute:

> He really lived his principle of tolerance and took Kant's Imperative seriously: to treat human beings, whether in one's own person or in that of any other, always as an end, never as a means only. Carnap would defend anybody whom I criticized by trying to understand and explain rationally other people's irrational feelings and behavior. He was a good model and when I have a problem I still catch myself thinking: I must ask Carnap.

Letters:
Dear Carnap, Dear Van: The Carnap-Quine Correspondence and Related Work, edited by Richard Creath (Berkeley, Los Angeles & London: University of California Press, 1990).

Interview:
Willy Hochkeppel, in *Mein Weg in die Philosophie,* edited by Hochkeppel (Stuttgart: Reclam, 1993), pp. 133–148.

Bibliographies:
Arthur J. Benson, "Bibliography of the Writings of Rudolf Carnap," in *The Philosophy of Rudolf Carnap,* edited by Paul Arthur Schilpp, The Library of Living Philosophers, volume 11 (La Salle, Ill.: Open Court / London: Cambridge University Press, 1963), pp. 1017–1070;

Friedrich Stadler, "Rudolf Carnap," in his *The Vienna Circle: Studies in the Origins, Development, and Influence of Logical Empiricism* (Vienna: Springer, 2001), pp. 617–623.

References:
Peter Achinstein and Peter Barker, eds., *The Legacy of Logical Positivism* (Baltimore: Johns Hopkins University Press, 1969);

A. J. Ayer, "The Vienna Circle," in his *The Revolution in Philosophy* (London: St. Martin's Press, 1963), pp. 70–87;

David Bell and Wilhelm Vossenkuhl, eds., *Science and Subjectivity: The Vienna Circle and Twentieth-Century Philosophy* (Berlin: Academie-Verlag, 1992);

Roger C. Buck and Robert S. Cohen, eds., *PSA 1970: In Memory of Rudolf Carnap. Proceedings of the 1970 Biennial Meeting, Philosophy of Science Association,* Boston Studies in the Philosophy of Science, volume 8 (Dordrecht, Netherlands: Reidel, 1971);

Richard Porter Butrick, *Carnap on Meaning and Analyticity,* Janua Linguarum, Series Minor, no. 85 (The Hague & Paris: Mouton, 1970);

J. Alberto Coffa, *The Semantic Tradition from Kant to Carnap,* edited by Linda Wessels (Cambridge: Cambridge University Press, 1991);

David DeVidi and Graham Solomon, "Tolerance and Metalanguages in Carnap's *Logical Syntax of Language,*" *Synthese,* 103 (1995): 123–139;

Michael Friedman, *Logical Positivism Reconsidered* (Cambridge: Cambridge University Press, 1999);

Friedman, *A Parting of the Ways: Carnap, Cassirer, and Heidegger* (Chicago: Open Court, 2000);

Peter Galison, "*Aufbau/Bauhaus:* Logical Positivism and Architectural Modernism," *Critical Inquiry,* 16 (1990): 709–752;

Ronald N. Giere and Alan Richardson, eds., *Origins of Logical Empiricism* (Minneapolis: University of Minnesota Press, 1996);

Rudolf Haller, *Neo-Positivismus: Eine historische Einführung in die Philosophie des Wiener Kreises* (Darmstadt: Wissenschaftliche Buchgesellschaft, 1993);

Haller and Friedrich Stadler, eds., *Wien-Berlin-Prag: Der Aufstieg der wissenschaftlichen Philosophie* (Vienna: Hölder-Pichler-Tempsky, 1993);

Jaako Hintikka, ed., *Rudolf Carnap, Logical Empiricist: Materials and Perspectives* (Dordrecht, Netherlands: Reidel, 1975);

B. H. Kazemier and D. Vuysje, eds., *Logic and Language: Studies Dedicated to Professor Rudolf Carnap on the Occasion of His Seventieth Birthday* (Dordrecht, Netherlands: Reidel, 1962);

Dirk Koppelberg, *Die Aufhebung der analytischen Philosophie: Quine als Synthese von Carnap und Neurath* (Frankfurt am Main: Suhrkamp, 1987);

Lothar Krauth, *Die Philosophie Carnaps* (Vienna & New York: Springer, 1970);

Alexandros Charles Michalos, *The Popper-Carnap Controversy* (The Hague: Nijhoff, 1971);

Thomas Mormann, *Rudolf Carnap* (Munich: Beck, 2000);

C. Ulises Moulines, "Making Sense of Carnap's Aufbau," *Erkenntnis,* 35 (1991): 263–286;

Arne Naess, *Four Modern Philosophers: Carnap, Wittgenstein, Heidegger, Sartre,* translated by Alastair Hannay (Chicago & London: University of Chicago Press, 1968);

Joelle Proust, *Questions of Form: Logic and the Analytic Proposition from Kant to Carnap,* translated by A. Brenner

(Minneapolis: University of Minnesota Press, 1989);

W. V. Quine, "Epistemology Naturalized," in his *Ontological Relativity and Other Essays* (New York: Columbia University Press, 1969), pp. 69–90;

Quine, "On Carnap's Views on Ontology," *Philosophical Studies*, 2 (1951): 65–72; republished in his *Ways of Paradox and Other Essays* (Cambridge, Mass.: Harvard University Press, 1976), pp. 203–211;

Quine, "Two Dogmas of Empiricism," *Philosophical Review*, 60 (1951): 20–43; republished in his *From a Logical Point of View* (Cambridge, Mass.: Harvard University Press, 1963), pp. 20–46;

Quine, *Word and Object* (Cambridge, Mass.: MIT Press, 1960);

Alan Richardson, *Carnap's Construction of the World: The Aufbau and the Emergence of Logical Empiricism* (Cambridge: Cambridge University Press, 1998);

Thomas Ricketts, "Carnap's Principle of Tolerance, Empiricism, and Conventionalism," in *Reading Putnam*, edited by Peter Clark and Bob Hale (Oxford: Blackwell, 1994), pp. 176–200;

Edmund Runggaldier, *Carnap's Early Conventionalism: An Inquiry into the Background of the Vienna Circle* (Amsterdam: Rodopi, 1984);

Sahotra Sarkar, "'The Boundless Ocean of Unlimited Possibilities': Logic in Carnap's *Logical Syntax of Language*," *Synthese*, 93 (1992): 191–237;

Werner Sauer, "On the Kantian Background to Neopositivism," *Topoi*, 8 (1989): 111–119;

Paul Arthur Schilpp, ed., *The Philosophy of Rudolf Carnap*, The Library of Living Philosophers, volume 11 (La Salle, Ill.: Open Court / London: Cambridge University Press, 1963);

Herbert Spiegelberg, *The Context of the Phenomenological Movement* (The Hague: Nijhoff, 1981);

Wolfgang Spohn, ed., *Erkenntnis Orientated: A Centennial Volume for Rudolf Carnap and Hans Reichenbach* (Dordrecht, Netherlands & London: Kluwer, 1991);

Friedrich Stadler, *The Vienna Circle: Studies in the Origins, Development, and Influence of Logical Empiricism* (Vienna: Springer, 2001);

Wolfgang Stegmüller, *Das Wahrheitsproblem und die Idee der Semantik: Eine Einführung in die Theorien von A. Tarski und R. Carnap* (Vienna & New York: Springer, 1968);

Thomas Uebel, "Anti-Foundationalism and the Vienna Circle's Revolution in Philosophy," *British Journal for the Philosophy of Science*, 47 (1996): 415–440;

Uebel, *Overcoming Logical Positivism from Within: The Emergence of Neurath's Naturalism in the Vienna Circle's Protocol Sentence Debate* (Amsterdam: Rodopi, 1992);

Jan Wolenski and Eckehart Köhler, eds., *Alfred Tarski and the Vienna Circle* (Dordrecht, Netherlands: Kluwer, 1998).

Papers:

The Rudolf Carnap Collection is part of the Archives for Scientific Philosophy in the Twentieth Century at Hillman Library of the University of Pittsburgh. It includes Carnap's papers, as well as his personal library. A microfilm of the collection is in the Special Collections Department at the Universität Konstanz in Germany. Many letters exchanged by Carnap and Otto Neurath are in the Otto Neurath Collection at the Rijksarchief Noord-Holland in Haarlem, the Netherlands.

Morris Raphael Cohen

(25 July 1880 – 28 January 1947)

Angelo Juffras
William Paterson University

BOOKS: *Reason and Nature: An Essay on the Meaning of Scientific Method* (Glencoe, Ill.: Free Press, 1931);

Law and the Social Order: Essays in Legal Philosophy (New York: Harcourt, Brace, 1933);

An Introduction to Logic and Scientific Method, by Cohen and Ernest Nagel (New York: Harcourt, Brace, 1934);

The Meaning of Marx: A Symposium, by Cohen, Bertrand Russell, John Dewey, Sidney Hook, and Sherwood Eddy (New York: Farrar & Rinehart, 1934);

Proposed Roads for American Jewry: A Symposium, by Cohen, Marvin Lowenthal, and Erich Gutkind (New York: National Council of Jewish Women, 1936);

Jewish Studies of Peace and Post-War Problems (New York: Research Institute on Peace and Post-War Problems of the American Jewish Committee, 1943);

A Preface to Logic (New York: Holt, 1944; London: Routledge, 1946);

The Faith of a Liberal: Selected Essays (New York: Holt, 1946);

The Meaning of Human History (La Salle, Ill.: Open Court, 1947);

A Source Book in Greek Science, by Cohen and I. E. Drabkin (New York: McGraw-Hill, 1948);

Studies in Philosophy and Science (New York: Holt, 1949);

A Dreamer's Journey: The Autobiography of Morris Raphael Cohen (Boston: Beacon, 1949);

Reason and Law: Studies in Juristic Philosophy (Glencoe, Ill.: Free Press, 1950);

King Saul's Daughter: A Biblical Dialogue (Glencoe, Ill.: Free Press, 1952);

American Thought: A Critical Sketch, edited by Felix S. Cohen (Glencoe, Ill.: Free Press, 1954).

OTHER: Charles Sanders Peirce, *Chance, Love, and Logic: Philosophical Essays by the Late Charles S. Peirce,* edited by Cohen (New York: Harcourt, Brace, 1923; London: Kegan Paul, Trench, Trubner, 1923);

Morris Raphael Cohen

Selected Readings in the Philosophy of Law, edited by Cohen and Felix S. Cohen (New York: Privately printed, 1930); enlarged as *Readings in Jurisprudence and Legal Philosophy* (New York: Prentice-Hall, 1951).

Morris Raphael Cohen is important for his writings on logic, philosophy of science, and legal philosophy and as a teacher. Abraham Edel says that "Cohen

Cohen and his wife, Mary Ryshpan Cohen, in 1932

grappled with nothing less than major intellectual problems of the 20th century. . . . He helped usher in directions of work that in later hands were to prove extremely fruitful." A centenary celebration of his life was held at a meeting of the Society for the Advancement of American Philosophy in 1980.

Although many important philosophers, including Ernest Nagel, Justus Buchler, Paul Weiss, Sidney Hook, Herbert Schneider, Morton White, Joseph Ratner, Sidney Ratner, Lewis S. Feuer, Philip W. Wiener, Joseph Lash, and Paul Goodman, were students of Cohen's, none of them could be described as followers of his philosophy. Despite his lack of followers, however, he had an important influence. His collection of Charles Sanders Peirce's essays in *Chance, Love, and Logic* (1923) introduced the largely forgotten Peirce to the philosophic community. Peirce's ideas on scientific inquiry, without the Peircean terminology, appear in Cohen and Ernest Nagel's *Introduction to Logic and Scientific Method* (1934). Cohen's enthusiasm for Peirce was also conveyed to his students: Buchler wrote *Charles Peirce's Empiricism* (1939) and was one of the founders of a journal devoted to Peirce studies, while Weiss joined Charles Hartshorne in editing Peirce's collected papers.

In his own philosophy Cohen was a realist, rejecting Romanticism, voluntarism, sentimentality, obscurantism, and excessive reductionism. He had a special antipathy toward nominalism. These positions were expressed in papers he read at meetings of the American Philosophical Association and in critical reviews.

Cohen was born in the Jewish ghetto of Minsk, Russia (today Belarus), on 25 July 1880 to Abraham Mordecai and Bessie Farfel Cohen. He was brought to

New York's Lower East Side as a twelve-year-old. In 1895 he entered the City College of New York. He graduated Phi Beta Kappa with a B.S. in 1900. From 1902 to 1904 he taught mathematics at City College while taking graduate philosophy courses at Columbia University, where he studied under Frederick J. E. Woodbridge and John Dewey and absorbed their naturalism. In 1904 he received a $750 scholarship from the New York Ethical Society to attend Harvard University. He received his Ph.D. from Harvard in 1906 and married Mary Ryshpan. They had three children: Felix Solomon, Victor William, and Leonora Davidson. Cohen taught mathematics at Townsend Harris Hall High School, the City College preparatory school, until 1912, when he secured an appointment in the philosophy department.

Despite his ability to produce outstanding students, Cohen was described by most of them as a terror in the classroom. He was acerbic and demanded thinking. In his autobiography Hook calls Cohen "one of the great teachers of the first third of our century" and "the first teacher to inspire my profound intellectual respect," but he also says,

Looking back on those days and years, I am shocked at the insensitivity and actual cruelty of Cohen's teaching method, and even more shocked at my indifference to its true character when I was his student. I was among those who spread the word about, in speech and writing, about his inspiring teaching and helped make him a legendary figure who was judged and admired for his reputation rather than his actual classroom performance. Only when I myself became a teacher did I realize that the virtues of his method could be achieved without the browbeating, sarcasm, and absence of simple courtesy that marked his dialectical interrogations.

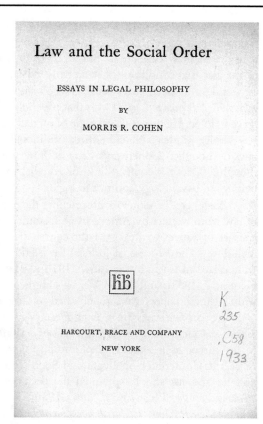

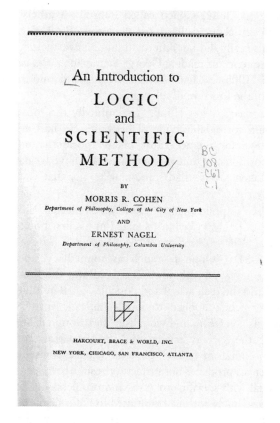

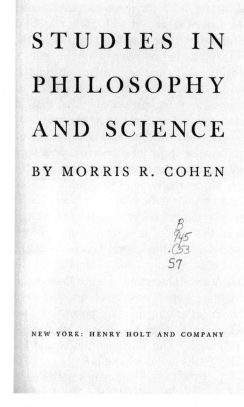

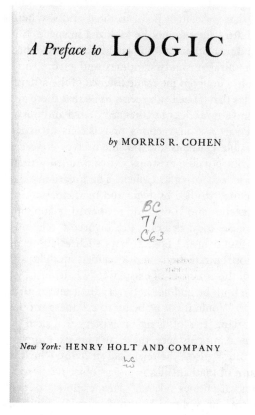

*Title pages for four of Cohen's books, published in (clockwise from top left) 1933, 1934, 1944, and posthumously in 1949
(Thomas Cooper Library, University of South Carolina)*

According to Hook, Cohen called himself an atheist and ironically claimed that most modernist Protestant theologians really did not differ with him. Nevertheless, as a consequence of reading George Santayana's *Reason in Religion* (1905) he had a sympathy for and understanding of the function of religion.

"He was," writes Hook, "undoubtedly the most incisive and formidable critic of his time. He had an unerring eye for the weakness of any position, and since all positions on fundamental questions have weaknesses, Cohen always had something to say that was unfailingly right."

Cohen's philosophical positions reflected his "principle of polarity," which is stated in his first book, *Reason and Nature: An Essay on the Meaning of Scientific Method* (1931): "Opposites such as immediacy and mediation, unity and plurality, the fixed and the flux, the ideal and the real, actual and possible . . . all involve each other when applied to any significant entity." Cohen was averse to individualism and nominalism, preferring the socially related and the universal. For Cohen, nominalism in law, physical science, and the social sciences produces unsatisfactory results because it fails to deal with specific processes and problems of the fields. Surprisingly for one committed to naturalism, he asserts the real existence of universals: "The vulgar prejudice against the reality of universals is really due to the fact that we cannot point to them and say here they are—that is, they cannot be localized in space. But for that matter, neither can our civil rights, our debts, our philosophical misunderstandings and errors; and yet no one has doubted the real existence of the latter." He concludes that "The truth seems to be that there are different kinds or modes of existence," actual and possible; "universals are abstractions or relations of order among possible existents and not themselves concrete existents." But possible existents exist more truly than anything else, according to Cohen. The invariant relational structures studied by logic and mathematics are possible existents, and "Logic and mathematics apply to nature because they describe the invariant relations which are found in it." Logical laws such as those of identity, noncontradiction, and excluded middle are indicative of the character of existence: "whatever is, is; nothing can both be and not be; everything must either be or not be. Would it not be better to call these propositions invariant laws of being or existence? Taken as affirmations about existence, these laws have a claim to empirical truth." Also, "the relational structure which is the structure of mathematics is just as objective as any of the physical entities related." Furthermore, science deals with such possible existents as frictionless engines, ideal gases, perfectly rigid bars, rational economic man, perfect vacuums, and so on. Cohen concludes that "when we consider natural objects as embodiments of such relations we are said to idealize these objects, or to consider them as ideal limits. But such idealization gives us the essential conditions of what truly exists."

Like the German logician Gottlob Frege, Cohen insists in *A Preface to Logic* (1944) that psychology has no place in logic. He wants to rid logic of mental terms and any vestige of idealism. "The three traditional so-called laws of thought," Cohen says, "say nothing at all about thought." How people think—or ought to think—belongs to psychology and not to logic.

Nagel credits Cohen with rescuing the philosophy of law from neglect by American philosophers through a series of papers written over the course of his career, including "The Process of Judicial Legislation" (1914), "The Place of Logic in the Law" (1916), "The Basis of Contract" (1933), and "Rule Versus Discretion" (1933). Most of these papers were republished in Cohen's *Law and the Social Order: Essays in Legal Philosophy* (1933) and *Reason and Law: Studies in Juristic Philosophy* (1950). Early in his career as a teacher of philosophy Cohen organized the Conference on Legal and Social Philosophy, and he and his son Felix edited the textbook *Selected Readings in the Philosophy of Law* (1930), which was enlarged as *Readings in Jurisprudence and Legal Philosophy* (1951). Cohen's papers deal principally with the place of logic in the law, the role of the courts in making laws, and the rationale for the substantive content of legal rules. Cohen disagreed with those who held that judicial decisions were based on precedent and tradition and that logic has no place in the law, pointing out that syllogistic reasoning is involved in applying general rules to individual cases; that analogical reasoning is involved in using precedents; and that judges who assess the social or legal import of a proposed ruling use probable inference. But he was also concerned to show that the rules of the legal system do not logically determine unambiguous answers to every problem that may arise. Moreover, he held that judicial legislation rightfully occurs when the courts interpret a law to extend to cases previously excluded from its range. Cohen championed the idea of a normative jurisprudence against those who held that moral beliefs should be excluded from the development and administration of the law. In "Rule Versus Discretion" Cohen finds sound impulses underlying both methods of deciding cases, thereby exhibiting the principle of polarity at work. Nagel assesses Cohen's legal writing as his chief contribution to philosophy, and Edel also thinks that Cohen's best work is in the philosophy of law.

In 1934 Cohen and Nagel published *An Introduction to Logic and Scientific Method*. The book changed the notion of scientific method from the then prevailing view, which deprecated hypotheses as unwarranted

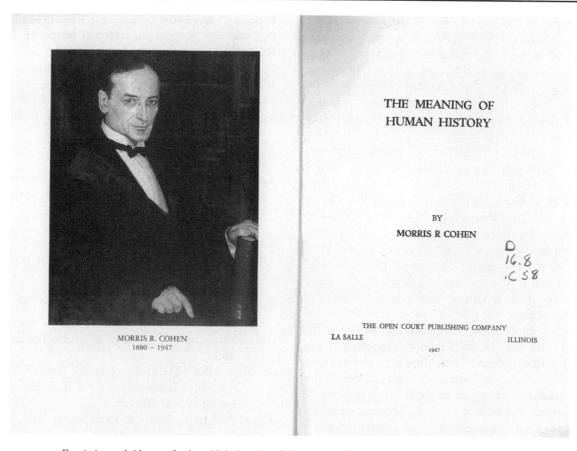

THE MEANING OF
HUMAN HISTORY

BY

MORRIS R COHEN

D
16.8
.C 58

THE OPEN COURT PUBLISHING COMPANY
LA SALLE   ILLINOIS
1947

MORRIS R. COHEN
1880 – 1947

*Frontispiece and title page for the published version of Cohen's 1944 Paul Carus Lectures, in which he criticizes
single-factor accounts of historical causation such as the "great man" and "social forces" theories
(Thomas Cooper Library, University of South Carolina)*

speculation. Cohen and Nagel showed the need for and the proper role of hypothetical reasoning and effected a revolution in teaching scientific method. This position has become such a commonplace that little awareness of Cohen and Nagel's accomplishment exists.

The preface to the work reiterates Cohen's view of the status of logical principles, attributing it to both authors: "We have taken the position that they are inherently applicable because they are concerned with ontological traits of utmost generality." The subject matter of the laws of identity, noncontradiction, and excluded middle "is certain general or generic traits of all things whatsoever. And the same thing may be said of all principles of logic. From this point of view, logic may be regarded as the study of the most general, the most pervasive characters of both what is and what ever may be." Apparently, however, the "we" is misleading, because one year later Nagel published an essay, "Toward a Naturalistic Conception of Logic," in which he says that logic "must not be construed as affirming . . . the view that mathematics is the articulation of the pervasive structures of natural processes. Indeed, pure mathematics when it is really 'pure' does not provide any analysis of natural structures . . . its pursuit involves nothing beyond the

construction and exploration of uninterpreted 'languages' or symbolic 'calculi.'"

After retiring from City College in 1938, Cohen taught at the University of Chicago for three years. In 1942 he suffered a stroke from which he never fully recovered. His wife died in June 1943. In *A Preface to Logic*, Cohen, apparently with Nagel's criticism in mind, complains that "contemporary logicians have insisted that the subject of their inquiry is simply marks on paper, or symbols without relevance to the objective realities that are explored by the natural and social sciences." Instead, according to Cohen, "The subject matter of logic is the formal aspect of all being." Nagel's essay "Logic without Ontology" appeared the same year as *A Preface to Logic*, as if in response to Cohen's book. Nagel argues that "a naturalistic philosophy must be consistent with its own assumptions. If it professes to accept the methods employed by the empirical sciences for obtaining knowledge about the world, it cannot with consistency claim to have a prior insight into the most pervasive structure of things." Using the example of the principle of noncontradiction, which holds that "the same attribute cannot at the same time belong and not belong to the same subject in the same respect," Nagel contends that such a principle cannot be an ontological norm. To have a status as a generic law of existence, it should be possible for it to be false; but according to Nagel, the qualification "in the same respect" makes it possible to defend the principle against all objections: "The interpretation of the principle as an ontological truth neglects its function as a norm or regulative principle for introducing distinctions and for instituting appropriate linguistic usage." Nagel goes on to criticize another thesis of Cohen's. In *A Preface to Logic* Cohen says, "Rules of logic are the rules of operation or transformation according to which all possible objects, physical, psychological, neutral, or complex can be combined. Thus logic is an exploration of the field of most general abstract possibility." Nagel answers that "it is not things and their actual relations which are said to be logically consistent or inconsistent with one another, but propositions or statements about them. . . . Inconsistency is something which can be located only in discourse, among statements, not among things in general"; and "there is no obvious warrant for the claim that" logical principles "are the rules in accordance with which all possible objects can be transformed or combined. . . . The interpretation of logical principles as ontological invariants seems therefore, on closer view, to be extraneous ornamentation upon the functions they actually exercise." Nagel's criticism did not persuade Cohen to change his position. The posthumous *Studies in Philosophy and Science* (1949) includes his 1930 essay "Faith of a Logician," in which he insists that "The fundamental laws or postulates of pure mathematics or logic are the invariant forms or relations which hold of all possible objects."

In 1944 Cohen delivered the Paul Carus Lectures at City College; they were published in 1947 as *The Meaning of Human History*. Cohen attacks single-factor accounts of historical causation such as the "great man" and "social forces" theories. According to Cohen, the "great men" of an age are those who "embody the aspirations of a large number of their fellow men, or who are fitted to the new technological capacities of the society into which they are born." As to patterns in history, Cohen believes that the pendulum of history oscillates back and forth between "a record of man's degeneration and the doctrine of perpetual progress." Morris Raphael Cohen died on 28 January 1947.

Bibliography:
Martin A. Kuhn, *Morris Raphael Cohen: A Bibliography* (New York: City College of New York Library, 1957).

Biography:
Leonora Cohen Rosenfield, *Portrait of a Philosopher: Morris R. Cohen in Life and Letters* (New York: Harcourt, Brace & World, 1962).

References:
Huntington Cairns, "The Legal Philosophy of Morris R. Cohen," *Vanderbilt Law Review,* 14 (1960): 239–262;

C. F. Delaney, *Mind and Nature: A Study of the Naturalistic Philosophies of Cohen, Woodbridge, and Sellars* (Notre Dame, Ind.: University of Notre Dame Press, 1969);

Abraham Edel, "The Unity of Morris Raphael Cohen's Thought," *Transactions of the C. S. Peirce Society,* 17 (Spring 1981): 107–127;

David Hollinger, *Morris R. Cohen and the Scientific Ideal* (Cambridge, Mass.: MIT Press, 1975);

Sidney Hook, "Educational Turning Point: Morris Cohen," in his *Out of Step: An Unquiet Life in the 20th Century* (New York: Harper & Row, 1987), pp. 53–79;

Thelma Z. Lavine, Introduction to "The Morris Raphael Cohen Centenary," *Transactions of the C. S. Peirce Society,* 17 (Spring 1981): 94–97;

Ernest Nagel, "The Dimensions of Cohen's Legal Philosophy," *Transactions of the C. S. Peirce Society,* 17 (Spring 1981): 98–106;

Nagel, "Logic without Ontology," in *Naturalism and the Human Spirit,* edited by Yervant H. Krikorian (New York: Columbia University Press, 1944), pp. 210–241.

Papers:
Morris Raphael Cohen's letters are at the University of Chicago.

Cadwallader Colden

(7 February 1688 – 28 September 1776)

Kevin J. Hayes
University of Central Oklahoma

See also the Colden entries in *DLB 24: American Colonial Writers, 1606–1734* and *DLB 30: American Historians, 1607–1865.*

BOOKS: *The Interest of the Country in Laying Duties: Or, A Discourse, Shewing How Duties on Some Sorts of Merchandize May Make the Province of New-York Richer than It Would Be without Them* (New York: Sold by J. Peter Zenger, 1726);

The History of the Five Indian Nations Depending on the Province of New-York in America (New York: Printed & sold by William Bradford, 1727); revised and enlarged as *The History of the Five Indian Nations of Canada, Which Are Dependent on the Province of New-York in America, and Are the Barrier between the English and French in That Part of the World* (London: Printed for Thomas Osborne, 1747);

An Explication of the First Causes of Action in Matter; and of the Cause of Gravitation (New York: Printed by James Parker, 1745; London: Printed for J. Brindley, 1746); revised and enlarged as *The Principles of Action in Matter, the Gravitation of Bodies, and the Motion of the Planets, Explained from Those Principles* (London: Printed for R. Dodsley, 1751);

An Abstract from Dr. Berkley's Treatise on Tar-Water: With Some Reflexions Thereon, Adapted to Diseases Frequent in America, as A Friend to the Country (New York: Printed & sold by J. Parker, 1745);

All Canada in the Hands of the English: Or, An Authentick Journal of the Proceedings of the Army, under General Amherst, from the Time It Embarked at Oswego, on the 10th of August (1760) to the Happy Reduction of Montreal, the 8th of September Following. Together with Several Other Particulars Relating to Canada (Boston: Printed and sold by B. Mecom, 1760);

The Philosophical Writings of Cadwallader Colden, edited by Scott Pratt and John Ryder (Amherst, N.Y.: Humanity Books, 2002).

OTHER: "An Introduction to the Study of Phylosophy Wrote in America for the Use of a Young

Gentleman," in *American Philosophic Addresses, 1700–1900,* edited by Joseph L. Blau (New York: Columbia University Press, 1946), pp. 289–311;

"A Summary of the Principles of Action," in *American Thought before 1900: A Sourcebook from Puritanism to Darwinism,* edited by Paul Kurtz (New York: Macmillan, 1966), pp. 113–121.

SELECTED PERIODICAL PUBLICATION–

UNCOLLECTED: "Plantae Coldenghamiae in provincia Noveboracensi Americes sponte crescentes," *Acta Societatis Regiae Scientiarum Upsaliensis,* 4 (1743): 81–135; 5 (1744–1750): 47–82.

Cadwallader Colden played many roles during his long life–philosopher, historian, naturalist, physicist, and statesman. His surviving papers hint that he would have preferred, above all, to be remembered for his discoveries in theoretical physics, but his work in that field, more than in any other, reveals his shortcomings. While the importance he attached to the powers of observation allowed him to excel as a naturalist and to write an original and influential history of the Iroquois, his overemphasis on the observable–and paradoxical neglect of the experimental–led him into error. Colden also applied his physical principles to human thought. Though his ideas have long been rejected as bad physics, they remain intriguing philosophy.

Colden was born in Ireland on 7 February 1688 and raised in Berwickshire, Scotland, where his father, Alexander Colden, ministered to the Presbyterian congregation at Duns. His mother's name is unknown. He attended the University of Edinburgh, where the anticlericalism and antischolasticism of the faculty strongly influenced him. He took the A.B. degree in 1705 and went to London to study medicine. With little chance of obtaining a lucrative medical practice in London, Colden returned to Scotland around 1708; two years later he immigrated to Philadelphia, where he engaged in the mercantile business. He married Alice Christie on 11 November 1715, during a brief visit to Scotland, then returned to Philadelphia with his bride and began to practice medicine. The couple eventually had eight children. Except for an acquaintanceship with the statesman and scholar James Logan, Colden found little intellectual camaraderie in the city. He began corresponding with the London intelligentsia and assembling a private library, for which he ordered many books in belles lettres, astronomy, botany, history, law, mathematics, and medicine.

In 1718, with encouragement from Robert Hunter, a fellow Scotsman who was governor of New York, Colden moved to that colony. He became surveyor general there in 1720. Hunter soon left the colony and was succeeded as governor by William Burnet. In 1721 Colden was appointed to the Governor's Council. He was involved in New York politics for the rest of his life.

Colden's official responsibilities during the 1720s gave him the opportunity to attend conferences that Governor Burnet held with the Iroquois nations. Colden quickly became intrigued with Native American government and social relations; the result of this fascination was *The History of the Five Indian Nations Depending on the Province of New-York in America;* the work, which contemporary historian John Huske calls in *The Present State of North American* (1755) "a masterly Performance," was published in 1727 and revised and enlarged in 1747.

According to J. A. Leo Lemay, Colden, in his history of the Iroquois, was the earliest American writer "to make sustained use of the comparative method and stage theory in a thoroughly Enlightenment manner." Colden believed that Europeans had gone through stages of development similar to those the Iroquois were undergoing. The behavior of the Iroquois–especially their eloquence and their form of government–was, therefore, analogous to that of the Europeans during an earlier stage. Colden justifies his lengthy discussion of Iroquois government on the grounds that it shows what government must have been like among the ancient Europeans: "As I am fond to think, that the present state of the *Indian Nations* exactly shows the *most Ancient* and *original Condition* of almost every Nation; so I believe, here we may with more certainty see the Original Form of all Government, than in the most *curious Speculations* of the Learned; and that the Patriarchal, and other *Schemes* in Politics are no better than *Hypotheses* in *Philosophy,* and as prejudicial to real Knowledge."

By observing the Iroquois, Colden believed, he could understand the origins of Western polity in a way that European philosophers could not. John Locke, for example, had written in his *Two Treatises of Government* (1689) that "in the primitive, patriarchal, Old Testament stage in Europe we once lived as the American Indians do now"; but Locke could only hypothesize what ancient European society might have been like, whereas Colden could see for himself what it was like.

In 1728 Colden moved with his wife and children from New York City to Coldengham, a country estate that he had begun developing earlier that decade. By 1739 he was spending most of his time there. He described his life in an undated letter to his frequent correspondent, the Boston physician William Douglass: "I hope I am now settled for some months free from the troublesome broils which mens passions occasion in all publick affairs. This gives me hopes of being able to amuse my self with more innocent & more agreeable speculations than usually attend intrigues of State." In the same letter Colden expressed the wish that "a certain

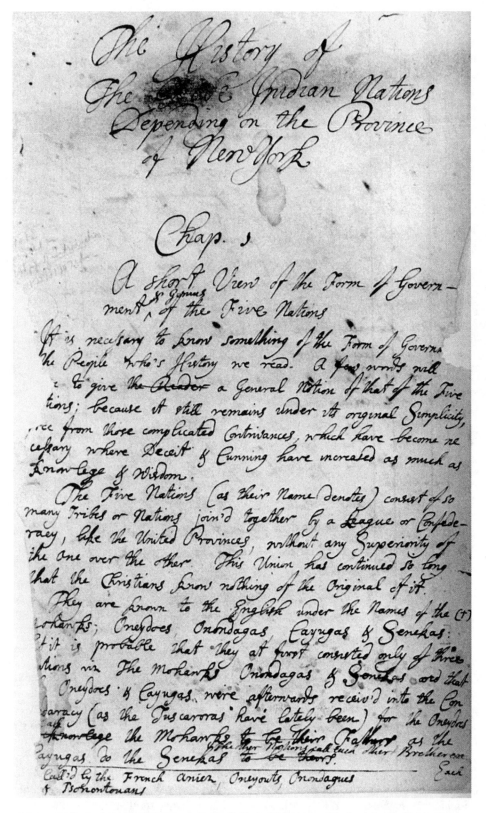

*Manuscript for the first page of the introduction to Colden's 1727 history of the Iroquois, in which he theorizes
that European nations had gone through stages of development similar to those the Native Americans
were undergoing during his time (The New-York Historical Society)*

Oil painting of Colden by an unknown artist, based on an original by Matthew Pratt (The New-York Historical Society)

allowed Colden to apply his acute powers of observation, it did not allow him, as *The History of the Five Indian Nations* had, to make the imaginative leap from observation to theory.

Colden soon indulged in a new field of inquiry that dominated his thought for the remainder of his life. This new direction becomes apparent in a series of letters between Colden and the Reverend Samuel Johnson of Connecticut that began in 1744, a correspondence that Woodbridge Riley characterized as "an interchange of ideas between the materialist and idealist which read like veritable dialogues between Hylas and Philonous." Johnson, the ablest advocate in America of the ideas of the Irish philosopher George Berkeley, the author of *Three Dialogues between Hylas and Philonous* (1713), hoped to persuade Colden to accept Berkeley's denial of the existence of matter; but Colden's many lengthy responses to Johnson reveal his fundamental and unshakable materialism.

Colden developed his thoughts most fully in *An Explication of the First Causes of Action in Matter, and, of the Cause of Gravitation* (1745). In this work he claims to have discovered something that Isaac Newton had not: the cause of gravity. As Brook Hindle has remarked, "No more audacious claim to intellectual eminence was ever made in colonial America." Colden had only a small number of copies printed, intending to distribute them to the American and European intelligentsia, receive their comments, and then publish a revised authoritative version. A pirated London edition, however, appeared in 1746, a German translation in 1748, and a French translation in 1751. Colden's enlarged edition was published in 1751 as *The Principles of Action in Matter, the Gravitation of Bodies, and the Motion of the Planets, Explained from Those Principles.* He completed the text for a third edition but was unable to find a publisher.

In *The Principles of Action in Matter* Colden describes action and motion as two distinct qualities. He then divides matter into three basic substances: resisting matter, that is, bodies having mass, occupying space, and capable of action; moving matter, which he equates with light; and ether, a reacting medium, contiguous everywhere with resisting and moving matter, that transmits action and movement between material bodies distant from each other. According to Colden, gravity is the force exerted by the ether on all planets and stars. He was attacked for what appeared to be an attempt to refute and go beyond Newton, but later scholars have tried to make sense of Colden's ideas. Hindle suggests that, far from a refutation of Newton, *The Principles of Action in Matter* was a response to and extension of the many queries that Newton had appended to his *Opticks* (1704). Colden, that is, essentially erected his system on ideas drawn from Newton's

number of Men would enter into a Voluntary Society for the advancing of Knowledge & that for this purpose such in the Neighbouring provinces as are most likely to be willing to promote this design be invited to enter in to it." In 1743 he became one of the original members of the American Philosophical Society.

Around 1742 Colden read Carolus Linnaeus's *Genera plantarum* (1737). He soon mastered the Linnaean classification system and began collecting the flora around Coldengham. A visit from the naturalist and explorer John Bartram in 1742 fueled Colden's newfound enthusiasm for botanical study. He also began corresponding with Linnaeus and the botanist Jan Fredrik Gronovius. He sent Gronovius a catalogue of the plants he had found near his home; Gronovius forwarded the work to Linnaeus, who published it as "Plantae Coldenghamiae in Provincia Noveboracensi Americes sponte crescentes" in two issues of the *Acta Societatis Regiae Scientiarum Upsaliensis* for 1743 and 1745–1750. The work remains Colden's most important scientific contribution. Still, he was dissatisfied with botany. He found Linnaeus's system faulty and wished for a more natural classification scheme. While botany

questions. Roy N. Lokken, on the other hand, argues that Colden's physics parallels his physiology. During the 1740s Colden's medical thought shifted from "iatrophysics" to "iatrochemistry": that is, he came to understand that organic life is based on chemical reactions, not mechanical movement. Mechanism by itself could produce no effects; matter must produce its own effects and, therefore, has to be an active substance.

In the preface to *The Principles of Action in Matter* Colden asserts that the physical processes he has identified are also responsible for thought: "all the primary or simple ideas we have of things external to us, arise from the impressions or actions of these things on our senses: and, therefore, that the properties and qualities of things are nothing else but their various actions, or modes of acting, either simple or complicated." Arguing that perception occurs as external objects act on the brain, he differed from the prevalent Lockean psychology. For Colden, Joseph L. Blau explains, "Knowledge could not be the cognition of inactive objects passively received by the senses. On the contrary, he asserted that all our primary ideas of external objects arise from the actions of the objects on our senses; that our knowledge of things is our perception of their actions; that thinking is a particular and unique kind of action. Thus, bodies and minds act jointly in perception. All knowledge is of action and its effects; passivity is cognitive nonexistence."

Around 1760 Colden wrote an introduction to the study of philosophy for Peter DeLancey, the nephew of Colden's son Alexander; he sent a revised and enlarged version to Alexander on 10 July 1760 under the title "An Introduction to the Study of Phylosophy Wrote in America for the Use of a Young Gentleman." It was first published in *American Philosophic Addresses, 1700–1900* (1946), edited by Joseph L. Blau, and is republished in *The Philosophical Writings of Cadwallader Colden* (2001), edited by Scott Pratt and John Ryder. Though historically a much less important work than *The Principles of Action in Matter,* the piece helps further to clarify Colden's philosophic thought. Since it was written for the beginning student, it assumes little knowledge of geometry and, therefore, avoids the more abstruse notions of *The Principles of Action in Matter.* "An Introduction to the Study of Phylosophy" begins with an explanation of the ancient origins of learning. Colden asserts that "Pythagoras was the best instructed of any of the Greeks in the Egyptian learning. It appears from the little which remains of his doctrine, that the Egyptians knew what of late times has been called the Copernican System, and that he knew the general apparent attraction between bodies, which has been rediscovered in the last century by Sʳ Isaac Newton. . . . It may be that we are now regaining the

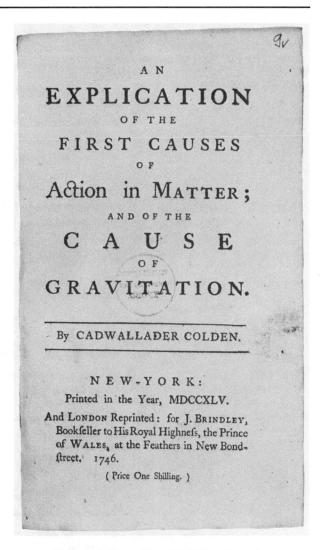

AN
EXPLICATION
OF THE
FIRST CAUSES
OF
Action in Matter;
AND OF THE
CAUSE
OF
GRAVITATION.

By CADWALLADER COLDEN.

NEW-YORK:
Printed in the Year, MDCCXLV.
And LONDON Reprinted: for J. BRINDLEY,
Bookſeller to His Royal Highneſs, the Prince
of WALES, at the Feathers in New Bond-
ſtreet. 1746.
(Price One Shilling.)

Title page for the work in which Colden claims to have discovered the cause of gravity (American Philosophical Society Library)

Principles of Physics, which were known many ages before the beginning of the Christian era." Colden's use of a theory of stages to describe the development of the Iroquois implied a belief in steady progress; in "An Introduction to the Study of Phylosophy" he offers a more cyclical theory of history.

After attacking the medieval scholastics for several pages, Colden devotes the remainder of the work to his physical ideas. He stresses for his youthful readers the importance of understanding these physical processes because, he asserts, the action of material objects on perception determines who one is and what one thinks: "Our life and health, our pleasure and pain all depend on the powers of those beings, which constitute the human system, and on the powers of other things, which are continually acting upon it. Not only the speculative sciences, the explaining of all the phenomena

Page from the 1760 manuscript for Colden's "An Introduction to the Study of Physics or Natural Philosophy for the Use of Peter De Lancey the Younger," which he rewrote the same year for his son Alexander as "An Introduction to the Study of Phylosophy Wrote in America for the Use of a Young Gentleman" (The New-York Historical Society)

which strike our senses, depend on the knowledge of these powers; but likewise all the practical arts depend on them. This knowledge is useful for us in every circumstance of life." Colden also reemphasizes the importance of observation. Knowledge of ether, for example, can be obtained only

> by an accurate observation of the effects or phenomena produced by it. I suppose none will affirm, that nothing exists, but what we either feel, see, hear, smell, or taste. The existence of some things may be as evident by reflexion on the phenomena, or on the effects produced by them, or by reasoning, as the existence of others is by immediate perception. Where effects are evidently perceived, it is with the greatest certainty concluded, that something exists which has sufficient power to produce these effects. In truth we have no other method to discover the existence of anything, but by its effects either mediately, or immediately on the senses.

The importance that Colden places on observation in his later writings is consistent with his earlier work. The skills, however, that allowed him to excel as a chronicler of the Iroquois and a botanist were not transferable to physics. A stamen or petal of a flower remains the same long enough for the botanist to describe its appearance accurately, but describing physical phenomena—a gunshot was one of Colden's favorite examples—requires imagination. In physics he made observations, thought creatively, and then put forth his theories. He failed to recognize that empiricism requires more than mere observation and therefore never performed experiments. Colden believed that for great thinkers such as Newton and Galileo imagination was crucial for comprehending the essential physical properties of the universe. Too much experimental drudgery cramped the imagination. As he told the youthful readers of "An Introduction to the Study of Phylosophy," "to be perpetually poring [on lines] and figures, and jumbling together algebraical characters, cramps the imagination." From *The Principles of Action in Matter* until the end of his life, imaginative thinking remained the most important step in Colden's own theoretical process.

In 1761 Cadwallader Colden became lieutenant governor of New York; he served as acting governor on several occasions. He died on 28 September 1776, loyal to the Crown.

Letters:

The Letters and Papers of Cadwallader Colden, 9 volumes (New York: New York Historical Society, 1918–1937; reprint, New York: AMS Press, 1973).

Biography:

Alice Mapelsden Keys, *Cadwallader Colden: A Representative Eighteenth Century Official* (New York: Columbia University Press, 1906).

References:

Joseph L. Blau, "Cadwallader Colden," in *American Philosophic Addresses, 1700–1900,* edited by Blau (New York: Columbia University Press, 1946), pp. 287–289;

Brook Hindle, "Cadwallader Colden's Extension of the Newtonian Principles," *William and Mary Quarterly,* third series 13 (1956): 459–475;

Alfred R. Hoermann, "Cadwallader Colden and the Mind-Body Problem," *Bulletin of the History of Medicine,* 50 (1976): 392–404;

Hoermann, "A Savant in the Wilderness: Cadwallader Colden of New York," *New York Historical Society Quarterly,* 62 (1978): 271–288;

J. A. Leo Lemay, "The Frontiersman from Lout to Hero: Notes on the Significance of the Comparative Method and the Stage Theory in Early American Literature and Culture," *Proceedings of the American Antiquarian Society,* 88 (1978): 187–223;

Roy N. Lokken, "Cadwallader Colden's Attempt to Advance Natural Philosophy beyond the Eighteenth-Century Mechanistic Paradigm," *Proceedings of the American Philosophical Society,* 122 (1978): 365–376;

Woodbridge Riley, *American Philosophy: The Early Schools* (New York: Dodd, Mead, 1907), pp. 329–372;

Herbert W. Schneider, *A History of American Philosophy,* second edition (New York: Columbia University Press, 1963), pp. 23–26;

Raymond Phineas Stearns, *Science in the British Colonies of America* (Urbana: University of Illinois Press, 1970), pp. 559–575;

Lawrence C. Wroth, *An American Bookshelf, 1755* (Philadelphia: University of Pennsylvania Press, 1934).

Papers:

Most of Cadwallader Colden's papers are held by the New York Historical Society in Albany. The manuscript for his third revision of *The Principles of Action in Matter* and some other items are in the library of the University of Edinburgh. Additional manuscripts are in the Newberry Library in Chicago; the Huntington Library in San Marino, California; and the Historical Society of Pennsylvania in Philadelphia. Colden's copybook for the years 1737 to 1753 is at the Rosenbach Museum and Library in Philadelphia.

John Dewey

(20 October 1859 – 1 June 1952)

Thomas M. Alexander
Southern Illinois University at Carbondale

and

Richard W. Field
Northwest Missouri State University

See also the Dewey entry in *DLB 246: Twentieth-Century American Cultural Theorists.*

BOOKS: *Psychology* (New York: Harper, 1887; revised, 1889; revised again, 1891);

Leibniz's New Essays Concerning the Human Understanding: *A Critical Exposition* (Chicago: Griggs, 1888);

The Ethics of Democracy, University of Michigan Philosophical Papers, second series no. 1 (Ann Arbor, Mich.: Andrews, 1888);

Applied Psychology: An Introduction to the Principles and Practice of Education, by Dewey and James Alexander McLellan (Boston: Educational Publishing, 1889);

Outlines of a Critical Theory of Ethics (Ann Arbor, Mich.: Register, 1891);

The Study of Ethics: A Syllabus (Ann Arbor, Mich.: Inland Press, 1894);

The Psychology of Number and Its Applications to Methods of Teaching Arithmetic, by Dewey and McLellan, International Education Series, volume 33 (New York: Appleton, 1895; London: Arnold, 1895);

Interest in Relation to Training of the Will, second supplement to the *Herbart Year Book for 1895* (Bloomington, Ill.: Public School Publishing Co., 1896); revised as *Interest as Related to Will,* edited by Charles A. McMurry (Chicago: University of Chicago Press, 1899); revised and enlarged as *Interest and Effort in Education* (Boston: Houghton Mifflin, 1913; Bath, U.K.: Chivers, 1969);

Hegel's Philosophy of Spirit: Lectures (Chicago: University of Chicago Press, 1897);

The Significance of the Problem of Knowledge (Chicago: University of Chicago Press, 1897);

My Pedagogic Creed (New York & Chicago: E. L. Kellogg, 1897);

John Dewey

Psychology and Philosophic Method: The Annual Public Address before the Union, May 15, 1899 (Berkeley: University of California Press, 1899);

The School and Society: Being Three Lectures by John Dewey, Supplemented by a Statement of the University Elementary

School (Chicago: University of Chicago Press, 1899; London: P. S. King, 1900; revised edition, Chicago: University of Chicago Press, 1915; Cambridge: Cambridge University Press, 1915);

Psychology and Social Practice, University of Chicago Contributions to Education, no. 11 (Chicago: University of Chicago Press, 1901);

The Child and the Curriculum (Chicago: University of Chicago Press, 1902);

The Educational Situation (Chicago: University of Chicago Press, 1902);

Studies in Logical Theory, by Dewey, H. B. Thompson, S. F. McLennan, M. L. Ashley, W. C. Gore, W. A. Heidel, H. W. Stuart, and A. W. Moore (Chicago: University of Chicago Press, 1903; London: Unwin, 1909);

Logical Conditions of a Scientific Treatment of Morality (Chicago: University of Chicago Press, 1903);

Ethics (New York: Columbia University Press, 1908);

Ethics, by Dewey and James H. Tufts (New York: Holt, 1908; London: Bell, 1909; revised edition, New York: Holt, 1932);

Moral Principles in Education (Boston: Houghton Mifflin, 1909);

How We Think (Boston: Heath, 1910; London: Harrap, 1910); revised and enlarged as How We Think: A Restatement of the Relation of Reflective Thinking to the Educative Processes (Boston: Heath, 1933; London: Harrap, 1933);

The Influence of Darwin on Philosophy and Other Essays in Contemporary Thought (New York: Holt, 1910; London: Bell, 1910);

German Philosophy and Politics (New York: Holt, 1915; republished, with a new introduction, New York: Putnam, 1942);

Schools of To-morrow, by Dewey and Evelyn Dewey (New York: Dutton, 1915; London: Dent, 1915);

Democracy and Education: An Introduction to the Philosophy of Education (New York: Macmillan, 1916; New York: Free Press / London: Collier-Macmillan, 1944);

Essays in Experimental Logic (Chicago: University of Chicago Press, 1916);

Creative Intelligence: Essays in the Pragmatic Attitude, by Dewey and others (New York: Holt, 1917)–includes "The Need for a Recovery of Philosophy," by Dewey, pp. 3–69;

Enlistment for the Farm, Columbia War Papers, series 1, no. 1 (New York: Division of Intelligence and Publicity of Columbia University, 1917);

Citizens of Tomorrow: The Contribution of the Public Schools to National Preparedness. Comprising Addresses Delivered at the Annual Meeting of the Public Education Association, by

Dewey and others (New York: Public Education Association of the City of New York, 1917);

Reconstruction in Philosophy (New York: Holt, 1920; London: University of London Press, 1921; revised and enlarged edition, with a new introduction, Boston: Beacon, 1948);

China, Japan, and the U.S.A.: Present-Day Conditions in the Far East and Their Bearing on the Washington Conference, New Republic Pamphlet, no. 1 (New York: Republic Publishing, 1921);

Human Nature and Conduct: An Introduction to Social Psychology (New York: Holt, 1922; London: Allen & Unwin, 1922; republished, with a new introduction, New York: Modern Library, 1930);

Ideals, Aims, and Methods in Education, by Dewey and others (London & New York: Pitman, 1922)–includes "Aims and Ideals of Education," by Dewey, pp. 1–9;

Outlawry of War: What It Is and Is Not (Chicago: American Committee for the Outlawry of War, 1923);

The Alexander-Dewey Arithmetic: Intermediate Book, by Dewey and Georgia Alexander (New York: Longmans, Green, 1925);

Experience and Nature (Chicago & London: Open Court, 1925; revised edition, New York: Norton, 1929; London: Allen & Unwin, 1929);

The Alexander-Dewey Arithmetic: Book Five, by Dewey and Alexander (New York: Longmans, Green, 1926);

What Mr. John Dewey Thinks of the Educational Policies of México (Mexico City: Talleres Gráficos de la Nación, 1926);

The Public and Its Problems (New York: Holt, 1927; London: Allen & Unwin, 1927); republished, with a new introduction, as The Public and Its Problems: An Essay in Political Inquiry (Chicago: Gateway, 1946);

Reflections on the Sacco-Vanzetti Tragedy, by Dewey, Edna St. Vincent Millay, William G. Thompson, and C. I. Claflin (Boston: Sacco-Vanzetti Defense Committee, 1927)–includes "Psychology and Justice," by Dewey;

Art and Education, by Dewey, Albert C. Barnes, Laurence Buermeyer, and others (Merion, Pa.: Barnes Foundation Press, 1929; revised and enlarged, 1947; revised and enlarged again, 1954);

Characters and Events: Popular Essays in Social and Political Philosophy, 2 volumes, edited by Joseph Ratner (New York: Holt, 1929; London: Allen & Unwin, 1929);

Impressions of Soviet Russia and the Revolutionary World, Mexico–China–Turkey (New York: New Republic, 1929);

The Quest for Certainty: A Study of the Relation of Knowledge and Action (New York: Minton, Balch, 1929; London: Allen & Unwin, 1930);

The Sources of a Science of Education (New York: Liveright, 1929);

Contrasts in Education (New York: Teachers College, Columbia University, 1929);

Construction and Criticism (New York: Columbia University Press, 1930; London: Oxford University Press, 1930);

Individualism, Old and New (New York: Minton, Balch, 1930; London: Allen & Unwin, 1931);

American Education Past and Future (Chicago: University of Chicago Press, 1931);

Context and Thought, University of California Publications in Philosophy, volume 12, no. 3 (Berkeley: University of California Press, 1931; London: Cambridge University Press, 1932);

Philosophy and Civilization (New York: Minton, Balch, 1931; London: Putnam, 1933);

The Way Out of Educational Confusion (Cambridge, Mass.: Harvard University Press, 1931; London: Oxford University Press, 1931);

Are Sanctions Necessary to International Organizations? by Dewey and Raymond Leslie Buell, Foreign Policy Pamphlets, nos. 82–83 (New York: Foreign Policy Association, 1932);

Art as Experience (New York: Minton, Balch, 1934; London: Allen & Unwin, 1934);

A Common Faith (New Haven: Yale University Press, 1934; London: H. Milford, Oxford University Press, 1934);

Education and the Social Order (New York: League for Industrial Democracy, 1934);

Liberalism and Social Action (New York: Putnam, 1935);

The Teacher and Society, by Dewey, William H. Kilpatrick, George H. Hartmann, Ernest O. Melby, and others (New York: Appleton-Century, 1937);

The Case of Leon Trotsky: Report of Hearings on the Charges Made against Him in the Moscow Trials by the Preliminary Commission of Inquiry, by Dewey and others (New York: Harper, 1937; London: Secker & Warburg, 1937);

Logic: The Theory of Inquiry (New York: Holt, 1938; London: Allen & Unwin, 1939);

Experience and Education (New York: Macmillan, 1938);

Not Guilty: Report of the Commission of Inquiry into the Charges Made against Leon Trotsky in the Moscow Trials, by Dewey, Suzanne La Follette, and Benjamin Stolberg (New York: Harper, 1938; London: Secker & Warburg, 1938);

Intelligence in the Modern World: John Dewey's Philosophy, edited by Ratner (New York: Modern Library, 1939);

Freedom and Culture (New York: Putnam, 1939; London: Allen & Unwin, 1940);

Theory of Valuation, volume 2, no. 4 of *International Encyclopedia of Unified Science,* edited by Otto Neurath, Rudolf Carnap, and Charles W. Morris (Chicago: University of Chicago Press, 1939);

What Is Democracy? Its Conflicts, Ends and Means, by Dewey, Boyd H. Bode, and T. V. Smith (Norman, Okla.: Cooperative Books, 1939);

Education Today, edited by Ratner (New York: Putnam, 1940; abridged edition, London: Allen & Unwin, 1941);

Problems of Men (New York: Philosophical Library, 1946); republished as *Philosophy of Education (Problems of Men)* (Ames, Iowa: Littlefield, Adams, 1956);

Knowing and the Known, by Dewey and Arthur F. Bentley (Boston: Beacon, 1949);

David Dubinsky: A Pictorial Biography, text by Dewey (New York: Inter-Allied Publications, 1951);

John Dewey: His Contribution to the American Tradition, edited by Irwin Edman (Indianapolis: Bobbs-Merrill, 1955);

Lectures in the Philosophy of Education, 1899, edited by Reginald D. Archambault (New York: Random House, 1966);

The Early Works of John Dewey, 1882–1898, 5 volumes, edited by Jo Ann Boydston (Carbondale: Southern Illinois University Press / London: Feffer & Simons, 1967–1972);

The Philosophy of John Dewey, 2 volumes, edited by John J. McDermott (New York: Putnam, 1973);

John Dewey: Lectures in China, 1919–1920, translated and edited by Robert W. Clopton and Tsuin-Chen Ou (Honolulu: University Press of Hawaii, 1973);

Lectures on Psychological and Political Ethics, 1898, edited by Donald F. Koch (New York: Hafner Press / London: Collier-Macmillan, 1976);

The Middle Works of John Dewey, 1899–1924, 15 volumes, edited by Boydston and others (Carbondale: Southern Illinois University Press / London: Feffer & Simons, 1976–1983);

The Poems of John Dewey, edited by Boydston (Carbondale: Southern Illinois University Press, 1977; London: Feffer & Simons, 1977);

The Later Works of John Dewey, 1925–1953, 17 volumes, edited by Boydston and others (Carbondale: Southern Illinois University Press / London: Feffer & Simons, 1981–1991);

Lectures on Ethics, 1900-1901, edited by Koch (Carbondale: Southern Illinois University Press, 1991);

Philosophy & Education in Their Historic Relations, transcribed by Elsie Ripley Clapp, edited by J. J. Chambliss (Boulder, Colo.: Westview Press, 1993);

Principles of Instrumental Logic: John Dewey's Lectures in Ethics and Political Ethics, 1895–1896, edited by Koch

(Carbondale: Southern Illinois University Press, 1998).

Editions and Collections: *The School and the Child: Being Selections from the Educational Essays of John Dewey,* edited by Joseph J. Findlay (London: Blackie, 1906);

Educational Essays, edited by Findlay (London: Blackie, 1910)–comprises *Ethical Principles Underlying Education, Interest in Relation to Training of the Will,* and *Psychology and Social Practice;*

The Philosophy of John Dewey, edited by Joseph Ratner (New York: Holt, 1928; London: Allen & Unwin, 1929);

The Wit and Wisdom of John Dewey, edited by A. H. Johnson (Boston: Beacon, 1949);

John Dewey: His Contribution to the American Tradition, edited by Irwin Edman (Indianapolis: Bobbs-Merrill, 1955);

The Child and the Curriculum; and, The School and Society, introduction by Leonard Carmichael (Chicago: University of Chicago Press, 1956);

Dewey on Education, edited by Martin S. Dworkin (New York: Bureau of Publications, Teachers College, Columbia University, 1959);

Dictionary of Education, edited by Ralph B. Winn, foreword by John Herman Randall Jr. (New York: Philosophical Library, 1959);

On Experience, Nature and Freedom: Representative Selections, edited by Richard J. Bernstein, Library of Liberal Arts, no. 41 (Indianapolis: Bobbs-Merrill, 1960);

Theory of the Moral Life, introduction by Arnold Isenberg (New York: Holt, Rinehart & Winston, 1960);

Philosophy, Psychology and Social Practice: Essays, edited by Ratner (New York: Putnam, 1963);

Selected Educational Writings, edited by F. W. Garforth (London: Heinemann, 1966);

Moral Principles in Education, preface by Sidney Hook (Carbondale: Southern Illinois University Press / London: Feffer & Simons, 1975);

The Moral Writings of John Dewey, edited by James Gouinlock (New York: Hafner, 1976; revised edition, Amherst, N.Y.: Prometheus, 1994);

John Dewey: The Essential Writings, edited by David Sidorsky (New York: Harper & Row, 1977);

The School and Society; and, The Child and the Curriculum, introduction by Philip W. Jackson (Chicago: University of Chicago Press, 1990);

John Dewey: The Political Writings, edited by Debra Morris and Ian Shapiro (Indianapolis: Hackett, 1993);

The Essential Dewey, 2 volumes, edited by Larry A. Hickman and Thomas M. Alexander (Bloomington: Indiana University Press, 1998)–comprises volume 1, *Pragmatism, Education, Democracy;* volume 2, *Ethics, Logic, Psychology;*

How We Think: A Restatement of the Relation of Reflective Thinking to the Educative Process, foreword by Maxine Greene (Boston: Houghton Mifflin, 1998).

OTHER: "Does Reality Possess a Practical Character?" in *Essays, Philosophical and Psychological: In Honor of William James, Professor in Harvard University, by His Colleagues at Columbia University* (New York: Longmans, Green, 1908), pp. 53–80;

"The Development of American Pragmatism," in *Studies in the History of Ideas,* by the Department of Philosophy of Columbia University, volume 2 (New York: Columbia University Press, 1925), pp. 353–377;

"The Rôle of Philosophy in the History of Civilization," in *Proceedings of the Sixth International Congress of Philosophy,* edited by Edgar Sheffield Brightman (New York: Longmans, Green, 1927), pp. 536–542;

"Philosophies of Freedom," in *Freedom in the Modern World,* edited by Horace Meyer Kallen (New York: Coward-McCann, 1928), pp. 236–271;

"From Absolutism to Experimentalism," in *Contemporary American Philosophy,* edited by G. P. Adams and W. P. Montague, volume 2 (New York: Macmillan, 1930), pp. 13–27;

"Creative Democracy–The Task before Us," in *John Dewey and the Promise of America,* Progressive Education Booklet, no. 14 (Columbus, Ohio: American Education Press, 1939), pp. 12–17;

The Living Thoughts of Thomas Jefferson, edited by Dewey (New York: Longmans, Green, 1940; London: Cassell, 1941);

The Bertrand Russell Case, edited by Dewey and Kallen (New York: Viking, 1941);

"Antinaturalism in Extremis," in *Naturalism and the Human Spirit,* edited by Y. H. Krikorian (New York: Columbia University Press, 1944), pp. 1–16;

"The Field of 'Value,'" in *Value: A Cooperative Inquiry,* edited by Ray Lepley (New York: Columbia University Press, 1949), pp. 64–77.

During his long life John Dewey contributed in profound and original ways to every field of academic philosophy: metaphysics, epistemology, ethics, political philosophy, aesthetics, and logic. Outside of philosophy, his ideas on education transformed pedagogical methods not only in the United States but throughout the world. He was actively engaged in causes ranging from getting the vote for women and unionizing teachers to defending persecuted intellectuals such as Bertrand Russell and Leon Trotsky, and his incisive, clear, and often impassioned statements on current events made his name familiar to the public at large. His collected works fill thirty-seven volumes, and his vast cor-

*George Sylvester Morris, one of Dewey's philosophy
professors at Johns Hopkins University*

respondence could fill many more. Pervading this work, from the most abstract to the most concrete, is Dewey's faith in the possibilities of democracy.

The third of four sons, the first of whom had died in infancy, Dewey was born on 20 October 1859 in Burlington, Vermont, to Archibald Sprague Dewey, a grocer, and Lucinia Rich Dewey, who was twenty years younger than her husband. Dewey's father had little formal education but was an avid reader of the works of John Milton and William Shakespeare; during the Civil War he served with the Union army as a quartermaster. Dewey was a bashful, bookish boy who loved hiking in the Adirondacks and boating on the nearby lakes and in Quebec.

While attending the University of Vermont, Dewey was caught up by the controversy over the theory of evolution and the questions it raised about the relationship between science and society; he was particularly impressed by Thomas Henry Huxley's textbook *Lessons in Elementary Physiology* (1866). He was also influenced by the American afterglow of German Romanticism, the Transcendentalist movement—in particular, by James Marsh's critical American edition (1829) of the poet Samuel Taylor Coleridge's *Aids to Reflection in the Formation of a Manly Character on the Several Grounds of Prudence, Morality, and Religion* (1825), which he later recalled as his spiritual emancipation. The effort to synthesize the biological concept of the organism with the organic thinking of German idealism drove Dewey into

philosophy and determined the development of his thinking. During his last year in college he attended H. A. P. Torrey's lectures on philosophical psychology, empiricism, and Plato; Torrey's Socratic personality made a strong impression on Dewey.

After graduating in 1879, Dewey taught high school for two years—first in Oil City, Pennsylvania, and then back home in Burlington. At the end of this period he submitted an article to *The Journal of Speculative Philosophy,* edited by the leader of the St. Louis Hegelians, William Torrey Harris. He included with the article a letter asking Harris's opinion as to whether the piece showed any philosophical aptitude. The article was accepted, as was another that Dewey subsequently sent, and Dewey, encouraged by Harris's response, borrowed $500 from an aunt and enrolled in the new graduate program in philosophy at Johns Hopkins University. A classmate was Thorstein Veblen, who later wrote *The Theory of the Leisure Class: An Economic Study of the Evolution of Institutions* (1899). Dewey's elder brother, Davis, enrolled a year later in the program in political economy and went on to teach at the Massachusetts Institute of Technology. At Johns Hopkins, Dewey was exposed to the dynamic idealism of George Sylvester Morris, who had studied in Germany and translated Friedrich Ueberweg's *A History of Philosophy: From Thales to the Present Time* (1872–1873). He presented Georg Wilhelm Friedrich Hegel's idealism as the resolution of the conflict between scientific materialism and moral values. Dewey embraced this version of idealism, and he and Morris became friends. Dewey was also influenced by G. Stanley Hall, whose courses on philosophical psychology reflected the most recent laboratory developments in Germany. He also took a course in philosophical logic taught by Charles Sanders Peirce, the founder of pragmatism, but was unimpressed with Peirce's formalistic conception of logic.

Dewey received his doctorate in 1884 with a dissertation on Immanuel Kant; the work has been lost, but its thesis was probably the same as that of Dewey's article "Kant and Philosophical Method," published in *The Journal of Speculative Philosophy* in April of that year.

In 1884 Dewey began teaching psychology at the University of Michigan at Ann Arbor. On 28 July 1886 he married Alice Chipman. She and her sister had been orphaned and raised by their maternal grandparents, Fred and Evelina Riggs. Fred Riggs had served as a judge in Dodge City, Kansas; prospected for gold in Colorado; and managed trading posts. An honorary member of the Chippewa tribe, he was fluent in their language and fought for their rights. His saying, "Some day these things will be found out, and not only found out, but *known,*" is frequently cited in Dewey's writings; it embodies Dewey's view that knowledge is a matter of public intelligence and not mere private understanding. Like her grandfather, Alice Dewey had a religious nature but was not attached to any doctrine. Years after her death, Dewey argued in *A Common Faith* (1934) that the religious quality of experience must be distinguished from any dogmatic or doctrinal claims. Here, as well as in Dewey's lifelong engagement with social issues, Alice's influence may be seen. The Deweys had six children: Frederick Archibald, born in 1887; Evelyn, born in 1889; Morris, born in 1892; Gordon Chipman, born in 1896; Lucy Alice, born in 1897; and Jane Mary, born in 1900.

Between 1884 and 1903, when he broke with the idealist movement, Dewey produced a vast body of writings, the importance of which has been eclipsed only because of the significance of Dewey's subsequent work. Dewey's early philosophy represents a sophisticated attempt to grapple with a range of issues; it was steadily recast until the late 1890s, by which time Dewey's appeal to the metaphysical presuppositions of idealism all but disappears.

Idealism as a philosophical term is to be contrasted with the ordinary sense of holding to high standards of conduct. With the rise of modern science during the Renaissance, the medieval reliance on the intellectual authority of Aristotle and other earlier thinkers was shattered, and two major schools of epistemology, or theory of knowledge, arose. One was rationalism, according to which truth is to be discovered by reason alone, as in mathematics; the information that comes from the senses is constantly changing and unreliable. Empiricism, on the other hand, claimed that the mind is originally a blank page, or tabula rasa, and that all of its ideas are derived from experience—of the workings of the mind itself, obtained through introspection, or of external reality, derived from sensation. The German philosopher Kant argued in his *Kritik der reinen Vernunft* (1781; revised, 1787; translated as *Critique of Pure Reason,* 1855) that pure concepts derived from reason establish nothing about the external world, but he also held that if the mind did not supply such concepts to organize sensations, experience would be a meaningless blur from which not even such concepts as space and time could be extrapolated. Thus, Kant concluded, reality cannot be known as it exists in itself but only as it appears to the mind. Experience, though it has a necessary structure imposed by the mind, is a no-man's-land between an unknowable external world and an unknowable internal self.

In response to this conclusion a succession of metaphysical systems were produced by Kant's German successors Johann Gottlieb Fichte, Friedrich Wilhelm Joseph von Schelling, and, most important, Hegel, all of which agreed that reality can be identified with the activity of "*Geist,*" or "Spirit," an all-embracing, universal self-consciousness. Cosmic and human history, Hegel argued in his *Die Phänomenologie des Geistes* (1807; translated as *The Phenomenology of Mind,* 1910), is the inner "dialectical" working out of Spirit's effort to understand itself on ever higher and more inclusive levels until it at last attains fully infinite, free, and rational self-understanding.

While British academic philosophy remained in the empiricist camp, German idealism had a great impact on the Romantic movement—especially on such intellectuals as Coleridge and the American Ralph Waldo Emerson. And although the Kantian philosophy gradually reasserted its dominance in German universities, by the middle of the nineteenth century, idealism, thanks largely to the writings of the philosopher T. H. Green, began to dominate British institutions such as the University of Oxford. By the end of the century ardent defenders of idealism included F. H. Bradley in England and Josiah Royce in the United States. One of the major appeals of idealism was its claim to reestablish a basis for moral and cultural values against the increasing materialistic and mechanistic view of nature and humanity offered by modern science. Moreover, it saw history as a process of development through ever higher stages, an idea that buttressed Victorian beliefs in progress and the superiority of European civilization.

When Dewey first entered the philosophical arena, he was attracted by the refusal of idealism to reduce the most significant aspects of human experience to a series of sensations caused by the actions of the physical environment on the bodily organs. In one of the early essays he sent to Harris he argued that the materialistic position does not need to be refuted, because it refutes itself: atoms in motion do not generate theories about atoms in motion. On the other hand, Dewey was dissatisfied with the idealist rejection of the methodology of empirical science in favor of a suspicious "dialectic" that could not be objectively tested but depended for its persuasiveness on the cleverness of the arguer. Just as he had desired a synthesis of Huxley's physiology with Coleridge's Romanticism in college and of Morris's idealism with Hall's psychology in graduate school, as a young lecturer Dewey wanted to preserve the metaphysical basis of idealism but to graft onto it the experimental psychology that was then emerging. This desire is the theme of several of Dewey's essays of the 1880s, most notably "The New Psychology" (*Andover Review,* September 1884), "The Psychological Standpoint" (*Mind,* January 1886), and "Psychology as Philosophic Method" (*Mind,* April 1886).

The same desire is the theme of Dewey's first book, *Psychology* (1887), a textbook in which he uses the latest psychological research to argue for the truth of absolute idealism. Though mostly of historical interest now, *Psychology* reveals several distinctly Deweyan concerns, not least his desire to integrate feeling and moral action with knowledge. Each factor, he contends, influences and determines the others in the fully complete "Absolute Self." Since psychology is the study of consciousness, it is also metaphysics, the study of reality. Rejecting Hegel's dialectic, Dewey argues that empirical psychology gives philosophy a legitimate methodology. Though he later abandoned the notion of the Absolute Self, he always retained the ideal of fully integrated experience. He described this ideal most fully in his accounts of aesthetic experience, and he regarded his books on education, ethics, social philosophy, and experimental inquiry—what he came to call "instrumentalism"—as means for realizing that ideal.

Dewey's critical embrace of idealism also appears in *Leibniz's* New Essays Concerning the Human Understanding: *A Critical Exposition,* a short volume he contributed in 1888 to a series introducing German philosophy to English-speaking readers that was edited by his former teacher Morris. The book is mainly an account of Gottfried Wilhelm Leibniz's "Nouveaux essais sur l'entendement humain" (1765), but Dewey concludes with a criticism of the formalistic logic in that work.

In 1888 Dewey accepted an offer to become the chairman of the philosophy department at the University of Minnesota in Minneapolis. His daughter Evelyn was born there in 1889. Dewey was only at Minnesota for a year, however: Morris died in 1889, and Dewey was asked to return to Michigan to replace him as the head of the philosophy department.

A textbook Dewey wrote to be used in his course in ethics, *Outlines of a Critical Theory of Ethics* (1891), shows him moving away from Morris's teachings. This movement had been made necessary by the appearance in 1890 of William James's *The Principles of Psychology.* James's functional analysis of consciousness as an emerging process developing out of biological action; his stress on the role of habit in determining thought, as well as conduct; and his critique of the notion of the self as an underlying substance rather than a creative process directly challenged the idealist psychology and metaphysics of Dewey's *Psychology* and offered a more satisfactory solution to the problems that had inspired Dewey's work from the start: it was the most extensive attempt to that time to integrate a functional understanding of the organism's behavior with a functional analysis of experience. Dewey revised his *Psychology* in 1891, but he was teaching James's text that same year. He wrote James a "confessional" letter (10 May 1891) in which he praised the book as a stimulus to "mental

freedom": "Many of my students, I find, are fairly hungering. They almost jump at any opportunity to get out from under the load and believe in their own lives."

Dewey's objections to traditional idealistic ethical theory are summarized in "Moral Theory and Practice," an essay that appeared in the *International Journal of Ethics* in January 1891. He says that ethics pertains to the whole of human conduct, not just a specifically "moral" side, and that moral insight is not the operation of a special faculty but employs "the same ordinary intelligence that measures dry-goods, drives nails, sells wheat, and invents the telephone." Moral ideals emerge in conduct to make it self-reflective and self-regulative; they serve as guides to action. Nevertheless, Dewey still sees ethics as a process of self-realization of a more complete self embodied in the community.

During this period Dewey attempted to recast Hegelianism in the terms of the naturalism he took from Charles Darwin and from James's *The Principles of Psychology.* Three of his early articles on logic adumbrate some of the problems and themes of his later writings in the field. One of these themes is his enduring interest in and respect for experimental science. In all of his logical writings Dewey expressed the view that science is the clearest and most significant contemporary exemplification of the fundamental structure of all intelligent inquiry. In these early essays he takes the position that because of the dominating importance of science in the development of intelligent inquiry in the modern age, the elucidation of scientific practice must be the central concern of logic. He is interested in clarifying not the specialized techniques or body of accumulated results of particular scientific disciplines but, rather, those pervasive features of science as a creative social activity that account for its success in explaining nature.

In "The Present Position of Logical Theory" (*Monist,* October 1891) Dewey sees the problem science poses for logic to be the relationship of observational fact or perception—the initial subject matter of scientific inquiry—to the thoughts or ideas by which these facts are explained. Traditional Aristotelian-Scholastic formal logic provides no answer to this problem but only exacerbates it, for in this tradition thinking is taken as subjective, as an internal aspect of the mind, with its own structure and rules that constitute a domain of reason independent of fact. In "The Logic of Verification" (*Open Court,* 24 April 1890) he contends that this dualism of fact and thought means that facts can never serve as the standard of verification for scientific hypotheses. If one supposes that the putative facts against which a hypothesis is to be tested are true and known prior to and independently of the formulation of the hypothesis, then the hypothesis is unnecessary: knowledge has already been achieved. On the other hand, if the facts are not known—if what are taken to be facts are simply guesses or opinions—then these apparent facts are useless for verification, since it is precisely such fallible opinions that scientific hypotheses are meant to correct.

Dewey's solution to this dilemma is that the dualism between fact and thought must be collapsed; the facts that are known cannot be thought of as existing independently of the ideas and hypotheses by which knowledge is achieved. The specifics of this solution are, however, presented within the framework of idealism: the factual or "real" world is imbued with the organizing influence of thought, of logical processes, from the beginning of inquiry; fact and thought are, therefore, not strictly distinguishable, for the former is part of the latter; the distinction is made within thought, not outside of it. As Dewey explains in "Is Logic a Dualistic Science?" (*Open Court,* 16 January 1890): "knowledge, experience, the material of the known world are one and the same all the way; it is one and the same world which offers itself in perception and in scientific treatment; and the method of dealing with it is one and the same—logic."

The extent of the influence exercised on Dewey by James's *The Principles of Psychology* is shown in "The Superstition of Necessity" (*Monist,* April 1893), where Dewey applies his interest in psychology to the concept of logical necessity, and in "Self-Realization as the Moral Ideal" (*Philosophical Review,* November 1893), where he rejects the notion that moral conduct is simply the empirical self following out the preestablished structure of the Absolute Self. One's concrete existential possibilities are real as possibilities, Dewey argues, and experience genuinely constitutes the realization of a self-in-process. Green, Dewey's former hero, is sharply criticized in this article.

In 1894 Dewey was asked to organize the department of philosophy and psychology at the newly established University of Chicago. Before moving to Chicago, he took his family on a trip to Europe, during which his son Morris died of diphtheria in Milan, Italy.

In Chicago, Dewey added pedagogy to the department of philosophy and psychology and established a laboratory school, popularly known as "the Dewey School," to experiment with educational methods. Dewey's associates in Chicago included the philosophers George Herbert Mead and James H. Tufts, both of whom had been with him at Michigan, as well as Chicago school superintendent Ella Flagg Young and the social worker Jane Addams, after whom Dewey's daughter was named.

Instead of revising *Outlines of a Critical Theory of Ethics* once again when the second edition was exhausted, Dewey overhauled his ethical theory. The

Dewey in the mid 1880s

result, *The Study of Ethics: A Syllabus* (1894), presents a position called "experimental idealism" that is close to Dewey's mature instrumentalism. Dewey describes ethical conduct as a continuing process of adjustment between agent and situation; the emphasis falls on aspects of ethical psychology rather than, as in *Outlines of a Critical Theory of Ethics,* on fundamental ethical concepts. Habit and impulse are given a central role in the development of character, and the book ends with a discussion of the virtues with no mention of the Absolute Self.

In the two-part article "The Theory of Emotion" (*Philosophical Review,* November 1894 and January 1895) Dewey reworks theories of the expression of emotion offered by James, Darwin, and C. J. Lange to develop a more integrated and functionalistic view of behavior. The culmination of the transformation in Dewey's thinking is found in "The Reflex Arc Concept in Psychology" (*Philosophical Review,* July 1896), which is his most profound contribution to the science of psychology and marks the breakthrough for his subsequent philosophical development. Dewey's immediate task in the article is to overcome the mechanistic and dualistic understanding of the relationship of the organism and its environment. Whereas the old reflex-arc theory argued for a chain of linear causality from the physical environment to the organism and then from the organism to consciousness, which then caused the organism to react on the environment, Dewey offers a dynamic

Letter in which Dewey accepts the offer of a professorship in philosophy at the University of Michigan, replacing the late George Sylvester Morris (James B. Angell Papers, Bentley Historical Library, University of Michigan)

view of the organism-environment relationship that he later termed "interaction" and, still later, "transaction." The organism does not passively wait to be acted on; it actively explores its environment, searching for stimuli. Stimuli, in turn, are determined by the organism's need to coordinate its activity with the environment. The result is that experience is not a series of mechanical cause-effect relations but a genuine process of intelligent learning and growth.

In *The Significance of the Problem of Knowledge,* a paper delivered to the Philosophical Club of the University of Michigan in the winter of 1897 and published the same year, Dewey locates the problem of the relation of observational fact and thought in the historical dissociation of the search for a proper method of theoretical inquiry from the problems of practical life that initially prompted the search. In Greek philosophy, he says, thought was separated from practice–thinking became a profession; this separation, which is both theoretical and social, has continued throughout the development of logical theory and still causes havoc for the modern theory of knowledge. The solution to the logical problem of the connection of thought and fact is to dissolve the historical dualism between theory and practice by recognizing that the search for secure knowledge is engendered by the exigencies of practical life.

The implications of this new model can be seen in the first of Dewey's mature writings on the theory of knowledge: the four introductory essays he contributed to the volume *Studies in Logical Theory* (1903) under the collective title "Thought and Its Subject-Matter." A cooperative effort by Dewey and seven colleagues and former students at the University of Chicago, *Studies in Logical Theory* is an attempt to develop a radically new approach to logic that solves some of the difficulties posed by traditional approaches such as the "transcendental" logic of Hegel and his followers and the empirically based logic of John Stuart Mill. Dewey's essays provide a general framework for the new approach, while the other seven articles deal with special topics in light of this framework.

The central theme of Dewey's essays is that unless inquiry is understood as an activity in the life process that has, like any other human activity, its own initiating preconditions, means of accomplishment, and objectives, the dualisms that have developed from the historical division of theory from practice cannot be eliminated from the theory of knowledge. Inquiry must be understood as a developing activity, the features of which play certain functional roles in this developmental process. Thus, facts, sensations, and perceptions, on the one hand, and ideas, concepts, and thoughts, on the other hand, are not to be regarded as independent preexistents that must be artificially combined in a logical

process; instead, they should be distinguished in the functional roles they play as instrumentalities in the accomplishment of completed inquiry.

Dewey distinguishes three phases in the development of inquiry. First, like any other human activity, inquiry is preceded by a situation that both stimulates activity and sets the general parameters to which the activity must conform. Dewey calls the situation antecedent to inquiry "problematic," since it is one in which uncertainty arises as to the meaning of the situation for action. The problematic situation, initially failing as a guide to practice, requires reconstruction through inquiry if it is to be restored as a reliable guide. Second, the development of the data or subject matter for thought involves isolating various elements of the situation and adapting them for use in inquiry. Finally, during the activity of reflective inquiry itself ideas, hypotheses, and rules of inference are developed with the direct aim of reconstructing the problematic situation in such a way as to remove the initial uncertainty and reestablish the fluency of activity.

Throughout his exposition Dewey takes Hermann Lotze as his philosophical antagonist. While admiring Lotze's logic for its avoidance of the inadequacies of the empiricism of Mill and David Hume and the rationalism of Kant and Hegel, Dewey contends that Lotze retains a dualism of fact and thought that renders his logic inconsistent. Since Lotze sees the distinction between fact and thought as basic and ontological, rather than as functional, he must find a way to show the relevance of the one to the other; in doing so, he transfers features of thought to his characterization of fact, in contradiction to the presumptive independence of the two.

Dewey criticizes Hegelian transcendental logic on similar grounds. The Hegelians avowedly do what Lotze attempts unsuccessfully to avoid doing: they attribute the organization of fact, prior to reflective inquiry, to the constitutive activity of thought. But if thought is active prior to reflective inquiry, Dewey argues, the question of what role reflective inquiry itself plays in the attainment of knowledge becomes acute: "For the more one insists that the antecedent situation is constituted by thought, the more one has to wonder why another type of thought is required; what need arouses it, and how it is possible for it to improve upon the work of previous constitutive thought." Dewey concludes that no satisfactory solution to this problem is available on Hegelian principles; he therefore rejects transcendental logic and, along with it, the views that he had defended in his early logical writings.

The critical response to the publication of *Studies in Logical Theory* was modest–ten reviews in various journals–but, on the whole, positive. In 1904, Peirce, writing in *The Nation,* and F. C. S. Schiller, writing in

Mind, expressed general sympathy with the views espoused by the contributors, although Peirce, in private correspondence with Dewey, admitted reservations about the adequacy of a developmental approach to logic. By far the most enthusiastic reception of the volume was by James: in the *Psychological Bulletin* in 1904 he proclaimed the birth of a new school of thought at the University of Chicago. One reason for James's enthusiasm is revealed in a 23 March 1903 letter to Dewey in which he noted with delight, and some surprise, that on reading *Studies in Logical Theory* he had discovered a close affinity between Dewey's thought and his own. As a consequence of this discovery, James cites Dewey as a coworker in the development of the pragmatic position in his later writings on the subject, including *Pragmatism, a New Name for Some Old Ways of Thinking: Popular Lectures on Philosophy* (1907) and *The Meaning of Truth: A Sequel to "Pragmatism"* (1909).

Increasingly strained relations with the president of the University of Chicago, William Rainey Harper, intensified by a misunderstanding between Dewey and Harper on Alice Dewey's role in the laboratory school, led Dewey to resign in 1904. He wrote to his friend James M. Cattel, chairman of the department of philosophy and psychology at Columbia University, about the prospects for an opening there. Cattel, fearing that other universities might make him an offer, took the matter up with the president, Nicholas M. Butler, who raised the money to create a position for Dewey. The resulting appointment included not only a position on the Faculty of Philosophy, a graduate division of the university, but also one on the Faculty of Teachers College.

During the summer before taking up his position at Columbia, Dewey lectured at the Summer School of the South in Knoxville, Tennessee. In July he took his family on another trip to Europe. In an uncanny repetition of what had occurred in 1889, his son Gordon died of diphtheria in Ireland. In 1905 the Deweys adopted a son, Sabino.

At Columbia, Dewey was relieved of the heavy administrative responsibilities he had assumed at Chicago. Also, whereas the department at Chicago, organized under Dewey's direction, had consisted of people whose philosophical views were closely aligned with his own—thus the appellation "The Chicago School"—at Columbia, Dewey entered a well-established department whose members had diverse backgrounds and interests. One of his new colleagues, F. J. E. Woodbridge, was concerned with developing a metaphysics based on Aristotelian principles but employing the modern insights of a scientific naturalism; another, Felix Adler, was primarily interested in religious and political issues; and a third, William P. Montague, endeavored in his writings to reinterpret the traditional

mind/body distinction according to modern physical principles. This diversity stimulated Dewey to work out his own position in more detail.

In essays written during his first years at Columbia, including "The Experimental Theory of Knowledge" (*Mind,* July 1906), "Reality and the Criterion for the Truth of Ideas" (*Mind,* July 1907), and "The Control of Ideas by Facts" (*Journal of Philosophy,* 4 April, 9 May, and 6 June 1907), Dewey develops the central tenets of his logic that he had first presented in *Studies in Logical Theory.* His main concern in these essays is to defend the pragmatic theory of truth, which was fundamental to the pragmatic school of thought and a principal target of critics. One gauge of the depth of this concern is an appeal Dewey made to James in 1909, when the latter was preparing to publish *The Meaning of Truth,* to omit the last two paragraphs from the essay "'Truth' *versus* 'Truthfulness.'" Dewey believed that James's proposal to substitute the word *truthful* for *truth* in the pragmatic theory would leave the theory open to criticism. James accepted Dewey's suggestion and changed the title of the essay to "The Existence of Caesar."

In "The Control of Ideas by Facts" Dewey accepts the most familiar formula for defining truth, that "a true idea in any situation consists in its agreement with reality." He suggests, however, as James does in *Pragmatism, a New Name for Some Old Ways of Thinking,* that the problem of the meaning of truth consists in settling what is meant by the "agreement" to which the definition refers. Dewey, like James, proposes that an idea agrees with reality insofar as its use in practice leads to the achievement of the goals one is pursuing in action. The truth of an idea is thus a consequence, not a precondition, of its usefulness; it presupposes the "problematic situation" of *Studies in Logical Theory,* in which activity is obstructed, requiring investigation to restore effective action. When this restoration is accomplished by the use of an idea, the idea is made true through its use. As James puts it in *Pragmatism, a New Name for Some Old Ways of Thinking,* "truth *happens* to an idea."

In other articles published during his first years at Columbia, most notably "The Postulate of Immediate Empiricism" (*Journal of Philosophy,* 20 July 1905), "What Does Pragmatism Mean by Practical?" (*Journal of Philosophy,* 13 February 1908), and "Does Reality Possess a Practical Character?" (1908), Dewey discusses the metaphysical implications of his instrumentalism. Unlike James, who regarded pragmatism as a methodology empty of metaphysical content, Dewey believed that the radical change of standpoint in the theory of knowledge effected by pragmatism was not consistent with traditional metaphysical views. The motivation behind tradi-

THE MICHIGAN ARGONAUT.

Psychology.

O what is the matter with yon, lank girl,
    A pale and wild and haggard she,
Oh, don't you know, the old man said,
    She's taking Dewey's Psychology.

Once she was fair to look upon,
    Fair as a morning in June was she,
And now the wreck you see to-day
    Is caused by Dewey's Psychology.

A year had passed, again I strayed
    By the Medic's hall; what did I see
But some whitened bones of a girl who died
    Taking Dewey's Psychology.

CHANNING GUILD.

The Channing Guild which has just

Poem that appeared in the University of Michigan student newspaper on 10 November 1888 (from Brian A. Williams,
Thought and Action: John Dewey at the University of Michigan, 1998)

tional metaphysics was, according to Dewey, the attempt to find a secure, immutable object of knowledge, isolated from the vicissitudes of empirically encountered states of affairs. By showing that knowledge is achieved through practice, that reflective inquiry is itself a type of human activity, and that knowledge is sought because of its instrumental value for practice, the pragmatic theory removes this motivation and not only opens the path to new metaphysical views but also requires a new view that takes full account of the empirical and practical character of reality. The metaphysical dimension of Dewey's instrumentalism has often been overlooked by critics but is essential to the position he was developing during this period.

In "The Postulate of Immediate Empiricism" Dewey argues that things experienced empirically "are what they are experienced as." This statement applies not only to the sophisticated experience of the scientist but also to the "naive" experience of people who lack any understanding of what they are experiencing. One of Dewey's examples is a noise in the dark that is expe-

rienced as fearsome but is found, on investigation, to be the innocuous tapping of a shade against a window. The later experience, shaped by the intervening inquiry, does not vitiate the previous status of the noise: the fearsome noise was just as real as the innocuous one. Thus, inquiry has not uncovered a reality underlying the appearance of the noise as fearsome but has effected a change in a concrete experiential reality: it has changed a situation fraught with practical uncertainty into one whose significance is settled.

The upshot of Dewey's position is that, although the factors of experience that have a cognitive function (sensations, ideas, hypotheses, and so forth) provide the means for the reconstruction of conflicting and puzzling elements of experience into a clarified and harmonious whole and thereby afford the basis for intelligent action, the objective and real in experience should not be identified exclusively with this cognitive function. In making this claim, Dewey throws into question the belief, going back to the ancient Greeks, that reality must be identified with the object of cognition. For Dewey, cognition is

SYLLABUS OF COURSE 5

INTRODUCTION TO PHILOSOPHY

PHILOSOPHICAL DEPARTMENT

UNIVERSITY OF MICHIGAN.

FEBRUARY, 1892.

SECTION 1.—Philosophy (science) is the conscious inquiry into experience. It is the attempt of experience to attain to its own validity and fullness; the realization of the meaning of experience.

Science and philosophy can only report the actual condition of life, or experience. Their business is to reveal experience in its truth, its reality. They state what *is*.

The only distinction between science and philosophy is that the latter reports the more generic (the wider) features of life; the former the more detailed and specific.

SECTION 2.—The separation of science and philosophy has reference to the incompleteness of knowledge. Although our experience goes on within the whole, the whole is the last thing of which we become conscious *as* a whole of included factors. Thus the trouble with philosophy is the difficulty of getting the whole, the generic, before consciousness in such a way that it may be naturally reported. The partial thing may be broken off from the whole and then described with comparative ease. But this process of multiplying pieces seems to leave the generic, the whole beyond and out of sight. It makes the whole remote, and capable of description only in unnatural ('metaphysical' 'transcendental') terms. Thus science, as relating to the part, and philosophy as referring to the whole, fall apart. Philosophy suffers by being made vague and unreal; science in becoming partial and thus rigid.

Syllabus for one of Dewey's courses (Bentley Historical Library, University of Michigan)

only one kind of experience; one's meaningful encounter with the world (with "reality") is also undergone in many other ways. Experience outside the context of inquiry can be perplexing and precarious, and these qualities stand, as components of reality, on an equal ontological footing with the clarifying products of cognitive activity. Thus, Dewey insists, inquiry effects a change within reality. It transforms a situation that is troubling and affords no sure guide for action into one whose significance is made intelligible; it does not substitute a reality for what was unreal or merely subjective.

One of the advantages of this view, Dewey contends, is that it provides the philosophical basis for a common-sense realism. In articles such as "The Realism of Pragmatism" (*Journal of Philosophy,* 8 June 1905), "Brief Studies in Realism" (*Journal of Philosophy,* 20 July and 28 September 1911), and "The Existence of the World as a Logical Problem" (*Philosophical Review,* July 1915) he argues that one is immediately aware of reality in experience. Only within the context of inquiry, when experience is in the process of reconstruction, do sensations and ideas play a mediating and inferential role in respect to a reality that transcends them; and even then, they do so only in respect to the specific elements of experience that generated doubt and stimulated the inquiry. When the aim of inquiry is accomplished, these mediating sensations and ideas "drop out, and things are present to the agent in the most naively realistic fashion" ("The Realism of Pragmatism").

Another advantage of this view, according to Dewey, is that it affords a way of restoring to empirical and immediately accessible reality those elements of experience that, because of a misleading logic, previous philosophers believed did not belong there. Of particular importance are the aesthetic and moral values experienced as qualities of things in the world. Because the philosophical tradition denied to what is immediately experienced, in all its richness of qualities and values, a place in the world of things—assigning it, instead, the status of appearance—value was detached from this world, taking a place either in the experiencing subject, for sensationalists such as Hume and John Locke, or in the ultimately real Absolute of Hegel and Bradley. Once the fallacy of identifying thought and reality is appreciated, the content of immediate experience in all its qualitative richness can be restored to an empirically encountered and real world. Dewey stresses this consequence of his position in several essays of this period, including "Beliefs and Realities" (*Philosophical Review,* March 1906), "Experience and Objective Idealism" (*Philosophical Review,* September 1906), and "Is Nature Good? A Conversation" (*Hibbert Journal,* July 1909).

The biological and behavioral roots of Dewey's logical and metaphysical views, first expressed in "The Reflex Arc Concept in Psychology," are brought into focus in "Does Reality Possess a Practical Character?" Dewey makes clear that in his view experience comprises a situation in which an organism is in a relationship of mutual dependency with its environment. When a problem occurs—when there is a conflict of behavioral tendencies that stultifies activity—the conflict is not located in the organism or the environment in isolation from one another but in the situation that includes both. When inquiry is successful in removing the initiating conflict, a change is effected in the situation, and, consequently, in both the organism and its environment. In his writings of this period Dewey uses the term *interaction* to describe this mutual involvement of organism and environment, but in his later works, such as *Knowing and the Known* (1949), he uses *transaction* to stress his view that the organism and the environment acquire many of their features by their mutual involvement and cannot be thought of in abstraction from one another without falsifying both.

Dewey's writings elicited many comments and criticisms; some, such as his colleague Woodbridge, were sympathetic to his philosophical aims, while others were antagonistic. Dewey believed that many of the criticisms resulted from misinterpretations; in particular, he thought that many critics interpreted the meanings of his terms in ways that were consistent with traditional epistemology and metaphysics but inconsistent with his own views. This concern remained with Dewey throughout his career. A desire to rid his vocabulary of any cause for misunderstanding was a central motivation behind his collaboration with Arthur F. Bentley that culminated in *Knowing and the Known.*

One of the most persistent criticisms of Dewey's instrumentalism and its metaphysical implications was that it was, at base, a subjectivism: that is, that it attributed characteristics to reality that are appropriately attributed only to the contents of consciousness. Dewey believed that this criticism was rooted in a misinterpretation of his use of the term *experience* in his analysis of the transformative nature of inquiry. In keeping with the empiricist tradition dating back to Locke and Hume, Dewey's critics understood the term to refer to a wholly subjective state having no essential connection with anything beyond the mind; but Dewey intended no such meaning. In responses to the criticisms of "The Postulate of Immediate Empiricism" and in articles such as "The Realism of Pragmatism" and "Reality as Experience" (*Journal of Philosophy,* 10 May 1906) he stresses that rather than denoting private or subjective sensations—"ideas" in Locke's sense, divorced from objective states of affairs—for him *experience* denotes the interactive relationship between an organism and its environment. As such, experience, independent of reflective inquiry, is immediately informative of the states and qualities of reality. Only when inquiry intervenes are certain aspects of experience–ideas and meanings–distinguished from this reality. In these contexts ideas and meanings are tentative and hypothetical, fulfilling a representative function in respect to those aspects of the preinvestigatory reality that have been brought into doubt. Thus, functional dualities between representational idea and represented object appear within experience in the process of inquiry; but such dualities should not, Dewey insists, be identified with a hard and fast dualism between experience as a whole, identified as the subjective mind, and reality as a whole, existing "outside" of the mind.

Dewey's efforts during his first decade at Columbia to develop, clarify, and defend his instrumental theory of knowledge and the broader themes of the pragmatic school culminated in two collected editions of his articles on logic and metaphysics. The first was published in 1910 as *The Influence of Darwin on Philosophy and Other Essays in Contemporary Thought*. The second, and more significant, collection resulted from a suggestion by C. J. Laing of the University of Chicago Press in the fall of 1915 that Dewey's four essays from *Studies in Logical Theory* be republished as a separate volume. Dewey replied in an 11 October letter that excluding the other contributors to *Studies in Logical Theory* from the new book would be "almost churlish," but he agreed to the plan after the consent of the others was obtained. In late 1915 and early 1916 he revised his essays from *Studies in Logical Theory* and added revised versions of eight previously published articles and a new and lengthy introduction. The volume was published in the summer of 1916 as *Essays in Experimental Logic*.

In his introduction Dewey summarizes the main themes of his instrumental logic and responds to some of the criticisms that had been brought against it. One criticism to which he was particularly sensitive was that his logic ignored the more traditional problems of the field relating to the nature of terms and propositions and their use in deductive and inductive reasoning. A development of his logical theory in the introduction to *Essays in Experimental Logic* is his attempt to answer this criticism by suggesting how terms and propositions are used as the bearers of meaning in formal logical procedures by which the implications of these meanings can be explored in abstraction from existential data. Another indication of Dewey's nascent interest in demonstrating the implications of instrumental logic for more-traditional logical questions is his unpublished paper "Logical Objects," delivered to the Philosophy Club of New York on 9 March 1916. In this paper Dewey discusses the status of what he calls "logical entities," such as the logical connectives *or, if, and,* and so

forth, and mathematical "entities," such as numbers and classes, in inferences. These writings include some insights that Dewey later developed into a theory of propositions and logical form in *Logic: The Theory of Inquiry* (1938).

Also in 1916 Dewey published his most important work on pedagogical theory, *Democracy and Education: An Introduction to the Philosophy of Education*. Dewey's background in psychology and his dynamic conception of experience explain his focus on education. In the history of Western philosophy only a handful of philosophers had concerned themselves with this issue–notably, Plato, Aristotle, Schiller, and Jean-Jacques Rousseau. While those thinkers tried to find absolute principles for the justification of knowledge, Dewey saw learning as more significant than knowing and described philosophy itself as "the general theory of education." Thus, his writings on education have a direct bearing on his theory of knowledge as inquiry and on his theory of the democratic community. At the time Dewey published his most important work in this area, the United States was experiencing one of the most dramatic and widespread transformations any society has undergone: technology was erasing past ways of life with new and ever-changing modes of behavior; large numbers of immigrants with diverse backgrounds, beliefs, and customs were struggling to adjust to the American melting pot; and the hard economic realities of unregulated industrialism were manifesting themselves. The question of education, then, not only presented Dewey with a new perspective on traditional philosophical problems but also offered, in his view, the only intelligent way in which a society could deal with such problems, transform itself, and resolve its tensions without resorting to oppression or revolution. The school must be the place where society develops the ability to change in a directed, cooperative, and foresighted fashion. This theory puts Dewey at odds with those, such as Karl Marx, who see violent revolution as the primary way a society can change itself and with those who regard education as the means whereby an existing social order indoctrinates its new members in the preexisting social habits.

Democracy and Education was the fruit of long reflection on the theory of democratic education; in his later years Dewey regarded it as one of the best expressions of his philosophy. He begins by looking at education as part of the process of life's need to renew itself: the certain death of each of society's members means that human culture can only continue to exist through transmission. Any community is constituted by the education of its members so that communication, cooperation, and shared life are possible. Human beings are learners by nature, and one of the major aims of education should be learning how to learn, how to keep growing, and how to acquire intelligent habits. This process requires both a structured context embodying the received knowledge and values of the past and the plasticity of mind to discover new truths and evaluate alternative possibilities. In Dewey's term, the aim of intelligence is "reconstruction," the dynamic but continuous development of social life.

A major point in Dewey's theory is that education is a social affair. Intelligence is not the personal property of the individual but a feature of cooperative and creative interaction. Thus, especially in a democratic society, educational methods should foster a spirit of shared inquiry and assistance, rather than competition among individuals. At the same time, instead of inculcating conformity and a blind respect for absolute values, a democratic society needs members who can integrate a complex range of values, imaginatively understand alternative points of view, and engage in a constructive dialogue with others about mutual problems. The ultimate ideal is that democratic society itself become a continuous process of shared learning. Dewey emphasized in many of his works that the pervasive culture of a society is the most powerful force in education; the institution of the school has only a limited ability to educate. If the customs of a society do not foster the habits necessary for democracy, then democracy as a political ideal will always be in jeopardy.

Dewey's writings on educational theory span most of his career. Two of the most impassioned and concise statements of his views are *The Child and the Curriculum* (1902) and *Experience and Education* (1938). In both works he explains that the problem of education is to avoid the extremes of forcing a completely alien subject matter on the child and being satisfied with rote memorization as "learning," at one extreme, and, at the other extreme, leaving the interests of the child with no development or guidance. The need is to use the child's current interests, capacities, and understanding as a means of gradually expanding his or her knowledge and range of concerns. One acquires a better understanding of abstract concepts by allowing them to emerge from a functional setting, such as learning geometry by having to measure and cut wood for building a house, than by memorizing formulas and then applying them as the occasion arises. Many of Dewey's experiments along this line are discussed in a series of lectures published in 1900 as *The School and Society,* one of Dewey's most influential and widely read books. Other important monographs on educational theory include *My Pedagogic Creed* (1897); *Interest in Relation to Training of the Will* (1896), revised and enlarged as *Interest and Effort in Education* (1913); *How We Think* (1910), which was extensively rewritten in 1933; and *Schools of To-morrow* (1915).

Dewey at the University of Chicago, where he taught from 1894 to 1904

Dewey's educational philosophy continues to be the subject of debate as fashions in education change. Dewey himself was critical of many of the excesses carried out in his name. But regardless of the specific recommendations he made during his career in response to the problems of his day, the moral of Dewey's position is that no pragmatic theory can dogmatically cling to an experiment that fails or that no longer meets current problems. One must constantly reexamine the needs of one's situation and try to formulate the most intelligent response to them.

While Dewey was working out his logical, metaphysical, and educational views during the 1890s and early 1900s, he was also formulating an ethical philosophy. His views on this topic are especially difficult to assess, since for Dewey "ethics" is concerned with every type of human conduct rather than being relegated to a somewhat arbitrary sphere known as "morality." Also, he continued to develop his ideas on this subject well into the 1940s. Nevertheless, broad features emerge. In the late 1890s, as he gradually abandoned idealism for a dynamic naturalism, he began to rework what he considered the major implications of the theory of evolution for moral theory. He faced a challenging task, since Herbert Spencer's influential "social Darwinism," a theory with which Dewey sharply disagreed, seemed to have presented the logical application of Darwin's "survival of the fittest" (a phrase Darwin himself had borrowed from Spencer) to a ruthless view of human life. Spencer argued that the efforts of society to sustain its weaker members ultimately betrayed the interests of the species: however much one's sympathies for the sick, the orphaned, the weak, and the crippled may be aroused, one is obliged to allow natural selection to operate without intervention. This philosophy was cheerful news, of course, to the captains of industry who were beginning to face political challenges to unrestrained capitalism. Dewey's major evaluation of Spencer is "The Philosophical Work of Herbert Spencer" (*Philosophical Review*, 1904), in which he undertakes to reveal the dogmatic assumptions Spencer dressed up in Darwinian garb—especially in his idea of evolution, which Dewey shows to be at odds with the Darwinian one. Spencer, says Dewey, assumes an unchanging environment to which an organism must adapt or perish, when, in fact, environments evolve as much as organisms do. Thus, to reduce human behavior to the most rudimentary criteria of animal survival is inappropriate. Morals evolve in the context of distinctive human needs and social control, where the code of "nature red in tooth and claw" may not assist the continuity of the group.

In "Evolution and Ethics" (*Monist*, April 1898) Dewey takes issue with Huxley's counterargument that although human beings had evolved naturally, morality is opposed to the principle of evolution and is, indeed, a struggle against it. This view is similar to the traditional approaches of Plato, Augustine, and Kant, which invoke a nonnatural principle to ground ethical values. Dewey tries to forge a middle path, arguing that the capacity of human beings to look out for each other as members of a group—especially the more helpless members, such as children—is precisely the sort of advantage that aids survival. By developing the capacity to use foresight, human beings were able to see the need for the immediate care of weaker members in the face of emergencies. The implication is that moral conduct represents a radical transformation of individual competition into social cooperation that is quite in line with the principles of evolution. "The environment is now a distinctly social one," says Dewey, "and the content of the term 'fit' has to be made with reference to social adaptation." Moreover, insofar as evolution does not, as Spencer thought, aim at some final, stable "end," ethics is part of the continuing struggle of human adaptation to changing situations—it is a process of growth, rather than a code of conduct grounded on fixed principles. Dewey points to the human capacity to create new environments that establish new patterns of behavior as quite in keeping with the evolutionary theory. With the advent of agriculture, for instance, the food environment was radically changed, which allowed for more nurturing and flourishing as well as requiring a higher degree of social organization.

Dewey's response to the dilemma posed by social Darwinism established the pattern of his subsequent moral theory. In 1902 he further explored the relationship of evolution to ethics in a two-part article in *The Philosophical Review*, "The Evolutionary Method as Applied to Morality," in which he argues that "evolution" cannot be read as a universal law applied to isolated instances. Rather, the implications of the "evolutionary method" are that one should look at any phenomenon, such as ethics, from the historical or "genetic" point of view—that is, as a developmental, contextualized process. Dewey tried to implement this program by looking at the history of Western ethical theory itself as a response to changing needs and contexts in culture. Instead of arguing for or against a particular ethical theory, he first attempted to see it in terms of his "genetic method," as in his brief historical synopsis *Ethics* (1908), the published version of a public lecture he delivered at Columbia in March 1908; it was revised and republished as "Intelligence and Morals" in *The Influence of Darwin on Philosophy and Other Essays in Contemporary Thought*.

The result was a radically novel approach to traditional philosophical questions in moral theory exemplified in another work titled *Ethics* and published in 1908, this one co-authored by Dewey and Tufts. Though meant as a college textbook, *Ethics* marks a philosophical development of major importance. It is divided into three major parts, the first and most of the third by Tufts, the second and the first two chapters of the third by Dewey. The first part consists of an historical examination of "the beginnings and growth of morality" from tribal life to the modern period. The second part, which moves from the empirical and descriptive to the theoretical level, is a philosophical discussion of "the theory of the moral life" that looks at types of ethical theories and argues for the dynamic, situational, and progressive view. The final section explores the applications of the theory to contemporary issues such as economics and the family.

Dewey's most important work on ethics, however, is *Human Nature and Conduct: An Introduction to Social Psychology* (1922). He takes up successively the roles of habit, impulse, and intelligence in conduct, concluding with a discussion of the function of ideals and freedom in human life. Habit constitutes the social world of culture into which each human being is born. Through education, plastic impulses are shaped and desires are directed to ends. Thus, Dewey sees in habit the foundation of intelligent activity—activity undertaken for the sake of, and guided by, an "end-in-view." Habit is not to be thought of as mere routine or custom, the mechanical repetition of the same act; habits are dynamic, growing patterns of organizing and responding to new experiences—the very tools of learning. They are, first and foremost, creative structures and are only minimally and degradedly present in meaningless repetition. Like Aristotle, Dewey locates the crux of morality in the acquisition of good habits, which make up one's character. He opposes both utilitarian and deontological (duty-oriented) ethics, which concentrate on the absolute ethical value of isolated rules or actions. Ethics, for Dewey, has to do with general dispositions toward intelligent activity rather with than rules or actions taken out of context.

Since situations may change, one needs to be able to probe them imaginatively so as to work out the best possible responses before acting. An essential moment of ethical reflection is the dramatic projection of oneself into the various possible alternatives. More important, one must be able to approach conflicts with a capacity to work out mutually sustaining solutions and compromises that preserve diverse and incommensurable values, instead of branding one side right and the other wrong. Dewey rejects the idea that some one value can be used to measure all others. In their actual lives, people have to adjust and integrate a complex range of values that gives the full meaning and sense of their existence. The role of intelligence and deliberation is to explore the meanings and values that are at play and potentially realizable in the present situation (since that is the situation in which one finds oneself and the only situation about which one can do anything). Dewey has been misread as a utilitarian, submitting all values to a calculation based on future consequences. Instead, he says that one tries to understand the future consequences of possible actions so as to understand and evaluate the meaning of the present, thereby finding the best possible mode of response. The embodiment of moral thinking, for Dewey, is not found in the individual subjective "conscience" fastening onto one principle and battling on, though the heavens may crash; it is found, rather, in a mutually undertaken, imaginatively heightened exploration of possible modes of response that can coordinate the conflicting values at issue and then constantly reevaluate the response chosen for its effectiveness in realizing its aim. While Dewey's ethics gives no absolute answers to abstract demands and enjoins no imperatives, it is far from being a subjective relativism. The task of intelligence is continuous, because the world changes and no recipe can replace

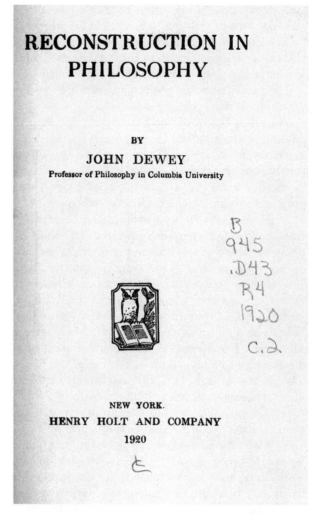

RECONSTRUCTION IN
PHILOSOPHY

BY
JOHN DEWEY
Professor of Philosophy in Columbia University

NEW YORK.
HENRY HOLT AND COMPANY
1920

Title page for the published version of a series of lectures Dewey gave at Imperial University in Japan in 1919, in which he argues against the separation of thought and practice that has historically characterized Western philosophy (Thomas Cooper Library, University of South Carolina)

long, careful experience. Dewey's ethical theory is intentionally oriented toward providing a basis for his political theory of the democratic life, later expressed in *The Public and Its Problems* (1927) and *Freedom and Culture* (1939), as well as illustrating the moral implications of his instrumentalism and his theory of education.

Dewey traveled in the Orient from 1919 to 1921, lecturing in Japan and China. While the authoritarian culture of imperial Japan did not attract Dewey, he was deeply impressed by the Chinese, who were struggling to reorganize their ancient Confucian bureaucracy into a modern, independent democratic nation. Dewey was particularly struck by the level of political involvement of the Chinese students, who organized a nationwide protest ("The May Fourth Movement"), as Dewey arrived, to prevent the government from making a concessionary treaty with the Japanese. On 20 June 1919 Dewey wrote to his children back home, "To think of kids in our country from fourteen on, taking the lead in starting a big cleanup reform politics movement and shaming merchants and professional men into joining them. This is sure some country."

In 1924 Dewey was invited to Turkey by the government of Kemal Atatürk to recommend improvements to the educational system. Dewey traveled extensively in the country, wrote several articles for *The New Republic* on the developing nation, and produced a report with progressive suggestions for the Turkish schools.

By the 1920s Dewey's national and international reputation had grown to such an extent that he became a much sought-after speaker and lecturer. As a consequence, many of his most important works of the 1920s and 1930s originated as lecture series. Chosen to deliver the first Paul Carus Lectures in 1922, he presented the talks "Existence as Stable and Precarious," "Existence, Ends, and Appreciation," and "Existence, Means and Knowledge" at the December meeting of the American Philosophical Association at the Union Theological Seminary in New York City. He expanded these lectures into a book in 1925 under the title *Experience and Nature*. Because of its breadth of approach and content, *Experience and Nature* is considered by many Dewey scholars his magnum opus, and it continues to be one of the most widely read of his philosophical works. It represents a crossroads in the development of his ideas, providing a distillation of his earlier views in logic, metaphysics, and ethics and a foreshadowing of his later thought.

The argument of *Experience and Nature* is a natural development of Dewey's earlier writings, in which he claimed that prereflective experience does not falsify the natural world, nor does reflective inquiry reveal a world that is more real than that experienced outside the context of inquiry. Rather, inquiry effects a change in reality in that it enables one to act productively within the natural environment without obstacle or inhibition. Thus, reflective inquiry is an instance of the human organism's involvement with its environing conditions and should be understood on a par with other such involvements—each with its peculiar preconditions, modes of development, and issues—that collectively comprise what Dewey calls "experience."

Experience in this broad and inclusive sense is Dewey's main concern in *Experience and Nature*. Experience so understood provides, he says, a method for metaphysical inquiry. As the sum of the many doings and sufferings of the organism in its life activity, experience is revelatory of the generic features of the natural world, of which it is itself a part. The task of the meta-

physician is to provide an account of these features that is faithful to the integrity of experience as a whole, without the introduction of falsifying dichotomies and dualisms. Here, as in his earlier writings, Dewey dissociates himself from the tradition in modern philosophy that identifies experience as a subjective and private possession of the individual, a matter of sensations and ideas existing separately from an objective "physical" world that is known only by inference. He holds that only when experience is taken more naively as a direct disclosure of nature is the traditional skepticism concerning the possibility of metaphysical understanding averted. Thus, whereas the prevalent approach in philosophical discussion had been psychological and personal, concerned primarily with describing the contents of the individual subjective mind, Dewey's approach in *Experience and Nature* is anthropological and social: he describes the generic traits of nature as they are revealed through shared human experience of the world of things.

Dewey begins by noting that the world, as it is experienced, exhibits an integral blend of what he calls "the precarious," that contingent aspect of things that entails risk and uncertainty, and "the stable," the rhythmic patterns of things that afford people prediction and control of changing states of affairs. These antipodal traits of nature are not only revealed in the course of individual lives but also acknowledged in cultural traditions and practices—the universal concern with luck and misfortune, magical intervention, and expiatory rites. Honest metaphysical description of these two aspects of the experienced world requires acknowledgment that natural processes admit of both order and disorder, regularity and contingency. On the negative side, any metaphysical system that postulates an unchanging, absolutely stable mode of being, whether it be called substance, universals, or the Absolute of the idealists, must be rejected. On the positive side, "every existence is an event": nature is composed of processes or occurrences that proceed through time. Stability in the course of changing events is afforded by their structure: the repetition of recognizable patterns based in the causal order.

The events that make up nature are both immediately possessed in their ineffable qualitative character within experience and related to one another in temporal and causal processes. The former character of events, their qualitative immediacy, accounts for the enjoyment, as well as the suffering, experienced in human beings' interactive involvement with environing conditions. Each event is also part of a temporal process and, as such, has conditions in relation to which it is an end or terminus and consequences in relation to which it is a beginning. In Dewey's terminology, events have "histories." In their immediate qualitative character they are not known but are simply suffered and enjoyed for what they are. When, however, some events are taken as signs or indications of other events that can be enjoyed or suffered–when they are abstracted from their immediacy and considered in terms of their use for the prediction and control of other events–then the concern for knowledge comes into play. Things are known insofar as they are related to one another as conditions and consequences.

This abstraction from the immediacy and unique individuality of things and concentration on the mathematical and causal relatedness of events accomplished by scientific inquiry gives science its defining character and its great success in predicting and controlling natural occurrences. But the objects of scientific inquiry–the generalized mathematical and causal relationships discovered by science–should not be identified with nature in toto; to do so would be to commit what Dewey calls the "philosophic fallacy" of identifying abstracted characteristics of nature with reality itself and excluding its immediate qualities, while at the same time disavowing the act of abstraction. Science has its unique instrumental value precisely in the facility it provides for controlling the immediacies of existence by controlling their conditions and consequences.

After this general description of experience, Dewey turns to experience transformed through the cultural use of symbols, the distinctively human world of communication, consciousness, reflection, art, and valuation–experience as "civilized." His discussion of communication is particularly significant. First, he expands the interactional model he worked out in "The Reflex Arc Concept in Psychology" to a social model. Insofar as an individual organism can coordinate its actions and responses to the environment, it does not need symbols and so does not have the capacity for self-reflection. But when a group of organisms must engage in cooperative behavior, each with a different part to play in achieving a common end, some form of communication is needed. Human beings developed a complicated mode of symbolic communication in which one individual could take the standpoint of another in terms of a commonly shared project and use that capacity to communicate with the other, who also had to take the standpoint of the one communicating. Thus, human beings not only gained self-reflection through symbolically mediated behavior but also began to develop the capacity for transforming experience far beyond the meager powers of the individual organism.

This account, sketched out in the fifth chapter of *Experience and Nature* and extensively developed by Dewey's friend and former colleague at Chicago, Mead–especially in the lectures that became *Mind, Self,*

JOHN DEWEY
LECTURES IN CHINA, 1919-1920

Edited and Translated from the Chinese by
ROBERT W. CLOPTON
AND TSUIN-CHEN OU

Dust jacket for the 1973 publication of lectures Dewey gave during his travels in the Far East

and Society from the Perspective of a Social Behaviorist (1934)– is also important as a theory of meaning. Meaning has been one of the primary concerns of twentieth-century philosophers. Most sought to locate it in a rigorously codified formal system grounded in self-evident intuitions either of sense-data or intentional essences, while others argued that meaning is reducible to the rules of ordinary language. Dewey and Mead reject both alternatives. Meaning, they say, to be sure, arises from the primary world of ordinary human activity, but such a world is not necessarily either explicitly cognitive nor codifiable into formal rules. The prereflective dimension of experience and its ambiguities are part of the world of meaning, as are the possibilities for meaning to grow and develop in ways not predictable by formal rules. The recognition of conflicts, the transformation of problematic situations, and poetic extensions of meaning are intrinsic to this theory.

Dewey proceeds to examine the emergence of individuality and subjective experience in this context. Individuality is not a preestablished given but a

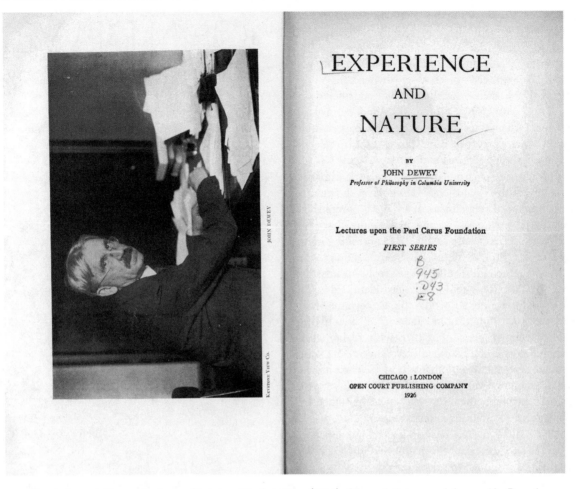

Frontispiece and title page for the second printing of the first edition (1925) of the work that many scholars consider Dewey's magnum opus, in which he argues that scientific inquiry is a specific instance of the human organism's involvement with its environment (Thomas Cooper Library, University of South Carolina)

gradually realized trait; it is, essentially, the distinctive ability of each member of a group to make a novel and potentially creative contribution to the social process. Whereas most cultures have traditionally tried to suppress novelty, creativity, and individuality for the sake of preserving conformity to previously set social patterns, Dewey argues that the modern emphasis on the importance of the individual must be seen from the perspective of the needs of a constantly changing world. Mind, which for Dewey is shared cultural patterns and habits of interpretation, must become individualized. Instead of seeing mind as a universal, impersonal rationality, Dewey sees it as a creative and transformative power to explore and extend the possibilities of one's culture through reconstructive imagination. Culture itself, he argues, should be a continuous dialogue between the unique and irreducible aspects of each individual and the shared needs of the community so that the society is a living, intelligent process.

Against the traditional attitude in most Western philosophy to regard the mind as radically opposed to the body and the senses, Dewey sees mind as "embodied," as something that emerges from the activities of a living being. Life itself, in turn, emerges from the physical universe. Mind cannot be reduced to biology, nor life to physics, but neither can they be understood in radical isolation. Dewey describes these three "plateaus"–the physical, the vital, and the conscious–as distinct, each needing its own categorical description for understanding but also standing in genetic or historical relationships to the others. This view, which is equally opposed to dualism, materialistic reductionism, and idealism, he calls "naturalistic emergentism." The qualitative world of feeling cannot be compartmentalized "inside" a subjective, nonphysical consciousness any more than it can be naively imposed on the real world as it is. The red of the rose is a quality neither of the rose nor of the conscious experience alone; it is the realization of a dynamic, interactive process between a sentient organism and a natural object in the organism's environment. The red is "in" the process of the interaction. For most practical purposes it can be pragmatically located in the object, but for others it may be treated as a function of the optical system of the living being. The qualitative feeling and the relational cognition both "intend" the inclusive transaction of the organism in its environment.

Consciousness as such and the having of those events termed "ideas" are part of this process: "Consciousness, an idea, is that phase of a system of meanings which at a given time is undergoing redirection, transitive transformation." One's immediate conscious experience is the dynamic hub of a relational and contextual field of experience, which is itself part of the interaction of the living organism and the world. The subconscious, for Dewey, is not a domain of "uncivilized" drives that must be deflected and sublimated, as Sigmund Freud maintained; rather, it is the sedimented body of organized habit and impulse that is capable of being either crude and unintelligent or eminently conducive to intelligent and perceptive experience. The prime manifestation of the latter type of unconscious can be found in the work of the artist, where a vast amount of training and experience feeds into the immediate perception and activity without becoming obtrusively evident. Against the blind materialistic energism of the Freudian view, Dewey restates his conviction that habit, education, and social practices shape the preconscious but meaningful contours of conscious experience.

This point leads Dewey to a discussion of two major topics in the philosophy of civilization that liberate experience: art and value. Art, in the sense of the intelligent control of a medium to secure a fulfilling end, is the civilization of experience itself. Between the two extremes of meaningless experience, one dominated by mechanized routine and the other by random, chaotic impulsiveness, art steps in to make experience a growth process of the realization of those meanings and values that give significance to human existence. Science may have banished ends on the level of physics, but insofar as human beings are part of nature, art reintroduces ends into an aspect of nature.

Though society has tried to separate the instrumental and the "consummatory" (Dewey's name for the fulfilling mode of experience illustrated by the arts) not merely intellectually but also in terms of social practice (the artisan producing for the aristocrat), the fundamental integration of these themes lies at the heart of Dewey's interpretation of experience. Thus, he wants to expand his readers' view of art from the cases of "fine art" to all activities that can assist in rendering human life worth living in the deepest and most complete sense and to eliminate the notion that the "instru-

mental" is concerned merely with means or with short-sighted, selfish ends. To view things instrumentally is to see all human activities and social institutions in terms of the general need of human beings to live well. Instead of being divorced from art, science and knowledge can be regarded as artistic enterprises when they are directed to this inclusive end.

In the final chapter of *Experience and Nature* Dewey discusses the role of philosophy as the criticism of valuations. Values, as they are immediately had, cannot be critically evaluated—they are simply enjoyed for what they are. The function of what Dewey calls "criticism" is to evaluate things valued in terms of their conditions and consequences—that is, in terms of the costs incurred in their attainment and the subsequent gain or loss of other values. He holds that such evaluation is vital for the development of a society in which human needs and wants are fulfilled in an intelligent and humane manner and that philosophers, because of the wide scope of their discipline, are in the ideal position to carry out this critical inquiry.

Experience and Nature received a great deal of critical attention. Thirty reviews appeared in professional journals, popular magazines, and newspapers. Many of the reviewers were sympathetic to Dewey's views, but, as was the case with many of his other philosophical writings, the difficulty of his style and the originality of his ideas generated many misunderstandings even among his supporters. As with his earlier work, Dewey believed that much of this misunderstanding stemmed from professional philosophers misinterpreting his ideas and vocabulary in the light of traditional philosophical discourse. In a 22 February 1926 letter to the art critic Leo Stein he remarked, "To a considerable extent, judging from personal letters, non-professional persons have got my meaning more readily than professional philosophers." And, also as with his earlier writings, Dewey was most concerned with the misunderstandings raised by his use of the term *experience*. To his friend Max Otto he wrote on 2 January 1926, "I am sure that in writing the book again, I could clear up some of the difficulties about 'experience' which others have felt beside the book, tho whether I could clear up the whole matter satisfactorily, I don't know."

In the summer of 1926 Dewey taught at the University of Mexico in Mexico City. He recorded his observations on the Mexican government's attempts to break up the country's agrarian feudalism.

Dewey's political theories are found throughout his writings and in a handful of specialized essays. But *The Public and Its Problems,* published in 1927, represents his most important and developed views on the relationship of democracy and political theory. Like the utilitarians, Dewey thinks that the natural-rights justification of representative democracy given by Locke is based on a metaphysics and epistemology that are no longer believable. The classic Lockean model of a "social contract" among free rational individuals as the quasi-historical basis of political society is equally flawed. The worst result, Dewey says, is that the fundamental conception of human beings is a social version of Newtonian atomism: independently complete "atomic" individuals are externally related to each other by rational "laws" according to which any right involves an equal and corresponding duty. The pragmatic effect of the doctrine is to oppose the individual to "society" and to government. Liberty is conceived as "freedom from" external intervention rather than "freedom to" do something based on actively developed, assisted capacities.

In the first place, Dewey notes, the social-contract model fails to recognize that human beings are born as helpless infants into cooperating, culturally educated human groups. The "individual" is, thus, a social being from the start. On the other hand, Dewey is critical of attempts by thinkers such as Rousseau, Hegel, and Marx to turn the state into a supraindividual organism in which each person surrenders his or her unique individuality to the "higher self" of the collective whole. Societies, he says, are constituted by individuals. His radical solution is to jettison the false dichotomy of the individual versus the social and to insist that humans are "social" beings from one perspective, while from another they are "individuals." Some interactions can be controlled and the results easily foreseen, but others cannot, and so careful control and supervision are required. These latter are "public" transactions and are what legitimately calls a state into being.

Thus, the state, for Dewey, arises from a pragmatic need: the need for "publics"—groups of individuals who are affected in common by important consequences—to regulate certain types of activities through the medium of officials. The state is the effort of people to apply the method of intelligence to a limited range of issues, though the range and the subject matter will vary from time to time and from place to place. The state has no all-inclusive interest in regulating private transactions; nor does it have a duty to allow destructive individuals and social institutions to exercise their freedom, any more than it has a "duty" to allow a river in flood to sweep away homes and destroy lives without some effort at control.

Dewey thinks that a limited and flexible amount of public planning for society is in keeping with the spirit of democracy. The primary need is to establish a genuinely democratic culture, a body of democratic social habits, rather than to try to specify an ideal set of formal institutional procedures. As the classical philoso-

phers often pointed out, laws are but words without citizens of wisdom and goodwill. The key lies in the ability of publics to recognize themselves. Before a problem can be controlled or solved, it must be identified as a problem and correctly analyzed through factual information and experiments, and an attempted solution must be undertaken and evaluated. For example, a community invites a plant to be built nearby to provide jobs. A gradual rise in cancer is eventually noticed. If the community is poorly equipped to identify the true cause, the deaths may be ascribed to chance, or the will of God, or a "miasma." An intelligent public will not only notice a statistical change in mortality from cancer but will also methodically search for the cause and, if it is attributed to toxic dumping by the plant, attempt to regulate it.

For this process to occur, several features must be present in the community. First, the community must recognize that it is potentially a responsive, intelligent organization. Effective means must be undertaken to acquire reliable information and disseminate it so that it can be truly known, not merely understood by isolated private individuals. Knowledge and inquiry must be recognized public aims. In other words, the primary condition of the democratic public is a total commitment to education and inquiry. Dewey's theory of education is, thus, a deeply integrated aspect of his political theory. Second, the community must allow communication and criticism as intrinsic parts of its way of life. For a community to have intelligence, it must engage in dialogue. It is enhanced by having within it a plurality of points of view, rather than a deadening uniformity of inculcated belief. Finally, the community must be prepared to undertake experiments in social practice and to evaluate their consequences. It cannot exist with an unshaken satisfaction that its customs and values are absolute.

The result, Dewey hopes, will be a community that can not only constantly adapt and evolve to changing circumstances but also actively, rather than haphazardly, search for those conditions on which fully satisfying, meaningful human lives can flourish. Democracy, in the end, means for him the capacity of each individual to participate as fully as possible in the realization of his or her capacities to lead a meaningful life and to experience the world in its aesthetic, even religious, qualities. The democratic individual will strive to accommodate a plurality of values and understand a variety of alternative points of view and will be ready to engage in informed dialogue and undertake experiments to resolve problems. In such a genuine community individuals will retain their uniqueness, which will actively contribute to the shared social context. Ultimately, Dewey argues, democracy must be a local affair of face-to-face relationships bonded by affection and rooted in attachment to the community. In such a situation individuals can see the direct consequences of their actions rather than lose them in the anonymity of abstractions and impersonal institutions.

Dewey's wife died in July 1927 after several years of declining health. After a brief trip to Hubbards, Nova Scotia, where he eventually bought a summer cottage, Dewey returned to New York City. Until his remarriage in 1946 one of his children always lived with him. In 1928 Dewey supported the Socialist presidential candidate, Norman Thomas. He went to the Soviet Union in 1928 to examine its new school system, which impressed him in many respects.

On 12 March 1928 Sir Alfred Ewing, principal of the University of Edinburgh in Scotland, had written to invite Dewey to be the Gifford Lecturer in Natural Theology for the academic year 1928–1929. Dewey delivered a set of ten lectures from 17 April to 17 May 1929 under the title "The Quest for Certainty." Although the purpose of the Gifford Lectureship, as stated in Lord Adam Gifford's will, was to advance the study of natural theology, no religious test was applied to prospective lecturers, and several previous lecturers had made only passing reference to religious topics. Thus, Dewey's agnosticism was not out of keeping with the provisions and practice of the Gifford Lectureship, although it did raise the eyebrows of some reviewers of *The Quest for Certainty: A Study of the Relation of Knowledge and Action* (1929), the book Dewey produced from his lectures.

Rather than attempting a narrow treatment of religious questions, Dewey explored in his lectures the history of Western thought so as to show the continuities and discontinuities of his philosophical views with traditional ideas. This project was not a new one for Dewey: in earlier writings, dating back to *The Significance of the Problem of Knowledge,* he had attempted an interpretation of the history of ideas from an instrumentalist perspective, concentrating on what he saw as the historical bifurcation between thought and practice and the philosophical dualisms to which it gave rise. In lectures he had delivered in 1919 at Imperial University in Japan and published in 1920 as *Reconstruction in Philosophy* he developed these themes in greater detail, anticipating many of the views expressed in *The Quest for Certainty.*

In his Gifford lectures Dewey suggests that the historical separation between theory and practice arose out of the situation in which primitive peoples found themselves. Because the environing conditions were in constant flux, actions taken to obtain safety and security were fraught with risks, and the people were only intermittently successful in obtaining their objectives. They hoped to attain certainty and security by tran-

Dewey in the early 1930s

scending the practical affairs of life through the cultivation of pure thought and reflection, but Dewey demonstrates that this hope was forlorn by tracing the many paths it has taken in the history of thought, from supernaturalism to classical and modern epistemology, and showing that these paths not only failed to provide the certainty and security they promised but actually inhibited the use of empirical and practical means to establish conditions that could satisfy basic human needs and desires. The rise of scientific investigation in the modern period represents a rejection of these traditional methods and of the goal of obtaining certain and unassailable knowledge, in favor of securing through empirical means beliefs that, while hypothetical and tentative in character, nevertheless have real practical import and, thus, concrete value for human affairs. Because of the emotional appeal of traditional beliefs, especially those of religion, however, an uneasy truce has arisen in modern times between science and tradition that gives authority to the former in respect of questions concerning the nature of the physical world, while reserving for the latter authority in matters concerning moral and social values. Thus, the transition

THE

Bertrand Russell
C A S E

Edited by John Dewey
and Horace M. Kallen

B
1649
·R94
D4

N E W Y O R K
The Viking Press
1 9 4 1

Ŀ

Title page for a collection of essays by Dewey and others on
the lawsuit that forced City College of New York to rescind
an offer of a teaching position to the British philosopher
Russell on moral grounds (Thomas Cooper Library,
University of South Carolina)

from traditional, nonempirical methods for securing belief to empirical methods has been incomplete, to the detriment of effective and intelligent social policy. Dewey advocates the adoption of an empirical methodology that he calls the "method of intelligence" to rectify this situation. In *The Quest for Certainty* and his later writings on social issues Dewey expresses his conviction that the application of scientific methods in matters of social welfare provides the only means to ensure the achievement of desirable social ends. His critique in the late 1930s of the totalitarian regimes of Nazi Germany and the Soviet Union in *Freedom and Culture* and other writings of the prewar period is based on this conviction. Dewey believed that the rise of totalitarianism was one of the most visible and deplorable consequences of the use of an absolutist and authoritarian, rather than a democratic, forward-looking, and experimental method of social organization and advancement.

In *The Quest for Certainty* Dewey assigns roles for religion and philosophy to play in the effort toward intelligent social action. Religion must relinquish supernaturalism as an outmoded and ineffective means of obtaining stability for moral and cultural values. Divorced from supernaturalism, religious values can serve a positive secular function by instilling devotion to the effort of attaining social goals. Dewey's discussion of this matter in *The Quest for Certainty* is vague, but in *A Common Faith* he says that even such central traditional religious concepts as "God" can fulfill a secular social role.

Dewey's discussion in *The Quest for Certainty* of the role of the philosopher in social reconstruction is a continuation of that in the last chapter of *Experience and Nature*. He argues that philosophy can perform the dual function of criticizing traditional intellectual habits and beliefs that inhibit social progress and of unifying the results of scientific investigation into a coherent program for social action. It can fulfill this role, however, only if philosophers renounce the traditional epistemological claim, motivated by the desire for sure and certain knowledge, to a privileged access to reality independent of the empirical findings of scientific inquiry.

In suggesting this new role for philosophy in social reconstruction, Dewey was advocating for other philosophers an involvement in social and political affairs that he himself practiced. Throughout his career he was engaged in various causes, and because of his growing reputation outside of academic philosophy he was asked with increasing frequency in the 1920s and 1930s to lend his name to committees and organizations that advanced positions on social policy issues. He often lent not only his name but also his talents as a writer and orator in the furtherance of causes he supported. During these decades he wrote many articles for the popular press concerning current political, social, and economic issues. (He contributed to *The New Republic* with such regularity that instead of remunerating him on an article-by-article basis, as was the normal practice, the magazine paid him a monthly stipend.) Dewey became a well-known social commentator in the public forum and was often sought out for his opinion on timely issues—a rare situation for an academic philosopher.

In 1929 Dewey revised *Experience and Nature,* rewriting the first chapter and adding a preface to explain the work as a whole. In the revised first chapter he attempts to clarify the empirical method employed in the book and the meaning he assigned to *experience*. This edition remains the standard version of the book.

In the wake of the stock market crash in the fall of 1929 Dewey unsuccessfully urged Senator George Norris of Nebraska to form a progressive party. His *Individualism, Old and New* (1930), which originally appeared as a series of articles in *The New Republic* after the crash, includes a searing indictment of a society that gambled away its social possibilities and squandered the lives and hopes of its struggling poor. Dewey's description of the "lost individual" of modern culture refutes the notion that he was a defender of technological progress or unregulated capitalism. It also includes Dewey's call for a new heroic individualism that will pioneer the social frontier of America.

Dewey's essays on his travels in the 1920s were collected in the volume *Impressions of Soviet Russia and the Revolutionary World, Mexico–China–Turkey* (1929). His emphasis throughout is on education as a means of democratic reform.

On 30 June 1930 Dewey retired from active teaching, but he continued to play an active role in the university community as professor emeritus of philosophy in residence. Freed from the demands of a full teaching schedule, he became even more involved in social and political affairs during the 1930s, largely in response to the economic dislocations of the Great Depression. As president of the People's Lobby, Dewey wrote many letters and articles calling for greater government action to relieve the effects of the depression on the unemployed and their children, and as chairman of the League for Independent Action he wrote articles arguing for a third political party to provide new leadership in the economic crisis. He also wrote essays for publications such as *The People's Lobby Bulletin*. In addition, he had to contend with militant communists gaining control of the teacher's union, Local No. 5, which he had helped to organize. After Franklin D. Roosevelt's election as president in 1932, Dewey believed that the New Deal was at best a halfway solution to the country's problems.

In 1932 a revised edition of Dewey and Tufts's 1908 *Ethics* appeared. Dewey's sections are so extensively rewritten as to constitute a new book that reflects the shifts in his thinking during the intervening years. The middle part of the revised edition (chapters 10 through 17) is, perhaps, the clearest introduction to Dewey's mature moral philosophy, which is most succinctly expressed in "Philosophies of Freedom" (1928) and "Three Independent Factors in Morals" (an address delivered in English to the French Philosophical Society in Paris on 7 November 1930, published in French translation in the society's *Bulletin* for October–December 1930, and translated into English by Jo Ann Boydston in the journal *Educational Theory* for July 1966).

Dewey had given the first series of William James Lectures at Harvard University in 1931; the ten lectures became *Art as Experience* (1934), one of his most important books. The work was the fruit of Dewey's effort to pay attention to the qualitative but noncognitive dimension of experience that had been present in his earliest work, though not always explicitly focused on the fine arts. This aspect of Dewey's philosophy had been the source of much misinterpretation, and with the appearance of the book Dewey was criticized by such eminent philosophers as Stephen C. Pepper, a sympathetic supporter of pragmatic contextualism, and the noted Italian neo-Hegelian Benedetto Croce for having lapsed into an idealistic aesthetic theory–a charge Dewey vigorously denied. The book is one of the best introductions to Dewey's general theory of experience in that it counters the traditional misreading of pragmatism as a form of utilitarianism concerned with technical problem-solving in the most limited and mundane sense.

The book also reflects the fruits of Dewey's friendship with Albert Barnes, an irascible millionaire industrialist who had assembled one of the most impressive collections of American and early modern art in the United States. Barnes had been impressed by *Democracy and Education* when it appeared and commuted to New York City to attend a class taught by Dewey. As their friendship blossomed, Barnes invited Dewey to become a member of the board of the Barnes Foundation and took him and his students to Europe to tour the art museums. Barnes, whose aesthetic theories were heavily influenced by Dewey, had dedicated *The Art in Painting* (1925) to him; Dewey reciprocated by dedicating *Art as Experience* to Barnes.

Art as Experience develops Dewey's analysis in *Experience and Nature*. The aesthetic experience, he says, is not a special type of experience confined to a special range of objects and exhibiting a simple, unique "aesthetic" quality. The roots of the aesthetic can be found wherever ordinary experience begins to develop an integration that gives it a suffused qualitative intensity that is consciously apprehended and used to organize the experience as it continues–from the enjoyment of tending a home garden to a child's absorption in watching construction machines or a baseball game. Dewey thus rejects any attempt to distinguish the fine from the practical arts on the basis of content. Experience at large has the capacity to be aesthetically developed, though most of that capacity remains latent. The techniques exhibited in the fine arts have realized the potentialities of their media in a particularly successful way, but the common tendency to idolize fine art and enshrine it with the trappings of high culture have alienated the aesthetic from society. This snobbish attitude is a vestige of the old social division in which the aristocracy was allowed to enjoy what the laboring class had produced. Dewey's solution is not to abolish art museums but to transform them from nationalistic monuments into public and educational institutions, a view that has become much more prevalent. More crucial, however, is his appeal that art not be separated from life but be understood as a development and essential part of it.

Of particular importance in the book are Dewey's discussions of aesthetic expression and form. Expression, he says, is the active relationship between the artist or appreciator and what Dewey calls the "art product"; it is not an internal state that must be projected onto some physical object. The work of art is this process of interaction; it is not the physical medium or art product. Aesthetic form is the interactive, temporal organization of the process of experience, not a fixed, underlying structure of the art product or a special aesthetic intuition. Thus, aesthetic experience reflects the dominant themes of Dewey's general theory of experience: he says not only that "esthetic experience is experience in its integrity" but also that "There is no text that so surely reveals the one-sidedness of a philosophy as its treatment of art and esthetic experience."

Published the same year as *Art as Experience, A Common Faith* was the result of the Terry Lectures that Dewey had given at Yale University earlier in 1934. His most explicit statement of his position on religion, the book can be viewed as a continuation of the discussions in *The Quest for Certainty* and *Art as Experience*. While initially *The Quest for Certainty* seems to be an argument against any form of religious ideal, it argues that ideals themselves, understood as ends used to guide action toward fulfilling activities rather than as a preexistent realm of actualities, have a key function in human existence. *Art as Experience* shows that the aesthetic quality of human existence is the result of realizing such potentialities, which give experience an intrinsic meaningfulness that transcends the cognitive dimension. *A Common Faith* describes the ideal of aesthetically funded human existence itself as a guiding social ideal.

Dewey begins by making a distinction between the religious quality of an experience and any particular doctrine that can be called a "religion." In doing so, he dispenses with any attempt to identify a genuine fulfilling feature of experience with a set of beliefs or claims about the nature of humanity, God, or the universe. Religious doctrines have become stumbling blocks to having religious experiences, Dewey says, and do not constitute legitimate forms of knowledge or inquiry. On the other hand, he argues against any attempt to dismiss or diminish the importance of the religious quality human experience can have. Leave the quest for truth to the experimental method, Dewey urges, but put the experimental method to the service of fulfilling human existence so that daily life becomes enriched and meaningful and bathed in "the light that never was on sea or land." The religious, then, is shared human experience illuminated by fulfilling ideals that guide practices so that the aesthetic possibilities of life are realized across the spectrum of existence. Such an enterprise involves a strenuous application of imaginative intelligence to see these possibilities of the actual world and devise the arts to realize them.

Dewey calls this imaginative transfiguration of the ordinary "God" and rejects atheism almost as strongly as he does theism. The kind of symbolically rich experience of genuine community sought in most religions should not be swept away for a cold, dispassionate, and value-neutral materialism. It should, rather, be taken from a mythic and supernatural realm and relocated in the dynamic processes of the world. The ideal is a possibility of the real to be actualized through the energetic application of human imagination and intelligence for the sake of creating the human community. Dewey's "common faith" is the shared faith of the community in struggling to realize its most meaningful possibilities through the application of intelligent idealism.

The book provoked a heated controversy, with theists heaping abuse on Dewey and his godless naturalism. A positive development of Dewey's views on religion, on the other hand, can be found in the work of Henry Nelson Wieman and other process philosophers.

Liberalism and Social Action (1935) is one of Dewey's most concise and trenchant analyses of political theory, examining the way in which liberalism has opted for one and then another philosophical ideology to justify itself, from natural-rights theory to utilitarianism to Romantic idealism. The problem is that an ideology used at one period to gain a specific kind of freedom eventually became a defense of the status quo when a new social struggle emerged. The natural-rights doctrine, for example, secured the freedom of the rising middle class of the eighteenth century against the claims of feudalism, but by the middle of the nineteenth century it was used to defend the rights of private capital against the new social classes created by the industrial revolution. Dewey urges liberalism to recognize that it is opposed to any ideology and is the movement of social reform itself and, therefore, that it must keep itself open to new needs and problems. At this time he thinks that democratic socialism is the form liberalism should take, but he sees this endorsement as his own tentative and historically localized suggestion and not as a dogmatic creed intrinsic to his theory. In general, "Liberalism is committed to an end that is at once enduring and flexible: the liberation of individuals so that realization of their capacities may be the law of their life."

Logic: The Theory of Inquiry is perhaps the most ambitious of Dewey's works. Thirteen years in preparation and comprising twenty-five chapters in four sections, the book is the culminating statement of his instrumentalist logic. None of his previous writings on the subject match it in the scope of topics discussed or the detail with which they are treated. His most important earlier work on the subject, *Essays in Experimental Logic,* had been compiled from his essays in *Studies in Logical Theory* and articles published in professional journals and so fell short of being a systematic statement of his views. By contrast, *Logic: The Theory of Inquiry* was conceived from the beginning as a continuous exposition employing a consistent terminology and a linear development of argument, and it constitutes a definitive text on instrumentalist logic.

Preparation of the work had begun in the fall of 1925, when Dewey mentioned in a letter to Barnes that he was attempting to commit some of his ideas in logical theory to writing in connection with a course he was teaching. During the intervening years leading to its publication in October 1938, Dewey worked on *Logic: The Theory of Inquiry* whenever his other commitments allowed. He sent drafts of parts of it to his former students Sidney Hook, Joseph Ratner, and Ernest Nagel and reformulated his ideas in response to their comments. At times he sought a wider audience for his ideas in the form of lectures or articles. Most notably, in 1936 he published a series of three articles in *The Journal of Philosophy:* "Characteristics and Characters: Kinds and Classes" (7 May), "What Are Universals?" (21 May), and "General Propositions: Kinds and Classes" (3 December).

Dewey's primary interest in *Logic: The Theory of Inquiry* is to explain by instrumentalist principles the genesis and function of logical form, the subject matter of logic since Aristotle. This subject matter includes the study of propositional forms (for example, "All As are Bs," "Some As are Bs") that classify the types of claims that can be made in declarative sentences, and argument forms ("If all As are Bs, and all Bs are Cs, then all As are Cs") that prescribe the rules for valid deductive inference. Traditionally, logicians had subscribed explicitly or implicitly to the view that logical forms are understood by intuition, independently of particular episodes of inquiry, and that such understanding is, in fact, a precondition of rational inquiry. This view is particularly evident in the idealist tradition to which Dewey had subscribed in his younger days. In *Logic: The Theory of Inquiry* Dewey argues that logical forms find their genesis in the historical development and increasing sophistication of inquiry as a peculiarly

Dewey with his friend and benefactor, the pharmaceutical manufacturer and art collector Albert C. Barnes, to whom he dedicated Art as Experience *(1934)*

human response to troublesome situations: "logical forms accrue to subject-matter when the latter is subjected to controlled inquiry."

As in his earlier works in the theory of knowledge, in *Logic: The Theory of Inquiry* Dewey takes his model for inquiry from the biological and behavioral sciences. The pattern of inquiry has its origin in the adaptive responses of prehuman organisms to their environment. In higher animals these responses take the form of searching and exploratory behaviors that, when successful, result in the organism's readjustment to or reintegration with its environment and the consequent reestablishment of effective activity. Inquiry on the human level is an evolutionary development continuous with these prehuman behaviors. The crucial difference is the use of language as a controlling factor in inquiry. Language serves to represent the existential connections of things in the form of symbolic meanings and implicatory relationships, abstracted from particular existential data, allowing adaptive behaviors to be rehearsed prior to being performed.

Dewey's account of what he calls the "pattern of inquiry" in *Logic: The Theory of Inquiry* is consistent with that in his earlier writings in logical theory. Inquiry commences in response to an "indeterminate situation," a situation the eventual issue of which is in question and the import of which for action is, therefore, unclear. The indeterminate situation becomes a "problematic" one when an attempt is made to respond to it through inquiry. The inquirer has two main tasks to perform: to gather facts so as to identify the nature of the problem and define the parameters for an eventual solution, and to formulate ideas of possible solutions and the operational means to test them. While the gathering and statement of facts ties inquiry to existential conditions, ideas deal with the exploration of abstract possibilities facilitated by the necessary implicatory relationships of discursively defined meanings. The sort of abstract hypothetical reasoning typified in scientific practice comes into play in the consideration of ideas or meanings without direct reference to existential conditions.

The goal of inquiry is the establishment of a "judgment," of which the subject matter is the situation that originally evoked inquiry. When inquiry is successful, judgment gives the initiating situation a unity and clarity that it originally lacked, such that its significance for life activity is made evident. To characterize what is attained in judgment Dewey uses the phrase "warranted assertibility" rather than *truth;* he limits his use of the latter term to the restricted sense proposed by Peirce, for whom truth is the ideal limit of scientific investigation. Dewey believes that terms such as *truth* and *knowledge* have connotations acquired by long association with the epistemological tradition that he rejects. In particular, they suggest that what is known to be true is certain and incorrigible. In contrast, Dewey, like Peirce, is a fallibilist—the results of inquiry are warranted only provisionally and are always open to revision in further inquiry.

The role of logical form in inquiry is most fully treated in "Propositions and Terms" and "The Logic of Scientific Method," parts 3 and 4, respectively, of *Logic: The Theory of Inquiry.* Dewey's fundamental claim is that logical forms are instituted in the course of inquiry as means of controlling the various factors involved in such a way as to reliably produce warranted assertions and, thus, that their ultimate value and justification depend on the results of their use. Consequently, rather than characterizing propositional and argument forms in terms of their linguistic syntactical structures, as was the common practice of logicians of the day who employed the symbolic techniques developed earlier in the century by Russell and Alfred North Whitehead, Dewey provides an analysis of logical forms in terms of the distinctive roles they play as means for the securing of judgment. For instance, consistent with his functional analysis of inquiry into factual and ideational elements, he distinguishes two classes of general propositions:

"generic" propositions used to establish observational facts and "universal" propositions used to develop and explore possible solutions to the problem at hand. Dewey cautions, however, that linguistic form is not a reliable guide for discerning which general propositions fulfill which of these roles.

Published in 1939, *Freedom and Culture* reflects the onset of World War II and the challenge presented to democracy by fascism and communism. As the title indicates, Dewey here resumes his inquiry into the cultural conditions that allow democracy as a way of life to be realized. In contrast to his earlier views, he now expresses the importance of a democratic imagination for organizing and inspiring a citizenry, in addition to more intellectual habits of inquiry. This work also indicates Dewey's disappointment in the Russian Revolution, which had led to Stalinism. He stresses more strongly the aim of democracy as the development of individual freedom. The influence of Thomas Jefferson, in particular, is present, perhaps because of Dewey's reacquaintance at that time with Jefferson's writings through his editing of *The Living Thoughts of Thomas Jefferson* (1940). Jefferson the revolutionary who saw government as a constant experiment, not Jefferson the agrarian individualist, attracts him. While Dewey does not withdraw his support for democratic socialism, *Freedom and Culture* exhibits his growing awareness of the dangers of totalitarianism and forms a counterweight to his views in *Individualism, Old and New* and *Liberalism and Social Action.*

In June 1939 Dewey retired from his position as professor emeritus in residence at Columbia. The 12 October 1939 issue of *The Journal of Philosophy* was devoted to a discussion of *Logic: The Theory of Inquiry,* with articles by such prominent philosophers as Evander Bradley McGilvery, a longstanding critic of Dewey's logical theory; C. I. Lewis of Harvard; and Dewey's colleague at Columbia and adviser on the writing of the work, Nagel. While Dewey's achievement in providing a comprehensive account of instrumentalist logic was widely admired, his critics either questioned the basic assumptions of his approach, as did McGilvery, or found fault with what were perceived to be ambiguities and obscurities in the statement of his views, which was Nagel's complaint concerning Dewey's account of universal propositions.

One of Dewey's severest critics was the British logician and philosopher Russell, a leading antagonist of the pragmatic movement and, in particular, the pragmatic theory of truth. In an article on Dewey's *Logic: The Theory of Inquiry* that he contributed to Paul Arthur Schilpp's *The Philosophy of John Dewey* (1939), the first volume of the Library of Living Philosophers series, and in his *An Inquiry into Truth and Meaning*

(1940) Russell criticized Dewey's emphasis on the process of inquiry and lack of attention to the objective truth-relation between beliefs and facts that he believed to obtain independently of inquiry. Dewey defended his position against Russell's criticisms in "Propositions, Warranted Assertibility, and Truth" in the 27 March 1941 issue of *The Journal of Philosophy*. The exchanges between Russell and Dewey are marked by an inability of the two great philosophers to discover any common ground or even to come to a proper understanding of each other's positions.

The philosophical differences with Russell did not prevent Dewey from coming to his defense when Russell's appointment on 26 February 1940 to a chair in philosophy at the College of the City of New York was attacked by Episcopalian bishop William T. Manning on the grounds that Russell's liberal social and moral views made him unfit for a teaching position. Other conservative clerics echoed Manning's complaints, and a suit seeking the recision of the appointment was brought against the New York City Board of Higher Education the following month. Dewey, throughout his career a vocal advocate of academic freedom, joined other philosophers and leaders of liberal opinion in defending Russell, but on 30 March the judge in the case ruled against the appointment in an opinion that was highly defamatory of Russell. Dewey and Horace Meyer Kallen co-edited and contributed to *The Bertrand Russell Case* (1941), a collection of essays about the affair and its implications.

Free of university duties, Dewey spent a good deal of his time in the early 1940s in the Florida Keys during the winter and at his cottage in Hubbards, Nova Scotia, during the summer. While he continued to publish in both professional journals and the popular press, a variety of illnesses slowed his writing and other activities from the pace that had been his custom throughout his academic career.

In 1946 Dewey married Roberta Lowitz Grant, forty-five years his junior, in a ceremony at his New York apartment attended by family and friends. In 1948 the couple adopted an orphaned brother and sister, whom they named John Jr. and Adrienne. Dewey had a great affection for children that was manifested in his lifelong interest in educational issues and his advocacy for federal action on behalf of children at the beginning of the Great Depression.

Intellectually, the 1940s and early 1950s were a period of reappraisal for Dewey. In articles such as "Propositions, Warranted Assertibility, and Truth," "Nature in Experience" (*Philosophical Review*, March 1940), and "Inquiry and Indeterminateness of Situations" (*Journal of Philosophy*, 21 May 1942) he attempted to clarify many of his philosophical views in

Dewey and Roberta Lowitz Grant the day before she became his second wife on 12 December 1946 (AP/Wide World Photos)

the light of the criticisms of other philosophers. Much of this reappraisal took the form not of direct replies to his critics but of a reexamination of the meanings of philosophical terms. One of his concerns throughout his career had been that the essential meaning of his views was lost to his readers because of the connotations that various terms had acquired through centuries of what he considered philosophical misuse. In many of his writings of the 1940s he cites the *Oxford English Dictionary* as a means of fixing the etymologies of various philosophical terms so as to furnish a common linguistic ground for discussion. Another manifestation of Dewey's linguistic concerns is found in several pages he wrote in 1951 for a new introduction to *Experience and Nature* (the introduction was never completed but was edited by Ratner and published in 1981 as an appendix to the edition of *Experience and Nature* in volume one of *The Later Works of John Dewey, 1925–1953*, 1981–1991). Here Dewey offers *culture* as a more adequate alternative to the previously favored

Dewey in 1949

experience to designate what is distinctively human, materially and ideally, within nature.

Dewey's interest in a reexamination of philosophical terminology is also evident in the most extensive of his intellectual projects during these years: the collaboration with Bentley on *Knowing and the Known*. Bentley had published a book on political theory and another on the philosophy of mathematics and was writing a third when he and Dewey began corresponding in the mid 1930s. By the early 1940s they were working together on the development of a vocabulary with which to formulate a theory of knowledge that was pragmatic and "transactional" in the sense of being founded in the concept of systematic wholes whose elements can only be understood within the context of the wholes. Bentley played the leading role in preparing the ten articles, published in *The Journal of Philosophy* from January 1945 to July 1947, that formed the nucleus of *Knowing and the Known,* which appeared in 1949–so much so that Dewey expressed his concern in his correspondence on several occasions that he was getting too much credit for work that was mostly Bentley's. A matter of some controversy among Dewey scholars is how much of the thought expressed in *Knowing and the Known* is attributable to Dewey.

In the late fall of 1951 Dewey suffered a fracture of the hip from which he was not able fully to recover. In late May 1952 he came down with pneumonia, and he died on 1 June.

The influence of Dewey's thought within the international philosophical community was increasingly eclipsed during his lifetime by a variety of other trends that were more readily embraced by Anglo-American and Continental philosophers for their promise of instituting a standard and systematic methodology akin to that of empirical science, by which a community of investigators might conjointly achieve a common set of results. In Germany and Austria the logical positivist movement, centered in the Vienna Circle, and phenomenology, led by Edmund Husserl, held this promise for many philosophers during the first decades of the twentieth century; phenomenology also became influential in France through the work of Maurice Merleau-Ponty and Jean-Paul Sartre. In England during this same period the analytic techniques of Oxford and Cambridge philosophers had a similar impact. All of these schools of thought found proponents in the United States, making the American philosophical scene a patchwork of methods and points of view. In this intellectual environment the pragmatic movement, which had seemed to hold great promise early in the century, waned in significance.

In the second half of the century, however, with the gradual dissolution of the other programs of philosophical inquiry, pragmatism in general and Dewey's thought in particular found a new audience and influence. W. V. Quine's views on the "naturalizing of epistemology" have unmistakable antecedents in the naturalism of Dewey's theory of inquiry. American phenomenologists such as James Edie and Sandra B. Rosenthal explored the affinities of phenomenological thought to the pragmatism of Dewey, Peirce, and James. The role of biological need and social interest in the sociohistorical development of systems of belief, first stressed by Dewey and the other pragmatists, found recognition in the writings of Richard Rorty, Hilary Putnam, and Jürgen Habermas. In this revitalized philosophical environment Dewey scholarship once again flourished, spurred by the editorial project at Southern Illinois University at Carbondale, headed by Jo Ann Boydston, that has made all of Dewey's writings available in new scholarly editions. This renewed interest in Dewey has once again brought his thought into the mainstream of philosophical discussion.

Letters:

John Dewey and Alice Chipman Dewey, *Letters from China and Japan,* edited by Evelyn Dewey (New York: Dutton, 1920);

John Dewey and Arthur F. Bentley: A Philosophical Correspondence, 1932–1951, edited by Sidney Ratner and Jules Altman (New Brunswick, N.J.: Rutgers University Press, 1964);

The Correspondence of John Dewey, CD-ROM, 3 volumes, edited by Larry Hickman and others (Charlottesville, Va.: Intelex Corporation, 1999–2002).

Bibliographies:

Milton Halsey Thomas, *John Dewey: A Centennial Bibliography* (Chicago: University of Chicago Press, 1962);

Jo Ann Boydston and Robert L. Andresen, *John Dewey: A Checklist of Translations, 1900–1967* (Carbondale: Southern Illinois University Press, 1969);

Boydston and Kathleen Poulos, *Checklist of Writings about John Dewey,* second edition (Carbondale: Southern Illinois University Press, 1978);

"Bibliography of the Writings of John Dewey" and "Addenda to the Writings of John Dewey," in *The Philosophy of John Dewey,* edited by Paul Arthur Schilpp and Lewis Edwin Hahn, The Library of Living Philosophers, volume 1, third edition (La Salle, Ill.: Open Court, 1989), pp. 609–683, 685–715;

Barbara Levine, *Works about John Dewey, 1886–1995* (Carbondale: Southern Illinois University Press, 1996).

Biographies:

Corliss Lamont, ed., *Dialogues on John Dewey* (New York: Horizon, 1959);

George Dykhuizen, *The Life and Mind of John Dewey,* edited by Jo Ann Boydston (Carbondale: Southern Illinois University Press, 1973);

Neil Coughlin, *Young John Dewey: An Essay in American Intellectual History* (Chicago: University of Chicago Press, 1973);

Charles F. Howlett, *Troubled Philosopher: John Dewey and the Struggle for World Peace* (Port Washington, N.Y.: Kennikat Press, 1977);

Boydston, Introduction to *The Poems of John Dewey,* edited by Boydston (Carbondale: Southern Illinois University Press, 1977; London: Feffer & Simons, 1977);

Jane M. Dewey and others, "Biography of John Dewey," in *The Philosophy of John Dewey,* edited by Paul Arthur Schilpp and Lewis Edwin Hahn, The Library of Living Philosophers, volume 1, third edition (La Salle, Ill.: Open Court, 1989), pp. 3–45;

Steven C. Rockefeller, *John Dewey: Religious Faith and Democratic Humanism* (New York: Columbia University Press, 1991);

Robert B. Westbrook, *John Dewey and American Democracy* (Ithaca, N.Y.: Cornell University Press, 1991);

Sidney Hook, *John Dewey: An Intellectual Portrait,* introduction by Richard Rorty (Amherst, N.Y.: Prometheus, 1995);

Alan Ryan, *John Dewey and the High Tide of American Liberalism* (New York: Norton, 1995);

Raymond D. Boisvert, *John Dewey: Rethinking Our Time* (Albany: State University of New York Press, 1998);

David Fott, *John Dewey: America's Philosopher of Democracy* (Lanham, Md.: Rowman & Littlefield, 1998);

Brian A. Williams, *Thought and Action: John Dewey at the University of Michigan* (Ann Arbor: Bentley Historical Library, University of Michigan, 1998).

References:

Thomas M. Alexander, *The Horizons of Feeling: John Dewey's Theory of Art, Experience, and Nature* (Albany: State University of New York Press, 1987);

Richard J. Bernstein, *John Dewey* (New York: Washington Square Press, 1966);

John Blewett, ed., *John Dewey: His Thought and Influence* (New York: Fordham University Press, 1960);

Raymond D. Boisvert, *Dewey's Mataphysics* (New York: Fordham University Press, 1988);

Jo Ann Boydston, ed., *Guide to the Works of John Dewey* (Carbondale: Southern Illinois University Press, 1970);

Gary Bullert, *The Politics of John Dewey* (Buffalo, N.Y.: Prometheus Books, 1983);

Stephen M. Cahn, ed., *New Studies in the Philosophy of John Dewey* (Hanover, N.H.: University Press of New England, 1977);

Harry M. Campbell, *John Dewey* (New York: Twayne, 1971);

Alfonso J. Damico, *Individuality and Community: The Social and Political Thought of John Dewey* (Gainesville: University Press of Florida, 1978);

Gérard Deledalle, *L'idée d'experience dans la philosophie de John Dewey* (Paris: University Press of France, 1967);

Robert D. Dewey, *The Philosophy of John Dewey: A Critical Exposition of His Method, Metaphysics, and Theory of Knowledge* (The Hague: Nijhoff, 1977);

Georges Dicker, *John Dewey's Theory of Knowing* (Philadelphia: Philosophical Monographs, 1976);

S. Morris Eames, *Experience and Value: Essays on John Dewey and Pragmatic Naturalism,* edited by Elizabeth R. Eames and Richard W. Field (Carbondale: Southern Illinois University Press, 2002);

Eames, *Pragmatic Naturalism: An Introduction* (Carbondale: Southern Illinois University Press, 1977);

Irwin Edman, *John Dewey: His Contribution to the American Tradition* (Indianapolis: Bobbs-Merrill, 1955);

Michael Eldridge, *Transforming Experience: John Dewey's Cultural Instrumentalism* (Nashville: Vanderbilt University Press, 1998);

Andrew Feffer, *The Chicago Pragmatists and American Progressivism* (Ithaca, N.Y.: Cornell University Press, 1993);

James W. Garrison, *Dewey and Eros: Wisdom and Desire in the Art of Teaching* (New York: Teachers College Press, 1997);

Garrison, ed., *The New Scholarship on Dewey* (Dordrecht, Netherlands & Boston: Kluwer, 1995);

George R. Geiger, *John Dewey in Perspective* (New York: Oxford University Press, 1958);

James Gouinlock, *John Dewey's Philosophy of Value* (New York: Humanities Press, 1972);

Casey Haskins and David I. Seiple, eds., *Dewey Reconfigured: Essays on Deweyan Pragmatism* (Albany: State University of New York Press, 1999);

Larry A. Hickman, *John Dewey's Pragmatic Technology* (Bloomington: Indiana University Press, 1990);

Robert Hollinger and David Depew, eds., *Pragmatism: From Progressivism to Postmodernism* (Westport, Conn.: Praeger, 1995);

Sidney Hook, *John Dewey: An Intellectual Portrait* (New York: John Day, 1939);

Hook, ed., *John Dewey: Philosopher of Science and Freedom* (New York: Dial, 1950);

Terry Hoy, *The Political Philosophy of John Dewey: Towards a Constructive Renewal* (Westport, Conn.: Praeger, 1998);

Philip W. Jackson, *John Dewey and the Lessons of Art* (New Haven: Yale University Press, 1998);

Victor Kestenbaum, *The Phenomenological Sense of John Dewey: Habit and Meaning* (Atlantic Highlands, N.J.: Humanities Press, 1977);

Morton Levitt, *Freud and Dewey on the Nature of Man* (New York: Philosophical Library, 1960);

Sidney Morgenbesser, ed., *Dewey and His Critics: Essays from* The Journal of Philosophy (New York: Journal of Philosophy, 1977);

Jerome Nathanson, *John Dewey: The Reconstruction of the Democratic Life* (New York: Scribners, 1951);

Lowell Nissen, *John Dewey's Theory of Inquiry and Truth* (The Hague: Mouton, 1966);

William Andrew Paringer, *John Dewey and the Paradox of Liberal Reform* (Albany: State University of New York Press, 1990);

Daniel F. Rice, *Reinhold Niebuhr and John Dewey: An American Odyssey* (Albany: State University of New York Press, 1993);

Robert J. Roth, *John Dewey and Self-Realization* (Englewood Cliffs, N.J.: Prentice-Hall, 1963);

Paul Arthur Schilpp, ed., *The Philosophy of John Dewey,* The Library of Living Philosophers, volume 1 (Evanston, Ill. & Chicago: Northwestern University Press, 1939);

Richard Shusterman, *Pragmatist Aesthetics: Living Beauty, Rethinking Art* (Oxford & Cambridge, Mass.: Blackwell, 1992);

Fernando M. Soares Silva, *John Dewey and Karl Jaspers: Main Philosophic Concepts and Educational Implications* (San Rafael, Cal.: Ecos Lusíadas, 1998);

Douglas J. Simpson and Michael J. B. Jackson, *Educational Reform: A Deweyan Perspective* (New York: Garland, 1997);

Malcolm Skilbeck, ed., *John Dewey* (London: Collier-Macmillan / Toronto & New York: Macmillan, 1970);

Ralph Sleeper, *The Necessity of Pragmatism: John Dewey's Conception of Philosophy* (New Haven: Yale University Press, 1987);

A. H. Somjee, *The Political Theory of John Dewey* (New York: Teachers College Press, 1968);

Jerome Paul Soneson, *Pragmatism and Pluralism: John Dewey's Significance for Theology* (Minneapolis: Fortress Press, 1993);

Laurel N. Tanner, *Dewey's Laboratory School: Lessons for Today* (New York: Teachers College Press, 1997);

H. S. Thayer, *The Logic of Pragmatism: An Examination of John Dewey's Logic* (New York: Humanities Press, 1952);

J. E. Tiles, *Dewey* (London: Routledge, 1988);

Tiles, ed., *John Dewey: Critical Assessments,* 4 volumes (London & New York: Routledge, 1992)—comprises volume 1, *Human Nature and Human Nurture;* volume 2, *Political Theory and Social Practice;* volume 3, *Value, Conduct, and Art;* and volume 4, *Nature, Knowledge, and Naturalism;*

Rodman B. Webb, *The Presence of the Past: John Dewey and Alfred Schutz on the Genesis and Organization of Experience* (Gainesville: University Press of Florida, 1976);

Jennifer Welchman, *Dewey's Ethical Thought* (Ithaca, N.Y.: Cornell University Press, 1995);

Morton White, *The Origin of Dewey's Instrumentalism* (New York: Columbia University Press, 1943).

Papers:

The John Dewey Papers are in Special Collections, Morris Library, Southern Illinois University at Carbondale.

Jonathan Edwards

(5 October 1703 – 22 March 1758)

George W. Stickel

See also the Edwards entry in *DLB 24: American Colonial Writers, 1606–1734.*

BOOKS: *God Glorified in the Work of Redemption, by the Greatness of Man's Dependance upon Him in the Whole of It: A Sermon Preached on the Publick Lecture in Boston, July 8, 1731* (Boston: Printed by S. Kneeland & T. Green for D. Henchman, 1731);

A Divine and Supernatural Light, Immediately Imparted to the Soul by the Spirit of God, Shown to Be Both a Scriptural, and Rational Doctrine: In a Sermon, Preach'd at Northampton, and Published at the Desire of Some of the Hearers, in the Year 1734 (Boston: Printed by S. Kneeland & T. Green, 1734);

Discourses on Various Important Subjects, Nearly Concerning the Great Affair of the Soul's Eternal Salvation, Viz. I. Justification by Faith Alone. II. Pressing into the Kingdom of God. III. Ruth's Resolution. IV. The Justice of God in the Damnation of Sinners. V. The Excellency of Jesus Christ. Delivered at Northampton, Chiefly at the Time of the Late Wonderful Pouring out of the Spirit of God There (Boston: Printed & sold by S. Kneeland & T. Green, 1734);

A Faithful Narrative of the Surprising Work of God in the Conversion of Many Hundred Souls in Northampton, and the Neighbouring Towns and Villages of New-Hampshire in New-England: In a Letter to the Reverend Dr. Benjamin Colman, of Boston. Written by the Reverend Mr. Edwards, Minister of Northampton, on Nov. 6, 1736. And Published, with a Large Preface, by Dr. Watts and Dr. Guyse (Edinburgh: Reprinted for J. Oswald, bookseller in London, and sold by J. Paton, J. Davidson, and others, 1736; Boston: Printed & sold by S. Kneeland & T. Green, 1738);

The Distinguishing Marks of a Work of the Spirit of God, Applied to That Uncommon Operation That Has Lately Appeared on the Minds of Many of the People in New-England: With a Particular Consideration of the Extraordinary Circumstances with Which This Work Is Attended. With a Preface by the Rev. Mr. Cooper of Boston, and Letters from the Rev. Dr. Coleman, Giving Some Account

Jonathan Edwards; painting by Joseph Badger
(Yale University Gallery)

of the Present Work of God in Those Parts (Boston: Printed & sold by S. Kneeland & T. Green, 1741; London: Reprinted by S. Mason, 1742);

The Resort and Remedy of Those That Are Bereaved by the Death of an Eminent Minister: A Sermon Preached at Hatfield, Sept. 2, 1741. Being the Day of the Interment of the Reverend Mr. William Williams, the Aged and Venerable Pastor of That Church. And Published at the United Request of Those Reverend and Honoured Gentlemen, the Sons of the Deceased. As also by the Desire and at the Expense of the Town (Boston: Printed by G. Rogers for J. Edwards, 1741);

Sinners in the Hands of an Angry God: A Sermon Preached at Enfield, July 8th 1741. At a Time of Great Awakenings;

and Attended with Remarkable Impressions on Many of the Hearers (Boston: Printed & sold by S. Kneeland & T. Green, 1741; Edinburgh: Reprinted by T. Lumisden & J. Robertson, 1745);

Some Thoughts Concerning the Present Revival of Religion in New-England, and the Way in Which It Ought to Be Promoted, Humbly Offered to the Publick, in a Treatise on That Subject (Boston: Printed & sold by S. Kneeland & T. Green, 1742; Edinburgh: Reprinted & sold by T. Lunisden & J. Robertson, 1743);

The Great Concern of a Watchman for Souls, Appearing in the Duty He Has to Do, and the Account He Has to Give, Represented & Improved, in a Sermon Preach'd at the Ordination of the Reverend Mr. Jonathan Judd, to the Pastoral Office over the Church of Christ, in the New Precinct at Northampton, June 8, 1743 (Boston: Printed by Green, Bushnell & Allen for G. Procter, 1743);

The True Excellency of a Minister of the Gospel: A Sermon Preach'd at Pelham, Aug. 30, 1744. Being the Day of the Ordination of the Revd. Mr. Robert Abercrombie to the Work of the Gospel Ministry in That Place (Boston: Printed by Rogers & Fowle for W. McAlpine, 1744);

An Expostulatory Letter from the Rev. Mr. Edwards of Northampton, to the Rev. Mr. Clap, Rector of Yale College in New-Haven, in Reply to His Late Printed Letter to Him, Relating to What He Reported Concerning the Rev. Mr. Whitefield, at Boston and Cambridge and Elsewhere, as from Mr. Edwards: Making the Falsity of That Report yet Much More Manifest (Boston: Printed & sold by S. Kneeland & T. Green, 1745);

Copies of the Two Letters Cited by Rev. Mr. Clap in His Late Printed Letter to a Friend in Boston, Concerning What He Has Reported, as from Mr. Edwards . . . Concerning the Rev. Mr. Whitefield. Communicated in a Letter to a Friend. With Some Reflections on the Affair Those Letters Relate to, and Rector Clap's Management Therein (Boston: Printed & sold by S. Kneeland and T. Green, 1745);

A Treatise Concerning Religious Affections in Three Parts: Part I. Concerning the Nature of the Affections, and Their Importance in Religion. Part II. Shewing What Are No Certain Signs That Religious Affections Are Gracious, or That They Are Not. Part III. Shewing What Are Distinguishing Signs of Truly Gracious and Holy Affections (Boston: Printed for S. Kneeland & T. Green, 1746; London: Printed for T. Fields, 1762);

The Church's Marriage to Her Sons, and to Her God: A Sermon Preached at the Instalment of the Rev. Mr. Samuel Buel as Pastor of the Church and Congregation at East-Hampton on Long-Island, September 19, 1746 (Boston: Printed & sold by S. Kneeland & T. Green, 1746);

True Saints, When Absent from the Body, Are Present with the Lord: A Sermon Preached on the Day of the Funeral of the Rev. Mr. David Brainerd, Missionary to the Indians . . . and Pastor of a Church of Christian Indians in New-Jersey; Who Died at Northampton in New-England, Octob. 9th, 1747 . . . Containing Some Account of His Character, and Manner of Life, and Remarkable Speeches and Behaviour at Death (Boston: Printed by Rogers & Fowle for D. Henchman, 1747);

An Humble Attempt to Promote Explicit Agreement and Visible Union of God's People in Extraordinary Prayer for the Revival of Religion and the Advancement of Christ's Kingdom on Earth, Pursuant to Scripture-Promises and Prophecies Concerning the Last Time: With a Preface by Several Ministers (Boston: Printed for D. Henchman, 1747; Northampton, England: Reprinted by T. Dicey, 1789);

A Strong Rod Broken and Withered: A Sermon Preached at Northampton, on the Lord's-Day, June 26. 1748. on the Death of the Honourable John Stoddard, Esq.; Often a Member of His Majesty's Council, for Many Years Chief Justice of the Court of Common Pleas for the County of Hampshire, Judge of the Probate of Wills, and Chief Colonel of the Regiment, &c. Who Died at Boston June 19. 1748. in the 67th Year of His Age (Boston: Printed by Rogers & Fowle for J. Edwards, 1748);

An Humble Inquiry into the Rules of the Word of God, Concerning the Qualifications Requisite to a Compleat Standing and Full Communion in the Visible Christian Church, appendix by Thomas Foxcroft (Boston: Printed & sold by S. Kneeland, 1749; Edinburgh: H. Inglis, 1790);

Christ the Great Example of Gospel Ministers: A Sermon Preach'd at Portsmouth, at the Ordination of the Reverend Mr. Job Strong, to the Pastoral Office over the South Church in That Place, June 28, 1749 (Boston: Printed & sold by T. Fleet, 1750);

A Farewel-Sermon Preached at the First Precinct in Northampton, after the People's Publick Rejection of Their Minister, and Renouncing Their Relation to Him as Pastor of the Church There, on June 22, 1750: Occasion'd by Difference of Sentiments, Concerning the Requisite Qualifications of Members of the Church, in Compleat Standing (Boston: Printed & sold by S. Kneeland, 1751);

Misrepresentations Corrected, and Truth Vindicated. In a Reply to the Rev. Mr. Solomon Williams's Book, Intitled, The True State of the Question Concerning the Qualifications Necessary to Lawful Communion in the Christian Sacraments (Boston: Printed by S. Kneeland, 1752);

True Grace, Distinguished from the Experience of Devils: In a Sermon, Preached before the Synod of New-York, Convened at New-Ark, in New-Jersey, on Sept. 28. n.s. 1752. (New York: Printed by James Parker, 1753);

A Careful and Strict Inquiry into the Modern Prevailing Notions of That Freedom of Will, Which Is Supposed to Be Essential to Moral Agency, Virtue and Vice, Reward and Punishment, Praise and Blame (Boston: Printed & sold by S. Kneeland, 1754; London: Reprinted for T. Field, 1762);

The Great Christian Doctrine of Original Sin Defended: Evidences of It's Truth Produced, and Arguments to the Contrary Answered. Containing, in Particular, A Reply to the Objections and Arguings of Dr. John Taylor, in His Book, Intitled, "The Scripture-Doctrine of Original Sin Proposed to Free and Candid Examination," &c. (Boston: Printed & sold by S. Kneeland, 1758; London: Reprinted for J. Johnson & G. Keith, 1766);

The Life and Character of the Late Reverend Mr. Jonathan Edwards, President of the College at New-Jersey: Together with a Number of his Sermons on Various Important Subjects, edited by Samuel Hopkins (Boston: Printed & sold by S. Kneeland, 1765); republished as *The Life and Character of the Late Reverend, Learned, and Pious Mr. Jonathan Edwards, President of the College of New-Jersey: Together with Extracts from His Private Writings and Diary. And also, Eighteen Select Sermons on Various Important Subjects* (London: Dilly / Glasgow: Printed by D. Niven for J. Duncan, 1785);

Two Dissertations: I. Concerning the End for Which God Created the World. II. The Nature of True Virtue (Boston: Printed & sold by S. Kneeland, 1765; Edinburgh: Printed by W. Darling, 1788);

A History of the Work of Redemption: Containing, the Outlines of a Body of Divinity, in a Method Entirely New, edited by John Erskine (Edinburgh: Printed for W. Gray and J. Buckland & G. Keith, 1774; New York: Printed by Shepard Kollock for Robert Hodge, 1786);

Sermons, on the Following Subjects: The Manner in Which Salvation Is to Be Sought. The Unreasonableness of Indetermination in Religion. Unbelievers Contemn the Glory of Christ. The Folly of Looking Back in Fleeing out of Sodom. The Warnings of Scripture in the Best Manner Adapted to the Awakening and Conversion of Sinners. Hypocrites Deficient in the Duty of Prayer. The Future Punishment of the Wicked Unavoidable and Intolerable. The Eternity of Hell-Torments. The Peace Which Christ Gives His True Followers, edited by Jonathan Edwards Jr. (Hartford, Conn.: Printed by Hudson & Goodwin, 1780);

Practical Sermons, Never before Published, edited by Jonathan Edwards Jr. (Edinburgh: M. Gray, 1788);

Miscellaneous Observations on Important Theological Subjects, edited by John Erskine (Edinburgh: Printed for M. Gray, 1793);

Remarks on Important Theological Controversies (Edinburgh: Galbraith, 1796);

The Works of President Edwards, 8 volumes, edited by Edward Williams and Edward Parsons (Leeds: Printed by Edward Baines, 1806–1811; London: Printed for James Black & Sons, 1817; supplement, 2 volumes, Edinburgh: Robert Ogle and Oliver & Boyd / Glasgow: M. Ogle & Son and William Collins / London: Hamilton, Adams, 1847);

Advice to Young Converts: A Letter from the Late Rev. Jonathan Edwards of Northampton, to a Young Lady at Suffield, Conn., to Which Is Added, a Discourse, Recommending Religious Conversation; and an Extract from a Sermon on Christian Conversation (Northampton: Printed & sold by Thomas M. Pomroy, 1807);

The Works of President Edwards, 8 volumes, edited by Samuel Austin (Worcester, Mass.: Isaiah Thomas Jr., 1808–1809; enlarged edition, 4 volumes, New York: J. Leavitt & J. F. Trow / London: Wiley & Putnam, 1843–1844);

The Theological Questions of President Edwards, Senior, and Dr. Edwards, His Son (Providence: Printed by Miller & Hutchens, 1822);

The Works of President Edwards: With a Memoir of His Life, 10 volumes, edited by Sereno E. Dwight (New York: S. Converse, 1829–1830);

Charity and Its Fruits; or, Christian Love as Manifested in the Heart and Life. Edited from the Original Manuscripts, edited by Tryon Edwards (London: Nisbet, 1852; New York: R. Carter, 1852);

Selections from the Unpublished Writings of Jonathan Edwards, of America, edited by Alexander B. Grosart (Edinburgh: Privately printed, 1865);

Observations Concerning the Scripture Oeconomy of the Trinity and Covenant of Redemption by Jonathan Edwards, edited by Egbert C. Smyth (New York: Scribners, 1880);

An Unpublished Essay of Edwards on the Trinity, with Remarks on Edwards and His Theology, edited by George P. Fisher (New York: Scribners, 1903);

The Philosophy of Jonathan Edwards from His Private Notebooks, edited by Harvey G. Townsend (Eugene: University of Oregon, 1955)—comprises "Of Being," "The Mind," and "Miscellanies."

Editions and Collections: *Selected Sermons of Jonathan Edwards,* edited by H. Norman Gardiner (New York: Macmillan / London: Macmillan, 1904);

Benjamin Franklin and Jonathan Edwards: Selections from Their Writings, edited by Carl Van Doren (New York: Scribners, 1920);

Jonathan Edwards: Representative Selections, edited by Clarence H. Faust and Thomas H. Johnson (New York & Cincinnati: American Book Co., 1935);

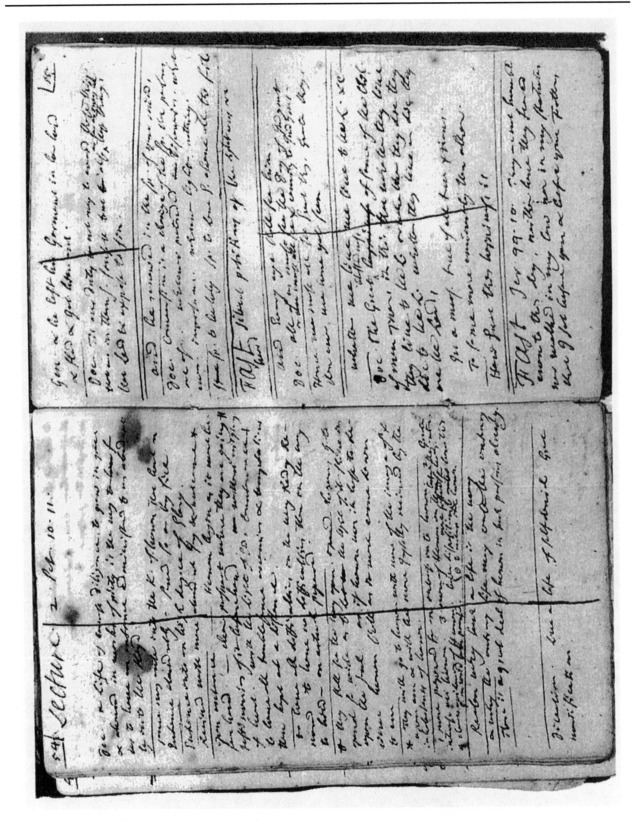

Pages from one of the notebooks in which Edwards composed his sermons
(Beinecke Rare Book and Manuscript Library, Yale University)

Images or Shadows of Divine Things, edited by Perry Miller (New Haven: Yale University Press, 1948);

Puritan Sage: Collected Writings of Jonathan Edwards, edited by Vergilius Ferm (New York: Library Publishers, 1953);

The Works of Jonathan Edwards, 20 volumes to date, Miller and John E. Smith, general editors (New Haven & London: Yale University Press, 1957–);

The Nature of True Virtue, foreword by William Frankena (Ann Arbor: University of Michigan Press, 1960);

Representative Selections, edited by Faust and Johnson (New York: Hill & Wang, 1962);

Treatise on Grace and Other Posthumously Published Writings, edited by Paul Helm (Cambridge: James Clark, 1971);

Jonathan Edwards: Apocalyptic Writings, edited by Stephen J. Stein (New Haven: Yale University Press, 1977);

A Jonathan Edwards Reader, edited by Smith, Harry S. Stout, and Kenneth P. Minkema (New Haven: Yale University Press, 1995);

The Sermons of Jonathan Edwards: A Reader, edited by Minkema, Wilson H. Kimnach, and Douglas A. Sweeney (New Haven: Yale University Press, 1999);

Standing in Grace: Jonathan Edwards's A Treatise on Grace, edited by Don Kistler (Morgan, Pa.: Soli Deo Gloria, 2002).

OTHER: "Part of a Large Letter from the Rev. Mr. Jonathan Edwards of Northampton: Giving an Account of the Late Wonderful Work of God in Those Parts," in *The Duty and Interest of a People, among Whom Religion Has Been Planted, to Continue Stedfast and Sincere in the Profession and Practice of It. From Generation to Generation. With Directions for Such as Are Concerned to Obtain a True Repentance and Conversion to God.—Preach'd at a Time of General Awakenings,* by William Williams (Boston: Printed & sold by S. Kneeland & T. Green, 1736);

An Account of the Life of the Late Reverend Mr. David Brainerd, Minister of the Gospel, Missionary to the Indians, from the Honourable Society in Scotland, for the Propagation of Christian Knowledge, and Pastor of a Church of Christian Indians in New-Jersey: Who Died at Northampton in New-England, Octob. 9th 1747, in the 30th Year of His Age: Chiefly Taken from His Own Diary, and Other Private Writings, Written for His Own Use; and Now Published, edited by Edwards (Boston: Printed for and sold by D. Henchman, 1749); republished as *An Account of the Life of Mr. David Brainerd: Missionary from the Society for Propagating Christian Knowledge, & Pastor of a Church of* *Christian Indians in New-Jersey* (Edinburgh: Printed by T. MacCliesh for J. Ogle, 1798).

Philosopher, theologian, preacher, historian, and scientist, Jonathan Edwards was the most prolific writer of the American colonial period and one of the most prolific authors in American history. John Dewey and William James are perhaps the only American philosophical contenders of note to surpass him in output. In terms of social and intellectual impact, no one except Benjamin Franklin and Thomas Jefferson equaled Edwards until the Civil War. The Puritanism he championed then fell into disfavor, being replaced by Unitarianism and New England Transcendentalism, and Edwards tended to be remembered as the harsh dogmatist who terrified his listeners with his fire-and-brimstone sermon *Sinners in the Hands of an Angry God* (1741) and was eventually rejected by his own congregation and sent into exile in the wilderness. In fact, he was a metaphysician and ethicist of some subtlety and originality, was conversant with the science and philosophy of his day, and was a theologian who both predates and postdates colonial Puritanism.

Born in East Windsor, Connecticut, on 5 October 1703, Edwards was the fifth of eleven children and the only son of the Reverend Timothy Edwards and Esther Stoddard Edwards. The family home had been purchased by Edwards's grandfather, Richard Edwards, a wealthy cooper and merchant. Edwards's paternal grandmother, Elizabeth Tuttle Edwards, seems to have been of unsound mind, as were some of her siblings: one of her brothers killed one of her sisters, while another sister killed her own child. Edwards's mother was the second of twelve children of the Reverend Solomon Stoddard and Esther Warham Mather Stoddard, who had previously been married to the Reverend Eleasar Mather, the brother of Increase Mather. When Mather died, Solomon Stoddard had been called to fill his pulpit in Northampton, Massachusetts, and, as was not unusual in the early New England church, he had also married the widow. Solomon Stoddard's mother was a niece of John Winthrop, the first governor of the Massachusetts Bay Colony.

Edwards's elementary schooling was provided by his father. At the age of twelve he recorded detailed observations of rainbows and spiders, drawing "conclusions about their flight." (Some species spin a gossamer to float in the breeze—today called "ballooning.") At thirteen he matriculated at Connecticut's Collegiate School, which had been founded in Killingworth in 1701 and had just settled in New Haven in 1716; in 1718 its name was changed to Yale College (it became Yale University in 1864). At Yale he was influenced by the works of the British empiricist philosopher John

Locke and the mathematician and physicist Sir Isaac Newton and wrote notes for treatises to be titled "Of Being," "The Mind," and "Of Atoms"; the notes were published posthumously in the 1829–1830 edition of his collected works. In "Of Being" he argues, in a manner similar to the pre-Socratic philosopher Parmenides, that nonbeing or nothingness is inconceivable and hence cannot exist; being therefore exists necessarily, eternally, and everywhere. It is not material, since the essence of a material thing is resistance to penetration by other things; but no other beings exist to penetrate the universal being. Being, furthermore, is identical with space, since space, like being, cannot be conceived or imagined as not existing. This necessary, eternal, omnipresent, incorporeal being, which is the only true substance, is God. A "body is nothing but a particular mode of perception," and "the material universe exists only in the mind."

In "The Mind" and "Of Atoms" Edwards agrees with Locke that the ideas of what Locke called "secondary qualities," such as colors, tastes, and odors, are not characteristics of external objects but are purely mental phenomena. But, like another British empiricist philosopher, George Berkeley, he goes on to argue the same is true of what Locke called "primary qualities," solidity, extension, shape, and motion. Locke thought that the ideas of those qualities were accurate representations of a reality outside the mind, but Edwards, like Berkeley—with whose writings Edwards seems not to have been familiar at this time—contends that these ideas, too, are purely mental. Edwards's argument is that all of the primary qualities are reducible to resistance: solidity is nothing but resistance, shape is the termination of resistance, and motion is the communication of resistance from one space to another; since "resistance is nothing else but the actual exercise of God's power," Edwards concludes—again like Berkeley—that the supposedly physical universe exists only as ideas in the mind of God, who created them by a free act of his will, and that those ideas are communicated in regular and orderly succession by God to the minds of human beings. God is the only true substance and the only true cause.

After graduating in 1720, Edwards remained at Yale for two years to study theology. During this time he overcame his intellectual objections to the Calvinist doctrine of predestination, according to which people are saved or damned from all eternity, regardless of their actions during their earthly existence, and early in 1721 he underwent a conversion experience, which led him to see predestination as positively beautiful and just. He preached in a Presbyterian church in New York City from August 1722 through March 1723. He

received his M.A. in 1723 and tutored at Yale from 1724 until he became seriously ill in September 1725.

In August 1726 Edwards was asked to preach at the Northampton church of his grandfather Stoddard; on 21 November he was invited to "settle" with the congregation and became his grandfather's assistant. He was ordained on 15 February 1727. On 28 July 1727 he married seventeen-year-old Sarah Pierrepont, the daughter of the Reverend James Pierrepont, one of the founders of Yale. Stoddard died on the following 22 February, and Edwards succeeded him as pastor at Northampton.

Like his own parents, Edwards and his wife had ten daughters and a son. Though infant mortality was high at that time, all eleven children survived infancy. The son, Jonathan Jr., was sent to school; Edwards tutored his daughters at home in Latin, Greek, rhetoric, and penmanship. The Edwards daughters also traveled far more than did most girls of the time, accompanying their father on his preaching tours and visiting relatives. The Edwards home had frequent visitors, including apprentice pastors; some of these guests stayed for months.

On 8 July 1731 Edwards gave a public lecture in Boston that became his first published book when it appeared that same year as *God Glorified in the Work of Redemption, by the Greatness of Man's Dependance upon Him in the Whole of It*. In this work he holds that the enterprising spirit and self-sufficiency of the colonists has made them susceptible to Arminianism, the notion propounded by the Dutch theologian Jacobus Arminius that human beings can earn salvation through virtue and good works. Edwards says that only God's grace, not human free will, can overcome the effects of original sin and result in salvation.

With sermons delivered in 1734 that were published as that same year as *A Divine and Supernatural Light, Immediately Imparted to the Soul by the Spirit of God, Shown to Be Both a Scriptural, and Rational Doctrine* and *Discourses on Various Important Subjects, Nearly Concerning the Great Affair of the Soul's Eternal Salvation*, Edwards set off a revival movement in New England that resulted in the conversion of at least three hundred people. Using his skill as an observer, he documented the movement in *A Faithful Narrative of the Surprising Work of God in the Conversion of Many Hundred Souls in Northampton, and the Neighbouring Towns and Villages of New-Hampshire in New-England* (1736). Edwards explains in detail the episodes of conversion, recording his own perceptions and those of others about the behavior of individuals before and after the conversion experience; his records about a single individual sometimes fill several pages. The book went through three editions and twenty printings in

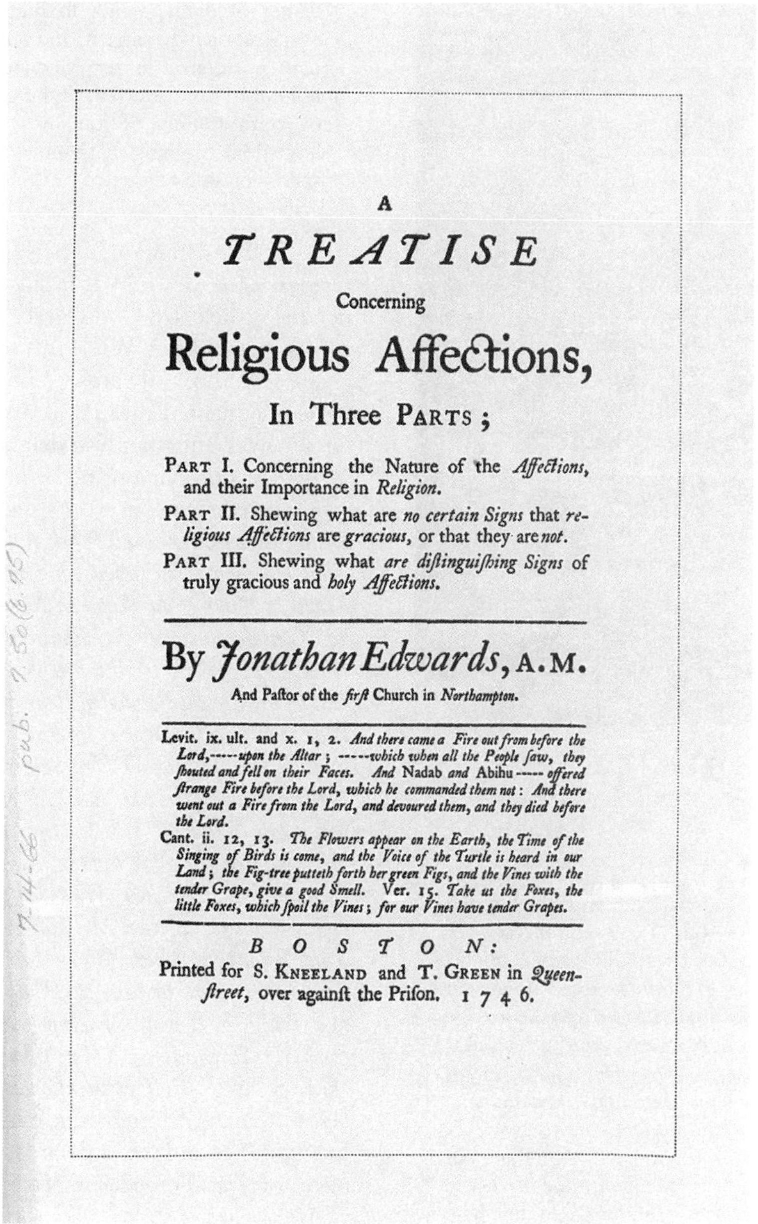

A

TREATISE

Concerning

Religious Affections,

In Three Parts;

PART I. Concerning the Nature of the *Affections*, and their Importance in *Religion*.

PART II. Shewing what are *no certain Signs* that religious *Affections* are *gracious*, or that they are *not*.

PART III. Shewing what *are distinguishing Signs* of truly gracious and *holy Affections*.

By *Jonathan Edwards*, A.M.

And Pastor of the *first* Church in *Northampton*.

Levit. ix. ult. and x. 1, 2. *And there came a Fire out from before the Lord,-----upon the Altar; -----which when all the People saw, they shouted and fell on their Faces. And Nadab and Abihu----- offered strange Fire before the Lord, which he commanded them not: And there went out a Fire from the Lord, and devoured them, and they died before the Lord.*

Cant. ii. 12, 13. *The Flowers appear on the Earth, the Time of the Singing of Birds is come, and the Voice of the Turtle is heard in our Land; the Fig-tree putteth forth her green Figs, and the Vines with the tender Grape, give a good Smell.* Ver. 15. *Take us the Foxes, the little Foxes, which spoil the Vines; for our Vines have tender Grapes.*

BOSTON:

Printed for S. KNEELAND and T. GREEN in *Queen-street*, over against the Prison. 1 7 4 6.

*Title page for Edwards's defense of emotionalism in religion
(Beinecke Rare Book and Manuscript Library, Yale University)*

three years and became the standard guide for church revivals for one hundred years.

Such observation and analysis should mark Edwards's book, rather than William James's *The Varieties of Religious Experience: A Study in Human Nature* (1902), as beginning the psychology of religion. Both Edwards and James deal with the essence of religious experiences and seek to understand the changes they produce in the persons involved, and both make the experiences of individuals central. James cites Edwards extensively in *The Varieties of Religious Experience* to show the relationship of internal experience to outward behavior.

Between 1740 and 1742 a wider revival movement, known as the Great Awakening, swept through the colonies. It was sparked by the emotional sermons of the English Methodist evangelist George Whitefield and the New Jersey Methodist preacher Gilbert Tenant. Edwards played a role in the movement with sermons such as *Sinners in the Hands of an Angry God,* which he preached in 1741 in Enfield, Massachusetts (the town was annexed into Connecticut in 1749). Edwards, whose sermons were usually rational and unemotional and delivered without the arm-waving histrionics employed by many evangelists, warned his hearers:

*Edwards's writing desk (Jonathan Edwards College,
Yale University; photograph by William K. Sacco)*

The God that holds you over the pit of hell, much as one holds a spider, or some loathsome insect over the fire, abhors you, and is dreadfully provoked: his wrath towards you burns like fire; he looks upon you as worthy of nothing else, but to be cast into the fire; he is of purer eyes than to bear to have you in his sight; you are ten thousand times more abominable in his eyes, than the most hateful venomous serpent is in ours. You have offended him infinitely more than ever a stubborn rebel did his prince; and yet it is nothing but his hand that holds you from falling into the fire every moment. It is to be ascribed to nothing else, that you did not go to hell the last night; that you were suffered to awake again in this world, after you closed your eyes to sleep. And there is no other reason to be given, why you have not dropped into hell since you arose in the morning, but that God's hand has held you up. There is no other reason to be given why you have not gone to hell, since you have sat here in the house of God, provoking his pure eyes by your sinful wicked manner of attending his solemn worship. Yea, there is nothing else that is to be given as a reason why you do not this very moment drop down into hell.

O sinner! Consider the fearful danger you are in: it is a great furnace of wrath, a wide and bottomless pit, full of the fire of wrath, that you are held over in the hand of that God, whose wrath is provoked and incensed as much against you, as against many of the damned in hell. You hang by a slender thread, with the flames of divine wrath flashing about it, and ready every moment to singe it, and burn it asunder; and you have no interest in any Mediator, and nothing to lay hold of to save yourself, nothing to keep off the flames of wrath, nothing of your own, nothing that you ever have done, nothing that you can do, to induce God to spare you one moment.

Such a definition of the sinner in relation, even in resistance, to the "only true substance"—that is, the sinner being held by God's grace—is consistent with his earlier metaphysics. While this sense of reality is Berkeleyan idealism, Edwards's epistemology is realistic—even pragmatic. Edwards not only participated in the Great Awakening but also defended it with analyses of systematic observations of the process of individual and group conversions, in works such as the following: *The Distinguishing Marks of a Work of the Spirit of God, Applied to That Uncommon Operation That Has Lately Appeared on the Minds of Many of the People in New-England: With a Particular Consideration of the Extraordinary Circumstances with Which This Work Is Attended* (1741); *Some Thoughts Concerning the Present Revival of Religion in New-England, and the Way in Which It Ought to Be Promoted, Humbly Offered to the Publick, in a Treatise on That Subject* (1742), *An Expostulatory Letter from the Rev. Mr. Edwards of Northampton, to the Rev. Mr. Clap, Rector of Yale College in New-Haven, in Reply to His Late Printed Letter to Him, Relating to What He Reported Concerning the Rev. Mr. Whitefield, at Boston and Cambridge and Elsewhere, as from Mr. Edwards: Making the Falsity of That Report yet Much More Manifest* (1745), *Copies of the Two Letters Cited by Rev. Mr. Clap in His Late Printed Letter to a Friend in Boston, Concerning What He Has Reported, as from Mr. Edwards . . . Concerning the Rev. Mr. Whitefield* (1745); and *A Treatise Concerning Religious Affections* (1746). Slicing through the emotion of conversion to functional responses, Edwards writes in the opening pages of *The Distinguishing Marks of a Work of the Spirit of God* he writes:

A Work is not to be judged of by any effects on the bodies of men; such as tears, trembling, groans, loud outcries, agonies of body, or the failing of bodily strength. The influence of minds or persons are under, is not to be judged of one way or the other, whether it be from the Spirit of God or no, by such effects on the body; and the reason is, because the Scripture nowhere gives us any such rule.

Again in *A Treatise Concerning Religious Affections* Edwards claims a utilitarian response that "the essence of all true religion lies in holy love," that "affections are no other, than the more vigorous and sensible exercises of the inclination and will of the soul," and that "Gracious and holy affections have their exercise and fruit in Christian

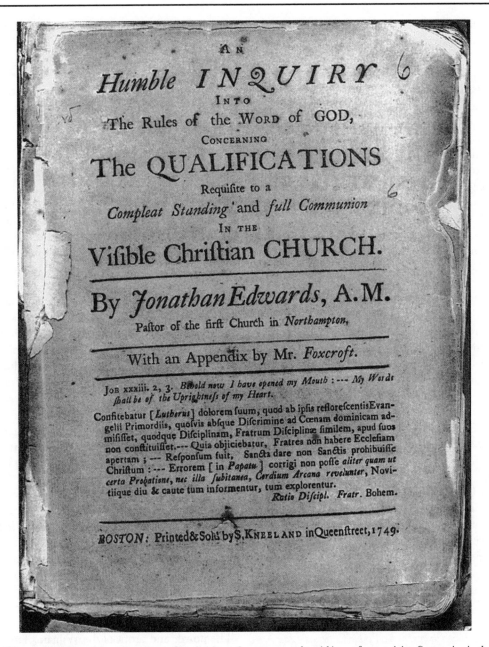

Title page for Edwards's announcement of his decision to bar unconverted parishioners from receiving Communion in the Congregational church in Northampton, Massachusetts, of which he was the pastor. The policy led to his dismissal in 1750 (Beinecke Rare Book and Manuscript Library, Yale University)

practice." That is, the converted soul will show the presence of God in its daily actions:

> There is no question whatsoever, that is of greater importance to mankind, and that it more concerns every individual person to be well resolved in, than this, what are the distinguishing qualifications of those that are in favor with God, and entitled to his eternal rewards? Or, which comes to the same thing, What is the nature of true religion? and wherein do lie the dis-

tinguishing notes of that virtue and holiness, that is acceptable in the sight of God?

In both *The Distinguishing Marks of a Work of the Spirit of God* and *A Treatise Concerning Religious Affections* Edwards defends what took place in these frontier revivals against those who doubted their authenticity or whose theological perspective was contrary to a Calvinist view. His arguments are biblically based and were intended to quiet opposition and doubt from Boston and Great Britain. He is careful to show that these revival experiences are consistent with his grandfather Stoddard's five "harvests" of souls in 1679, 1683, 1696, 1712, and 1718, as well as with New Testament descriptions of conversion experiences.

Schisms in New England churches generally concerned the issue of pastoral versus congregational authority, and the situation in Northampton was no exception. Although what Edwards scholars call the "bad book incident" of 1744 was a particularly visible event that engaged a large number of people, tensions had arisen between Edwards and his congregation as early as 1734 over the pastor's salary. The church members felt that the Edwardses did not live frugally enough; a hat purchased in Boston became a sore point. Furthermore, Edwards was an intellectual, and many of his sermons were not understood by his parishioners. Additionally, although he was always ready to comfort the sick and afflicted, Edwards did not observe the custom of paying regular visits to parishioners' homes.

The "bad book incident" began in March 1744 when Edwards discovered that some young people in the congregation had read a prohibited book, Thomas Dawkes's *The Midwife Rightly Instructed; or, The Way, Which All Women Desirous to Learn, Should Take, to Acquire the True Knowledge and Be Successful in the Practice Of, the Art of Midwifery* (1736). After he explained the offense, and the congregation voted to form a committee to investigate, Edwards read a list of the names of teenagers who were to report to the committee; the list included both the alleged offenders and the witnesses against them—some of the latter were from leading families in the community—with no indication of which was which. The congregation was enraged, and no new members joined the church for four years.

The breaking point came in 1749, when Edwards published *An Humble Inquiry into the Rules of the Word of God, Concerning the Qualifications Requisite to a Compleat Standing and Full Communion in the Visible Christian Church*. Edwards was reneging on a practice that had been begun at Northampton by his grandfather Stoddard and had become common in New England churches of allowing church members to partake in the Eucharist even if they had not undergone a conversion experience. Edwards argued that to take Communion, a person had to profess such a conversion—an "experience of the heart." Led by Joseph Hawley, whose father had committed suicide during the first of Edwards's revivals, the congregation dismissed Edwards on 22 June 1750. On 1 July he preached his parting sermon, which was published in 1751 as *A Farewel-Sermon Preached at the First Precinct in Northampton, after the People's Publick Rejection of Their Minister, and Renouncing Their Relation to Him as Pastor of the Church There, on June 22, 1750: Occasion'd by Difference of Sentiments, Concerning the Requisite Qualifications of Members of the Church, in Compleat Standing*. Nevertheless, Edwards remained in Northampton for a year, even filling in as interim pastor as needed. Edwards's position on Communion ultimately prevailed in the New England congregationalist churches.

Edwards received calls to several churches in America and in Scotland but accepted the one to Stockbridge, Massachusetts, a small community on the frontier, closer to Albany, New York, than to Northampton. While many commentators have stated that Edwards was exiled to Stockbridge, he thought that the lighter workload there would allow him more time for writing. Also, Stockbridge was where David Brainerd had served as a missionary to the Indians. Brainerd had been engaged to Edwards's daughter Jerusha but had died of tuberculosis on 9 October 1747; Jerusha, who had nursed him during his illness, had died the following February at age seventeen. Edwards had preached at Brainerd's funeral and had edited Brainerd's diary for publication in 1749; the work was well received.

Edwards worked at Stockbridge during the summer before his installation as missionary on 16 October 1751; his family arrived later in October. He reported to the church commission on missions in Boston early and often about his administrative problems and the tensions among the local Native Americans and between them and the whites. The mission had been established for the Houstunnocks, but Mohawks, who were enemies of the Houstunnocks, had moved into the area. While Edwards's family became fluent in the Indians' language, and Edwards could use it for ordinary communication, he could not preach in it. Furthermore, the town leaders, many of whom were members of the Williams family, were making profits from the mission; Edwards became an advocate for the Indians, but his letters did little good until the boys' school was burned in 1753, and the commission reexamined his reports. The power and profit of the Williams family then came to an end. The Williamses were cousins of Edwards on his mother's side; other members of the family in Northampton had worked for his dismissal. Many of the Williamses had coveted Stoddard's pastorate, which had gone to Edwards. During this period, however, Edwards received an apology from Hawley, who had been his main nemesis in Northampton, for his actions against Edwards.

The French and Indian War, in which the Houstunnocks took the side of the French against the British, broke out in 1754; it did not end until 1763. When several whites were murdered nearby, area residents moved in with the Edwardses, and a fort was quickly built around their home; four soldiers were also billeted with the family. The Edwardses turned in a bill for 800

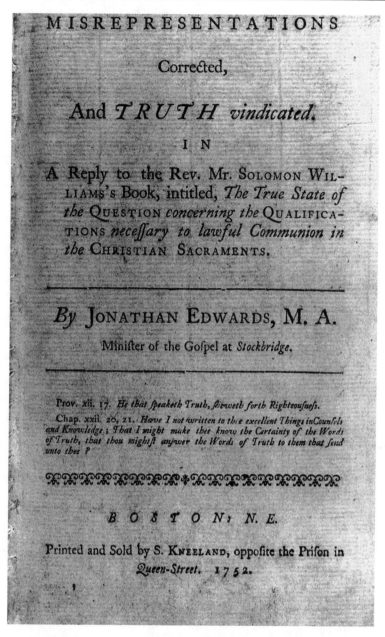

MISREPRESENTATIONS

Corrected,

And *TRUTH* vindicated.

IN

A Reply to the Rev. Mr. SOLOMON WIL-
LIAMS's Book, intitled, *The True State of
the* QUESTION *concerning the* QUALIFICA-
TIONS *necessary to lawful Communion in
the* CHRISTIAN SACRAMENTS.

By JONATHAN EDWARDS, M. A.

Minister of the Gospel at *Stockbridge.*

Prov. xii. 17. *He that speaketh Truth, sheweth forth Righteousness.*

Chap. xxii. 20, 21. *Have I not written to thee excellent Things in Counsels
and Knowledge; That I might make thee know the Certainty of the Words
of Truth, that thou mightst answer the Words of Truth to them that send
unto thee?*

BOSTON, N.E.

Printed and Sold by S. KNEELAND, opposite the Prison in
Queen-Street. 1752.

*Title page for Edwards's defense of his Communion policy (Beinecke Rare Book
and Manuscript Library, Yale University)*

meals during this period, plus another 180 that they had provided during the construction of the fort.

Despite these distractions, Edwards produced several major works during his time in Stockbridge. *Misrepresentations Corrected, and Truth Vindicated. In a Reply to the Rev. Mr. Solomon Williams's Book, Intitled, The True State of the Question Concerning the Qualifications Necessary to Lawful Communion in the Christian Sacraments* was published in 1752, followed by *A Careful and Strict Inquiry into the Modern Prevailing Notions of That Freedom of Will, Which*

Is Supposed to Be Essential to Moral Agency, Virtue and Vice, Reward and Punishment, Praise and Blame on 17 October 1754. *The Great Christian Doctrine of Original Sin Defended: Evidences of It's Truth Produced, and Arguments to the Contrary Answered* was in the press at the time of his death and was available late in 1758. *Two Dissertations: I. Concerning the End for Which God Created the World. II. The Nature of True Virtue* was not published until 1765. *A History of the Work of Redemption: Containing, the Outlines of a Body of Divinity, in a Method Entirely New* had begun as a

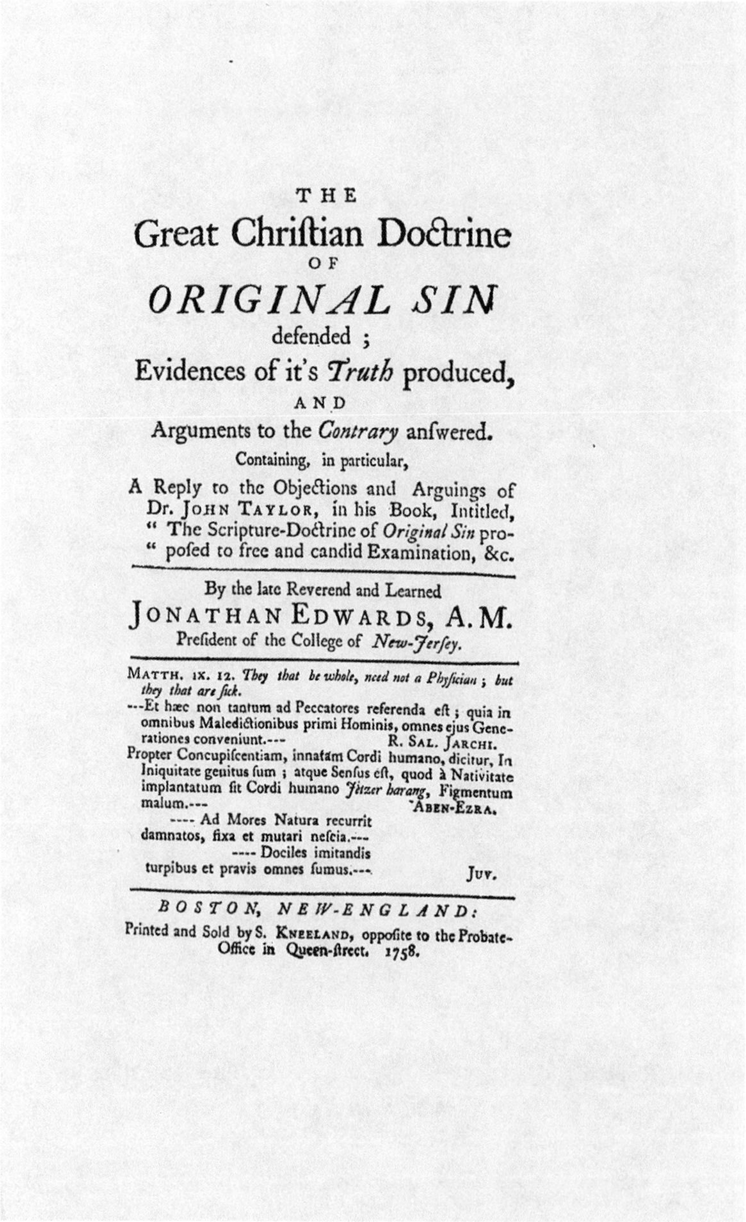

THE

Great Christian Doctrine
OF

ORIGINAL SIN

defended ;

Evidences of it's *Truth* produced,

AND

Arguments to the *Contrary* anſwered.

Containing, in particular,

A Reply to the Objections and Arguings of
Dr. JOHN TAYLOR, in his Book, Intitled,
" The Scripture-Doctrine of *Original Sin* pro-
" poſed to free and candid Examination, &c.

By the late Reverend and Learned

JONATHAN EDWARDS, A.M.
Preſident of the College of *New-Jerſey.*

MATTH. IX. 12. *They that be whole, need not a Phyſician ; but
they that are ſick.*
---Et hæc non tantum ad Peccatores referenda eſt ; quia in
omnibus Maledictionibus primi Hominis, omnes ejus Gene-
rationes conveniunt.---   R. SAL. JARCHI.
Propter Concupiſcentiam, innatam Cordi humano, dicitur, In
Iniquitate genitus ſum ; atque Senſus eſt, quod à Nativitate
implantatum ſit Cordi humano *Jetzer harang*, Figmentum
malum.---   ABEN-EZRA.
---- Ad Mores Natura recurrit
damnatos, fixa et mutari neſcia.---
---- Dociles imitandis
turpibus et pravis omnes ſumus.---   JUV.

BOSTON, NEW-ENGLAND :

Printed and Sold by S. KNEELAND, oppoſite to the Probate-
Office in Queen-ſtreet. 1758.

*Title page for the posthumous work in which Edwards argues that the human race did not inherit original sin
from Adam but can be viewed as having participated with him in his act of disobedience to God
(Beinecke Rare Book and Manuscript Library, Yale University)*

series of sermons in 1739; Edwards worked on it in Stockbridge but never completed it, and John Erskine edited it for publication in 1774.

In *A Careful and Strict Inquiry into the Modern Prevailing Notions of That Freedom of Will, Which Is Supposed to Be Essential to Moral Agency, Virtue and Vice, Reward and Punishment, Praise and Blame,* Edwards argues that the notion of free will, as applied to human beings, is incoherent. If every deliberate action must be preceded by an act of free will, then the act of willing itself must be preceded by another act of willing, and so on, leading to an infinite regress that would mean that no action could ever occur—which is absurd. On the other hand, if actions happen spontaneously, with no antecedent cause, then no one could be praised or blamed for his or her actions. Furthermore, all human actions are necessitated by God's foreknowledge of them: if an action that God knows will occur were not to occur, then God would be mistaken—which is, of course, impossible. Nevertheless, in spite of this theological determinism, and in spite of the fact that people are naturally inclined to evil by original sin, from which only God's freely given grace can release them, an individual may still be justly blamed and condemned to hell for his or her wrongful actions, since the individual was not hindered from performing them and takes pleasure in them.

In *The Great Christian Doctrine of Original Sin Defended* Edwards argues against the Arminians that God has not "imputed" Adam's sin to his offspring. According to Edwards, God determines what counts as a "species" or kind of thing; thus, God can count Adam and his progeny as one thing, so that all of humanity participated with Adam in the sinful inclination that led to his act, and all are therefore justly punished. Edwards buttresses his argument with biblical passages and with empirical evidence of human sinfulness.

In *The Nature of True Virtue* Edwards says that rational self-love, parental love, conscience, patriotism, and pity, which are commonly taken as virtues, are mere "shadows" of true virtue, because they are directed at portions of reality. True virtue consists of the love of universal benevolence for its own sake and the love of being itself, or God. Only benevolence is truly beautiful, and only God's benevolence is perfect; thus, only God is beautiful without qualification, and "All the beauty to be found throughout the whole creation is . . . the reflection of the diffused beams of that Being who hath an infinite fullness of brightness and glory." Only the saints or "elect"—those to whom God has granted an unearned absolution from original sin—can act from motives of true virtue, fully understand the hatefulness of sin, and appreciate true beauty.

Edwards's last call was to serve as president of the College of New Jersey (which was founded by the Tenants—Gilbert and William—and later became Princeton University in 1896), following the death of the former president, Edwards's son-in-law Aaron Burr, in September 1757. Edwards was inaugurated on 16 February 1758. He received an inoculation on 23 February against a smallpox epidemic in the Princeton area but died of a secondary fever on 22 March. Two weeks later his daughter Esther Burr, Aaron Burr's widow, who had been inoculated at the same time as her father, also died. Edwards's wife, Sarah, died on 2 October after arriving in Philadelphia to care for Esther's two children. One of those children, two-year-old Aaron, grew up to tie Jefferson in the presidential election of 1800 and serve as his vice president from 1801 to 1805.

Edwards's tenure as president of a reformed institution, albeit brief, places him within a larger reformed tradition valuing education, which included the development of Harvard, Yale, and a vast number of smaller colleges that followed on the westward expansion of the frontier. It also shows a consistency in the valuation of education in his theology, which is also evidenced in his education of his daughters and in his own lifelong scholarship.

Perry Miller sums up Edwards's importance in his 1956 biography:

> He was one of America's five or six major artists, who happened to work with ideas instead of with poems or novels. He was much more a psychologist and a poet than a logician, and though he devoted his genius to topics derived from the body of divinity—the will, virtue, sin—he treated them in a manner of the very finest speculators, in a manner of Augustine, Aquinas, and Pascal.

While Jonathan Edwards was a significant intellectual and the first comprehensive American philosopher, he saw his role as that of a theologian. His was a "voice in the wilderness," but not a lone voice: he was part of a continuum of reformed theologians that extends from John Calvin through John Witherspoon during the American Revolution and Lyman Beecher during the early republic to Karl Barth. Moreover, while his epistemology is realistic, even pragmatic, like that of William James and John Dewey, his metaphysics is idealistic, which makes him more akin to the "objective idealism and logical realism" of the founder of pragmatism, Charles Sanders Peirce. Thus, while more comparative studies are warranted, perhaps instead of "the last Puritan" a better title for Edwards would be "the first pragmatist."

Biographies:
Arthur C. McGiffert Jr., *Jonathan Edwards* (New York & London: Harper, 1932);

Perry Miller, *Errand into the Wilderness* (Cambridge, Mass.: Belknap Press of Harvard University Press, 1956);

Edward H. Davidson, *Jonathan Edwards: The Narrative of a Puritan Mind* (Cambridge, Mass.: Harvard University Press, 1968);

David Levin, ed., *Jonathan Edwards: A Profile* (New York: Hill & Wang, 1969);

Elisabeth D. Dodds, *Marriage to a Difficult Man: The "Uncommon Union" of Jonathan and Sarah Edwards* (Philadelphia: Westminster Press, 1971);

Miller, *Jonathan Edwards* (Westport, Conn.: Greenwood Press, 1973);

Ola Elizabeth Winslow, *Jonathan Edwards, 1703–1758: A Biography* (New York: Octagon, 1973).

References:
David C. Brand, *Profile of the Last Puritan: Jonathan Edwards, Self-Love, and the Dawn of the Beatific* (Atlanta: Scholars Press, 1991);

Conrad Cherry, *The Theology of Jonathan Edwards: A Reappraisal* (Garden City, N.Y.: Anchor, 1966; revised edition, Bloomington: Indiana University Press, 1990);

Stephen H. Daniel, *The Philosophy of Jonathan Edwards: A Study in Divine Semiotics* (Bloomington: Indiana University Press, 1994);

Roland André Delattre, *Beauty and Sensibility in the Thought of Jonathan Edwards: An Essay in Aesthetics and Theological Ethics* (New Haven: Yale University Press, 1968);

Douglas J. Elwood, *The Philosophical Theology of Jonathan Edwards* (New York: Columbia University Press, 1960);

Clarence H. Faust, "Jonathan Edwards as a Scientist," *American Literature,* 1 (1930): 393–404;

Norman Fiering, *Jonathan Edwards's Moral Thought and Its British Context* (Chapel Hill: University of North Carolina Press, 1981);

William James, *The Varieties of Religious Experience: A Study in Human Nature* (New York & London: Longmans, Green, 1902);

Robert W. Jenson, *America's Theologian: A Recommendation of Jonathan Edwards* (New York: Oxford University Press, 1988);

Hugh T. Kerr and John M. Mulder, eds., *Conversions* (Grand Rapids, Mich.: Eerdmans, 1983), pp. 67–70;

Virginia A. Peacock, *Problems in the Interpretation of Jonathan Edwards'* The Nature of True Virtue (Lewiston, N.Y.: Edwin Mellen Press, 1990);

John E. Smith, *Jonathan Edwards: Puritan, Preacher, Philosopher* (Notre Dame, Ind.: University of Notre Dame Press, 1992);

William J. Wainwright, "Jonathan Edwards and the Language of God," *Journal of the American Academy of Religion,* 48 (1980): 520–530;

Wainwright, "Jonathan Edwards, Atoms, and Immaterialism," *Idealistic Studies,* 12 (1982): 79–89;

Wainwright, "Jonathan Edwards, William Rowe, and the Necessity of Creation," in *Faith, Freedom, and Rationality: Philosophy of Religion,* edited by Jeff Jordan and Daniel Howard-Snyder (Lanham, Md.: Rowman & Littlefield, 1996), pp. 119–133;

Wainwright, "Original Sin," in *Philosophy and the Christian Faith,* edited by Thomas V. Morris (Notre Dame, Ind.: University of Notre Dame Press, 1988);

Wainwright, *Reason and the Heart: A Prolegomenon to a Critique of Passional Reason* (Ithaca, N.Y.: Cornell University Press, 1995).

Papers:

The Yale Collection in the Yale University Library has 568 of Jonathan Edwards's sermons, his notebooks, and an annotated list of books that he read or hoped to read. The Andover Collection of the Andover-Harvard Theological Seminary in Boston has sermons, letters, and early writings by Edwards.

Ralph Waldo Emerson

(25 May 1803 – 27 April 1882)

Richard A. Hutch
University of Queensland

See also the Emerson entries in *DLB 1: The American Renaissance in New England; DLB 59: American Literary Critics and Scholars, 1800–1850; DLB 73: American Magazine Journalists, 1741–1850; DLB 183: American Travel Writers, 1776–1864;* and *DLB 223: The American Renaissance in New England, Second Series.*

BOOKS: *Nature,* anonymous (Boston: Munroe, 1836);

An Oration, Delivered before the Phi Beta Kappa Society, at Cambridge (Boston: Munroe, 1837);

An Address Delivered before the Senior Class in Divinity College, Cambridge (Boston: Munroe, 1838); republished as *Man Thinking: An Oration* (London: C. E. Mudie, 1843);

An Oration, Delivered before the Literary Societies of Dartmouth College (Boston: Little & Brown, 1838);

Essays (Boston: Munroe, 1841; London: James Fraser, 1841); republished as *Essays: First Series* (Boston: Munroe, 1847);

The Method of Nature: An Oration, Delivered before the Society of the Adelphi (Boston: Samuel G. Simpkins, 1841; London: C. E. Mudie, 1844);

Nature: An Essay. And Lectures on the Times (London: H. G. Clarke, 1844); unauthorized enlarged edition published as *Nature, An Essay; Lectures on the Times; and On War* (London: George Slater, 1850);

Orations, Lectures, and Addresses (London: H. G. Clarke, 1844; unauthorized enlarged edition, London: George Slater, 1849);

Essays: Second Series (Boston: Munroe, 1844; London: Chapman, 1849);

An Address Delivered in the Court-House in Concord, Massachusetts . . . on the Anniversary of the Emancipation of the Negroes in the British West Indies (Boston: Munroe, 1844; London: Chapman, 1844);

Poems (Boston: Munroe, 1847; London: Chapman 1847);

Poems (London: Chapman, 1847; Boston: Munroe, 1847);

Nature: Addresses and Lectures (Boston: Munroe, 1849); republished as *Miscellanies: Embracing Nature,*

Ralph Waldo Emerson

Addresses, and Lectures (Boston: Phillips, Sampson, 1856; London: Macmillan, 1884);

Representative Men: Seven Lectures (Boston: Phillips, Sampson, 1850; London: Chapman, 1850);

English Traits (Boston: Phillips, Sampson, 1856; London: Routledge, 1856);

The Conduct of Life (Boston: Ticknor & Fields, 1860; London: Smith, Elder, 1860);

May-Day and Other Pieces (Boston: Ticknor & Fields, 1867; London: Routledge, 1867);

Society and Solitude: Twelve Chapters (Boston: Fields, Osgood, 1870; London: Sampson Low, Son & Marston, 1870);

Letters and Social Aims, edited by James Elliot Cabot and Edward Waldo Emerson (Boston: Osgood, 1876; London: Chatto & Windus, 1876);

Fortune of the Republic: Lecture Delivered at the Old South Church (Boston: Houghton, Osgood, 1878);

Miscellanies, edited by Cabot and Edward Waldo Emerson (Boston: Houghton, Mifflin, 1884);

Lectures and Biographical Sketches, edited by Cabot and Edward Waldo Emerson (Boston: Houghton, Mifflin, 1884; London: Routledge, 1884);

Natural History of Intellect, edited by Cabot and Edward Waldo Emerson (Boston: Houghton, Mifflin, 1893);

The Journals of Ralph Waldo Emerson, edited by Edward Waldo Emerson and Waldo Emerson Forbes, 10 volumes (Boston & New York: Houghton Mifflin, 1909–1914);

Uncollected Writings, edited by Charles C. Bigelow (New York: Lamb, 1912);

Young Emerson Speaks: Unpublished Discourses on Many Subjects, edited by Arthur Cushman McGiffert (Boston & New York: Houghton Mifflin, 1938);

The Early Lectures of Ralph Waldo Emerson, 3 volumes, edited by Stephen E. Whicher, Robert E. Spiller, and Wallace E. Williams (Cambridge, Mass.: Harvard University Press, 1959–1972);

The Journals and Miscellaneous Notebooks of Ralph Waldo Emerson, 16 volumes, edited by William H. Gilman, Alfred R. Ferguson, George P. Clark, Merrell R. Davis, A. W. Plumstead, Harrison Hayford, Ralph H. Orth, J. E. Parson, Linda Allardt, Susan Sutton Smith, Merton M. Sealts Jr., David W. Hill, Ruth H. Bennett, Ronald A. Bosco, and Glen M. Johnson (Cambridge, Mass.: Harvard University Press, 1960–1982);

The Poetry Notebooks of Ralph Waldo Emerson, edited by Orth and others (Columbia: University of Missouri Press, 1986);

The Complete Sermons of Ralph Waldo Emerson, 4 volumes, edited by Albert J. von Frank and others (Columbia: University of Missouri Press, 1989–1992);

The Topical Notebooks of Ralph Waldo Emerson, 3 volumes, edited by Orth and others (Columbia: University of Missouri Press, 1990–1994).

Collections: *The Complete Works of Ralph Waldo Emerson,* 12 volumes, edited by Edward Waldo Emerson (London: Routledge, 1902–1903; Boston & New York: Houghton, Mifflin, 1903–1904);

The Collected Works of Ralph Waldo Emerson, 5 volumes, edited by Robert E. Spiller, Alfred R. Ferguson, Joseph Slater, Jean Ferguson Carr, Douglas Emory Wilson, Ralph H. Orth, Wallace E. Williams, Philip L. Nicoloff, and Robert E. Burkholder (Cambridge, Mass.: Harvard University Press, 1971–1994);

Emerson in His Journals, edited by Joel Porte (Cambridge, Mass.: Belknap Press of Harvard University Press, 1982);

Ralph Waldo Emerson: Collected Poems and Translations, edited by Harold Bloom and Paul Kane (New York: Library of America, 1994);

Emerson's Antislavery Writings, edited by Len Gougeon and Joel Myerson (New Haven: Yale University Press, 1995);

The Later Lectures of Ralph Waldo Emerson, 2 volumes, edited by Ronald A. Bosco and Myerson (Athens: University of Georgia Press, 2000).

OTHER: Thomas Carlyle, *Sartor Resartus,* edited by Emerson (Boston: Munroe, 1836);

Carlyle, *Critical and Miscellaneous Essays,* 4 volumes, edited by Emerson (Boston: Munroe, 1838–1839);

Jones Very, *Essays and Poems,* edited by Emerson (Boston: Little & Brown, 1839);

Memoirs of Margaret Fuller Ossoli, edited by Emerson, James Freeman Clarke, and William Henry Channing (2 volumes, Boston: Phillips, Sampson, 1852; 3 volumes, London: Bentley, 1852);

Henry David Thoreau, *Excursions,* edited by Emerson (Boston: Ticknor & Fields, 1863);

Thoreau, *Letters to Various Persons,* edited by Emerson (Boston: Ticknor & Fields, 1865);

Parnassus, edited by Emerson (Boston & New York: Houghton, Mifflin, 1874).

Ralph Waldo Emerson is perhaps the most influential and pivotal figure in American literary history. As a writer he was a major nineteenth-century craftsman of American cultural identity. Emerson brought about an awareness of what it could mean to be an American, as distinct from being a colonial subject of the British Empire. While his philosophical notions may blur into common themes of the American Romantic period, the parallel between his mature philosophical thought and the emergence of the American republic stands out. His early life reveals a struggle to achieve an identity of his own and to seal it with an appropriate vocational commitment; few significant models were available to guide him. Emerson's personal struggle has a parallel in the struggle of American institutional and cultural life to become autonomous on the world scene. His mature philosophical writings, most of which appeared in the 1850s, reflect thematic reverberations of his first thirty-five years. As a representative version of the emergence of the republic and the national culture of the United States of America, that philosophy reigned supreme as a statement of national achievement during the second half of the nineteenth century. Emerson remains a central ideologist of American self- understanding during the nineteenth and early twentieth centuries.

The first thirty-five years of Emerson's almost eighty years of life were a tumultuous time of personal conflict, primarily over the question of vocation. The influence of ministers was greater than it had ever been when Emerson undertook to pursue that career in 1825, but the profession of the ministry was on the wane in Boston in the mid nineteenth century. As theology ceased to dominate the New England mind, literature and philosophy attracted more attention, and no other denomination in the country devoted as much energy to them as Boston's Unitarians. Emerson's thirteen-year conflict over a career in the Unitarian ministry, however, constituted more than mere resistance to changing professional trends in the society of his day. The young man was also tormented by ambivalence over being a perpetual son. This personal ambivalence paralleled the budding nation's continuing connections to Britain. If one did not cast aside all other sorts of consciousness but one's own, Emerson said in his journal at the end of his crisis, on 18 March 1838, then one would be like a "son who should always suck at his mother's teat."

Emerson's protracted crisis consisted of coming to grips with his feelings about his mother, Ruth Haskins Emerson, and her expectations for his professional development after his father, William Emerson, the minister of Boston's First Unitarian Church, died on 12 May 1811. Her impact on Emerson was twofold. On the one hand, he sought to separate himself from his mother on more than one occasion, but, on the other hand, he abided by her hard-won expectations that he walk the well-trodden path of his father toward a ministerial career, a path taken briefly by Emerson's older brother, William, but not at all by his younger ones, Edward, Charles, and Robert Bulkeley (three other siblings died in infancy or early childhood). As he walked this path, he found his sense of personal autonomy and strength wanting. Also, inasmuch as he sensed that he was able to stand by himself without feeling obligated to please his mother, he felt the ministry to be an antiquated profession that did not merit his best and most thoughtful efforts. This change constitutes a shift from his sense of being a mother's son to a sense of being born again as a native American son—an expansion of consciousness of considerable magnitude.

Three events, each several years long, stand out during the period from Emerson's birth on 25 May

Emerson's father, the Unitarian minister William Emerson, who died in 1811 (from Gay Wilson Allen, Waldo Emerson: A Biography, *1981)*

1803 until his renunciation of the Unitarian pulpit in 1838. Together they suggest how Emerson's self-awareness of being a perpetual son shifted from focusing on his mother to emphasizing his native land. The first two events highlight his confusion over conflicting senses of sonship, while the third draws attention to the lessening of such confusion in terms of his discovery of new vocational and cultural identity—an identity he himself designed and built as a way of making his world more intellectually and emotionally habitable. Thus, Emerson's struggle as a young man took him from the oppressive mantle of the inherited ministry to the expanding vistas of native lecturing and Romantic philosophical thought. Emerson celebrates the uniqueness of the self and relates all external reality to that unified and autonomous self.

The first of the three events is the most unusual acquaintance Emerson seems ever to have had, if only because of its one-sidedness: his college relationship with Martin Gay from 1820 to 1822. His ambivalence about Gay prefigures Emerson's vocational conflict. The second event began with his entrance into the Harvard Divinity School in 1825 and continued through his resignation in 1832 from his position at Second Church in Boston, where he had served since early 1829. The third event was Emerson's first marriage, which lasted from September 1829 until February 1831, when his wife died of tuberculosis. By her death, Emerson's wife paid the price for his personal autonomy and professional and intellectual independence. Together, these events represent Emerson's transition to maturity as a man, as a philosopher, and as a symbol of an American culture ready to take its place in the world.

Emerson went to Boston Public Latin School when he was nine and entered Harvard College in 1817. On 25 January 1820, when he was a junior, he started keeping a journal. He was, perhaps, prompted to this sort of self-examination by noticing what he calls in the 8 August entry "a strange face in the Freshman class whom I should like to know very much. He has a great deal of character in his features & should [be] either a fast friend or a bitter enemy. His name is Gay. I shall endeavour to become acquainted with him & wish if possible that I might be able to recall at a future period the singular sensations which his presenc[e] produced at this." Later, he tried to scratch out the name "Gay" here and in almost every other passage where it occurs. Being haunted by such a face was not easily dismissed by an adolescent with an unsure sexual identity. On 1 April 1821 Emerson notes that he and Gay have not "exchanged above a dozen words" during their one year of acquaintance. The relationship was confined to "seeing" and "being seen"; Emerson was free to see Gay as he wished to see him, and though the process of seeing Gay was silent, it was not, he reflects on 29 November 1822, a glance between "indifferent persons." On a date that cannot be precisely determined in 1821 or 1822 he wrote a "song to one whose unimproved talents and friendship have interested the writer in his character and fate":

> By the unacknowledged tie
> Which binds us to each other
> By the pride of feeling high
> Which friendship's name can mother
> By the cold encountering eyes
> Whose language deeply thrilling
> Rebelled against the prompt surmise
> Which told the heart was willing;
>
> By all which you have felt and feel
> My eager gaze returning
> I offer you this silent zeal
> On youthful altars burning . . .

Emerson attempted to keep Gay at arm's length by means of a visual fantasy expressed in poetic reverie. This way of reacting to others was the seedbed of Emerson's embrace of Romantic philosophical idealism, in which the "real" is juxtaposed to and surpassed intellectually by the "ideal" form it represents. Having never talked to Gay, Emerson prevented himself from becoming intimate with the boy. "Why do you look after me?" Emerson wrote rhetorically to Gay in his journal in 1821 or 1822. "I cannot help looking out as you pass." Emerson was perplexed by being unable to avoid staring at the passing figure.

The journal record illustrates how Emerson unconsciously constructed his worldview in terms of "face-to-face" encounters. This personal style forms a template for his mature philosophical idealism: the desire of the true philosopher to see into Nature and behold its essence. On 1 May 1821 Emerson records that "I am more puzzled than ever with [Gay]'s conduct. He came out to meet me yesterday and I observing him, just before we met turned another corner and most strangely avoided him. This morning I went out to meet him in a different direction and stopped to speak to a lounger so as to be directly in [Gay]'s way, but [he] turned into the first gate and went towards Stoughton. All this baby play persists without any apparent design, and as soberly as if both were intent on some tremendous affair." He immediately goes on to note that "With a most serious expectation of burning this book I am committing to it more of what I may by and by think childish sentiment than I should care to venture on vagabond sheets which Somebody else may light upon. (Mr. Somebody, will it please your impertinence to be conscience-struck!)" Evidently, Emerson's own conscience had been stricken "without any apparent design." He found himself caught between what he believed to be the real and the ideal. Looking back on the relationship on 7 May 1822, Emerson recalled feeling "pride in being a collegian, & a poet, & somewhat romantic in my queer acquaintance with [Gay]."

While the relationship was unsettling, it supplied a point of enduring personal stability that anchored Emerson's mature Romantic speculations about Nature, the "feminine" partner in his work as a philosophical visionary. Fixing his sight on Gay enabled Emerson to see his way free from ever-renewed conflict. "Seeing" was the way Emerson controlled his psychological ambivalence between 1820 and 1822. Distancing himself from such conflict until the terms of it grew dull in his sight became a convenient psychological tactic, and he continued to use it. Indeed, seeing his way beyond the mundane world was the underlying philosophical platform of the "Transcendentalism" he and others founded in New England in the middle of the nineteenth century. The pattern of his philosophical labor was thus set during Emerson's adolescence, and it had to do with the psychological–later, philosophical–

management of "face-to-face" encounters. (Gay went on to become a respected physician in Boston; he died in January 1850. No evidence exists that Emerson ever met him again after Emerson left Harvard.)

In September 1821 Emerson graduated from Harvard College thirtieth in a class of fifty-nine and took a job teaching in his brother William's School for Young Ladies in Boston. When his brother left in 1823, Emerson was left in charge. School-keeping, he said in an 8 November 1821 letter to his aunt, Mary Moody Emerson, was his "*Gehenna*." He was intimidated by his young female pupils; when a disciplinary problem arose, the only recourse he had was to send the student to his mother, who resided upstairs; she would administer sufficient "rustication." Turning twenty-one in 1824, he compared himself with his peers, peers whom he thought included the girls attending his school: "What is called a warm heart, I have not," he says in a journal entry for 18 April 1824. He confesses in the same entry a "sore uneasiness in the company of most men & women, a frigid fear of offending & jealousy of disrespect, an inability to lead & an unwillingness to follow the current conversation." He was pained by "infirmities of the cheek"–the blushing that the young ladies provoked. His ideal relationship with Gay had been replaced by the real experience of relating to young women in a professional setting in which he was hesitant, at best.

Emerson closed the school in December 1824, convinced that he was not a teacher. An alternative profession was at hand that relieved his uncertainty, carried on the family tradition, and commanded public respect: his father's prestigious footsteps as a Unitarian minister seemed a reasonable path to follow. In the 18 April 1824 entry, one of the longest, most torturously self-assessing passages in the journals, he predicts that "if I devote my nights & days *in form,* to the service of God & the War against sin,–I shall soon be prepared to do the same *in substance.*"

Each time Emerson made a commitment to the Unitarian tradition, he simultaneously undercut it by becoming physically ill, withdrawing from his parish duties, and traveling for his health. The ministry obviously elicited his psychological ambivalence. In this respect, Emerson's relationship to the ministry was similar to his relationship to Gay: he had to put psychological distance between himself and both Gay and the ministry. Again, the real and the ideal were juxtaposed. An exemplary instance of the coincidence between commitment, sickness, and withdrawal occurred in early March 1825: Emerson had been studying at the Harvard Divinity School for barely a month when he suffered the loss of his eyesight. Professor of biblical theology Andrews Norton gave Emerson permission to

Emerson's mother, Ruth Haskins Emerson (from Gay Wilson Allen, Waldo Emerson: A Biography, *1981)*

forgo the usual class recitations, but Emerson dropped out of Harvard toward the end of March and retreated to the rural environs of Newton and Chelmsford, Massachusetts. Only when he returned to Cambridge with the loosely defined status of "graduate resident" in January 1826 does he report in his journal (8 January) that his eyes have mended.

A licensure service before the Middlesex Association was scheduled for 10 October 1826. As the time for the service neared, Emerson was racked by rheumatism of the hip and noticed with anguish the dreaded signs of tuberculosis, of which his father had died fifteen years previously. Nevertheless, when the licensure service took place, the Middlesex Association was pleased with Emerson's sermon.

Instead of making up for lost time, however, Emerson dropped out again. He sailed to Charleston, South Carolina, in November and proceeded to St. Augustine, Florida, early in 1827, ostensibly for the benefit of his health. In a 15 March letter to his brother William he reported that his weight had shot from 141 1/2 pounds at the end of January to 152 pounds. He returned to New England in June with few of the sermons he had hoped to write but with restored health and a bright outlook. He turned down a request in July 1827 to take a pulpit in western Massachusetts for a long period of time, believing it better "to consult my health by remaining in the country, & preaching only half days in Boston." Only a few weeks later, however, he journeyed to the same area and took a pulpit for about as long a period as the first offer had requested him to stay. On 3 April of the following year he wrote his brother William, who had abandoned ministerial training in 1825, that he was "embarrassed at present whenever any application is made to me that may lead to permanent engagements. For I fancy myself dependent for my degree of health on a lounging capricious unfettered mode of life." At the same time as he was relishing vocational detachment, however, he was reflecting in a journal entry for 30 July on a deeper, more personal attachment: "a child is connected to the womb of its mother by a cord from the navel. So it seems to me is man connected to God by his conscience."

In June 1828 Emerson's brother Edward suffered a recurrence of the delusions of persecution that had afflicted him several years earlier. Emerson had to seek employment to support all of his brothers—Charles and William were poverty-stricken legal apprentices in Boston and New York, respectively, and Bulkeley was mentally retarded—and their mother. When Edward was placed in the asylum in Charlestown, the family's financial resources shrank even further. Under these circumstances, Emerson, after a year of occasional preaching throughout Massachusetts, told William in a 30 June 1828 letter that he had agreed to supply the pulpit of the ailing Henry Ware at Second Church in Boston starting in August "but shall probably relinquish it." The unwilling schoolmaster had become the unwilling minister.

When he took Edward along on a preaching trip to New Hampshire in December 1828 for the benefit of his brother's health, Emerson not only withdrew from Boston but also temporarily eased his mother's distress. Ruth Emerson's favorite son seemed to be taking charge of family necessities, at least in regard to Edward. While out of reach, however, Emerson acted decisively for perhaps the first time in his life. His sudden decision served to offset the daily grim realities he faced by establishing an ideal personal connection that he could believe was permanent and that, thus, partook of eternity: to the surprise of the family, he became engaged to Ellen Louisa Tucker of New Concord, New Hampshire. Plans for a September wedding forced Emerson to view his new job as a financial necessity. Encouraged by the "strong expression of confidence & goodwill" of the congregation, he accepted the "solemn office" of junior pastor of Second Church on 30 January 1829 without "any sanguine confidence in my abilities, or in my prospects" and "in weakness, and not in strength." Thus, Emerson allowed circumstances and family financial necessities to press him into a long-resisted vocational commitment.

Ellen Tucker had suffered from tuberculosis for a long time before Emerson met her. Her illness was much more serious than the one that had prompted him to sail southward for recovery in 1828. During their engagement he excused himself from his parish duties several times to take her riding in the fresh air of the mountains of western New England. Ellen's sickness was, thus, a pretext for removing himself temporarily from the church; the pretext, if carried to its logical conclusion, implied that if Ellen became extremely sick or died, then the young minister would have the excuse he needed to leave the church permanently. Ellen had two major bleeding attacks just before the wedding, after visiting her fiancé. After the wedding on 30 September 1829 the couple took up residence with Emerson's mother. While Emerson wrote his sermons, Ellen tried her hand at housekeeping, in spite of her rapidly worsening condition.

In August 1830 Ellen underwent her third violent bleeding attack since early 1829, but she seemed quite well after a brief excursion to New Concord. A decision about what to do with Ellen in the face of the approaching New England winter was needed; according to Emerson in a 6 September letter to William, the family pondered "many plans," one of which was a journey to the south. Emerson added that the Reverend William Ellery Channing's situation was, coincidentally, much like his own: "Dr. Channing, I learn goes to Cuba this winter for his *wifes* health!!" In fact, Channing spent the winter of 1830–1831 in St. Croix in the Virgin Islands, and the purpose was to restore his own health. But even if Emerson was mistaken about Channing's actual situation, he implied that men of moral stature see to it that their sick wives get well, whatever the price.

The idea of a southern journey, however, was sabotaged by Ellen's optimistic inclination, as Emerson put it in his letter to William, "to stay at home this winter" and by her doctor's advice that she not undertake a journey southward unless she was prepared to stay there for ten years. He also cautioned the family about the dangers of sea travel, especially during the winter months. The family seized on the second point and put aside the idea of the couple's sailing south. The doctor's point, however, was not what the family took it to be. They continued to think in terms of a short-term restorative journey for the couple; the doctor had suggested that such a journey would not suffice to cure Ellen, but he also implied that relocating in warmer and drier latitudes might prolong her life. Thus, though the doctor

Well, I am sorry to have learned that my friend is dissolute; or rather the anecdote which I accidentally heard of him shews him more like his neighbours than I should wish him to be. But I shall have to throw him up, after all, as a cheat of fancy. Before I ever saw him, I wished my friend to be different from any individual I had seen. I invested him with a solemn cast of mind, full of poetic feeling, & an idolater of friendship, & possessing a vein of rich sober thought. When I saw *[crossed out]* the *[crossed out]* with the complete character which fancy had formed and though entirely *[crossed out]* was pleased to observe the notice which *[crossed out]* for a year I have entertained towards him the *[crossed out]* feelings I should be sorry to lose him altogether before we have ever exchanged above a dozen words.

NB   By the way this book is of an inferiour character & contains so much doubtful matter that I believe I shall have to burn the second number of the Wide World immediately upon its completion.

Page from the journal Emerson began keeping when he was a junior at Harvard College, showing his attempt to obliterate the name of a fellow student, Martin Gay (Houghton Library, Harvard University)

*Emerson at twenty-six; miniature by Sarah Goodrich
(from Robert E. Spiller, Alfred R. Ferguson, and
others,* The Collected Works of Ralph
Waldo Emerson, *1971–1994)*

cautioned against a sea voyage, he did not rule out a move by chaise to Baltimore or South Carolina.

It was mainly Emerson's mother who would hear no medical advice that implied that her son would have to leave home permanently. She had wanted at least one of her five sons to follow in their father's footsteps; three of them had opted for legal careers, and the other was feebleminded, making Emerson her last hope. Charles told William in an 11 August letter that he doubted that any climate could save Ellen, implying that he thought that the couple should stay in Boston. No action was taken, and Emerson reported to William on 4 October that "Ellen is pretty well & we hope in a fortnight to begin our housekeeping & are busy buying carpets & the like."

Late in 1830 Edward Emerson, who was staying with William in New York City, began showing signs of tuberculosis. He considered sailing southward and taking up residence in St. Croix. His relatives in Boston were convinced, however, that he should return home to be nursed back to health not only by his mother but, Emerson wrote William on 29 November, also by Ellen. To volunteer the services of his mother was one thing: she was a tower of strength. But to suggest that

Ellen was able to care for Edward was to be blind to his wife's actual condition in the fall of 1830. Prone to delusions of persecution in the past, Edward fled from these new pressures from the north and left for St. Croix in December. Detained for two days en route to New York City to retrieve Edward, his mother discovered, Emerson told his grandfather Ezra Ripley, in a 15 December letter, that he had sailed out of the harbor "about half an hour before she arrived." She had not been upset when Emerson went to Charleston in 1826–1827, because she knew that he would return home within the year; but the thought that Edward was considering making St. Croix his permanent home, breaking up the family she had held together with great difficulty after her husband's death, was beyond her comprehension. Ruth Emerson was more concerned for her son's professional life than for the health of her daughter-in-law; had her presence been less commanding, Emerson and Ellen might have taken the possibility of a southern relocation more seriously than they did.

Ellen wished that she had sailed with Edward: "Hug yourself for your timely retreat," she wrote him on 24 December, since she herself was unable to embrace the "beautiful balm" of the southern air. She asked Edward to "speak kindly of kith and kin" to people in St. Croix and to "pick out a pretty spot for Waldo and wife to live." She spoke "so strongly," she said, because her requests were more than mere sisterly politeness. A few days before her death, Emerson wrote Edward on 20 April 1831, she had expressed a hope "to live to hear of Edward's safe arrival" in St. Croix. She never did: Ellen Emerson died on 8 February 1831, leaving her widower, as he wrote to his aunt Mary a few hours later, "alone in the world & strangely happy." Ellen's death triggered a restructuring of Emerson's vocational cultural identity; his acquiescence of 1830–1831 led to a sense of self-reliance in 1832–1833 and to his subsequent philosophical idealism and New England "Transcendentalism."

The transformation began with the sacrament of the Lord's Supper. Toward the end of 1831 Emerson began having pangs of conscience over administering the rite. Jesus, he thought, never intended the supper as a memorial to himself, and to consider it sacred and holy was hypocritical. In the early summer of 1832 he wrote in his journal that "I have sometimes thought that in order to be a good minister it was necessary to leave the ministry. The profession is antiquated. In an altered age, we worship the dead forms of our forefathers," and he began making a major issue of Communion. He asked the society to permit him to forgo the ceremony, just as he had asked Norton to excuse him from classroom recitations years before. The request was denied: Emerson would have to administer the sacrament, as his father and seven generations of Emerson clergymen had done. That was the reality, but Emerson sought something that was, to his mind, more ideal. To refuse to follow form was to state a declaration of independence. In 1832, however, his future turned on this insight: in the past he had tried to accept the church by reluctantly becoming a minister. Now, however, he realized that it was the church that had accepted him. Thus, his first step toward independence was to make himself unacceptable to the church by questioning the foundation of the Christian tradition represented by the sacrament of the Lord's Supper. Emerson's autonomous self thus commenced its appearance in his personal and, more significantly, in his professional affairs. That summer he suffered from a persistent diarrhea that left him, as he recorded in his journal for 11 August, as "weak . . . as a reed" and unable to preach. He told his aunt Mary in a 19 August letter that he considered the condition, coming when it did, a "divine plan," and said that because he was of a "mind not prepared to eat or drink religiously," and "seeing no middle way, I apprehend a separation" from the church. In early September he preached a sermon about what he was by then convinced was a misconstrued ceremony. On 11 September he sent in his letter of resignation, and on 28 October the society voted to accept it. They agreed to continue his salary to the end of the year and to bid him farewell with "affectionate regret." In a 19 November letter to William, Emerson said that he considered the result of his initiative a "mutual relief" to the congregation and to himself and that he could now "walk firmly toward a peace & a freedom which I plainly see before me albeit afar."

Once he effected separation from the Unitarian Church, his conscience became attached to a calling as a philosophical thinker that only he was able at this time to see. Following the precedents when he dropped out in 1825 and 1826–1827, he journeyed abroad in 1833.

One effect of Emerson's resignation was renewed and permanent health. On 18 April 1833 he wrote his aunt from Rome that he was in better health than he had enjoyed since he had been in college. From his graduation in 1821 until 1833 he had felt weak and continually subject to illness; those twelve years had literally made him sick. Not coincidentally, those years were a time when his vocational identity was staked on precedents that had been in his family for a long time—teaching and, most of all, the ministry. As he moved from Italy to France to Scotland and, finally, to England, where he met Samuel Taylor Coleridge, William Wordsworth, and Thomas Carlyle, Emerson realized that he no longer had to face those precedents. His future could be crafted unaided by the past. This realization was the source of his philosophical idealism and

Emerson's first wife, Ellen Louisa Tucker, around the time of their marriage on 30 September 1829; miniature by Sarah Goodrich (from Joel Porte, ed., Emerson in His Journals, *1982)*

New England "Transcendentalism." Returning home, he felt proud of his newfound autonomy and strength, and he resolved never to be fastened to the Unitarian ministry again. Waiting in Liverpool to depart from England, he wrote in his journal on 2 September: "Glad I bid adieu to England, the old, the rich, the strong nation, full of arts & men & memories[;] nor can I feel any regret in the presence of the best of its sons that I was not born here. I am thankful that I am an American as I am thankful that I am a man." The "best merit" of England "to my eye," he says, is "that it is the most resembling country to America which the world contains." As he stood on the deck of the New York–bound ship, watching England shrink from view as the western horizon expanded ahead, he was aware for the first time of a shift from the sense of being only a mother's son, set to repeat the realities of his paternal past, to being something new and different. He had become a true and aspiring native son of America.

Emerson had weathered a protracted transition to personal maturity, the prelude to his professional success as an American philosopher. The pillar of his new faith in himself was his sense of self-reliance. With this inner conviction in place, Emerson could finally express

Emerson in 1842, the year he began editing the Transcendentalist magazine The Dial

continental Europe; its chief influences were the poet Coleridge, the German idealist philosopher Freidrich Wilhelm Joseph von Schelling, and orientalism. While it was a general attitude rather than a systematically worked-out philosophy, it was, nonetheless, distinctive. Transcendentalism opposed Lockean empiricism, materialism, rationalism, Calvinism, Deism, Trinitarianism, and middle-class commercialism. The metaphysics it espoused generally followed that of post-Kantian idealism, which posited the immanance of the divine in finite existence and tended toward pantheism. These themes establish the concept of self-reliance in Emerson's works. Its epistemological position was idealistic and intuitive, and its ethics embraced idealism, individualism, mysticism, reformism, and optimism regarding human nature. If it could be said to have a theological slant, Transcendentalism was autosoteric (that is, it held that human beings are responsible for their own salvation), unitarian, and broadly mystical.

Emerson always used his own life as a means of thinking through an answer to his central question: "How shall I live?" His mature thought addresses this question by building on the concept of self-reliance. His philosophy is not methodology, logic, systematic analysis, or inquiry; it is the organic construction of a pattern of thought and observation in reasonable harmony with certain accepted axioms of intuited belief. This philosophy stands in opposition to the doctrine of incarnation he reluctantly espoused during his years as a Unitarian minister. The Christian Incarnation draws mind and spirit downward into the body; for the post-1831 Emerson, the motion is upward, cyclical, opposing and circling into a spiral of awareness. This awareness occurs through the power of every individual soul as it participates in the unifying force of the one soul, the "Over-Soul," of which everything is composed. The positive energy of this process involves visual and intuitive horizons that unite the earthly and the heavenly in Nature.

In 1838 Emerson, who had temporarily administered the East Lexington pulpit since 1836, gave up those duties; on 19 February he wrote his wife that the "froward man" was "cutting the last threads that bind him to that prized gown & band the symbols black & white of old & distant Judah." At the same time as he was cutting those last clerical threads, he was also giving thought to shaping his attitudes—the budding American consciousness. As he noted in his journal for 18 March 1838, to "accept another man's consciousness" for one's own was for Americans to be like "permanent embryos which received all their nourishment through the umbilical cord" that continued to be fruitlessly attached to Mother England. The sons of the first generation of American fathers had to grow up; they had

in his mature philosophical thought the hard-won lessons he had learned about how to live as an autonomous self and visionary. Around the concept of self-reliance turned the attitudes that thereafter shaped his lectures and writings.

In 1834 Emerson moved from Boston to Concord, Massachusetts. On 14 September of the following year he married Lydia Jackson of Plymouth; he always called her "Lidian." They had four children: Waldo, born on 30 October 1836; Ellen, born on 24 February 1839; Edith, born on 22 November 1841; and Edward, born on 10 July 1844. Waldo Emerson died of scarlet fever on 27 January 1842.

The feeling of finally being "alone in the world & strangely happy," as he put it only hours after his first wife died, is reflected throughout Emerson's mature thought about self-reliance. In his work Emerson revived philosophical idealism and made it the basis of what he and others who gathered in Boston in 1836 called "Transcendentalism." The so-called Transcendental Club, which also included George Putnam, George Ripley, Frederic Hedge, Orestes Brownson, James Freeman Clarke, Convers Francis, Bronson Alcott, Theodore Parker, Margaret Fuller, Elizabeth Peabody, and Henry David Thoreau, stemmed intellectually from the Romantic movement in England and

to go beyond the past, to transcend old styles of thought. To cling to a colonial consciousness after the severance brought about by the War of Independence begun in 1776 was merely for sons to mimic "sincere persons who live in shams." Again, the real and the ideal are juxtaposed and used to frame matters at hand. Besides, Emerson assured his mother in a 14 March 1838 letter, lecturing as a part of the new American lyceum movement "promises to be good bread."

Emerson expressed his views in his sermons, lectures, poems, and such important and popular works as *Nature* (1836) and his two series of *Essays* (1841 and 1844). He, Ripley, and Alcott launched a magazine, *The Dial,* edited by Fuller, on 1 July 1840; Emerson edited the magazine from July 1842 until it ceased publication after sixteen issues in 1844. In 1847–1848 Emerson spent nine months in England and France, lecturing in England. His mother, who had been living with Emerson and his family, died at the age of eighty-five on 16 November 1853.

Emerson continued writing and lecturing, with special emphasis on the Civil War and the new science, until his death of pneumonia on 27 April 1882, but his mature philosophical thought is presented in *Representative Men* (1850), *English Traits* (1856), and *The Conduct of Life* (1860). These three works represent the core of Emerson's philosophy.

The fundamental question "How shall I live?" is central to *Representative Men*. Emerson writes about six men–the philosopher Plato, the mystic Emanuel Swedenborg, the skeptic Michel de Montaigne, the poet William Shakespeare, the man of the world Napoleon Bonaparte, and the writer Johann Wolfgang von Goethe–each of whom is representative of a cluster of traits of thought, or characteristic mind-sets, of humankind. In the introductory essay, "Uses of Great Men," Emerson advises the reader that great men address the basic question "How shall we live?" if one assumes that they live for "us." Emerson's interpretive style in the work grows out of the experimental manner of scrutinizing Gay: "It is natural to believe in great men. . . . Nature seems to exist for the excellent. The world is upheld by the veracity of good men: they make the earth wholesome. . . . The search after the great man is the dream of youth, and the most serious occupation of manhood. . . . Each man seeks those of different quality from his own, and such as are good of their kind; that is, he seeks other men, and the *otherest*." When such human qualities are abstracted, Emerson's philosophical idealism is at its most evident. Great men serve others indirectly, by representation; each is "connected with some district of nature, whose agent and interpreter he is; as Linnaeus, of plants; Huber, of bees . . . Euclid, of lines; Newton, of fluxions. . . . Every ship

Emerson in 1846

that comes to America got its chart from Columbus. Every novel is a debtor to Homer." Lest these men become mere models whom one would slavishly imitate in detail, a natural checks-and-balances system in nature elicits spiritual aspiration from the individual: "In some other and quite different field the next man will appear; not Jefferson, not Franklin, but now a great statesman; then a road-contractor; then a student of fishes; then a buffalo-hunting explorer; or a semi-savage Western general. . . . With each new mind, a new secret of nature transpires; nor can the Bible be closed until the last great man is born."

Plato "represents the privilege of the intellect, the power, namely, of carrying up every fact to successive platforms, and so disclosing, in every fact, a germ of expansion." About mystics such as Swedenborg he writes, "The privilege of this caste is an access to the secrets and structure of nature by some higher method than by experience. In common parlance, what one man is said to learn by experience, a man of extraordinary sagacity is said, without experience, to divine." Of Montaigne he says, "Who shall forbid a wise skepticism, seeing that there is no practical question on which any thing more than an approximate solution can be had?" From Shakespeare one learns that "The greatest genius is the most indebted man. A poet is no rattle-brain, saying what comes uppermost, and, because he says everything, saying at last something good; but a heart in unison with his time and country." Napoleon "had a directness of action never before combined with so much comprehension." And from Goethe one learns "courage, and the equivalence of all times; that the disadvantages of any epoch exist only to the faint-hearted." Emerson scrutinizes character much in the same way as he looked at his own commitment to what he called the "sham" of the Unitarian ministry. He judged people as bearers of spiritual benefit.

Emerson traveled to England three times: in 1832, 1847, and 1783. *English Traits* reflects his fascination with England and English culture, as well as with what—by contrast—*not* being English means to him and his countrymen. Again, he asks, "How shall I live?" But here he puts the question to a country to which America was only recently opposed, yet from which it descended. Opposition is the key: oppose England, he recommends, and learn from the complex warp and woof of opposition how to craft an American national and cultural identity.

Emerson asks, "Why is England England?" He answers in a series of chapters: "Land," "Race," "Ability," "Manners," "Truth," "Character," "Cockayne" (humor), "Wealth," "Aristocracy," "Universities," "Religion," "Literature," and "Result." The chapters are interconnected: for instance, the land locates the race; aristocracy locates the wealth; and humor locates the character in its particular English context. Each chapter has a theme: "England is a garden"; "The English composite character betrays a mixed origin. Everything English is a fusion of distant and antagonistic elements"; "The Norman has come popularly to represent in England the aristocratic, and the Saxon the democratic principle"; "I find the Englishman to be him of all men who stands firmest in his shoes"; "The Teutonic tribes have a national singleness of heart, which contrasts with the Latin races"; "The English race are reputed morose"; "The English are a nation of humorists"; "There is no country in which so absolute a homage is paid to wealth"; "The feudal character of the English state, now that it is getting obsolete, glares a little, in contrast with the democratic tendencies"; "The logical English train a scholar as they train an engineer. Oxford is a Greek factory, as Wilton mills weave carpet and Sheffield grinds steel"; "The religion of England is part of good-breeding"; "England is the best of actual nations. . . . Broad-fronted, broad-bottomed Teutons, they stand in solid phalanx foursquare to the points of the compass; they constitute the modern world, they have earned their vantage ground and held it through the ages of adverse possession. . . . They cannot see beyond England."

According to Emerson, the English have learned much by opposing, and Americans will learn even more by opposing them. The upward sweep of awareness from the real to the ideal is activated by such mental opposition, which harks back to Emerson's return from England in 1833 with no regrets and a fresh sense of personal and vocational independence. He had realized that he was an autonomous moral unity, not split by yearning for Mother England, while, at the same time, putting distance—a concealed form of opposition—between himself and his real mother in Boston. This psychodynamic usually worked to stall his attempts to create the kind of professional future he actually forged for himself in the end. Emerson shifted his sense of being an autonomous moral unity from person to object, to representative men, to nation and type, and through all of these variations ran the active and creative power of his sense of the inner divinity of intuition. As he once phrased it in his journal, "faith is a telescope" that shapes the natural forces of heredity, geography, and history along an axis of vision stretching from the close horizon of the individual soul to the widest horizon of the "Over-Soul," or the sum total of Neoplatonic forms of which the universe is composed. English traits are English fate: within them move the powers of human beings. Form, change, and purpose are organic for Emerson in the classic sense: part of a pattern, not a romantic caprice. Thus, the England of *English Traits* strengthened his beliefs, as his beliefs informed that Saxon substance.

The nine chapters of *The Conduct of Life* are based on lectures Emerson gave in Boston in the 1850s: "Fate," "Power," "Wealth," "Culture," "Behavior," "Worship," "Considerations by the Way," "Beauty," and "Illusions." Emerson's hearers might well have wondered at the nonreligious nature of the lectures, which lack biblical texts and allusions. His list of topics spans the centuries with moral generalizations that link together the ideal and the real and refer specifically to daily living. Throughout, Emerson advocates self-reliance as the key to perceiving the true nature of living.

"How shall I live?" is the central question of *The Conduct of Life,* which is Emerson's clearest philosophical statement. His early problem of vocation resurfaces in that general query, and it implies the need to be self-reliant. He does not ask "What is the spirit of the times?" or "What is the dominant theory of the age?" or "What can be done to reform society?" "What" is replaced by the more significant "how"—how to live. And "we" are not involved in finding an answer together; instead, "I" need to find out how to live. This question and Emerson's answers foreshadow themes of existentialist philosophy: "I" shall live with fate (the limitations of my inheritance and the natural world); with power (my abilities and energies); with wealth (my gains and losses); with culture (my widest sympathies and affinities); with considerations (the positive centers for my action); with beauty (the underlying likenesses of the beautiful); and with illusions (the games and masks of self-deception). The essays move in the direction of increasing self-reliance based on the intuitive assertion that chance and anomaly do not exist in the universe; that all is an ideal system and gradation, dissonances and negations notwithstanding; and that the young mortal, the pure in heart, survives with the true, beautiful, and mortal gods. This work shows Emerson at his best as a literary Romantic.

According to Emerson, a person addresses fate in six steps of self-understanding in which the aim is to perceive that life includes no contingencies. First, one accepts limitations, brute facts, negations, and the daily tyrannies of life. Second, one accepts the force of these limitations, facts, negations, and tyrannies:

> Nature is, what you may do. There is much you may not. . . . Once we thought, positive power was all. Now we learn that negative power, or circumstance, is half. Nature is the tyrannous circumstance, the thick skull, the sheathed snake, the ponderous, rock-like jaw; necessitated activity; violent direction; the conditions of a tool, like the locomotive, strong enough on its track, but which can do nothing but mischief off of it; or skates, which are wings on the ice, but fetters on the ground. The book of Nature is the book of Fate.

Third, thought has power, in that it unites "god and devil, mind and matter, king and conspirator, belt and spasm, riding peacefully together in the eye and brain of every man." Fourth, thought not only counters fate but uses it for a higher purpose: fate is "a name for facts not yet passed under the fire of thought." Fifth, the interrelations of fate and thought are manifold. Finally, thinking about the spirit of the age is the interworking of event and person, the advance out of fate into freedom, and their rebalancing. Thus, the world "contains the event that shall befall it, for the event is only the actualization of its thoughts; and what we pray to ourselves for is always granted." In short, "Beautiful Necessity" educates one to the perception that nothing happens by coincidence.

Fate leads to power, which emphasizes the potential force in humankind. Power is enhanced by wealth, which is "applications of the mind to nature, from the rudest strokes of spade and axe, up to the last secrets of art." Culture moderates the ideas of power and wealth by expanding them. The books one reads, the travels one undertakes, the people one meets, and one's own solitude carry one from focused energy to widening thought, from quadruped to human. Hence, the "how" of one's life is none other than the how of "Manners," or the question of one's behavior and the

THE

CONDUCT OF LIFE.

BY

R. W. EMERSON.

BOSTON:
TICKNOR AND FIELDS.
M DCC LX.

Title page for the published texts of Emerson's lectures "Fate," "Power," "Wealth," "Culture," "Behavior," "Worship," "Considerations by the Way," "Beauty," and "Illusions," all of which were delivered in Boston during the 1850s (from Joel Myerson, Ralph Waldo Emerson: A Descriptive Bibliography, *1982)*

best and gentlest ways of doing things. This question raises the attitude of worship, or the way of invigorating the natural body with spirit:

> In our large cities, the population is godless, materialized,—no bond, no fellow-feeling, no enthusiasm. These are not men, but hungers, thirsts, fevers, and appetites walking. How is it people manage to live on,—so aimless as they are? After their peppercorn aims are gained, it seems as if the lime in their bones alone held them together, and not any worthy purpose.

Emerson thinks that the "last lesson of life, the choral song which rises from all elements and all angels, is, a voluntary obedience, a necessitated freedom. Man

Emerson in his late fifties

is made of the same atoms as the world is, he shares the same impressions, predispositions, and destiny. When his mind is illuminated, when his heart is kind, he throws himself joyfully into the sublime order, and does, with knowledge, what the stones do structure."

The final essays in the volume–"Considerations by the Way," "Beauty," and "Illusions"–describe the sublime order in all things. Relations of harmony pervade the descriptions. This assumption about reality is based biographically on the resolution of Emerson's relationships to his mother and his deceased wife. Empathy carried him beyond family conflict to something of a mystical connection to Nature, which he unwittingly personifies as the mother of humankind. "Considerations by the Way" relates individuals and groups to questions of true and false bonds, true and false allegiances, and centers of value: "Our chief want in life, is, somebody who shall make us do what we can. This is the service of a friend." It also is the service of a good minority in government or elsewhere: a service of loosening false ties and of giving one courage to be what one truly is. "Beauty" moves one from surface appearances to the depths of living. A beautiful thing has no superfluous parts, is valuable in itself, is related to all things, and is the standard of extremes. The highest power of beauty is the human capacity to relate to all things in a spirit of openness and fluidity of mutual apprehension. Beauty beckons the would-be nature mystic. Finally, in "Illusions" he cautions the reader

about deception, false fronts, and masks. The forms of life are ever changing, so that "If we must accept Fate, we are not less compelled to affirm liberty, the significance of the individual, the grandeur of duty, the power of character." Thus, *The Conduct of Life* ends as it began, based on Emerson's intuition that all things are in an ideal harmony, notwithstanding appearances to the contrary. Empathetic awareness of all things natural characterizes the personal impact Emerson expected his philosophy to make. In this respect he anticipated aspects of modern psychotherapeutic practice and much of the idealism surrounding the emergence of global environmental awareness.

These three major volumes, written in the decade of Emerson's philosophical maturity, the 1850s, stemmed from his personality as it sought expression and resolution through his times. The writings that blossomed late in his life were already entrenched in the hearts of New England readers through the two series of *Essays* and the *Poems* (1847) of the 1840s. Together, these six collections offer Emerson's most formal and formulated wisdom. The striking assertions of such individual essays as "Self-Reliance" and "The Over-Soul" and the combined force of the poems "Woodnotes" and "Threnody" find a center of gravity in various forms of the question "How shall I live?"

Emerson's philosophy is the outcropping of his creative response to long-standing tensions related to standing on his own feet as a young man, schoolmaster, minister, and, finally, lecturer. He achieved in his person and mature philosophical thought the autonomous self, the central theme of nineteenth-century Romanticism and its intellectual foundation of philosophical idealism.

Contemporary postmodern theory holds that the "autonomous self" of Romantic idealism is not the reified entity that Emerson believed it to be but an ideological construct articulated in language available to an individual at a particular historical moment. According to this theory, the coherent and stable human self who originates and perpetuates the meaning of experience and history is the construct of modern philosophical thought. This view originates in the assumption of empiricism that knowledge is the product of experience and the assumption of idealism that a universal human nature exists outside the confines of history. Thinkers such as Jacques Lacan, Michel Foucault, and Louis Althusser have substituted for the universal essence of human nature a human subject constituted by history, language, and culture. This reformulated self is a product of specific discourse and of social processes. That is, individuals construct themselves as subjects through language, but the individual–rather than being the source of his or her own meaning—can only adopt positions within the language available at a given moment.

The poststructuralist concept of the self redefines the self as a position—a locus where discourses intersect. The person may believe that the various positions make an autonomous whole, but that feeling of constancy and consistency occurs only because of memory. If human subjects attend to inconsistencies and contradictions, the theory holds, the self may seem less self-evident. Although postmodernism criticizes Emerson's concept of the self, the moral impact of his example of self-reliance continues to have an important impact on many people's lives. The success Ralph Waldo Emerson enjoyed in establishing a position of selfhood in language, history, and culture during his times served his audiences then, as they may serve his readers today, as an inspiration to be self-reliant. This wider horizon of public enthusiasm for Emersonian philosophy, both in the United States and in England and continental Europe, helped to establish a distinctive national culture and a unique American philosophical spirit based on Emerson's personal and professional moral stature as a self-reliant man.

Letters:

The Correspondence of Thomas Carlyle and Ralph Waldo Emerson 1834–1872, 2 volumes, edited by Charles Eliot Norton (Boston: Osgood, 1883; London: Chatto & Windus, 1883);

A Correspondence between John Sterling and Ralph Waldo Emerson, edited by Edward Waldo Emerson (Boston & New York: Houghton, Mifflin, 1897);

Letters from Ralph Waldo Emerson to a Friend, 1838–1853, edited by Norton (Boston & New York: Houghton, Mifflin, 1899; London: Watt, 1899);

Correspondence between Ralph Waldo Emerson and Herman Grimm, edited by Frederick William Holls (Boston & New York: Houghton, Mifflin, 1903);

Records of a Lifelong Friendship, 1807–1882: Ralph Waldo Emerson and William Henry Furness, edited by Horace Howard Furness (Boston & New York: Houghton Mifflin, 1910);

Emerson-Clough Letters, edited by Howard F. Lowry and Ralph Leslie Rusk (Cleveland: Rowfant Club, 1934);

The Letters of Ralph Waldo Emerson, 6 volumes, edited by Rusk (New York: Columbia University Press, 1939);

One First Love: The Letters of Ellen Louisa Tucker to Ralph Waldo Emerson, edited by Edith W. Gregg (Cambridge, Mass.: Harvard University Press, 1962);

The Correspondence of Emerson and Carlyle, edited by Joseph Slater (New York: Columbia University Press, 1964).

Bibliographies:

George Willis Cooke, *A Bibliography of Ralph Waldo Emerson* (Boston: Houghton, Mifflin, 1908);

Frederic Ives Carpenter, *Emerson Handbook* (New York: Hendricks House, 1953);

Jacob Blanck, *The Bibliography of American Literature,* volume 3 (New Haven: Yale University Press, 1959), pp. 16–70;

Jackson R. Bryer and Robert A. Rees, *A Checklist of Emerson Criticism 1951–1961* (Hartford, Conn.: Transcendental Books, 1964);

Floyd Stovall, "Ralph Waldo Emerson," in *Eight American Authors,* edited by James Woodress, revised edition (New York: Norton, 1971), pp. 37–83;

Joel Myerson, *Ralph Waldo Emerson: A Descriptive Bibliography* (Pittsburgh: University of Pittsburgh Press, 1982);

Myerson and Robert E. Burkholder, *Emerson: An Annotated Secondary Bibliography* (Pittsburgh: University of Pittsburgh Press, 1985);

Manfred Putz, *Ralph Waldo Emerson: A Bibliography of Twentieth-Century Criticism* (New York: Peter Lang, 1986).

Biographies:

Moncure Daniel Conway, *Emerson at Home and Abroad* (Boston: Osgood, 1882);

James Elliot Cabot, *A Memoir of Ralph Waldo Emerson,* 2 volumes (Boston & New York: Houghton, Mifflin, 1889);

Denton J. Snider, *A Biography of Ralph Waldo Emerson* (St. Louis: William Harvey Miner, 1921);

Townsend Scudder, *The Lonely Wayfaring Man: Emerson and Some Englishmen* (New York: Oxford University Press, 1936);

Ralph Leslie Rusk, *The Life of Ralph Waldo Emerson* (New York: Columbia University Press, 1949);

Henry F. Pommer, *Emerson's First Marriage* (Carbondale: Southern Illinois University Press, 1967);

Edward Wagenknecht, *Ralph Waldo Emerson: Portrait of a Balanced Soul* (New York: Oxford University Press, 1974);

Joel Porte, *Representative Man: Ralph Waldo Emerson in His Times* (New York: Oxford University Press, 1979);

Gay Wilson Allen, *Waldo Emerson: A Biography* (New York: Viking, 1981);

Richard A. Hutch, *Emerson's Optics: Biographical Process and the Dawn of Religious Leadership* (Lanham, Md.: University Press of America, 1983);

John McAleer, *Ralph Waldo Emerson: Days of Encounter* (Boston & Toronto: Little, Brown, 1984);

Evelyn Barish, *Emerson: The Roots of Prophecy* (Princeton: Princeton University Press, 1989);

Albert J. von Frank, *An Emerson Chronology* (New York: G. K. Hall, 1994);

Robert D. Richardson Jr., *Emerson: The Mind on Fire* (Berkeley: University of California Press, 1995).

References:

Sacvan Bercovitch, *The Rites of Assent* (New York: Routledge, 1993);

Edmund G. Berry, *Emerson's Plutarch* (Cambridge, Mass.: Harvard University Press, 1961);

Jonathan Bishop, *Emerson on the Soul* (Cambridge, Mass.: Harvard University Press, 1964);

Richard Bridgman, "From Greenough to 'Nowhere': Emerson's *English Traits,*" *New England Quarterly,* 59 (December 1986): 469–485;

Lawrence Buell, *Literary Transcendentalism* (Ithaca, N.Y.: Cornell University Press, 1973);

Kenneth Walter Cameron, ed., *Emerson among His Contemporaries* (Hartford, Conn.: Transcendental Books, 1967);

Stanley Cavell, *Conditions Handsome and Unhandsome: The Constitution of Emersonian Perfectionism* (Chicago: University of Chicago Press, 1990);

Mary Kupiec Cayton, *Emerson's Emergence: Self and Society in the Transformation of New England, 1800–1845* (Chapel Hill: University of North Carolina Press, 1989);

John Jay Chapman, *Emerson and Other Essays* (New York: Scribners, 1898);

William Charvat, *Emerson's American Lecture Engagements* (New York: New York Public Library, 1961);

Stephen Donadio, Stephen Railton, and Ormond Seavey, eds., *Emerson and His Legacy: Essays in Honor of Quentin Anderson* (Carbondale: Southern Illinois University Press, 1986);

Julie Ellison, *Emerson's Romantic Style* (Princeton: Princeton University Press, 1984);

Charles Feidelson Jr., *Symbolism and American Literature* (Chicago: University of Chicago Press, 1961);

Benjamin Goluboff, "Emerson's *English Traits*: 'The Mechanics of Conversation,'" *American Transcendental Quarterly,* 3 (June 1989): 153–167;

Maurice Gonnaud, *Individu et societé dans l'oeuvre de Ralph Waldo Emerson: Essai de biographie spirituelle* (Paris, 1964); translated by Lawrence Rosenwald as *An Uneasy Solitude: Individual and Society in the Work of Ralph Waldo Emerson* (Princeton: Princeton University Press, 1987);

Len Gougeon, *Virtue's Hero: Emerson, Antislavery, and Reform* (Athens: University of Georgia Press, 1990);

Walter Harding, *Emerson's Library* (Charlottesville: University Press of Virginia, 1967);

Kenneth Marc Harris, *Carlyle and Emerson: Their Long Debate* (Cambridge, Mass.: Harvard University Press, 1978);

Alan D. Hodder, *Emerson's Rhetoric of Revelation: Nature, the Reader, and the Apocalypse Within* (University Park: Pennsylvania State University Press, 1989);

Oliver Wendell Holmes, *Ralph Waldo Emerson* (Boston: Houghton, Mifflin, 1885);

Vivian C. Hopkins, *Spires of Form: A Study of Emerson's Aesthetic Theory* (Cambridge, Mass.: Harvard University Press, 1951);

George S. Hubbell, *A Concordance to the Poems of Ralph Waldo Emerson* (New York: Wilson, 1932);

Mary Alice Ihrig, *Emerson's Transcendental Vocabulary: A Concordance* (New York: Garland, 1982);

Eugene F. Irey, *A Concordance to Five Essays of Ralph Waldo Emerson* (New York: Garland, 1981);

Michael Lopez, *Emerson and Power: Creative Antagonism in the Nineteenth Century* (DeKalb: Northern Illinois University Press, 1996);

F. O. Matthiessen, *American Renaissance: Art and Expression in the Age of Emerson and Whitman* (New York: Oxford University Press, 1941);

John Michael, *Emerson and Skepticism: The Cipher of the World* (Baltimore: Johns Hopkins University Press, 1988);

Perry Miller, ed., *The Transcendentalists: An Anthology* (Cambridge, Mass.: Harvard University Press, 1950);

Wesley T. Mott, *"The Strains of Eloquence": Emerson and His Sermons* (University Park: Pennsylvania State University Press, 1989);

Mott and Robert E. Burkholder, eds., *Emersonian Circles: Essays in Honor of Joel Myerson* (Rochester, N.Y.: University of Rochester Press, 1997);

Joel Myerson, ed., *Emerson Centenary Essays* (Carbondale: Southern Illinois University Press, 1982);

Myerson, ed., *A Historical Guide to Ralph Waldo Emerson* (New York: Oxford University Press, 2000);

Philip L. Nicoloff, *Emerson on Race and History: An Examination of "English Traits"* (New York: Columbia University Press, 1961);

Richard R. O'Keefe, *Mythic Archetypes in Ralph Waldo Emerson: A Blakean Reading* (Kent, Ohio: Kent State University Press, 1995);

B. L. Packer, *Emerson's Fall: A New Interpretation of the Major Essays* (New York: Continuum, 1982);

Sherman Paul, *Emerson's Angle of Vision: Man and Nature in the American Experience* (Cambridge, Mass.: Harvard University Press, 1952);

John Peacock, "Self-Reliance and Corporate Destiny: Emerson's Dialectic of Culture," *Emerson Society Quarterly,* 29, no. 2 (1983): 59–72;

Joel Porte, *Emerson and Thoreau: Transcendentalists in Conflict* (Middletown, Conn.: Wesleyan University Press, 1966);

Porte, *Representative Man: Ralph Waldo Emerson in His Time* (New York: Columbia University Press, 1979; revised, 1988);

Porte and Saundra Morris, eds., *The Cambridge Companion to Ralph Waldo Emerson* (New York: Cambridge University Press, 1999);

David Porter, *Emerson and Literary Change* (Cambridge, Mass.: Harvard University Press, 1978);

Susan L. Roberson, *Emerson in His Sermons: A Man-Made Self* (Columbia: University of Missouri Press, 1995);

David M. Robinson, *Apostle of Culture: Emerson as Preacher Lecturer* (Philadelphia: University of Pennsylvania Press, 1982);

Robinson, *Emerson and The Conduct of Life* (New York: Cambridge University Press, 1993);

Lawrence Rosenwald, *Emerson and the Art of the Diary* (New York: Oxford University Press, 1988);

F. B. Sanborn, ed., *The Genius and Character of Emerson* (Boston: Osgood, 1885);

Merton M. Sealts Jr., *Emerson on the Scholar* (Columbia: University of Missouri Press, 1992);

Sealts and Alfred R. Ferguson, eds., *Emerson's Nature—Origin, Growth, Meaning* (Carbondale: Southern Illinois University Press, 1969; revised, 1979);

William W. Stowe, "Ralph Waldo Emerson: the Reluctant Traveler," in his *Going Abroad: European Travel in Nineteenth-Century American Culture* (Princeton: Princeton University Press, 1994), pp. 72–101;

Richard F. Teichgraeber, *Sublime Thoughts/Penny Wisdom: Situating Emerson and Thoreau in the American Market* (Baltimore: Johns Hopkins University Press, 1995);

Gustaaf Van Cromphout, *Emerson's Ethics* (Columbia: University of Missouri Press, 1999);

Van Cromphout, *Emerson's Modernity and the Example of Goethe* (Columbia: University of Missouri Press, 1990);

Albert J. von Frank, *The Trials of Anthony Burns: Freedom and Slavery in Emerson's Boston* (Cambridge, Mass.: Harvard University Press, 1998);

Hyatt Waggoner, *Emerson as Poet* (Princeton: Princeton University Press, 1974);

Stephen E. Whicher, *Freedom and Fate: An Inner Life of Ralph Waldo Emerson* (Philadelphia: University of Pennsylvania Press, 1953);

Donald Yannella, *Ralph Waldo Emerson* (Boston: Twayne, 1982);

R. A. Yoder, *Emerson and the Orphic Poet in America* (Berkeley: University of California Press, 1978);

Charles L. Young, *Emerson's Montaigne* (New York: Macmillan, 1941);

Christina Zwarg, *Feminist Conversations: Fuller, Emerson, and the Play of Reading* (Ithaca, N.Y.: Cornell University Press, 1995).

Papers:

Most of Ralph Waldo Emerson's papers—including letters, journals, and manuscripts—are in the Ralph Waldo Emerson Memorial Association Collection of the Houghton Library at Harvard University. More manuscripts and letters are in The Joel Myerson Collection of Nineteenth-Century American Literature in the Department of Rare Books and Special Collections, Thomas Cooper Library, University of South Carolina.

William Torrey Harris

(10 September 1835 – 5 November 1909)

Dorothy G. Rogers
Montclair State University

BOOKS: *The First Reader,* by Harris, Andrew J. Rickoff, and Mark Bailey (New York: Appleton, 1878);

The Second Reader, by Harris, Rickoff, and Bailey (New York: Appleton, 1878);

The Fifth Reader, by Harris, Rickoff, and Bailey (New York: Appleton, 1878);

The Advanced Reader, by Harris, Rickoff, and Bailey (St. Paul, Minn.: D. D. Merrill, 1878);

Method of Study in Social Science: A Lecture Delivered before the St. Louis Social Science Association, March 4, 1879 (St. Louis: G. I. Jones, 1879);

The Third Reader (New York: Appleton, 1880);

Philosophy in Outline: Being a Brief Exposition of the Method of Philosophy, and Its Results in Obtaining a View of Nature, Man, and God (New York: Appleton / London: Trübner, 1883);

Introductory Fourth Reader (New York & Boston: Appleton, 1884);

The Right of Property and the Ownership of Land (Boston: Cupples, Hurd, 1887);

How to Teach Natural Science in Public Schools (Syracuse, N.Y.: Bardeen, 1887);

Word-Manual to Accompany Appletons' Introductory Fourth Reader (New York: Appleton, 1888);

Memoirs of Members of the Social Circle in Concord, by Harris, John Shepard Keyes, Ebenezer Rockwood Hoard, and Edward Waldo Emerson (Cambridge, Mass.: Privately printed, 1888);

Thoughts on Educational Psychology (Bloomington, Ill., 1889);

Introduction to the Study of Philosophy, edited by Marietta Kies (New York: Appleton, 1889);

Morality in the Schools (Boston: Christian Register Association, 1889);

Hegel's Logic: A Book on the Genesis of the Categories of the Mind (Chicago: Griggs, 1890);

Report of the Committee of Fifteen of the National Education Association of the United States, by Harris, Andrew Sloan Draper, and Horace Sumner Tarbell (Boston: New England Publishing Co., 1895);

Horace Mann (Syracuse, N.Y.: Bardeen, 1896);

The Spiritual Sense of Dante's Divina Commedia (Boston & New York: Houghton, Mifflin, 1896; London: Kegan Paul, Trench, Trübner, 1901);

Psychologic Foundations of Education: An Attempt to Show the Genesis of the Higher Faculties of the Mind (New York: Appleton, 1898);

Women in the Legal Profession: An Address Delivered at the Third Annual Commencement of the Washington College of Law, May 22, 1901 (Washington, D.C.: B. S. Adams, 1901);

The Difference between Efficient and Final Causes in Controlling Human Freedom (Bloomington, Ill.: Public-School Publishing Co., 1902);

The United States of America: A Pictorial History of the American Nation from the Earliest Discoveries and Settlements to the Present Time, 5 volumes, by Harris, Edward Everett Hale, Oscar Phelps Austin, Nelson Appleton Miles, and George Cary Eggleston (New York: Imperial, 1906–1909);

Horace Mann and Our Schools, by Harris, Payson Smith, and A. E. Winship (New York & Cincinnati: American Book Co., 1937)—includes "Horace Mann: Educational Missionary," by Harris;

The Record Book of the St. Louis Philosophical Society, Founded February 1866, edited by Kurt F. Leidecker, Studies in the History of Philosophy, volume 14 (Lewiston, N.Y.: Edwin Mellen Press, 1990).

OTHER: Georg Wilhelm Friedrich Hegel, *Hegel's First Principle: An Exposition of Comprehension and Idea (Begriff und Idee)*, edited and translated by Harris (St. Louis: Printed by G. Knapp, 1869);

"Essay on the System of Classification," in *Catalogue, Classified and Alphabetical, of the Books of the St. Louis Public School Library: Including, Also, the Collections of the St. Louis Academy of Science, and St. Louis Law School*, by John Jay Bailey (St. Louis: Democrat Book and Job Printing House, 1870);

C. R. Barns, ed., *The Commonwealth of Missouri: A Centennial Record*, contributions by Harris (St. Louis: Bryan, Brand, 1877);

Hegel, *Hegel's Doctrine of Reflection: Being a Paraphrase and a Commentary Interpolated into the Text of the Second Volume of Hegel's Larger Logic, Treating of "Essence,"* edited and translated by Harris (New York: Appleton, 1881);

Karl Rosenkranz, *The Philosophy of Education*, translated by Anna C. Brackett, edited by Harris, International Education Series, volume 1 (New York: Appleton, 1886);

"Goethe's *Faust*," in *The Life and Genius of Goethe: Lectures at the Concord School of Philosophy*, edited by Franklin Benjamin Sanborn (Boston: Ticknor, 1886), pp. 368–445;

Edward Gardiner Howe, *Systematic Science Teaching: A Manual of Inductive Elementary Work for All Instructors*, edited by Harris (New York: Appleton, 1894);

Johann Gottlieb Fichte, *The Science of Ethics as Based on the Science of Knowledge*, translated by A. E. Kroeger, edited by Harris (New York: Appleton, 1897; London: Kegan Paul, Trench, Trübner, 1897);

Webster's International Dictionary of the English Language: Being the Authentic Edition of Webster's Unabridged Dictionary, Comprising the Issues of 1864, 1879, and 1884, edited by Harris and Noah Porter (Springfield, Mass.: Merriam, 1900; revised, 1909);

The Autralasian Supplement to Webster's International Dictionary, Containing a Vocabulary of 25,000 Additional Words, Phrases, and Definitions, edited by Harris, Fred J. Bromfield, Edward Pulsford, and Joseph Finney (Springfield, Mass.: Merriam, 1905).

The leader of the idealist movement in American philosophy, William Torrey Harris exercised great influence over social and intellectual life in the United States during the last thirty years of the nineteenth century. Members of this movement were the first to translate and interpret the works of German thinkers such as Georg Wilhelm Friedrich Hegel, Friedrich Wilhelm Joseph von Schelling, and Johann Gottlieb Fichte; they were also the first to establish a periodical devoted exclusively to philosophy, *The Journal of Speculative Philosophy*. Harris and the majority of his followers were professional educators who believed in the applicability of philosophy to education and other practical matters; therefore, much of what they found most useful in German thought had to do with pedagogical theories and practices, many of which they imported to the United States. As superintendent from 1868 until 1880, Harris made the St. Louis, Missouri, public schools a model school system. Drawing on developments in German pedagogy, he established the nation's first free public kindergarten, instituted the graded school system, standardized curricula at all grade levels, promoted the spread of public libraries, developed a method of cataloguing library books, supported normal schools for teacher training, encouraged instruction in art and music, advocated equal education for African Americans, and insisted on the value of the coeducation of men and women. Such innovative projects brought Harris a good deal of recognition in the educational world, and he served as United States Commissioner of Education from 1890 until 1906.

It is almost impossible to assess Harris's career and influence without taking into consideration the immense impact his egalitarian views and policies had on his female colleagues. His support of equity for women was invaluable to the female members of his intellectual circle in St. Louis and beyond. He did not merely pay lip service to such causes as equal education, equal employment opportunity, and equal pay for women but was committed to achieving gender equity in social and political life, and he acted on this commitment throughout his career. He supported the efforts of his female colleagues as both educators and intellectuals and in many cases helped facilitate their professional development. The most prominent women in Harris's circle included the kindergarten educator and pedagogical theorist Susan E. Blow; the normal-school educator, pedagogical theorist, and feminist Anna C. Brackett; the normal-school educator and feminist Grace C. Bibb; the philosopher, literary theorist, and feminist Ellen M. Mitchell; the political philosopher Marietta Kies; and the educator and pacifist theorist Lucia Ames Mead. Each of these women either worked with Harris in the St. Louis schools or studied with him at the Concord Summer School of Philosophy he established in Massachusetts. Each of them also wrote works that Harris either published in *The Journal of Speculative Philosophy* or endorsed for publication elsewhere. They capitalized on the recognition that Harris's support brought them, publishing and lecturing widely, and in doing so brought Harris even more visibility. As a result, Harris and his intellectual community came to be seen as trendsetters who were transplanting the newest and best European intellectual and social movements into American soil.

Harris was born in Putnam, Connecticut, about forty miles from Providence, Rhode Island, on 10 September 1835, the first of nine children of William Harris, a farmer who had failed at several business ventures, and Zilpah Torrey Harris. He was descended from early English settlers, Thomas Harris and Captain William Torrey, who had arrived in America in 1637 and 1640, respectively. Other prominent early settlers in the family tree included Roger Williams, the founder of Rhode Island, and Daniel Mowry, a member of the Continental Congress in 1780–1781. Harris's mother and maternal grandmother instilled in Harris the sense that the family legacy of leadership was his to carry on. He often credited these women with his success as a student, teacher, and administrator.

Harris's earliest education took place in a classic one-room schoolhouse in North Killingly (today part of Putnam), where his Aunt Catherine was the teacher. When the family moved to Providence in 1844, he had a great deal of difficulty making the transition to an urban school, where learning was conducted by rote and punishments were severe. Harris attended at least four preparatory schools before finishing at Phillips Academy in Andover, Massachusetts. There he first encountered philosophy, reading John Locke's *Essay Concerning Human Understanding* (1689) and Immanuel Kant's *Kritik der reinen Vernunft* (1781; revised, 1787; translated as *Critique of Pure Reason,* 1855). He found philosophy, particularly modern German philosophy, more captivating than the ancient languages and classical literature in the preparatory-school curriculum. He left Phillips at the end of the fall term of 1853 and taught school in Thompson, Connecticut, in the winter of 1853–1854. By the time he entered Yale University in the fall of 1854, he had begun reading the works of

modern thinkers on his own and attending lectures by radical thinkers such as Theodore Parker, the Unitarian minister and radical abolitionist, and Amos Bronson Alcott, a Transcendentalist freethinker and the father of the novelist Louisa May Alcott. His professors' warnings that the ideas of such men were morally corrupting intrigued him all the more.

Against his parents' wishes, Harris left Yale at the end of his junior year and moved to St. Louis. Arriving in the summer of 1857, he roomed with Robert Moore, a friend from Yale. The two tried giving stenography lessons, selling pens door to door, and private tutoring, all unsuccessfully. In March 1858 Moore gave up on the adventure and borrowed money from Harris to go back east. In April, Harris reluctantly accepted an offer to teach at the Franklin Grammar School. Having a full-time job meant that he would be able to support a family, and on 27 December he married Sarah Tully Bugbee in Providence. They had four children: Theodore in 1859; Charlotte in 1862 and Ethan in 1864, both of whom died of childhood illnesses; and Edith in 1875. In 1859 Harris was promoted to principal of the newly opened Clay School.

Harris had joined the St. Louis Philosophical and Literary Society when he arrived in the city. The members of the group held radical religious, social, and political views, and they readily accepted Harris's youthful attraction to alternative ideas and schools of thought such as vegetarianism, Swedenborgianism, and phrenology. Many society members were atheists and proponents of free love who wanted to reorder social structures or even overturn them. Harris was surprised to hear himself criticized by the group for making presentations that were too biblically centered, and he found himself defending many orthodox positions that he had criticized in debates at Phillips and Yale.

The Philosophical and Literary Society was responsible for introducing Harris to Henry Conrad Brockmeyer, who had immigrated to the United States as a teenager in the late 1840s to escape the tyranny of his parents, as he put it, as well as political unrest in Prussia. At Brown College, rather than at home in Prussia, he had encountered Hegel's philosophy, which he read in the original German. Harris and two friends, George Stedman and John Watters, struck a bargain with Brockmeyer: they paid the rent for his room in downtown St. Louis, where he slept on a pallet on the floor; in return, he instructed them in Hegel's philosophy and worked on a translation of Hegel's *Wissenschaft der Logik* (1812–1816; translated as *Hegel's Science of Logic,* 1929) that they planned to publish. But Brockmeyer proved to be a poor translator. Since he had learned English relatively late in life, he could communicate Hegel's ideas well in speech but only clumsily in

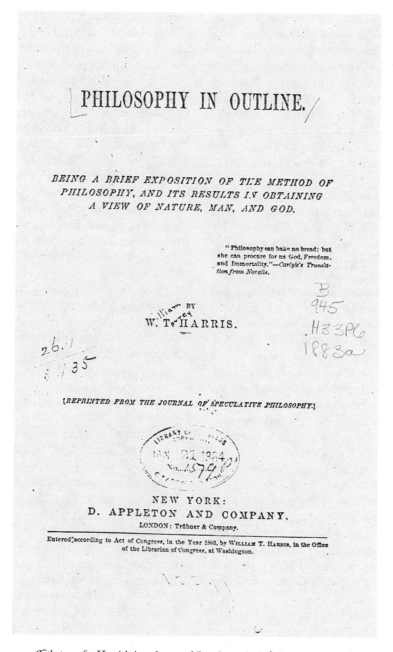

PHILOSOPHY IN OUTLINE.

BEING A BRIEF EXPOSITION OF THE METHOD OF PHILOSOPHY, AND ITS RESULTS IN OBTAINING A VIEW OF NATURE, MAN, AND GOD.

" Philosophy can bake no bread; but she can procure for us God, Freedom, and Immortality."—*Carlyle's Translation from Novalis.*

BY

W. T. HARRIS.

[REPRINTED FROM THE JOURNAL OF SPECULATIVE PHILOSOPHY.]

NEW YORK:
D. APPLETON AND COMPANY.
LONDON: Trübner & Company.

Entered according to Act of Congress, in the Year 1883, by WILLIAM T. HARRIS, in the Office of the Librarian of Congress, at Washington.

Title page for Harris's introductory philosophy textbook (Library of Congress)

writing. He also had a brusque personality and scoffed at conventions of all kinds—including grammatical ones. Harris once decided against inviting Brockmeyer on an Eastern lecture tour for fear that he would offend his Boston audience by uttering some "diablery or profanity." Harris and his friends still had their sights set on publishing a Brockmeyer translation of *Wissenschaft der Logik,* however, until Brockmeyer signed up to fight with the Union army in the Civil War. Harris, who had suffered an injury as a teenager that left him with a glass eye, was exempt from combat and remained in St. Louis as the principal of Clay School.

As the St. Louis schools weathered budget cuts and other hardships that the war brought on, Harris and his friends focused on developing a coherent philosophy of education that would help them in their work. Education continued to be the central concern for Harris and his colleagues throughout the existence of the St. Louis philosophical movement. In 1863 Brackett was hired as the principal of the normal school, and she and Harris developed a good working relationship. Brackett became deeply involved in the St. Louis group's philosophical work and was able to hold her own in debates with her male contemporaries.

Harris and his colleagues were acutely aware of current social and political issues. They analyzed the Civil War as a conflict that manifested a Hegelian dialectic in real life, with bondage as the thesis and freedom as the antithesis. A synthesis must and would emerge, they believed, as the forces of history took hold. After the war ended, Harris and others in his circle, including Brackett; Bibb, who taught in the normal school; and Mitchell, began to be more vocal about feminist causes such as pay equity and voting rights for women.

In 1868 Harris became superintendent of the St. Louis school system and began to be known as a national leader in philosophy and education. He brought improvements and reforms to the schools as quickly as possible, including a strengthened normal school. In 1873 he hired Blow to initiate and direct a kindergarten program, an educational innovation that she had studied in Germany. Blow, too, became a major force in the philosophy group and was called "almost the heroine of the movement" by historian Cleon Forbes. Vowing never to let his students undergo the trials he had endured in the Providence schools, he banned the use of corporal punishment throughout the St. Louis school system: children were not intimidated into learning or behaving properly but were encouraged to do their best by the use of what is today called "positive reinforcement." Harris also effected pay equity for women in the school system. When he had been hired as a principal, he had received the standard beginning salary for a man of $1,100 annually, while female principals were paid $750. As superintendent he persuaded the St. Louis school board to put women's salaries on a par with men's. Under Harris's administration, for example, Brackett was paid $2,000 yearly as principal of the normal school, while George McClellan earned $1,500 as a teacher.

By focusing on education, Harris and his colleagues were being true to Hegel's ideas, since Hegel himself had been a rector at a school in Nuremberg that specialized in classical studies for boys. The *Philosophische Propädeutik* (1887; translated as *The Philosophical Propaedeutic*, 1986), compiled by Hegel's disciple, Karl Rosenkranz, constitutes the bulk of Hegel's lectures to his Nuremberg students.

As part of their effort to advance idealist philosophy in both theory and practice, Harris and his associates established several societies and organizations, some of which grew into or merged with national movements: the Missouri State Teachers' Association, the Art Society, the Public School Library Association, the Pedagogical Society, the Pen and Pencil Club, and the Aristotle Club. Two organizations stand out as the venues through which the St. Louis circle did its most strictly philosophical work: the Kant Club and the Philosophical Society. The Kant Club actually focused on the thought of Hegel more than on that of Kant, but its name was never changed to reflect the reality. Harris's first philosophical book, *Hegel's Logic: A Book on the Genesis of the Categories of the Mind* (1890), grew out of the work he did with this group, although he did not publish it until well after he had left St. Louis and the group had dispersed. The Philosophical Society had a more lasting influence. Distinct from the group that Harris had joined shortly after he arrived in St. Louis, the Philosophical Society had begun meeting in 1866. The members of this group were some of Harris's closest and most trusted friends and colleagues: Brockmeyer, the lawyer, politician, and would-be Hegel translator; Thomas Davidson, a high-school teacher and scholar of ancient thought, particularly of Greek philosophy; George Holmes Howison, a Washington University philosophy professor and "personal idealist"; Alfred Kroeger, a Fichte scholar; Denton J. Snider, a high-school teacher and William Shakespeare scholar; Louis Soldan, a high-school teacher and Hegel translator; and Gabriel Woerner, a lawyer and later a judge in St. Louis. Women were never official members of the Philosophical Society, even though they actively participated in its meetings. Bibb, Blow, Brackett, Mitchell, Ella Morgan, and two of Harris's sisters—most likely Sarah and Ellen, both of whom taught in St. Louis—are among the women known to have attended St. Louis Philosophical Society meetings.

After the society had been meeting for a year, Harris suggested that they begin publishing a journal devoted exclusively to philosophy. According to Snider, the group's self-appointed historian, Harris was motivated to start his own journal because his paper on Herbert Spencer had been rejected by the *North American Review*. Snider recounts in his *The St. Louis Movement in Philosophy, Literature, Education, Psychology: With Chapters of Autobiography* (1920) the moment the idea for the journal was born: Harris read aloud from his rejection letter, interspersing sarcastic comments throughout, as the other members laughed and cheered him on; after reading the closing lines, he exclaimed, "We'll start our own journal, then!" Plans for the first issue of *The Journal of Speculative Philosophy* began shortly thereafter.

Although Snider believed that the society should have delayed publishing the journal until the members' ideas had matured, *The Journal of Speculative Philosophy* influenced American intellectual life immensely. Some of the most prestigious American philosophers—including Davidson, John Dewey, Frederick Henry Hedge, William James, Charles Sanders Peirce, and Josiah Royce—had their early writings published in it. As the journal gained recognition, it brought together several

HEGEL'S LOGIC.

A BOOK ON THE

GENESIS OF THE CATEGORIES OF THE MIND.

A CRITICAL EXPOSITION.

By WILLIAM T. HARRIS, LL.D.,

U. S. COMMISSIONER OF EDUCATION.

'Η διαλεκτικὴ μέθοδος μόνη πορεύεται τὰς
ὑποθέσεις ἀναιροῦσα ἐπ' αὐτὴν τὴν ἀρχήν, ἵνα
βεβαιώσηται . . . . καὶ τὸ τῆς ψυχῆς ὄμμα ἠρέμα
ἕλκαι καὶ ἀνάγει ἄνω.

PLATO'S REPUBLIC, 533—D.

CHICAGO:

S. C. GRIGGS AND COMPANY.

1890.

Title page for Harris's discussion of the logical theory of the German idealist philosopher Georg Wilhelm Friedrich Hegel (Main Library, Indiana University, Bloomington)

previously disparate groups of philosophers. Followers of Hegel who disagreed about how to interpret his work were invited to become "associate" members of the St. Louis Philosophical Society and receive a subscription to *The Journal of Speculative Philosophy*. The majority did join, and many contributed articles to the journal. Harris's journal thus represented a much wider range of thought and broader interpretations of idealism than had ever appeared together before. In Germany, where interest in Hegel had dwindled and partisanship among the remaining Hegelians ran rampant, such a development would have been impossible.

Harris's philosophy of education focused on three major themes: culture, self-estrangement, and self-activity. Following Hegel's lead, Harris and the majority in the St. Louis group were opposed to Jean-Jacques Rousseau's theory of education. Rousseau would have had his ideal student, "Emile," educated in isolation, far from the corrupting influences of society; only in this way could the boy discover his own talents and flourish freely. For Harris and his followers, Rousseau's perspective on education was fatally flawed, because education brings culture–or, more properly, acculturation (in German, *Bildung*)–to children. The purpose of the school is to acquaint children with the history of the human race, the greatest human achievements, and the deepest human longings. True education ushers children into the world of social progress. In isolation, capriciousness and even malice creep into a child's mind. The controlled social setting that the school provides ensures that minds of children will be nurtured and ennobled, the St. Louis group believed.

From the kindergartner to the young adult, education triggers a process of Hegelian self-estrangement and return to a self that is transformed by the estranging experience. For small children this process is put in motion by fairy tales and childhood games. Children lose themselves in the world of fantasy and make-believe, imagining themselves to be heroes or rescued maidens, then return to their original selves when the story or game has ended. In the process of getting "lost" and "returning" to the self the child grows and expands in both intellectual ability and self-understanding. A similar process takes place in youths and young adults who immerse themselves in the classic tales and literature.

Self-activity was Harris's translation of the word *Selbsttätigkeit* in *Hegel's First Principle: An Exposition of Comprehension and Idea (Begriff und Idee)* (1869), his selections from the *Philosophische Propädeutik,* and over time the group used it to refer both to the self-determining power of the Absolute as a wholly independent, self-motivated, and motivating force and to that same power–to the degree that it exists–in human beings. The group focused most on human self-activity, because it is central to the educative process. Blow was particularly interested in applying the term to early-childhood education; but she, Harris, and Kies also discussed self-activity in the contexts of labor laws, the relation of humanity to the Divine, and the nature of the Trinity.

Harris promulgated his educational theories in several short but important articles between 1870 and 1880: "German Reform in American Education" in *The Western Review* (September 1872), "The Three Stages of Theoretical Culture" in the *Pennsylvania School Journal* (December 1872), "On the Relation of Education to the Individual, to Society, and to the State" in the *Wisconsin Journal of Education* (January 1874), and "Pedagogics as a Province of Education" in the St. Louis *Journal of Education* (June 1877). He also published articles that provide a sketch of his social and political ideals, such as "The Co-education of the Sexes" in *The Western Review* (March 1871) and "The Idea of the State and Its Necessity" in *The Western Review* (April 1877).

In 1878 Harris held an experimental summer-school session at the home of Amos Bronson Alcott in Concord, Massachusetts. The main speaker was Hiram K. Jones, a well-known Platonist from Jacksonville, Illinois, where Harris's brother David had settled and had also become a school superintendent. The experiment was a great success, and Harris joined forces with Franklin Benjamin Sanborn to organize a continuing summer school in Concord to begin the following year. The Concord Summer School of Philosophy and Literature ran only until 1888 but was a huge success while it lasted. More than two hundred participants registered the first year, and academic philosophers as well as public intellectuals presented papers and lecture series. Concord School lectures featured the older generation of thinkers, such as the well-respected Transcendentalists Hedge, Thomas Wentworth Higginson, Julia Ward Howe, and Elizabeth Peabody, as well as an up-and-coming generation of academics including James of Harvard, Nicholas Murray Butler of Columbia, James McCosh of Princeton, George Sylvester Morris of Michigan, and Noah Porter of Yale. Public intellectuals from Harris's own circle also lectured at Concord, among them Davidson, Mitchell, Snider, and Soldan.

For women the Concord School provided an opportunity for informal but challenging postbaccalaureate work at a time when most universities refused to open graduate programs to them. Mitchell, Kies, and Mead each undertook serious academic work at the Concord School. Mitchell studied with Harris, Snider, and W. R. Alger and wrote *A Study of Greek Philosophy* (1891). Kies studied with Harris and Morris and compiled Harris's lectures and papers into *Introduction to the Study of Philosophy* (1890), which she used as a textbook in her classes at Mount Holyoke Seminary. She then applied to the University of Michigan, where in 1891 she became the first woman to earn a doctorate in philosophy at the institution. Mead studied with Harris, reading Kant thoroughly and becoming acquainted with his theory of perpetual peace. She went on to become a leader of the women's peace movement prior to World War I and a strong proponent of the League of Nations. More than half of the participants in the school were women, for whom it was a rare opportunity to be taken seriously as intellectuals by Harris and his male colleagues.

Harris retired as superintendent of the St. Louis school system in 1880. Without the responsibility of public-school administration to take up his time, he was able to publish more and longer works on philosophy and education, including "The Church, the State, and the School" in the *North American Review* (September 1881), *Hegel's Doctrine of Reflection: Being a Paraphrase and a Commentary Interpolated into the Text of the Second Volume of Hegel's Larger Logic, Treating of "Essence,"* (1881), "New England Lectures on Pedagogy" in the Boston *Journal of Education* (1882–1883), *Philosophy in Outline: Being a Brief Exposition of the Method of Philosophy, and Its Results in Obtaining a View of Nature, Man, and God* (1883), and "English and German: A Study in the Philosophy of History" in the *Andover Review* (December 1886). Neither of the books on philosophy that Harris published at this time were profound, though they were by no means failures. *Philosophy in Outline* served as a helpful introductory guidebook for students or beginning philosophy teachers. Similarly, in *Hegel's Doctrine of Reflection* Harris does a fair job of analyzing Hegel's view of knowledge and identity, but he could have been more thorough. This is the main criticism that has been made of Harris: that his philosophical work did not go deep enough, that he sacrificed depth for breadth. Harris himself believed that he was guilty of making this error in his book on Hegel's logic. But in his fervor to publish and promulgate Hegel's ideas, he rushed the writing of the book, and ultimately it suffered. He never got the chance to complete the rewritten and enlarged version of the work he had intended, and this failure was a point of frustration for him.

Yet, Harris's success as a philosopher has to be put into context. He might not have been the best interpreter of Hegel and other German idealists, but he was the first to make a significant effort to do so. The Scottish thinker James Hutchison Stirling had produced the first work of this sort in *The Secret of Hegel* (1865), though critics joked that he seemed to have done a good job at keeping the secret to himself. Harris was the first American to undertake an interpretation and to do so in two full-length books on different aspects of Hegel's thought.

Toward the end of the 1880s the Concord School began to wane in popularity. Other summer programs that offered more-general liberal arts programs had begun springing up across the country. The Concord School's focus on philosophy made it less accessible to a general audience than its rivals, the best known of which was the one in Chautauqua, New York. In addition, philosophy was becoming more highly professionalized, and academics were less interested in participating in philosophic forums for amateurs. Finally, in the late 1880s Michigan, Cornell, Johns Hopkins, and Boston universities began to admit women to graduate study, and by 1895 they had granted the first doctorates to them. Although Harris applauded the admission of women to the highest levels of academia, this development meant that the Concord School no longer served the distinctive purpose it once had. The last session was held in 1888.

In 1890 Harris became the United States Commissioner of Education. Even the demands of this position did not curtail his productivity. He continued to write articles and present papers on educational and social and political philosophy. Some of these works continued his advocacy for women's equality: "The Relation of Women to the Trades and Professions" in the *Education Review* (October 1900); "Women in the Legal Profession," the Washington College commencement address for 1901; and "Why Women Should Study Law" in the *Ohio Educational Monthly* (July 1901).

He also served as the general editor of the International Education Series, in which he republished the works of Blow, Brackett, and others.

But in the philosophical world, Harris was beginning to lose influence. Former associates who participated in his projects in St. Louis and Concord had begun to branch off in different directions. James and Dewey found idealism too abstract and detached from everyday experience and real-world applications and established their own school of thought, pragmatism. Dewey shared with Harris an interest in education, but his approach was far more empirical than Harris's, and his pedagogical theories diverged widely from those Harris had espoused and worked to promote.

Another of Harris's colleagues, Howison, remained within the idealist fold but took his philosophy into a more progressive domain than Harris. As a personal idealist, Howison saw personality as being at the core of all reality, particularly divine reality. Harris did not object to this aspect of Howison's thought; it was simply a more systematic and metaphysical version of Harris's own philosophy. Harris did, however, object to the pluralistic nature of Howison's theory. Harris and Blow were adamant that the universe must be essentially monistic–there must be one transcendent force or Absolute–otherwise, reality would consist of unrelated individual entities and thus be reduced to chaos. Since a rational order obviously exists in the universe–an order that human beings are able to comprehend and to articulate as a single order–the world must, they held, be essentially monistic, not pluralistic.

Those who maintained essentially the same viewpoints that they had held along with Harris at the height of his influence also faded from prominence. Brockmeyer, Snider, and Soldan continued to work in law and politics, literature, and education, respectively. Blow continued to write and lecture on education but began encountering opposition in regard to the proper path for the kindergarten to take. She came to be considered old-fashioned and her ideas obsolete. Brackett and Mitchell wrote and lectured about and advocated for women's rights, but neither pursued the more philosophical aspects of their ideas as vigorously as they had in earlier years. Finally, Kies and Davidson met early deaths: Kies in 1899 from tuberculosis and Davidson in 1900 from cancer.

Harris, however, was an effective education commissioner. By the turn of the twentieth century he could see the educational policies–if not the educational philosophy–he had instituted being applied more and more uniformly throughout the nation: kindergarten, graded schools, teacher education, and coeducation in particular. He did encounter opposition: he favored equal–though not necessarily integrated–education for both African Americans and Native Americans and continued to press for more educational opportunities for women, and each of these issues continued to be controversial in the late nineteenth century. In addition, many of his philosophically based ideas about education were beginning to be supplanted by more sophisticated psychological theories, empirical observation, and data gathering. His pedagogical work was, thus, beginning to be regarded as outdated by the time he retired and moved back to Providence in 1906. Even so, he was a respected and influential member of the national administration at the end of his career. He died at his home on 5 November 1909.

Biography:

Kurt F. Leidecker, *Yankee Teacher: The Life of William Torrey Harris* (New York: Philosophical Library, 1946).

References:

Thomas Henry Clare, *The Sociological Theories of William Torrey Harris* (Belleville, Ill.: C. Hepp Printing Co., 1935);

John Walton Colcord, *William Torrey Harris: The Commemoration of the One Hundredth Anniversary of His Birth, 1835–1935* (Washington, D.C.: U.S. Government Printing Office, 1937);

Cleon Forbes, "The St. Louis School of Thought," 5 parts, *Missouri Historical Review,* 25 (October 1930): 83–101; (January 1931): 289–305; (April 1931): 461–473; (July 1931): 609–622; 26 (October 1931): 68–77;

Frances B. Harmon, "The Social Philosophy of the St. Louis Hegelians," dissertation, Columbia University, 1943;

John Ross Kinzer, "A Study of the Educational Philosophy of William Torrey Harris with Reference to

the Education of Teachers," dissertation, George Peabody College for Teachers, 1940;

Neil Gerard McCluskey, *Public Schools and Moral Education: The Influence of Horace Mann, William Torrey Harris, and John Dewey* (New York: Columbia University Press, 1958);

Charles M. Perry, ed., *The St. Louis Movement in Philosophy: Some Source Material* (Norman: University of Oklahoma Press, 1930);

Henry A. Pochmann, *German Culture in America: Philosophical and Literary Influences, 1600–1900* (Madison: University of Wisconsin Press, 1957), pp. 257–304;

Pochmann, *New England Transcendentalism and St. Louis Hegelianism; Phases in the History of American Idealism* (Philadelphia: Carl Schurz Memorial Foundation, 1948);

John S. Roberts, *William T. Harris: A Critical Study of His Educational and Related Philosophical Views* (Washington, D.C.: National Education Association of the United States, 1924);

Edward Leroy Schaub, ed., *William Torrey Harris, 1835–1935: A Collection of Essays* (Chicago & London: Open Court, 1936);

Denton J. Snider, *The St. Louis Movement in Philosophy, Literature, Education, Psychology: With Chapters of Autobiography* (St. Louis: Sigma, 1920);

Studies in Honor of William Torrey Harris on the Occasion of the Hundredth Return of His Birthday, September 10th, 1935 (Berlin: Weidmann, 1935).

Papers:

William Torrey Harris's papers are in the Library of Congress; the Conford Free Library in Concord, Massachusetts; and the Missouri Historical Society in St. Louis.

Charles Hartshorne

(5 June 1897 – 9 October 2000)

Donald Wayne Viney
Pittsburg State University

BOOKS: *The Philosophy and Psychology of Sensation* (Chicago: University of Chicago Press, 1934);

Beyond Humanism: Essays in the New Philosophy of Nature (Chicago & New York: Willett, Clarke, 1937; republished with new preface, Lincoln: University of Nebraska Press, 1968);

Man's Vision of God, and the Logic of Theism (Chicago & New York: Willett, Clarke, 1941);

The Divine Relativity: A Social Conception of God (New Haven: Yale University Press, 1948);

Reality as Social Process: Studies in Metaphysics and Religion, foreword by William Ernest Hocking (Glencoe, Ill.: Free Press, 1953);

The Logic of Perfection and Other Essays in Neoclassical Metaphysics (La Salle, Ill.: Open Court, 1962);

Anselm's Discovery: A Re-examination of the Ontological Argument for God's Existence (La Salle, Ill.: Open Court, 1965);

A Natural Theology for Our Time (La Salle, Ill.: Open Court, 1967);

Creative Synthesis and Philosophic Method (La Salle, Ill.: Open Court, 1970; London: SCM Press, 1970);

Whitehead's Philosophy: Selected Essays, 1935–1970 (Lincoln: University of Nebraska Press, 1972);

Born to Sing: An Interpretation and World Survey of Bird Song (Bloomington: Indiana University Press, 1973);

Aquinas to Whitehead: Seven Centuries of Metaphysics of Religion (Milwaukee: Marquette University Publications, 1976);

Whitehead's View of Reality, by Hartshorne and Creighton Peden (New York: Pilgrim Press, 1981);

Insights and Oversights of Great Thinkers: An Evaluation of Western Philosophy (Albany: State University of New York Press, 1983);

Omnipotence and Other Theological Mistakes (Albany: State University of New York Press, 1984);

Creativity in American Philosophy (Albany: State University of New York Press, 1984);

Wisdom as Moderation: A Philosophy of the Middle Way (Albany: State University of New York Press, 1987);

The Darkness and the Light: A Philosopher Reflects upon His Fortunate Career and Those Who Made It Possible (Albany: State University of New York Press, 1990);

The Zero Fallacy and Other Essays in Neoclassical Philosophy, edited by Mohammad Valady (Chicago: Open Court, 1997);

The Unity of Being, edited by Randall E. Auxier and Hyatt Carter (Chicago: Open Court, forthcoming 2003).

OTHER: *Collected Papers of Charles Sanders Peirce,* 6 volumes, edited by Hartshorne and Paul Weiss (Cambridge, Mass.: Harvard University Press, 1931–1935; Bristol, U.K.: Thoemmes Press, 1998);

"Santayana's Doctrine of Essence," in *The Philosophy of George Santayana,* edited by Paul Arthur Schilpp, The Library of Living Philosophers, volume 2 (Evanston & Chicago: Northwestern University Press, 1940), pp. 135–182;

"Whitehead's Idea of God," in *The Philosophy of Alfred North Whitehead,* edited by Schilpp, The Library of Living Philosophers, volume 3 (Evanston & Chicago: Northwestern University Press, 1941), pp. 513–539;

"Radhakrishnan on Mind, Matter, and God," in *The Philosophy of Sarvepalli Radhakrishnan,* edited by Schilpp, The Library of Living Philosophers, volume 8 (New York: Tudor, 1952), pp. 315–322;

Philosophers Speak of God, edited by Hartshorne and William L. Reese (Chicago: University of Chicago Press, 1953);

"Replies to Interrogation of Charles Hartshorne, Conducted by William Alston," in *Philosophical Interrogations,* edited by Sydney Rome and Beatrice Rome (New York: Holt, Rinehart & Winston, 1964), pp. 321–354;

"A New Look at the Problem of Evil," in *Current Philosophical Issues: Essays in Honor of Curt John Ducasse,* edited by Frederick C. Dommeyer (Springfield, Ill.: Charles C. Thomas, 1966), pp. 201–212;

"Martin Buber's Metaphysics," in *The Philosophy of Martin Buber,* edited by Schilpp and Maurice Friedman, The Library of Living Philosophers, volume 12 (La Salle, Ill.: Open Court, 1967), pp. 49–68;

"Lewis's Treatment of Memory," in *The Philosophy of C. I. Lewis,* edited by Schilpp, The Library of Living Philosophers, volume 13 (La Salle, Ill.: Open Court, 1968), pp. 395–414;

"A Philosophy of Death," in *Philosophical Aspects of Thanatology,* volume 2, edited by Florence M. Hetzler and A. H. Kutscher (New York: MSS Information Corporation, 1978), pp. 81–89;

"Mysticism and Rationalistic Metaphysics," in *Understanding Mysticism,* edited by Richard Woods (Garden City, N.Y.: Image, 1980), pp. 415–421;

"Understanding as Seeing to Be Necessary," in *The Philosophy of Brand Blanshard,* edited by Schilpp, The

Library of Living Philosophers, volume 15 (La Salle, Ill.: Open Court, 1980), pp. 629–635;

"Marcel on God and Causality," in *The Philosophy of Gabriel Marcel,* edited by Schilpp and Lewis Edwin Hahn, The Library of Living Philosophers, volume 17 (La Salle, Ill.: Open Court, 1984), pp. 353–366;

"Toward a Buddhisto-Christian Religion," in *Buddhism and American Thinkers,* edited by Kenneth K. Inada and Nolan P. Jacobson (Albany: State University of New York Press, 1984), pp. 1–13;

John C. Moskop, *Divine Omniscience and Human Freedom: Thomas Aquinas and Charles Hartshorne,* foreword by Hartshorne (Macon, Ga.: Mercer University Press, 1984);

Existence and Actuality: Conversations with Charles Hartshorne, edited by John B. Cobb Jr. and Franklin L. Gamwell (Chicago: University of Chicago Press, 1984);

Santiago Sia, *God in Process Thought: A Study in Charles Hartshorne's Concept of God,* Studies in philosophy and Religion, volume 7, postscript by Hartshorne (Dordrecht, Netherlands: Nijhoff, 1985);

Sia, ed., *Process Theology and the Christian Doctrine of God,* includes Hartshorne's replies to critics (Petersham, Mass.: St. Bede's, 1986);

"Mind and Body: A Special Case of Mind and Mind," in *A Process Theory of Medicine: Interdisciplinary Essays,* edited by Marcus Ford (Lewiston, N.Y.: Edwin Mellen Press, 1987), pp. 77–88;

"A Metaphysics of Universal Freedom," in *Faith and Creativity: Essays in Honor of Eugene H. Peters,* edited by George Nordgulen and George W. Shields (St. Louis: CBP Press, 1987), pp. 27–40;

"Some Principles of Procedure in Metaphysics," in *The Nature of Metaphysical Knowledge,* edited by G. F. McLean and Hugo Meynell (Lanham, Md.: University Press of America, 1988), pp. 69–75;

"Sankara, Nagarjuna, and Fa Tsang, with Some Western Analogues," in *Interpreting across Boundaries: New Essays in Comparative Philosophy,* edited by G. J. Larson and Eliot Deutsch (Princeton: Princeton University Press, 1988), pp. 98–115;

Robert Kane and Stephen H. Phillips, eds., *Hartshorne, Process Philosophy and Theology,* includes Hartshorne's replies to critics (Albany: State University of New York Press, 1989);

"Von Wright and Hume's Axiom," in *The Philosophy of Georg Henrik von Wright,* edited by Schilpp and Hahn, The Library of Living Philosophers, volume 19 (La Salle, Ill.: Open Court, 1989), pp. 59–76;

"Some Causes of My Intellectual Growth" and "The Philosopher Replies," in *The Philosophy of Charles*

Hartshorne, edited by Hahn, The Library of Living Philosophers, volume 20 (La Salle, Ill.: Open Court, 1991), pp. 3–45, 567–731.

SELECTED PERIODICAL PUBLICATIONS– UNCOLLECTED: "Ethics and the Assumption of Purely Private Pleasures," *International Journal of Ethics,* 40, no. 4 (July 1930): 496–515;

"Contingency and the New Era in Metaphysics," *Journal of Philosophy,* 29 (4 August 1932): 421–431; (18 August 1932): 457–469;

"The Intelligibility of Sensations," *Monist,* 44 (July 1934): 161–185;

"Metaphysics for Positivists," *Philosophy of Science,* 2 (July 1935): 287–303;

"Are All Propositions about the Future either True or False?" *Program of the American Philosophical Association: Western Division, April 20–22* (1939): 26–32;

"The Formal Validity and the Real Significance of the Ontological Argument," *Philosophical Review,* 53 (May 1944): 225–245;

"On Hartshorne's Formulation of the Ontological Argument: A Rejoinder," *Philosophical Review,* 54 (January 1945): 63–65;

"Professor Hartshorne's Syllogism: Rejoinder," *Philosophical Review,* 54 (September 1945): 506–508;

"The Logic of the Ontological Argument," *Journal of Philosophy,* 58 (17 August 1961): 471–473;

"Thinking about Thinking Machines," *Texas Quarterly,* 7 (Spring 1964): 131–140;

"The Meaning of 'Is Going to Be,'" *Mind,* 74 (January 1965): 46–58;

"Psychology and the Unity of Knowledge," *Southern Journal of Philosophy,* 5 (Summer 1967): 81–90;

"Charles Hartshorne's Recollections of Editing the Peirce Papers," *Transactions of the Charles S. Peirce Society,* 6 (Summer 1970): 149–159;

"Pensées sur ma vie" and "Thoughts on My Life," *Bilingual Journal: Lecomte du Nouy Association,* 5 (Fall 1973): 26–32, 60–66;

"Creativity and the Deductive Logic of Causality," *Review of Metaphysics,* 27 (September 1973): 62–74;

"John Hick on Logical and Ontological Necessity," *Religious Studies,* 13 (June 1977): 155–165;

"Bell's Theorem and Stapp's Revised View of Space-Time," *Process Studies,* 7 (Fall 1977): 183–191;

"Concerning Abortion: An Attempt at a Rational View," *Christian Century,* 98 (21 January 1981): 42–45;

"Hegel, Logic, and Metaphysics," *CLIO,* 19, no. 4 (1990): 345–352;

"Communication from Charles Hartshorne," *Proceedings of the American Philosophical Association,* 65 (November 1991): 69–70;

"An Open Letter to Carl Sagan," *Journal of Speculative Philosophy,* 5, no. 4 (1991): 227–232;

"Can Philosophers Cooperate Intellectually? Metaphysics as Applied Mathematics," *Midwest Quarterly,* 35 (Autumn 1993): 8–20;

"A Psychologist's Philosophy Evaluated after Fifty Years: Troland's Psychical Monism," "God as Composer-Director and Enjoyer, and in a Sense Player, of the Cosmic Drama," "Thomas Aquinas and Three Poets Who Do Not Agree With Him," and "Darwin and Some Philosophers," edited by Donald Wayne Viney, *Process Studies,* 30 (Fall–Winter 2002): 237–241, 242–253, 261–275, 276–288.

Charles Hartshorne was the leading representative of process philosophy during the second half of the twentieth century; but his career spanned the better part of the century, and his influence extended beyond philosophy to theology, psychology, and ornithology. He traveled widely, and he knew or corresponded with many seminal figures in twentieth-century philosophy. His publications–including books, articles, and reviews in professional journals–number more than five hundred. The journal *Process Studies,* founded in 1971, is devoted in part to the study and critique of his work.

Hartshorne (the name, which means "deer's horn," is pronounced "hart's horn") was born on 5 June 1897 in Kittanning, Pennsylvania, to Francis Cope Hartshorne, an Episcopal minister, and Marguerite Haughton Hartshorne. He was named for a grandfather who had helped design a transcontinental railroad; the town of Hartshorne, Oklahoma, was named after the grandfather. He had one older sister, Frances, and four younger brothers: identical twins Henry and James, Richard, and Alfred. Richard, who was born in 1899, became a well-known geographer; he died in 1992.

From his parents Hartshorne learned a tolerant and liberal form of Christianity. In his autobiography, *The Darkness and the Light: A Philosopher Reflects upon His Fortunate Career and Those Who Made It Possible* (1990), he recalls his mother telling him, "Charles, life is big!" The family moved to Phoenixville, Pennsylvania, in 1909. From 1911 to 1915 Hartshorne attended Yeates Boarding School in Lancaster County, Pennsylvania, where he read Ralph Waldo Emerson's *Essays* (1841) and *Essays: Second Series* (1844) and Matthew Arnold's *Literature and Dogma: An Essay towards a Better Apprehension of the Bible* (1873). After reading Emerson, he says in the preface to *The Logic of Perfection and Other Essays in Neoclassical Metaphysics* (1962), he resolved to "trust reason to the end." In *Existence and Actuality: Conversations with Charles Hartshorne* (1984), edited by John B. Cobb Jr. and

Hartshorne's parents, Marguerite Haughton Hartshorne and Francis Cope Hartshorne

Franklin L. Gamwell, he says that "Arnold's book was almost like an explosion in my mind" and, to the distress of his parents, was the catalyst for his break with orthodox Christianity. He did not become an atheist, however: throughout his career he attempted to formulate a concept of God that is at once rationally defensible and religiously satisfying. While at Yeates he also developed his lifelong interest in birdsong.

Hartshorne entered Haverford College in 1915. There he studied with the Quaker mystic Rufus Jones, who gave him a sense of the limitations of philosophy by telling him that an impasse exists somewhere in every philosophical system. Jones also argued that the difference between mystics, who claim a direct experience of the divine, and other people is only a matter of degree. God, if truly omnipresent, cannot be totally absent from any experience; the question is the extent to which one is aware of what one is experiencing. This idea became a distinctive feature of Hartshorne's theism.

Under Jones's influence, Hartshorne read Josiah Royce's *The Problem of Christianity* (1913). Royce's essay on community persuaded Hartshorne that self-interest is not the only or even the most basic human motiva-

tion: an individual's identity is partly the product of sharing in the lives of others; hence, the self in whom one is interested cannot be separated from the selves of others. Self-interest, then, necessarily involves interest in others. Thus, Hartshorne rejected the theory of psychological egoism, according to which all of one's actions are undertaken with the motive of benefiting oneself. Hartshorne later saw that Royce's view further implies that self-identity is not absolute. To say that one is "the same person" throughout one's life is an abstraction from the fact that one changes from moment to moment. In Hartshorne's mature philosophy these insights are generalized into the claim that all of reality, including God, has an essentially social structure.

World War I cut Hartshorne's study at Haverford short: he volunteered as a medical orderly in 1917. Crossing the Atlantic, he had a near-mystical experience while reading H. G. Wells's defense of a finite God in the novel *Mr. Britling Sees It Through* (1916). The relative peace of the hospital where he worked near Le Tréport, France, some distance from the front lines, afforded him time to read William James's *The Varieties of Religious Experience: A Study in Human Nature*

(1902). James respected the demands of reason without assuming that religious experience should be explained away. This position, and James's attack on traditional theology, helped Hartshorne in his attempt to think clearly about God. He reached the conclusion that the world is always experienced in emotional terms, though sometimes the affective dimension of experience is so subtle that it goes unnoticed. Experience never reveals the world as the materialist describes it, devoid of affective coloring. Thus, by this point in his development Hartshorne had rejected both psychological egoism and materialism.

In 1919 Hartshorne entered Harvard University, where he majored in philosophy and minored in English literature. He helped to reinstate the Liberal Club and, as president of the Philosophy Club, invited Mary Whiton Calkins to speak to the group. His teachers included James Haughton Woods, William Ernest Hocking, H. M. Sheffer, Ralph Barton Perry, and C. I. Lewis. Hartshorne claimed that he learned the most from Lewis, with whom he had five courses. Hocking, however, convinced Hartshorne that the future might be open, even for God: if the future exists as a realm of possibilities, then God must know it as such; to know possibilities as already settled would be ignorance, not knowledge, and God cannot be ignorant.

In 1923 Hartshorne submitted his dissertation, which will be published posthumously in 2003 as *The Unity of Being*. In *Creativity in American Philosophy* (1984) he describes the work as "a more or less systematized and energetically defended, but on the whole somewhat naive and best forgotten, form of process philosophy." In the dissertation he defends "teleological monism," the view that all things are contained within the unity of God, who is the supreme instance of value; value, moreover, is relational or social. Several more years were required for Hartshorne to refine and clarify his position.

From 1923 to 1925 Hartshorne was a Sheldon Traveling Fellow in Europe. He spent most of his time in Germany but also visited England, France, and Austria. Of the many philosophers he met, the best known were the phenomenologists Edmund Husserl and Martin Heidegger. Husserl's ideal of a presuppositionless beginning in philosophy struck Hartshorne as naive, and he says in "Some Causes of My Intellectual Growth" in *The Philosophy of Charles Hartshorne* (1991) that he sided with Heidegger in believing that "*being in the world* is indeed the basic datum, present even in dreams." Since he believed that all experience is suffused with affective tones, Hartshorne also objected to Husserl's dualism of sensation and feeling. When he asked Husserl about this matter, he says in "Some Causes of My Intellectual Growth," the phenomenolo-

gist replied, "Vielleicht haben Sie Etwas" (Perhaps you have something). In 1929 Hartshorne published in *The Philosophical Review* the first English review of Heidegger's *Sein und Zeit* (1927; translated as *Being and Time*, 1962); the review was incorporated into the seventeenth chapter of his second book, *Beyond Humanism: Essays in the New Philosophy of Nature* (1937).

Hartshorne was a member of the junior faculty of the Harvard philosophy department from 1925 to 1928. During this period he was exposed to the ideas of two philosophers who, more than any others, helped him refine his thinking: Charles Sanders Peirce, who had died in 1914 and whose papers Hartshorne was assigned to edit; and Alfred North Whitehead, who came from England to join the philosophy department at Harvard in 1924. Editing Peirce's papers was a major undertaking that, Hartshorne says in "Some Causes of My Intellectual Development," he considered an "obligation to the profession"; he had no intention of becoming a Peirce scholar. During this time he had a dream in which he was introduced to Peirce, who looked at him disapprovingly and said, "What makes you think you are competent to edit my writings when you don't know science and mathematics?" In 1927 Paul Weiss joined him in the project. The papers were published in six volumes between 1931 and 1935.

Hartshorne found kindred philosophic spirits in Peirce and Whitehead. Although he had briefly accepted psychological determinism after seeing a play in which a character seemed to be completely controlled by certain drives, he abandoned it after reading James's "The Dilemma of Determinism" (1884). Peirce reinforced this rejection. Hartshorne was particularly impressed with Peirce's theory that "time is objective modality." Peirce did not think of time as a series of moments through which things pass or as a way of measuring change; he claimed that past, present, and future correspond to actuality, the becoming of actuality, and possibility, respectively.

Whitehead was also friendly to the doctrines of indeterminism and objective becoming. In contrast to Peirce and the French philosopher Henri-Louis Bergson, James had said that experience—indeed, the universe itself—grows in "drops and buds"; Whitehead concurred with James and called the discrete units of process the "concrescence" (growing together) of "actual entities." Hartshorne, too, stressed the atomicity of becoming, but he conceded that, with the exception of the deepest sleep, experience seems to be continuous rather than atomic. Thus, he accepted this view not as a description of experience but as the only account that makes sense of a world in process.

Hartshorne was not, however, willing to accept Whitehead's theory of possibility—in this respect, he

Hartshorne (second from left) and his siblings in 1909: Frances, the twins James and Henry, Richard, and Alfred

was more Peircean than Whiteheadian. Whitehead called pure possibilities "eternal objects" to stress their nontemporal character and their existence as distinct forms. According to Whitehead, when a leaf changes color in the fall, the greenness of the leaf does not itself undergo any change. Hartshorne rejected this view, at least insofar as contingencies–possibilities that may or may not be actualized–are concerned. The particular shade of green of the leaf, he thought, does not haunt the universe eternally waiting to find exemplification; instead, it comes to exist simultaneously with the leaf. Hartshorne accepted Peirce's view that possibilities form a continuum that, like a line, can be "cut" by novel actualities in an infinite number of ways. What existed prior to the leaf was not the possibility of its particular shade of green but only the possibility of its somehow being green. In *Creative Synthesis and Philosophic Method* (1970) he says that "possibilities are determinable not determinates."

Hartshorne's metaphysics allows for future ways that the actual world could be, but it denies the reality of fully determinate sets of possible worlds. According to Hartshorne, the idea of possible worlds destroys the contrast between possibility and actuality; a fully determinate possibility would be no different than an actuality. He calls the mistake of thinking of the future as a realm of real entities, rather than as generalities, "the

fallacy of possible worlds." In Hartshorne's view, one should speak of "possible world states" instead of "possible worlds."

Hartshorne found Whitehead's concept of "prehension" particularly helpful. Whitehead said that the actualities of which the world is composed are related to each other by means of prehensions–indeed, the actualities *are* their prehensions. To "prehend" is to "grasp" or take account of other actualities. Prehending is not limited to human beings: as nonhuman forms of experience exist, so do nonhuman forms of prehension. Every actual entity, including nonhuman ones, is related to the world by means of prehensions. The particular way in which each actual entity prehends the world, Whitehead called the "subjective form" of the prehension, by which he meant its affective tone. Thus, a prehension is a "feeling of feeling."

In *Creativity in American Philosophy* Hartshorne calls the concept of prehension "one of the most original, central, lucid proposals ever offered in metaphysics." The notion of prehension as a relation that necessarily involves emotional qualities coincided with Hartshorne's conviction that human beings are related to the world by affective bonds. He also saw in prehension a way of understanding perception, including memory, and causation as two aspects of the same thing. If X prehends Y, then X perceives and is affected by Y. Further, the relation between X and Y is temporal: Y precedes X. The most concrete illustrations in human experience of these ideas are introspection and sensory awareness. Hartshorne rejected the notion that an experience could have only itself as an object: that is, what philosophers call "sense-data" do not exist. Hence, in introspection one is aware of or "feels" previous states of oneself; in sensory awareness one is directly aware of the immediate past of the body, and through it, of the surrounding world. In *Whitehead's Philosophy: Selected Essays, 1935–1970* (1972) Hartshorne later drew the distinction between introspection and perception in terms of personal memory and impersonal memory, respectively.

By the time he came under Whitehead's influence, Hartshorne already believed that God is social and, though existing necessarily, cannot be divorced from the temporal processes of the world. In his dissertation he refers to his "*social* view of the Good" and says, "we hold it a contradiction to suppose a Perfect Being who determines all." Like Whitehead, but independently, Hartshorne rejected traditional theism.

Hartshorne had, however, already adopted positions that distinguish his brand of theism from Whitehead's. The most obvious is his defense of the ontological argument for God's existence, an argument Whitehead rejected. Another difference concerns the proper analogy for the relationship of God to the world. In *Adventures of Ideas* (1933) Whitehead objects to the Platonic World-Soul analogy as the parent of "puerile metaphysics." According to this analogy, God is related to the world somewhat as a person is related to his or her body. Hartshorne, on the contrary, enthusiastically embraced the analogy and claimed in "The Philosopher Replies" in *The Philosophy of Charles Hartshorne* that Whitehead rejected it for "weak reasons."

In 1928 Hartshorne became a professor at the University of Chicago. Shortly after his arrival he received a dinner invitation from Dorothy Eleanore Cooper, a Chicago resident whom he had met in 1926 when she was a student at Wellesley College. They were married on 22 December 1928. Hartshorne credited her with improving his writing through her diligent proofreading; she also published bibliographies of her husband's works. The Hartshornes' only child, Emily, was born in 1940.

In his first book, *The Philosophy and Psychology of Sensation* (1934), Hartshorne argues against the prevailing paradigm of the day that sensory modalities are isolated, irreducible, and sui generis. The physiologist Hermann von Helmholtz, for example, claimed that while comparisons of sensory qualities within a modality are possible, comparisons between modalities are not. For instance, one could say that orange is more

similar to red than to yellow, but to say—except as a matter of poetic license—that a sound was more like red than like yellow would be meaningless. Hartshorne marshals anecdotal evidence, empirical studies, and philosophical arguments against Helmholtz's view. Ordinary language knows nothing of the incomparability of sensory qualities, he says: people speak of warm colors, bright sounds, smooth tastes, hot fragrances, and bitter cold. In some cases, the differences between sensory modalities are difficult to discern. The taste of wine is mostly in its fragrance; the apparent aroma of sugar is in the intensity of its taste. Helen Keller, blind and deaf from an early age, claimed to be able to understand colors and sounds by means of analogies drawn from her experiences of touch and smell. Hartshorne argues that meaningful analogies among the senses are possible because sensory qualities exist along an "'affective continuum' of aesthetically meaningful, socially expressive, organically adaptive and evolving experience functions." He concedes that the entire continuum is not found in experience; nevertheless, he maintains that the differences among the senses are matters of degree.

The central point in Hartshorne's theory is that all sensations are feelings, whereas not all feelings are sensations—hence, the "affective continuum." Hartshorne calls the dominant view in philosophy and psychology, that affective tones are associated with or added to bare sensations through experience, the "annex view of value." His counterexamples to the annex view are mainly drawn from touch, taste, and smell, senses in which the felt relevance of the body is most immediate. He asks, for instance, whether a pain could be anything but unpleasant. That in ordinary language a pain is both a sensation and a feeling is not insignificant, he says. The emotional qualities of colors and sounds are, Hartshorne admits, not as obvious, but they are no less real: "Thus, the 'gaiety' of yellow (the peculiar highly specific gaiety) is the yellowness of the yellow."

Hartshorne does not deny that feelings can be annexed to sensations; he denies that sensations have no intrinsically affective dimensions. In a 1934 article, "The Intelligibility of Sensations," he notes that he acquired a fondness for the odor—if not too strong—given off by a skunk, while never failing to perceive it as distinctly disagreeable. Environment, history, and culture can affect the emotions associated with sensory qualities, but it does not follow that feelings are arbitrarily "added on" to sensations. Wayne Viney notes in his contribution to *The Philosophy of Charles Hartshorne* that evolutionary considerations support Hartshorne's theory: sensations must have adaptive value for the organism, but how sensation, stripped of

*Hartshorne in his U.S. Army Medical Corps
uniform during World War I*

feeling, could help an animal adapt is difficult to understand. Viney concludes that Hartshorne's theory of the affective continuum is "more clearly biological than many of its predecessors."

After 1934 Hartshorne returned to metaphysics and philosophical theology, concerns he had addressed in his dissertation; but the decade of the 1930s was the heyday of the Vienna Circle and its philosophy of logical positivism, which dismissed metaphysical statements as incapable of being either true or false and, therefore, as cognitively meaningless. Hartshorne argued against the logical positivists; nevertheless, when he was secretary of the University of Chicago philosophy department in 1936–the only administrative position he ever held–he was instrumental in hiring Rudolf Carnap, the most prominent member of the Vienna Circle. In his second book, *Beyond Humanism,* Hartshorne attempts to show that humanistic philosophies, among which he numbers logical positivism, yield inadequate accounts of nature. Hartshorne's preferred alternative is a blend of panpsychism (the claim that all things have a mental aspect), indeterminism, and theism. Hartshorne's views did not change substan-

tially after *Beyond Humanism;* his later writings present his position more systematically and offer more thorough critiques of both humanistic and nonhumanistic philosophies. Most of the differences between the earlier and later works are terminological: he ceased calling his views "theistic naturalism," "pantheism," and "panpsychism."

Hartshorne's stated purpose in *Man's Vision of God, and the Logic of Theism* (1941) is to add precision and logical rigor to discussions of theism. Citing the eleventh-century archbishop St. Anselm of Canterbury's definition of God as "that than which nothing greater can be conceived," Hartshorne notes that various meanings can be given to the concepts of "nothing" and "greater than." He asks whether the statement that nothing can surpass God includes God among the things by which God cannot be surpassed. Only two possibilities exist: either God is unsurpassable by any being, including the divine self, or he is unsurpassable by any being, excluding the divine self. Hartshorne calls the first alternative "A-perfection," for absolute perfection, and the second alternative "R-perfection," for relative perfection. The two kinds of perfection are compatible, provided that one distinguishes different respects in which God has them. For example, God could be A-perfect with respect to moral categories (that is, ethically perfect) and R-perfect with respect to aesthetic categories (that is, capable of indefinite increase in richness of experience).

Classical theists held that God is A-perfect in all respects. *Man's Vision of God, and the Logic of Theism* is an extended argument for the view that God is A-perfect in some respects but R-perfect in others. Hartshorne calls this position "panentheism" (literally, "all-in-God"). He maintains that God includes the universe in a way analogous to that in which persons include the cells of their bodies:

> God's volition is related to the world as though every object in it were to him a nerve-muscle, and his omniscience is related to it as though every object were a muscle-nerve. A brain cell is for us, as it were a nerve-muscle and a muscle-nerve, in that its internal motions respond to our thoughts, and our thoughts to its motions. . . . God has no separate sense organs or muscles, because all parts of the world body directly perform both functions for him. In this sense the world is God's body.

Daniel A. Dombrowski summarizes Hartshorne's view in *Analytic Theism, Hartshorne, and the Concept of God* (1996): "it makes sense to say both that the cosmos is ensouled and that God is embodied."

Hartshorne argues that persons are not identical with their bodies, but neither can their experiences be divorced from their bodies. Similarly, God is not identical with the universe—which is why Hartshorne stopped calling his view pantheism—but events in the universe have effects on God. Unlike a human body, the divine body has no external environment, only an internal one. But God's internal environment, which is the universe, is in constant flux: time, change, and contingency are not illusions. Hence, God is, in some respects, temporal, mutable, and contingent.

Panentheism does not entail a denial of God's power, love, knowledge, or creativity, but these attributes must be interpreted differently than classical theists understood them. Hartshorne accepts Whitehead's view that God cannot make creatures' decisions for them; since decision is creation, the world is a joint product of God and the creatures. If the world is God's body, then the creature is, as far as God's accidental qualities are concerned, "part-creator of God." In *Beyond Humanism* Hartshorne agreed with Peirce that laws of nature are habits. Here, however, he argues that God creates the laws of nature and that no creature could exist without them. Divine love is understood in terms of God's sympathetic participation in the feelings of the creatures. This idea is foreign to classical theology, which understands God's love as devoid of emotion.

Hartshorne considered God's knowledge as a form of prehension—a feeling of the feelings of the creatures. Therefore, it would be impossible for God to know the future free decisions of the creatures, since, before the decisions are made, they do not exist to be known. Nevertheless, Hartshorne had some doubts about how to represent future-tense propositions. Aristotle seems to have held that propositions about future contingents (events that may or may not occur) are neither true nor false, but indeterminate. Hartshorne defended the Aristotelian idea in a short article, "Are All Propositions about the Future either True or False?" (1939). The problem with Aristotle's theory, Hartshorne says, is that it sacrifices the logical law of excluded middle.

By 1941 Hartshorne had abandoned the Aristotelian view. Instead of speaking of a third truth value, he introduced the idea of a triad of predicates that reflect temporal and causal modalities. For any event E, causal conditions either require E (definitely E), exclude E (definitely not-E), or leave E undecided (indefinite with respect to E). If any one of these is true of an event, the other two are false. Thus, no violation of the law of excluded middle occurs. These distinctions are marked in ordinary language with expressions such as "will be," "will not," and "may or may not be." For example, in Charles Dickens's *A Christmas Carol* (1843) Ebenezer Scrooge asks the Ghost of Christmas Yet to Come, "Are these the shadows of the things that Will be, or are they shadows of the things that May be, only?" Thus, the indeterminacy of the future is represented by Hartshorne not in the truth values of propositions but in predicates pertaining to the future.

Some philosophers criticize Hartshorne's position on the grounds that truth is eternal and that propositions about what may or may not occur are concessions to human ignorance about the future. From the limited human point of view, they say, the probability of some event occurring in the future is 1 (necessity), 0 (impossibility), or some value between 1 and 0; from a perspective of omniscience, such as God's, all probabilities would reduce to 1 or 0. Hartshorne rejects this view. He says in "The Meaning of 'Is Going to Be'" (1965) that "the notion that dates can be assigned from eternity is one of the fairy tales—or controversial assumptions—which haunt this subject." According to Hartshorne, the indeterminateness of the future is not a function of human lack of knowledge: the future really is indeterminate.

Hartshorne also denies the traditional view that God created the universe ex nihilo. To be sure, God, by creating order in the cosmos, is the eminent creator; but nondivine beings also have creative power. By constantly adding new definiteness to reality, the temporal process itself is creative. Creation always presupposes a prior world out of which new definiteness arises. Hartshorne argues, by way of illustration:

> Either my parents were genuinely causative of me, or they were not. If they were, then God plus nothing was not the cause; if my parents were not part-causes of me, then, by the same reasoning, the creatures are never causes of anything.

A consequence of Hartshorne's view is that the universe had no beginning. He does not deny the theory, currently popular among scientists, that the present universe began with the Big Bang. Hartshorne maintains, however, that the beginning of this universe does not represent an absolute beginning.

A common objection to belief in God is the problem of evil: if God is all-good and all-powerful, then why does apparently unjustified suffering exist? God should have both the motive and the means to ensure that suffering is never undeserved. In response, Hartshorne questions the ability of any being, including God, to decide the events of the world unilaterally. He says that the traditional concept of omnipotence is not even coherent enough to be false. If X and Y are two individuals making decisions, and X decides A and Y decides B, then the combination AB is decided by neither X nor Y taken singly. The logic of the situation does not change if one of the decision makers is God. Therefore,

*Hartshorne around the time he became a professor
at the University of Chicago in 1928*

what occurs is not wholly the result of divine decisions. Cooperation among the decision makers can eliminate some but not all of the risks of undesirable consequences. Even so, cooperation among the agents is not guaranteed. Suffering and tragedy are the inevitable consequences of multiple creativity. Because the deity is affected by creatures' decisions, tragedy exists even for God. Hartshorne quotes Whitehead's statement that God is the fellow sufferer who understands: because all suffering occurs within the context of divine sympathy, tragedy is never simply meaningless. The redemption of the world is in its valuation by God.

After reading *Man's Vision of God, and the Logic of Theism,* Hartshorne's father asked why he had not written more about sin. Hartshorne pointed out that he had a paragraph on sin in the book. His father replied by slowly repeating, "A . . . paragraph." Sin does not, in fact, play a central role in Hartshorne's thought, largely because he denies that God is primarily concerned about moral values. Hartshorne's God is not a cosmic judge who keeps a tally of human deeds but a cosmic artist who appreciates and contributes to the beauty of the universe. While not denying that terrible evils exist, Hartshorne cannot see how promises of rewards in heaven or threats of punishment in hell would help the situation either at a practical or a theoretical level. He is inclined to agree with Whitehead, who said that the

power of God is the worship that God inspires. Nevertheless, much later in his career, Hartshorne writes in *Wisdom as Moderation: A Philosophy of the Middle Way* (1987) of the "truly monstrous evils" in the world and concedes at least a functional equivalent of original sin.

In 1947 Hartshorne received a joint appointment in the philosophy department and the Meadville/Lombard Theological Seminary of the University of Chicago. Thus, he knew the central figures in the so-called Chicago School of theology: Henry Nelson Wieman, Daniel Day Williams, Bernard Meland, and Bernard Loomer. Like Hartshorne, they found Whitehead's philosophy useful, stressed the dynamic aspects of nature, and denied supernaturalism. But he emphatically rejected their empirical approach to theology. Over the years Hartshorne's defense of his version of theism attracted more attention than other aspects of his thought.

In *The Divine Relativity: A Social Conception of God* (1948) Hartshorne disagrees with classical theists, such as St. Thomas Aquinas, who claim that God is unaffected in any way by creatures—that God is wholly necessary and the world is wholly contingent. Because God is all-inclusive, Hartshorne says, God is affected by, and, thus, related to, all that exists. Hartshorne offers a proof of this idea—and, a fortiori, a disproof of the classical theistic idea—that Carnap helped him to formulate more rigorously: if W is contingent (that is, if it could be otherwise), then knowledge of W must be contingent. Thus, if God knows the world, and the world is contingent, then God is contingent, at least in respect to God's knowledge of the world.

Aquinas and other classical theists argue that if God is contingent, then God might cease to exist, which is absurd. Hartshorne replies that God need not be conceived as contingent in all respects: "That God exists is one with his essence and is an analytic truth . . . but how, or in what actual state of experience or knowledge or will, he exists is contingent in the same sense as is our existence." God's essence (defining characteristic) may be to exist. But the particular way in which that existence is realized—for instance, as knowing, loving, and influencing this world state rather than some other possible world state—is not necessary. One could think of the existence of God as a set whose members are the divine experiences: to say that God necessarily exists is to say that the set of divine experiences can never be empty, but the specific experiences that fill the set are not necessary. This distinction is that between existence, or the fact that a thing is, and actuality, or the particular way in which the existence is realized. David Tracy calls this distinction "Hartshorne's discovery." It allows one to say, without contradiction, that God's existence is necessary but God's actuality is contingent.

The Divine Relativity characterizes God as the "self-surpassing surpasser of all" and thereby makes a clean break with the dominant theological tradition. Aristotle's and Aquinas's idea of God as the unmoved mover Hartshorne calls "A perfect example of a half-truth parading as the whole truth. A God who loves and is loved by the creatures is anything but unmoved." The existence of God is unmoved in the sense that it is unchanging; but the actuality of God is constantly changing as it adjusts with infinite patience to the creative advance of the world. The set of divine experiences is constantly gaining new members as the temporal process continues.

In his introduction to Rabbi Abraham Heschel's *Between God and Man* (1959) Fritz Rothschild describes Heschel's God as the "most moved mover," in contrast to Aristotle's "unmoved mover." In later works Hartshorne speaks of God as "the most and best moved mover," a deliberate appropriation of Rothschild's description of Heschel's God.

Addressing the issue of religious language, Hartshorne asks in what sense, if any, concepts rooted in human discourse can apply literally to God. He answers that one is speaking literally when one says that God is all-inclusive, an individual with strictly universal functions. No more than one all-inclusive being can exist: the term *human being* does not specify how many human beings could exist, but *all-inclusive being* can apply to only one individual; polytheism, therefore, is false. Unlike other individuals, God is definable by concepts alone. Furthermore, the attributes applied to God, such as *supreme love, power,* and *knowledge,* signify the eminent exemplifications of these qualities. For example, the love of a nondivine being is mixed with selfishness, stubbornness, and lack of sympathy; divine love is not. Hence, the quality of love as ascribed to God is an unqualified concern for the welfare of others. Divine love is love in its most literal sense. Thus, "theology (so far as it is the theory of the essence of deity) is the most literal of all sciences of existence. It is anthropology (including theological anthropology) that is shot full of metaphors and statements never literally true."

Schubert Ogden, one of Hartshorne's students at Chicago who became a well-known theologian, observes that in *Existence and Actuality* Hartshorne's position on religious language requires apparently incompatible claims. First, he says, Hartshorne argues that human beings' understanding of language about God must be grounded in their understanding of themselves. For instance, one can say that God is love, because one understands the meaning of love in human life. On the other hand, Hartshorne often argues that people understand divine qualities not by finding them within human experience but by imagina-

tively subtracting the specifically human defects and extrapolating to God. Hartshorne concedes that unresolved tensions exist in his theory of religious language. He argues, however:

> The analogy from us to God implies a reverse analogy from God to us. In learning the meaning of words we appear necessarily to follow the us-to-God path, but then we must be able to follow conceptually the reverse path to understand fully what we have done. This is a matter of logical coherence.

For Hartshorne, logical coherence is the final test of metaphysical truth. Thus, the question becomes whether it makes logical sense to follow the conceptual God-to-us path. To answer this question, more is required than a theory of religious language.

That Hartshorne spoke with great confidence about God has not escaped the notice even of his admirers. The popular science writer Martin Gardner, another of Hartshorne's students at Chicago, writes in *The Whys of a Philosophical Scrivener* (1983): "Hartshorne's writings are stimulating to read and seldom opaque, but I am always made uncomfortable by the fact that he seems to know so much more about God than I do."

Hartshorne was not oblivious to this criticism. In "Charles Hartshorne's Letters to a Young Philosopher: 1979–1995" (2001) he explains:

> Concerning M. Gardner & my knowing too much about God, what he, & so many, miss is that what I claim to know is *very little.* The mystery is not what *extreme abstractions* apply to God, but what the divine life concretely is, how God prehends you or me or Hitler, or the feelings of bats, ants, plant cells, atoms. The one "to whom all hearts are open" knows, or loves the *concrete concretely.* We know nothing in that way.

Hartshorne took seriously the claims of mystics to have a direct and more adequate access to God than is available through intellectual reflection. He ends his discussion of mysticism in "Mysticism and Rationalistic Metaphysics" (1980): "Possibly we need to devote more time to meditation and less (though at present it is no vast amount) to rationalistic metaphysics."

In 1948–1949 Hartshorne lectured in German at the University of Frankfurt am Main and in French at the Sorbonne in Paris. During this time he met Anders Nygen, Karl Barth, Karl Jaspers, and Jean Wahl. On his return to the United States he took up his duties as president of the Western Division of the American Philosophical Association. His friend Charner Perry advised him that in his presidential address "You must not talk about God." Hartshorne obliged and gave a talk titled "Chance, Love, and Incompatibility," a lively

Hartshorne's wife, Dorothy Cooper Hartshorne

repeat the same song without interspersing other songs. The theory behind the hypothesis is that birds have a primitive aesthetic sense. The theory does not depend on his metaphysical view that feeling is pervasive and efficacious throughout nature, but it is clearly in accord with such a view. As Hartshorne and his wife traveled around the globe, he continued his study of birds and made many recordings of their songs. He published his major statement on birdsong, *Born to Sing: An Introduction and World Survey of Bird Song*, in 1973.

In 1955 Hartshorne left Chicago for Emory University in Atlanta. He traveled to Hawaii, the Philippines, Japan, and Taiwan in 1958. In 1962 he moved to the University of Texas at Austin. He visited India and Japan in 1966, Australia in 1974, Belgium in 1978, Japan and Hawaii in 1984, and England in 1988. At Emory and Texas he concentrated on defending his version of the ontological argument, developing his metaphysical system, reexamining the history of philosophy, and writing his autobiography.

Hartshorne's best-known but least-understood work is his defense of the ontological argument. He probably wrote more on the subject than any other philosopher has; but despite his many remarks to the contrary, the supposition that he considered the argument to be a definitive proof of God's existence is widespread. The final chapter of his dissertation is devoted to the argument; two decades later he returned to it in the penultimate chapter of *Man's Vision of God, and the Logic of Theism* and in the article "The Formal Validity and Real Significance of the Ontological Argument" (1944). In *Philosophers Speak of God* he distinguished two forms of the argument in Anselm's work–seven years before Norman Malcolm made the same point in "Anselm's Ontological Arguments" (1960), an article that caused a minor stir among analytic philosophers. Hartshorne discussed Malcolm's article in "The Logic of the Ontological Argument" (1961). In that same article he first formulated the ontological argument using the notation of modal logic. He gave a more elaborate formalization and defense of the argument in *The Logic of Perfection and Other Essays in Neoclassical Metaphysics*. In *Anselm's Discovery: A Re-examination of the Ontological Argument for God's Existence* (1965) he defends Anselm's second argument and gives detailed analyses of historical treatments of the argument. Finally, he presents it as part of a cumulative case for God's existence in *Creative Synthesis and Philosophic Method*.

Hartshorne contends that Anselm discovered something important about the idea of deity: that any being that exists with the possibility of not existing (that is, contingently) cannot be God. Therefore,

defense of his metaphysics that makes no explicit mention of God. When he published the speech in *Reality as Social Process: Studies in Metaphysics and Religion* (1953), however, he revised it to restate his case for theistic metaphysics and, as in *Beyond Humanism,* to point to the limitations of both religious and nonreligious humanistic philosophies.

Philosophers Speak of God was also published in 1953. Hartshorne and his student William L. Reese collected writings on the nature of God by well-known and obscure Western and Eastern philosophers throughout history; commentaries from the standpoint of panentheism follow each selection.

While at Chicago, Hartshorne began the serious study of birdsong. In 1951–1952 he visited Australia and New Zealand to pursue his interest in oscines and met philosophers such as J. J. C. Smart and J. L. Mackie. He spent the summers of 1952 and 1953 studying ornithology in northern Michigan. During the first summer he hit on the idea of a "monotony threshold," which he tested the following summer. The hypothesis is that birds that repeat the same song will have marked pauses between songs, and birds with more varied repertoires will not

either God exists without the possibility of not existing, or God cannot exist. In other words, God's existence is either necessary or impossible: a contingent divine existence is a contradiction. It does not follow that God exists—one reason Hartshorne denied that the argument is a proof of God's existence. The argument shows, however, that any argument for or against the existence of God that assumes that God is equally conceivable either as existent or nonexistent is fallacious. Thus, Hartshorne holds that the ontological argument is the key to the logic of any theistic or atheistic argument.

According to Hartshorne, the premise of the ontological argument that Anselm failed to justify is that God's existence is not impossible. The medieval Scholastic John Duns Scotus and the German rationalist philosopher Gottfried Wilhelm Leibniz also made this criticism of Anselm. Philosophers as diverse as the logical positivists and the existentialist Jean-Paul Sartre have claimed that the concept of God involves some incoherence or contradiction. The concept of God to which they deny consistency, however, is that of classical theism; in that respect, Hartshorne agrees with them: "All my difficulty in believing in theism, all of it, turns on the not easily disproved suspicion that every available formulation of the idea of God involves some more or less well hidden absurdity." But he argues that the panentheistic concept of God is not self-contradictory.

Some philosophers criticize Hartshorne's ontological argument for equivocating on the modal concepts of necessity and possibility. For example, John Hick in "A Critique of the 'Second Argument'" and David A. Pailin in *God and the Processes of Reality* claim that saying that God has always existed and always will exist (ontological necessity) is different from saying that the proposition "God exists" is necessarily true (logical necessity). Hick and Pailin, both theists, hold that God's existence is ontologically but not logically necessary. Hartshorne replies that as far as the ontological argument is concerned, the difference between logical and ontological necessity is merely verbal: "modal distinctions are ultimately coincident with temporal ones. The actual is the past, the possible is the future." Thus, he refers to God's "modal coincidence," the idea that God's existence is coextensive with actuality and possibility.

Hartshorne does not believe that the ontological argument, by itself, is sufficient to make a convincing case for theism. For this purpose he employs what he calls "the global argument," which consists of six mutually supportive arguments: in addition to the ontological argument, Hartshorne develops versions of the cosmological, design, epistemic, moral, and aesthetic arguments. The ontological argument is meant to show that God's conceivability implies God's existence; the other arguments are meant to show that God is conceivable. The global argument is prefigured in many of Hartshorne's writings, beginning with the dissertation, but is fully presented only in *Creative Synthesis and Philosophic Method* and in Donald Wayne Viney's *Charles Hartshorne and the Existence of God* (1985).

None of the elements of the global argument are "empirical" in the sense Karl Popper gave the term: that is, none of them presupposes that the proposition "God exists" could be falsified. Hartshorne makes clear in *A Natural Theology for Our Time* (1967) that the global argument is metaphysics, not science. The nearest historical parallel to Hartshorne's argument is Duns Scotus's *De Primo Principio*, but, of course, Hartshorne denies Scotus's classical theism. Moreover, Hartshorne does not claim to have demonstrated the existence of God—not long after publishing *Creative Synthesis and Philosophic Method*, he ceased to call the arguments proofs. Each of the arguments is presented as a logically exhaustive set of alternatives, one of which is panentheism; in each case Hartshorne argues that panentheism is the most rationally defensible position. Disagreeing with him, he says, does not mean that one is irrational; one will have understood, however, the rational price to be paid by rejecting theism.

An objection to panentheism that has probably troubled Hartshorne more than any other comes from relativity physics. According to Albert Einstein's special theory of relativity, no single time line exists for the entire universe. Temporal relations among events can only be fixed relative to an inertial reference frame. Two events may occur simultaneously in one frame of reference but successively in another frame of reference. The problem is that relativity physics does not permit one to say that any one reference frame is any more privileged than another. Therefore, the question whether the events are really simultaneous does not make sense. Without a single time line for the universe, what does it mean to say, as Hartshorne does, that there is a divine time?

Some hope for escaping the problem comes from quantum physics. According to Bell's theorem (named for J. S. Bell), one event may influence another event before a light signal has had time to traverse the distance between them. The importance of Bell's theorem for Hartshorne's theism is that it opens the possibility that, contrary to relativity physics, a single time line for the universe does exist. At first Hartshorne greeted Bell's theorem with excite-

in its necessary features. True metaphysical statements are, therefore, in principle not falsifiable by any conceivable experience. Some philosophers argue that if no experience could count against a statement, then the statement is meaningless. Hartshorne accepts verifiability by some conceivable experience, divine or nondivine, as a criterion for meaning in general; but he holds that falsifiability is the criterion only for empirical meaning. Metaphysics is similar to mathematics in that it deals with highly abstract concepts; but, unlike mathematics, its subject matter extends beyond quantity to include the qualitative dimensions of reality. For Hartshorne, the notion of empirical metaphysics is self-contradictory. Metaphysics is the study of concreteness as such—or, somewhat paradoxically, "the study of the abstraction 'concreteness.'"

One might object to Hartshorne's claim that no experience can count against the truth of a metaphysical statement by citing the statement "Nothing exists": it is nonrestrictive and existential and, therefore, seems to be a metaphysical statement; but it also seems to be refuted by experience. Hartshorne responds that "Nothing exists" is false not empirically, or as a matter of fact, but necessarily. According to Hartshorne, a negative statement can only be made true by some positive state of affairs. To say, for example, that there is no life on the planet Pluto is to presuppose the existence of Pluto. But nothing could make the statement "Nothing exists" true; it is a mere verbal formula describing no conceivable state of affairs. Therefore, the old question "Why is there something rather than nothing?" is bad metaphysics, for it presupposes that there might have been nothing.

Hartshorne maintains that metaphysical ideas have an inherent pragmatic value. They are not only universally applicable but also universally useful. He criticizes pragmatists such as James for failing to see that an idea that is good only for some purposes need not be true to be useful. But metaphysical ideas are categorically different: their pragmatic value is in their indispensability, not in their temporary utility. Furthermore, an ugly metaphysical truth is not possible: negative valuations suggest things to be avoided or prevented, but metaphysical truths can be neither prevented nor avoided; their only value is positive. The poet John Keats's phrase "Beauty is truth, truth beauty" is exactly correct where metaphysical ideas are concerned. It follows that extreme pessimism is pragmatically meaningless. This notion is illustrated by the story of the man who complains, "Would that I had never existed!" to which his companion replies, "Ah, but who is so lucky? Not one in a thousand."

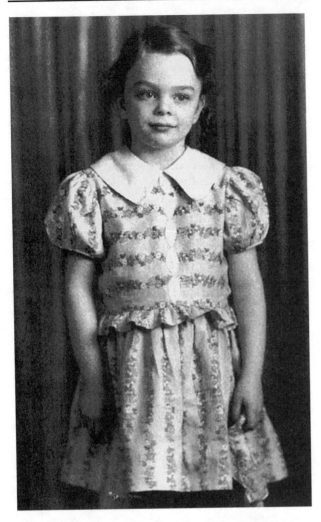

Hartshorne's only child, Emily, who was born in 1940

ment as a possible way out of his difficulty. Later, in his reply to critics in *Charles Hartshorne's Concept of God: Philosophical and Theological Responses* (1990) he said he knew "too little physics to be confident in such topics" and suggested that this is the kind of "impasse" in philosophical systems of which Jones had spoken.

The most complete statement of Hartshorne's neoclassical metaphysics is found in *Creative Synthesis and Philosophic Method*. He rejects the understanding of metaphysics as a search for a reality behind the veil of experience, and he has little patience with dogmatism, special claims to insight, or the search for indubitable truths. He characterizes metaphysics as "the study which evaluates *a priori* statements about existence." True metaphysical statements are nonrestrictive, in that they exclude no conceivable state of affairs; they are existential, in that they describe the world not in its contingent aspects but

Hartshorne's metaphysical position is indeterministic, psychicalist, and theistic. The most pervasive fact of experience, according to Hartshorne, is creativity, the becoming of novel actualities. Whitehead said that the "many become one and are increased by one." Hartshorne expresses the same idea by saying that "*To be is to create*." The extent of novelty is a matter of degree, ranging from a minimum in the nearly exact repetition of pattern at the inorganic level to the maximum in artistic creation at the human level. Of course, experience is also marked by law-like regularities, and science is largely occupied in discovering "laws of nature." Hartshorne insists, however, that the determinist's view that sufficient causal conditions can, in principle, be found for every event is not warranted by experience. The regularities perceived are never so exact as to eliminate novelty. Causes provide the necessary, not the sufficient, conditions for the emergence of new actual entities. When causes severely limit the possible range of effects, one finds the stability of order that is reflected in the laws of nature.

Indeterminism can, thus, account for nature's regularities, whereas determinism cannot account for its novelties. This point is often missed, because indeterminism is mistakenly identified with the view that events are never causally conditioned. Hartshorne argues that the becoming of an actual entity is always causally conditioned, but that causes never guarantee every detail of their effects. Therefore, an effect is always "more than" its causes; the surplus is the measure of novelty in the world. Perfect knowledge would allow one to deduce causes from an effect, but no amount of knowledge would allow one to deduce an effect from its causes. It is not simply a limitation of knowledge that prevents one from predicting a poet's next poem: such a prediction would amount to composing the poem oneself.

Human experience provides the clearest example of the novel actualities that emerge in the "creative advance." Of course, many nonhuman forms of experience exist. The title of Thomas Nagel's article "What Is It Like to Be a Bat?" (1974) poses a meaningful, if unusual, question. Hartshorne takes the question a step further, generalizing beyond both human and animal experience and claiming that everything that is concrete has some degree of sentience or feeling. He says "concrete" because he does not mean to suggest that literally everything has feeling:

Of course tables do not feel; but it does not follow that there is no feeling in them. There is feeling in a flock of birds or in a swarm of bees, but the flock or the swarm feels nothing. So there can be feeling in a swarm of molecules, though the swarm does not feel.

The distinction between "concrete entities"–that is, individuals–and the wholes of which they can be parts allows Hartshorne to formulate an intelligible panpsychism, or, as he prefers to call it, "psychicalism."

An obvious objection to Hartshorne's psychicalism is that attributing feelings to creatures with central nervous systems is one thing, while saying that molecules or atoms have primitive forms of feeling is quite another. Hartshorne responds to this argument, first, by noting that no conceptual or a priori criterion limits feelings to higher organisms: a brain may be no more necessary to feeling than lungs and a stomach are to oxygenating and digesting, as in one-celled organisms. Second, he points out that the only way the simplest entities could show themselves to have primitive feelings is by responding to stimuli, and in that case, "any evidence there logically could be for very low-level sentience there actually seems to be." Psychic qualities are cosmic variables admitting unlimited kinds of instantiations, ranging from the most primitive forms of feeling through the highly integrated and complex mental states found in some primates and other large-brained mammals to the mind of God.

Hartshorne's psychicalism goes against the dominant tradition in philosophy that defines mind as a nonphysical substance. He argues that no non-question-begging criteria exist for the total absence of mind. Being physical is not the same as having no mind-like qualities. Moreover, many qualities traditionally ascribed to minds have physical dimensions: feelings, for example, are located at various places in the body. He admits that higher-order cognition, such as thinking, is not felt as a localized phenomenon (except, perhaps, in extreme mental exertion that results in headaches); but this fact does not constitute evidence that thinking is not a physical process.

Hartshorne offers psychicalism as an alternative to dualism and materialism. Dualism posits an autonomous realm of mind, independent of insentient matter. The interaction between mind and matter has long been an embarrassment for dualism; with the advent of an evolutionary worldview, the dualist is faced with the additional mystery of the emergence of mind from matter. Materialists face a similar problem: they assume that the only relationships that exist are among objects from which subjectivity is entirely missing. But experience, whatever else it may be, is a relationship involving a subject and its object—what the phenomenologists call "intentionality." Explain-

Hartshorne and his wife recording birdsongs at their home in Atlanta, Georgia, in 1961

ing how this relationship is possible is the bane of materialism. Hartshorne argues that materialists are committed to a temporal dualism in attempting to account for the emergence of mind in the course of evolution. For Hartshorne, on the other hand, being a center of experience, and thus subjective, is part of what it means to be actual. On this view, what emerges in the course of evolution are not minds as such but only minds of varying levels of awareness. Hartshorne was fond of pointing out that the geneticist Sewell Wright, his friend and colleague at Chicago, shared his psychicalist view of nature.

Hartshorne follows Leibniz in believing that many errors are hidden in what philosophers deny: "with properties of which there can be varying degrees, the zero degree, or total absence, is knowable empirically only if there is a known least quantum, or finite minimum, of the property," as with Planck's constant. To claim to know empirically that such a property is totally absent is to commit the "zero fallacy." Hartshorne finds the fallacy committed in the denial of all creative activity to some causal processes,

in the idea of matter devoid of all mind-like qualities, and in the notion of sensation stripped of all affect.

God is required by Hartshorne's metaphysics of indeterminism and psychicalism. Ordered or law-like relations in nature must be explained, if at all, by the creativity of one or many of the actualities comprising the universe. The order in question, however, is cosmic in scope. Therefore, the cosmic order cannot be explained by a mutual adjustment among entities within the universe. Nor can it be explained by the currently fashionable chaos theory, for this theory presupposes a cosmos in which new forms of order appear. Only a being whose influence extends to all times and places—an all-inclusive being—could account for order on a cosmic scale. Thus, Hartshorne says, "metaphysics is no more and no less than natural theology."

Hartshorne argues that neither the various orders within the universe nor the order of the universe itself is absolute. Indeterminism implies that ordered relations in nature are best expressed as probabilities (what scientists call "stochastic laws").

Furthermore, the laws themselves are not absolute: God determines the cosmic order not for eternity but for an extensive but limited time. The laws of nature that exist are contingent, but that natural laws exist is not contingent. A necessary truth requires no explanation; therefore, divine activity does not explain order per se but only the particular laws that obtain in the endless sequence of universes—what Whitehead called "cosmic epochs."

Hartshorne contends that the progression of cosmic epochs occurs for aesthetic reasons: the universe as a whole has a beauty that God alone can fully appreciate; beauty requires unity and contrast; the laws of nature provide the unity of the universe. If the counterpoint of rhythms—the activity of the creatures—allowed by those laws were ever exhausted, the result would be, from God's perspective, monotony. Like the birds of which Hartshorne was so fond, the divine being has a monotony threshold; therefore, new patterns of order, new universes must be created.

A key to Hartshorne's metaphysics is the distinctive way he treats the polar contrasts relative and absolute, subject and object, effect and cause, becoming and being, temporal and eternal, concrete and abstract, actual and potential, contingent and necessary, finite and infinite, and complex and simple. He makes four claims about these sets of contrasts. First, considered as extreme abstractions, they are correlative, in that each member of a pair requires the other for its meaning; that is, symmetry of meaning exists between them. Second, when the contrasts are exemplified, they are related asymmetrically. For example, while *cause* and *effect* must be defined in terms of each other, actual effects are related asymmetrically to their causes: the man depends, in part, on the boy he once was, but the boy does not depend on the man. Third, in each case the first term is proportional to the second: for instance, effects are to causes as subjects are to objects. Finally, the contrasts are ultimate in that they cannot fail of exemplification: the ultimate contrasts are metaphysical categories that describe every conceivable universe or state of affairs.

Traditional theism is hampered, Hartshorne contends, by what he calls a "monopolar prejudice": God and the world are put on opposite sides of polar contrasts. The neoclassical alternative is to speak of God as dipolar, as in different respects finite and infinite, temporal and eternal, complex and simple, and so on. The qualification "in different respects" refers to the asymmetrical ways in which these categories apply to God. According to Hartshorne, God's actual states are contingent, and all of these states have in common the necessity of God's existence. The polar

contrasts, when applied to God, result in the doctrine of dual transcendence (or, if one prefers, dual immanence), the view that the contrasts apply to God in an eminent fashion. When he was accused of denying God's transcendence, Hartshorne would reply that he believed in twice as much transcendence as classical theists.

Only after his ninetieth birthday did Hartshorne arrive at what he considered a fully satisfactory way of representing the possible relations between the polar contrasts as applied to God and the world. In "Can Philosophers Cooperate Intellectually? Metaphysics as Applied Mathematics" (1993) he represented the formal possibilities in a matrix of four columns and four rows. Uppercase letters represent divine modalities, and lowercase letters represent the modalities as applied to the world; the zeros represent either impossibility or having no modal status. Using, for example, the polar contrasts of necessity and contingency, God is either necessary in all respects (Column I), contingent in all respects (Column II), necessary and contingent in diverse respects (Column III), or impossible or without modal status (Column IV). Similarly, the world is either necessary in all respects (Row 1), contingent in all respects (Row 2), necessary and contingent in diverse respects (Row 3), or impossible or lacking in modal status (Row 4). According to Hartshorne, only one of the sixteen possibilities can be true, and at least one must be true.

Hartshorne notes that the table represents not only the logical possibilities but also the historically significant options: the Hindu Advaita Vedanta (N.0), early Buddhist thought (0.cn), Aristotle's theism (N.cn), Aquinas's theism (N.c), the pantheism of the Stoics or Baruch Spinoza (N.n), the atheism of Pierre-Simon Laplace (0.n), John Stuart Mill's doctrine of a purely finite God (C.c), Jules Lequyer's theism (NC.c), Sartre's atheism (0.c), and Hartshorne's neoclassical theism (NC.cn). The table serves as an argument for Hartshorne's position, insofar as it illustrates that only his view preserves the ultimate contrasts as applied, in different respects, to God and the world.

In *The Zero Fallacy and Other Essays in Neoclassical Philosophy* (1997) Hartshorne says that "the sixteen options become thirty-two if each is subdivided into those accepting and those not accepting Plato's mind-body analogy" (he denies that the mind-body distinction is a polar contrast). The number of formal alternatives leaps to 256 (16 x 16) if one combines any two pairs of contrasts—for example, between relative and absolute, finite and infinite, and so forth. More generally, if n represents the number of polar contrasts that apply to both God and the world, then 16^n represents the number of formally possible concepts

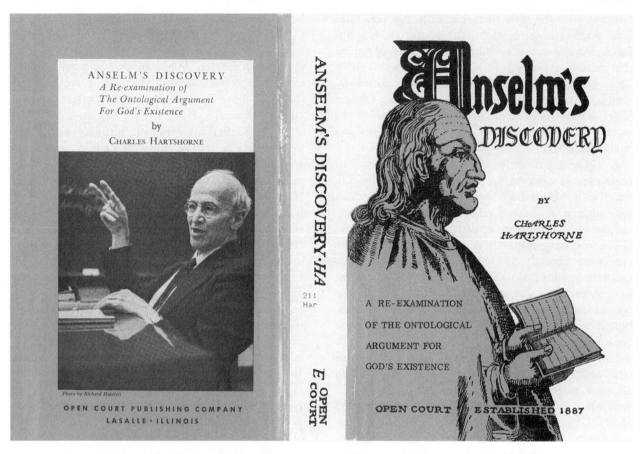

Dust jacket for Hartshorne's 1965 book, in which he defends St. Anselm's argument that God, as a being than which nothing greater can be conceived, necessarily exists (Richland County Public Library)

of God and God's relation to the world (16^n x 2, if one includes those that accept and those that reject the mind-body analogy).

When Hartshorne says that the polar contrasts apply to both God and the world, he may seem to be blurring the distinction between the divine and the nondivine. In fact, however, he distinguishes the two in a different way than classical theists do. The difference between God and a creature is not a difference between the infinite and the finite but between the whole and the fragment. According to Hartshorne, any realization of value, even within the life of God, is a finite realization. The realization of all possible values is impossible, since some positive values exclude each other. For instance, the child at the smorgasbord fills his plate with more than he can eat and discovers that one's eyes can be bigger than one's stomach. The creature is identified not by its finitude but by its fragmentariness, the fact that it is part of the universe and not the whole. The fragmentariness includes both spatial and temporal limitations. Unlike God, no creature exists in all times and all places.

Hartshorne says that religion is the acceptance of one's fragmentariness.

The only form of immortality for creatures that Hartshorne admits is what Whitehead called "objective immortality." God's memory is the measure of the reality of the past. Hence, everything a creature has been, all of its joys and sorrows, achievements and failures, are preserved in the mind of God as objectively immortal. To want more than this sort of immortality, says Hartshorne, is to want to be God. Hartshorne's counsel is to accept one's fragmentariness, not to hope for a posthumous career but to find meaning by contributing to the divine whole of which one is a part. He calls this doctrine "contributionism." In *Wisdom as Moderation* he says, "God's possession of us is our final achievement, not our possession of God."

Traditionally, the doctrine of personal survival of death played an important role in solving the problem of evil: the innocent who suffer unjustly in this life may be compensated in the next life. Hartshorne's "objective immortality" provides no basis for this hope. Thus, some philosophers sympathetic to Hartshorne's views, such as David Ray Griffin and Marjorie Hewitt Suchocki, have explored ways of supplementing objective immortality with some form of personal survival. In *Evil Revisited: Responses and Reconsiderations* (1991) Griffin claims that a doctrine of an afterlife would help Hartshorne answer Hick's charge that process theology is elitist because the unfortunate and downtrodden of the earth may not believe that they can make a significant contribution to the divine life.

Hartshorne, however, frequently pointed out that the Book of Job addresses the problem of evil without appeal to an afterlife. Furthermore, the tragedy inherent in multiple creativity cannot, in Hartshorne's view, be rectified in an afterlife without eliminating freedom. Doctrines of the afterlife framed for the purposes of theodicy are elaborately orchestrated affairs in which God imposes a moral order that the creatures are too ignorant or too wicked to achieve for themselves. Hartshorne endorses Sigmund Freud's observation that life is not a kindergarten.

According to Hartshorne, the most inclusive values are aesthetic. As Aristotle maintained that virtue is a mean between extremes, Hartshorne says that beauty is a mean between the double extremes of order and disorder and complexity and simplicity. Too much order results in neatness, too little order in ugliness; too much simplicity yields prettiness, too much complexity yields sublimity. Hartshorne notes that aesthetic sensibilities possess a certain relativity—one must always ask, "Too much or too little for whom?" A melody that is profound for a bird may be trivial to a human being. Nevertheless, Hartshorne maintains that every being's sense of beauty preserves the basic contrasts. Hartshorne advocated a situation aesthetic, or what John Hospers calls "contextualism." He summarized his aesthetic theory in *Creative Synthesis and Philosophic Method* in a circle diagram that Max Dessoir and Kay Davis helped him develop.

Hartshorne concedes that his aesthetic theory cannot easily accommodate some of the counterexamples that can be offered. For example, a simple melody may be of surpassing beauty; if one changes a note here or there, it becomes mundane or even ugly. He resists, however, the facile relativism that says that aesthetic judgments lack any objective component; he denies that beauty is merely "in the eye of the beholder." Furthermore, his work on sensation and in ornithology made him sensitive to the biological and nonhuman dimensions of aesthetics that connect human beings to the world from which they evolved. Hartshorne's theory thus provides aesthetic reasons—in addition to economic, ethical, and ecological ones—to oppose the wholesale destruction of the environ-

ment. In *The Philosophy of Charles Hartshorne* he says that he believes that the circle diagram survives most critiques and "says vastly more, almost at a glance, than even a large number of words alone can convey."

Hartshorne continued his remarkable productivity into his nineties. *Whitehead's Philosophy: Selected Essays, 1935–1970,* a collection of previously published pieces, was followed by two shorter works that treat Whitehead in historical context: *Aquinas to Whitehead: Seven Centuries of Metaphysics of Religion* (1976), a succinct historical overview and defense of dipolar theism, and *Whitehead's View of Reality* (1981), which he co-authored with Creighton Peden (Hartshorne contributed the first three chapters).

In *The Logic of Perfection* Hartshorne maintained that "Objectivity is not in the individual thinker but in the process of mutual correction and inspiration." This ideal of objectivity was most nearly realized for Hartshorne personally in his eighth and ninth decades, during which he published dozens of articles, reviews, and forewords, and seven major books. In addition, he contributed to four books devoted to his thought, giving detailed replies to sixty-two essays by fifty-six scholars; his responses fill approximately one fourth of the pages in these books. In his late nineties he gave editorial advice on the first published volume of his correspondence, that with Edgar Sheffield Brightman (2001). With good reason he expressed concern that philosophers might find it difficult to stay abreast of his writing.

In *Insights and Oversights of Great Thinkers: An Evaluation of Western Philosophy* (1983) and *Creativity in American Philosophy* Hartshorne carries on a dialogue with the great European and American philosophers. His concern is not to report the history of philosophy but to see what can be learned from other thinkers about how to solve philosophical—and, in particular, metaphysical—problems. Hartshorne never agreed with those who see the history of philosophy as a gradual fall from some era of greatness in the past. He never doubted that philosophers of the past have important things to teach, although they often do so by way of their mistakes. To suppose, however, that progress does not occur—that Aristotle, Aquinas, or Immanuel Kant would have nothing to learn from James, Whitehead, or Hartshorne—is unreasonable. According to Hartshorne, philosophy makes halting progress that is marked by false starts, blind alleys, and flashes of insight. The history of philosophy is a laboratory for testing the truth of ideas; which system of thought is nearest the truth is no more important than which philosophers have succeeded or failed in framing and answering particular questions. The book on American philosophy makes a special case

	I	**II**	**III**	**IV**
1.	N.n	C.n	NC.n	0.n
2.	N.c	C.c	NC.c	0.c
3.	N.cn	C.cn	NC.cn	0.cn
4.	N.0	C.0	NC.0	0.0

Hartshorne's matrix (as revised slightly by Joseph Pickle) of the possible relationships of necessity and contingency as applied to God (uppercase N and C, respectively) and the world (lowercase n and c). The columns represent the possibilities for God, the rows for the world. Zero represents impossibility or lack of modal status.

for the importance of philosophy in the United States: "one might about as easily reach great heights in philosophy without benefit of the work done in modern America as to reach them in physics without using the work of modern Germans."

Hartshorne also saw Eastern traditions as an essential source of philosophic wisdom. *Philosophers Speak of God* includes some of his views on Oriental thought, as do his anthologized articles "Toward a Buddhisto-Christian Religion" (1984) and "Sankara, Nagarjuna, and Fa Tsang, with Some Western Analogues" (1988). *Charles Hartshorne's Concept of God* and *The Philosophy of Charles Hartshorne* include Hartshorne's responses to Hindu and Buddhist scholars.

Two of Hartshorne's most accessible works are *Omnipotence and Other Theological Mistakes* (1984) and *Wisdom as Moderation.* For the most part, these books are nontechnical and were written with an intelligent but nonacademic audience in mind. *Omnipotence and Other Theological Mistakes* came about as a result of conversations Hartshorne had with two educated women who were troubled by what they considered absurdities in traditional ideas of God. The book discusses these absurdities and offers dipolar theism as a reasonable alternative. *Wisdom as Moderation* is a collection of essays, about half of which previously appeared in periodicals. The main theme is that speculative philosophy, ethics, and aesthetics should avoid extremes and strive to preserve concepts that express a legitimate contrast. For example, indeterminism, unlike determinism, expresses the contrast between order and disorder. These short volumes

present no new metaphysical doctrines; if anything besides style sets them apart from the rest of Hartshorne's corpus, it is their practical wisdom. Hartshorne addresses within the framework of neoclassical metaphysics issues as diverse as abortion, illiteracy, near-death experiences, fundamentalism, animal rights, drugs (including nicotine and caffeine), nuclear arms, and even furniture size. *Wisdom as Moderation* has a chapter on the relationship between his work in metaphysics and in ornithology.

Hartshorne's openness to new perspectives, even late in his life, was nowhere more evident than in his treatment of feminism. He regarded the movement to make abortion illegal as a remnant of male chauvinism. In *The Darkness and the Light* he says, "My sympathy for actual persons, including pregnant mothers, is far stronger than my sympathy for fertilized eggs." Inverting the Aristotelian-Thomistic idea that women are incomplete men, he argues in *The Philosophy of Charles Hartshorne,* following the anthropologist Ashley Montague, that physiologically men, not women, are incomplete: only a woman can provide life support for the unborn and milk for the infant. He also argues, in *Omnipotence and Other Theological Mistakes,* that women are wiser than men, citing as evidence the fact that women commit far fewer crimes and antisocial acts. In *Hartshorne and Brightman on God, Process, and Persons* (2001) he said that, if given the chance, he would retitle his third book "Our Vision of God." Finally, recognizing the bias of traditional theology in speaking and conceiving of deity in exclusively male terms, he adopted inclusive lan-

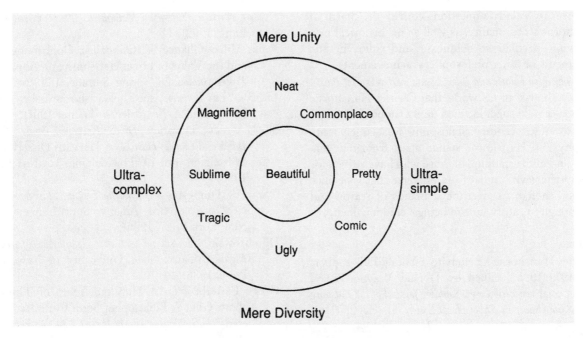

*Hartshorne's aesthetic theory as summarized in a diagram that he devised
with the assistance of Max Dessoir and Kay Davis*

guage for God. He said, however, that in some respects the female rather than the male furnishes the best symbol for deity: the nearest approximation in human experience to the existence of human beings as part of the body of God (the universe) and of divine love is the relationship between the mother and the developed fetus.

Hartshorne published several articles on his life and thought, but the most complete account is his autobiography, *The Darkness and the Light: A Philosopher Reflects upon His Fortunate Career and Those Who Made It Possible,* published in 1990. The title reflects the elements of his philosophy: "the darkness and the light" is from a poem by William Wordsworth that conveys the idea that bonds of mutual feeling among the elements, creatures, and God unify nature. The reference in the subtitle to "his fortunate career and those who made it possible" points to the theme, reiterated throughout the book, that life is a gamble and that success or failure is as much due to good or bad self-management as to good or bad luck. The idea that chance is only a name for ignorance or that everything that happens must have a precise reason is, he says, "only ignorance posing as knowledge." In the preface he calls the book "a celebration of life." Anecdotes sprinkled throughout illustrate what he calls his "strange flair for preserving foibles and witticisms."

The Philosophy of Charles Hartshorne, volume 20 in the prestigious Library of Living Philosophers series, appeared in 1991. Hartshorne had contributed to

eight of the previous volumes in the series—more than any other philosopher. As Hartshorne's former student Cobb says, the philosophical community had recognized "a strange and alien greatness."

Hartshorne's wife died on 21 November 1995. *The Zero Fallacy and Other Essays in Neoclassical Philosophy* was published shortly before Hartshorne's one-hundredth birthday. The editor, Mohammad Valady, selected both new and previously published essays to show the breadth of Hartshorne's thought. The familiar themes are present: the metaphysical necessity of God's existence, the emphasis on divine love over brute force, and the eminent ways in which God receives influence from the world. On the other hand, Hartshorne's assessment of the specifically human contribution to the divine life now joins cosmic perspective with moral and aesthetic condemnation. Human beings' destruction of the environment, penchant for driving other species to extinction, and cruelty to each other on a mass scale make the species the "bullies of the planet." Hartshorne asks whether the placing of the "billions of other solar systems out of our reach" is a providential arrangement. Suggesting that it is "our very selves that we need to recreate," he advises human beings to take their isolation in the vastness of the cosmos seriously and develop a sense of world citizenship. A unique feature of the book is the forty-two-page "Points of View: A Brisk Dialogue," based on conversations Hartshorne and Valady had between 1986 and 1988. Hartshorne's responses to Valady's questions convey the charm of Hartshorne's personality, as well as his historical perspective, speculative boldness, and idiosyncratic assessments of other philosophers' achievements.

The Zero Fallacy and Other Essays in Neoclassical Philosophy was the last of his works that Charles Hartshorne lived to see published. He died on 9 October 2000.

Twentieth-century philosophy was largely antimetaphysical. Hartshorne stands apart from that tendency and in the tradition of those who have striven for a comprehensive vision of the universe that is at once rigorous enough to meet the demands of reason and rich enough to satisfy human beings' emotional nature.

Letters:

"Charles Hartshorne's Letters to a Young Philosopher: 1979–1995," edited by Donald Wayne Viney, special issue of *Logos-Sophia: Journal of the Pittsburg State University Philosophical Society*, 11 (Fall 2001);

Hartshorne and Brightman on God, Process, and Persons: The Correspondence, 1922–1945, edited by Randall E. Auxier and Mark Y. A. Davies (Nashville: Vanderbilt University Press, 2001).

Bibliographies:

Dorothy C. Hartshorne, "Charles Hartshorne: Secondary Bibliography," *Process Studies*, 3 (Fall 1973): 179–277;

Dean R. Fowler, "Bibliography of Dissertations and Theses on Charles Hartshorne," *Process Studies*, 3 (Winter 1973): 304–307;

Hartshorne, "Charles Hartshorne: 1980 Bibliographical Addenda," *Process Studies*, 11 (Summer 1981): 108–150;

Fowler, "Addenda to Bibliography of Dissertations and Theses on Charles Hartshorne," *Process Studies*, 11 (Summer 1981): 151–152;

Hartshorne, "Charles Hartshorne: Primary Bibliography," in *The Philosophy of Charles Hartshorne*, edited by Lewis Edwin Hahn, The Library of Living Philosophers, volume 20 (La Salle, Ill.: Open Court, 1991), pp. 735–766;

Hartshorne, Donald Wayne Viney, and Randy Ramal, "Charles Hartshorne: Primary Bibliography of Philosophical Works," *Process Studies*, 30 (Fall–Winter 2001): 374–409.

References:

American Journal of Theology and Philosophy, special Hartshorne issue, edited by J. Wesley Robbins and Jennifer G. Jesse, 22 (May 2001);

Gregory A. Boyd, *Trinity and Process: A Critical Evaluation and Reconstruction of Hartshorne's Di-Polar Theism towards a Trinitarian Metaphysics* (New York: Peter Lang, 1992);

Anita Miller Chancey, "Rationality, Contributionism, and the Value of Love: Hartshorne on Abortion," *Process Studies*, 28 (Spring–Summer 1999): 85–97;

Creative Transformation, special Hartshorne issue, edited by William A. Beardslee, 6 (Winter 1997);

Sheila Greeve Davaney, *Divine Power: A Study of Karl Barth and Charles Hartshorne*, Harvard Dissertations in Religion, no. 19 (Philadelphia: Fortress Press, 1986);

Daniel A. Dombrowski, *Analytic Theism, Hartshorne, and the Concept of God* (Albany: State University of New York Press, 1996);

Dombrowski, *Hartshorne and the Metaphysics of Animal Rights* (Albany: State University of New York Press, 1988);

Gregg Easterbrook, "A Hundred Years of Thinking about God: A Philosopher Soon to Be Rediscovered," *U.S. News & World Report*, 124 (23 February 1998): 61, 65;

Lewis S. Ford, ed., *Two Process Philosophers: Hartshorne's Encounter with Whitehead* (Tallahassee, Fla.: American Academy of Religion, 1973);

Martin Gardner, *The Whys of a Philosophical Scrivener* (New York: Quill, 1983), p. 251;

George L. Goodwin, *The Ontological Argument of Charles Hartshorne* (Missoula: Montana Scholars Press, 1978);

Alan Gragg, *Charles Hartshorne, Maker of the Modern Theological Mind*, edited by Bob E. Patterson (Waco, Tex.: Word Books, 1973);

David Ray Griffin, *Evil Revisited: Responses and Reconsiderations* (Albany: State University of New York Press, 1991);

Lewis Edwin Hahn, ed., *The Philosophy of Charles Hartshorne*, The Library of Living Philosophers, volume 20 (La Salle, Ill.: Open Court, 1991);

John Hick, "A Critique of the 'Second Argument,'" in *The Many-Faced Argument*, edited by Hick and Arthur C. McGill (New York: Macmillan, 1976), pp. 341–356;

Ralph E. James, *The Concrete God: A New Beginning for Theology—The Thought of Charles Hartshorne* (Indianapolis: Bobbs-Merrill, 1967);

Robert Kane and Stephen H. Phillips, eds., *Hartshorne, Process Philosophy and Theology* (Albany: State University of New York Press, 1989);

Tomasz Komendzinski, ed., *God, Nature and Process Thought: Essays on the Philosophy and Theology of Charles Hartshorne* (forthcoming);

William S. Minor, ed., *Charles Hartshorne and Henry Nelson Wieman* (Lanham, Md.: University Press of America, 1969);

Randall C. Morris, *Process Philosophy and Political Ideology: The Social and Political Thought of Alfred North Whitehead and Charles Hartshorne* (Albany: State University of New York Press, 1991);

John C. Moskop, *Divine Omniscience and Human Freedom: Thomas Aquinas and Charles Hartshorne* (Macon, Ga.: Mercer University Press, 1984);

David A. Pailin, *God and the Processes of Reality: Foundations of a Credible Theism* (London: Routledge, 1989);

Personalist Forum, special Hartshorne issue, edited by William Myers, 14 (Fall 1998);

Eugene H. Peters, *Hartshorne and Neoclassical Metaphysics* (Lincoln: University of Nebraska Press, 1970);

Peters, "Philosophic Insights of Charles Hartshorne," *Southwestern Journal of Philosophy,* 7 (1976): 157–170;

Process Studies, special Hartshorne issue, edited by Marjorie Hewitt Suchocki and John B. Cobb Jr., 21 (Summer 1992);

Process Studies, special Hartshorne issue, 30 (Fall–Winter 2001);

Andrew J. Reck, "The Philosophy of Charles Hartshorne," *Tulane Studies in Philosophy,* 10 (May 1961): 89–108;

George W. Shields, "Hartshorne and the Analytic Philosophical Tradition," in *Faith and Creativity: Essays in Honor of Eugene H. Peters,* edited by Shields and George Nordugulen (St. Louis: CBP Press, 1987), pp. 197–228;

Shields, ed., *Process and Analysis: Essays on Whitehead, Hartshorne, and the Analytic Tradition* (Albany: State University of New York Press, 2002);

Santiago Sia, *God in Process Thought: A Study in Charles Hartshorne's Concept of God* (Dordrecht, Netherlands: Nijhoff, 1985);

Sia, ed., *Charles Hartshorne's Concept of God: Philosophical and Theological Responses* (Dordrecht, Netherlands: Kluwer, 1990);

Sia, ed., *Process Theology and the Christian Doctrine of God* (Petersham, Mass.: St. Bede's, 1986);

David Tracy, "Analogy, Metaphor and God-Language: Charles Hartshorne," *Modern Schoolman,* 62 (May 1985): 249–264;

Donald Wayne Viney, *Charles Hartshorne and the Existence of God* (Albany: State University of New York Press, 1985);

Viney, "Does Omniscience Imply Foreknowledge? Craig on Hartshorne," *Process Studies,* 18 (Spring 1989): 30–37;

Viney, "How to Argue for God's Existence: Reflections on Hartshorne's Global Argument," *Midwest Quarterly,* 28 (Autumn 1986): 36–49;

Viney, "In Defense of the Global Argument: A Reply to Professor Luft," *Process Studies,* 16 (Winter 1987): 309–311;

Viney and Rebecca Viney, "For the Beauty of the Earth: A Hartshornean Ecological Aesthetic," in *Proceedings of the Institute for Liberal Studies Science, Technology and Religious Ideas* (Frankfort: Kentucky State University, 1993), pp. 38–44;

Barry L. Whitney, *Evil and the Process God* (Toronto & New York: Edwin Mellen Press, 1985);

Forest Wood Jr. and Michael DeArmey, eds., *Hartshorne's Neo-Classical Theology,* Tulane Studies in Philosophy, no. 34 (New Orleans: Tulane University, 1986).

Papers:

Charles Hartshorne's philosophical papers and letters are at the Center for Process Studies in Claremont, California. His ornithological papers and letters are at the Florida Museum of Natural History in Gainesville.

William Ernest Hocking

(10 August 1873 – 12 June 1966)

John Howie
Southern Illinois University at Carbondale

BOOKS: *A Union for Ethical Action,* by Hocking and Howard Woolston (Cambridge, Mass.: Privately printed, 1904);

The Necessary and Sufficient Conditions of Human Happiness (Stanford, Cal.: Stanford University Press, 1907);

The Meaning of God in Human Experience: A Philosophic Study of Religion (New Haven: Yale University Press / London: Humphrey Milford, Oxford University Press, 1912);

Human Nature and Its Remaking (New Haven: Yale University Press / London: Humphrey Milford, Oxford University Press, 1918; revised, 1923);

Morale and Its Enemies (New Haven: Yale University Press, 1918);

Present Status of the Philosophy of Law and of Rights (New Haven: Yale University Press / London: Humphrey Milford, Oxford University Press, 1926);

Man and the State (New Haven: Yale University Press / London: Humphrey Milford, Oxford University Press, 1926);

The Self, Its Body and Freedom (New Haven: Yale University Press / London: Humphrey Milford, Oxford University Press, 1928);

Types of Philosophy (New York: Scribners, 1929; revised, 1939; revised, by Hocking and Richard Boyle O'Reilly Hocking, 1959);

The Spirit of World Politics: With Special Studies of the Near East (New York: Macmillan, 1932);

Evangelism: An Address on Permanence and Change in Church and Mission (Chicago: Movement for World Christianity, 1935);

George Herbert Palmer, 1842–1933: Memorial Address (Cambridge, Mass.: Harvard University Press, 1935);

Thoughts on Death and Life (New York & London: Harper, 1937); revised and enlarged as *The Meaning of Immortality in Human Experience, Including Thoughts on Death and Life, Revised* (New York: Harper, 1957);

The Lasting Elements of Individualism (New Haven: Yale University Press, 1937);

William Ernest Hocking

Living Religions and a World Faith (New York: Macmillan, 1940; London: Allen & Unwin, 1940);

What Man Can Make of Man (New York & London: Harper, 1942);

Arab Nationalism and Political Zionism (Flint, Mich.: League of American-Arab Committee for Democracy, 1944);

The Church and the New World Mind, by Hocking and others (St. Louis: Bethany Press, 1944);

Science and the Idea of God (Chapel Hill: University of North Carolina Press, 1944);

The Immortality of Man (Lancaster, Pa., 1945);

Preface to Philosophy: Textbook, by Hocking, Brand Blanshard, Charles William Hendel, and John Herman Randall Jr. (New York: Macmillan, 1946);

Freedom of the Press: A Framework of Principle. A Report from the Commission on Freedom of the Press (Chicago: University of Chicago Press, 1947);

Freedom of the Press in America: Inaugural Address Delivered on His Entrance into Office as Guest Professor at the University of Leyden on Friday, 24 October 1947 (Leiden: Leiden University Press, 1947);

Experiment in Education: What We Can Learn from Teaching Germany (Chicago: Regnery, 1954);

The Coming World Civilization (New York: Harper, 1956; London: Allen & Unwin, 1958);

Strength of Men and Nations: A Message to the USA vis-à-vis the USSR (New York: Harper, 1959).

OTHER: "The Postulates," in *Immanuel Kant, 1724–1924,* edited by E. C. Wilm (New Haven: Yale University Press, 1925), pp. 37–49;

"Mind and Near-Mind," in *Proceedings of the 6th International Congress of Philosophy, 1926,* edited by Edgar Sheffield Brightman (New York: Longmans, Green, 1927), pp. lxxv–lxxvii;

"Religion of the Future," in *Religion and Modern Life,* edited by L. B. R. Briggs (New York: Scribners, 1927), pp. 343–370;

"What Philosophy Says," in *An Anthology of Recent Philosophy,* edited by D. S. Robinson (New York: Crowell, 1929), pp. 33–44;

"Some Second Principles," in *Contemporary American Philosophy: Personal Statements,* volume 1, edited by George Plimpton Adams and William Pepperell Montague (New York: Macmillan, 1930);

Charles A. Bennett, *The Dilemma of Religious Knowledge,* edited by Hocking (New Haven: Yale University Press / London: Humphrey Milford, Oxford University Press, 1931);

"The Ontological Argument in Royce and Others," in *Contemporary Idealism in America,* edited by Clifford Barrett (New York: Macmillan, 1932), pp. 45–66;

Commission of Appraisal of the Laymen's Foreign Missions Inquiry, *Re-Thinking Missions: A Laymen's Inquiry after One Hundred Years,* edited, with contributions, by Hocking (New York: Harper, 1932);

"Can Values Be Taught?" in *The Obligation of Universities to the Social Order,* edited by Henry Pratt Fairchild (New York: New York University Press, 1933), pp. 332–350;

"Josiah Royce (1855–1916)," in *Encyclopedia of the Social Sciences,* volume 13, edited by Edwin R. A. Seligman and Alvin Johnson (New York: Macmillan, 1934), pp. 451b–452a;

"Christianity and Intercultural Contacts," in *Modern Trends in World Religions,* edited by A. E. Haydon (Chicago: University of Chicago Press, 1934), pp. 141–152;

George Herbert Palmer, 1842–1933: Memorial Addresses, edited, with a contribution, by Hocking (Cambridge, Mass.: Harvard University Press, 1935);

"Ways of Thinking about Rights: A New Theory of the Relation between Law and Morals," in *Law: A Century of Progress, 1835–1935,* volume 2 (New York: New York University Press, 1937), pp. 242–265;

"Outline-Sketch of a System of Metaphysics," in *Philosophical Essays in Memory of Edmund Husserl,* edited by Marvin Farber (Cambridge, Mass.: Harvard University Press, 1940), pp. 251–261;

"Whitehead on Mind and Nature," in *The Philosophy of Alfred North Whitehead,* edited by Paul Arthur Schilpp, The Library of Living Philosophers, volume 3 (Evanston, Ill.: Northwestern University Press, 1941), pp. 383–404;

"The Cultural and Religious Organization of the Future," in *Toward International Organization,* edited by Ernest Hatch Wilkins (New York: Harper, 1942), pp. 162–188;

"The Mystical Spirit," in *Protestantism: A Symposium,* edited by William K. Anderson (Nashville, Tenn.: Methodist Church Commission on Courses of Study, 1944), pp. 185–195;

"Value of the Comparative Study of Philosophy," in *Philosophy–East and West,* edited by Charles A. Moore (Princeton: Princeton University Press, 1944), pp. 1–11;

"The Treatment of Ex-Enemy Nations," in *Christianity Takes a Stand: An Approach to the Issues of Today,* edited by William Scarlett (New York: Penguin, 1946), pp. 42–56;

"Justice, Law, and the Cases," in *Interpretations of Modern Legal Philosophies,* edited by Paul Sayre (New York: Oxford University Press, 1947), pp. 332–351;

James Bissett Pratt, *Reason in the Art of Living,* foreword by Hocking (New York: Macmillan, 1949);

"The Binding Ingredients of Civilization," in *Goethe and the Modern Age,* edited by Arnold Bergstraesser (Chicago: Regnery, 1950), pp. 252–283;

Charles Hartshorne, *Reality as Social Process: Studies in Metaphysics and Religion,* foreword by Hocking (Glencoe, Ill.: Free Press, 1953);

Gabriel Marcel, *Royce's Metaphysics,* translated by V. Ringer and G. Ringer, foreword by Hocking (Chicago: Regnery, 1956);

"History and the Absolute," in *Philosophy, Religion, and the Coming World Civilization,* edited by Leroy S. Rouner (The Hague: Nijhoff, 1966), pp. 423–463.

SELECTED PERIODICAL PUBLICATIONS–
UNCOLLECTED: "What Is Number?" *Intelligence: A Journal of Education,* 18 (15 May 1898): 360–362;

"The Function of Science in Shaping Philosophic Method," *Journal of Philosophy, Psychology and Scientific Methods,* 2 (30 August 1905): 477–486;

"The Transcendence of Knowledge," *Journal of Philosophy, Psychology and Scientific Methods,* 3 (4 January 1906): 5–12;

"The Group Concept in the Service of Philosophy," *Journal of Philosophy, Psychology and Scientific Methods,* 3 (2 August 1906): 421–431;

"The Religious Function of State Universities," *University of California Chronicle,* 10 (October 1908): 454–466;

"How Can Christianity Be the Final Religion?" *Yale Divinity Quarterly,* 5 (March 1909): 266–288;

"Two Extensions of the Use of Graphs in Elementary Logic," *University of California Publications in Philosophy,* 2 (17 May 1909): 31–44;

"On the Law of History," *University of California Publications in Philosophy,* 2 (17 September 1909): 45–65;

"Analogy and Scientific Method in Philosophy," *Journal of Philosophy, Psychology and Scientific Methods,* 7 (16 March 1910): 161;

"The Significance of Bergson," *Yale Review,* 3 (January 1914): 303–326;

"Political Philosophy in Germany," *Journal of Philosophy,* 12 (14 October 1915): 584–586;

"Instinct in Social Psychology," *Journal of Abnormal and Social Psychology,* 18 (July–September 1923): 153–166;

"Illicit Naturalizing in Religion," *Journal of Religion,* 3 (November 1923): 561–599;

"Leaders and Led," *Yale Review,* 13 (July 1924): 625–641;

"The Working of the Mandates," *Yale Review,* 19 (December 1929): 244–268;

"Social Censorship," *Outlook and Independent,* 153 (11 December 1929): 579;

"Action and Certainty," *Journal of Philosophy,* 27 (24 April 1930): 225–238;

"Religion and the Alleged Passing of Liberalism," *Advance,* 126 (3 May 1934): 86–88;

"What Has Philosophy to Say about Education?" *Harvard Alumni Bulletin,* 37 (2 November 1934): 161–164;

"Does Civilization Still Need Religion?" *Christendom,* 1 (October 1935): 31–43;

"Chu Hsi's Theory of Knowledge," *Harvard Journal of Asiatic Studies,* 1 (April 1936): 109–127;

"Philosophy–the Business of Everyman," *Journal of the American Association of University Women,* 30 (June 1937): 212–217;

"Fact and Destiny," *Glasgow Herald,* 18 January 1938, 21 January 1938, 28 January 1938, 4 February 1938, 11 February 1938, 18 February 1938, 25 February 1938, 4 March 1938, 11 March 1938, 17 March 1938, 30 November 1938, 3 December 1938, 7 December 1938, 10 December 1938, 14 December 1938, 17 December 1938, 11 January 1939, 14 January 1939, 18 January 1939, 21 January 1939;

"Dewey's Concepts of Experience and Nature," *Philosophical Review,* 49 (March 1940): 228–244;

"The Nature of Morale," *American Journal of Sociology,* 47 (November 1941): 302–320;

"Fact and Destiny (I)," *Review of Metaphysics,* 4 (September 1950): 1–12;

"Fact and Destiny (II)," *Review of Metaphysics,* 4 (March 1951): 319–342;

"Marcel and the Ground Issues of Metaphysics," *Philosophy and Phenomenological Research,* 14 (June 1954): 439–469.

An "objective idealist" philosopher who spent the largest portion of his long career at Harvard University, William Ernest Hocking was an influential teacher and a prolific writer. His interests and writings in philosophy left hardly any facet of the subject untouched–philosophy of religion, human nature, political and social philosophy, comparative religion, and philosophy of law. While standing in the idealist tradition and strongly influenced by Josiah Royce, Hocking appropriated elements from William James's radical empiricism and incorporated the chief insights of mysticism. He believed that experience in its most primitive form is already social, involving a knowledge of other human minds and an immediate awareness of God as Other Mind.

Hocking was never narrowly concerned with intellectual issues. He underscored repeatedly, in word and deed, that philosophy is no armchair endeavor. "If the teachings of a philosopher seem esoteric or divorced from reality," he remarked, "it's the fault of the philosopher." Hocking often applied his philosophical views to action in the public realm: he participated in the rebuilding of San Francisco after the 1906 earthquake and fire; tried to get the United States to join the League of Nations; cofounded with his wife the Shady Hill experimental school in Cambridge, Massachusetts, in 1915; and supported the Arab cause against Israel and wrote a book on the social and political problems of the Middle East. With others he undertook a careful study of Protestant missionary work in the Far East and served as the author of its final report that advocated extensive changes. He served as chairman and author of the report of the Commission on Freedom of the Press. After extensive investigation and research, he published a book on post–World War II education in Germany, emphasizing where the United States could improve its perspective and treatment. His last book encouraged dialogue and cooperation in areas of common concern between the United States and the Soviet Union. He relished talking to labor-union schools in Oakland and Boston, because he admired the honesty of the workers.

Hocking's writing style was discursive, dialectical, and spiced with poetry quotations. Leaving aside the usual philosophical arguments for proving or disproving a view, he relied on a "negative pragmatism" to disclose the falsity of a belief and a more thorough questioning procedure he called "empirical dialectic" to convince a doubter of the truth of a position. The task, as he saw it, was to explain ideas and to permit one's listener or reader to reach his or her own conviction. The process involves no coercion; no genuine belief was possible apart from the inner assent that the individual alone must grant.

Hocking was born in Cleveland, Ohio, on 10 August 1873, the first child and only son of William Francis Hocking, a homeopathic physician, and Julia Carpenter Pratt Hocking, a teacher. When he was eight the family moved to Joliet, Illinois, where he and his four sisters were brought up as Methodists. The parents were devoutly religious: every day, after breakfast, the family knelt in a circle for prayers. Each of the children would recite a Bible verse committed to memory the previous day.

Hocking described his conversion to Leroy S. Rouner as occurring at the age of twelve during a Methodist "special meeting" held on a Sunday evening in Joliet. "A presence felt, a reality perceived" brought Hocking, with tears streaming, to the altar. The experience included a vision of himself as a part of a "great procession" of humankind, each member having an immortal soul, and left him with a sense of relief and assurance.

After graduating from Joliet High School at fifteen, Hocking earned money for college as a surveyor for a railroad, a mapmaker, and a printer's devil. After the Panic of 1893 he joined his family in Newton, Iowa, where he worked for the summer teaching Latin at Newton Normal School. In 1894 he entered Iowa State College of Agriculture in Ames as an engineering student.

At the suggestion of the librarian at Ames, Hocking read James's *The Principles of Psychology* (1890) and was enthralled by James's description of a world that is experimental and lively, full of excitement and adventure. Here, Hocking thought, was a scholar who

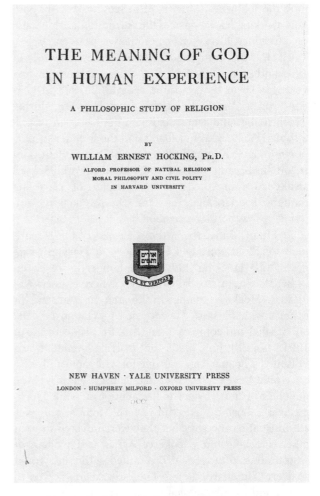

THE MEANING OF GOD
IN HUMAN EXPERIENCE

A PHILOSOPHIC STUDY OF RELIGION

BY

WILLIAM ERNEST HOCKING, Ph.D.
ALFORD PROFESSOR OF NATURAL RELIGION
MORAL PHILOSOPHY AND CIVIL POLITY
IN HARVARD UNIVERSITY

NEW HAVEN · YALE UNIVERSITY PRESS
LONDON · HUMPHREY MILFORD · OXFORD UNIVERSITY PRESS

Title page for the 1912 book in which Hocking counters the then-dominant philosophy of absolute idealism with his more personalistic view of God (Thomas Cooper Library, University of South Carolina)

was well acquainted with facts and yet admitted that humans had creative possibilities. Hocking decided that whatever the cost, he must go to Harvard to study with the author. He left Iowa State at the end of his second year and took a job teaching business mathematics at Duncan's Business College in Davenport, Iowa. A year later he was made principal of Public School Number 1 in Davenport. As principal he published in an education journal his first philosophical essay, "What Is Number?" (1898). It was a criticism of the John Dewey-James Alexander McLellan method of teaching arithmetic. After serving in the post for four years, he had earned enough to undertake his studies at Harvard.

Hocking enrolled at Harvard in 1899, only to find James away delivering Gifford Lectures. His disappointment was assuaged when he took some courses from Royce, whose idealistic philosophy Hocking found compatible with his own experiences and beliefs. Hocking took the following summer off to see the Paris Exposition, working his way across the Atlantic as a cattle hand on a freighter. It was the first of many trips overseas.

Hocking completed his undergraduate work in 1901 and earned his A.M. from Harvard the following year. He spent the academic year 1902–1903 in Germany on a Walker Fellowship from Harvard, during which he became acquainted with the historian of philosophy Wilhelm Windelband and the founder of phenomenology, Edmund Husserl, whose student and friend he became. His personal contact with Husserl awakened him to the mental agony of clarifying thought. For Hocking, this task requires "creative suffering" or "suffering in creation."

Hugo Münsterberg, the chairman of the Department of Philosophy and Psychology at Harvard, suggested that Hocking study at the University of Berlin rather than at provincial Göttingen, where Husserl was located. Hocking complied, although he kept up his contact with Husserl. He returned to Harvard in the fall of 1903 and completed the work for his doctorate in 1904. On 28 June 1905 he married Agnes Boyle O'Reilly. The marriage was one for which most observers would have predicted dismal failure: Agnes was the daughter of an Irish poet and revolutionist, while Hocking was a business-like Midwestern Methodist. It was an unusual partnership, but they were devoted to each other. Hocking often spoke of Agnes as a woman of "astounding courage." When asked why, he would answer: "She married me." Their interaction served to enrich and to enlarge their creativity; Agnes is reputed to have required Hocking to rewrite the first chapter of *The Meaning of God in Human Experience: A Philosophic Study of Religion* (1912) thirteen times, and she claimed, with justification, that the chapter on prayer was "her chapter." They also worked together in the founding of Shady Hill School in Cambridge. It was a notable success in which he served as the formulator of principles and she as the dynamic spirit. They had three children: Richard, Hester, and Joan. Richard followed his father into the field of philosophy and became chairman of the department at Emory University. Agnes Hocking died in May 1955.

Hocking taught comparative religion at Andover Seminary from 1904 to 1906 and then, on an invitation from George Holmes Howison, spent two years at the University of California at Berkeley. In 1908 he joined the philosophy department at Yale University. Four years later he attracted widespread attention with the publication of *The Meaning of God in Human Experience,* in which he sets forth the major outline of his philosophical perspective. The book was written to meet a widely felt demand. The dominant philosophy of the time was absolute idealism, which had been brought from Germany to England by T. H. Green and F. H. Bradley and had the impressive support of Royce in the United States. To many religious people this view was overintellectual and took no account of the personal God of traditional Christianity. Against the charge of intellectualism, Hocking insists pragmatically that what does not "work" is not true. To counter the second difficulty he says that the absolute enters into personal religious life through mystical experience. He was able to win more assent to the first proposition than to the second.

From James, Hocking adopts what he calls a "negative pragmatism," the methodological principle that whatever does not work is not true: any theory that brings about no difference in people's lives, has no results, or has only undesirable consequences is in some way false. Hocking does not, however, accept pragmatism as a positive principle: the notion that whatever works is true he considers useless and invalid. A proposition is true not because it works but because it meets the standards of what Hocking calls the "empirical dialectic," the chief of which is coherence.

Hocking understands the term *empirical* in an inclusive sense. It is not restricted to what is given in human experience as described by the natural sciences; it includes the rational activity of mind, making possible a solution to the problem of creativity. This problem, as Hocking remarked in an unpublished letter to John Howie of 4 September 1961, is "the central mystery of metaphysics and the occasion of many a philosophical shipwreck." The empirical aspect of Hocking's method requires that one proceed from part to whole, but it does not assume that any account of the parts can provide an understanding of the whole. To understand the whole one must understand its origin and its goal or destination, but no mere account of the parts can provide this understanding. Hocking's empiricism calls for a preliminary attitude of acceptance of the given—an acknowledgment of the importance of sense-data—but insists that further questions must be asked and answered. Hocking's empiricism is not opposed to system building; in fact, a system is required for the placing of new experiences. System is the "inner coherence" of assent to propositions and "understanding-through-experience."

Hocking uses the term *dialectic* to designate "conceptual reasoning" as a process for understanding, rather than merely describing, the world. Understanding requires insight into the deductive relationships of entities. To understand, he says, is to explain in a "heterotypal" manner: to account for something in terms of what it is not rather than in terms of what it is. Heterotypal understanding will account for newness, as well as difference. For Hocking, dialectic is the midwife of understanding.

Empirical dialectic enables the thinker to test hypotheses by observing the positive and negative effects of experience when the hypothesis is taken as the basis for action. Any partially false position will provide a tendency toward a more reliable viewpoint. The empirical dialectic can help one to eliminate erroneous presuppositions and definitions and to confirm a priori truths that are indispensable prerequisites of experience itself. The empirical dialectic proceeds by an alternation of attention and interests that is dictated by human nature itself: prolonged and uninterrupted attention to the parts or details generates fatigue, which leads to a concern for the whole; by the same token, a focus on the whole will, in time, foster a desire to know about the parts or details. "Empirical knowledge," Hocking explains, "grows from a sketch, in which the whole is outlined and parts are placed by internal development of structure and detail."

Feeling, Hocking says, is the undifferentiated consciousness out of which the intellect and will develop. Feeling in this deep, pervasive, undifferentiated sense is aroused in religious or mystical experience. At this level feeling and idea are fused. In returning to this combined feeling-idea state one connects with the "will-circuit" of God or Reality. Love, a complex form of feeling, is the forerunner of the idea, and the idea is the forerunner of action.

The core of *The Meaning of God in Human Experience,* and of Hocking's philosophy as a whole, is the account in chapters 17 through 20 of how communication is possible. Hocking argues that the knowledge that one would desire to have of other people's minds is precisely the knowledge one actually has. One wants to know nature as it is experienced by the other mind. "Nature," Hocking explains, "may be interpreted . . . as the visible pledge and immediate evidence of our living contact." In knowing the commonality of space, time, and motion, one knows other minds. One's experience of nature is always a social experience; even the experience of solitariness, Hocking points out, presupposes commonality of sensible barriers. Social experience is inseparable from physical experience. This world of nature held in common makes communication possible. The "idea" of other minds has special qualities; it is not built up by extending or enlarging or combining other known relations. The idea of other minds is, at the same time, the experience of other minds. It is "a concrete a priori knowledge."

Thus, human knowledge is triadic. It involves knowing natural objects as those objects are known by another mind, knowing the self reflexively, and knowing (having an "idea" of) the other mind. The "reflexive turn of consciousness which takes notice of the self, as of something always present, must, if we are right, dis-

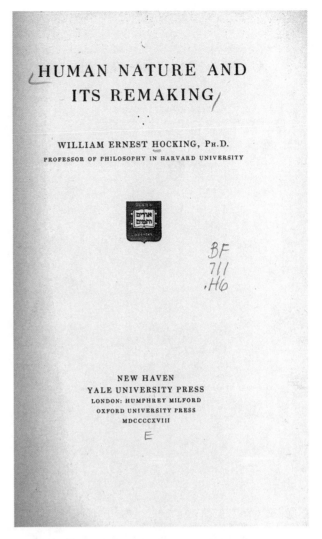

Hocking's second major book, in which he discusses the principles involved in educating, civilizing, and converting human beings (Thomas Cooper Library, University of South Carolina)

cover the other also, my other I, perpetual sustainer of universality in my judgments of experience." Hocking extends this argument to the mind of God: "Space and Nature are numerically one, and I by my community with Other Mind, am born inheritor of that one identical object; in so far, I have an infallible element in my knowledge of my finite comrades, as well as in my knowledge of God."

The book led to Hocking's appointment in 1914 as professor of philosophy at Harvard. His service there was interrupted by World War I. Enlisting in the army in the summer of 1916, he underwent basic training at Plattsburgh, New York, and in 1917 was sent to England and France with the first American military engineers. On leave in London he met the historian Arnold Toynbee. He returned to the States

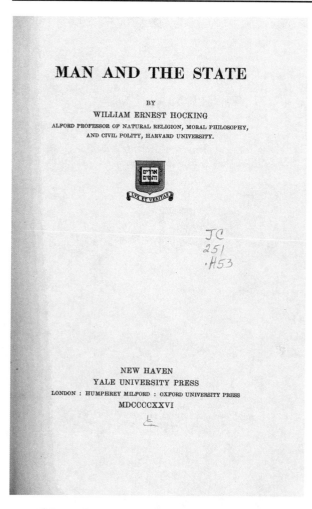

MAN AND THE STATE

BY
WILLIAM ERNEST HOCKING
ALFORD PROFESSOR OF NATURAL RELIGION, MORAL PHILOSOPHY,
AND CIVIL POLITY, HARVARD UNIVERSITY.

NEW HAVEN
YALE UNIVERSITY PRESS
LONDON : HUMPHREY MILFORD : OXFORD UNIVERSITY PRESS
MDCCCCXXVI

Title page for a work in which Hocking proposes a political philosophy of "organic pluralism" that steers a middle ground between atomistic individualism and an organic view of the state (Thomas Cooper Library, University of South Carolina)

when he was appointed inspector of war issues. His military experiences provided the basis for his *Morale and Its Enemies* (1918).

Hocking's second major book, *Human Nature and Its Remaking* (1918), deals with the principles that govern the process of educating, civilizing, and converting human beings. Human beings, he says, consist of a set of urges or instincts seeking fulfillment. All of these urges, which include curiosity, play, pugnacity, and fear, are channels for a single "will to suffer in creation." Creators must be "hard," as the German philosopher Friedrich Nietzsche said, but their toughness, according to Hocking, is a "power *for*," not a "power *over*." Nature has made human beings, but social actions and their own efforts continually remake them. Holding before it an idea of the good, the self, through its activities and experiences, forms an "ideal" that enables it to develop a stable policy.

Experience is the cooperation of inner and outer factors of change. The outer factor is social experience, which provides data and tools essential for interaction; the inner factors are will and conscience. Society extends the vestibule of satisfaction and limits the range of objects with which one can be concerned. The state, as an expression of society, is essential for the noncompetitive satisfaction of the will. Religion provides the social cohesion and loyalty that are indispensable for the maintenance of society.

The "dialectic of will" consists of the alternation of focus between the public order, symbolized by ambition, and the private order, epitomized by love. Ambition seeks to express the will to power in public actions. Love wants a mutuality of life in which each appreciates in the other what the other essentially is, rather than what the other does.

Art and religion increase the energies of creativity. Religion is motivated by a craving for a restoration of creative power; the source of this power is a perception of reality. This perception is what the mystic attains. Religion remakes or transforms human nature by satisfying the whole will to power and fulfilling the final meaning of love by conferring immortality. Religion both demands and provides for the complete transformation or remaking of human nature: "If God exists as a good will, that will must do its work in the world of time and event as a will to power not wholly unlike our own, and so coming to itself, as we must, through the saving of others." If Christianity is to remake human nature, it must transform sexuality, pugnacity, and ambition by sublimation so that the human will to power may find creative expression. Christianity reforms sex-love into a nurture of the creative potentiality in the beloved. It remakes pugnacity into an opposing of an enemy's ill will in the name of an ideal self. It converts worldly ambition into the spiritual aim of serving all. What begins as a power over finds its ultimate fulfillment as a power for. The will to power changes into a will to confer spiritual life.

In 1920 Hocking was named to the Alford Chair of Natural Religion, Moral Philosophy, and Civil Polity at Harvard. In *Present Status of the Philosophy of Law and of Rights* (1926), which originated in joint seminars with professor of jurisprudence Roscoe Pound, Hocking says that "legal rights are presumptive rights": people are treated as though they are equal. Differences between persons that are obvious and relevant can be ignored, because the legal right aims at a condition that is not yet in existence, and ignoring the obvious and relevant characteristics may help to produce it. Rights are "a set of conditions, *which promote the development of powers*" of individuals. The only natural right is the right to develop one's human powers, but even it can be forfeited. Human beings have a right to a society wherein self-fulfillment is not excluded, but this right has as its corollary that the individual provide what is indispensable for the life of society itself. Following Rudolf Stammler's *Theorie der Rechtswissenschaft* (Theory of Jurisprudence, 1911), Hocking insists that no rights can exist apart from a community of wills. A community of wills is a union of wills that, apart from the community relationship, would clash with each other; each will would treat its own ends as of overriding importance, ignoring the ends of fellow citizens and considering those citizens means or tools for the realization of the will's own goals.

This community, Hocking explains in the more comprehensive volume *Man and the State* (1926), is a group-forming activity that is "com-motive"–a moving together, as well as a willing together or a common choosing. He argues that experience reveals the inadequacy of both the atomistic and organic views of the state; he proposes a theory of "organic pluralism" that combines the merits of the two extreme views, while avoiding their defects. Hocking's psychology is entirely individualistic: he espouses no group mind such as Royce defends and of which even James admits the possibility. Although he denies the existence of a group mind numerically distinct from the minds of individuals, Hocking acknowledges that the state provides a context beyond the individual boundaries of self that is indispensable to the full development of the self.

These extensions of the self include physical objects, surroundings, and social commitments of the self. Hocking calls them "vital circuits," or, when he wants to stress their volitional character, "will-circuits." The state is the embodiment of these will-circuits in a particular national community. The state has a will to power of its own, dependent on but not identifiable with its individual constituent wills. For Hocking, individual wills to power require nation-states, with their particular geographies, climates, natural resources, and so forth, rather than a world state. This particularity makes the contract notion of the state inappropriate if conceived as struck by human beings in general. The state is an artificial construct, but it is also natural, since humans are by nature its artificer. A world faith is required precisely because a world state is not desirable.

According to Hocking, the state possesses three kinds of power: physical power, bargaining power, and the power of prestige. Of these, the most important is the power of prestige. Bargaining power is involved in the state's efforts to provide the protection and peace its citizens need because of their "desires to have," while prestige power depends on the citizens' "desires to be." "Desires to be" are what the citizens desire to become and can become on account of the state.

The democratic state is based on the universal human right to learn, to share in governing, to earn a living, and to become someone worth being–"the right to become a whole man." In *Present Status of the Philosophy of Law and of Rights* Hocking referred to this right as "the right of liberty" exercised in self-management, social control, and control of nature. Democracy is to be esteemed because it honors this universal right.

In *The Self, Its Body and Freedom* (1928) and *What Man Can Make of Man* (1942) Hocking employs his empirical dialectic to show that behavioristic psychology is self-defeating: the laws offered by the behaviorists would have to apply also to their makers and would thereby invalidate their claim to be true. In *The Spirit of World Politics: With Special Studies of the Near East* (1932) he applies the method to colonialism; he concludes that political independence corresponds roughly with national distinctness and that cultural creativity is the criterion of such independence. In *The Lasting Elements of Individualism* (1937) he brings together insights from John Stuart Mill and Karl Marx to propose a "co-agent state" that provides for group activity (the "commotive function") while allowing for a wide range of individual expression and development.

In his Hibbert Lectures, delivered at the University of Oxford in 1938 and published as *Living Religions and a World Faith* (1940), Hocking says that the development of a "world faith" requires an alternation between "excursive" (acquisitional) and "reflective" (assimilative) phases. In its excursive phase, faith would concentrate on the communication of religious truths in specific historic contexts. In its reflective phase it would focus on the universal, on whatever is independent of localism and historical accidents. Through "reconception," a balancing-in-process of particularity and universality, false beliefs and partial truths would have their falsity or fragmentary character exposed and their elements of truth embodied in a new conception.

Hocking defines religion as "a passion for righteousness, and for the spread of righteousness as a cosmic demand." By "righteousness" he means the search for a law or principle to govern the good life. As a "passion" it is in earnest about its search and is closely identified with feeling in its deeper reaches.

Religion differs from morality in two important ways: it is a quest for righteousness as a "cosmic demand," giving it an ardor and a ground that mere dutifulness does not have, and it has a depth of feeling that is based in an expectancy. This feeling is not a disturbed emotional state; rather, it is a deep, inescapable tension of concern and urgency. The tension arises in part because religion embraces the paradox of being both universal and particular. Grounded in the essential truth of human psychology, religion is necessarily

Hocking (back row, far right) and the other members of the Harvard University philosophy department in 1929:
(front row) Ralph Barton Perry, Alfred North Whitehead, James Houghton Woods, James W. Miller,
John Wild, and Henry Sheffer; (back row) C. I. Lewis, Kerby Sinclair Miller,
Ralph M. Blake (visiting professor), and Ralph Eaton

universal in its hope, passion, fear, and awe. But because it must be communicated, religion is also particular. Idea must take conceptual shape and must realize itself in deed. Only by conceptualizing his or her insights and acting on them can the discoverer be united with his or her fellow believers.

The definition of religion as a "passion for righteousness" is not intended to replace Hocking's earlier definition in *The Meaning of God in Human Experience* of religion as "anticipated attainment." In the earlier work the emphasis is on the individual's efforts to realize his or her potential without excluding similar realization by other individuals. The "attainment" is righteous living; it is "anticipated" because it is never fully attained but serves as a constant goal for the con-

tinual striving of the devotee. The passion for righteousness gives emphasis to the work of religion in the human community and is compatible with the stress in the earlier work on the importance of prophecy alternating with mystical experience.

The definition of religion as a "passion for righteousness" implicitly recognizes that the mystic needs the community, even as the community needs the mystic. The mystic provides the spirit or "morale" that is essential to the vitality of the religious community. But, equally, the mystic needs the community. The mystic needs to share his or her insights and ideas with his or her fellow humans and have the group acknowledge the new insights and provide experimental corroboration and development of them.

The insights and feelings of the mystic are often incorporated into the rituals of the religious community. Rituals conserve feelings that might otherwise be lost and are thereby made accessible to individuals in crises. The mystic's religious feeling is evanescent and transient; it requires the community to achieve its proper dimension, conceptual structure, and imaginative scope. To conserve his or her own emotion the mystic needs to invest it "in communal observance, where it can reflect to him, through local symbols, the adequate response of mankind to the inner glory of the world." Finally, the mystic needs the community "for the *prolongation of his deed*." Hocking notes that "As a matter of biography, the great mystics have inclined to alternate in the roles of teacher and hermit."

In seeking a "world faith" Hocking rejects the ways of "radical displacement" and "synthesis" in favor of "the way of reconception." Displacement of one faith by another assumes an exclusive monopoly on religious truth. Synthesis is a preliminary rather than a solution to the problem of differences among religions. Reconception as a way to a world faith requires a broadening of the base of religion and is a continuing process. It is an attempt to discover the essence of religion. As each religion understands its own essence, it begins to understand the essence of all religion. Reconception is a conservative approach, since it conserves what is worthwhile in other faiths. To have a world faith, religion must be reconceived through world culture and world culture, in turn, reconceived through the revised religious perspective. If Christianity is to fulfill its promise of universality, it must carry out the work of reconception without claiming exclusivity and without confining itself within Western cultural limitations. What is required is an inward dialogue among the world's religions: a conversation between one's enlarged understanding of other religions and one's awareness of the relation of other religions to the core of one's own faith. For Hocking, the germ of world faith exists in every religion.

In 1938–1939 Hocking was the Gifford Lecturer at the University of Glasgow, an honor accorded previously only to Royce, James, and Dewey among American philosophers. The lectures, titled "Fact and Destiny," have never been published in book form in their entirety. At the time he presented them, they appeared in fairly complete but condensed form in the *Glasgow Herald* and in an even more abbreviated version in *The Scotsman*. An outline of their argument, somewhat revised, was published in *The Review of Metaphysics* in 1950–1951. But in spite of laboring on them time and again, he never could revise them to his satisfaction for book publication.

In his McNair Lectures, published as *Science and the Idea of God* (1944), Hocking argues against the proposition that traditional belief in God must be abandoned in the light of modern psychology, sociology, astronomy, and physics. Psychoanalysis, an application of "causal" psychology, provides no substitute for religious affection and confession. God alone, Hocking argues, bestows meaning on human beings' personal attachments and provides integration for the disordered mind. Sociology cannot claim society as a substitute for God, because society cannot provide the sympathetic understanding, knowledge, and power human beings require to revive their creative potency. Religion undergirds society's ascription to each individual of intrinsic worth and equality, which is necessary for society's cohesiveness. Astronomy and physics, with their focus on the measurable, neglect qualities and meanings. They deal with sense-data; but data are, literally, things that are given, which suggests a "Giver"–God–who is active in the world in a noncausal mode. As an object of affection, this Giver is the source of psychological and social health, both individually and historically, and the joint creator with human beings of all new qualities and new truth. Experience as interpreted by the empirical dialectic thus indicates that scientific views taken by themselves are inadequate and that human beings cannot get along without God.

In *The Coming World Civilization* (1956) Hocking delineates the roles of state and church. Through its laws, "the coinage of custom constantly criticized," the state sanctions certain expressions of human nature and specific adjustments for resolving conflicting impulses of its citizenry. But the state depends for its vitality on a motivation that it cannot by itself command. This motivation, with its standards of self-judgment not only for behavior but also for motive and principle, is supplied by Christianity. For example, the state can apply penalties, but it cannot punish. Only the person who has enough good within himself or herself to grasp the justice of the penalty can be punished. This sensitivity to the good is the task of religion. Similarly, the state cannot educate either the mind or the will of its citizens. Education occurs through personal qualities of teachers and family members, and these personal qualities are beyond the state's power to produce or to control. Even with regard to obedience to law itself, the state must assume a disposition among its citizenry to comply that it cannot produce.

The relationship of religion to the state is "a natural symbiosis." Religious consciousness, in its primal form, involves a summoning of the will to think by the universal other-mind. Philosophy, as an organ of such thought, keeps religion from being "a blind survival impulse." But, although religion cannot do without

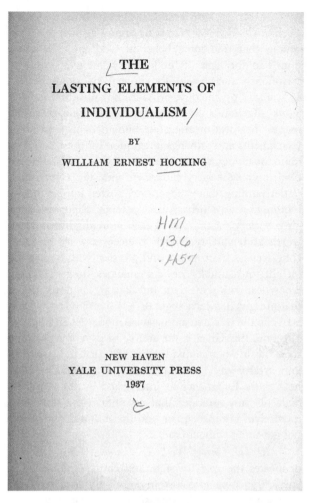

THE

LASTING ELEMENTS OF

INDIVIDUALISM

BY

WILLIAM ERNEST HOCKING

HM
136
.H57

NEW HAVEN
YALE UNIVERSITY PRESS
1937

Title page for a work in which Hocking combines insights from John Stuart Mill and Karl Marx to propose a form of government that provides for group activity and individual expression (Thomas Cooper Library, University of South Carolina)

ers what one would have others do unto oneself unless one knows what one prefers done unto oneself. Fourth, the Golden Rule requires control of one's feelings, a seemingly impossible task. It can make this demand because the Golden Rule itself is a standard for self-judgment.

The "master induction" of Christianity is the principle of losing one's life to save it: if one loses one's life through an affirmative power of a purposeful devotion, the same devotion shall save one's life. This induction, Hocking claims, is found in all great religious traditions, so that the approaches of the other religious traditions can be reconceived in their own contexts within this larger Christian induction. Similarly, Hocking suggests that Christianity will find in these other great religious traditions a reconception of broader scope—for example, the Chinese Ming, or mandate of heaven.

To this common moral/religious foundation the mystic, properly understood, contributes a recognition that there are finalities in religion and the awareness that these finalities are subject to enlargement and revision through mystical experience and reconception. This recognition and awareness Hocking labels "the unlosable intuitions." In its most universal ideal Christianity is "a creative fanaticism." By this phrase Hocking means that Christianity, after its reconception through a deeper understanding of Eastern religions, will be the needed foundation of world faith.

World faith, Hocking explains, recognizes the growing unity of "unlosable essences," while understanding and accepting the variety of religions. It will provide for the integrity of volition that the state must assume, uphold the dignity of the individual human being, and assure its proponents that the way of duty is also a way of happiness in loving and being loved. World faith will provide for the full employment of one's powers and inner peace, the path of a will to create through suffering.

To make the dialogue among the world's religions effective in progressing toward a world faith, three postulates intended to ameliorate conflicts among world religions need to be considered. First, the genuine mystic in any religion must recognize the genuine mystic in any other religion. Second, each religion has its own essence and historical integrity; no religion can claim to be the only way to God. Third, "to every man belongs the full truth of religion": each devotee knows something in his or her own tradition that demands total and exclusive loyalty. To the extent that this claim of universality is present in all religions, it is a part of the germinal world faith. No faith is entitled to claim this universality until it has justified it by showing it to be present in a germinal form in all religions.

thought, it involves a great deal more. Hocking asks whether Christianity can present the valid essences of religion in such a way as to give them relevance to the issues of contemporary humankind, and he answers with a qualified "yes." If Jesus' teaching as a whole can be conceived as an "inductive reconception" of the Hebrew lawgivers, prophets, and poets, then Christianity can accomplish its ambition of serving as the foundation of a world faith required by the emerging world civilization. Hocking contends that the Golden Rule of Jesus provides this required inductive reconception for four reasons. First, its categorical form places it beyond literal compliance: no one can truly treat others as he or she would want to be treated by them. Second, it summarizes what the law and the prophets require. Third, the rule requires self-judgment: one cannot do unto oth-

Hocking says that the "filaments" of a world faith can be discerned. They are belief in righteousness as an obligation with cosmic bearing, belief that the ultimate source of things is good, and belief in the kind of permanence for what is real in selfhood. In its ideal form Christianity may provide a symbol for the conquest of estrangement among the genuine seekers of God, while in its actual form it acknowledges its failures to solve such problems as war and poverty and recognizes values in non-Christian religions that ought not to perish. Because it has faced modern secularism and recognized its possibilities, Christianity can lend its "maturity" to all other religions. It is equipped to venture "beyond modernity" and to unite the natural and the supernatural.

Hocking's conversion experience, in which he had a vision of human beings with their immortal souls, is reflected in *Thoughts on Death and Life* (1937) and the revised and enlarged edition, *The Meaning of Immortality in Human Experience, Including Thoughts on Death and Life, Revised* (1957), which includes a new preface and three additional chapters, as well as Hocking's Ingersoll Lectures, delivered at Harvard in 1935, and his Hiram W. Thomas Lectures, delivered at the University of Chicago in 1936. The revised edition can be taken as a guide to his mature thinking on immortality. The self is a bipolar entity with an excursive and a reflective pole. The bipolar character of the self means that a "single-space" concept of immortality is erroneous: immortality is not simply moving at death from an earthly existence "here" to a heavenly existence "there." A single-space concept is inadequate for two reasons: it is inaccurate concerning the versatility of the self, and it misconstrues the character of immortality. The self is versatile in that it not only lives in more than one space during its earthly life but is also capable of making the transition from one space to another. For example, it can function in dream space, the space of imagination, and actual physical space. Metaphorically speaking, the self is a "field of fields"; the present space is only one "field" in which the self acts. If space and time are interrelated, as the theory of relativity maintains, one can frame the insight in terms of time, as well: "Time is within the reflective self, whereas the dated self is in time." The self, as a "vinculum" that relates these fields or contexts, is superior to any one of them. This versatility carries with it the possibility of immortality. Recognition of the self as a hinge of transition from one space to another gives the self a destiny separate from the causally governed field or context of the world of nature. The body through which a person acts is a member of two worlds: the world of possibility and the world of actuality. In choosing to execute a specific deed, the self dictates the transition from possibility to

LIVING RELIGIONS
AND A
WORLD FAITH

by
WILLIAM ERNEST
HOCKING
Alford Professor of Philosophy in
Harvard University

New York
THE MACMILLAN COMPANY
1940

Title page for the published version of Hocking's 1938 Hibbert Lectures, in which he defines religion as "a passion for righteousness, and for the spread of righteousness as a cosmic demand" (Thomas Cooper Library, University of South Carolina)

actuality. This choice is "actual creation." Creation has a dual effect: the self creates the idea, and the idea creates the self. Those who die for a cause illustrate that the excursive self (the physical body) has less value than the cause. In rejecting bodily life, the reflective self is laying hold on something of greater value.

Hocking admits that philosophical analysis and argument cannot prove that humans are immortal. Rather, they suggest that death may be "relative" and not final. Immortality has meaning in the human experiences of love and of death itself. The impulse of love, understood in its deeper reaches, requires that the beloved be held immune to "the accidents of time and death." Hocking says that

SCIENCE
AND THE IDEA OF GOD

By
WILLIAM ERNEST HOCKING

BL
240
.H715

CHAPEL HILL
THE UNIVERSITY OF NORTH CAROLINA PRESS
1944

Title page for the published version of Hocking's McNair Lectures, in which he argues that belief in God is compatible with modern science (Thomas Cooper Library, University of South Carolina)

the life of the lover—aware not alone of what is, but of what is unborn possibility in the beloved—is in bringing that possibility to birth under the egis of the shared (though undefined) goal. Thus love becomes the energy of a continuous creativity in time. And since the unrealized but germinal self has the dimension of infinitude, *the Mission of love in time is never done.* Unless such love holds in itself an assurance of its own perpetuity, it moves under the shadow of a cosmic deceit.

Those who have observed the dying often report a yielding to nature or death that is other than simple resignation. Hocking, of course, is speaking of natural deaths, rather than accidents that befall the young; the premature death of a talented young person is likely to bring forth the protest that such a self ought to have a fulfillment that has been denied. What are today called "out-of-body" experiences do not provide any proof of immortality; they have the function of provoking questions concerning the finality of death.

For Hocking, the final answers to these questions are to be found, if at all, in the common experiences of humankind. A clue is provided by one's awareness of freedom. People know themselves to be both creature and creator; their earthly lives, Hocking says, are "an *apprenticeship in creativity.*" Humans' "task" or "destiny" is theirs to bring into being. "God himself," Hocking insists, "has not prethought your conception; your creation, within its bounds, is as real as his." Death may be "relative" to the "body" as a participant within a specific "field" or context. No conclusive evidence exists that the reflective pole of the self falls victim to the same fate as its body in any given field. Out-of-body experiences, experiences of love, and mystical experiences all hint that the death of the physical body does not terminate the self.

Hocking's final book, *Strength of Men and Nations: A Message to the USA vis-à-vis the USSR* (1959), was written at the height of the Cold War, before the fall of communism in Russia and the breakup of the Union of Soviet Socialist Republics. In *Strength of Men and Nations* Hocking sketches a world community in which competitiveness is transformed into cooperation, nationalism is largely displaced by global pride, individualism yields to urgent communal needs, and optimism is balanced by a patient realism. He again relies on a principle that has served as the cornerstone of his entire philosophy: "the *universality of private experience.*" This principle assumes that everyone's experience has universality by virtue of being grounded in an experience of a purposive, nonintrusive Other Self. What is true for the individual is true for all others. Hocking applies the principle to advocate a third type of diplomacy. He rejects appeasement, which would sacrifice principle for the sake of peace, and he rejects a rigidity of principle that fails to acknowledge the malleability of motives. What is needed is "creative diplomacy" based on common elements of purpose implied by human nature itself. The United States needs to take a "creative risk" to evoke the democratic will of the Soviet people. This justified risk, which will break the vicious circle of distrust and armament races, is a challenge to the USSR to compete in the world arena for human fulfillment. To take this venturesome risk is the final test of national strength or "moral virility." Emphasis in both the United States and the USSR must be on creativity, rather than on economic productivity. Creativity allows individual freedom of thought and its expression in action: "The foundation of all national strength lies in the conviction of the individual thinker." This creative task requires continuing dialogue and the acceptance of certain principles of interaction among peoples: the right of national entities to exist; the right of existing federal unions to continue practicing their experiments in social order, provided that their peoples freely cooperate; and the right of unfederated nations to exist in free neutrality and free alliance, unencumbered by contractual agreements for economic aid and guidance.

Hocking was one of America's most notable and prolific philosophers. In addition to the Gifford, McNair, Ingersoll, and Hiram M. Thomas Lectures, he gave the Dudleian Lectures at Harvard in 1920, the Terry Lectures at Yale in 1925–1926, the James W. Richards Lectures at the University of Virginia in 1935, the Hibbert Lectures at the University of Oxford in 1938, and the William James Lectures at Harvard in 1947. As president of the American Philosophical Association he gave an address of welcome to delegates of the World Congress of Philosophy, which met at Harvard in 1926. He was elected to the American Philosophical Society in 1943. He was awarded honorary doctorate degrees by Williams College in 1923, the University of Glasgow and the University of Chicago in 1933, Oberlin College in 1934, Duke University in 1941, the University of Leiden in 1948, Colby College in 1950, and the University of California in 1952. He received the Lecomte du Nouy Award for *The Coming World Civilization* in 1957. In 1958, still vigorous at eighty-five, he presented a presidential address to the American Metaphysical Society.

But Hocking was always disappointed that he was unable to publish his Gifford Lectures. He provided a revised summary of the second series of the lectures for publication in the festschrift edited by Rouner, *Philosophy, Religion, and the Coming World Civilization* (1966), as "History and the Absolute." This summary was published the year of Hocking's death: he died on 12 June. In a 1958 letter to Blanshard, Hocking had remarked: "I shan't regret the delay, if it means that I can do more perfectly what I then intended to do. It was 1939 when I got through, and our heads were immersed in the preludes to Britain's war, gas masks for every person including visitors . . . in the preludes to a new wave of nihilism, bringing the world-view to the judgment of raw 'fact.'" No doubt Hocking realized that his own "world-view" needed rethinking, with all the disclosures of man's inhumanity to man, the new developments in physics, and new directions in philosophy.

Hocking was concerned about the course philosophy was taking by the end of his life. In regard to the "linguistic turn," he would have agreed with Bertrand Russell that the task of philosophy is to understand the world, not merely to understand sentences. He had much to say through the years concerning the one-sidedness and inadequacies of Marxism; to Marx's often-quoted statement in *Theses on Feuerbach* (1888), "The philosophers have only interpreted the world in various ways; the point, however, is to change it,"

Hocking responded in his *Types of Philosophy* (1929): "The alternative is spurious; for any world-changing, not preceded and shot-through with reflection, can only be mischievous." Although skeptical of their antisystematic bias, he had more sympathy for existentialism and phenomenology. Bruce Kuklick notes that Hocking's style and comprehensive sweep, interest in mysticism, and concern for world problems mark him as a man swimming against the current of present-day philosophical specialties. But Hocking's confidence in the vitality of philosophy and his hope for its eventual return to its traditional concerns never waned.

Letters:

"Nine Letters of William Ernest Hocking," in *Royce and Hocking, American Idealists: Introduction to Their Philosophy, with Selected Letters,* edited by Daniel Summer Robinson (Boston: Christopher, 1968), pp. 157–169.

Bibliography:

Richard C. Gilman, "The Bibliography of William Ernest Hocking," in *Philosophy, Religion, and the Coming World Civilization: Essays in Honor of William Ernest Hocking,* edited by Leroy S. Rouner (The Hague: Nijhoff, 1966), pp. 465–504.

Biographies:

Leroy S. Rouner, "The Making of a Philosopher: Ernest Hocking's Early Years," in *Philosophy, Religion, and the Coming World Civilization,* edited by Rouner (The Hague: Nijhoff, 1966), pp. 5–22;

Rouner, "Chronology," in his *Within Human Experience: The Philosophy of William Ernest Hocking* (Cambridge, Mass.: Harvard University Press, 1969), pp. 325–327;

Brand Blanshard, Preface to *The Wisdom of William Ernest Hocking,* edited by Rouner and John Howie (Washington, D.C.: University Press of America, 1978).

References:

Neal Bond Fleming, "Hocking's Philosophy of the Human Self," dissertation, Boston University, 1941;

Richard Carleton Gilman, "The General Metaphysics of William Ernest Hocking," dissertation, Boston University, 1952;

John Howie, "Creativity in the Thought of William Ernest Hocking and Henry Nelson Wieman," dissertation, Boston University, 1965;

Howie, "Metaphysical Elements of Creativity in the Philosophy of W. E. Hocking," *Idealistic Studies,* 2

(September 1972): 249–264; 3 (January 1973): 52–71;

Howie and Leroy S. Rouner, eds., *The Wisdom of William Ernest Hocking* (Washington, D.C.: University Press of America, 1978);

Jacquelyn A. Kegley, Barbara Mackinnon, and Eugene Mayers, eds., *Theory of Community in the Philosophies of Royce and Hocking* (Hayward: California State University, 1979);

Bruce Kuklick, "Ernest Hocking," in *The Rise of American Philosophy, Cambridge, Massachusetts, 1860–1930* (New Haven & London: Yale University Press, 1977), pp. 481–495;

A. R. Luther, *Existence as Dialectical Tension* (The Hague: Nijhoff, 1968);

James Alfred Martin Jr., *Empirical Philosophies of Religion, with Special Reference to Boodin, Brightman, Hocking, Macintosh, and Wieman* (New York: King's Crown Press, 1945);

Andrew J. Reck, "The Empirical Idealism of William Ernest Hocking," in his *Recent American Philosophy: Studies of Ten Representative Thinkers* (New York: Pantheon, 1964), pp. 42–83;

Roland Preston Rice, "Mysticism in the Philosophy of William Ernest Hocking," dissertation, Boston University, 1954;

Rouner, "The Surveyor as Hero: Reflections on Ernest Hocking's Philosophy of Nature," in *Contemporary Studies in Philosophical Idealism,* edited by Howie and Thomas O. Buford (Cape Cod, Mass.: Claude Stark, 1975), pp. 53–68;

Rouner, *Within Human Experience: The Philosophy of William Ernest Hocking* (Cambridge, Mass.: Harvard University Press, 1969);

Rouner, ed., *Philosophy, Religion, and the Coming World Civilization* (The Hague: Nijhoff, 1966);

James L. Arnold Snedden, "A Critical Examination of the Systematic Philosophy of William Ernest Hocking," dissertation, University of Buffalo, 1956;

Edmund Jabez Thompson, "An Analysis of the Thought of Alfred North Whitehead and William Ernest Hocking Concerning Good and Evil," dissertation, University of Chicago, 1933;

W. H. Werkmeister, "Hocking's 'Individualistic Idealism,'" in his *A History of Philosophical Ideas in America* (New York: Ronald Press, 1949), pp. 293–307.

William James
(11 January 1842 – 26 August 1910)

Gary Alexander
Illinois Board of Higher Education

BOOKS: *The Principles of Psychology,* 2 volumes (New York: Holt, 1890; London: Macmillan, 1890); abridged by James as *Psychology: Briefer Course* (New York: Holt, 1892; London: Macmillan, 1892);

Is Life Worth Living? (Philadelphia: S. B. Weston, 1896);

The Will to Believe, and Other Essays in Popular Philosophy (New York, London & Bombay: Longmans, Green, 1897);

Louis Agassiz: Words Spoken by Professor William James at the Reception of the American Society of Naturalists by the President and Fellows of Harvard College, Cambridge, on December 30, 1896 (Cambridge, Mass.: Printed for the University, 1897);

Human Immortality: Two Supposed Objections to the Doctrine (Boston & New York: Houghton, Mifflin, 1898; London: Constable, 1903);

Talks to Teachers on Psychology; and to Students on Some of Life's Ideals (New York: Holt, 1899; London: Longmans, Green, 1899);

The Varieties of Religious Experience: A Study in Human Nature. Being the Gifford Lectures on Natural Religion Delivered at Edinburgh in 1901–1902 (New York & London: Longmans, Green, 1902);

Pragmatism: A New Name for Some Old Ways of Thinking. Popular Lectures on Philosophy (New York & London: Longmans, Green, 1907);

The Meaning of Truth: A Sequel to "Pragmatism" (New York & London: Longmans, Green, 1907);

A Pluralistic Universe: Hibbert Lectures at Manchester College on the Present Situation in Philosophy (New York & London: Longmans, Green, 1909);

Some Problems of Philosophy: A Beginning of an Introduction to Philosophy, edited by Horace M. Kallen (New York & London: Longmans, Green, 1911);

Memories and Studies (New York & London: Longmans, Green, 1911);

On Vital Reserves; The Energies of Men; The Gospel of Relaxation (New York: Holt, 1911);

Essays in Radical Empiricism, edited by Ralph Barton Perry (New York & London: Longmans, Green, 1912); enlarged as *Essays in Radical Empiricism; A Pluralistic Universe* (New York: Longmans, Green, 1947);

Selected Papers on Philosophy, edited by C. M. Bakewell (London & Toronto: Dent / New York: Dutton, 1917);

Collected Essays and Reviews, edited by Perry (New York: Longmans, Green, 1920);

William James on Psychical Research, edited by Gardner Murphy and Robert O. Ballou (New York: Viking, 1960; London: Chatto & Windus, 1961);

The Writings of William James: A Comprehensive Edition, edited by John J. McDermott (New York: Random House, 1968).

Collections: *The Philosophy of William James, Drawn from His Own Works,* edited by Horace M. Kallen (New York: Modern Library, 1925);

As William James Said: Extracts from the Published Writings of William James, edited by Elizabeth Perkins Aldrich (New York: Vanguard, 1942);

Essays on Faith and Morals, edited by Ralph Barton Perry (New York & London: Longmans, Green, 1943);

Essays in Pragmatism, edited by Alburey Castell (New York: Hafner, 1948);

William James: The Essential Writings, edited by Bruce Wilshire (New York: Harper & Row, 1971).

OTHER: *The Literary Remains of the Late Henry James,* edited by James (Boston: Houghton, Mifflin, 1884);

John Edward Maude, *The Foundations of Ethics,* edited by James (New York: Holt, 1887).

William James made significant contributions to the disciplines of psychology and philosophy. His book *The Principles of Psychology* (1890) ushered in the modern era of American psychology by demonstrating that a truly scientific discipline has no need for such metaphysical or religious notions as a transcendental ego or a substantial soul. Although most of the specific doctrines of *The Principles of Psychology* have been superseded, James's pioneering work in such areas as the relationship of the brain to the mind, consciousness, emotion, habit, will, and belief continues to have influence. As a philosopher, James advocated the discipline's independence from dogmatic theology and worked to improve its teaching in American universities and colleges.

James's impact on his own generation went beyond the strength of his intellect. He was one of the most engaging characters of the day, numbering among his friends, acquaintances, and correspondents such luminaries as the jurist Oliver Wendell Holmes Jr. and the philosophers Charles Sanders Peirce, Chauncey Wright, Josiah Royce, Charles Renouvier, Henri Bergson, George Santayana, and F. H. Bradley. On James's death H. Addington Bruce wrote in the *Boston Evening Transcript* (5 October 1910), "certainly no other of his

generation exercised such an international influence as did William James," and Bertrand Russell wrote in the British magazine *The Nation* (3 September 1910) that James was "one of the most eminent, and probably the most widely known, of contemporary philosophers." The 1960s brought about a revival of interest in James's humanistic psychology and psychology of religion. Phenomenologists have begun to consider the implications of *The Principles of Psychology* for their philosophical orientation, and his theories of pragmatism and radical empiricism, on the basis of which he argued that truth must be understood in relation to experience and that no absolute standpoint exists from which to interpret the world, are debated today as vigorously as when he first presented them.

It is tempting, but incorrect, to view James's career as developing in an orderly progression from his early studies in anatomy and physiology, leading to the M.D.—the highest academic degree he attained—then to his pioneering work in psychology, and concluding with his philosophical output. In fact, from the time James began to consider a career, all of these interests were woven into a complex fabric reflecting the eye of a painter, the vocation for which he first studied as a young man. In the words of James's biographer Ralph Barton Perry, "if genius implies continuous, frictionless, outpouring spontaneity, then James was not a genius. Periods of outpouring alternated with periods of painful effort." This pattern was produced in part by James's frequent episodes of ill health but in large measure by his habit of intensely examining a topic, leaving it for a time, and then returning to it. Most of the material in his books had either been previously published in articles or delivered as addresses to academic or general audiences. In these articles and addresses he returns repeatedly to such topics as free will, belief, morality, experience, and truth, usually introducing new ways of looking at the subject. Much of James's popularity derived from his overriding concern that philosophy make a difference to human experience—that the philosopher speak in terms available to the general audience as well as to the discipline's practitioners.

James was born in New York City on 11 January 1842, the eldest of five children of Henry and Mary Robertson Walsh James. The son of a wealthy businessman, Henry James had had difficulty in settling on a vocation. After graduating from Union College, he had studied law and then bookkeeping, but neither had held his attention. He attended Princeton Theological Seminary but withdrew in 1838, according to Perry, "permanently alienated from the Church." He remained intensely religious, however, and finally turned to the theology of the Swedish mystic Emanuel Swedenborg to balance his stern Calvinist upbringing.

James's parents, Mary Robertson Walsh James (Collection of Henry James Vaux) and Henry James Sr.
(Houghton Library, Harvard University and Alexander R. James)

His career problems were solved when a lawsuit broke his father's will, which had stipulated that the $3 million estate be held in trust until the youngest grandchild reached the age of twenty-one, and provided him with an annual income of $10,000. William James's brother Henry Jr., a year younger than William, went on to achieve fame as a novelist. The two brothers corresponded regularly throughout their lives, often discussing and criticizing each other's work. Their sister Alice died in 1892 at forty-four; her diary, published in 1934, established her as an interesting figure in her own right and provided insights into the lives of her two famous brothers. The two remaining siblings, Garth Wilkinson (Wilky) and Robertson, served in the Civil War: Wilky, an adjutant in the all-black Forty-fourth Massachusetts Regiment, was wounded leading his troops into battle; Robertson achieved the rank of captain in the Forty-fifth Massachusetts Regiment. After the war the two younger brothers were partners in a failed effort to run a Florida plantation with emancipated blacks as workers.

Henry James Sr. constantly moved his children from the United States to Europe and from school to school; William James rarely spent an entire year in one place, and by eighteen he had attended nine schools in four countries. Nor did his father make his eldest son's choice of a career easy. When the eighteen-year-old James demonstrated a talent for painting and expressed the desire to become a professional artist, his father opposed the idea while praising science. Yet, when William switched his interest to science, Henry Sr. expressed a concern that this course of study might damage his son's moral development. When James finally turned to philosophy, his father sharply criticized academic philosophers. Nevertheless, the bond between father and son is demonstrated in a 14 December 1882 letter in which James confesses to Henry Sr., who was then on his deathbed, "All my intellectual life I derive from you; and though we have often seemed at odds in the expression thereof, I'm sure there's a harmony somewhere, and that our strivings will combine. What my debt to you is goes beyond all my power of

James's sister, Alice, in 1869 (Houghton Library, Harvard University)

estimating,—so early, so penetrating, and so constant has been the influence."

James entered Lawrence Scientific School, which was loosely associated with Harvard University, in the fall of 1861, bringing the brilliant but erratically educated young man, who had seldom been separated from his parents for more than a few days, into contact with such prominent American scientists as Louis Agassiz, Jeffries Wyman, and Asa Gray. Lawrence had no required curriculum; students selected the faculty members under whom they wanted to study. James chose to study chemistry under Charles William Eliot, who recorded in a memorandum to James's son Henry after James's death that he found James "a very interesting and agreeable pupil . . . not wholly devoted to the study of Chemistry," who "possessed unusual mental powers, remarkable spirituality, and great personal charm."

James withdrew from Lawrence in the middle of his second year, complaining of backaches, headaches,

eyestrain, and nervousness. While convalescing, he read widely in literature, science, and philosophy and decided to study medicine as a compromise between his interest in science and a more practical career, such as becoming a printer. Returning to Lawrence in the fall of 1863, he switched from chemistry to comparative anatomy under Wyman. His studies provided a solid biological foundation for his later psychological studies of the mind-body relationship.

Following an eight-month research expedition to Brazil led by Agassiz, James resumed his medical education in the summer of 1866. Problems with his back and eyes recurred, however, and he left for Europe in April 1867 for a year of study and of visits to mineral baths for his back. His biographer Howard M. Feinstein observes that "Of the seven years between his return from Brazil and the start of his career as a teacher at Harvard, two were devoted to medical school and five to the search for health." James received his medical degree on 21 June 1869 with a thesis on the common cold.

His physical and educational travails had not prevented James from producing his first publication, an unsigned review in *The North American Review* for January 1865 of Thomas Henry Huxley's *Lectures on the Elements of Comparative Anatomy* (1865). Most of his publications between 1865 and 1878 were unsigned essays and reviews in the two magazines for which his brother Henry also wrote, *The Nation* and *The Atlantic Monthly*.

James's physical health and emotional difficulties played a central role in one of his most dramatic observations about free will, which he later described in *The Varieties of Religious Experience: A Study in Human Nature. Being the Gifford Lectures on Natural Religion Delivered at Edinburgh in 1901–1902* (1902) as an account provided by an anonymous French "sufferer"; in fact, it is an account of James's own experience with depression in late 1869 or early 1870. His "French" alter ego reports a state of "philosophic pessimism and general depression of spirits about my prospects . . . a horrible fear of my own existence" such that "I became a mass of quivering fear. . . . In general I dreaded being left alone." In a notebook entry dated 30 April 1870 James says that his recovery from this severe state of anxiety was assisted by his encountering Renouvier's definition of free will as "the sustaining of a thought *because I choose to* when I might have other thoughts"; his first act of free will, he decided, "shall be to believe in free will." The importance of this famous account has been somewhat exaggerated: in an 18 March 1873 letter to Henry Jr., Henry Sr. reported that he had inquired about the causes of his son's recovery and that James had mentioned not only Renouvier but also his reading of the poetry of William Wordsworth and "more than anything else, his having given up the notion that all mental disorder requires to have a physical basis."

James wrote his parents in July 1872 that the physiologist Henry P. Bowditch had offered to let James take over his teaching position at Harvard University if James's former chemistry professor Eliot, who had become president of Harvard in 1869, consented. Mary James paid a visit to Eliot, who was by then a neighbor and friend of the Jameses, and on 26 July she wrote Henry Jr. that she had "little doubt of his agreeing." In August, James agreed to share teaching responsibilities for an elective course in comparative anatomy and physiology with the anatomist Timothy Dwight for a salary of $600 a year. James proved to be a stimulating lecturer and found his own spirits lifted by the experience of preparing for classes. When Eliot offered him a permanent position teaching anatomy and physiology beginning in 1873, James hesitated because he wanted to concentrate on the more philosophically oriented study of the "mental sciences." Finally, however, he accepted Eliot's offer on the basis of a "feeling that philosophical activity as a *business* is not normal for most men, and not for me." Nevertheless, in a diary entry around this time he says that while he has decided to continue teaching biology, "philosophy I will nevertheless regard as my vocation and never let slip a chance to do a stroke of it."

By the fall of 1874 James was a full member of Harvard's psychology program and was responsible for its Museum of Comparative Anatomy. At the time, psychology at Harvard continued to be grounded in the Cartesian distinction between body and mind defended by Frances Bowen, Alford Professor of Philosophy. Under Bowen's leadership, too, the philosophy department, in which the psychology faculty was housed, remained tied to the assumption that philosophical studies should be directed to the promotion of eternal Christian truths. James's rise in the Harvard philosophy department coincided with the overthrowing of this Cartesian and Christian dominance.

What John J. McDermott terms the "earliest statement of the central features" of James's philosophy is a review in *The Atlantic Monthly* for September 1875 of *Problems of Life and Mind,* by the English philosopher George Henry Lewes. James assails an excessive concern for either "flawless accuracy" or radical subjectivism—that is, simply consulting one's "prophetic soul"—in philosophy. James asserts that the world is not such that absolute certainty can be attained before one adopts a believing attitude, nor can truth be found merely by waiting for all of the facts to appear before making a decision. These attitudes resurfaced in his famous essay "The Will to Believe" (1896) and remained central to James's later reflections on the

nature of consciousness and reality in a pluralistic, relational universe.

Learning in December 1875 that he was being considered for promotion to assistant professor of physiology, James wrote Eliot a letter in which he stated his "firm belief" that a "living science" of psychology cannot be taught by anyone lacking "a first-hand acquaintance with the facts of nervous physiology." James considered himself the appropriate person to redirect the teaching of psychology at Harvard away from its traditionalist orientation and toward a thoroughly modern stance. James was promoted to assistant professor of physiology with a salary of $1,200 a year and a promise of $2,000 the following year.

In an unsigned letter in the 21 September 1876 issue of *The Nation* James charged that the teaching of philosophy in American colleges was most often "in the hands of the president, who is usually a minister of the Gospel." Consequently, he went on, "*safeness*" becomes the chief characteristic of the philosophical classroom, with students forced to memorize "flabby formulas" and endure "lifeless discussions."

In April 1877 James notified Eliot of his desire to be considered for Harvard's next vacancy in philosophy. He also informed Daniel Coit Gilman, the president of Johns Hopkins University, that he was willing to consider new job opportunities. Gilman invited James to give a series of lectures in February 1878. The lectures, on the mind-body connection, received a positive reception and were published as "Remarks on Spencer's *Definition of Mind and Correspondence*" in *The Journal of Speculative Philosophy* (January 1878), "Quelques Considérations sur la méthode subjective" in the French journal *Critique Philosophique* (24 January 1878), and "The Sentiment of Rationality" in the British journal *Mind* in 1879. James subsequently informed Gilman that "I think I can now say I should not decline" a permanent appointment were the "salary and duties agreeable." To entice James to remain at Harvard, Eliot allowed him to offer his first course exclusively in philosophy and in 1880 formally changed his appointment to assistant professor of philosophy.

James's father had returned from a meeting of the Radical Club of Boston one evening early in 1876 with the announcement that he had seen William's future wife. James attended the next meeting with his father and met Alice Howe Gibbens, whose "unreserved candor," according to James's biographer Gay Wilson Allen, could be "rather startling." For two years the two maintained a troubled courtship, James agonizing over inflicting his physical weaknesses on Alice and she doubting that she was the right woman for him. Finally, in the spring of 1878, she accepted his proposal of marriage; the wedding took place on 10

James's younger brothers: Garth Wilkinson (Wilky) in 1869; Robertson in the 1890s
(Houghton Library, Harvard University)

July. Their son Henry was born in 1879. In the summer of 1880 James visited his brother Henry in London; the meeting accentuated the growing differences between the successful novelist and the emerging teacher and scholar. Hard at work on *The Portrait of a Lady* (1881), Henry complained that William "takes himself, and his nerves, and his physical condition too hard and too consciously," while William accused Henry of being "better suited by superficial contact with things at a great many points than by a deeper one at a few points." James's mother died in January 1882. His and Alice's second son, William, was born in June of the same year.

James had begun working on *The Principles of Psychology* during his honeymoon. He had signed a contract with Henry Holt and Company in June 1878 to write a psychology textbook, about five hundred pages in length, for use in American universities and colleges. Holt had first asked John Fiske, an amateur psychologist, to write the book, but Fiske had decided that he could not complete the project and had recommended James as his replacement. Holt wanted the work to be available for the opening of classes in the fall of 1880,

but James was determined to produce the best possible text on the subject; his scrupulousness, combined with his delicate health, resulted in the manuscript taking twelve years to complete. During that period James published sixteen articles that he revised for use in *The Principles of Psychology* and one, "The Association of Ideas," published in *Popular Science Monthly* in 1880, that he included virtually without revision.

Having secured Royce as a substitute, James left for a year in Europe in the fall of 1882. Henry Sr. died on 18 December; his health had steadily failed since his wife's death. That month James met in London with a group of English philosophers and psychologists who called themselves the "Scratch Eight Club." Among the group were Edmund Gurney and Henry Sidgwick, who had founded the Society for Psychical Research the previous February. Two months later James delivered a paper to the Scratch Eight in which he discussed the ideas of a "fringe" of consciousness and the distinction between the "feeling" of knowing something by acquaintance as opposed to knowing about it objectively, concepts that he incorporated in *The Principles of Psychology* and carried into his later work.

James's third son, Herman, was born in January 1884, two months after the death in Milwaukee of James's brother Wilky. Herman died of pneumonia at eighteen months.

James was named professor of philosophy at Harvard in 1885. A daughter, Margaret Mary (Peggy), was born in 1887. Most of his students found him a personable and stimulating teacher, although one of them, Santayana, could never understand James's "muscular" approach to philosophy. On the other hand, Gertrude Stein found James "a man among men . . . embodying all that is strongest and worthiest in the scientific spirit." A well-known anecdote recounts Stein turning in a final examination book that contained only the note, "Dear Professor James, I am so sorry but really I do not feel like an examination paper in philosophy today." The next day she received a reply: "Dear Miss Stein, I understand perfectly how you feel. I often feel like that myself." James gave her the highest grade in the class.

In the fall of 1889 the James family moved into a newly built house at 95 Irving Street in Cambridge, which was James's home for the rest of his life. By January 1890 Holt had received 350 pages of the manuscript for *The Principles of Psychology;* James assured him that the rest would be completed by 1 May and encouraged him to begin typesetting. The long-suffering publisher refused to do so without having the entire text in hand. On 9 May, James wrote Holt, "No one could be more disgusted than I at the sight of the book," which, he claimed, testified only to the facts that "there is no such thing as a *science* of psychology" and that "W. J. is an incapable." James completed *The Principles of Psychology* on 22 May and finished reading the proofs in August. The work was published in the fall, not long before the birth of the Jameses' fifth child, Alexander Robinson. It is a survey of the state of psychology in the late nineteenth century, combined with James's description of and commentary on the major issues then being debated by psychologists. The distinction between psychology and philosophy as fully separate disciplines did not occur until well into the twentieth century, but James argues for the independence of psychology and metaphysics. In the preface he asserts that when psychology "has ascertained the empirical correlation of the various sorts of thought or feeling with definite conditions of the brain," then psychology "can go no farther" without becoming "metaphysical."

Steering a course between materialism and idealism, James demands that body and mind be clearly distinguished in a scientific psychology. He rejects materialism by stressing that the conscious human being pursues "future ends" by selecting the means to obtain them, an ability not present in the purely mechanical activity of the brain and nervous system. At the same time, he

James at eighteen (Houghton Library, Harvard University)

rejects idealism by claiming that biology is the best foundation for the investigation of consciousness.

An emphasis that sets James apart from most other modern psychologists is his confidence that introspection is a trustworthy means of investigating consciousness. He maintains that through introspection one can feel one's experiences of attention, will, and so forth and that the subjective aspect of experience makes a real difference in the way one understands experience and in the choices that one makes. In his assertion that the subjective element makes a difference, especially when a person is faced with conflicting hypotheses based on incomplete data, can be seen elements of the doctrine of pragmatism that later emerged as one of his principle philosophical contributions.

The Principles of Psychology quickly became a leading textbook in American institutions of higher education. Since the two-volume work proved unwieldy for classroom use, James revised it in 1892 as the one-volume *Psychology: Briefer Course,* nearly half of which was new or rewritten material. This book, for many years the most popular psychology text in English, was popularly dubbed "Jimmy" because of its relatively small size.

While James was not unknown prior to the publication of *The Principles of Psychology,* the work, translated into German, French, Italian, and Russian,

James in 1865 on a research expedition to Brazil led by the naturalist Louis Agassiz (Houghton Library, Harvard University and Alexander R. James)

brought him international recognition. And while virtually all critics found the book disorderly, they unanimously agreed on its impressive scope and unique contribution to the field. Psychologist James Sully, writing in *Mind* (1891), declared *The Principles of Psychology* a work of great importance, gracefully and enthusiastically written, and delightful in its lack of reverence for "authorities." Still, he found himself wishing "here and there for just a soupçon of the old spirit which has prompted mankind at all stages to pay reverence to ancestors." James's former graduate student G. Stanley Hall wrote in *The American Journal of Psychology* (1891) that James was "an *impressionist* of psychology . . . a veritable storm-bird, fascinated by problems most impossible of solution, and surest where specialists and experts . . . are most in doubt" and described *The Principles of Psychology* as "on the whole . . . the best work in any language" on the subject. Peirce, writing in *The Nation*

(1891), considered *The Principles of Psychology* "the most important contribution that has been made to the subject for many years" but was disturbed by an "uncritical acceptance of data" that he believed too sharply separated James's psychology from accepted scientific standards. In *The Atlantic Monthly* (April 1891) Santayana expressed the opinion, shared by many, that James had "outdone the materialists themselves" by surrendering psychology to their domain. This criticism reflects James's theory of the emotions; his introduction of the theory in an article in *Mind* in April 1884 had been followed a year later by a paper in the same journal proposing similar ideas that the Danish psychologist Carl G. Lange had developed independently. As a result, the theory was dubbed the James-Lange theory of emotions. It states that emotions are not only embodied but are also effects of bodily excitation.

Late-twentieth- and early-twenty-first-century philosophers have taken a renewed interest in *The Principles of Psychology*. Phenomenologists are especially interested in James's chapters on the stream of thought and the consciousness of self. Others have found in *The Principles of Psychology* anticipations of Gestalt psychology and Freudian psychoanalysis. Still others have turned to *The Principles of Psychology* in response to the concern for philosophical psychology created by the works of Gilbert Ryle and Ludwig Wittgenstein.

James's next significant publication, *The Will to Believe, and Other Essays in Popular Philosophy* (1897), a controversial collection of essays written between 1879 and 1896, occasioned a dispute with his publisher, Holt. James informed Holt that he had been in contact with two other publishers, Charles Scribner's Sons and Longmans, Green, and intended to send all three the manuscript to "see if any one promises to make me richer than another. Wealth is now my only ideal." Holt replied that publishers of their stature did not engage in bidding wars, but James suspected collusion when Scribner also rejected the plan. James finally chose Longmans, Green, telling Holt that since he was "cut off from Scribner, I thought I would just cut myself off from you," as well. Nevertheless, he promised to send Holt his next manuscript.

In September 1898 James wrote his brother Henry that *The Will to Believe, and Other Essays in Popular Philosophy* was in its fourth printing of 1,000 copies and that Longmans, Green had sent him a check for "nearly $900 above the four hundred which I paid for the plates." The book went through twelve printings during James's lifetime, with posthumous printings from the original plates in 1910 and 1927. Available records indicate that between 1897 and 1912 royalties were paid to James or his heirs on British sales of some 4,442 copies.

The Will to Believe, and Other Essays in Popular Philosophy consists of ten essays delivered as lectures during the time James was teaching physiology and psychology. The first four emphasize the reasonableness and significance of religious belief. James says that belief must come into play where evidence is limited and that "there is really no scientific or other method by which men can steer safely between the opposite dangers of believing too little or of believing too much." When faced with having to choose between believing the truth and avoiding error at all cost, James recommends "a certain lightness of heart," a recognition that the world is so constituted that errors are certain to occur "in spite of all our caution." He is not saying that one may adopt any belief whatever, only that belief is a valid element of human experience.

James presents his defense of belief in both a weak and a strong form. The weak version, which asserts an individual's right to believe in situations where the evidence is lacking, owes a debt to Wright, who had criticized his friend's implication that the individual has a duty to believe in certain situations. Wright persuaded James that the only duty an individual has is to consider the available evidence impartially. The strong version—the assertion that emotion plays a legitimate role in all decision-making processes, including scientific ones—reflects Renouvier's continuing influence on James's thought.

In his essays on moral and social philosophy James argues that determinists, by rejecting the concept of chance, are doomed either to an all-encompassing pessimism about the universe or to abandoning any notion of regret about instances of evil. James argues instead for a pluralistic, indeterminate cosmos in which chance plays a constitutive role. Some of James's critics thought that his indeterminism eliminated the basis of human morality; Bradley accused him of making humans responsible only for the "mere accidents," the very thing for which he had supposed himself not to be arguing. James replied to such criticisms that he was concerned solely with the question of an open or closed future, not with the issue of human agency in moral affairs. According to James, an open future entails moral responsibility; a closed one does not. Other critics attacked James's notion of a finite God. E. L. Godkin said that he had an inadequate definition of religion, and thus of God; George Holmes Howison accused him of atheism; and Bradley noted that a finite deity was hardly compatible with Christianity.

James considered "The Moral Philosopher and the Moral Life" the most important essay in *The Will to Believe, and Other Essays in Popular Philosophy,* although the

address had not elicited much response when he first presented it to the Yale Philosophical Club in 1891. He begins by rejecting the idea that any ethical philosophy can be developed in advance of actual events and apart from human experience. There can be no final ethical truth, according to James, until the last individual has spoken; therefore, the best act is one "which makes for the *best whole,* in the sense of awakening the least sum of dissatisfactions." In this essay, his most important discussion of ethical theory, James proposes the adoption of the "strenuous mood," which enables one to endure "present ill, if only the greater ideal be attained." He asserts that the moral life involves a willingness to measure the vicissitudes of the present against a higher ideal. For this reason, he argues, humanity must posit a God, if only "as a pretext for the living hard, and getting out of the game of existence its keenest possibilities of zest." In this way James posits a transcendental ideal that enables people to make some sense out of the cacophony of conflicting needs and desires that is human experience.

James concludes *The Will to Believe, and Other Essays in Popular Philosophy* with "What Psychical Research Has Accomplished," in which he assails "the intolerance of science for such phenomena as we are studying," its "peremptory denial either of their existence or of their significance." His interest in psychic research, which was encouraged by his wife and his mother-in-law, is one of the most controversial aspects of James's thought. Some of his Harvard colleagues, such as the psychologist Hugo Münsterburg, found him too sympathetic to the claims of psychics, while others, including Royce, were amused by his openness to the claims of psychic researchers. One reason for James's interest in psychic research was his desire to deal with his own depression. In his letter to Frederic Myers accepting the presidency of the Society of Psychical Research in December 1893, he reported that an improvement in his mental state "may be due" to his visits to a "mind-curer with whom I tried eighteen sittings." A second source of James's interest in psychic phenomena was his hope that spiritualists might provide substantive information about the moral and religious dimensions of experience. As early as 1885 he had visited the well-known medium Leonora Evelina Piper, and he continued to patronize such practitioners throughout his life. While always skeptical of the psychics' claims, James was sufficiently convinced of their potential value that he opposed efforts in the Massachusetts legislature to curtail their activities. In an 1894 letter to the *Boston Transcript* he said that he held "no brief for any of these healers" but did believe that "their *facts* are patent and startling, and anything that interferes with the multiplication of such facts, and with our freest opportunity of

Pencil self-portrait by James, circa 1866 (Houghton Library, Harvard University)

observing and studying them, will . . . be a public calamity." James's position is more understandable when one recalls that medicine at that time was in a crude state, with quack remedies readily available; quackery was not limited to "mind-curers" alone.

James's interest in psychic research was both moral and experimental. As a medical student, he had written in a 21 February 1864 letter that in most cases "a doctor does more by the moral effect of his presence on the patient and family than by anything else." In his opinion spiritual healers could convey this moral presence just as well as practitioners who had undergone medical training. His experimental interest was reflected in his belief that the mediums should not be rejected simply because their standards did not conform to the norms of established science; the possibility always remained that their "experiments" might bear fruit. Despite the difficulties some colleagues had with James's interest in psychic phenomena, he was held in such esteem that in 1893 he was elected not only to the presidency of the British Society for Psychical Research but also to that of the American Association of Psychologists.

Because of his interest in psychic research, James was invited to give the 1897 Ingersoll Lecture on the Immortality of Man at Harvard. In this lecture he drew on Myers's idea of a "subliminal consciousness" to argue that at least the possibility of a consciousness that is independent of the brain–and, therefore, of immortality–cannot be denied. The lecture was published in 1898 as *Human Immortality: Two Supposed Objections to the Doctrine.*

Paul Henry Hanus, who had been appointed assistant professor of the history and art of teaching at Harvard in 1891, invited instructors in other departments who responded to his encouragement that they develop courses on the methods appropriate to teaching their respective disciplines. James and Royce were among those who responded. James's 1892 lectures to an audience of Cambridge teachers, dealing with such topics as stream of consciousness, habit, the association of ideas, interest, attention, memory, and will, were published individually in *The Atlantic Monthly* in 1899 before being collected that same year, together with three addresses to undergraduates at various women's colleges, as *Talks to Teachers on Psychology; and to Students on Some of Life's Ideals.* James's audience was eager to discern in the new psychology principles and techniques to apply in the classroom, but James cautions them that "psychology is a science, and teaching is an art; and sciences never generate arts directly out of themselves." Rather, James says, the teacher must gain attention by evoking the student's innate interests through concrete examples, anecdotes, illustrations, and stories. He encour-

James in 1869 (Houghton Library, Harvard University)

ages teachers to instruct students in the philosophy of habit and draws on his discussions in *The Principles of Psychology* to argue that the more elements of life that can be consigned to the realm of habit, the greater the scope that will be opened for voluntary behavior. Despite asserting the biological foundations of behavior and will, James asserts his belief in "free will and purely spiritual causation" and echoes his earlier denial of materialism in claiming that the production of consciousness by the nervous system remains a mystery. The act of free will seems to entail a feeling of agency not explainable by material means.

One of the concluding essays in *Talks to Teachers on Psychology; and to Students on Some of Life's Ideals,* "On a Certain Blindness in Human Beings," cites the human inability to understand things from the perspectives of "creatures and people different from ourselves." James has in mind the war against Spain that followed the destruction of the battleship *Maine* in Havana harbor in February 1898. Soon after this event James had joined the Anti-Imperialist League and had begun writing letters and making speeches against efforts by the U.S. government to annex the territory of other nations. He believed that an imperialist social policy represented a

*James in 1873, the year he accepted a position as a teacher
of anatomy and physiology at Harvard University
(Houghton Library, Harvard University)*

denial of the value of the individual that he considered essential both to democracy and to improving the human condition. James was severely criticized from many quarters for his opposition to what he perceived as the expansionist tendencies of the United States.

Talks to Teachers on Psychology; and to Students on Some of Life's Ideals went through at least twelve printings during James's lifetime and at least thirteen more from 1910 to 1929. Again, however, James entered into a controversy with Holt. In 1901 the Holt firm ordered a supply of the book from the printer, Ellis, requesting that they be sent to its Chicago office. Through a clerical error, James received a bill for the shipment from Ellis but no royalties from Holt. A vitriolic exchange of letters ensued, with James accusing Holt of fraud. Although James later acknowledged that he had been in the wrong and apologized, his relationship with Holt was permanently soured, and he never again sent Holt a manuscript.

In 1896 Edinburgh University had invited James to give the Gifford Lectures on Natural Religion. James annoyed his wife by initially rejecting the invitation, hoping that it would be repeated later, and by recommending Royce in his stead. Alice James fumed in an April 1897 letter to her brother-in-law Henry: "Royce! *He* will not refuse, but over he will go with his Infinite under his arm, and he will not even do honor to William's recommendation. William overrates him." James finally did accept, and two series of lectures were scheduled: one in 1899 and the other in 1901. In the fall and winter of 1896 he delivered eight talks on abnormal mental states at Boston's Lowell Institute that provided a background for the Gifford Lectures. These unpublished addresses covered such subjects as dreams and hypnotism, hysteria, automatisms, multiple personality, demoniacal possession, witchcraft, degeneration, and genius. In February he delivered the address on demoniacal possession to the Neurological Society at the New York Academy of Medicine.

While preparing for an August 1898 lecture series at the University of California, James went alone to the Adirondacks. The year had been a difficult one for him, beginning with sleeplessness and nervous exhaustion in early January, followed by the necessity to escort his brother Robertson to a sanitarium in hopes of finding a cure for his drinking. February brought the explosion of the *Maine* and James's stressful involvement with the anti-imperialist movement. His preferred method of relaxation was vigorous hiking in the mountains, which, he later discovered, had caused permanent damage to his heart. One experience, however, provided a boost to his preparation for the Gifford Lectures. Unable to sleep after a day of strenuous activity at high altitude, James wrote his wife on 9 July that he had experienced an intense "state of spiritual alertness" such that "it seemed as if the Gods of all the nature-mythologies were holding an indescribable meeting in my breast with the moral Gods of the inner life." He reported that this experience led him to see that "the two kinds of Gods have nothing in common," a realization that, he wrote, gave his Gifford Lectures "quite a hitch ahead."

In November 1898 James experienced chest pains that were severe enough to convince him to begin consulting doctors. Vacationing in the Adirondacks the next summer, he fainted twice while lost in the woods. James joked about the experience on returning to Cambridge, but his heart was seriously damaged. His continuing ill health prompted him to write to Edinburgh University offering to resign the appointment as Gifford Lecturer. Instead, the invitation was extended for two years to allow him more time to prepare.

The Gifford Lectures began on 16 May 1901; they were published as *The Varieties of Religious Experi-*

ence: A Study in Human Nature on 9 June 1902, the day James delivered the last lecture in the second series. His original intention had been to divide the subject matter into two equal parts, one descriptive and the other metaphysical. He found, however, that "the unexpected growth of the psychological matter" made such a balance impossible, and his metaphysical observations were largely confined to the "Conclusions" and a "Postscript" added for readers of the book.

In *The Varieties of Religious Experience* James emphasizes the experiences of extraordinary individuals such as saints and mystics, on the assumption that theirs are the "pattern-setters" for the great mass of ordinary religious experiences. Anticipating criticism for this emphasis on extreme cases, he admits that he was led to examine them by an "irrepressible curiosity" but also maintains that they provide the best means of understanding all other forms of religion: the significance of a subject is always best understood by considering its "exaggerations and perversions, its equivalents and substitutions and nearest relatives elsewhere." To those who might fear that scientific study would "discredit the religious side of life," James replies that the biological and psychological bases of religious experience must be distinguished from their results and, further, that such experience must be judged not by its origins, as revealed by critical study, but "by its results exclusively."

James's famous definition of religion reflects his belief that its institutional and theological aspects are secondary to individual experience: "Religion . . . shall mean for us *the feelings, acts and experiences of individual men in their solitude, so far as they apprehend themselves to stand in relation to whatever they may consider the divine.*" This position is no mere subjectivism, since James understands "experience" to be *of* something—in this case, of a broadly defined "divine" object. He further requires that this object be taken with absolute seriousness: the truly religious person does not trivialize faith.

The subtitle of the book, *A Study in Human Nature,* reflects James's conviction that religious experience is but one aspect of human experience in general, to be compared and classified within that broader domain. The various states of religious happiness, sadness, mystical trance, and the like "are each and all of them special cases of kinds of human experience of much wider scope." Each instance of an experience in a particular religious tradition must be examined within the general category to which it belongs and in light of the way in which other religions interpret it. In the chapter "Philosophy" James calls for a "Science of Religions" that will classify and judge religion objectively, apart from the emotion-laden struggles that occur within and among the world's many religious sects.

James considers mysticism the basis for personal religious experience. He does not mean that all religion is mystical or that mystics' claims must be uncritically accepted. Nonetheless, the nature of mystical experience is to "break down the authority of the non-mystical or rationalistic consciousness, based upon the understanding and the sense alone. They show it to be only one kind of consciousness. . . . the existence of mystical states absolutely overthrows the pretension of non-mystical states to be the sole and ultimate dictators of what we may believe." He argues for the possibility of being connected through Myers's "subliminal consciousness" to a larger cosmic reality than one ordinarily perceives. So understood, religious experience testifies not necessarily to the existence of God as traditionally conceived but, at least, to the existence of "*something* larger than ourselves" with which we "have business" and in union with which we can "find our greatest peace."

The Varieties of Religious Experience has been critically examined by psychologists, theologians, philosophers, and ordinary readers. Some have found in it justification for their religious beliefs; others have criticized James's emphasis on individual and extreme cases; still others have objected that James's subjectivism denies the validity of rational justification of religion. In *Psychoanalysis and Religion* (1950) Erich Fromm said that James's use of the concept of "subliminal consciousness" anticipated Carl Gustav Jung's interpretation of religion as a function of the unconscious. On the other hand, F. R. Tennant objected in his *Philosophical Theology* (1935) to what he considered James's denigration of ordinary religious experience as compared to the supposedly superior subconscious dimension. James's colorful examples and vivid language made *The Varieties of Religious Experience* the most widely read and discussed of his writings to that time, and it remains one of the most important works in the psychology of religion. The manner in which it draws on both psychological and philosophical theory marks the book as a pivotal moment in James's intellectual life. While he by no means abandoned his interests in psychology and religion, the philosophical concerns that underlay all of his thought now surfaced in a series of books, two published posthumously, devoted to his theories of pragmatism and radical empiricism.

Although he had published little in the field of philosophy, James strongly desired to be recognized as a philosopher. From 1904 through 1907 he published many articles articulating his philosophical views, culminating in the 1907 publication of *Pragmatism: A New Name for Some Old Ways of Thinking. Popular Lectures on Philosophy.* The book was an immediate success, going through ten printings in the first three years and at least twenty-five printings, using the original plates, until 1948.

James had introduced his theory of pragmatism in an 1898 lecture to the Berkeley Philosophical Union, "Philosophical Conceptions and Practical Results."

Alice Howe Gibbens around the time she and James became engaged in 1878 (Houghton Library, Harvard University)

There he gave Peirce credit for first enunciating the doctrine, although, as many commentators have noted, the two men's conceptions are markedly different: whereas for Peirce pragmatism is a means of clarifying concepts, for James it is a theory of truth.

James spent the first five months of 1906 teaching at Stanford University. On 25 February he delivered to the entire university community the address "The Psychology of the War Spirit," in which he suggested that society substitute for "military conscription a conscription of the whole youthful population" into an army that would work to improve society rather than engage in its characteristic bloodshed. Young people could thus learn such virtues as self-denial, humility, honor, and discipline in an organization that would be morally equivalent to the military but would lack the latter's violent nature. The address served as the basis for one of his best-known essays, "The Moral Equivalent of War," published in 1910.

The San Francisco earthquake occurred on 18 April; James went to San Francisco that morning and spent the day observing the destruction. Later that year, in his presidential address to the American Philosophical Association, James drew on his experiences in the California earthquake to discuss the way in which a crisis can evoke from individuals previously unexpressed powers of will and discipline.

James returned to Harvard in the fall of 1906. On 11 January 1907 he officially resigned his position. Eliot granted him emeritus status with a stipend of $2,600 a year. Allen describes James's final class at Harvard: "As Professor James began his last lecture on January 22, he was surprised to see his wife and several colleagues slip into seats at the rear of the room, but he proceeded to teach his class in his usual informal manner. At the end of the period there was an enthusiastic ovation and then the class presented him with a silver loving cup." James felt relief at leaving the classroom, writing his brother Henry on 4 May 1907, "You can't tell how happy I am at having thrown off the nightmare of my 'professorship.' As a 'professor' I always felt myself a sham, with its chief duties of being a walking encyclopedia of erudition. I am now at liberty to be a *reality,* and the comfort is unspeakable–literally unspeakable, to be my own man, after 35 years of being owned by others. I can now live for truth pure and simple, instead of for truth accommodated to the most unheard-of requirements set by others." At last James felt free to explore the implications of philosophy for human existence. The immediate task at hand was turning his lectures on pragmatism into a book.

The formal lectures on which the text of *Pragmatism* is based were delivered at Boston's Lowell Institute in late 1906 and at Columbia University in New York City in the weeks just after his final classroom lecture. James envisions pragmatism as "primarily a method of settling metaphysical disputes that otherwise might be interminable" in order to determine the implications of such disputes for everyday existence. Although he disclaims any logical connection between pragmatism and his doctrine of radical empiricism, James makes it clear that pragmatism "represents . . . the empiricist attitude" that challenges the dogmatism of more-rationalistic philosophies. The most controversial aspect of the book is his proposal that truth is never final: "truth *happens* to an idea. It *becomes* true, is *made* true by events. Its verity *is* in fact an event, a process: the process namely of its verifying itself." Verification of truth is a "function of agreeable leading" that requires that attention be paid to the relations among things and not simply to the momentary definitions created by the human mind. This understanding of truth calls to mind James's claims in *The Principles of Psychology* that definitions are merely stopping points within the stream of thought, from which the individual can proceed to reconsider, alter, and redefine the meaning of reality. No final or absolute truth is available to human consciousness. Truth has practical value when it leads from "one moment of experience . . . towards other moments which it will be worth while to have been led to. Primarily, and on the common-sense level, the truth of a state of mind means this function of a *leading that is worth-while.*" James's confidence in his work is apparent in his 4 May 1907 letter to his brother Henry, written just after he finished checking the proofs: "I shouldn't be surprised if ten years hence it should be rated as 'epoch-making,' for of the definitive triumph of that way of thinking I can entertain no doubt whatever—I believe it to be something quite like the protestant reformation."

In 1907 James published *The Meaning of Truth: A Sequel to "Pragmatism"* with the intention of clarifying his controversial theory of truth. Unlike its predecessor, the sequel was addressed to professional philosophers. Unfortunately for James, *The Meaning of Truth* did not persuade his detractors that he had clarified his position or satisfied their criticisms. The book was viewed as mainly a restatement of his earlier claims rather than a response to the questions it had raised. One of the most common criticisms was that he confused the question of the substance of truth with the means of arriving at it. Whatever one's assessment of James's view, in *Pragmatism* and *The Meaning of Truth* he stimulated an energetic and creative debate that continues to the present day.

In 1909 James published *A Pluralistic Universe,* based on the Hibbert Lectures he delivered at Manchester College of the University of Oxford in 1908 and 1909 on the topic "The Present Situation in Philosophy." James had accepted the invitation despite his increasingly painful angina. In the lectures, which were so popular that many were turned away at the door, he espoused the idea of an open, unfinished universe. "Radical empiricism and pluralism stand out for the legitimacy of the notion of *some:* each part of the world is in some ways connected, in some other ways not connected with the other parts, and the ways can be discriminated, for many of them are obvious, and their differences are obvious to view," he says in *A Pluralistic Universe.* Absolutism rejects this relational perspective in favor of a unified cosmos whose parts are subordinate to some Higher Truth. James, opting for a reality that is continuously in process, depicts human beings as moral actors bound by their very nature to participate in the creation and discovery of new truths and new realities. In its presentation of this attitude *A Pluralistic Universe* serves well as a coherent statement of James's mature philosophy.

James heard Sigmund Freud lecture at Clark University in Worcester, Massachusetts, in early September 1909. While professing difficulty with Freud's "dream theories" and pronouncing "'symbolism' . . . a

most dangerous method" in a 28 September letter to Théodore Flournoy, James said that "I hope that Freud and his pupils will push their ideas to their utmost limits, so that we may learn what they are." In *An Autobiographical Study* (1935) Freud recalled walking with James: "He stopped suddenly, handed me a bag he was carrying and asked me to walk on, saying that he would catch me up as soon as he had got through an attack of angina pectoris which was just coming on. He died of that disease a year later; and I have always wished that I might be as fearless as he was in the face of approaching death."

James's last few months were physically difficult. On 25 October 1909 he recorded in his diary, "Dreadful angina on going to bed." The symptoms were so severe that he began visiting a Christian Science practitioner. Still, he kept up his professional relationships, spoke out for his anti-imperialist stance, and continued to draw criticism for his interest in psychic research. Royce and Münsterberg lost some of their professional respect for James as a result of his tolerance for an Italian medium, Eusapia Paladino, whom everyone, including James, knew to be a fraud. When Münsterberg published an article in *Metropolitan Magazine* in February 1910 calling psychic researchers pseudoscientists who were taken in by the performances of mediums such as Paladino, James stormed in his diary, "buffoon article!"

After a trip to Europe to see his brother Henry, who was ill, and to try "a certain medical experiment" in Paris, James returned to the family's summer home in Chocorua, New Hampshire. On Friday, 26 August 1910, Alice James recorded in her diary that "William died just before 2:30 in my arms. . . . No pain at the last and no consciousness." In his eulogy one of James's former students, the Reverend George A. Gordon, pastor of Boston's New Old South Church, declared that "after all is said and done, it is the human aspect that lasts the longest. The scholar, thinker, teacher is merged at last in the human being. The man is the ultimate and everlasting value." Biographer Allen comments that "these were William James's own strongest convictions, and what the words lacked in originality they made up in appropriateness." James was cremated at Mount Auburn Cemetery, and his ashes were scattered on the mountain stream at Chocorua, where he had often bathed on his summer visits.

Two important books appeared after James's death. *Some Problems of Philosophy: A Beginning of an Introduction to Philosophy* (1911) represents his efforts to state his philosophical position systematically. He had worked on the book until a few weeks before his death; in a memorandum dated 26 July 1910 he directed that it be published with a notice to the reader that it is

*James with his brother, the novelist Henry James, in 1905
(Houghton Library, Harvard University
and Alexander R. James)*

"fragmentary and unrevised. . . . Call it 'A beginning of an introduction to philosophy.' Say that I hoped by it to round out my system, which now is too much like an arch built only on one side." James's student and friend Horace M. Kallen prepared the text from two available versions, with assistance from Perry. While reviewers commonly noted that the book for the most part restated James's earlier views, some found new ideas in the text, especially the discussions of infinity, causality, and the breakdown of rationalism. *Essays in Radical Empiricism* (1912) is a collection of James's scattered writings on the topic assembled by Perry. James had announced "radical empiricism" as his philosophical attitude in the preface to *The Will to Believe*: "I say 'empiricism,' because it is contented to regard its most assured conclusions concerning matters of fact as hypothesis liable to modification in the course of future experience; and I say 'radical,' because it treats the doctrine of monism itself as an hypothesis." One of the most striking claims in the text is James's assertion that consciousness, as an entity, "is fictitious." He proposes instead a doctrine of "pure experience" that does not distinguish between consciousness and its object. "'Pure' experience" is "the instant field of the present" that simply is; it is potentially either subject or object,

but in the present moment it is simply "*there*" to be acted on. Although *Essays in Radical Empiricism* did not receive as great a critical reception as had *Pragmatism,* it stimulated a vigorous debate that has yet to run its course. Some have viewed James's radical empiricism as essentially solipsistic, while others have debated the uncertain relationship between radical empiricism and pragmatism. Phenomenologists have produced much literature on the phenomenological character of both James's psychology and his radical empiricism; it is known that James influenced Edmund Husserl, the founder of phenomenology. A. J. Ayer spoke positively of radical empiricism, and Russell claimed that this aspect of James's thought exercised the main influence on his theory of "neutral monism."

William James played a central role in both philosophy and psychology at a time when American intellectual life was struggling into the modern era. His popularity in his day was evident in his success as an author and lecturer. He continues to be widely read in the twenty-first century, particularly by philosophers and psychologists concerned with human behavior, experience, and consciousness. As he was in his lifetime, James is still regarded as an original thinker whose vision has the power to stimulate popular and academic audiences alike.

Letters:

The Letters of William James, Edited by His Son, 2 volumes, edited by Henry James (Boston: Atlantic Monthly Press, 1920; London: Longmans, Green, 1920);

The Selected Letters of William James, edited by Elizabeth Hardwick (New York: Farrar, Straus & Cudahy, 1961);

The Letters of William James and Théodore Flournoy, edited by Robert C. Le Clair (Madison: University of Wisconsin Press, 1966);

William James: Selected Unpublished Correspondence, 1885–1910, edited by Frederick J. Down Scott (Columbus: Ohio State University Press, 1986);

The Correspondence of William James, 12 volumes projected, 9 volumes published to date, edited by Ignas K. Skrupskelis, Elizabeth M. Berkeley, Bernice Grohskopf, and Wilma Bradbeer (Charlottesville: University Press of Virginia, 1992–);

William and Henry James: Selected Letters, edited by Skrupskelis and Berkeley (Charlottesville: University Press of Virginia, 1997).

Bibliographies:

Ralph Barton Perry, "Annotated Bibliography of the Writings of William James," in *The Writings of William James: A Comprehensive Edition,* edited by

John J. McDermott (New York: Random House, 1968), pp. 811–858;

Ignas K. Skrupskelis, *William James: A Reference Guide* (Boston: G. K. Hall, 1977).

Biographies:

Alice James, *Alice James: Her Brothers, Her Journal,* edited by Anna Robeson Burr (New York: Dodd, Mead, 1934);

Ralph Barton Perry, *The Thought and Character of William James,* 2 volumes (Boston: Little, Brown, 1935);

F. O. Mathiessen, *The James Family: A Group Biography* (New York: Knopf, 1947);

Gay Wilson Allen, *William James: A Biography* (New York: Viking, 1967);

Howard M. Feinstein, *Becoming William James* (Ithaca, N.Y. & London: Cornell University Press, 1984);

R. W. B. Lewis, *The Jameses: A Family Narrative* (New York: Farrar, Straus & Giroux, 1991);

Linda Simon, ed., *William James Remembered* (Lincoln: University of Nebraska Press, 1996);

Simon, *Genuine Reality: A Life of William James* (New York: Harcourt Brace, 1998).

References:

Gordon W. Allport, "The Productive Paradoxes of William James," *Psychological Review,* 50 (1943): 95–119;

A. J. Ayer, *The Origins of Pragmatism: Studies in the Philosophy of Charles Sanders Peirce and William James* (San Francisco: Freeman, Cooper, 1968);

G. William Barnard, *Exploring Unseen Worlds: William James and the Philosophy of Mysticism* (Albany: State University of New York Press, 1997);

Jacques Barzun, *A Stroll with William James* (New York: Harper & Row, 1983);

Graham Bird, *William James* (London & New York: Routledge & Kegan Paul, 1986);

Julius Seelye Bixler, *Religion in the Philosophy of William James* (Boston: Marshall Jones, 1926);

Daniel W. Bjork, *The Compromised Scientist: William James in the Development of American Psychology* (New York: Columbia University Press, 1983);

Bjork, *William James: The Center of His Vision* (New York: Columbia University Press, 1988);

Brand Blanshard and Herbert W. Schneider, eds., *In Commemoration of William James, 1842–1942* (New York: Columbia University Press, 1942; republished, New York: AMS Press, 1967);

Emile Boutroux, *William James* (New York: Longmans, Green, 1912);

Don S. Browning, *Pluralism and Personality: William James and Some Contemporary Cultures of Psychology* (Lewis-burg, Pa.: Bucknell University Press / London: Associated University Press, 1980);

Milic Capek, "The Reappearance of the Self in the Last Philosophy of William James," *Philosophical Review,* 62 (October 1953): 526–544;

George Cotkin, *William James, Public Philosopher,* New Studies in American Intellectual and Cultural History (Baltimore: Johns Hopkins University Press, 1990);

Paul Jerome Croce, *Science and Religion in the Era of William James,* volume 1: *Eclipse of Certainty, 1820–1880* (Chapel Hill: University of North Carolina Press, 1995);

Michael H. Dearmey and Stephen Skousgaard, eds., *The Philosophical Psychology of William James,* Current Continental Research, volume 5 (Washington, D.C.: Center for Advanced Research in Phenomenology & University Press of America, 1986);

Margaret E. Donnelly, ed., *Reinterpreting the Legacy of William James* (Washington, D.C.: American Psychological Association, 1992);

Patrick Kiaran Dooley, *Pragmatism as Humanism: The Philosophy of William James* (Chicago: Nelson-Hall, 1974);

James M. Edie, *William James and Phenomenology,* Studies in Phenomenology and Existential Philosophy (Bloomington: Indiana University Press, 1987);

Craig R. Eisendrath, *The Unifying Moment: The Psychological Philosophy of William James and Alfred North Whitehead* (Cambridge, Mass.: Harvard University Press, 1971);

Théodore Flournoy, *The Philosophy of William James* (New York: Holt, 1917);

Eugene Fontinell, *Self, God and Immortality: A Jamesian Investigation* (Philadelphia: Temple University Press, 1986);

Marcus Peter Ford, *William James's Philosophy: A New Perspective* (Amherst: University of Massachusetts Press, 1982);

Sigmund Freud, *An Autobiographical Study* (London: Leonard & Virginia Woolf at the Hogarth Press and the Institute of Psychoanalysis, 1935);

Erich Fromm, *Psychoanalysis and Religion* (New Haven: Yale University Press, 1950), pp. 20, 49, 403;

William Joseph Gavin, *William James and the Reinstatement of the Vague* (Philadelphia: Temple University Press, 1992);

George P. Graham, *William James and the Affirmation of God,* American University Studies, Series VII: Theology and Religion, volume 110 (New York: Peter Lang, 1992);

Richard A. Hocks, *Henry James and Pragmatistic Thought: A Study in the Relationship between the Philosophy of*

William James and the Literary Art of Henry James (Chapel Hill: University of North Carolina Press, 1974);

Michael G. Johnson and Tracy B. Henley, eds., *Reflections on* The Principles of Psychology: *William James after a Century* (Hillsdale, N.J.: L. Erlbaum Associates, 1990);

Henry S. Levinson, *The Religious Investigations of William James* (Chapel Hill: University of North Carolina Press, 1981);

Levinson, *Science, Metaphysics, and the Chance of Salvation: An Interpretation of the Thought of William James* (Missoula, Mont.: Published by Scholars Press for the American Academy of Religion, 1978);

Hans Linschoten, *On the Way toward a Phenomenological Psychology: The Psychology of William James* (Pittsburgh: Duquesne University Press, 1968);

David W. Marcell, *Progress and Pragmatism: James, Dewey, Beard, and the American Idea of Progress* (Westport, Conn.: Greenwood Press, 1974);

Joshua I. Miller, *Democratic Temperament: The Legacy of William James,* American Political Thought (Lawrence: University Press of Kansas, 1997);

Gerald E. Myers, *William James: His Life and Thought* (New Haven: Yale University Press, 2001);

Robert J. O'Connell, *William James on the Courage to Believe* (New York: Fordham University Press, 1984);

Doris Olin, ed., *William James: Pragmatism in Focus* (London & New York: Routledge, 1992);

Ralph Barton Perry, *In the Spirit of William James* (New Haven: Yale University Press, 1938);

Ross Posnock, *The Trial of Curiosity: Henry James, William James, and the Challenge of Modernity* (New York: Oxford University Press, 1991);

Ruth Anna Putnam, ed., *The Cambridge Companion to William James* (Cambridge & New York: Cambridge University Press, 1997);

Bennett Ramsey, *Submitting to Freedom: The Religious Vision of William James,* Religion in America (New York: Oxford University Press, 1993);

Andrew Reck, "Dualisms in William James's *Principles of Psychology,*" *Tulane Studies in Philosophy,* 21 (1972): 24–38;

Frederick J. Ruf, *The Creation of Chaos: William James and the Stylistic Making of a Disorderly World,* SUNY

Series in Rhetoric and Theology (Albany: State University of New York Press, 1991);

Charlene Haddock Seigfried, *Chaos and Context: A Study in William James* (Athens: Ohio University Press, 1978);

Seigfried, *William James's Radical Reconstruction of Philosophy* (Albany: State University of New York Press, 1990);

John J. Shea, *Religious Experiencing: William James and Eugene Gendlin* (Lanham, Md.: University Press of America, 1987);

Skousgaard, "The Phenomenology of William James's Philosophical Psychology," *Journal of the British Society of Phenomenology,* 7 (May 1976): 86–95;

Richard Stevens, *James and Husserl: The Foundations of Meaning* (The Hague: Nijhoff, 1974);

Ellen Kappy Suckiel, *Heaven's Champion: William James's Philosophy of Religion* (Notre Dame, Ind.: University of Notre Dame Press, 1996);

Suckiel, *The Pragmatic Philosophy of William James* (Notre Dame, Ind.: University of Notre Dame Press, 1982);

Eugene Taylor, *William James on Consciousness beyond the Margin* (Princeton: Princeton University Press, 1996);

Taylor, *William James on Exceptional Mental States: The 1896 Lowell Lectures* (New York: Scribners, 1983);

F. R. Tennant, *Philosophical Theology,* volume 1 (Cambridge: Cambridge University Press, 1935), p. 120;

Kim Townsend, *Manhood at Harvard: William James and Others* (New York: Norton, 1996);

James C. S. Wernham, *James's Will-to-Believe Doctrine: A Heretical View* (Kingston, Ont.: McGill-Queen's University Press, 1987);

John Wild, *The Radical Empiricism of William James* (Garden City, N.Y.: Doubleday, 1969);

Bruce Wilshire, *William James and Phenomenology: A Study of* The Principles of Psychology (Bloomington: Indiana University Press, 1968).

Papers:

Most of William James's papers are at the Houghton Library of Harvard University.

Marietta Kies

(31 December 1853 – 20 July 1899)

Dorothy G. Rogers
Montclair State University

BOOKS: *The Ethical Principle and Its Applications in State Relations* (Ann Arbor, Mich.: Inland Press, 1892);

Institutional Ethics (Boston: Allyn & Bacon, 1894).

OTHER: William Torrey Harris, *Introduction to the Study of Philosophy,* edited by Kies (New York: Appleton, 1890).

Marietta Kies distinguished herself as one of the first American women to earn a Ph.D. in philosophy. She was also one of the first women to become a professional academic philosopher in the United States, teaching at the college level at four institutions. She was a member of the idealist movement in American philosophy, which imported into the United States the basic principles of German thought, particularly that of Georg Wilhelm Friedrich Hegel and his contemporaries, along with their progressive educational ideas. While Kies's female colleagues in the idealist movement focused almost solely on pedagogy or on feminist theory in their published work, she discussed matters unrelated to education or to women's issues and developed a political philosophy in which altruism is a central concept.

Kies was born on 31 December 1853 in Killingly, a small town in the northeast corner of Connecticut, to William Knight and Miranda Young Kies. She was descended from Scottish immigrants who arrived in America in the mid 1700s. Though her immediate family was not particularly prominent or well-to-do, there were several influential figures in her extended family. A great-great-aunt, Mary Dixon Kies, was the first woman in America to be granted a patent–in 1809, for an innovative weaving technique–and was recognized by Dolly Madison for this achievement. Dixon Kies's legacy continued to be lauded in Marietta Kies's day and is still remembered by Kies family descendants. Other relatives included an aunt, Mary Ann Kies, who was a social worker in New York City, and a second cousin, Edwin W. Davis, an educator in Colorado.

Marietta Kies (Mount Holyoke College Archives)

As the second oldest of five girls, Kies was expected to help support the family as soon as she was able. She alternated between factory work and school, a common practice for working-class children during the period. In her mid teens she began teaching in public schools in Killingly and nearby Putnam. Because she needed to earn money for college, her higher education was delayed. She began her studies at Mount Holyoke Female Seminary (now Mount Holyoke College) in South Hadley, Massachusetts, when she was nearly twenty-five. After graduating from Mount Holyoke in

1881, she became the assistant principal at the public high school in Putnam, Connecticut. In 1883 she accepted a teaching position in the women's division of Colorado College in Colorado Springs. She returned to the East in 1885 to serve as professor of ethics and mental and moral philosophy at Mount Holyoke, though she was allowed to take a three-month leave of absence each year in order to continue her studies.

Kies began to develop her philosophical ideas at Mount Holyoke. She used texts by thinkers who were popular at the time: Noah Porter, the president of Yale University; the personalist philosopher Borden Parker Bowne of Boston University; and, most notably, William Torrey Harris, the recognized leader of the American idealist movement. Kies attended the Summer School of Philosophy in Concord, Massachusetts, which Harris had established in 1879 with Franklin Sanborn and Amos Bronson Alcott. The school was an experimental adult-education program that drew hundreds of participants to Concord each summer until 1888. Since many universities refused to admit women, more than half of those in attendance were women who were eager to study with famous men such as Harris and Porter.

Kies studied with Harris at the Concord School between 1882 and 1888, and she collected his essays and lectures into a volume for use as a textbook in her philosophy courses. She also attended lectures by George Sylvester Morris, another early American idealist philosopher, who taught at the University of Michigan. By 1887 Harris and Morris recognized that Kies was a serious thinker who could contribute a great deal to the development of American philosophy. Harris wrote her a strong letter of recommendation for admission to the doctoral program at the University of Michigan, one of the first universities to admit women at both the undergraduate and graduate levels, and addressed it to Morris. Morris forwarded it to the university's president, James B. Angell, and Kies became the first woman to study philosophy at the doctoral level at the University of Michigan (and the sixth in the nation) in the fall of 1887.

At Michigan, Kies was part of a lively and intellectually stimulating environment that had been open to women undergraduates for nearly twenty years when she became a student there. Her professors, Morris and the soon-to-be-famous John Dewey, were involved in student life, holding classes at their homes and leading clubs and discussion groups. Both men were supportive of women's education at Michigan and provided an egalitarian environment in which women could fully participate in debates and discussions. This attitude was the exception to the rule at Michigan and many other universities at the time, because male stu-

dents and faculty members often felt resentful of women's sudden entry into the academic world. In 1890, while still a student, Kies published her collection of Harris's works as *Introduction to the Study of Philosophy*.

Kies and two other women completed their degrees in philosophy at Michigan in the early 1890s: Kies in 1891 and Eliza Read Sunderland and Caroline Miles Hill in 1892. Several other women completed master's degrees in the field at the university during this period.

After completing her Ph.D., Kies accepted a position as an instructor of moral and mental philosophy at Mills College, a women's school in Oakland, California. She played an active role in the college and the surrounding academic community by attending the Philosophical Union meetings of George Holmes Howison, a friend and colleague of Harris's in St. Louis in the 1860s who had joined the faculty of the University of California at Berkeley in 1884. The independent-minded Kies got into a dispute with Howison over his interpretation of Hegel at a Philosophical Union meeting in 1891. Harris had often argued philosophical points with Howison, favoring monism over Howison's pluralism, for example, and Kies took up the debate in place of her mentor. Kies argued fiercely on behalf of monism and, as noted by her close friend Georgiana Hodgkins in a eulogy published in *In Memoriami Marietta Kies, A.M., Ph.D.* (1900), established herself as "a Modern Hypatia" among her female colleagues for this "incomparable defense" of her views.

In 1892 Kies published her first original book, *The Ethical Principle and Its Applications in State Relations,* a discussion of the feasibility of altruism as a political theory. An ethical society, Kies says, requires both "justice" and "grace" if it is to be truly fair to all of its members. Justice, in Kies's understanding, is the principle that guides individualistic, or egoistic, thinking. Justice provides only a thin veil of protection for individuals in society—what are called "negative freedoms" in political philosophy. The society that operates on a justice-based principle ensures only that individuals have "freedom from" interference by others. Justice considers the needs of the individual first, of the whole later. Grace, on the other hand, is the principle of action that guides charitable or altruistic thinking. Grace does not simply protect individuals from harm but actually ensures that both individuals and groups within society can thrive. Laws based on grace provide "positive freedoms." Rather than "freedoms from," positive freedoms are "freedoms to": to get a good education, to work in the field of one's choice, and the like. In contrast to justice, grace considers the needs of the whole first and of individuals afterward. In Kies's view, the ability to demonstrate grace toward others makes one truly human. A Progressivist and a Christian Socialist, Kies believed that political decision makers were increasingly taking grace, or altruism, into account in public life. *The Ethical Principle and Its Applications in State Relations* received a brief and unenthusiastic review by Josiah Royce in *The International Journal of Ethics*. Royce, a contemporary of Kies, thought her ideas were too close to those of Harris, whom Royce saw as a member of the old guard, and he claimed that she merely echoes Harris rather than providing original material. Another critic, Charles Cook, gave the book a more thorough, favorable review in *The Philosophical Review*.

Kies studied at the Universities of Zurich and Leipzig during the 1892–1893 academic year; European universities were beginning to be more open to female students, and even the top institutions welcomed American women. When she returned to the United States, Kies became principal of a high school in Plymouth, Massachusetts.

Kies's second and last book, *Institutional Ethics*, was published in 1894. It deals with the same general theme as *The Ethical Principle and Its Applications in State Relations:* the need for justice and grace to complement each other in the political world. Yet, Kies expands her discussion by analyzing the roles in society of the law, the family, the school, and the church. She distinguishes two kinds of law, corresponding to the two kinds of freedom. "Protective" laws ensure individual rights; they prevent people from harming others by threatening to impose penalties on those who do so. These laws provide negative freedoms—from theft or injury, for instance. But for a society and the individuals within it to thrive, more than negative freedoms are required; laws are needed that enable people to have the "freedom to" pursue greater goals. Kies calls these "constructive laws." Constructive laws underlie provisions such as public education, labor reform, and social welfare.

In *Institutional Ethics* Kies's commitment to the progressive political and social movements of her day is clear. For instance, her "constructive" laws place an immense burden on the government both to curb industrial monopolies and to uplift and support the poor so that they can eventually help themselves. Even so, Kies remains true to her idealist roots. Like her mentor Harris, she sees Hegel as the model philosopher; and for Hegel, society is an organic whole, and the "State" is necessarily rational. Therefore, the State can and should ensure balance and harmony within society. Yet, Kies differs from Hegel in advocating welfare benefits to the poor: Hegel feared that too much assistance would discourage individual effort and initiative among the "rabble." Kies holds that legislation that requires people to behave "as if" they care about the poor will change individuals and, eventually, society as

Kies in 1881, the year she graduated from Mount Holyoke College (Mount Holyoke College Archives)

a whole, so that helping the poor will become a commonly accepted practice.

With Hegel, Kies sees the family as the fundamental institution in society. A person is born into a certain concrete family situation and is shaped and directed by the care provided there. The family is meant to nurture and protect its members but also to prepare them to fend for themselves in "civil society"– the business office, the marketplace, the courtroom, and so on. In civil society an individual differentiates himself or herself from others. The State–the government– ensures that competition among individuals in civil society does not destroy the unity of the whole. The family, civil society, and the State are the fundamental social institutions, while the school and the church are mediating institutions. The school supplements the family's educative role, teaching children respect and collaboration but also independence. Ideally, the church should help individuals to attain Christian ideals of goodness, but at the very least it allows self-development for all individuals.

Kies was writing more than fifty years after Hegel presented his theories of society and its primary institutions, and her ideas were shaped by historical differences. First, public education was widespread in Kies's day, and the mediating influence of the school was therefore much more visible to her than it had been to Hegel. In addition, most school districts provided equal education for elementary-school children, so that even if girls and boys were not in classes together, each group was exposed to similar academic challenges and social pressures. Kies therefore assumes that the school provides the same bridge from family life to civil society for girls that it does for boys, while Hegel thought that girls and young women would be satisfied to remain in the home. Related to this notion is Kies's departure from the Hegelian view of the family. Hegel saw the family as a unity in which it is impossible to be truly individuated, while Kies assumes individuality within the family and even holds that its members can have competing interests. She saw that the growing education of women and girls and their resulting ability to make independent decisions had affected family life. While maintaining a Hegelian ideal of family unity overall, she recognizes its evolving nature. In this sense she is being truly Hegelian, in that Hegel regarded social and political structures as being in a constant state of evolution.

Surprisingly enough, Kies is not strongly in favor of women's voting rights. She says that only certain issues, such as education, temperance, and some labor matters, are sufficiently relevant to women to justify the extension of the vote to them. Whether women should vote or simply continue to be represented by the votes of men is a question of expediency; and in Kies's view it is not particularly expedient for women to vote alongside men, because the act of casting a ballot is just the culminating act in a long process of public discourse and debate. It is sufficient for women to participate in political life by contributing to the discussion of policy; they do not need to be involved in enacting it. Kies does not deny that, in the abstract, women have at least as much of a right to vote as men do. But in her view an abstract right is not particularly valuable or meaningful. Women's concrete situation is more important. They are already able to join in public discourse on matters of interest to them, and they thereby influence the outcome of elections. How, Kies asks, would voting advance their interests any further?

The book received a favorable notice from W. B. Elkin in *The Philosophical Review*. An anonymous review in *The Dial* (October 1895) was less positive, but it could not have harmed Kies professionally. The reviewer was not well versed in academic philosophy,

expressing disappointment that Kies does not focus on some spiritual and rather esoteric ideas about the unity of the earth and heavens—ideas barely tangential to the Hegelian unity Kies discusses in her introduction to the book.

In 1896 Kies assumed her most important academic position when she became the professor of rhetoric at Butler College, a coeducational institution in Indianapolis. Although she was subject to the common inequities imposed on women at the time, such as being passed over for promotion and receiving lower pay than her male colleagues, she thrived at Butler. She was thoroughly engaged in campus life, teaching rhetoric (then considered a branch of philosophy) and serving as adviser to the debate team.

Had Kies lived into the twentieth century, as the women's voting rights movement gained momentum, she might have changed her views on women's suffrage. But during the 1898–1899 academic year she contracted tuberculosis, and by the end of the spring semester she was extremely worn down physically and emotionally. Planning to convalesce at the home of her cousin Davis and his wife, May, she took the train from Indianapolis to Pueblo, Colorado, in mid June. Her health declined further, however, and she died on 20 July.

Because of her early death and the increased emphasis on professional academic philosophy since the turn of the twentieth century, Kies is barely remembered today. Yet, she made an important contribution by applying a complex philosophical theory—Hegelian idealism—to some important social and political questions of her day. While she recognized that her altruistic political ideal might be unattainable, she maintained that it should be pursued. Altruism is the highest stage in ethics, in her view, because it is modeled after the Christian religion, which links the human and the divine. Kies's theory of "justice" and "grace" continues to be relevant to political philosophy. Since the 1980s feminist thinkers have made serious and substantive critiques of traditional political and moral theory, charging it with gender bias. Feminists have insisted that another model of political and ethical action is needed that will include women in the dialogue. Kies provides precisely this sort of model, one that applies traditional ideas and concepts in a new way.

Reference:
Sherberne S. Mathews, ed., *In Memoriam: Marietta Kies, A.M., Ph.D.* (Boston: Printed by Frank Wood, 1900).

Susanne K. Langer
(20 December 1895 – 17 July 1985)

Donald Dryden
Duke University

BOOKS: *The Cruise of the Little Dipper and Other Fairy Tales,*
illustrated by Helen Sewell (New York: Norcross,
1923; second edition, with new introduction by the
author, Greenwich, Conn.: New York Graphics
Society, 1963);

The Practice of Philosophy (New York: Holt, 1930);

An Introduction to Symbolic Logic (Boston: Houghton Mifflin, 1937; London: Allen & Unwin, 1937);

*Philosophy in a New Key: A Study in the Symbolism of Reason,
Rite and Art* (Cambridge, Mass.: Harvard University Press, 1942; second edition, with new preface
by the author, Cambridge, Mass.: Harvard University Press, 1951; London: Geoffrey Cumberlege, Oxford University Press, 1951; third
edition, with new preface by the author, Cambridge, Mass.: Harvard University Press, 1957);

Feeling and Form: A Theory of Art Developed from Philosophy in a New Key (New York: Scribners, 1953;
London: Routledge & Kegan Paul, 1953);

Problems of Art: Ten Philosophical Lectures (New York:
Scribners, 1957; London: Routledge & Kegan
Paul, 1957);

Philosophical Sketches (Baltimore: Johns Hopkins University Press, 1962; London: Oxford University
Press, 1962);

Mind: An Essay on Human Feeling, 3 volumes (Baltimore &
London: Johns Hopkins University Press, 1967–
1982).

Edition: *Mind: An Essay on Human Feeling,* abridged by
Gary Van Den Heuvel, foreword by Arthur C.
Danto (Baltimore & London: Johns Hopkins University Press, 1988).

OTHER: Ernst Cassirer, *Language and Myth,* translated
by Langer (New York: Harper, 1946);

"On Cassirer's Theory of Language and Myth," in *The
Philosophy of Ernst Cassirer,* edited by Paul Arthur
Schilpp, The Library of Living Philosophers, volume 6 (Evanston, Ill.: Library of Living Philosophers, 1949), pp. 381–400;

*Susanne K. Langer (photograph by Philip A. Biscuti; from
the dust jacket for* Mind: An Essay on Human
Feeling, *volume 1, 1967)*

*Structure, Method, and Meaning: Essays in Honor of Henry M.
Sheffer,* edited by Langer, Paul Henle, and Horace
M. Kallen (New York: Liberal Arts Press, 1951);

*Reflections on Art: A Source Book of Writings by Artists, Critics,
and Philosophers,* edited by Langer (Baltimore:
Johns Hopkins University Press, 1958);

"The Great Shift: Instinct to Intuition," in *Man and
Beast: Comparative Social Behavior,* edited by J. F.
Eisenberg and Wilton S. Dillon (Washington,
D.C.: Smithsonian Institution Press, 1971), pp.
315–332.

SELECTED PERIODICAL PUBLICATIONS–
UNCOLLECTED: "Confusion of Symbols and Confusion of Logical Types," *Mind,* 35 (1926): 222–229;

"Form and Content: A Study in Paradox," *Journal of Philosophy,* 23 (1926): 435–438;

"A Logical Study of Verbs," *Journal of Philosophy,* 24 (1927): 120–129;

"The Treadmill of Systematic Doubt," *Journal of Philosophy,* 26 (1929): 379–384;

"Facts: The Logical Perspectives of the World," *Journal of Philosophy,* 30 (1933): 178–187;

"On a Fallacy in 'Scientific Fatalism,'" *International Journal of Ethics,* 46 (1936): 473–483;

"The Lord of Creation," *Fortune,* 29 (January 1944): 127–154;

"Why Philosophy?" *Saturday Evening Post,* 234 (13 May 1961): 34–35, 54, 56;

"Henry M. Sheffer," *Philosophy and Phenomenological Research,* 25 (1964): 305–307.

Susanne K. Langer was one of the first women to pursue an academic career in philosophy in the United States and the first to receive both professional and popular recognition as an American philosopher. After writing one of the first introductory textbooks on symbolic logic, she turned her attention to a general study of symbolic forms–language, scientific knowledge, ritual, myth, and the arts–and their role in the formation of knowledge and experience under the influence of the German philosopher Ernst Cassirer. Her first book in that field, *Philosophy in a New Key: A Study in the Symbolism of Reason, Rite and Art,* was published in 1942 but became a best-seller when it was released in paperback six years later. It remains Langer's best-known work, especially among readers outside professional philosophy.

Philosophy in a New Key included a chapter on music, which Langer developed into a systematic and comprehensive philosophy of art with the publication of *Feeling and Form: A Theory of Art Developed from* Philosophy in a New Key in 1953, and within a few years she became known primarily as a philosopher of art. But she soon took on the more ambitious project of working out a naturalistic theory of mind to account for the uniquely human activities of language, dreaming, ritual, myth, and art within a broadly biological framework that she hoped would support an evolutionary account of the nature and origin of human mentality and human society. The results of this project are recorded in the three volumes of *Mind: An Essay on Human Feeling* (1967–1982), the last of which was published three years before her death. Although Langer considered this work her magnum opus, the book received a mixed critical response and failed to attract any significant attention

from professional philosophers in the years following its publication. There are indications, however, that Langer's work may still have something valuable to contribute to the scientific study of consciousness, which has attracted a great deal of attention since the beginning of the 1990s in philosophy, psychology, and the biological sciences. Her theory of knowledge, for example, is based on what some researchers in cognitive science have described as the metaphysical structure of the human conceptual system.

Susanne Katherina Knauth was born in New York City on 20 December 1895 to Antonio Knauth, a prosperous corporation lawyer and partner in the banking firm of Knauth, Nachod and Kuehne, and Else M. Ulich Knauth. The parents had immigrated to the United States from Germany in the 1880s. Susanne Knauth had an older sister, Ilse; a younger sister, Ursula; and two younger brothers, Peter and Berthold. The father was an accomplished amateur musician who played both cello and piano; his friends included professional musicians, and he often joined them in informal musical performances in his home. Else Knauth, the daughter of a wealthy textile manufacturer, had strong literary interests. As a child Susanne Knauth learned to play the piano; wrote poetry and stories, which she illustrated; and put on plays with her brothers and sisters for family and friends. The family had a summer home, "Felseck," on Lake George; because she spent hours exploring the nearby woods, Susanne was affectionately called "*Waldhexe*" (witch of the woods) by her family.

Knauth grew up speaking German at home and retained a slight German accent throughout her life. She attended the Veltin School for Girls, a private day school on the Upper West Side of Manhattan, where she learned to speak English and French. She also required frequent instruction at home as a result of chronic health problems stemming from cocaine poisoning she suffered in infancy when a pharmacist made an error in filling a prescription. As a girl she already showed serious philosophical interests, for she was reading Immanuel Kant's *Kritik der reinen Vernunft* (1781; revised, 1787; translated as *Critique of Pure Reason,* 1855) in German–along with Louisa May Alcott's *Little Women; or, Meg, Jo, Beth and Amy* (1868, 1869)–by the time she was twelve.

For reasons that are not clear, Knauth began her undergraduate studies relatively late: she entered Radcliffe College in the fall of 1916, when she was nearly twenty-one years old. In addition to her academic courses, she studied the cello and took courses in music theory and composition. She continued to play the cello throughout most of her life; it was one of the few activities that she would allow to compete seriously with her work.

At Radcliffe, which had been chartered in 1894 to offer the equivalent of a Harvard University degree for women, Knauth came under the influence of the Harvard logician Henry M. Sheffer, who introduced her to the rapidly developing field of formal logic. Sheffer had inherited from his teacher, the American philosopher Josiah Royce, an expansive vision of logic as the science of order or of forms in general, which Royce had pursued as an alternative to the more restricted view held by many of his contemporaries—and most fully developed by the British philosophers Bertrand Russell and Alfred North Whitehead in their *Principia Mathematica* (1910–1913)—that treated logic as the study of the principles of inference. In "The Principles of Logic" (1913) Royce had defined logic as "the General Science of Order, the Theory of the Forms of any Orderly Realm of Objects, real or ideal," and he believed that its study would lead to an understanding of more and more comprehensive systems of order that were prior to and inclusive of logic in the more restricted sense, and from which the more specialized order systems of the various branches of knowledge could be derived. Sheffer does not appear to have shared his teacher's metaphysical interests, but he found in Royce's logical investigations the means to pursue a study of relations, systems, and principles of order that went far beyond the confines of traditional logic. In Sheffer's hands symbolic logic became a general theory of structure, form, or pattern; Whitehead later called this approach one of the great advances in modern logic. In an unpublished manuscript in Harvard's Houghton Library, "Henry Sheffer's Legacy to His Students," Langer recalls that she was inspired by the power of Sheffer's logical imagination "to see logic as a field for invention, and to learn that in this traditionally stiff and scholastic pursuit" there was "as much scope for originality as in metaphysics." Under Sheffer's tutelage she acquired confidence in her power to deal with difficult intellectual problems: "I remember the growing sense of mental power that came with following his expositions, expecting to understand, even before the end of a discourse, a whole intricate conceptual structure with the same clarity as its simplest initial statements." Knauth's abilities were evident to Sheffer, who wrote in a letter of recommendation on her graduation that she had "a firmer grasp of philosophy problems than many a Harvard Ph.D."

Knauth received her B.A. in philosophy in 1920. On 3 September 1921 she married William L. Langer, who had been born in Boston to German immigrant parents and had received a master's degree in history from Harvard in the spring. William Langer recalled in his autobiography, *In and Out of the Ivory Tower* (1977),

AN INTRODUCTION TO SYMBOLIC LOGIC

by SUSANNE K. LANGER
Tutor in Philosophy in Radcliffe College

LONDON
GEORGE ALLEN & UNWIN LTD
MUSEUM STREET

Dust jacket for Langer's 1937 work, one of the earliest textbooks on its subject (Connecticut College Library)

that when they had met during her senior year at Radcliffe, his future wife had impressed him as "by temperament a scholar, if there ever was one, deeply engrossed in philosophy and especially logic, as well as whole-heartedly devoted to music." They had "many common interests," he said, though he was "less addicted than she to long tramps in the woods and mountains."

William had been awarded a fellowship to the University of Vienna to explore the alliances that had led up to World War I. The couple left for Europe soon after their wedding and spent the 1921–1922 academic year in Vienna. When they returned to Cambridge, William began writing his dissertation, and Susanne started graduate work in philosophy at Radcliffe. Their son Leonard Charles Rudolph Langer was born on 30 August 1922. In 1923 William received his doctorate from Harvard and joined the history department at Clark University in Worcester, Massachusetts, and Susanne published a book of her own fairy tales, *The Cruise of the Little Dipper and Other Fairy Tales,* with illustrations by her childhood friend Helen Sewell.

Langer received her M.A. in philosophy from Radcliffe in June 1924 with a thesis titled "Eduard von Hartmann's Notion of Unconscious Mind and Its Metaphysical Implications." That same year Whitehead joined the Harvard philosophy department and became Langer's dissertation adviser. Langer traveled the forty miles from Worcester to Cambridge by train each week to attend Whitehead's graduate seminar on metaphysics and Sheffer's lectures on modern logic; she met with Whitehead for an individual conference about once a month. On 6 May 1925 she gave birth to a second son, Bertrand Walter Langer. The following year she completed her dissertation, "A Logical Analysis of Meaning," and was awarded the Ph.D. in philosophy from Radcliffe. That same year her first published article, "Confusion of Symbols and Confusion of Logical Types," a criticism of the theory of types that Russell had developed in the first volume of the second edition of *Principia Mathematica* (1925), appeared in the British journal *Mind,* after Whitehead submitted it with his endorsement to the editor, G. E. Moore. Other articles on logic and epistemology, as well as many book reviews, soon followed in other journals.

In 1927 William Langer joined the history department at Harvard, and Susanne Langer became a part-time tutor in philosophy at Radcliffe. The Langers built a house at 72 Raymond Street in Cambridge; they had a live-in maid to help with the housework and care of the children. Susanne Langer's *The Practice of Philosophy* appeared in 1930 with a prefatory note by Whitehead, who called it "an admirable exposition of the aims, methods, and actual achievements of philosophy." William began to study the viola in 1930, and they reserved Friday evenings to play chamber music with friends or students they invited to dinner in their home. Throughout the 1930s the Langers spent their summers at the beach in Annisquam, a village on the western side of Cape Ann, about forty-five miles northeast of Boston.

In the mid 1930s Susanne Langer was one of the founders, along with the philosophers C. I. Lewis, Alonzo Church, W. V. Quine, and other pioneers in the development of formal logic in the United States, of the Association for Symbolic Logic. She served as a consulting editor for the association's *Journal of Symbolic Logic* from its first issue in 1936 until the end of 1939, contributing regular reviews of the German, French, and Italian literature in the field. In 1937 she published her own *Introduction to Symbolic Logic,* one of the earliest textbooks on the subject; the third edition, published in 1953, was still in print in 2002.

Langer is best known for her contributions to the philosophy of culture, and in particular to the philosophy of art. Readers are often puzzled, therefore, by her early preoccupation with symbolic logic and her frequent use of logical concepts in her theory of artistic meaning, as when she calls art the "logical expression" of feelings or describes music as offering "a 'logical picture' of sentient, responsive life" in *Philosophy in a New Key.* Langer's conception of logic, however, was the wide one inherited from Sheffer and modified in the light of her concern with the epistemological significance of the arts. In Langer's view logic is not limited to the principles of inference but includes a study of the structures, forms, or patterns exhibited by objects, events, and processes of all kinds; the articulation of logical patterns in this wider sense can be achieved in any medium that can be manipulated to exhibit complex combinations of distinguishable elements—the tonal materials in a musical composition or the pigments in a painting as well as the words or mathematical symbols in a piece of discursive reasoning.

Langer follows Sheffer in using the term *form* in its most general sense to mean a complex relational structure. In *An Introduction to Symbolic Logic* she points out that in this wider sense, "anything may be said to have form that follows a pattern of any sort, exhibits order, internal connection." On this view it is the business of logic, which is the science of forms or patterns, to study the "types and relations among abstracted forms, or concepts." Everything exemplifies some form, and any given form might also be exemplified by some other thing. When two things are put together in the same way, they are "analogous"—they exemplify the same relational structure or logical form. "The value of analogy is that a thing which has a certain logical form may be *represented* by another which has the same structure, i.e. which is analogous to it." When two things exhibit a common logical form, one may serve as a "logical picture" of the other. One may attend only to the form, pattern, configuration, or complex relational structure that various objects, events, or situations have in common, thereby "consciously, deliberately abstracting the form from all things which have it." Scientific concepts "are forms which are exemplified in some general and important part of reality"; but beyond the patterns that are the objects of scientific study is a "great storehouse of forms which may be interpretable physically, psychically, or for any realm of experience whatever." Logic is concerned with "abstracted patterns as such—the orders in which any things whatever may be arranged, the modes under which anything whatever may present itself to our understanding." In this sense, "logic applies to everything in the world." The study of logic, therefore, includes but is not restricted to the study of the

Susanne K. Langer

[Project for a philosophy of mind]

The aim of philosophy is to clarify, ~~and~~ develop, and interconnect our ideas, so that the ~~most~~ great general ones, and the ~~most special~~ small immediate ones shall somehow belong together, and no matter how far we carry reflection on any serious subject it shall not end in self-contradiction or ~~hopeless~~ ~~confusion~~ confusion.

The value of philosophy is not ^that^ it provides a comforting faith, but that it gives mental security, ~~confidence in one's~~ ~~own mind,~~ and makes for mental freedom and daring.

Philosophy might be called the process of making sense out ~~of ~~~~~~~ of experience ~~~~~~~~~ of our own ideas. It deals with ideas, not facts. Facts cannot contradict each other; only our ~~conceptions of them, and the ways we draw~~ ways of breaking them down and stating them, can be incoherent or contradictory. ~~Philosophy~~ Philosophy is the critique, and often the reconstruction, of basic ideas. ~~~~~~~ Certain basic ideas are ^always^ implicit in our descriptions, and even our observations, of fact.

The direct purpose of philosophizing is not ~~~~~~~~~~~~, to achieve an ultimate world-view ^is^ (that is ~~always~~ a rare reward of ^the^ intellectual ^life~~force~~), but to construe concepts in terms of which some important but elusive problems ~~~~~~~ may be stated so they become ~~more~~ amenable to solution. Every philosophy has a particular orientation, because every philosophy starts from some central problem.

My own work started from ^my^ semantic problems, ~~that~~ ~~was need in my youth~~ Training in logic and music, and a natural penchant for poetry, ~~and for the~~ convinced me ~~too but~~ ~~science~~ made the contrast of two kinds of ~~thought and~~ expression patent. ~~At the same time deepened the realization~~ that both discursive and artistic activity were ~~essentially~~ expressive of ideas, Ernst Cassirer's work offered a clue to their difference : a

Page from a manuscript by Langer, probably written around 1959 for a symposium. The title is not Langer's but was added by a person who was inventorying her papers. A typescript that is nearly identical to the manuscript is titled "Art, Feeling, and Mind." The work has not been published (Houghton Library, Harvard University).

forms of discourse—of logical inference and the structure of propositions—"logic" in the common understanding of the term.

In *The Practice of Philosophy* Langer uses these conceptions of logic and logical patterns as a basis for her theory of knowledge, at the center of which is the capacity of the human mind to apprehend forms or patterns in the material furnished by experience. "By the recognition of forms we find *analogies,* and come to understand one thing in terms of another." Ideally, she believes, some symbolic medium could be devised for the apprehension of every sort of configuration that is the object of a possible experience. "There is no knowledge without form, and probably no form is unique; therefore all knowledge can find symbolic expression." Although the elements of spoken and written language are the most familiar symbolic materials, the human mind is capable of apprehending configurations that are too intricate to be adequately expressed in the medium of language. In a painting, for example, "the balance of values, line and color and light, and . . . other elements, is so highly adjusted that no verbal proposition could hope to embody its pattern"; and the patterns found in music might correspond to "the endlessly intricate yet universal pattern of emotional life." People who are responsive to the arts live "through the eye, the musical hearing, the bodily senses," and "see more meaning in artistic wholes, i.e. in things, situations, feelings, etc., than they can ever find in propositions." There is no reason, Langer argues, to suppose that the apprehension of artistic significance is any more "irrational" or "alogical" than the process of understanding propositional knowledge, provided that reason and logical insight are defined in the broadest possible sense as the appreciation of patterns. Langer's belief that the general power of "seeing" one thing in terms of another is the key to understanding human mentality reappears as a central theme in her later writings and forms the basis for her claim that each of the products of human culture—language, myth, ritual, and the arts—makes a unique and indispensable contribution to the achievement of knowledge.

Toward the end of the 1930s strains began to appear in the Langers' marriage. In the fall of 1939 William took a sabbatical and traveled alone to Mexico and Central America. In 1942 he requested a divorce, and Susanne did not contest it. She traveled to Reno with their son Bertrand that summer of 1942, spending the six weeks required to establish residency in Nevada to expedite the divorce, which became final in August.

The publication of *Philosophy in a New Key* that same year marked a major shift in Langer's interests from formal logic to a more general theory of the human capacity for what she called "symbolic transfor-

mation," a concept that was influenced by the German neo-Kantian philosopher Cassirer, whose three-volume *Philosophie der symbolischen Formen* (1923–1929) Langer had read in the 1920s, long before its translation into English as *The Philosophy of Symbolic Forms* (1953). With the development of the theory of symbolic transformation, Langer was able to treat the discursive uses of language as only one among a wide variety of cultural resources—including myth, ritual, and the arts—that were central to the constitution of human experience.

Cassirer's work suggested that abstractions, and the patterns they make available to the human understanding, are dependent on the symbolic materials that are used to formulate them, and that the possibilities for the appreciation of patterns must include far more than what is available through the resources of language alone—even if language is broadly defined to include the notational systems of formal logic and mathematics. Under Cassirer's influence, and in response to her own literary and artistic sensibilities, Langer expands the definitions of *knowledge* and *reason* in *Philosophy in a New Key* to encompass nondiscursive formulations of experience embodied in the spontaneous activity of dreaming and in the cultural productions of myth, ritual, and the arts.

Symbolic transformation is "a natural activity, a high form of nervous response" that is "characteristic of man among the animals" and is an expression of "the impulse toward symbolic formulation, expression, and understanding of experience" that ultimately serves the fundamental human need for orientation within the natural and social worlds that are the setting for human life. The human mind "is constantly carrying on a process of symbolic transformation of the experiential data that come to it," causing it to be "a veritable fountain of more or less spontaneous ideas"; but only some of the products of the symbol-making brain figure in the discursive uses of language. There is also an enormous output of other symbolic materials that are constantly being produced but are put to different uses. These essentially nondiscursive formulations furnish the material for dreaming, myth, ritual, and the arts.

The most primitive expression of the fundamental human need for conception is found in the spontaneous activity of dreaming. Langer says that "the riotous symbolism of dreams" provides the most elementary conceptions of objects of desire and of the personal drama of their frustration and gratification. Behavioral acts, and the gestures that are their abbreviated forms, provide the symbolic materials for ritual, which formulates and records the responses of a human group to "the basic facts of human existence, the forces of generation and achievement and death." The ultimate product of ritual is "a complex, permanent *attitude* . . . toward 'first and last things'" that serves "man's ceaseless quest for conception and orientation." A further domain for the production and elaboration of symbolic material is myth, which provides an "organized and permanent envisagement of a world-drama" and a "serious envisagement of its fundamental truths." Myth presents, "however metaphorically, a world-picture, an insight into life generally," and, therefore, it tends to become systematized. Because myth can be considered "the primitive phase of metaphysical thought, the first embodiment of general ideas," its thrust is ultimately philosophical; and together with ritual, myth is ultimately taken up in the service of religion, whose purpose is to provide "a gradual envisagement of the essential pattern of human life."

The remaining product of symbolic transformation that Langer considers in *Philosophy in a New Key* is music. She rejects theories that treat music as either a stimulus to feeling or a symptomatic expression of emotion: "Music is not self-expression, but formulation and representation of emotions, mood, mental tensions and resolutions—a 'logical picture' of sentient, responsive life," and therefore, like all symbolic presentations, a source of insight and understanding, albeit by means other than language. For "the limits of language are not the last limits of experience, and things inaccessible to language may have their own forms of conception, that is to say, their own symbolic devices." Music may be said, with certain reservations, to be "about" feeling; and the recognition that such nondiscursive forms may be "charged with logical possibilities of meaning . . . broadens our epistemology to the point of including not only the semantics of science, but a serious philosophy of art."

Philosophy in a New Key made publishing history. It became one of the first books written for a major academic press to be picked up by a mass-market publisher when Penguin Books released a thirty-five-cent paperback edition in 1948. By 1951 it had sold more than 110,000 copies, and by the mid-1980s sales had reached almost 450,000. The book was translated into eleven languages and used as a text for courses in a wide variety of academic disciplines. In 1971 Harvard University Press brought out its own paperback edition, which was still in print in 2002. Total sales for *Philosophy in a New Key,* in all of its editions, have probably been close to 570,000 copies.

At the end of the fall term of 1942 Langer resigned from her position at Radcliffe and took the first of a series of temporary appointments that supported her over the next twelve years. In the winter and spring terms of 1943 she taught in the philosophy department at the University of Delaware. In the fall of 1944 she moved to New York City, where she maintained an apartment at 112 East Thirty-first Street until

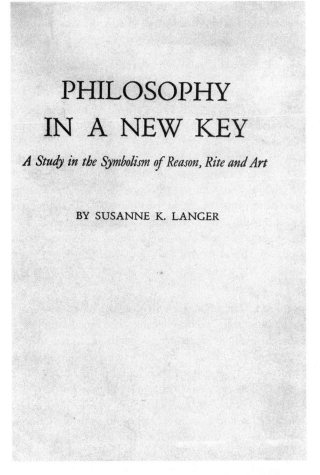

PHILOSOPHY
IN A NEW KEY

A Study in the Symbolism of Reason, Rite and Art

BY SUSANNE K. LANGER

Dust jacket for Langer's best-known work, in which she develops her philosophy of symbolic forms. Published in 1942, it became a best-seller when it appeared in paperback six years later (Bruccoli Clark Layman Archives).

1954. She was a lecturer in philosophy at the Dalton School in 1944–1945, a visiting assistant professor at New York University in 1945–1946, a lecturer in philosophy at Columbia University from 1945 to 1950, a lecturer on the teaching of English and foreign languages at Teachers College of Columbia University in 1949–1950, and a visiting professor at the New School of Social Research in 1950.

Many of the ideas in *Feeling and Form* were worked out during her years in New York City. Langer had met Cassirer in the winter of 1941, soon after his emigration from Sweden to assume a professorship at Yale. Recognizing a common ground between them, Cassirer took an interest in Langer's work, and they remained in close contact until his death in 1945, less than a year after he had moved to New York City to teach at Columbia University. For nearly four years beginning in 1946 Langer held a research grant from the Rockefeller Foundation that allowed her to devote much of her time to the research that went into the writing of

Feeling and Form. The grant also enabled her to hire a research assistant, Eugene T. Gadol, whose contribution she acknowledged in the introduction to the book.

Langer spent the winter term of 1951 at Northwestern University in Evanston, Illinois, and in the spring she taught philosophy and literature at Ohio State University. After taking a year off to finish *Feeling and Form,* she spent the academic year 1952–1953 in the philosophy department at the University of Washington in Seattle. After another break she taught at the University of Michigan during the spring of 1954. In the fall of that year she accepted her first permanent academic appointment, in the philosophy department at Connecticut College. Although Langer received a grant two years later that freed her from her teaching responsibilities, she remained affiliated with the department. In 1962 she assumed the title Professor of Philosophy Emeritus and Research Scholar.

With the publication in 1953 of *Feeling and Form,* a systematic and comprehensive theory of the arts, Langer achieved widespread recognition in the field of aesthetics. Her mature philosophy of art is developed in that book, *Problems of Art* (1957), and *Philosophical Sketches* (1962). The expanded concept of logical form, which she had acquired from Sheffer and transformed under Cassirer's influence into a general concept of symbolic form, is further developed in these works as the concept of "expressive form." The analogy of form, or correspondence of configuration between relational structures, which she had first proposed as the fundamental pattern of all meaning situations in her dissertation and had continued to regard as the indispensable condition for symbolization, remains the basis for what she defines as the "expressiveness" of works of art. And the theory that she proposed in *Philosophy in a New Key* to explain the significance of music is generalized to apply to all the arts, which she defines in *Philosophical Sketches* to include "painting, sculpture, architecture, music, dance, literature, drama, and film."

In *Philosophical Sketches* Langer defines works of art as "forms expressive of human feeling" and defines *form* to include "a permanent form like a building or a vase or a picture, or a transient, dynamic form like a melody or a dance, or even a form given to imagination, like the passage of purely imaginary, apparent events that constitutes a literary work." A work of art is a complex relational structure—that is, as she writes in *Feeling and Form,* "a much more intricate thing than we usually think of as a form, because it involves *all* the relationships of its elements to one another, all similarities and differences of quality, not only geometric or other familiar relations." In *Problems of Art* she uses the example of a painting, in which "a visible, individual form" is produced by "the interaction of colors, lines, surfaces, lights and shadows."

As a physical object, the work of art is just an arrangement of materials—pigments on a canvas in the case of a painting, gestures and other movements in a dance, words in a literary work, or tonal materials in a musical composition. What emerges from the arrangement of colors, gestures, words, or tones, however, is a complex array of qualities that seems to be charged with life and feeling, an object that appears to have a kind of substantial reality, although it is given primarily to only one of the senses or even to the imagination alone. Such an object Langer calls a "virtual entity"—it exists only for perception or imagination, like a rainbow or an image in a mirror, and plays no ordinary part in the physical world as common objects do.

Langer notes that what is most compelling about works of art is often described, by critics and artists alike, with metaphors drawn from the realm of life and feeling. "Every artist," she observes in *Problems of Art,* "finds 'life,' 'vitality,' or 'livingness' in a good work of art. He refers to the 'spirit' of a picture, not meaning the spirit in which it was painted, but its own quality; and his first task is to 'animate' his canvas. An unsuccessful work is 'dead.' Even a fairly good one may have 'dead spots.'" Similarly, in a musical composition "melodies move and harmonies grow and rhythms prevail, with the logic of an organic living structure." In music one hears, with apparent immediacy, "a flow of life, feeling, and emotion in audible passage." The virtual image created by the arrangement of tonal materials in music is a powerful illusion of movement that seems in some way to be charged with life and feeling.

In Langer's theory a work of art formulates an idea of feeling, which Langer defines quite broadly in *Problems of Art* as "inner life," "subjective reality," or "consciousness." "Feeling" for Langer is thus a generic term for conscious experiences, or what William James in *The Principles of Psychology* (1890) calls "mental states at large, irrespective of their kind." What a work of art expresses, or formulates for one's conception, is not actual feeling, she argues in *Feeling and Form,* "but ideas of feeling; as language does not express actual things and events but ideas about them." Art serves an indispensable function in human life, because language is poorly suited to articulate what she calls in *Problems of Art* "the subjective aspect of experience, the direct feeling of it." In *Philosophical Sketches* she argues that the "inward life" of human beings "is something language as such—as discursive symbolism—cannot render." What defies verbal expression, however, "may nevertheless be known—objectively set forth, publicly known" by means of other symbolic materials. The products of artistic creation, she argues in *Problems of*

Art, are "congruent with the dynamic forms of our direct sensuous, mental, and emotional life; works of art are projections of 'felt life,' as Henry James called it, into spatial, temporal, and poetic structures. They are images of feeling, that formulate it for our cognition."

Langer's interests had begun to shift significantly within a few years of the publication of *Feeling and Form,* as some of her correspondence indicates. She began to suspect connections between the studies in the philosophy of art that had occupied her for more than a decade and problems in the nature and evolution of the mind; and although she was nearly sixty years old, she began reading widely in evolutionary biology, developmental biology, and the neurosciences and audited courses from her colleagues in the biology department at Connecticut College.

Probably in the early 1950s Langer had met the man who played a major role in supporting the culminating work of her philosophical career. Edgar Kaufmann Jr. was the heir to a Pittsburgh department-store fortune who became one of the country's leading scholars of architecture and design, as well as an art collector and philanthropist. Kaufmann, who never attended college, spent several years studying painting in Europe before returning to the United States, where, at twenty-four, he became an apprentice to the architect Frank Lloyd Wright. Kaufmann's father met Wright during his son's apprenticeship, and in 1935 he commissioned Wright to build the house that came to be known as Fallingwater in the woods near Bear Run, Pennsylvania. In 1946 Kaufmann Jr. settled in New York City and became director of the Museum of Modern Art's department of industrial design and later an adjunct professor of architecture and art history at Columbia University. In 1956 Kaufmann, who by then had become one of Langer's closest friends and an admirer of her work, arranged for her to become the recipient of a grant from the philanthropic foundation that had been endowed by his father. The grant, which supported her for the next twenty-five years, enabled her to give up teaching and devote all of her time to research and writing; and her last work, the three volumes of *Mind: An Essay on Human Feeling,* began to take shape.

By the time Langer wrote the introductory essay to *Philosophical Sketches,* the overall plan of *Mind* and her reasons for undertaking the project had fallen into place. Consciousness, or subjectivity, she argues in that essay, is the proper subject matter of psychology. The difficulties of dealing with mental phenomena, however, had forced psychology to divert its attention to other things, such as overt behavior or the activity of the brain and nervous system, which were thought to be more amenable to scientific investigation. Although

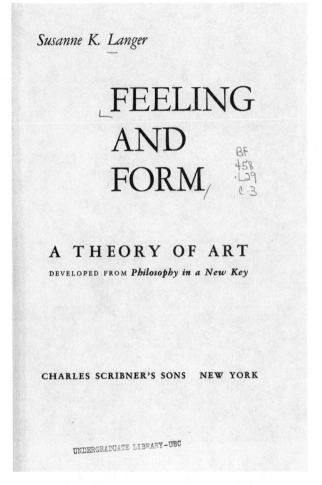

Susanne K. Langer

FEELING AND FORM

A THEORY OF ART
DEVELOPED FROM *Philosophy in a New Key*

CHARLES SCRIBNER'S SONS   NEW YORK

Title page for the 1953 work in which Langer presents her systematic and comprehensive aesthetic theory (Thomas Cooper Library, University of South Carolina)

"the most pressing need of our day," she writes, is "to bring mental phenomena into the compass of natural fact," psychology has been unable to deal conceptually with its own essential subject matter.

In the introduction to the first volume of *Mind* Langer argues that "our basic philosophical concepts are inadequate to the problems of life and mind in nature," including what she considers "the central problem of . . . the nature and origin of the veritable gulf that divides human from animal mentality, in a perfectly continuous course of development of life on earth that has no breaks." The most serious problem facing a naturalistic study of the mind, Langer believes, is the lack of suitable images of the objects of biology and psychology. Images borrowed from the physical sciences, although suitable to the realm of inorganic nature, do "not fit the forms of life very far above the level of their organic chemistry." Works of art, however, can provide "images of the forms of feeling" that "can rise to the presentation of all aspects

Dust jacket for the first volume (1967) of the work Langer considered her magnum opus, in which she attempted to elaborate a naturalistic theory of mind to account for the uniquely human activities of language, dreaming, ritual, myth, and art. The third and final volume was published in 1982, three years before her death (Bruccoli Clark Layman Archives).

of mind and human personality" and are, therefore, an invaluable source of insight into the dynamics of subjective experience that can serve as a measure of the adequacy of theories and "a touchstone to test the scope of our intellectual constructions."

One of the outstanding intellectual challenges of the late twentieth century, in Langer's view, is the construction of "a conceptual framework for the empirical study of mind" that will be grounded in the biological sciences. Given the right working concepts, she believes, the study of mind should lead "down into biological structure and process . . . and upward to the purely human sphere known as 'culture.'" Drawing on Whitehead's metaphysics and on her extensive reading in the biological sciences, Langer offers a reconstruction of the conceptual framework of biological thought that she hopes will provide the basis for an evolutionary

account of the nature and origin of human mentality and human society that will, in turn, support advances in psychology, the social sciences, and the humanities, including ethics and political philosophy.

The critical response to the publication of the first volume of *Mind* was mixed. Reviewers were unable to agree on what Langer was trying to do. Richard M. Liddy, writing in the *International Philosophical Quarterly* (1970) saw the work as evidence of Langer's commitment to the reduction of psychology and the biological sciences to physics, while an unidentified reviewer for the *Yale Review* (Summer 1968) saw it as the work of a romantic holist with a commitment to "an arbitrary indeterminism" and "a philosophical antagonism to scientific analysis."

The work received its most sympathetic reading from some members of the scientific community. The reviewer for *Science* (29 September 1967), Robert B. MacLeod, saw the book as exhibiting "the kind of careful and reflective observation which the scientist admires," while calling at the same time for "a radically revised conception of the nature of the reality which all sciences are trying to describe." Langer was invited by the biologist C. H. Waddington to join fifteen other biologists, physicists, and mathematicians in an interdisciplinary symposium on the theoretical foundations of biology held in 1968 in Bellagio, Italy.

Langer herself understood *Mind* primarily as a contribution to psychology and the biological sciences. In a review of the first volume of *Mind* in the *Saturday Review* (15 July 1967) the English philosopher Sir Herbert Read referred to the book as "a metaphysical system"; and according to an unpublished manuscript by her friend Wes Wehr, Langer was incensed. "I should think," she told him, "that by now Sir Herbert would know the difference between 'a metaphysical system' and a scientific line of inquiry."

In the second volume of *Mind,* published in 1972, Langer develops a theory of instinct and argues for a radical departure–which she calls "the great shift"–in the evolution of the human mind from the instinctual basis of animal behavior. Work on the third volume went even more slowly, as Langer struggled with diabetes and failing eyesight. After laboring for several years to develop a theory of the evolution of human society, she realized that she would be unable to write the chapters on epistemology with which she had planned to conclude the work. With the help of a research assistant, Linda Legassie, Langer managed to write the essay dealing with "the new intellectual standard, the concept of fact, and its impact on a human age which has but lately opened with the brilliant rise of mathematics" and the physical sciences that serves as the final chapter of the book. The Kaufmann Foundation continued to support her until 1982, when the final volume appeared. Susanne K. Langer died on 17 July 1985 at her home in Old Lyme, Connecticut. Her ashes were scattered in the woods near the cabin in the Catskills that had been her favorite retreat for many years.

Bibliography:

Rolf Lachmann, "Susanne K. Langer: Primär- und Sekundärbibliographie," *Studia Culturologica,* 2 (1993): 91–114.

References:

Thomas M. Alexander, "Langer, Susanne (1895–1985)," in *A Companion to Aesthetics,* edited by David E. Cooper (Oxford & Cambridge: Blackwell, 1992), pp. 259–261;

Ann E. Berthoff, "Susanne K. Langer and the Process of Feeling," in her *The Mysterious Barricades: Language and Its Limits* (Toronto: University of Toronto Press, 1999), pp. 112–124;

Peter A. Bertocci, "Susanne K. Langer's Theory of Feeling and Mind," *Review of Metaphysics,* 23 (1970): 527–551;

Vincent Colapietro, "Susanne Langer on Artistic Creativity and Creations," in *Semiotics 1997,* edited by C. W. Spinks and John Deeley (New York: Peter Lang, 1998), pp. 3–12;

Donald Dryden, "Susanne K. Langer and American Philosophic Naturalism in the Twentieth Century," *Transactions of the Charles S. Peirce Society,* 33 (1997): 161–182;

Dryden, "Susanne Langer and William James: Art and the Dynamics of the Stream of Consciousness," *Journal of Speculative Philosophy,* 15 (2001): 272–285;

Dryden, "Whitehead's Influence on Susanne Langer's Conception of Living Form," *Process Studies,* 26 (1997): 62–85;

Alexander Durig, "What Did Susanne Langer Really Mean?" *Sociological Theory,* 12 (1994): 254–265;

Ranjan K. Ghosh, *Aesthetic Theory and Art: A Study in Susanne K. Langer* (Delhi: Ajanta Prakashan, 1979);

Jerry H. Gill, "Langer, Language, and Art," *International Philosophical Quarterly,* 34 (1994): 419–432;

Max Hall, *Harvard University Press: A History* (Cambridge, Mass.: Harvard University Press, 1986), pp. 79–80, 116–117, 161, 181;

Robert E. Innis, "Perception, Interpretation, and the Signs of Art," *Journal of Speculative Philosophy,* 15 (2001): 20–33;

Bruce Kuklick, "Women Philosophers at Harvard," in his *The Rise of American Philosophy: Cambridge, Massachusetts* *1860–1930* (New Haven: Yale University Press, 1977), pp. 590–594;

Rolf Lachmann, *Susanne K. Langer: Die lebendige Form menschlichen Fühlens und Verstehens* (Munich: Fink, 2000);

William L. Langer, *In and Out of the Ivory Tower: The Autobiography of William L. Langer* (New York: Neale Watson, 1977);

Richard M. Liddy, "Art and Feeling: An Analysis and Critique of the Philosophy of Art of Susanne K. Langer," dissertation, Pontificia Universitas Gregoriana, 1970;

Beatrice K. Nelson, "Susanne K. Langer's Conception of 'Symbol': Making Connections through Ambiguity," in *Presenting Women Philosophers,* edited by Cecile T. Tougas and Sara Ebenreck (Philadelphia: Temple University Press, 2000), pp. 71–80;

Kingsley Price, "Philosophy in a New Key: An Interpretation," *Philosophy of Music Education Review,* 1 (1993): 34–43;

Process Studies, special Langer and Alfred North Whitehead issue, edited by Lachmann, 26 (1997): 57–150;

Mary J. Reichling, "Susanne Langer's Theory of Symbolism: An Analysis and Extension," *Philosophy of Music Education Review,* 1 (1993): 3–17;

Joseph R. Royce, "The Implications of Langer's Philosophy of Mind for a Science of Psychology," *Journal of Mind and Behavior,* 4 (1983): 491–506;

Lloyd E. Sandelands, "The Sense of Society," *Journal for the Theory of Social Behaviour,* 24 (1994): 305–338;

Winthrop Sargeant, "Philosopher in a New Key," *New Yorker* (3 December 1960): 67–100;

Cameron Shelley, "Consciousness, Symbols and Aesthetics: A Just-So Story and Its Implications in Susanne Langer's *Mind: An Essay on Human Feeling,*" *Philosophical Psychology,* 11 (1998): 45–66;

Donald W. Sherburne, "Meaning and Music," *Journal of Aesthetics and Art Criticism,* 24 (1966): 579–583;

Robert Frederick Snyder, "Cognition and the Life of Feeling in Susanne K. Langer," dissertation, Harvard University, 1991;

Christine P. Watling, "The Arts, Emotion, and Current Research in Neuroscience," *Mosaic,* 31 (1998): 107–124.

Papers:

A collection of Susanne K. Langer's manuscripts and correspondence is in the Houghton Library of Harvard University.

C. I. Lewis

(12 April 1883 – 3 February 1964)

Murray G. Murphey
University of Pennsylvania

BOOKS: *A Survey of Symbolic Logic* (Berkeley: University of California Press, 1918; revised edition, New York: Dover, 1960; Bristol, U.K. & Sterling, Va.: Thoemmes Press, 2001);

Mind and the World Order (New York: Scribners, 1929);

Symbolic Logic, by Lewis and Cooper Harold Langford (New York & London: Century, 1932);

An Analysis of Knowledge and Valuation (La Salle, Ill.: Open Court, 1946);

The Ground and Nature of the Right, Woodbridge Lectures, no. 5 (New York: Columbia University Press, 1955);

Our Social Inheritance (Bloomington: Indiana University Press, 1957);

Values and Imperatives: Studies in Ethics, edited by John Lange (Stanford, Cal.: Stanford University Press, 1969);

Collected Papers of Clarence Irving Lewis, edited by John D. Goheen and John L. Mothershead Jr. (Stanford, Cal.: Stanford University Press, 1970).

OTHER: "Kant, Immanuel," in *Colliers Encyclopedia,* volume 11 (New York: Collier, 1950), pp. 519–523;

"Critique of Pure Reason," in *The Encyclopedia Americana* (New York: Americana, 1958), pp. 212–213;

"Philosophy," in *The Encyclopedia Americana,* volume 21 (New York: Americana, 1958), pp. 769–777;

"Autobiography" and "Replies to My Critics," in *The Philosophy of C. I. Lewis,* edited by Paul Arthur Schilpp, The Library of Living Philosophers, volume 13 (La Salle, Ill.: Open Court, 1968), pp. 1–21, 653–676.

SELECTED PERIODICAL PUBLICATIONS–
UNCOLLECTED: "The Calculus of Strict Implication," *Mind,* 23 (April 1913): 240–247;

"Interesting Theorems in Symbolic Logic," *Journal of Philosophy,* 10 (24 April 1913): 232–239;

"A New Algebra of Implications and Some Consequences," *Journal of Philosophy,* 10 (31 July 1913): 428–438;

C. I. Lewis

"Review of A. N. Whitehead and Bertrand Russell, *Principia Mathematica,*" *Journal of Philosophy,* 11 (27 August 1914): 497–502;

"The Matrix Algebra for Implications," *Journal of Philosophy,* 11 (18 October 1914): 589–600;

"A Too Brief Set of Postulates for the Algebra of Logic," *Journal of Philosophy,* 12 (16 September 1915): 523–525;

"The Issues Concerning Material Implication," *Journal of Philosophy,* 14 (21 June 1917): 350–356;

"Strict Implication—an Emendation," *Journal of Philosophy,* 17 (20 May 1920): 300–302;

"Review of John Maynard Keynes, *A Treatise on Probability,*" *Philosophical Review,* 31 (March 1922): 180–186;

"La Logique de la méthode mathématique," *Revue de Métaphysique et de Morale,* 29 (October–December 1922): 455–474;

"Review of D. Nys, *La Notion d'espace,*" *Journal of Philosophy,* 20 (10 May 1923): 277–278;

"Review of Charles S. Peirce, *Chance, Love, and Logic,* Edited by Morris R. Cohen," *Journal of Philosophy,* 21 (31 January 1924): 71–74;

"Review of C. D. Broad, *Scientific Thought,*" *Philosophical Review,* 34 (July 1925): 406–411;

"Review of Harold R. Smart, *The Philosophical Presuppositions of Mathematical Logic,*" *Journal of Philosophy,* 23 (15 April 1926): 220–223;

"Review of N. O. Losokij, *Handbuch der Logic,*" *Journal of Philosophy,* 24 (24 November 1927): 665–667;

"Reply to Mr. Ushenko" and "Reply to Mr. Ushenko's Addendum," *Monist,* 43 (April 1933): 292–293, 295–296;

"Note Concerning Many-Valued Logical Systems," *Journal of Philosophy,* 30 (6 July 1933): 364;

"Paul Weiss on Alternative Logics," *Philosophical Review,* 43 (January 1934): 70–74;

"Emch's Calculus and Strict Implication," *Journal of Symbolic Logic,* 1 (1936): 77–86;

"Review of *Royce's Logical Essays,* Edited by Daniel S. Robinson," *Philosophy and Phenomenological Research,* 12 (March 1952): 431–434;

"Paul Carus–1852–1919," *Proceedings of the American Philosophical Association,* 24 (1953): 62–63;

"Santayana at Harvard," *Journal of Philosophy,* 51 (January 1954): 29–31.

Having been a student of William James and Josiah Royce, C. I. Lewis carried on the tradition of Harvard pragmatism and became its foremost exponent. He made important contributions to logic, epistemology, and the theory of values, and had he lived to complete his book on ethics, he might well have made an important contribution to that field, as well. As a professor at Harvard from 1920 to 1953 he taught many of those who became the leading American philosophers of the generation after his; but his greatest influence was exerted through his writings, which included six books published during his lifetime and many articles.

The oldest of five children of Irving and Hannah Dearth Lewis, Clarence Irving Lewis was born in Stoneham, Massachusetts, on 12 April 1883. Irving Lewis was a socialist whose support of the Knights of Labor led to his being blacklisted from his trade as a shoemaker, leaving his family in poverty. C. I. Lewis worked in a shoe factory during his high-school years to earn money for college. In 1902 he entered Harvard University, where he majored in philosophy and took a course in which James and Royce critiqued each other's views. Although he was influenced by James, Royce became Lewis's ideal of a philosopher, and he was an adherent of idealism when he graduated in 1906. For the next two years he taught English at the University of Colorado. During this time—on 1 January 1907—he married his high-school sweetheart, Mabel Maxwell Graves, and their first child, Irving, was born.

In 1908 Lewis returned to Harvard to do graduate study in philosophy. His chief interest was in epistemology, and he was particularly impressed by the German philosopher Immanuel Kant, whose influence is clear throughout his work. He received his Ph.D. in 1910, and in 1911 he served as an assistant to Royce in a course on logic. Royce introduced him to *Principia Mathematica* (1910–1913), by Alfred North Whitehead and Bertrand Russell, and encouraged him to pursue work in logic.

Later in 1911 Lewis was appointed an instructor in philosophy at the University of California at Berkeley. Soon afterward he was promoted to assistant professor. His daughter Margaret (Peggy) was born in 1911; his son, Irving, died of diphtheria in 1913.

Most of Lewis's early papers were devoted to logic and to what he considered the faults of *Principia Mathematica.* He recognized the magnitude of Whitehead and Russell's achievement and accepted their thesis that mathematics is derivable from logic, but he could not accept material implication as a basis for inference. He regarded the relation of implication in ordinary logic as being equivalent to deducibility: that is, "p implies q" means "q is deducible from p." Since such was manifestly not the case with material implication, in which "p implies q" is true not only when p and q are both true but whenever p is false, Lewis believed that *Principia Mathematica* was built on a false foundation and that the proofs it presented were invalid.

Starting in 1912, Lewis published a series of papers attacking the identification of material implication with inference and developing an alternative system based on "strict implication," which he defined as "not-possibly-(p and not-q)." In these papers Lewis tried first to develop a system different from that of *Principia Mathematica* and then to construct a more general system from which both the *Principia Mathematica* system and his own could be derived. In the course of doing so, he discovered that he could derive all of the

Lewis as a private in the U.S. Army during World War I.
He served as an artillery instructor and rose to the rank
of captain (Collection of Mabel Lewis).

postulates and theorems of *Principia Mathematica* within his system of strict implication, thus showing that the theorems of *Principia Mathematica* really did follow from its premises–something that, he claimed, had never been shown before.

Another son, David, was born in 1915. Lewis served in World War I as an artillery instructor but did not see combat; he left the army with the rank of captain.

In 1918 Lewis published his first book, *A Survey of Symbolic Logic*. The early chapters are an historical survey of the development of symbolic logic beginning with Gottfried Wilhelm Leibniz in the late seventeenth and early eighteenth centuries. In chapter 6 he introduces his system of strict implication, and in the

final chapter he proposes Royce's formalist approach to logic as an alternative to that of Whitehead and Russell. But shortly after the book was published, he received a letter from E. L. Post pointing out that within Lewis's system one could prove that not-possibly-p was equivalent to not-p, which would reduce the system to a redundant form of material implication. This situation resulted from a single postulate that Lewis was able to replace, thus preserving his system; but many of the theorems and proofs in the book had to be revised or abandoned.

In 1920 Lewis returned to Harvard as a lecturer in philosophy; he was promoted to assistant professor the following year. His office was a room in which the unpublished manuscripts of Charles Sanders Peirce were stored. Lewis claims in his "Autobiography" in the Library of Living Philosophers volume devoted to him (1968) that he read many of the papers and that they helped to stimulate his memory of James's teaching and of what Royce called "Absolute Pragmatism," which brought him to the realization that his own beliefs were pragmatic. While this account is no doubt true in part, Lewis also faced the problem that he had created a logic that was an alternative to the one in Principia Mathematica and had to choose between them. He saw this problem as analogous to that of choosing between Euclidean and non-Euclidean geometries, and it gradually dawned on him that the only basis for such a choice had to be pragmatic.

Although Lewis had considered himself an idealist when he went to Berkeley, he became convinced that the new logical and mathematical analyses of infinity and continuity disproved Kant's arguments for the ideality of appearances, and by the time he returned to Harvard he was reexamining his position. In the 1920s he published a series of articles in which he broke with idealism, attacked its doctrines of monism (the idea that there is only one reality) and reaffirmation through denial (the assertion that not-p implies that not-p implies p), and developed his concept of the pragmatic a priori. This decade was the most creative period of Lewis's life.

Traditionally, the a priori has been seen as truths that prescribe the form of experience. Lewis reverses the traditional picture: the given experience is what cannot be repudiated; the a priori is true just because it prescribes nothing to experience. It is legislative for one's attitude toward experience, representing one's determination to view experience in a certain way; but as the mind's legislation for itself, it is necessarily true. Thus, for example, the logical law of excluded middle represents a decision to dichotomize; but human beings could equally well choose to trichotomize or to make some other type of division. The a priori is an arbitrarily chosen conceptual system that can be applied to experience; but many a priori systems are possible, and the choice among them is purely pragmatic: if a given conceptual system does not serve to bring order to experience, it can be abandoned and another adopted; the rejected system is not thereby proven false, merely useless. Just as Nikolay Lobachevsky's non-Euclidean geometry is a consistent system that does not apply to real space, so, Lewis holds, the logic of *Principia Mathematica* is consistent but not useful in dealing with standard forms of thought. This view of the a priori was revolutionary.

Lewis's son Andrew was born in 1925. In 1929 Lewis, who had been promoted to associate professor, published *Mind and the World Order,* his first book in epistemology. The model of human knowledge that he presents is based on five components: awareness of the given, knowledge of objects and objective properties, the analytic a priori, the categorical a priori, and universal generalizations that are not a priori. By "the given" Lewis means that element in experience that is not created and cannot be altered by thought. Experience consists of the given as interpreted; the given as it is in itself can only be obtained by abstraction from experience. One cannot, Lewis holds, be wrong about the given; but one's statements about it can be wrong, because they are in language, and language inherently involves interpretation. Since empirical knowledge consists of statements that can be either true or false, awareness of the given is not part of such knowledge; but it is, nevertheless, the foundation of empirical knowledge.

The analytic a priori is best illustrated by mathematics and logic: it depends only on the meanings of the terms involved and cannot be falsified by empirical facts. It can, however, prove to be useless, in which case, as prescribed by Lewis's theory of the pragmatic a priori, it is withdrawn. The categorical a priori consists of the criteria by which experience is categorized into the real and the unreal. Such criteria are a priori, Lewis says, because they cannot be refuted by experience; any experience that does not fit the criteria of the real—such as dreams, hallucinations, illusions, and so on—is classified as unreal. Like the analytic a priori, however, any such system of categories may prove to be less useful in making sense of experience than some other, in which case it will be withdrawn and the other substituted for it. Thus, the categorical a priori also falls within the pragmatic a priori.

Objects and objective properties are known through the conceptual interpretation of experience. A given presentation serves as a sign of other presenta-

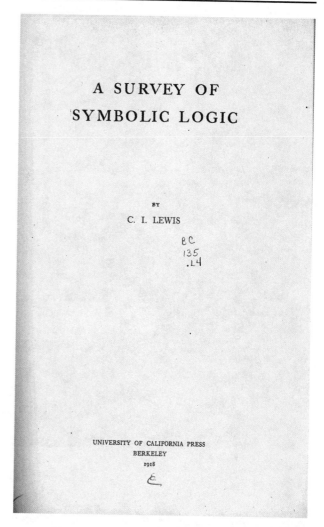

Title page for Lewis's first book, in which he proposes an approach to logic that is an alternative to that of Alfred North Whitehead and Bertrand Russell's 1910–1913 Principia Mathematica *(Thomas Cooper Library, University of South Carolina)*

tions that can be realized in future experience by appropriate action. These regularities in experience are the signs of real objects and real objective properties. Thus, having presentation "A," one predicts that if one performs action "B," then one will experience "C"; if this prediction is verified in experience, one explains this fact by the hypothesis that "A" and "C" are effects of a real object or real property. Finally, empirical generalizations concern the behavior of real things and are verified by predictions of future experience. Such generalizations are, however, only probable, and Lewis devotes a chapter to a discussion of probability based on John Maynard Keynes's *A Treatise on Probability* (1921).

These five elements combine to create the knowledge that people have, both a priori and a poste-

Lewis circa 1930 (Collection of Mabel Lewis)

two systems of strict implication, one stronger than the other, that he calls S1 and S2; in the appendix he sets out S3, the system of *A Survey of Symbolic Logic* amended to eliminate the problems found by Post, and S4 and S5, stronger systems that use postulates discovered by others. The systems S1 through S5 have become known as the Lewis modal logics, that is, logics that include the notions of possibility and necessity. Lewis uses numerical matrices to demonstrate that these systems are consistent, and he shows that they are not reducible to any form of material implication. These systems earned Lewis the title of the modern founder of modal logic, and subsequent work has taken off from his. Lewis considered S2 the preferred form of strict implication. When Ruth C. Barcan (later Ruth Barcan Marcus) demonstrated in 1946 that the deduction theorem does not hold for S2, she raised the question whether or not strict implication really captures what is meant by deducibility. Lewis did not reply.

When Lewis finished *Symbolic Logic,* he intended never to write on logic again: the rapid development of the field and its increasingly technical nature convinced him that he had either to specialize in logic or to abandon it, and he had other issues he wanted to pursue. He had believed from the beginning of his career that ethics was the most important branch of philosophy, and he intended to concentrate on that subject. But the work of the logical positivist Vienna Circle was just then becoming known in the United States. Lewis was greatly attracted by Rudolph Carnap's *Der logische Aufbau der Welt* (1928; enlarged edition, 1961; translated as "The Logical Structure of the World," 1967), Moritz Schlick's early writings, and Hans Reichenbach's work. But as the publications of the logical positivists clarified their position, he found himself strongly opposed to their view that ethical, aesthetic, and valuational statements have no cognitive meaning but are only expressions of emotion. Throughout the 1930s he became ever more opposed to the positivists' views and tried to answer them as he worked out his own position.

Lewis's sons David and Andrew served in the army in World War II; both ended up in the Pacific, preparing for the expected invasion of Japan, but were spared by the dropping of atomic bombs on Hiroshima and Nagasaki in August 1945. Shortly after returning home, David fell ill with encephalitis that he had contracted on Okinawa and nearly died. He was largely confined to a wheelchair for the rest of his life. Of the four Lewis children, Andrew was thus the only one who survived to adulthood in good health.

By the late 1930s Lewis had become convinced that valuation is a form of empirical knowledge,

riori. But Lewis goes further: he wants to demonstrate the validity of knowledge, and to do so he attempts to prove the validity of induction by arguing that any possible experience will contain regularities. Lewis takes these regularities to be caused by real objects, but the argument as posed identifies the regularity with the real object. A real object cannot cause a regularity if it is the regularity; hence Lewis's position becomes either idealism or phenomenalism (the doctrine that knowledge is limited to phenomena), neither of which is what he intended.

Mind and the World Order made Lewis's reputation as an epistemologist. It also established him as a pragmatist second only to John Dewey among living philosophers (James had died in 1910). It was a highly influential work for the next two decades.

By 1932 Lewis was a full professor; that year his daughter Peggy died of leukemia. Also in 1932 he and Cooper Harold Langford published *Symbolic Logic,* in which Lewis presents his own ideas and brings together some of the work that others had done since the appearance of *A Survey of Symbolic Logic.* In the main text of *Symbolic Logic* he presents

although he believed that ethics was not—or not purely—empirical. Although he had presented a theory of empirical knowledge in *Mind and the World Order,* he had said nothing there about valuation; accordingly, he found it necessary to go back to epistemology to justify his view of valuation. But by 1940 he was also facing a new challenge: logicians such as W. V. Quine and Alfred Tarski had expressed doubts about the validity of the distinction between analytic and synthetic statements, and the controversy over this problem had become heated. For Lewis, the distinction was fundamental, and he wanted to defend it. All of these issues come together in 1946 in *An Analysis of Knowledge and Valuation.*

The "*AKV,*" as it is usually called, consists of an introductory section and three "books": the first on analytic truth, the second on empirical knowledge, and the third on valuation. In book 1 Lewis presents a theory of meaning that is far more developed than any in his earlier writings. With respect to terms, he distinguishes the denotation, the class of all existing things to which the term applies; the comprehension, the class of all the possible things—including actual ones—to which the term applies; the signification, the property of the referent by virtue of which the term applies to it; and the connotation or intension, all the terms applicable to anything to which the given term is applicable. Thus, *human being* denotes existing people, comprehends all possible people (such as Hercules), signifies animality and rationality, and connotes "rational," "animal," and so forth. He extends this theory to propositions by holding that propositions are terms: "Mary baking pies now" or "that Mary is baking pies now" are propositions for Lewis. Propositions denote the actual world, signify states of affairs, comprehend the possible worlds in which the propositions would be true, and connote all the propositions logically entailed by them. Lewis distinguishes the proposition, as something entertained by the mind, from the uses of the proposition: thus, "Mary is baking pies now" is the assertion of the proposition "that Mary is baking pies now." The proposition can be questioned, hoped for, hypothesized, and so on. In other words, Lewis distinguishes what would now be called the "speech act" from the proposition. A proposition does not imply its own truth, but the act of asserting a proposition implies that the proposition is true. Lewis later made important use of this distinction in his ethics.

Lewis divides the intension of a proposition or term into its "linguistic meaning"—all the other propositions entailed, or terms implied, by it—and its "sense meaning." The sense meaning is a schema (in the Kantian sense) for the application of the term, together

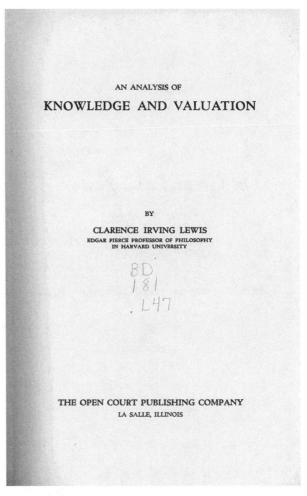

AN ANALYSIS OF

KNOWLEDGE AND VALUATION

BY

CLARENCE IRVING LEWIS
EDGAR PIERCE PROFESSOR OF PHILOSOPHY
IN HARVARD UNIVERSITY

THE OPEN COURT PUBLISHING COMPANY
LA SALLE, ILLINOIS

Title page for Lewis's 1946 book, in which he discusses the analytic/synthetic distinction, meaning in terms and propositions, the nature of empirical knowledge, and values (Thomas Cooper Library, University of South Carolina)

with an imagined result of the application. Sense meaning ties language to the world and permits verification of propositions—the imagined result allows one to recognize the predicted object in experience when one meets it. Without such an imagined result, one could never know what objects of experience satisfy a proposition or term. Sense meaning also supplies Lewis's answer to the problem of analytic truth. The statement "All squares are rectangles" is analytic because the sense meaning of *square* includes that of *rectangle;* one could not verify that something is a square without simultaneously verifying that it is a rectangle.

Book 2 deals with empirical knowledge. Lewis recasts his theory from *Mind and the World Order,* singling out three classes of empirical statements that are involved in empirical knowledge. The first is "expres-

*Title page for the published version of Lewis's Woodbridge
Lectures, delivered at Columbia University in
November 1954 (Thomas Cooper Library,
University of South Carolina)*

sive statements of the given." Lewis now holds these statements to be certain, even though they are in language. "This is red," used as an expressive statement, is not a classificatory statement and does not refer to an objective property; rather, it asserts that the presented quale in experience is identical with some quale that is classified as red. That this theory assumes that one already knows some quale so classified is not a problem for Lewis, because the expressive statement is not temporally prior to other statements. An expressive statement cannot be in error; the knower knows whether or not the statement is true. But it can be false, since the knower can lie.

For Lewis, given experience contains a heterogenous content, much of which will be classified as dreams, illusions, and so forth. Hence, there is no requirement of consistency for statements of the given. Inconsistencies occur in experience; they cannot be eliminated without falsifying the data. The problem is to explain them by appropriate classifications.

The second class of statements are "non-terminating statements"; this class includes all statements about real things and properties. They are non-terminating because they imply an infinite number of possible verifying experiences, and so their verification can never be complete. All such statements are probable, at best, since some predictions of future experience may be false. The third class is "terminating judgments," which constitute the sense meaning of the non-terminating statements. Lewis holds that terminating judgments are implied by non-terminating judgments, as they should be if they are part of the meaning of the latter. Terminating judgments are statements of the form "S being given, then if A then probably B," where "S," "A," and "B" are phrased in expressive terms. Thus, the terminating judgment is a prediction that, given some presentation "S," if one performs action "A," then, with probability P, one will experience quale "B." This prediction can be decisively confirmed or falsified; hence, its verification terminates when the relevant experience occurs. The consequent can only be probable, since if it were certain, verification would not be needed. But the connection between antecedent and consequent is not expressive; Lewis says that it is a "real" connection. What he means by this phrase is not clear, but, following the British empiricist philosopher George Berkeley, he probably means that "S" must be such that it is a sign of "B." And Lewis is insistent that "A" must stand for actions taken by the knower. Scientific observations do not just happen; one has to look for them or create the conditions for their occurrence.

Lewis sees knowledge as requiring the prediction of future experience on the basis of present experience. But he also requires that statements be justified, and justification can only be in terms of probabilities based on prior experience. He makes no attempt here to prove the validity of induction; instead, he adopts Reichenbach's position that one must assume the validity of enumerative induction—the principle that, if the frequency of an event E in a series of K trials has been n/m in the past, then the frequency of E over the course of future trials will continue to be n/m (within a negligible margin of error)—because it will lead to truth if there is a truth to be found; and if there is not, nothing will help. But Lewis attempts to marry an a priori theory of probability like that of Keynes to the frequency theory by holding that a probability is an estimate of a frequency based on premises that supply the data for the estimate. This position has not been adopted by others.

Lewis then provides what is generally regarded as a brilliant analysis of the problem of memory. He points out that one requirement for memory statements is that they should be "congruent"—that is, the probability of any one statement is increased if the others can be taken as premises. But this requirement alone would result in a coherence theory of memory, which he regards as inadequate. Lewis adds the stipulation that memory statements must be accorded prima facie probability. That requirement will permit any given statement, but not the whole of one's "memorial knowledge," to be impeached. His argument is that without memorial knowledge of some credibility, there can be no knowledge at all; one could not classify something as "red" without memorial knowledge of other red things. Thus, in the case of memory and induction, Lewis thinks, one is left with only a Kantian type of deduction: they must be assumed, because unless they are we have no knowledge at all. (Lewis labels this section "'Deduction' of the basic validity of memory and of induction.")

Book 3 deals with valuation. What has intrinsic value, Lewis says, is immediate experience; as experience comes to one, one loves it or hates it, finds it gratifying or grievous. Thus, the value-qualities of experience are simply given and, like other given qualia, are formulated linguistically in expressive statements. As with expressive statements, one cannot be in error about these value qualia, although, since one could lie, the statements could be false. The object of experience that one regards as responsible for the intrinsic value one experiences has what Lewis calls an "inherent value," which is an extrinsic value. Lewis divides extrinsic values into the inherent and the instrumental, the latter being the value of something that is a means to experiencing something that provides an intrinsic value. Thus, a painting may have inherent value, which causes experiences in the observer that have intrinsic value. Walking to the art museum will have an instrumental value, since it allows the person to experience the painting.

Statements of intrinsic value are expressive statements. Statements that something has inherent value are non-terminating statements, because the capacity of an object to produce experiences of intrinsic value must be tested by future experience and can never be certain. Therefore, terminating judgments of value must exist in which the quality of future experience is predicted and that can be decisively confirmed or refuted. Thus, Lewis extends to valuation the analysis of empirical knowledge he gave in book 2, but with certain differences. Nonvaluational properties such as "red" can be defined in terms of the wavelength of light, and such definitions can come to be preferred

Dust jacket for the published version (1957) of Lewis's Powell Lectures, delivered at Indiana University in the spring of 1956 (Bruccoli Clark Layman Archives)

even over the testimony of the senses. But valuational properties cannot be so defined: what *seems* good to a person *is* good, and there is no objective definition that can be contrasted to it.

The summum bonum, Lewis says, is "a life found good in the living of it." Lewis rejects any sort of Benthamite "calculus" as a way of determining the goodness of a life; he denies that intrinsic goods are additive. What constitutes the goodness of a whole life is, rather, a "gestalt" that combines all the goods and bads of experience into a structure that has its own quality and so its own intrinsic good. This position does not create a double standard for intrinsic goods, since although the goodness or badness of an experience is intrinsic and not subject to correction, the value of having that experience is subject to critique. The particular intrinsic goods one experiences contribute to the total gestalt—they have what Lewis calls "contributory value"—but the value of the gestalt is not merely the sum of the particular intrinsic goods of life. Lewis is left with the problem of how the intrinsic value of a temporally extended whole is to be determined. He cannot rely here on analogies to hearing a symphony or reading a book, because, since death is not an event in life, there can be no final appraisal. He takes the solution to be some sort of synthetic grasping of the whole, though exactly how it is to be done is left vague.

Much of book 3 is addressed to the question of why, if valuation is as Lewis says it is, so much disagreement about values should exist. Lewis argues that the value of some valuable things cannot be realized, because the de facto conditions do not allow it: the "gem of purest ray serene" may possess inherent value, but so long as it lies at the bottom of the sea, the value cannot be realized. He extends this point to include factors that may preclude an individual from realizing the intrinsic values available in an object: Helen of Troy surely possessed inherent value, but she is not available today. Lewis deploys this strategy to explain why some who lack the training may not be able to experience the value of a symphony or a painting, whereas others can.

The *AKV* is Lewis's most important work. It was at once an attempt to defend the notion of analytic truth against Quine and his allies, to revise his theory of empirical knowledge, and to extend that theory to valuation. In the face of the logical positivist attack, Lewis sought to show that knowledge of values was, indeed, cognitive knowledge. But he saw the *AKV* as a preparation for what he intended to be his last major work: a book on ethics. Valuation, he believed, was a question of empirical fact; but ethics was not—or not only—an empirical subject. Thus, having finished the *AKV,* he turned to ethics.

Lewis retired from Harvard in 1953 and spent a year as a visiting scholar at Princeton University. He and his wife then moved to Menlo Park, California. Lewis was immediately appointed to the faculty of Stanford University, where he taught until 1957. Much in demand as a lecturer, in November 1954 he gave the Woodbridge Lectures at Columbia University, which were published as *The Ground and Nature of the Right* (1955); in spring 1956 he delivered the Powell Lectures at Indiana University, which were published as *Our Social Inheritance* (1957). His lectures at Wesleyan University in 1959 on the foundations of ethics were not published until after his death, when they were included in *Values and Imperatives: Studies in Ethics* (1969).

Lewis never finished his book on ethics, but his public lectures and his unpublished manuscripts on the subject allow his position to be pieced together at least in outline. Any action, Lewis held, must be appraised in terms of the goodness or badness of its consequences. To perform an act the consequences of which will be good is to do right, and to perform an act the consequences of which will be bad is to do wrong. The goodness or badness of an act are thus necessary conditions for its rightness or wrongness; but they are not sufficient conditions, because as Lewis put it in "Pragmatism and the Roots of the Moral," an article collected in *Values and Imperatives,* "the good solicits but the right commands." Lewis believed that underlying ethical actions—indeed, all actions—are imperatives that are binding on human beings.

Here one comes to the heart of Lewis's philosophic vision. For Lewis, what is special about human beings is that they are aware that they are of their temporality. They are also free to act, and as they do so they find their experience to be gratifying or grievous. They must, therefore, act, in terms of the future they foresee, to try to attain "a life that is good in the living of it." In an uncertain world they must deliberate and make decisions about what to do. This responsibility is the cause of the concern or anxiety that drives humans to think, plan, hope, and strive. Facing a dangerous and partially indeterminate future, people have only their minds and their experience to guide them. To act successfully in such a situation, one must be consistent: if one makes a plan, one must be able to carry it through, despite distractions and interruptions. There is, therefore, a fundamental imperative to be consistent, and from this imperative logic springs. But consistency is not enough: one must act in terms of the world as it really is if one is to achieve any goal. Such action requires empirical knowledge that is accurate, that conforms to the criteria of empirical knowledge elaborated in the *AKV.* Lewis calls this imperative "the imperative of cogency." The imperatives of consistency and cogency have to do with one's mental actions; other imperatives govern physical action, and Lewis, borrowing his terminology from Kant, calls them technical, prudential, and moral imperatives.

Technical imperatives are specific to the particular end sought; unless adequate means are employed, the end will not be achieved. The only general imperative here is, perhaps, an injunction to efficiency. The prudential imperative is to act so as to maximize one's own good in the long run. The moral imperative is Kant's Categorical Imperative: to act so that one could wish the maxim of one's act (the principle on which one is acting) to be a universal law. These five imperatives together make up what Lewis terms "human rationality"; to violate them is to be irrational.

68 Yale Road, Menlo Park, Calif.
Nov. 5, 1961

Dear Professor Schilpp,

I enclose copy for one alteration I should like to make in my autobio-
graphic notes.

Recently I entertained a visiting colleague
who inquired about your projected Lewis
volume.

It is not my business to speak of that; and
I should like you to know my settled policy
in case of such inquiry. I make it clear
that I do not feel concerned about the
date of its appearance. But on inquiry, I
say that I have read the contributions and my
part of it is in your hands. Any other or
further questions, I evade and manage
to allow no basis for inference about
them.

Yours very truly
Clarence Lewis

Letter from Lewis to Paul Arthur Schilpp, the editor of the Library of Living Philosophers volume devoted to Lewis
(from Schilpp, ed., The Philosophy of C. I. Lewis, *1968)*

One might ask, however, what the justification is for having just these imperatives and not others. In the early 1950s Lewis thought that he could prove that they were analytic, but by the middle of the decade he realized that he could not do so. Instead, he invented a proof he called the "pragmatic contradiction." His favorite example of it is the old paradox of Epimenides the Cretan, who said that all Cretans are liars. Lewis notes that there is no contradiction in this statement; had a non-Cretan said it, it would have been unremarkable. But drawing on his theory of propositions, Lewis argues that since the act of assertion asserts the truth of what is asserted, Epimenides does contradict himself—not logically but pragmatically, for in asserting that all Cretans are liars he pragmatically implies that his statement is true, which contradicts the statement. Similarly, the Cyrenaic who says that one should take no thought for the morrow pragmatically contradicts himself by asserting a principle for the morrow. Lewis tried to show that all of the imperatives could be proven by pragmatic contradiction.

Yet, in the end, Lewis recognized that the argument from pragmatic contradiction was circular: it assumes that the person to whom the argument is addressed already accepts the imperative of consistency. Lewis concluded that human nature is as it is, and that the imperatives are requirements of human nature. This claim assumes that his theory of human nature is true, but Lewis accepted this circularity as irremediable.

Lewis was a pragmatist in a deep sense of that word. Like James, Dewey, Peirce, and all other pragmatists, he started from the notion of a particular kind of organism seeking to gratify its needs in a particular environment. More than any other pragmatist except Peirce, who greatly influenced him, Lewis sought to show how knowledge of the world is built up from first-person experience. Like other pragmatists, he understood that knowledge itself was normative. But unlike the others, Lewis probed deeply into just what that claim meant. People govern themselves by rules, and those rules have imperative force; but how and why do they have that force? Lewis's philosophy is normative through and through: logic is the right way to reason; empirical knowledge is the correct form of knowledge; and one's actions must be right if one is to achieve "a life worth the living." Lewis found his answer in the fundamental imperatives without which he thought human thought and action were unintelligible. The problem that he could never solve was how to reconcile prudence and justice—that is, self-regard and regard for others. He wanted a system in which each was given its due but in which justice would, finally, override prudence. He never found a way to accomplish this goal.

Lewis received an honorary degree from the University of Chicago in 1941; he was given the Nicholas Murray Butler Medal in 1950; the American Council of Learned Societies awarded him a $10,000 tax-free prize in 1961; he was elected to the American Philosophical Society, British Academy as a corresponding member, and Phi Beta Kappa as an honorary member. These honors were indications of his stature as the leading systematic philosopher of his generation in the United States. Yet, even before his death on 3 February 1964, many of his doctrines were under attack. Quine led the assault on the notion of analytic truth, others criticized his notion of the given, and still others argued against his claim that valuation is a form of empirical knowledge. Lewis rarely answered his opponents; he believed that in time his views would be vindicated. The underlying issue in most of these arguments is the question of intension. Lewis believed that human knowledge is conceptual: that concepts are mental and constitute the meanings of words and propositions. Concepts can be expressed in language but are prior to and independent of language. Thought, therefore, is not necessarily linguistic; one could think without language and express thought in nonlinguistic ways. Analytic statements are true because they state relations among meanings, and those relations are directly known and are as they are, regardless of language. Similarly, awareness of the given is independent of language; since language is largely restricted to the description of external objects and properties, the linguistic statement of what is given in experience is difficult and requires a special use of language. But Lewis considered it absurd to deny the existence of a given element in experience merely because its description in language is difficult. In the heyday of linguistic philosophy and of behaviorism, many philosophers found Lewis's views antiquated and pursued an opposite path. But behaviorism is defunct, and cognitive scientists talk freely of mental representations that function as concepts. Whether or not time will vindicate Lewis remains to be seen.

Bibliography:

E. M. Adams, "The Writings of C. I. Lewis," in *The Philosophy of C. I. Lewis*, edited by Paul Arthur Schilpp, The Library of Living Philosophers, volume 13 (La Salle, Ill.: Open Court, 1968), pp. 677–689.

References:

Alice Ambrose, "A Critical Discussion of *Mind and the World Order*," *Journal of Philosophy,* 28 (2 July 1931): 365–381;

Charles Baylis, "C. I. Lewis's Theory of Value and Ethics," *Journal of Philosophy,* 59 (1964): 559–567;

Robert Browning, "On Professor Lewis's Distinction between Ethics and Valuation," *Ethics,* 59 (1949): 95–111;

Elizabeth Flower and Murray Murphey, *A History of Philosophy in America,* volume 2 (New York: Putnam, 1977), pp. 891–958;

Bruce Kuklick, *The Rise of American Philosophy, Cambridge, Massachusetts, 1860–1930* (New Haven: Yale University Press, 1977), pp. 533–562;

Vincent Luizzi, *A Naturalistic Theory of Justice: Critical Commentary on, and Selected Readings from, C. I. Lewis' Ethics* (Washington, D.C.: University Press of America, 1981);

Ruth Barcan Marcus, "The Deduction Theorem in a Functional Calculus of the First Order Based on Strict Implication," *Journal of Symbolic Logic,* 11 (1946): 115–118;

Marcus, "Strict Implication, Deducibility and the Deduction Theorem," *Journal of Symbolic Logic,* 18 (1953): 234–236;

Bernard Peach, "C. I. Lewis on the Foundations of Ethics," *Noûs,* 9 (1975): 211–225;

Sandra Rosenthal, "C. I. Lewis and the Pragmatic Rejection of Phenomenalism," *Philosophy and Phenomenological Research,* 41 (1980): 204–215;

Rosenthal, "The 'World' of C. I. Lewis," *Philosophy and Phenomenological Research,* 29 (1969): 589–597;

J. Roger Saydah, *The Ethical Theory of Clarence Irving Lewis* (Athens: Ohio University Press, 1969);

Paul Arthur Schilpp, ed., *The Philosophy of C. I. Lewis,* The Library of Living Philosophers, volume 13 (La Salle, Ill.: Open Court, 1968);

Morton White, "Value and Obligation in Dewey and Lewis," in *Readings in Ethical Theory,* edited by Wilfrid Sellars and John Hospers (New York: Appleton-Century-Crofts, 1952), pp. 332–339.

Papers:

The papers of C. I. Lewis are at Stanford University.

Arthur O. Lovejoy

(10 October 1873 – 30 December 1962)

Anthony J. Graybosch
California State University, Chico

BOOKS: *Handbook of the War for Public Speakers,* by Lovejoy and Albert Bushnell Hart (New York: National Security League, 1917);

Essays in Critical Realism: A Co-operative Study of the Problem of Knowledge, by Lovejoy, Durant Drake, James Bissett Pratt, Arthur Kenyon Rogers, George Santayana, Roy Wood Sellars, and Charles Augustus Strong (London: Macmillan, 1920)–includes "Pragmatism versus the Pragmatist," by Lovejoy;

The Revolt against Dualism: An Inquiry Concerning the Existence of Ideas, The Paul Carus Lectures, series 2 (Chicago: Open Court / New York: Norton, 1930; London: Allen & Unwin, 1930);

Hitler as Pacifist (Baltimore: American Jewish Conference, Baltimore Branch, 1934);

Primitivism and Related Ideas in Antiquity, by Lovejoy, George Boas, W. F. Albright, and P. E. Dumont (Baltimore & London: Johns Hopkins University Press, 1935);

The Great Chain of Being: A Study of the History of an Idea. The William James Lectures Delivered at Harvard University, 1933 (Cambridge, Mass.: Harvard University Press, 1936);

Can We Prevent Future Wars? U.S. War Department Education Manual EM 12, GI Roundtable Series (Madison, Wis.: USAFI, 1944);

The Dumbarton Oaks Proposals: The Enforcement of Peace. Analysis (Boston: Universities Committee on Post-War International Problems, 1944);

Essays in the History of Ideas (Baltimore: Johns Hopkins University Press, 1948);

The Reason, the Understanding, and Time (Baltimore: Johns Hopkins University Press, 1961);

Reflections on Human Nature (Baltimore: Johns Hopkins University press, 1961);

The Thirteen Pragmatisms and Other Essays (Baltimore: Johns Hopkins University Press, 1963).

Edition: *The Revolt against Dualism: An Inquiry Concerning the Existence of Ideas,* introduction by Jonathan B. Imber (New Brunswick, N.J.: Transaction, 1996).

Arthur O. Lovejoy

OTHER: "Academic Freedom," in *Encyclopaedia of the Social Sciences,* volume 1, edited by Edwin R. A. Seligman and Alvin Johnson (New York: Macmillan, 1930), pp. 384–388;

"A Temporalistic Realism," in *Contemporary American Philosophy: Personal Statements,* volume 2, edited by

George P. Adams and William P. Montague (New York: Macmillan, 1930), pp. 85–105.

SELECTED PERIODICAL PUBLICATIONS–
UNCOLLECTED: "The Dialectic of Bruno and Spinoza," *University of California Publications in Philosophy*, 1 (1904): 141–174;

"The Origins of Ethical Inwardness in Jewish Thought," *American Journal of Theology*, 11 (1907): 228–249;

"The Argument for Organic Evolution before 'The Origin of the Species,'" *Popular Science Monthly*, 75 (1909): 499–514, 537–549;

"The Association of University Professors," *Science*, 40 (1914): 744–745;

"The Profession of the Professorate," *Johns Hopkins Alumni Magazine*, 2 (1914): 181–195;

"Organization of the American Association of University Professors," *Science*, 41 (1915): 151–154;

"On Some Conditions of Progress in Philosophical Inquiry," *Philosophical Review*, 26 (1917): 123–163;

"To Conscientious Objectors," *New Republic*, 11 (1917): 187–189;

"Academic Freedom in War Time," *Nation*, 106 (1918): 401–402;

"Is a 'Peace of Conciliation' Possible?" *New Republic*, 16 (1918): 257–259;

"German Peace Drives Rightly Named 'Traps,'" *New York Times Magazine* (28 July 1918): 4, 15;

"The Historiography of Ideas," *Proceedings of the American Philosophical Society*, 78 (1938): 529–543;

"Reflections on the History of Ideas," *Journal of the History of Ideas*, 1 (1940): 3–23;

"Communism versus Academic Freedom," *American Scholar*, 18 (1949): 332–337.

A philosopher and historian of ideas, Arthur O. Lovejoy was largely responsible for the acceptance of intellectual history as a separate discipline. He cofounded with Philip P. Wiener *The Journal of the History of Ideas* in 1940. Lovejoy's professional career combined academic philosophy and extraordinary service to both academic life and his country. He was an early advocate of academic freedom, a founder of the American Association of University Professors (AAUP), and an articulate defender of American engagement in two world wars. True to the pragmatic tradition, Lovejoy in his engagement as a public intellectual rejected moral absolutes. He sought to combine academic freedom with a rejection of communism as an ideology opposed to freedom; a love of peace with an awareness of the importance of military engagement with violators of human rights. Lovejoy's 1927 Paul Carus Lectures for the American Philosophical Association (APA) were

published in 1930 as *The Revolt against Dualism: An Inquiry Concerning the Existence of Ideas,* and his William James Lectures at Harvard in 1933 appeared in 1936 as *The Great Chain of Being: A Study of the History of an Idea.*

Arthur Schauffler Lovejoy was born in Berlin on 10 October 1873 to Wallace William Lovejoy, a Boston physician who was in Germany for postgraduate study after completing his medical degree at Harvard, and Sara Oncken Lovejoy, the daughter of a Hamburg Baptist missionary and religious publisher with whom Wallace Lovejoy had boarded on arriving in Germany. Arthur Lovejoy's middle name was taken from that of his mother's widowed sister, Margaret Oncken Schauffler; sometime before 1890 he exchanged it for his mother's maiden name. Wallace Lovejoy could trace his ancestors in the United States to a John Lovejoy who had arrived in Massachusetts as an indentured servant in 1630.

Wallace Lovejoy returned to Boston with his family in May 1874. On 26 April of the following year his wife died from an overdose–whether accidental or deliberate has never been determined–of gelsemium, which she had been taking from her husband's medicine cabinet, without his knowledge, to help her sleep. Devastated by her death, Lovejoy's father was no longer able to care for him. His paternal grandmother and several of his father's sisters took the child back to Germany. He was reunited with his father in Boston in 1878; shortly afterward, Wallace Lovejoy moved to Germantown, Pennsylvania, where he abandoned medicine and became an Episcopal minister. His son, his mother, and several of his sisters joined him there. In January 1881 Wallace Lovejoy married Emmeline Dunton. The family moved to Irontown, Ohio, for a short time, after which Lovejoy and his stepmother returned to Germantown while Wallace Lovejoy continued his theological studies in Boston. They also lived in Palmyra and Trenton, New Jersey. In 1891 the family moved to Oakland, California.

From 1891 to 1895 Lovejoy attended the University of California at Berkeley, where he studied classics, humanities, languages, and philosophy. One of his professors was George Holmes Howison, an idealist philosopher who carried on an extensive correspondence with William James. Howison was concerned with many of the problems of philosophical theology that occupied James and Josiah Royce, especially the conflict between human freedom and divine omnipotence and omniscience.

Lovejoy went to Harvard in the fall of 1895 and spent the next three years studying philosophy with Royce, James, Hugo Münsterberg, George Herbert Palmer, and George Santayana. After receiving his M.A., he went to Paris for an additional year of postgraduate study. In 1899 he became the first philosopher on the faculty of Stanford University.

In 1900 the statements of Edward Ross, an economics professor at Stanford, criticizing the importation of Asian workers and advocating public ownership of utility companies led Jane Stanford, the widow of the founder of the university, to demand that President David Starr Jordan dismiss Ross. Lovejoy refused the "invitation" of Stanford's administration to the faculty to support the action against Ross. Lovejoy had been active in settlement work at Berkeley, Harvard, and Stanford and had come to recognize a special role for professors as active advocates of social change. He believed that without some sort of collective action and protection of faculty rights, the tenuousness of academic appointments would make it difficult for faculty members to express unpopular views. He wrote Jordan that a lack of respect for the free speech of professors would discredit their positions and thwart the social change that universities could foster. At the beginning of the 1901 spring semester he published a statement condemning the action against Ross as a violation of academic freedom and offered his resignation. The latter was accepted, effective immediately. After resigning from Stanford, Lovejoy taught at Washington University in St. Louis for six years, at Columbia University for one year, and at the University of Missouri for two years.

In 1908 Lovejoy published "The Thirteen Pragmatisms" in *The Journal of Philosophy;* it was republished in 1963 in the posthumous collection *The Thirteen Pragmatisms and Other Essays.* In this article Lovejoy analyzes the concept of pragmatism in the work of James, Charles Sanders Peirce, John Dewey, and F. C. S. Schiller and uncovers thirteen uses of the term grouped into four types: theories of meaning, theories of the nature of truth, theories of the criterion of truth, and ontologies. The three theories of meaning are that the meaning of a judgment is the future experiences predicted by it, the future consequences of believing it, and "the apprehension of the relation of some object to a future purpose." The galleys for the essay in Harvard University's Houghton Library collection of James's papers include marginal notations by James, with replies by Lovejoy; at this point James writes that the distinction between the first two theories of meaning is "crucial especially in relation to the *Will to Believe.*" Lovejoy notes that a criterion of the meaning of a claim may not be a means of determining its truth and that one must have a criterion for accepting a belief as a plan of action long before the future date on which its satisfactory role as a plan of action verifies it as true. If these three claims cannot be separated, then pragmatism will be useful only after the fact. Pragmatist theories of meaning, however, hold that a belief loses its meaning

in being confirmed: meaning is in the future consequences of a belief, and the belief now refers to the past.

As a theory of truth, pragmatism holds that propositions are not true but become true: "The truth of a judgment 'consists in' the complete realization of the experience (or series of experiences) to which the judgement had antecedently pointed." Lovejoy argues that this theory of truth is distinct from and independent of the three theories of meaning and that the pragmatic view of the nature of truth is faulty because a test of truth cannot be derived from it. He comments that the only true proposition is a dead one (a remark that displeased James).

Lovejoy finds eight pragmatic theories of the criterion of truth. They hold that propositions should be accepted as true if, in the past, the predictions they made for future experience were realized; if they have had biological survival value to the individuals who relied on them; if they meet a psychological need and enable a person to pass from doubt to conviction; if they provide the "maximum bulk of satisfaction," where satisfaction is understood in James's multidimensional sense; if their adoption provides theoretical satisfactions, such as consistency and conservatism; if they are put forth as postulates that turn out to have practical usefulness, and it is understood that there are no necessary truths; if they are practically useful, and there are a limited number of additional necessary truths; and if they are practically useful, where "usefulness" is understood to include moral, religious, and aesthetic satisfactions on an equal level with those of science and common sense.

Finally, pragmatism as an ontology recognizes temporal becoming as a fundamental characteristic of reality. The future is open, in the sense that it is not already decided in every detail, its outcome can be affected by conscious choices, and it can be fully known only as it becomes present. Lovejoy concludes the essay by stating that he has offered a prolegomenon to a future pragmatism that has made its key positions clear and avoided inconsistencies.

Lovejoy was particularly amenable to pragmatism as an ontology. In "Pragmatism and Theology," published in 1908 in *The American Journal of Theology* and republished in *The Thirteen Pragmatisms and Other Essays,* he calls the "open future" James's "characteristic metaphysical doctrine." He praises the postulate as a presupposition of all rational action and endorses James's rejection of a universe in which "God's in his Heaven, all's well with the world." Lovejoy insists that philosophers not adopt the idealist fashion of the day and optimistically assert that some perspective exists from which the dichotomy of good and evil disappears into a higher unity in which all is good. With James, Lovejoy asserts the stubborn reality of unredeemed evils and uncompensated losses: "Our business with these is not to harmonize them, or even to explain how they came to be there; our business is to get rid of them, and to devote our powers to eliminating them from the world that is to be." James's finite God and grudgingly optimistic meliorism, Lovejoy believes, are central to the rational theology of the future.

In 1910 Lovejoy moved to Johns Hopkins University. In 1913 Lafayette College in Easton, Pennsylvania, terminated a philosopher, John Mecklin, for his liberal views. Mecklin protested to the American Philosophical Association and the American Psychological Association. The president of Lafayette College refused to cooperate with the two associations, demonstrating to Lovejoy the powerlessness of professional academics. At Lovejoy's instigation, senior faculty at Johns Hopkins invited nine other universities to send faculty representatives to a meeting for the establishment of a professional union. Seven universities, in addition to Johns Hopkins, participated in the organizational meeting on 17 November 1913. The philosophy department at Harvard wanted to hire Lovejoy in 1914, but the appointment was blocked by the president, A. Lawrence Lowell, because of Lovejoy's role in the union movement. In January 1915 the American Association of University Professors was formed, with Dewey as president and Lovejoy as secretary.

Lovejoy was an influential member of the committee that developed the AAUP position on academic freedom, which was ratified by the membership in 1916. The AAUP position reflected Lovejoy's belief in the university as a source of social change and as the community of scientific scholars envisioned by Royce, Howison, and Peirce. The committee declared that a "scholar must be absolutely free not only to follow his investigations but to declare the results of his researches, no matter where they may lead him or to what extent they may come in conflict with accepted opinion." Academic freedom was crucial to a society interested in expanding human knowledge and providing competent instruction to students. The committee also stated that academic freedom belonged to those who carried out their jobs in the scientific spirit and presented their views in a noninflammatory manner. Professors could express their own opinions but should also provide all other significant perspectives on the issue. Dispassionate, critical, and careful inquiry before forming an opinion was to be practiced both inside and outside the classroom. Lovejoy later returned to this notion, that one had to earn academic freedom by embodying the virtues of the good scientist, when he argued for limits on academic freedom

Lovejoy's parents, Sara Oncken and Wallace William Lovejoy

for Communists and on academic freedom in general during wartime.

During World War I Lovejoy worked for various organizations dedicated to improving American morale, including the War Department and the National Security League. His writings included *Handbook of the War for Public Speakers* (1917), in which he and Albert Bushnell Hart assembled documents purportedly demonstrating the injustice of the German war effort, together with an introduction and commentary. Lovejoy explains that the major reason for limiting freedom in times of emergency is that the democratic form of government is not the most efficient in waging wars. During wartime, democracies must consolidate power in the head of government, act in the interests of expediency without public consultation, and restrict some liberties while resolving to restore them to their full extent after the war. Lovejoy says that he is puzzled that anyone would hold that there are no causes worth fighting for, but he argues that the nation can afford to tolerate conscientious objectors.

In 1916 the AAUP appointed Lovejoy to chair a committee on academic freedom during wartime. The committee said that professors could be terminated if they interfered with the war effort by disobeying laws related to the war, including draft laws; participated in activities designed to influence others to disobey such laws; attempted to persuade others not to make voluntary efforts in support of the war; or made public statements in support of the German war effort. The AAUP approved the committee's report.

Lovejoy had been active in the American Philosophical Association since its founding in 1901. His concept of the professorate as an army of dispassionate inquirers influenced his view of the association: he thought that philosophers would profit by imitating scientific societies; they would join in cooperative investigation of significant philosophical problems framed by agreed-on definitions and common assumptions. As president of the APA in 1916, Lovejoy delivered an address titled "On Some Conditions of Progress in Philosophical Inquiry." He advised philosophers to avoid haste in reaching conclusions, to enumerate all relevant considerations on the issues they pursued, to engage in cooperative inquiry, to work from common terms and postulates, to isolate specific problems within a nest of hypothetical issues, and to survey all other philosophical issues relevant to the one at hand. Lovejoy served on the APA Committee on Definitions, which sought to facilitate discussions at the annual meetings by proposing definitions and precise statements of the problems to be addressed. The APA gradually abandoned Lovejoy's vision of scientifically organized philosophical research teams, but Lovejoy still engaged in cooperative publications such as *Essays in Critical Realism: A Co-operative Study of the Problem of Knowledge* (1920) and *Primitivism and Related Ideas in Antiquity* (1935).

In "Pragmatism versus the Pragmatist," first published in *Essays in Critical Realism,* Lovejoy says that a consistent pragmatism must recognize four theses that amount to a joining of realism and dualism. The first thesis is that instrumental knowledge "is, or at least includes and requires, 'presentative' knowledge, a representation of not present existents by present data." Lovejoy is committing himself to a representative realism and implicitly rejecting naive realism. The second claim is that "knowledge is thus necessarily and constantly conversant with entities which are existentially 'transcendent' of the knowing experience, and frequently with entities which transcend the total experience of the knower." Lovejoy thus accepts the commonsense notion that knowledge extends to objects

that one has never directly experienced, such as the distant past. Knowledge, that is, is not just knowledge of present objects and present memories. Lovejoy's third thesis is that once one accepts—as one should—the existence of the physical world proposed by the natural sciences, then "certain of the contents of experience, and specifically the contents of anticipation and retrospection, cannot be assigned to that world, and must be called 'psychical.'" The world of the physical sciences has no place for the various psychical qualities by which objects are represented to the knower. The existence of two worlds, containing different kinds of entities—physical and mental—must be admitted. Hence, pragmatists must accept dualism. Finally, Lovejoy maintains that "knowledge is mediated through such psychical existences and would be impossible without them." This claim is more than a summation of the other three; Lovejoy is saying that pragmatic dualism has provided an account of the commonsense notion of knowledge and that other attempts to explain knowledge without accepting dualism have failed.

Lovejoy upholds epistemological naturalism, according to which knowledge is a natural event that is taken for granted by biology and all other sciences. Psychology may seem to be an exception to this generalization, but Lovejoy remarks that psychologists do not usually investigate acts of knowing as thoroughly as philosophers do. Such acts, along with judging and doubting, provide the phenomena that allow philosophy its own distinctive objects that qualify it as a science. Lovejoy is aware that his dualism commits him to an analysis of knowledge in which physical objects are known by a physical knower through the representation of nonphysical entities. Philosophy is, therefore, a peculiar science.

In "The Anomaly of Knowledge," published in 1923 in *University of California Publications in Philosophy* and republished in *The Thirteen Pragmatisms and Other Essays,* Lovejoy makes the tensions in his dualism explicit in two anomalies. The "lesser anomaly" arises from regarding knowledge from the perspective of the physical sciences. Acts of knowing physical objects by physical organisms involve experienced items that are not themselves part of what the natural sciences place in the physical world. The "greater anomaly" is that knowing involves having within one's experience objects that one places outside the world of one's present experience. When one knows a past object, it is within one's experience at the same time as one's knowledge places it outside one's experience. Lovejoy solves the greater anomaly by interpreting knowledge as being about its objects and not a direct acquaintance with them: "Knowledge . . . is a salutation, not an embrace." But his escape from the greater anomaly requires him to accept the lesser: knowledge is mediated by representative ideas and qualities that have psychical existence.

The epistemology Lovejoy advocates in *The Revolt against Dualism* is a combination of the "animal faith" of Santayana with the transcendental arguments from the nature of communication advocated by Royce. Lovejoy acknowledges five expectations of naive knowers: many objects of knowledge exist in external space, humans have knowledge of past and future objects, humans have knowledge of things as they are in themselves, humans have knowledge of each other's experiences, and the world of objects of knowledge is a public, shared world. His major departure from naive dualism is in denying the complete qualitative identity of the object of knowledge and its representation. Although Lovejoy offers arguments to establish that object and representation differ in important respects, such as their temporal and physical locations, his major motive for denying the identity of object and representation is the Roycean concern to provide room for error: if the representation of the object of knowledge were a direct apprehension of it, knowledge claims could not fail.

Lovejoy's method of philosophizing is to proceed in a piecemeal fashion to solve specific problems within a nest of assumptions. For instance, in "The Anomaly of Knowledge" he assumes pragmatism as a working hypothesis and asks whether pragmatists must be idealists or realists. He tacitly assumes that by working together and solving enough of these problems over time, philosophers will uncover a system in which the necessity of each position will be obvious from its agreement with each of the others. This notion of philosophy is surprising for those who live after philosophy made its analytic turn under the influence of the logical positivists in the 1930s. But a combination of idealism, close analysis of the meaning of philosophical issues, and respect for scientific method was Lovejoy's heritage from Peirce and Royce, and this notion of what philosophy should aspire to accomplish was shared by many of his contemporaries. In his own time, Lovejoy's approach to philosophy was most at odds with that of James. James grounded his philosophy on what he called "the sentiment of reason." This sentiment encompassed more than an appreciation of the usual scientific virtues of consistency among beliefs, empirical exhaustiveness, and faithfulness to experience: James elevated the aesthetic, moral, and religious impulses to equal status with the data of the senses as forms of satisfaction. He paid lip service to the primacy of intellectual concerns in selecting the true hypothesis, but he was honest enough to admit that when faced with two hypotheses that were equally

Lovejoy's stepmother, Emmeline Dunton Lovejoy, whom his father married in 1881 after his first wife's death in 1875

supported by the facts, he felt free—in fact, obligated—to choose the one that satisfied his other needs.

James's attempt to wed truth to what satisfied broader human needs was no more agreeable to Lovejoy than it had been to Peirce. Most of the problems significant enough to occupy philosophers, he pointed out, would not be settled on empirical grounds. Lovejoy believed that James had not fully understood the philosophy he had founded, and he set out to rescue pragmatism from the pragmatists.

Lovejoy's best-known book, *The Great Chain of Being,* is a study of the historical development of theism in Western thought. Lovejoy contrasts the notion of a God of absolute otherworldliness, self-sufficiency, and completed perfection with that of a God whose chief characteristic is generativeness manifested in a diversity of created organisms. Lovejoy locates the source of the two Gods in the writings of Plato and traces the history of the attempt to wed the two together. Paying special attention to the works of the Romantics and to the introduction of the idea of divine evolution into reli-

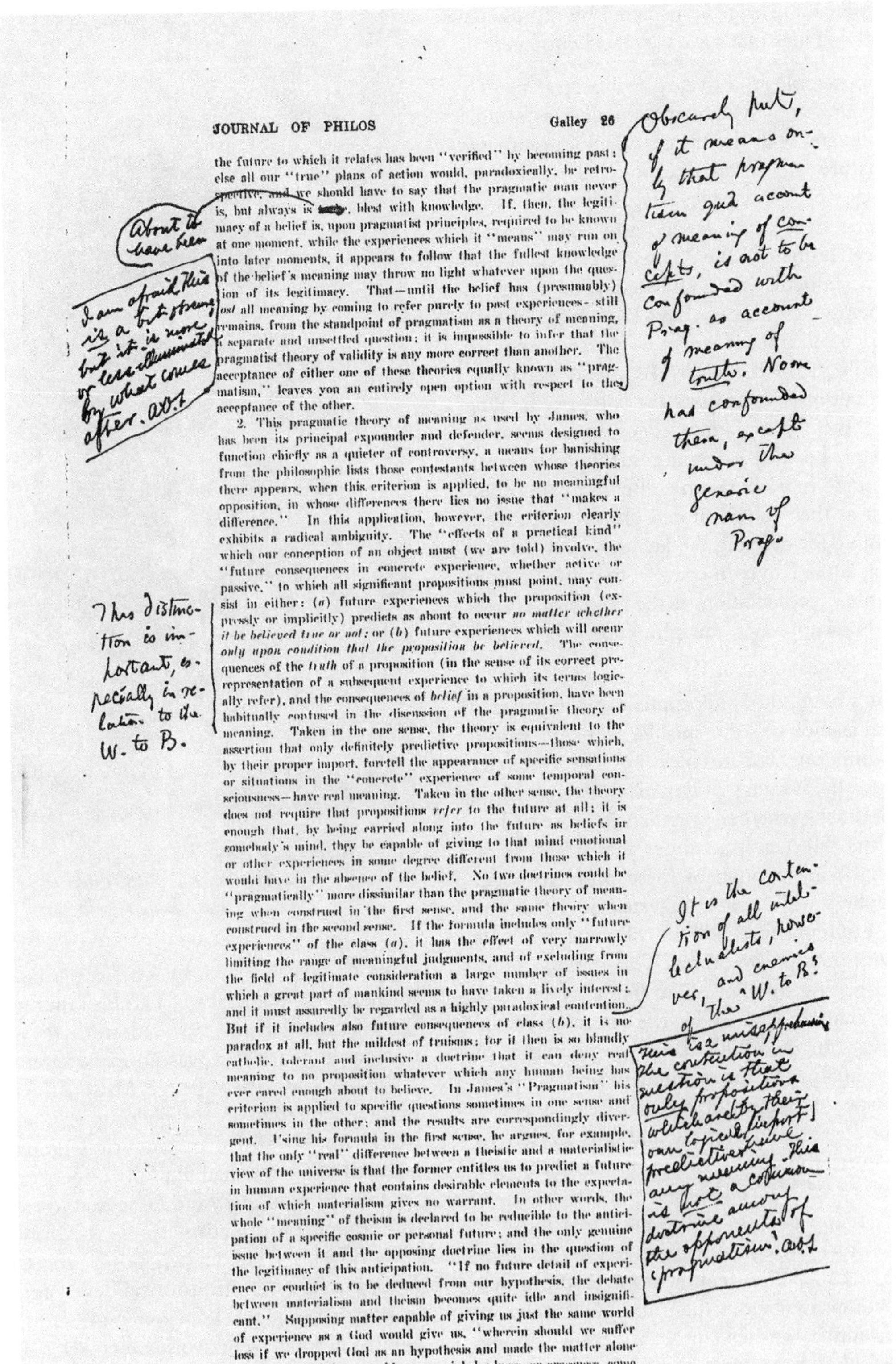

JOURNAL OF PHILOS　　　　　　　　　　　Galley 26

the future to which it relates has been "verified" by becoming past; else all our "true" plans of action would, paradoxically, be retrospective, and we should have to say that the pragmatic man never is, but always is ~~tardy~~, blest with knowledge. If, then, the legitimacy of a belief is, upon pragmatist principles, required to be known at one moment, while the experiences which it "means" may run on into later moments, it appears to follow that the fullest knowledge of the belief's meaning may throw no light whatever upon the question of its legitimacy. That—until the belief has (presumably) lost all meaning by coming to refer purely to past experiences—still remains, from the standpoint of pragmatism as a theory of meaning, a separate and unsettled question; it is impossible to infer that the pragmatist theory of validity is any more correct than another. The acceptance of either one of these theories equally known as "pragmatism," leaves you an entirely open option with respect to the acceptance of the other.

2. This pragmatic theory of meaning as used by James, who has been its principal expounder and defender, seems designed to function chiefly as a quieter of controversy, a means for banishing from the philosophic lists those contestants between whose theories there appears, when this criterion is applied, to be no meaningful opposition, in whose differences there lies no issue that "makes a difference." In this application, however, the criterion clearly exhibits a radical ambiguity. The "effects of a practical kind" which our conception of an object must (we are told) involve, the "future consequences in concrete experience, whether active or passive," to which all significant propositions must point, may consist in either: (a) future experiences which the proposition (expressly or implicitly) predicts as about to occur no matter whether it be believed true or not; or (b) future experiences which will occur only upon condition that the proposition be believed. The consequences of the truth of a proposition (in the sense of its correct representation of a subsequent experience to which its terms logically refer), and the consequences of belief in a proposition, have been habitually confused in the discussion of the pragmatic theory of meaning. Taken in the one sense, the theory is equivalent to the assertion that only definitely predictive propositions—those which, by their proper import, foretell the appearance of specific sensations or situations in the "concrete" experience of some temporal consciousness—have real meaning. Taken in the other sense, the theory does not require that propositions refer to the future at all; it is enough that, by being carried along into the future as beliefs in somebody's mind, they be capable of giving to that mind emotional or other experiences in some degree different from those which it would have in the absence of the belief. No two doctrines could be "pragmatically" more dissimilar than the pragmatic theory of meaning when construed in the first sense, and the same theory when construed in the second sense. If the formula includes only "future experiences" of the class (a), it has the effect of very narrowly limiting the range of meaningful judgments, and of excluding from the field of legitimate consideration a large number of issues in which a great part of mankind seems to have taken a lively interest; and it must assuredly be regarded as a highly paradoxical contention. But if it includes also future consequences of class (b), it is no paradox at all, but the mildest of truisms; for it then is so blandly catholic, tolerant and inclusive a doctrine that it can deny real meaning to no proposition whatever which any human being has ever cared enough about to believe. In James's "Pragmatism" his criterion is applied to specific questions sometimes in one sense and sometimes in the other; and the results are correspondingly divergent. Using his formula in the first sense, he argues, for example, that the only "real" difference between a theistic and a materialistic view of the universe is that the former entitles us to predict a future in human experience that contains desirable elements to the expectation of which materialism gives no warrant. In other words, the whole "meaning" of theism is declared to be reducible to the anticipation of a specific cosmic or personal future; and the only genuine issue between it and the opposing doctrine lies in the question of the legitimacy of this anticipation. "If no future detail of experience or conduct is to be deduced from our hypothesis, the debate between materialism and theism becomes quite idle and insignificant." Supposing matter capable of giving us just the same world of experience as a God would give us, "wherein should we suffer loss if we dropped God as an hypothesis and made the matter alone responsible? Where would any special deadness or crassness come

Marginal notes (handwritten):

[left margin] About it have been

[left margin] I am afraid this is a bit obscure but it is more or less illuminated by what comes after. A.O.L.

[left margin] This distinction is important, especially in relation to the W. to B.

[right margin] Obscurely put, if it means only that pragmatism qua account of meaning of concepts, is not to be confounded with Prag. as account of meaning of truth. No one has confounded them, except under the generic name of Prag.

[right margin] It is the contention of all intellectualists, however, and enemies of the "W. to B."

[right margin] This is a misapprehension the contention in question is that only propositions which are by their own topical import predictive have any meaning. This is not a contention about the opponents of "pragmatism." A.O.L.

Pages from the galley proofs for Lovejoy's 1908 essay "The Thirteen Pragmatisms," with marginal notations by Lovejoy and William James (Houghton Library, Harvard University)

218

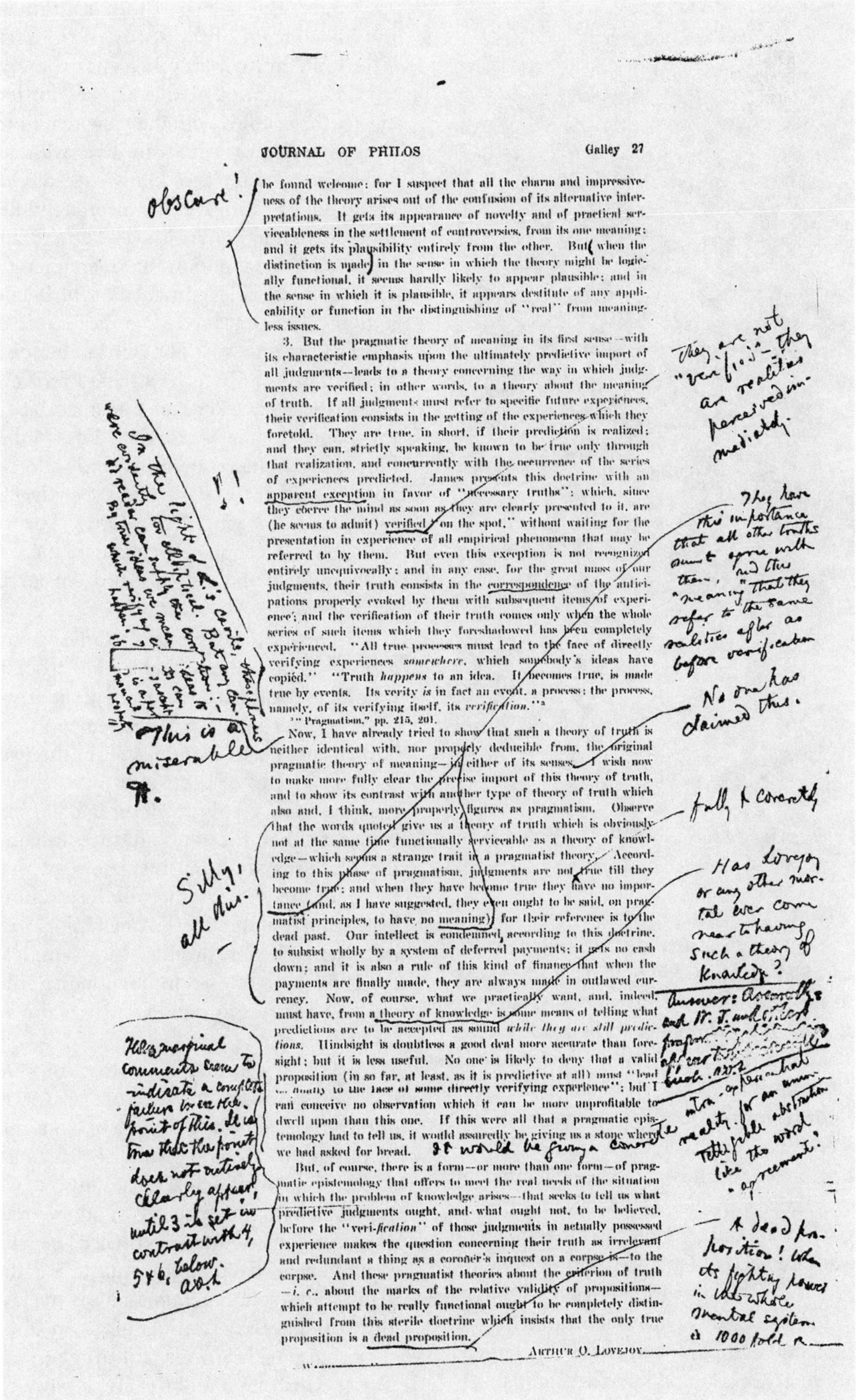

JOURNAL OF PHILOS   Galley 27

be found welcome; for I suspect that all the charm and impressiveness of the theory arises out of the confusion of its alternative interpretations. It gets its appearance of novelty and of practical serviceableness in the settlement of controversies, from its one meaning; and it gets its plausibility entirely from the other. But when the distinction is made in the sense in which the theory might be logically functional, it seems hardly likely to appear plausible; and in the sense in which it is plausible, it appears destitute of any applicability or function in the distinguishing of "real" from meaningless issues.

3. But the pragmatic theory of meaning in its first sense—with its characteristic emphasis upon the ultimately predictive import of all judgments—leads to a theory concerning the way in which judgments are verified; in other words, to a theory about the meaning of truth. If all judgments must refer to specific future experiences, their verification consists in the getting of the experiences which they foretold. They are true, in short, if their prediction is realized; and they can, strictly speaking, be known to be true only through that realization, and concurrently with the occurrence of the series of experiences predicted. James presents this doctrine with an apparent exception in favor of "necessary truths"; which, since they coerce the mind as soon as they are clearly presented to it, are (he seems to admit) verified "on the spot," without waiting for the presentation in experience of all empirical phenomena that may be referred to by them. But even this exception is not recognized entirely unequivocally; and in any case, for the great mass of our judgments, their truth consists in the correspondence of the anticipations properly evoked by them with subsequent items of experience; and the verification of their truth comes only when the whole series of such items which they foreshadowed has been completely experienced. "All true processes must lead to the face of directly verifying experiences somewhere, which somebody's ideas have copied." "Truth happens to an idea. It becomes true, is made true by events. Its verity is in fact an event, a process; the process, namely, of its verifying itself, its verification."

Now, I have already tried to show that such a theory of truth is neither identical with, nor properly deducible from, the original pragmatic theory of meaning—in either of its senses. I wish now to make more fully clear the precise import of this theory of truth, and to show its contrast with another type of theory of truth which also and, I think, more properly figures as pragmatism. Observe that the words quoted give us a theory of truth which is obviously not at the same time functionally serviceable as a theory of knowledge—which seems a strange trait in a pragmatist theory. According to this phase of pragmatism, judgments are not true till they become true; and when they have become true they have no importance (and, as I have suggested, they even ought to be said, on pragmatist principles, to have no meaning) for their reference is to the dead past. Our intellect is condemned, according to this doctrine, to subsist wholly by a system of deferred payments; it gets no cash down; and it is also a rule of this kind of finance that when the payments are finally made, they are always made in outlawed currency. Now, of course, what we practically want, and, indeed, must have, from a theory of knowledge is some means of telling what predictions are to be accepted as sound while they are still predictions. Hindsight is doubtless a good deal more accurate than foresight; but it is less useful. No one is likely to deny that a valid proposition (in so far, at least, as it is predictive at all) must "lead ... finally to the face of some directly verifying experience"; but I can conceive no observation which it can be more unprofitable to dwell upon than this one. If this were all that a pragmatic epistemology had to tell us, it would assuredly be giving us a stone where we had asked for bread.

But, of course, there is a form—or more than one form—of pragmatic epistemology that offers to meet the real needs of the situation in which the problem of knowledge arises—that seeks to tell us what predictive judgments ought, and what ought not, to be believed, before the "veri-fication" of those judgments in actually possessed experience makes the question concerning their truth as irrelevant and redundant a thing as a coroner's inquest on a corpse is—to the corpse. And these pragmatist theories about the criterion of truth—i. e., about the marks of the relative validity of propositions—which attempt to be really functional ought to be completely distinguished from this sterile doctrine which insists that the only true proposition is a dead proposition.

ARTHUR O. LOVEJOY

"Pragmatism," pp. 215, 201.

Handwritten marginalia:

obscure!

!!

This is a miserable ¶.

Silly! all this.

His marginal comments seem to indicate a complete failure to see the point of this. It is true that the point does not outline clearly after ... until 3 is set in contrast with 4, 5 & 6, below. A.O.L

They are not "verified"—they are realities perceived immediately.

They have this importance that all other truths come & agree with them, and the "meaning" that they refer to the same realities after as before verification.

No one has claimed this.

fully & correctly

Has Lovejoy or any other mortal ever come near to having of such a theory of knowledge?

Answer: Assuredly ... W. J. ...

A dead proposition! When its fighting power in the whole mental system is 1000 fold ...

Lovejoy visiting the front lines during World War I

Lovejoy discusses four unit-ideas in illustrating his concept of the study of the history of ideas. The first, human simplicity, is the eighteenth century's acceptance of the inaccessibility of theological truth, coupled with the view that human beings are simple creatures who can live without such truth; self-knowledge replaces knowledge of God as the basic epistemological source of a meaningful life. The second unit-idea is the nominalist desire to "reduce the meaning of all general notions to an enumeration of the concrete and sensible particulars which fall under those notions," which played a significant role in the development of pragmatism. The third unit-idea is "metaphysical pathos," in which a characterization of reality automatically awakens an empathetic acceptance; Lovejoy points to the work of Georg Wilhelm Friedrich Hegel and Henri Bergson and quotes approvingly James's wonder that so many people take such great satisfaction in saying, "All is One." The fourth unit-idea is that of philosophical semantics: the uncovering and explicating of the sacred words of an historical time such as *nature*.

The history of ideas studies a unit-idea in all aspects of a culture, traces the processes by which unit-ideas influence various disciplines and institutions, studies intellectual movements across languages and cultures, and is interested in the use of unit-ideas by large groups of people, not just by cultural leaders. The secondary cultural figures of a period aspire to transcend their time and produce universal works, and their failures are often revelatory of the unit-ideas of their culture. For instance, an historian of ideas might learn much about the Soviet Union from a study of the science fiction produced by significant authors of the 1930s, as opposed to the popular culture's fixation on westerns in translation, such as the works of Zane Grey.

The three unit-ideas that produce the Great Chain of Being are the Idea of the Good, the Principle of Plenitude, and the Principle of Continuity. The genesis of the two Gods is found in Plato's assertion that a perfect God would not be jealous; it would offer no impediment to the existence of other entities and organisms. An "otherworldly existence" in which true value is permanent, fixed, and complete is radically opposed to the values found in human life. Lovejoy characterizes this-worldliness as "an identification of the chief value of existence with process and struggle in time, an antipathy to satisfaction and finality, a sense of the 'glory of the imperfect.'" The value of both worlds is preserved by Plato's avoidance in his later work of characterizing the world of becoming as an illusion. Instead, the perfection of an absolute, perfect, and complete God becomes the ground, through lack of impediment, to

gious thought, he combines analytic technique, close attention to historical detail, and hypothetical reasoning in an attempt to tease out useful morals from the unfolding story of the two Gods. His conclusions address the hope for a rational theism and the ultimate role of reason in human life.

Lovejoy conceives the history of ideas as being different from both philosophy and the history of philosophy. It is like analytic chemistry in its initial move of breaking systematic worldviews down into their simplest elements, which he calls "unit-ideas." God is not a unit-idea: beneath the idea of God are more-basic units of meaning, such as "otherworldliness" and "this-worldliness." The arrangement of unit-ideas into the claims that animate philosophies and cultures is largely an historical product, not a logical inference. The historian of ideas comes to realize that novelty is rare in human thought and that when it occurs, it is the result of a creative pattern of arrangement of unit-ideas; just as cultures adopt fashions in clothing, they are dominated by basic assumptions and mental habits.

the creation of the entities of the temporal world. The Principle of Plenitude articulates the realization that such a being would not obstruct any possible existence, so that all possible entities must exist. This principle provides a way of understanding the connection between the two worlds and, eventually, between the two Gods. Aristotle completed the Great Chain of Being by proposing the Principle of Continuity as a necessary consequence of the Principle of Plenitude: all possible intermediary types must be realized. Thus, species must overlap at their limits; existences and organisms make up a continuum.

When God was identified with the temporal process at the end of the eighteenth century, it became apparent that the temporally developing God was in the process of becoming perfect. Evolution's entrance into intellectual interpretations of God resulted in an awareness that God was in the process of evolving from a lower to a higher form. At this point the two ideas of God could no longer be rationally held together. With the separation of the two Gods came the realization that if the experienced temporal world had value, it was not based in the value of an otherworldly Idea of the Good: "an Absolute which is self-sufficient and forever perfect and complete cannot be identified with a God related to and manifested in a world of temporal becoming and alteration and creative advance."

Aristotle's derivation of the Principle of Continuity from the Principle of Plenitude rested on the assumption that the universe is rational. The sundering of the temporal from the absolute world leads to the realization that the temporal world is one of contingent events in which the will is prior to intellect. The reinterpretation by modern theists, such as Alfred North Whitehead, of God as the ultimate limitation makes God's existence the ultimate irrationality. Continual philosophical insistence on an ultimate divine ground for existence revealed through the study of the idea of the Great Chain of Being stands as an example of a craving peculiar to the philosophic mind. Lovejoy concludes that the nonrational is primary in philosophy.

Lovejoy was a visiting professor at Harvard in 1937–1938. He retired from his professorship at Johns Hopkins in May 1938. In 1939 he gave a series of lectures at Princeton University that were published in 1961 as *The Reason, the Understanding, and Time*. In 1940 he and Wiener, a philosopher at the City College of New York, founded the *Journal of the History of Ideas*. In 1941 Lovejoy presented a series of lectures at Swarthmore College that were published in 1961 as *Reflections on Human Nature*.

After World War II Lovejoy was an active anti-Communist; he worked in organizations such as the Academic Freedom Committee of the American Com-

Lovejoy in 1940

mittee for Cultural Freedom, where he served with Sidney Hook. Lovejoy believed that Communists should be excluded from the faculties of American universities, because they surrendered to the Communist Party the objectivity–or attempt at objectivity–that he saw as essential to the role of the university. By committing themselves to the success of Communist revolution by any means necessary, they violated the professional ethic of dispassionate inquiry. Furthermore, he held, advocates of freedom ought not to tolerate those who sought to end freedom. Communism could be taught, he contended, but not by Communists.

One of Lovejoy's last public appointments was to the board of regents of the Maryland university system in 1951. The committee that reviewed his appointment initially wanted to reject him because of his unorthodox views on God; but when the governor let the committee know that the next nominee would be an African American, Lovejoy was accepted.

Lovejoy never married. He died on 30 December 1962. In his 1979 presidential address to the Eastern

THE THIRTEEN PRAGMATISMS and Other Essays / Arthur O. Lovejoy

Dust jacket for the 1963 posthumous collection of Lovejoy's writings (Richland County Public Library)

Division of the APA, published as "Pragmatism, Relativism, and Irrationalism" in his *Consequences of Pragmatism: Essays, 1972–1980* (1982), Richard Rorty bemoaned the triumph of Lovejoy's vision of scientific philosophy over James's rejection of a search for objectivity. James, Rorty claims, thought that philosophy should pursue edifying beliefs over a dispassionate search for objective truths. Rorty describes Lovejoy's explanation of the philosopher's divorce from the rest of culture:

> the gap between philosophers and the rest of high culture is of the same sort as the gap between physicists and laymen. The gap is not created by the artificiality of the problems being discussed, but by the development of technical and precise ways of dealing with real problems.

Bibliography:

Daniel J. Wilson, "Bibliography," in his *Arthur O. Lovejoy and the Quest for Intelligibility* (Chapel Hill: University of North Carolina Press, 1980), pp. 233–241.

Biography:

Daniel J. Wilson, *Arthur O. Lovejoy and the Quest for Intelligibility* (Chapel Hill: University of North Carolina Press, 1980).

References:

George Boas, "A. O. Lovejoy: Reason-in-Action," *American Scholar,* 29 (1960): 535–542;

Boas, "A. O. Lovejoy as Historian of Philosophy," *Journal of the History of Ideas,* 9 (1948): 404–411;

Lewis S. Feuer, "Arthur O. Lovejoy," *American Scholar,* 46 (1977): 358–366;

Edwin B. Holt and others, *The New Realism: Cooperative Studies in Philosophy* (New York: Macmillan, 1901);

Maurice Mandelbaum, "Arthur O. Lovejoy and the Theory of Historiography," *Journal of the History of Ideas,* 9 (1948): 412–423;

W. P. Montague, "Professor Lovejoy's Carus Lectures," *Journal of Philosophy,* 25 (1928): 293–296;

Richard Rorty, "Pragmatism, Relativism, and Irrationalism," in his *Consequences of Pragmatism: Essays, 1972–1980* (Minneapolis: University of Minnesota Press, 1982), pp. 160–175;

H. A. Taylor, "Further Reflections on the History of Ideas: An Examination of A. O. Lovejoy's Program," *Journal of Philosophy,* 40 (1943): 281–299;

Philip P. Wiener, "Lovejoy's Role in American Philosophy," in *Studies in Intellectual History,* by the Johns Hopkins History of Ideas Club (Baltimore: Johns Hopkins University Press, 1953), pp. 161–173.

Papers:

Arthur O. Lovejoy's papers are in the Special Collections department of the Johns Hopkins University Library. A copy of the galleys of "The Thirteen Pragmatisms," with annotations by Lovejoy and William James, is included in the William James Papers, Houghton Library, Harvard University.

George Herbert Mead

(27 February 1863 – 26 April 1931)

George Cronk
Bergen Community College

BOOKS: *Creative Intelligence: Essays in the Pragmatic Attitude,* by Mead, John Dewey, Addison W. Moore, Harold Chapman Brown, Boyd H. Bode, Henry W. Stuart, James H. Tufts, and Horace M. Kallen (New York: Holt, 1917)–includes Mead's "Scientific Method and Individual Thinker," pp. 176–227;

The Philosophy of the Present, edited by Arthur E. Murphy (Chicago & London: Open Court, 1932);

Mind, Self and Society from the Perspective of a Social Behaviorist, edited by Charles W. Morris (Chicago & London: University of Chicago Press, 1934);

Movements of Thought in the Nineteenth Century, edited by Merritt H. Moore (Chicago & London: University of Chicago Press, 1936);

The Philosophy of the Act, edited by Morris, John M. Brewster, Albert M. Dunham, and David L. Miller (Chicago & London: University of Chicago Press, 1938);

The Social Psychology of George Herbert Mead: Selected Writings of an American Pragmatist, edited by Anselm Strauss (Chicago: University of Chicago Press, 1956); revised as *George Herbert Mead on Social Psychology: Selected Papers,* edited by Anselm Strauss (Chicago & London: University of Chicago Press, 1964);

George Herbert Mead: Selected Writings, edited by Andrew J. Reck (Indianapolis, New York & Kansas City: Bobbs-Merrill, 1964);

George Herbert Mead: Essays on His Social Philosophy, edited by John W. Petras (New York: Teachers College Press, 1968);

The Individual and the Social Self: Unpublished Work of George Herbert Mead, edited by Miller (Chicago & London: University of Chicago Press, 1982);

Play, School and Society, edited by Mary Jo Deegan, American University studies, series 11: Anthropology and Sociology, volume 71 (New York: Peter Lang, 1999);

Essays on Social Psychology, edited by Deegan (New Brunswick, N.J. & London: Transaction, 2001).

George Herbert Mead

OTHER: "The Objective Reality of Perspectives," in *Proceedings of the Sixth International Congress of Philosophy, Harvard University, Cambridge, Massachusetts, United States of America, September 14, 15, 16, 17, 1926,* edited by Edgar Sheffield Brightman (New York & London: Longmans, Green, 1927), pp. 75–85;

"A Pragmatic Theory of Truth," in *Studies in the Nature of Truth,* University of California Publications in Philosophy, volume 11 (Berkeley: University of California Press, 1929), pp. 65–88;

"The Nature of the Past," in *Essays in Honor of John Dewey*, edited by John Coss (New York: Holt, 1929), pp. 235–242.

SELECTED PERIODICAL PUBLICATIONS–
UNCOLLECTED: "A Theory of Emotions from the Physiological Standpoint," *Psychological Review*, 2 (1895): 162–164;

"The Relation of Play to Education," *University of Chicago Record*, 1 (1896): 140–145;

"The Working Hypothesis in Social Reform," *American Journal of Sociology*, 5 (1899): 367–371;

"Suggestions towards a Theory of the Philosophical Disciplines," *Philosophical Review*, 9 (1900): 1–17;

"A New Criticism of Hegelianism: Is It Valid?" *American Journal of Theology*, 5 (1901): 87–96;

"The Definition of the Psychical," *Decennial Publications of the University of Chicago*, first series, 3 (1903): 77–112;

"Image or Sensation," *Journal of Philosophy, Psychology and Scientific Method*, 1 (1904): 604–607;

"The Relation of Psychology and Philology," *Psychological Bulletin*, 1 (1904): 375–391;

"The Imagination in Wundt's Treatment of Myth and Religion," *Psychological Bulletin*, 3 (1906): 393–399;

"The Relation of Imitation to the Theory of Animal Perception," *Psychological Bulletin*, 4 (1907): 210–211;

"Concerning Animal Perception," *Psychological Review*, 14 (1907): 383–390;

"The Philosophical Basis of Ethics," *International Journal of Ethics*, 18 (1908): 311–323;

"Social Psychology as Counterpart to Physiological Psychology," *Psychological Bulletin*, 6 (1909): 401–408;

"The Psychology of Social Consciousness Implied in Instruction," *Science*, 31 (1910): 688–693;

"Social Consciousness and the Consciousness of Meaning," *Psychological Bulletin*, 7 (1910): 397–405;

"What Social Objects Must Psychology Presuppose?" *Journal of Philosophy, Psychology and Scientific Methods*, 7 (1910): 174–180;

"The Mechanism of Social Consciousness," *Journal of Philosophy, Psychology and Scientific Methods*, 9 (1912): 401–406;

"The Social Self," *Journal of Philosophy, Psychology and Scientific Methods*, 10 (1913): 374–380;

"Natural Rights and the Theory of the Political Institution," *Journal of Philosophy*, 12 (1915): 141–155;

"Josiah Royce–a Personal Impression," *International Journal of Ethics*, 27 (1917): 168–170;

"A Translation of Wundt's 'Folk Psychology,'" *American Journal of Theology*, 23 (1919): 533–536;

"A Behavioristic Account of the Significant Symbol," *Journal of Philosophy*, 19 (1922): 157–163;

"Scientific Method and the Moral Sciences," *International Journal of Ethics*, 33 (1923): 229–247;

"The Genesis of the Self and Social Control," *International Journal of Ethics*, 35 (1925): 251–277;

"The Nature of Aesthetic Experience," *International Journal of Ethics*, 36 (1925–1926): 382–393;

"Bishop Berkeley and His Message," *Journal of Philosophy*, 26 (1929): 421–430;

"National-Mindedness and International-Mindedness," *International Journal of Ethics*, 39 (1929): 385–407;

"The Philosophies of Royce, James, and Dewey in Their American Setting," *International Journal of Ethics*, 40 (1929–1930): 211–231;

"Cooley's Contribution to American Social Thought," *American Journal of Sociology*, 35 (1930): 693–706.

Along with Charles Sanders Peirce, William James, James H. Tufts, and John Dewey, George Herbert Mead was one of the founders of pragmatism, a distinctively American philosophical movement that called for an empirical and experimental approach to philosophical problems in which ideas and theories are evaluated on the basis of their practical consequences. Mead published many articles but no books (except a collaboration with several other authors) during his lifetime; after his death, several of his students produced four books in his name from his unpublished–and even unfinished–notes and manuscripts, from students' notes, and from stenographic records of some of his courses at the University of Chicago. The closest Mead came to completing a book during his lifetime was his Carus Lectures, delivered at the American Philosophical Association Meeting in Berkeley, California, in December 1930. These lectures, together with several supplementary essays, were edited by Arthur E. Murphy as *The Philosophy of the Present* (1932)–the first of Mead's posthumous works.

Mead exercised a significant influence on twentieth-century social theory. His theory of the emergence of mind and self out of the social process of significant communication became the foundation of the symbolic interactionist school of sociology and social psychology. Mead's thought also includes important contributions to the philosophy of nature, philosophy of science, philosophical anthropology, philosophy of history, and "process philosophy." Such eminent philosophers as Dewey and Alfred North Whitehead regarded Mead as a thinker of the highest order.

Mead was born in South Hadley, Massachusetts, on 27 February 1863 to Hiram and Elizabeth Storrs Billings Mead. He had a sister, Alice, who was born in 1859. Hiram Mead, a Congregationalist minister, was descended from a long line of New England farmers and clergymen. In 1870 the family moved to Oberlin, Ohio, where Hiram Mead became professor of homiletics at the newly founded Oberlin Theological Seminary.

Mead entered Oberlin College in 1879. There he and his best friend, Henry Northrup Castle, a scion of a wealthy Honolulu family, studied the Greek and Latin classics, rhetoric, literature, Christian ethics, mathematics, and science. Mead's first publication, an article on the relation of art to morality, appeared in the *Oberlin Review* in 1881. After receiving his B.A. in 1883, Mead taught in a local elementary school but was fired after a few months because he dealt with disruptive pupils by sending them home. He worked from the end of 1883 through the summer of 1887 as a surveyor for the Wisconsin Central Rail Road Company.

In 1887 Mead enrolled at Harvard University to pursue graduate studies in philosophy. Among his professors were George H. Palmer and Josiah Royce. Mead was most influenced by Royce's Romanticism and philosophical idealism. Although he later became one of the major figures in the pragmatist movement, he did not study under James—but he did live in James's home as tutor to James's children.

Mead received his M.A. in 1888 and went to Germany to pursue a Ph.D. in philosophy and physiological psychology at the University of Leipzig. He became strongly interested in Darwinism and studied with Wilhelm Wundt and G. Stanley Hall, major figures in the rise of experimental psychology; Wundt's concept of "the gesture" had a profound influence on Mead's later work. In the spring of 1889 Mead transferred to the University of Berlin, where he concentrated on physiological psychology and economic theory.

Castle and his sister, Helen, had traveled to Europe in the summer of 1888 and were living in Leipzig when Mead arrived there. Mead and Helen Castle fell in love in Germany and were married in Berlin on 1 October 1891. They immediately returned to the United States because Mead had accepted an instructorship in philosophy and psychology at the University of Michigan to replace Tufts, who was leaving to complete his Ph.D. at the University of Freiburg. At Michigan, Mead—who never completed his own Ph.D.—taught the history of philosophy, philosophy of science, general psychology, and physiological and experimental psychology. His colleagues included the sociologist Charles Horton Cooley, the psychologist Alfred Lloyd, and Dewey, who became a close friend.

The Meads' only child, Henry Castle Albert Mead, was born in 1892. The Meads also raised an orphan. In addition to sharing their home with countless students,

Mead as a student at Oberlin College in 1882

they entertained such notables as the social reformer Jane Addams and the composer Sergei Prokofiev.

In 1892, having completed his doctoral studies, Tufts was invited to assist President William Rainey Harper in organizing the new University of Chicago, which had been endowed by John D. Rockefeller. Tufts recommended Dewey for the chairmanship of the philosophy department, and Dewey accepted on the condition that Mead be given a position as assistant professor. Thus, the University of Chicago became the new center of American pragmatism, which had originated with Peirce and James at Harvard.

Mead joined Dewey in many of his ventures in progressive education and wrote eight articles on the subject between his joining the Chicago faculty and World War I. He was active from its inception in the experimental school Dewey founded at Chicago. He was also president of the School of Education's Parents' Association and edited its journal, *The Elementary School Teacher.* A close friend of Addams's, he was also associated with Addams's Hull House, giving lectures there frequently (as did Dewey), and was a member and, for a time, president of the City Club of Chicago, a group of reform-minded businessmen and professionals.

Mead was promoted to associate professor in 1902. In 1904 Dewey moved to Columbia University, leaving Tufts and Mead as the major spokesmen for the pragmatist movement at the University of Chicago. Mead became a full professor in 1907.

In 1929 Robert Maynard Hutchins became president of the University of Chicago. He brought with him the Aristotelian and Neo-Thomist philosopher Mortimer J. Adler, whom he appointed professor of the philosophy of law in the law school. Advocating the "Great Books of the Western World" as the heart of a college education, Hutchins and Adler began radically reorganizing undergraduate and graduate study at Chicago. Hutchins wanted to appoint Adler to the philosophy department, but the members of the department regarded Hutchins's and Adler's philosophical classicism and traditionalism as antiscientific and obscurantist and resisted the move.

Helen Mead died on 25 December 1929. Mead was grief-stricken, and his own health began to deteriorate. Nonetheless, when Tufts retired in 1930, Mead assumed the chairmanship of the philosophy department and continued the struggle with Hutchins. When it appeared that Hutchins would prevail in his effort to force Adler on the department, Mead submitted his resignation and accepted an appointment, arranged by Dewey, at Columbia University, to begin in the fall of 1931. But he became seriously ill in late January 1931, and he died in Chicago on 26 April. Mead's son, Henry, had become a physician and had married Tufts's daughter, Irene, a psychiatrist. Mead had often sent his manuscripts to Irene and discussed his ideas with her. Henry and Irene looked after Mead during his last illness, and after his death they called on Mead's students to prepare his unpublished work for publication. Irene played the principal role in arranging financial backing for the project.

Mead had begun teaching his course in social psychology at the University of Chicago in the fall of 1900 and had continued to do so, at more and more advanced levels, until the winter quarter of 1930–1931. *Mind, Self and Society from the Perspective of a Social Behaviorist* (1934), edited by Charles W. Morris, is based on a stenographic record of the 1927 course, two sets of student notes on the 1930 course, stenographic notes on some of Mead's related courses, and several unpublished manuscripts by Mead.

In *Mind, Self, and Society* Mead contends that the individual mind arises within the social process of communication and cannot be understood apart from that process. The communication process has two phases: the "conversation of gestures" and the "conversation of significant gestures," or language. Mead introduces the notion of the "conversation of gestures" with the example of a dogfight:

> Dogs approaching each other in hostile attitude carry on such a language of gestures. They walk around each other, growling and snapping, and waiting for the opportunity to attack. . . . The act of each dog becomes the stimulus to the other dog for his response. There is then a relationship between these two; and as the act is responded to by the other dog, it, in turn, undergoes change. The very fact that the dog is ready to attack another becomes a stimulus to the other dog to change his own position or his own attitude. He has no sooner done this than the change of attitude in the second dog in turn causes the first dog to change his attitude. We have here a conversation of gestures. *They are not, however, gestures in the sense that they are significant.* We do not assume that the dog says to himself, "If the animal comes from this direction he is going to spring at my throat and I will turn in such a way." What does take place is an actual change in his own position due to the direction of the approach of the other dog.

In the conversation of gestures, the individual is unaware of the response that his or her gestures elicit in others; the individual is communicating but does not know that he or she is communicating. That is, the conversation of gestures is unconscious communication. Language–conscious communication–emerges out of the conversation of gestures. Language supersedes but does not replace the conversation of gestures; it marks the transition from nonsignificant to significant interaction.

Mead defines language as communication through "significant symbols." Gestures "become significant symbols when they implicitly arouse in an individual making them the same responses which they explicitly arouse, or are supposed to arouse, in other individuals, the individuals to whom they are addressed." For example, "You ask somebody to bring a visitor a chair. You arouse the tendency to get the chair in the other, but if he is slow to act, you get the chair yourself. The response to the gesture is the doing of a certain thing, and you arouse that same tendency in yourself."

The concept of conversation of significant symbols provides the basis for Mead's theory of mind: "Only in terms of gestures as significant symbols is the existence of mind or intelligence possible; for only in terms of gestures which are significant symbols can thinking–which is simply an internalized or implicit conversation of the individual with himself by means of such gestures–take place." Mind is a form of participation in a social process: it is the result of adopting the attitudes of others toward one's own gestures. Mead says that there is no "mind or thought without language" and that language—the content of mind—"is only a development and product of social interaction." Mind is not reducible to the neurophysiology of the individual but emerges in "the dynamic, ongoing social process" that constitutes human experience.

Like the mind, the self is a product of social interaction: "The self is something which has a development; it is not initially there, at birth, but arises in the process of social experience and activity, that is, develops in the given individual as a result of his relations to that process as a whole and to other individuals within that process." The self "is an object to itself"; this reflexivity of the self "distinguishes it from other objects and from the body," for they are not objects to themselves:

It is perfectly true that the eye can see the foot, but it does not see the body as a whole. We cannot see our backs; we can feel certain portions of them, if we are agile, but we cannot get an experience of our whole body. There are, of course, experiences which are somewhat vague and difficult of location, but the bodily experiences are for us organized about a self. The foot and hand belong to the self. We can see our feet, especially if we look at them from the wrong end of an opera glass, as strange things which we have difficulty in recognizing as our own. The parts of the body are quite distinguishable from the self. We can lose parts of the body without any serious invasion of the self. The mere ability to experience different parts of the body is not different from the experience of a table. The table presents a different feel from what the hand does when one hand feels another, but it is an experience of something with which we come definitely into contact. The body does not experience itself as a whole, in the sense in which the self in some way enters into the experience of the self.

Mead distinguishes two uses of the term *consciousness*. It may refer to "a certain feeling consciousness" that is the outcome of an organism's sensitivity to its environment; animals are conscious in this sense. *Consciousness* may also denote a form of awareness that "always has, implicitly at least, the reference to an 'I' in it"—that is, self-consciousness. Human consciousness is of this type. In self-consciousness the individual appears as an object within his or her own experience but does so "only on the basis of social relations and interactions, only by means of his experiential transactions with other individuals in an organized social environment." Self-consciousness is the result of a process in which the individual attempts to view himself or herself from the standpoint of others. Thus, the self as an object arises from the individual's experience of other selves.

Three major forms of intersubjective activity are language, play, and games. All are types of "symbolic interaction" in that they take place by means of shared symbols such as words, definitions, roles, gestures, rituals, and so forth. In language, or communication via "significant symbols," the individual responds to his or her own gestures in terms of the symbolized attitudes of others. This "process of taking the role of the other" is the primal form of self-objectification. In play and in games, as in linguistic activity, role-playing is the main process that generates self-consciousness. In playing, the child acts as though he or she were the other person—mother, doctor, nurse, Indian, and countless other symbolized roles. Play involves taking on a single role at a time. "If we contrast play with the situation in an organized game, we note the essential difference that the child who plays in a game must be ready to take the attitude of everyone else involved in the game, and that these different roles must have a definite relationship to each other." The attitudes of all the participants in the game are brought together in "an organized and generalized attitude" that Mead calls the "generalized other." The individual defines his or her own conduct with reference to the generalized other. When the individual is able to view himself or herself from the standpoint of the generalized other, Mead says, "self-consciousness in the full sense of the term" is attained.

According to Mead, the self has two phases: "The 'I' is the response of the organism to the attitudes of the others; the 'me' is the organized set of attitudes of others which one himself assumes." The "me" is "a conventional, habitual individual," while the "I" is the "novel reply" of the individual to the generalized other. The "me" constitutes the principle of conformity, while the "I" is the foundation of individuality: "both aspects of the 'I' and the 'me' are essential to the self in its full expression." The "me" is a symbolic structure that makes the action of the "I" possible: "without this structure of things, the life of the self would become impossible." The generalized other, internalized in the "me," is the mechanism by which the community gains control over the conduct of its members.

Social control, however, is limited by the "I" phase of the self. Furthermore, Mead distinguishes two types of social groups: "concrete social classes or subgroups," in which "individual members are directly related to one another," and "abstract social classes or subgroups," in which "individual members are related to one another only more or less indirectly, and which only more or less indirectly function as social units, but which afford unlimited possibilities for the widening and ramifying and enriching of the social relations among all the individual members of the given society as an organized and unified whole." Abstract groups

Mead and his wife, Helen Castle Mead, at the time of their marriage in Berlin on 1 October 1891

allow for a vast expansion of the "definite social relations" that constitute the individual's sense of self: the individual may identify with a "larger" community than the one in which he or she has been involved—for example, a nation rather than a tribe.

Mead presents two models of the relationship between consensus and conflict in societies: intragroup consensus combined with extragroup conflict and intragroup conflict combined with extragroup consensus. In the first model the members of a group are united in opposition to another group that is characterized as the "enemy." Mead points out that many organizations derive their sense of solidarity and even their raison d'être from the actual or putative existence of an "enemy"—communists, fascists, infidels, liberals, conservatives, or whatever the case may be. The second model describes the situation in which an individual opposes his or her own group by appealing to a "higher sort of community," such as "all of humanity"; thus, intragroup conflict is carried on in terms of an extragroup consensus, even if the consensus is only imagined.

The Philosophy of the Act (1938), a systematic compilation by Morris, John M. Brewster, Albert M. Dun-

ham, and David L. Miller of unpublished papers composed by Mead during the last ten or fifteen years of his life, addresses issues in epistemology, cosmology, philosophy of nature, philosophy of science, and theory of value. The influence of Whitehead and Albert Einstein is evident throughout the book.

Mead has two models of the act: the "act-as-such," or organic activity in general; and the "social act," which is a special case of organic activity. The act-as-such determines "the relation between the individual and the environment." Reality, Mead says, is a field of situations that "are fundamentally characterized by the relation of an organic individual to his environment or world. The world, things, and the individual are what they are because of this relation." The relationship between the individual and his or her world is defined and developed by means of the act.

The act develops in four stages: the stage of impulse, in which the organic individual responds to "problematic situations" in his or her experience (for example, the approach of an enemy); the stage of perception, in which the individual defines and analyzes his or her problem (the direction of the enemy's attack is sensed, and a path leading in the opposite direction is chosen as a route of escape); the stage of manipulation, in which action is taken with reference to the individual's perceptual appraisal of the problematic situation (the individual runs along the path away from the enemy); and the stage of consummation, in which the encountered difficulty is resolved and the continuity of organic existence reestablished (the individual escapes and returns to his or her ordinary affairs). In this description the individual is not merely a passive recipient of external influences but is capable of taking action in response to such influences; he or she reconstructs his or her relation to the environment through selective perception and through the use of the objects selected in perception (for example, the escape route). The objects in the environment are created through the activity of the individual: the path along which the individual escaped did not exist in his or her thoughts or perceptions until it was needed. Perception is not something that occurs within the organism but is an objective relationship between the organism and its environment; and the perceived object is not an entity independent of the organism but is one pole of the interactive perceptual process.

Objects of perception arise in the individual's attempt to solve problems that have arisen in his or her experience and are determined by the individual himself or herself: the character of the environment is determined by the individual's sensory capabilities. Objects "are what they are in the relationship between the individual and his environment, and this relationship is that of conduct."

The act-as-such, Mead's model of individual biological activity, is not adequate as an analysis of social experience. For the latter, he uses his concept of the social act. The human individual is a member of a social organism, and his or her acts occur in the context of social acts that involve other individuals. Society is not the mere collection of preexisting atomic individuals described by Thomas Hobbes, John Locke, and Jean-Jacques Rousseau, but a whole within which individuals define themselves by participating in social acts: "For social psychology, the whole (society) is prior to the part (the individual), not the part to the whole; and the part is explained in terms of the whole, not the whole in terms of the part or parts." The social act is a "dynamic whole" or "complex organic process" within which the individual is situated, and individual acts are possible and have meaning only within this situation.

The social act is a collective act involving two or more individuals, and the "social object" is a collective object that has a common meaning for all of the participants in the act. Social acts range from the relatively simple interaction of two individuals, as in dancing, lovemaking, or a game of handball, through more complex acts involving more than two individuals, such as a play, a religious ritual, or a hunting expedition, to highly complex acts carried on in the form of social organizations and institutions, such as law enforcement, education, or economic activity. The life of a society is the totality of such acts.

People in a society construct their sense of reality by means of social acts. The objects of the social world, from common ones such as clothes, furniture, and tools, to scientific objects such as atoms and electrons, are the objects they are as a result of being defined and used within the context of specific social acts. Thus, an animal skin becomes a coat in the experience of people such as barbarians or pretenders to aristocracy who perform the social act of covering or adorning their bodies, and the electron is a hypothetical object introduced in the scientific community's investigation of the nature of physical reality.

Communication through significant symbols makes the intelligent organization of social acts possible by creating a world of common symbolic meanings within which further acts are possible. Significant communication is also involved in the construction of social objects, since humans indicate to one another the objects relevant to their collective acts by means of significant symbols. Social objects emerge in social experience and are constructed in social action and organization, and the symbolization process is an essential aspect of this construction. For example, if a group of people are going to the zoo, and one of them offers to drive the others in his car, and the others follow the driver to his vehicle, the car has thus become an object for all of the members of the group. Prior to the project of the trip to the zoo, the car was, no doubt, an object in some other social act; but it was not a means of transportation to the zoo. What it was would have been determined by its role in some other social act, such as the owner's project of getting to work. The decision to go to the zoo and to use the car to get there were made through a conversation involving significant symbols. In human society individual acts must be viewed in the context of social acts, for the problems, objects, and goals confronting individuals are socially constructed. The individual must act not only in response to difficulties that arise in the biological environment but also in response to problems in the social world; and the individual's perceptions, definitions, and behavior in regard to social problems will be conditioned by those of other individuals in response to the same problems. This taking account of others' attitudes is, according to Mead, the essence of intelligent conduct.

Mead's concepts of the act and sociality form the basis of his epistemology and metaphysics. In *The Philosophy of the Act* he presents a vision of reality as situational or perspectival. A perspective is "the world in its relationship to the individual and the individual in his relationship to the world." Obviously, many such perspectives exist. They are not, Mead says, imperfect representations of some "absolute reality"; instead, "these situations are the reality" that is the world.

Perceptual objects arise within an act and are instrumental in the performance of the act. At the perceptual stage of the act, the objects are spatially and temporally distant from the perceiver: they are "not here" and "not now." Such objects invite the perceiving individual to "make contact" with them. Thus, perceptual objects are "plans of action" that "control" the "action of the individual." "Distance experience" implies "contact experience"; perception leads to manipulation.

Mead calls the individual's readiness to make contact with distant objects a "terminal attitude." Terminal attitudes "are beginnings of the contact response that will be made to the object when the object is reached." Such attitudes, "if carried out into overt action, would lead to movements which, if persevered in, would overcome the distances and bring the objects into the manipulatory sphere." A terminal attitude is an implicit manipulation of a distant object; present in the beginning of the act, the terminal attitude contains the later stages of the act in that perception implies manipulation and manipulation is aimed at the solving of a problem. In acting, the individual approaches distant objects in terms of the "values of the manipulatory sphere"; he or she perceives distant objects "with the dimensions they would have if they were brought within the field in which we could both handle and see them." For example, a distant object is seen as having a certain size, weight, texture, and so on. In perception the distant object becomes, hypothetically, a "contact object."

In immediate perceptual experience the distant object is in the future. Contact with the distant object is anticipated: "The percept is there as a promise." But insofar as the act of perception involves terminal attitudes, the "promise" or futurity of the distant object is "collapsed" into a hypothetical "now" in which the perceiving individual and the object exist simultaneously. The temporal distance between individual and object is suspended; this suspension of time allows alternative contact reactions to the object to be "tested" in the imagination. This imagined testing of alternative responses to distant objects is, according to Mead, the essence of reflective conduct.

Early modern accounts of perception by such thinkers as Galileo and Locke distinguished between the "primary qualities" and "secondary qualities" of objects. The primary qualities were those that are subject to measurement and mathematical calculation, such as number, position, size, and shape, and were thought to be in the external objects; the secondary qualities, such as color, sound, odor, and taste, were not quantifiable and were thought to be in the mind of the perceiver. Because they are objective, the primary qualities were considered to be more "knowable" than the secondary qualities.

The distinction between primary and secondary qualities was attacked by George Berkeley in *A Treatise Concerning the Principles of Human Knowledge* (1710). Berkeley pointed out that the primary, as well as the secondary, qualities are apprehended in sensation; moreover, primary qualities are always perceived in conjunction with secondary qualities. Both primary and secondary qualities, therefore, are "in the mind"; the primary qualities are as dependent on the perceiver as are the secondary qualities. Berkeley's radical subjectivism was carried to its logical conclusion in the skepticism of David Hume.

Mead finds the basis of the distinction between primary and secondary qualities in the acting individual's tendency to reduce distant objects to the contact area: "It is this collapsing of the act which is responsible for the so-called subjective nature of the secondary qualities." The "contact characters" of the object are focused on, while the "distance characters" are ignored. For the purposes of action, "the reality of what we see is what we can handle." The distinction between contact and distance characters is roughly equivalent to that between primary and secondary qualities, respectively. For Mead, however, the distance characters of an object are just as objective as the contact characters: "In the manipulatory area one actually handles the colored, odorous, sounding, sapid object. The distance characters seem to be no longer distant, and the object answers to a collapsed act."

Mead's theory of perspectives is an attempt to make clear the mutual determination of organism and environment. Opposing environmental determinism, Mead points out that perceptual objects are perspectively determined, and perspectives are determined by perceiving individuals:

> Even when we consider only sense data, the object is clearly a function of the whole situation whose perspective is determined by the individual. There are peculiarities in the objects which depend upon the individual as an organism and the spatio-temporal position of the individual. It is one of the important results of the modern doctrine of relativity that we are forced to recognize that we cannot account for these peculiarities by stating the individual in terms of his environment.

In addition to denying the existence of independent objects, Mead also denies the existence of the independent psyche. Perceptual experience has nothing subjective about it: objects exist with reference to perceiving individuals, but those individuals exist with reference to objects. Where the relationship between the world and the perceiving individual led Berkeley to a radical subjectivism, Mead's relationism leads him to an equally radical objectivism. Perspectives, he says, are real: they are "there in nature," and natural reality is the overall "organization of perspectives." As far as can be known, no reality exists beyond the organization of perspectives.

Mead distinguishes between perceptual and reflective perspectives. A perceptual perspective is rooted in the world of immediate perceptual experience and unreflective action; a reflective perspective is a response to the world of perceptual perspectives. The perspectives of fig trees and wasps are perceptually independent, "But in the reflective perspective of the man who plants the fig trees and insures the presence of the wasps, both life-histories run their courses, and their intersection provides a dimension from which their interconnection maintains their species." Reflectively, the fig-tree perspective and the wasp perspective combine to form a single perspective "that includes the perspectives of both." The world of reflective perspectives is the world of reflective thought and action, distance experience, and of scientific inquiry. The hypothetical objects of the "collapsed act" arise within the reflective perspective.

Corresponding to the two types of perspective are two attitudes toward perceptual objects. Corresponding to the perceptual perspective is "the attitude of immediate experience," which is grounded in "the world that is there." "The world that is there"—a phrase Mead uses repeatedly—includes one's own acts, one's body, and one's psychological responses to the things that emerge in one's activity. Perceptual objects in "the world that is there" are what they appear to be in their relationship to the perceiving individual.

Corresponding to the reflective perspective is the attitude of reflective analysis, which attempts to set forth the preconditions of perceptual experience. Scientific objects are constructed through reflective analysis of perceptual objects. Scientific objects include absolute space and time and absolute simultaneity, as well as atoms, electrons, and so on. Such objects are hypothetical abstractions that arise in the scientific attempt to explain immediate experience: "The whole tendency of the natural sciences, as exhibited especially in physics and chemistry, is to replace the objects of immediate experience by hypothetical objects which lie beyond the range of possible experience."

A danger in the reflective analysis of "the world that is there" is that the perceptual world may come to be conceived of as a product of organic sensitivity, including human consciousness, and the world of scientific objects "as entirely independent of perceiving individuals." The separation of scientific and perceptual objects leads to a "bifurcated nature" in which experience is cut off from reality. Mead's critique of the doctrine of primary and secondary qualities, however, has shown that "the organism is a part of the physical world we are explaining" and that the perceptual object, with all of its qualities, is objectively present in the relationship between organism and world. The scientific object, moreover, ultimately refers to the perceptual world: the act of reflective analysis within which the scientific object arises presupposes "the world that is there" in perceptual experience. Scientific objects are abstractions that occur in the attempt to account for the objects of perceptual experience, and the scientist must go to "the world that is there" to confirm or disconfirm the existence of these hypothetical objects.

The reification of scientific objects at the expense of perceptual experience results from an "uncritical scientific imagination." Mead does not, however, deny the reality of scientific objects: he says that they are hypothetical objects that are real insofar as they render the experiential world intelligible and controllable. As Harold N. Lee explains Mead's position,

Mead's wife with their only child, Henry Castle Albert Mead, in 1896

the task of science is to understand the world we live in and to enable us to act intelligently within it; it is not to construct a new and artificial world except in so far as the artificial picture aids in understanding and controlling the world we live in. The artificial picture is not to be substituted for the world.

A central theme in Mead's thought is the temporal character of human existence. Temporality arises with the occurrence in experience of "emergent" events: unexpected disruptions of continuity that constitute a problem for action. The emergent event arises in the present; the person, blocked in his or her activity, looks to the future as the locus for a potential resolution of problem. The future is a temporally and, frequently, a spatially distant place that is to be reached through intelligent action; human action is, thus, inherently "action-in-time." Mead notes that without the distance created by the blocking of action, no experience of time would be possible; experience presupposes change. Change does not mean the total annihilation of continuity: a "persisting non-passing content" is required, against which the emergent event can be experienced as a change. Continuity itself cannot be experienced unless it is interrupted by the emergence of discontinuous events: "The now is contrasted with a then and implies that a background which is irrelevant to the difference between them has been secured within which the now and the then may appear. There must be banks within which the stream of time may flow."

The role of emergence in experience is the basis of Mead's controversial rejection of the notion of the irrevocability of the past in his article "The Nature of the Past" (1929) and in *The Philosophy of the Present*. The idea of a "real" past makes no sense, according to Mead, because the past is continually being reformulated from the point of view of the newly emergent situation. Every new discovery alters the picture of the past. In "The Nature of the Past" Mead writes, "Every generation rewrites its history—and its history is the only history it has of the world. While scientific data maintain a certain uniformity within these histories, so that we can identify them as data, their *meaning* is dependent upon the structure of history as each generation writes it." Mead does not deny that historical accounts can be valid, but he holds that their validity is not absolute but relative to a specific emergent context. In *The Philosophy of the Present* he says that accounts of the past "become valid in interpreting" the world insofar as "they present a history of becoming" in the world "leading up to that which is becoming today." Historical interpretation is valid insofar as it makes change intelligible and the continuation of activity possible. An "absolutely correct" account of the past is not only impossible but also irrelevant: historical inquiry is "subjective" in that it aims at an interpretation of the past that will be useful for action in the present and for the foreseeable future. Historical inquiry is the imaginative but honest and intelligent reconstruction of the past on the basis of all the available relevant evidence.

The dialectical relationship of the emergent event and the past is important not only in historical research but in all scientific inquiry. A scientific hypothesis is based on an account of the past that reduces an emergent event to intelligibility. If the hypothesis "anticipates that which occurs," Mead says in *The Philosophy of the Present*,

> it then becomes the account of what has happened. If it breaks down, another hypothesis replaces it and

another past replaces that which the first hypothesis implied. The long and the short of it is that the past (or the meaningful structure of the past) is as hypothetical as the future.

The emergent event, then, is an unexpected occurrence that "in its relation to other events gives structure to time." Emergence, in turn, is grounded in the "sociality" or relatedness of natural processes. The environment of any organism contains a multiplicity of processes, perspectives, and systems, any one of which may become a factor in the organism's activity. The organism's ability to act with reference to such a multiplicity of situations is an example of the sociality of nature. The organism is able to deal with novel occurrences by virtue of this "capacity of being several things at once." A bee, for example, can relate to other bees, to the flowers from which it draws nectar, to bears who try to steal its hive's honey, and to boys who try to catch it. Sociality is not a property only of animate objects: a mountain, for example, may be simultaneously a geographical feature, an item in a landscape, an object of religious worship, the opposite of a valley, and so forth. In Mead's view, sociality is a universal characteristic of nature.

Sociality has two modes. First, "the temporal mode of sociality," or "sociality in passage," is "given in immediate relation of the past and present" and is the "process of readjustment" by which an organism incorporates an emergent event into its experience. Second, a natural object is social by virtue of its simultaneous membership in various systems: in any given present, "the location of the object in one system places it in the others as well." The second mode of sociality is the context within which emergent events arise.

In the spring quarter of 1898 Mead initiated an undergraduate course titled "Movements of Thought in the Nineteenth Century"; by 1930 he had taught it no fewer than twenty-five times. During the 1920s several of his students arranged for his lectures to be stenographically recorded. On the basis of the stenographic record, supplemented by some student notes, Merritt H. Moore produced the volume *Movements of Thought in the Nineteenth Century* (1936), an intellectual and cultural history into which are woven many of Mead's own perspectives in social theory, philosophy of science, metaphysics, epistemology, and the philosophy of history. It includes significant treatments of Immanuel Kant, Johann Gottlieb Fichte, Friedrich Wilhelm Joseph von Schelling, Georg Wilhelm Friedrich Hegel, Henri Bergson, evolutionism, the Industrial Revolution, utilitarianism, Marxism, developments in science, and the rise of pragmatism. Mead presents the Romantic movement of the late eighteenth and early nineteenth centuries as an illustration of the way in which inquiries into the past are oriented to the present and the future. Confronted with the political, social, and cultural revolutions of the sixteenth, seventeenth, and eighteenth centuries, the Romantics turned to the medieval past in an effort to redefine European historical and cultural identity.

According to Mead, the revolt against arbitrary authority "came on the basis of a description of human nature as having in it a rational principle from which authority could proceed." The doctrine of natural rights and the notion of the social contract were combined by Hobbes, Locke, and Rousseau in an attempt to give political authority a purely human foundation, in contrast to the medieval theory of the divine right of kings. Society was reconceived as a voluntary association of individuals formed for the purpose of preserving the natural rights of its members to life, liberty, and property of the members; political authority was derived from the agreement of these individuals to live together and to pursue this goal: "When men came to conceive the order of society as flowing from the rational character of society itself; when they came to criticize institutions from the point of view of their immediate function in preserving order, and criticized that order from the point of view of its purpose and function; when they approached the study of the state from the point of view of political science; then, of course, they found themselves in opposition to the medieval attitude which accepted its institutions as given by God to the church."

But the outcome of the revolution was not what the philosophers of the Age of Reason had anticipated. The medieval institutions of monarchy, theocracy, and feudalism were eliminated or drastically limited; but in the new bourgeois society, class divisions reappeared in the division of capital and labor, people were viewed as economic units, and liberty became the freedom to compete in the market: "When labor was brought into the factory centers, there sprang up great cities in which men and women lived in almost impossible conditions. And there sprang up factories built around the machine in which men, women, and children worked under ever so hideous conditions." The rights and liberties that the revolution was supposed to have produced were ideological rather than real.

While the revolution attained its goals at least partially in England and America, it was a complete failure in continental Europe. The French Revolution descended into the Terror and ultimately led to Napoleon's imperialism. The ideals of liberty, equality, and fraternity proved to be inadequate bases for a rational society, in Mead's view, because they were politically naive. The Age of Reason's concept of liberty was negative: it demanded "that the individual shall be free from restraint." In the real political world, where conflict of wills occurs, the freedom of some individuals or groups will infringe on that of other individuals or groups. Fraternity, the notion of comradeship of all humanity, was "much too vague to be made the basis for the organization of the state" and ignored the fact that "people have to depend upon their sense of hostility to other persons in order to identify themselves with their own group." Finally, equality, the demand that "each person shall have . . . the same political standing as every other person," was an ideal to be pursued, not a description of what actually existed in society. The abstract ideals of liberty, fraternity, and equality could not survive in the postrevolutionary struggles for political and economic power.

The failure of the revolution led to the emergence of the Romantic movement: "There came a sense of defeat, after the break down of the Revolution, after the failure to organize a society on the basis of liberty, equality, and fraternity. And it is out of this sense of defeat that a new movement arose, a movement which in general terms passes under the title of 'romanticism.'" Europeans' ties to their medieval past had been severed, but their revolutionary hopes had not been realized; their sense of self was in crisis. The Romantic movement was an attempt to overcome this crisis by reconstructing the past to reestablish the continuity of European culture.

Early modern theories of the self were based on associationist psychology. The self, as Hume said in *A Treatise of Human Nature* (1739–1740), is "nothing but a bundle or collection of different perceptions, which succeed each other with an inconceivable rapidity, and are in a perpetual flux and movement." The fragmentation of consciousness in psychological theory paralleled the cultural fragmentation that was occurring in the seventeenth and eighteenth centuries. The Romantic conception of the unified self was formulated in opposition to this fragmentation.

Kant began the attack on associationism. Mead notes that Kant was not a Romantic philosopher, but he holds that Kant's theory of self provided the basis for philosophical Romanticism. Kant contends in his *Kritik der reinen Vernunft* (1781; revised, 1787; translated as *Critique of Pure Reason,* 1855) and *Kritik der praktischen Vernunft* (1788; translated as *Critique of Practical Reason,* 1956) that associationism cannot adequately account for science or ethics. Associationism is restricted to an empirical investigation of psychological phenomena, but actual knowing and acting presuppose a self that transcends phenomena. Knowing, for Kant, involves more than perception: it also involves judgment, and judging implies a judge. Kant calls this judge the "transcendental unity of apperception" and says that it is a necessary

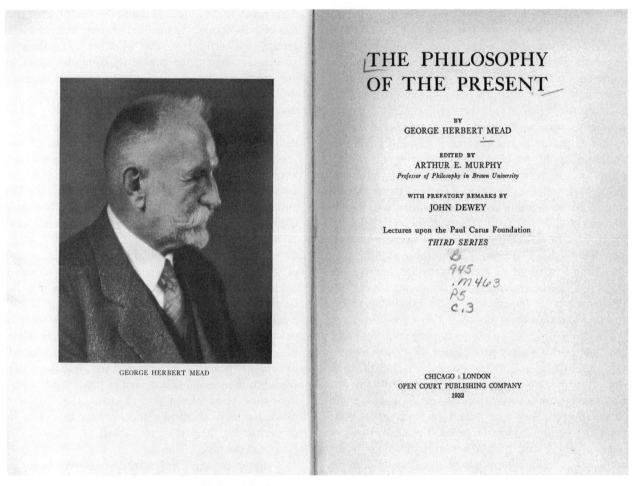

THE PHILOSOPHY
OF THE PRESENT

BY
GEORGE HERBERT MEAD

EDITED BY
ARTHUR E. MURPHY
Professor of Philosophy in Brown University

WITH PREFATORY REMARKS BY
JOHN DEWEY

Lectures upon the Paul Carus Foundation
THIRD SERIES

B
945
.M463
P5
c.3

CHICAGO : LONDON
OPEN COURT PUBLISHING COMPANY
1932

GEORGE HERBERT MEAD

Frontispiece and title page for the first of Mead's posthumously published books, in which he says that an absolutely correct account of the past is impossible (Thomas Cooper Library, University of South Carolina)

precondition of knowledge. As Mead puts it, the "I judge" is "something given in advance of perception" and organizes perceptions into knowledge. As a precondition of knowledge, the transcendental unity of apperception, or self, cannot be an object of knowledge—that is, it cannot be known—but it must be presupposed to account for the unity and structure of perceptions. In ethics, Kant argues that the sense of moral responsibility presupposes that human action is free: "ought" implies "can." Thus, Kant postulates the existence of a nonphenomenal or "noumenal" self that is not subject to the causal necessity of the phenomenal world. Like the transcendental unity of apperception, the noumenal self cannot be known but must be presupposed to make moral experience intelligible. Mead says that the noumenal self is a postulate that "cannot be proved but which we cannot avoid."

The Romantic conception of the self grew out of Kant's critique of associationist psychology, but the Romantic self was not conceived of as transcendental; it was, Mead says, "something which is directly given in experience." For the Romantics, knowledge of the self was not only possible but was the supreme form of knowledge.

The Romantic preoccupation with self-consciousness raises the question of the relationship of subject and object, which is a central concern of Mead's. The Romantic analysis of the subject-object relationship arose in regard to what Mead calls "the age-old problem of knowledge: How can one get any assurance that that which appears in our cognitive experience is real?" The early modern revolt of reason against authority had resulted in a skepticism that "shattered all the statements, all the doctrines, of the medieval philosophy. It had even torn to pieces the philosophy of the Renaissance." With Hume's skeptical analysis of the cause-and-effect relationship, "It had shattered the natural structure of the world which the Renaissance science

234

had presented in such simplicity and yet such majesty, that causal structure that led Kant to say that there were two things that overwhelmed him, the starry heavens above and the moral law within." In response to this skepticism, the Romantics made the self the precondition of experience: experience, including the experience of external objects, was to be understood in relation to the self. The objective world was to be encompassed within the subjective world; the universe was to be made an intimate part of self-consciousness. In self-consciousness the self appears as both subject and object: "the self does not exist except in relation to something else." The subject-object relationship is "a primary relation to experience." Every subject has an object, and every object has a subject: "There cannot be one without the other." According to Mead, "The romantic attitude is . . . the externalizing of the self. One projects one's self into the world, sees the world through the guise, the veil, of one's own emotions. That is the essential feature of the romantic attitude." For the Romantics, too, the self is a dynamic process; the polarity of self and not-self is not static but is "something that is going on":

> The very existence of the self implies a not-self; it implies a not-self which can be identified with the self. You have seen that the term "self" is a reflexive affair. It involves an attitude of separation of the self from itself. Both subject and object are involved in the self in order that it may exist. The self must be identified, in some sense, with the not-self. It must be able to come back at itself from the outside. The process, then, as involved in the self is the subject-object process, a process within which both of these phases of experience lie, a process in which these different phases can be identified with each other—not necessarily as the same phase but at least as expressions of the same process.

The Romantic point of view, according to Mead, leads to a pragmatic conception of knowledge: knowledge is the result of a process in which the self appropriates the not-self. The similarity of Romantic epistemology to Mead's "philosophy of the act" is apparent.

Self-consciousness and historical consciousness are closely connected in Romantic thought. The bourgeois revolution, though it had failed to realize the hopes of the philosophers of the Age of Reason, did create a new concept of the individual, one who "looked at himself as having his own rights, regarded himself as having his own feet to stand on. . . . This gave him a certain independence which he did not have before; it gave him a certain self-consciousness that he never had before." The Romantic view of the Middle Ages was an attempt by Europeans to reconstruct the continuity of

their experience. Romanticism, Mead says, "is a reconstruction of the self through the self's assuming the roles of the great figures of the past":

> That is, the self looked back at its own past as it found it in history. It looked back at it and gave the past a new form as that out of which it had sprung. It put itself back into the past. It lived over again the adventures and achievements of those old heroes with an interest which children have for the lives of their parents—taking their roles and realizing not only the past but the present itself in that process.

From the Romantic search for the "historical connections" between past and present emerged a new past and a new sense of "how the present had grown out of the past." Romantic self-consciousness reconstructed the past and made it one of the main foundations of the self.

Mead never managed to incorporate his philosophy into a systematic treatise. An humble and unassuming man, he apparently had little faith in his own ability and much doubt concerning the profundity of his own ideas. Dewey said that Mead "was always dissatisfied with what he had done; always outgrowing his former expressions, and in consequence so reluctant to fix his ideas in the printed word that for many years it was [only] his students and his immediate colleagues who were aware of the tremendous reach and force of his philosophical mind." George Herbert Mead would no doubt be greatly surprised to find that he is now considered one of the giants of American philosophy and social theory.

Bibliography:

"Mead Documents," *George's Page,* http://spartan.ac. brocku.ca/%7Elward/mead/mead_biblio. html.

Biographies:

Henry Castle Arthur Mead, "Biographical Notes," in Mead's *The Philosophy of the Act,* edited by Charles W. Morris, John M. Brewster, Albert M. Dunham, and David L. Miller (Chicago: University of Chicago Press, 1938), pp. lxxv–lxxix;

David L. Miller, "Introduction: Biographical Notes," in his *George Herbert Mead: Self, Language, and the World* (Chicago: University of Chicago Press, 1938), pp. xi–xxxviii.

References:

Reuben Abel, "Pragmatism and the Outlook of Modern Science," *Philosophy and Phenomenological Research,* 27 (1966): 45–54;

Mitchell Aboulafia, "Habermas and Mead: On Universality and Individuality," *Constellations,* 2 (1995): 95–113;

Aboulafia, "Mead, Sartre: Self, Object & Reflection," *Philosophy and Social Criticism,* 11 (1986): 63–86;

Aboulafia, *The Mediating Self: Mead, Sartre and Self-Determination* (New Haven: Yale University Press, 1986);

Aboulafia, ed., *Philosophy, Social Theory and the Thought of George Herbert Mead* (Albany: State University of New York Press, 1991);

Van Meter Ames, "Buber and Mead," *Antioch Review,* 27 (1967): 181–191;

Ames, "Mead and Husserl on the Self," *Philosophy and Phenomenological Research,* 15 (1955): 320–331;

Ames, "Mead and Sartre on Man," *Journal of Philosophy,* 53 (1956): 205–219;

Ames, "Zen to Mead," *Proceedings and Addresses of the Amererican Philosophical Association,* 33 (1959–1960): 27–42;

John D. Baldwin, *George Herbert Mead: A Unifying Theory for Sociology* (Beverly Hills: Sage, 1986);

Baldwin, "George Herbert Mead and Modern Behaviorism," *Pacific Sociological Review,* 24 (1981): 411–440;

Mary-Ellen Batiuk, "Misreading Mead: Then and Now," *Contemporary Sociology,* 11 (1982): 138–140;

Bedrich Baumann, "George H. Mead and Luigi Pirandello," *Social Research,* 34 (1967): 563–607;

Herbert Blumer, "Mead and Blumer: Social Behaviorism and Symbolic Interactionism," *American Sociological Review,* 45 (1980): 409–419;

Blumer, "Sociological Implications of the Thought of G. H. Mead," *American Journal of Sociology,* 71 (1966): 535–544;

Patrick L. Bourgeois and Sandra B. Rosenthal, "Role Taking, Corporeal Intersubjectivity and Self: Mead and Merleau-Ponty," *Philosophy Today,* 34 (1990): 117–128;

Richard Burke, "George Herbert Mead and the Problem of Metaphysics," *Philosophy and Phenomenological Research,* 23 (1962): 81–88;

Gary A. Cook, "The Development of George Herbert Mead's Social Psychology," *Transactions of the C. S. Peirce Society,* 8 (1972): 167–186;

Cook, *George Herbert Mead: The Making of a Social Pragmatist* (Urbana: University of Illinois Press, 1993);

Cook, "Whitehead's Influence on the Thought of George Herbert Mead," *Transactions of the C. S. Peirce Society,* 15 (1979): 107–131;

Walter R. Corti, ed., *The Philosophy of George Herbert Mead* (Winterthur, Switzerland: Amriswiler Bucherei, 1973);

Lewis Coser, "George Herbert Mead," in his *Masters of Sociological Thought* (New York: Harcourt Brace Jovanovich, 1971), pp. 333–355;

Leonard S. Cottrell Jr., "George Herbert Mead and Harry Stack Sullivan," *Psychiatry,* 41 (1978): 151–162;

George Cronk, *The Philosophical Anthropology of George Herbert Mead* (New York: Peter Lang, 1987);

Cronk, "Symbolic Interactionism: A 'Left-Meadian' Interpretation," *Social Theory and Practice,* 2 (1973): 313–333;

Cronk, "A Symbolic Interactionist Interpretation of the Process of Psychotherapy," *Darshana International: An International Quarterly,* 14 (Spring 1974): 17–25;

John Dewey, "George Herbert Mead," *Journal of Philosophy,* 28 (1931): 309–314;

Ellsworth Faris, "The Social Psychology of G. H. Mead," *American Journal of Sociology,* 43 (1937–1938): 391–403;

Sing-Nan Fen, "Present and Re-Presentation: A Discussion of Mead's Philosophy of the Present," *Philosophical Review,* 60 (1951): 545–550;

Thomas Goff, *Marx and Mead: Contributions to a Sociology of Knowledge* (Boston: Routledge & Kegan Paul, 1980);

Peter Hamilton, *George Herbert Mead: Critical Assessments* (New York: Routledge & Kegan Paul, 1993);

Karen Hanson, *The Self Imagined: Philosophical Reflections on the Social Character of Psyche* (New York: Routledge & Kegan Paul, 1987);

Hans Joas, "The Creativity of Action & the Intersubjectivity of Reason: Mead's Pragmatism and Social Theory," *Transactions of the C. S. Peirce Society,* 26 (1990): 165–194;

Joas, *George Herbert Mead: A Contemporary Re-Examination of His Thought* (Cambridge, Mass.: MIT Press, 1997);

Joas, *Pragmatism and Social Theory* (Chicago: University of Chicago, 1993);

Grace Chin Lee, *George Herbert Mead: Philosopher of the Social Individual* (New York: King's Crown Press, 1945);

Harold N. Lee, "Mead's Doctrine of the Past," *Tulane Studies in Philosophy,* 12 (1963): 52–75;

J. David Lewis, "G. H. Mead's Contact Theory of Reality," *Symbolic Interaction,* 4 (1981): 129–141;

Bernard N. Meltzer, "Mead's Social Psychology," in *Symbolic Interaction,* edited by Meltzer and J. G. Manis (Boston: Allyn & Bacon, 1972): 4–22;

David L. Miller, *George Herbert Mead: Self, Language, and the World* (Chicago: University of Chicago Press, 1973);

Miller, "G. H. Mead's Conception of the Past," *Philosophy of Science,* 10 (January 1943): 29–39;

Miller, "G. H. Mead's Conception of the Present," *Philosophy of Science*, 10 (January 1943): 40–46;

Miller, "The Nature of the Physical Object," *Journal of Philosophy*, 44 (1947): 352–359;

Charles Morris, *Signification and Significance: A Study of the Relations of Signs and Values* (Cambridge, Mass.: MIT Press, 1964);

Morris, *Signs, Language, and Behavior* (Englewood Cliffs, N.J.: Prentice-Hall, 1946);

Maurice Natanson, "George H. Mead's Metaphysics of Time," *Journal of Philosophy*, 50 (1953): 770–782;

Natanson, *The Social Dynamics of George Herbert Mead* (Washington, D.C.: Public Affairs Press, 1956);

Paul E. Pfeutze, *Self, Society, Existence: Human Nature and Dialogue in the Thought of George Herbert Mead and Martin Buber* (New York: Harper, 1961);

Konrad Raiser, *Identität und Sozialität: George Herbert Meads Theorie der Interaktion und ihre Bedeutung für die theologische Anthropologie* (Munich: Kaiser / Mainz: Grünewald, 1971);

Andrew J. Reck, "The Philosophy of George Herbert Mead," *Tulane Studies in Philosophy*, 12 (1963): 5–51;

Sandra Rosenthal, "Mead and Merleau-Ponty," *Southern Journal of Philosophy*, 28 (1990): 77–90;

Rosenthal, *Mead and Merleau-Ponty: Toward a Common Vision* (Albany: State University of New York Press, 1991);

Darnell Rucker, *The Chicago Pragmatists* (Minneapolis: University of Minnesota Press, 1969);

Israel Scheffler, *Four Pragmatists: A Critical Introduction to Peirce, James, Mead and Dewey* (London: Routledge & Kegan Paul / New York: Humanities Press, 1974);

T. V. Smith, "The Social Philosophy of G. H. Mead," *American Journal of Sociology*, 37 (1931): 368–385;

Anselm Strauss, "Mead's Multiple Conceptions of Time and Evolution," *International Sociology*, 6 (1991): 411–426;

Alfred Tonness, "A Notation on the Problem of the Past–with Especial Reference to George Herbert Mead," *Journal of Philosophy*, 24 (1932): 599–606.

Papers:

The University of Chicago Library has George Herbert Mead's manuscripts, students' notes on and stenographic records of courses given by Mead, and letters between Mead and Henry Northrup Castle. The library also has the Henry Northrup Castle Papers, which include approximately 1,500 Mead items; most are letters written between 1889 and 1901 from Mead to members of the Castle family and from them to him.

Charles Sanders Peirce

(10 September 1839 – 19 April 1914)

George W. Stickel

BOOKS: *Chance, Love, and Logic: Philosophical Essays by the Late Charles S. Peirce, the Founder of Pragmatism. With a Supplementary Essay on the Pragmatism of Peirce by John Dewey,* edited by Morris R. Cohen (London: Kegan Paul, Trench, Trübner / New York: Harcourt, Brace, 1923);

Collected Papers of Charles Sanders Peirce, 8 volumes, volumes 1–6 edited by Charles Hartshorne and Paul Weiss, volumes 7 and 8 edited by Arthur W. Burks (Cambridge, Mass.: Harvard University Press, 1931–1958);

The Philosophy of Peirce: Selected Writings, edited by Justus Buchler (New York: Harcourt, Brace / London: Kegan Paul, Trench, Trübner, 1940);

Values in a Universe of Chance: Selected Writings of Charles S. Peirce, edited by Philip P. Wiener (Stanford, Cal.: Stanford University Press, 1958);

Charles S. Peirce: The Essential Writings, edited by Edward C. Moore (New York: Harper & Row, 1972);

Contributions to The Nation, 4 volumes, edited by Kenneth Laine Ketner and James Edward Cook (Lubbock: Texas Tech Press, 1975–1987);

The New Elements of Mathematics, 4 volumes in 5, edited by Carolyn Eisele (The Hague: Mouton / Atlantic Highlands, N.J.: Humanities Press, 1976);

The Writings of Charles S. Peirce: A Chronological Edition, 1857–1886, 6 volumes published, edited by Max H. Fisch, Nathan Houser, and Christian J. W. Kloesel (Bloomington: Indiana University Press, 1982–   );

Peirce on Signs: Writings on Semiotic by Charles Sanders Peirce, edited by James Hoopes (Chapel Hill: University of North Carolina Press, 1991);

The Essential Peirce: Selected Philosophical Writings, 2 volumes, edited by Kloesel and Houser (Bloomington: Indiana University Press, 1992, 1998);

Reasoning and the Logic of Things: The Cambridge Conferences Lectures of 1898, edited by Ketner (Cambridge, Mass.: Harvard University Press, 1992);

Pragmatism as a Principle and Method of Right Thinking: The 1903 Harvard Lectures on Pragmatism, edited by

Charles Sanders Peirce

Patricia Ann Turrisi (Albany: State University of New York Press, 1997);

His Glassy Essence: An Autobiography of Charles Sanders Peirce, edited by Ketner (Nashville: Vanderbilt University Press, 1998).

OTHER: *Studies in Logic by Members of the Johns Hopkins University,* edited, with a contribution, by Peirce (Boston: Little, Brown, 1883)–includes "A Theory of Probable Inference," by Peirce;

Victor Schumann, *On the Absorption and Emission of Air and Its Ingredients for Light of Wave-Lengths from 250 μμ to 100 μμ,* translated by Peirce (Washington, D.C.: Smithsonian Institution, 1903).

Charles Sanders Peirce (pronounced "purse"), the polymath founder of pragmatism, was for some time after his death mainly known in the United States as William James's friend and John Dewey's logic instructor. He was more highly regarded in countries other than his own: one could find Peirce scholars in China, Canada, throughout Europe (including Russia), and in South America. Two of Peirce's most renowned students today are the Italian linguist, semiotician, and novelist Umberto Eco and the Russian-born Belgian 1977 Nobel laureate in physical chemistry and chaos theory, Ilya Prigogine. Eco has written and spoken extensively on Peirce and has used Peirce's theory of semiotics (the study of signs) in his own works in language and communication theory and practice. Eco's novels are also implicitly filled with Peirce's philosophy and logic. For example, in Eco's medieval murder mystery *Il nome della rosa* (1980; translated as *The Name of the Rose,* 1983) the methods used by the protagonist, William of Baskerville, are not based on the ideas of Roger Bacon, as indicated in the text, but on the philosophy of logic and science of Peirce. "Abduction," the logical process of forming hypotheses, which Max H. Fisch suggests is Peirce's greatest discovery, is employed by Eco's William in precise Peircean style.

In the same year that the Italian edition of *The Name of the Rose* was published, Eco's friends and colleagues Thomas A. Sebeok and Jean Umiker-Sebeok published *"You Know My Method": A Juxtaposition of Charles S. Peirce and Sherlock Holmes.* The book opens with a true mystery story that began in Boston on 20 June 1879 when Peirce boarded the steamship *Bristol* bound for New York. When he disembarked, Peirce left behind an expensive watch and an overcoat; when he returned for them, they were missing. A Pinkerton detective could not solve the case, but Peirce, using the science of semiotics that he had developed, retrieved his possessions. In *Order out of Chaos* (1984) Prigogine and Isabelle Stengers write that "today Peirce's work appears to be a pioneering step toward the understanding of the pluralism involved in physical laws." Peirce was struggling with the same issues as modern cosmologists such as Stephen Hawking and George Smoot. Barbara von Eckardt uses Peirce's semiotic logic as a foundation for cognitive science, while neuropsychia-

trist Phillip Epstein has been interested in Peirce's semiotic as he explores alternative medicines. Patricia Churchland refers to Peirce in her *Neurophilosophy: Toward a Unified Science of the Mind-Brain* (1986).

Peirce's biographer, Joseph Brent, notes that Peirce's "philosophical manuscripts and letters . . . number in the tens of thousands of pages, his published works in the thousands." Among his publications were his reviews for *The Nation* from 1869 to 1908 and his many major contributions to the *Century Dictionary* and to James Mark Baldwin's *Dictionary of Philosophy and Psychology.* Late in his life Peirce lamented in his notes: "It is a pity my best articles cannot be reprinted in one volume. It is perfectly heart-breaking to hear people tell me to my face, as they do, that they are perfectly unintelligible. If they were collected in a volume, philosophers would in some future generation get the benefit of them." Brent quotes Lewis Mumford:

The mere failure to publish the greater parts of Peirce's thought has obscured the fact that, in the very dregs of the Gilded Age, a large and universal mind quietly filled itself, a mind whose depth and impact have still to be felt and fathomed. If one is to condemn the Gilded Age for Peirce's lack of influence, one must equally condemn the glorious thirteenth century for the comparative obscurity of Roger Bacon, or the sixteenth century for not publishing the notes of Leonardo da Vinci. Doubtless the condemnation would be deserved, but the glory of their positive achievements still remains.

In an introductory note to Sebeok's *The Play of Musement* (1981) Fisch summarizes Peirce's achievements:

Who is the most original and the most versatile intellect that the Americans have so far produced? The answer "Charles S. Peirce" is uncontested, because any second would be so far behind as not to be worth nominating. Mathematician, astronomer, chemist, geodesist, surveyor, cartographer, metrologist, spectroscopist, engineer, inventor; psychologist, philologist, lexicographer, historian of science, mathematical economist, lifelong student of medicine; book reviewer, dramatist, actor, short story writer; phenomenologist, semiotician, logician, rhetorician and metaphysician. He was, for a few examples, the first modern experimental psychologist in the Americas, the first metrologist to use a wave-length of light as a unit of measure, the inventor of the quincuncial projection of the sphere, the first known conceiver of the design and theory of an electric switching-circuit computer, and the founder of "the economy of research." He is the only system-building philosopher in the Americas who has been both competent and productive in logic, in mathematics, and in a wide range of sciences. If he has had any equals in that

Portrait of Peirce's father, the mathematician and astronomer Benjamin Peirce (from Collected Papers of Charles Sanders Peirce, *volume 3, edited by Charles Hartshorne and Paul Weiss, 1933)*

respect in the entire history of philosophy, they do not number more than two.

Fisch might have added that Peirce was the first American to attend an international scientific conference.

Peirce was born in Cambridge, Massachusetts, on 10 September 1839, the second son of Benjamin Peirce, Perkins Professor of Mathematics and Astronomy at Harvard University, and Sarah Hunt Mills Peirce, the daughter of a U.S. senator (whose seat, after he retired, was taken by a family friend, Daniel Webster). Peirce's older brother, James Mills "Jem" Peirce, became a professor of mathematics and dean of the graduate school at Harvard. His younger siblings were Benjamin Mills Peirce, who became a mining engineer and died at age twenty-six; Helen Huntington Peirce; and Herbert Henry Davis Peirce, who had a distinguished career in the foreign service. The Peirce home was filled with the visiting intellectual leaders of the day.

The precocious Peirce claimed to be able to remember a visit to Salem in 1841, when he would have been about two. His father spent hours helping

him sharpen his mathematical prowess; he became interested in chemistry at age seven or eight and claimed to have written a history of the subject in 1850, when he was ten or eleven. He began the serious study of logic at twelve and of the philosophy of Immanuel Kant at sixteen.

During his senior year at Harvard, Peirce began suffering attacks of trigeminal neuralgia, an excruciatingly painful disorder of the facial nerves. He would spend days unable to work; when he did work, he was intensely driven, since he did not know when the affliction would return. His father suffered from the same disorder, and both men used ether and tincture of opium to manage the pain; Charles Peirce later also took morphine and, probably, cocaine. Brent says that "It is to the extreme pain of this disease—described as unbearable by its sufferers—and his use of drugs as palliatives that much of Peirce's erratic behavior can be attributed."

Also during his senior year Peirce wrote an account of his life in the "Class-Book," in which he recorded his recollection of the Salem visit and the composition of the history of chemistry. Most of the entries, however, are the arrogant braggadocio of a cocky young man who had been indulged by his parents. Peirce was always self-centered, bent equally on pleasure and on intellectual pursuits. That self-centeredness drove him to excellence in science, mathematics, and philosophy but made him ineffective in political and personal relationships. At one point he was asked not to return to France because of a disagreement with French scientists concerning instruments and procedures to measure gravity; he was later proven correct and invited to return. His promiscuity caused rifts in both of his marriages, and his extravagant tastes created financial problems for himself and his wives.

Peirce graduated from Harvard in 1859. In July 1861 he was hired as his father's "assistant computer" by the U.S. Coast and Geodetic Survey, of which Benjamin Peirce was one of the founders. He spent the next thirty years working for the agency—most of that time under protection of his father, who became superintendent in 1867.

Peirce completed a master of arts at Harvard in 1862. On 16 October 1862 he married Harriet Melusina "Zina" Fay, the granddaughter of the first Episcopal bishop of Vermont. Peirce earned a bachelor of science in chemistry, summa cum laude, from Harvard's Lawrence Scientific School in 1863. Through the efforts of his friend James, he gave lectures at Harvard in 1865, 1869–1870, 1898, 1903, and 1907. In spite of James's pleas, however, Harvard president Charles Eliot refused to offer Peirce a position at the university:

as an undergraduate Peirce had alienated Eliot, who had been his chemistry teacher.

Peirce's wife traveled extensively with him on his scientific field studies, including the observation of a solar eclipse in Sicily on 22 December 1870. They separated in 1876. In 1879 Peirce was hired as a lecturer in logic at Johns Hopkins University, but tensions existed between him and Benjamin Gilman, the president of the university. Peirce and his wife were divorced on 24 April 1883; six days later Peirce married Juliette Froissy. Peirce's relationship with Froissy before his divorce might have caused the final break with Gilman at Johns Hopkins: Peirce was dismissed from the lectureship in 1884. While affairs were not unknown in the 1880s, Peirce was anything but discreet.

His father's death in 1880 had left Peirce without political support at the Coast and Geodetic Survey, and he had made many enemies. His work was without peer, but he kept poor records and often left his reports unfinished. In 1885 congressional investigations were held into his management of Coast and Geodetic Survey funds; he offered his resignation, but it was not accepted. The charges were eventually reduced to "extravagance."

In 1889 Thomas Conwin Mendenhall became superintendent of the Coast and Geodetic Survey. Simon Newcomb, then director of the Nautical Almanac Office, was a former professor of Mendenhall's; a mediocre scientist and a religious fundamentalist, he believed, according to Brent, that "Peirce's evil character infected the results of his science." Newcomb had been responsible for Peirce's dismissal from Johns Hopkins, and his contempt for Peirce seems certain to have influenced Mendenhall. Peirce was forced to retire from the Coast and Geodetic Survey on 31 December 1891.

The loss of his Coast and Geodetic Survey income did not lead Peirce and his wife to moderate their lifestyle. They had an apartment in New York and a two-thousand-acre tract of land near Milford, Pennsylvania, which they had purchased in increments between 1888 and 1889. Peirce hoped to build a school of philosophy on the land, which he called "Arisbe" after the Greek source of cosmology, philosophy, and science on the Selleis River in Asia Minor. Arisbe was only one of his schemes to gain wealth; Brent says that "only a few were successful, and those did not produce enough money to support the life he insisted on." Arisbe drained the Peirces financially; all of their assets were tied up in it, but they refused to sell it at a loss. By 1897 they were on the verge of starvation, and Peirce was stealing food to survive.

Some of Peirce's most profound work was produced during his years at Arisbe. His later lectures at Harvard and some that he delivered in private homes

in Cambridge beginning in 1898 were written there, and much of his work on ethics and the culmination of his study of logic was completed there.

Peirce died of cancer at Arisbe on 19 April 1914. Juliette Peirce died twenty years later, and Arisbe was sold to pay her debts. She had sent some of Peirce's papers to Harvard; but no one wanted what remained, and many were burned in the front yard of Arisbe in 1936. Today the home and land are maintained by the Pennsylvania Park Service.

Peirce is recognized as the founder of pragmatism. He first discussed the philosophy at the Harvard Metaphysical Club in the fall of 1872, and he stated the pragmatic maxim in the essay "How to Make Our Ideas Clear," published in *Popular Science Monthly* in January 1878: "Consider what effects, which might conceivably have practical bearings, we conceive the object of our conception to have. Then, our conception of these effects is the whole of our conception of the object." James claimed in an 1898 address that while Peirce did not use the word *pragmatism* in the essay, he had used it in his presentation at the Metaphysical Club. Peirce adopted the name *pragmaticism* for his theory because he did not like the use others were making of pragmaticism, and he wanted a word that was "ugly enough to be safe from kidnappers."

Peirce's pragmatism is more systematic, comprehensive, and mathematically oriented than that of the other three founding pragmatists—James, Dewey, and George Herbert Mead. Peirce envisioned the maxim as applying far more broadly than to human experience: he saw it as a process of the universe, and he sought to explicate that process from as comprehensive a perspective as the human mind allowed. His ultimate intention, he wrote in the fall of 1887 or the winter of 1888 in "A Guess at the Riddle," which was first published in *Collected Papers of Charles Sanders Peirce* (1931–1958), was "to outline a theory so comprehensive that . . . the entire work of human reason . . . shall appear as the filling up of its details."

"A Guess at the Riddle" was intended as a book, but many of the ideas in it found their way into articles Peirce contributed to *The Monist* between 1891 and 1893. Peirce discusses the notion of habit, by which he means a consistent or regular response to some mental or physical stimulus. Physical laws can be considered "habits" of nature:

> Moreover, all things have a tendency to take habits. For atoms and their parts, molecules and groups of molecules, and in short every conceivable real object, there is a greater probability of acting as on a former like occasion than otherwise. This tendency itself constitutes a regularity, and is continually on the increase. . . .

According to this, three elements are active in the world: first, chance; second, law; and third, habit taking.

When the universe originated in what is today called the Big Bang–Peirce calls it the "first flash" or the "original chaos"–habits had not yet been formed: "The existence of things consists in their regular behavior. . . . Not only substances, but events, too, are constituted by regularity. The original chaos, therefore, where there was no regularity, was in effect a state of mere indeterminacy, in which nothing existed or really happened." Human knowing, Peirce argues, is a natural outgrowth of the process of habit formation within the universe.

In "The Fixation of Belief," published in *Popular Science Monthly* in November 1877, Peirce contrasts the pragmatic method, which he calls "the method of science," with three other ways of knowing: tenacity, authority, and a priori. Tenacity involves "taking any answer to a question which we may fancy, and constantly reiterating it to ourselves, dwelling on all which may conduce to that belief, and learning to turn with contempt and hatred from anything which might disturb it." Authority is the belief system of a group; it is better than individual tenacity and has served to create great cultures, but it also makes people slaves to a system. Moving beyond authority, people can develop beliefs that are "in harmony with natural causes" and seem "agreeable to reason." Such belief systems "have not usually rested upon any observed facts, at least not in any great degree." This "a priori" way of knowing is the most reasonable of the three and is used in philosophy, but doubts can still arise in regard to such knowledge. Therefore, Peirce says,

the method must be such that the ultimate conclusion of every [one] shall be the same. Such is the method of science. Its fundamental hypothesis, related in more familiar language, is this: There are real things, whose characters are entirely independent of our opinions about them; those realities affect our senses according to regular laws, and, though our sensations are as different as our relations to the objects, yet, by taking advantage of the laws of perception, we can ascertain by reasoning how things really are, and any, if he have sufficient experience and reason enough about it, will be led to the one true conclusion.

Truth, however, does not always come with the first hypothesis or first trial. In an October 1908 letter to a Columbia University professor, Cassius J. Keyser, Peirce wrote: "To say 'we don't know,' is sloth! *The business of a [person] of science is to guess,* and disprove guess after guess, being guided by the particular way the last guess failed in forming the next one. A scientific genius has seldom had to guess as many times as Keppler [*sic*] did."

Several of Peirce's works, including "A Guess at the Riddle," address what he called his "architectonic theory of thought." Such a theory, he says in "The Architecture of Theories," published in *The Monist* (January 1891), "should first of all make a complete survey of human knowledge." The attempt to develop such a theory, which today is known as the Grand Unification Theory, occupied Albert Einstein's later life and is the quest of particle physicists, astrophysicists, and cosmologists. Peirce's architectonic, which centers around his "categories" of Firstness, Secondness, and Thirdness, appears at first sight to be a form of numerology. In "A Guess at the Riddle" he says:

For my part, I am a determined foe of no innocent number; I respect and esteem them all their several ways; but I am forced to confess to a leaning to the number three in philosophy. In fact, I make so much use of three-fold divisions in my speculations, that it seems best to commence by making a slight preliminary study of the conceptions upon which all such divisions must rest. I mean no more than the ideas of First, Second, Third,–ideas so broad that they may be looked upon rather as moods or tones of thought, than as definite notions, but which have great significance for all that.

During the summer or fall of 1886 Peirce wrote:

I am going in this book to propound a hypothesis about the constitution of the universe. The hypothesis is constructed from three elementary conceptions,– or . . . tones,–the ideas of First, Second, Third.

By the First, I do not at all mean the philosophical notion of the One, as a synthetizing unity or Whole. I mean simply what presents itself as first, fresh, immediate, free, spontaneous. An object at first blush, unreflectively taken. Undifferentiated. What Adam on first opening his eyes thought of the world before examining it.

The Second, last or term or end is in the fact otherness, relation, force (not abstract, but as it feels when one gets hit), effect, dependence, occurrence, reality, upshot.

The Third is the medium, or that which mediates between the absolute first and absolute last. Continuity. Process. Flow of time. Sympathy. Comparison, Exchange. Modification, compromise (an outward shallow sort of third). Sign, representative. Combination, mixture. . . . Coherence. Whole.

For example, a fork in a road is a First, the road is a Second, and a place is a Third. Possibility is a First, actuality is a Second, and necessity is a Third. A beginning is a First, an end is a Second, and a means is a Third. In physics, position is a First, velocity is a Second, and acceleration is a Third. In mathematics, a straight line is a First, a broken line is a Second, and a curve is a Third. In theology, the Holy Spirit is a First, the Father is a Second, and the Son is a Third. In semiotics, the existence of an object, in and of itself and apart from anything else, is a First. When one observes an object, the initial image formed of that object–the first sensation of the redness of a robin's breast or the warmth of a sun-baked stone–is a First and a sign of the object. The object being perceived–the robin being seen or the stone being felt–is a Second. The thoughts called to the observer's mind by the robin or the rock are interpreting signs or interpretants; signs mediate between the object and what anyone thinks about the object, so they are Thirds. Further, the sign can be an icon, an index, or a symbol, resulting in degrees of Firstness, Secondness, and Thirdness. Peirce scholars have discussed concepts such as First Firstness or Second Thirdness. Particularly when addressing signs and the objects they signify, and how they signify those objects, they use numerical codes such as "111" for a First First Firstness (which Peirce calls a "Rhematic Iconic Qualisign"), a pure feeling of some quality. Michael Cabot Haley uses Peirce's categories to understand metaphor, and Donna Orange uses them theologically for conceptualizing God. Haley and Orange both quote a dense passage from one of Peirce's manuscripts, Haley to explain the need for metaphor and Orange to confirm that the "deity is the reasonable aspect of the whole evolutionary process":

Peirce circa 1860 (Houghton Library, Harvard University)

> but as I am at present advised the aesthetic Quality appears to me to be the total unanalizable [*sic*] impression of a reasonableness that has expressed itself in a creation. It is a pure Feeling, but a feeling that is the impress of a Reasonableness that Creates. It is the Firstness that truly belongs to a Thirdness in its achievement of a Secondness.

In *Frontiers in Semiotics* (1986) John Deely, Brooke Williams, and Felicia Kruse present some of the many works that use the categories in fields from language to zoology. Sebeok, one of the authors inclued in *Frontiers in Semiotics,* has spent a lifetime showing the value of the Peircean categories. Once the language is understood, scholars have been able to use Peirce's ideas in many areas; language, in particular, has been examined quite thoroughly in this way.

If the categories are the framework of the universe and the framework of knowledge, then semiotics is the detail of the universe and the objects of knowledge, and Peirce's semiotic logic is the process whereby the frame blossoms into complexity, people grow, and civilization develops. The categories, the semiotics, and the logic are a united whole and provide for a comprehensive philosophy.

In 15 July 1902 Peirce submitted an application to the Carnegie Foundation for funding for a comprehensive scientific work in which he would present a "*unitary system of logic in all its parts*" and classify scientific research. The project would explicate his architectonic theory (the categories), his semiotics, and his logic. The project was never funded, but in the application Peirce defined logic

> as *formal semiotic*. A definition of a sign will be given which no more refers to human thought than does the definition of a line as the place which a particle occupies, part by part, during a lapse of time. Namely, a sign is something, *A,* which brings something, *B,* its *interpretant* sign determined or created by it, into the same sort of correspondence with something, *C,* its *object,* as that in which itself stands to *C.* It is from this definition, together with a definition of "formal," that I deduce mathematically the principles of logic. I also make a historical review of all the definitions and conceptions of logic, and show, not merely that my defini-

Peirce (standing, fourth from left) and others gathered to observe a solar eclipse in Sicily on 22 December 1870.
Peirce's father is to his left, and his younger brother Herbert Henry Davis Peirce
is seated in front of them (Collection of Mrs. Peirce Prince).

tion is no novelty, but that my non-psychological conception of logic has *virtually* been quite generally held, though not generally recognized.

For Peirce, semiotics, the study of signs, includes much more than linguistics, since the universe is replete with signs:

> It seems a strange thing, when one comes to ponder over it, that a sign should leave its interpreter to supply a part of its meaning; but the explanation of the phenomenon lies in the fact that the entire universe,—not merely the universe of existents, but all that wider universe, embracing the universe of existents as a part, the universe which we are all accustomed to refer to as "the truth,"—that all this universe is perfused with signs, if it is not composed exclusively of signs.

Peirce presented a series of lectures on pragmatism in Cambridge in 1903 that James describes in *Pragmatism: A New Name for Some Old Ways of Thinking* (1907) as "flashes of brilliant light relieved against Cimmerian darkness." In the manuscript for one lecture Peirce says:

> Therefore, if you ask me what part Qualities can play in the economy of the universe, I shall reply that the universe is a vast representamen, a great symbol of God's purpose, working out its conclusions in living realities. Now every symbol must have, organically attached to it, its Indices of reactions and these qualities

play in an argument that, they of course, play in the universe—that Universe being precisely an argument.

Peirce was clear that all thought was semiotic and was defined logically. In "Some Consequences of Four Incapacities," published in *The Journal of Speculative Philosophy* in 1868, Peirce argues:

> We have no power of Intuition, but every cognition is determined logically by previous cognitions. . . . We have no power of thinking without signs. . . . whenever we think, we have present to the consciousness some feeling, image, conception, or other representation, which serves as a sign. . . . We have seen that the content of consciousness, the entire phenomenal manifestation, is a sign resulting from inference.

The whole universe is signs becoming signs, with growing complexity. In "The Architecture of Theories" Peirce says: "The one intelligible theory of the universe is that of objective idealism, that matter is effete mind, inveterate habits becoming physical laws." The mind functions with a semiotic logic framed in the categories of First, Second, and Third.

Peirce's two best-known definitions of *sign* are: "A sign, or *representamen,* is something which stands to somebody for something in some respect or capacity" and "A *Sign,* or *Representamen,* is a First which stands in such a genuine triadic relation to a Second, called its

Object, as to be capable of determining a Third, called its *Interpretant,* to assume the same triadic relation to its Object in which it stands itself to the same Object." For example, the words *American Flag* are a sign that calls forth in the minds of readers an image of a red, white, and blue cloth object. Each will interpret the image in a unique way: an American veteran of World War II will interpret it differently from an anti–Vietnam War protester, although the sign and the object are the same. Because of the interpretation, the object–the flag–becomes different to each. The qualities of the object–its colors, the texture of the cloth–are the same for all, but individuals' emotions, actions, and conceptions will be different depending on their experience with the object. Likewise, the flag as a sign representing the nation called "The United States" calls forth a different interpretation in each individual according to that individual's experience. "E = mc²"; the club, diamond, heart, and spade symbols in a deck of playing cards; the word *agape* written in Greek characters; and the chemical formula or the combination of hydrogen and oxygen to form water are signs, as are feelings, sounds, and colors. Indeed, everything is a sign, even the vibrations of molecules (which can be read by instrumentation), the force of an automobile accelerating (which is "read" by the body of a driver as a response to the depression of the accelerator), and the gaseous explosion of a distant nebula (which is "read" by the Hubble Space Telescope). In each of these cases the reading is interpreted by a human observer; but signs are not limited to human observation. The molecular vibration is also read by another molecule; the car interprets the acceleration in ways described in physics; and the plasma from the nebular explosion responds in ways consistent with plasma in other gaseous explosions in other parts of the universe.

The diversity of signs even in language, let alone in the universe, led Peirce to establish several classification systems and coin many terms to aid in their study. His ten-class system is the simplest, relatively speaking; he also developed a sixty-six-class system. The ten-class system is based on three trichotomies: the nature of the sign; the relation of the sign to the object; and the interpretant's representation of the sign. In the first trichotomy the sign's nature can be a quality, or *qualisign;* an actually existing thing, or *sinsign;* or a law, which Peirce calls a *legisign.* The second trichotomy is the relationship of the sign to the object, which can be an *icon,* "by virtue of characters of its own"; an *index,* which is "really affected by that object"; or a *symbol,* "by virtue of a law, usually an association of general ideas." In the third trichotomy the interpretant can represent the object as a possibility, or *rheme;* as an actually existing thing, or *dicent sign* (also called a *dicisign*); or as a sign of law, an

argument. The first member of each category is a First, the second is a Second, and the third is a Third. For example, qualisign, icon, and rheme are all Firsts and can be represented numerically by a "1." The classes of signs are formed by taking the three trichotomies in the order nature of the sign, relation of the sign to the object, and interpretant's representation of the sign. The first class of signs would then be a "qualisign iconic rheme"–or "Qualisign," for short–with a numerical representation of "111," where the first "1" represents the nature of a sign, the second the relation of the sign to the object, and the last the interpretant's representation of the sign.

While the number of permutations of the three trichotomies is greater than ten, Peirce requires that the nature of the sign dictate the range of the sign's relationship to the object and the interpretant's representation of the sign. The sign's relation to the object, in turn, defines the options for the interpretant's representation. Therefore, the numerical code of subsequent trichotomies must be the same or higher in each category; that is, from left to right the numbers can only be the same or higher than those that precede them. The numerical code of a class could be "111," "112," or "223," but never "121." Thus, a qualisign could only be iconic, never indexical or symbolic; a sinsign could be iconic or indexical but never symbolic, and it could be a rheme or a dicent sign, never an argument. Given these requirements, the Qualisign (111) has to be first. That is why the short name "Qualisign" can be used, since a qualisign (nature of the sign) can never be anything but iconic and rhemetic.

The Ten Classes, then, are: Qualisign (111), a quality as a sign, such as "the feeling red"; Iconic Sinsign (112), "an object of experience in so far as some quality of it makes it determine the idea of the object," such as "an individual diagram"; Rhematic Indexical Sinsign (122), a direct experience directing attention to something, such as a "spontaneous cry"; Dicent Sinsign (222), "any object of direct experience," such as a weathercock; Iconic Legisign (113), a sign referring to some general type, as "H₂O" refers iconically to two hydrogen atoms bonded to an oxygen atom to represent a water molecule in general but no one molecule in particular; Rhematic Indexical Legisign (123), a sign that is "really affected" by the object, a "demonstrative pronoun," as in "This puppy is really cute!" where the dog is affecting the sign *this,* which is a word in English but as a sign is merely a possibility; Dicent Indexical Legisign (223), where specific information is presented in a instant, and the sign and the sign's nature to the object are existential, as in a "street cry" such as "Get your newspapers!"; Rhematic Symbol (133), where the sign and object are associated generally, because of

On the Algebraic Principles of Formal Logic. By.
C. S. Peirce.

There are two purposes of a logical algebra, viz: —
1st. The mathematical purpose of solving problems, of
finding the conclusion [to be drawn] from given premises, and
2nd. The logical purpose of analyzing inferences and showing
precisely upon what their validity depends.
The latter is to my mind the first object to be fulfilled.
After an algebra has been constructed to do that, it will
probably need various modifications [to be used with]
[to fit it for] a mathematical ~~convenience~~ uses. These modifications
though improvements from a mathematical point of
view will [appear] be defects [when viewed] from a logical or analytical
standpoint. At present I seek only logical per-
fection in the algebra of logic.

Page from a manuscript written by Peirce in 1879 (Houghton Library, Harvard University)

habit, "a common noun" where the sign is still a possibility, as in "flag," which could refer to several different images in the mind, all of them "flag-like"; Dicent Symbol (233), "a sign connected with its object by an association of general ideas," for example, an ordinary proposition or premise in logic; and Argument (333), "a sign whose interpretant represents its object as being an ulterior sign through a law . . . that the passage from all such premises to such conclusions tends to the truth."

The sixty-six-class system is more comprehensive and has an additional variety of technical terms. For the sixty-six classes the trichotomies include the natures of the objects, the interpretants, and the various relationships within the triadic—that is, the sign, object, and interpretant.

The semiotic dynamic results in the triadic relation between a sign, an object, and an interpretant. The interpretant within the human mind may be a feeling, which is a Firstness; it may be an action, a Secondness; or it may be an idea, a Thirdness. That feeling, action, or idea could become more refined with further experiences with the object and the sign representation of the object. So, over time the interpretant, whether feeling, action, or idea, changes in relation to the object. The final interpretant is the habit that is established as the individual repeatedly responds to an object in a certain way that is brought about by the sign. This final interpretant is a result of the logic of the semiotic action and is the ultimate interpretant for that individual. It can also be the ultimate interpretant for the society, which is "taught" in school. So, for example, a child responds verbally (an action), or conceptually (an idea), with "4" when given the sign "2 + 2 = ____."

Is there ever an absolutely final interpretant? The brief answer is no. For example, in the arithmetic problem the sign can be changed slightly to "2 + 2 = ____ (base 3)." Now the logical interpretant is no longer "4" but "11," which is not "eleven" but a number in the base 3 system. In this manner, there can be continual growth of the individual, of society, and even of the universe, which, for Peirce, is an increase in the order of mind.

Peirce was a logician from around the time of his twelfth birthday, when he went into his older brother's room and picked up his brother's new college textbook: Richard Whately's *Elements of Logic* (first published in 1826). Peirce devoted the next several days to "absorbing" its contents; Fisch writes of this experience in *The Writings of Charles S. Peirce: A Chronological Edition, 1857–1886* (1982–): "Since that time, he often said late in life, it had never been possible for him to think of anything, including even chemistry, except as an exercise in logic. And so far as he knew, he was the only man since the Middle Ages who had completely devoted his life to

logic." Peirce applied his logic to the physiology and neurology of thought. Logic defines how habits form and how they are executed neurologically: "The irritation of the brain, in another aspect, appears as the uneasy sense of doubt; and the end of all thinking is the removal of doubt, just as the end of all nervous action is the removal of the source of irritation."

Thinking and the process of removing doubts rely on habits. Habits are rules of action for the individual; they are systems of logic, and Peirce defines their biological application with a valid syllogism in the form ("mood") that has traditionally been named with the mnemonic device "Barbara" (signifying that it consists of three "A," or universal affirmative, statements): *Rule:* All men are mortal; *Case:* Enoch was a man; *Result:* Enoch was mortal. Peirce continues:

> The cognition of a rule is not necessarily conscious, but is of the nature of a habit, acquired or congenital. The cognition of a case is of the general nature of a sensation; that is to say, it is something which comes up into present consciousness. The cognition of a result is of the nature of a decision to act in a particular way on a given occasion. In point of fact, a syllogism in Barbara virtually takes place when we irritate the foot of a decapitated frog. The connection between the afferent and efferent nerve, whatever it may be, constitutes a nervous habit, a rule of action, which is the physiological analogue of the major premise. The disturbance of the ganglionic equilibrium, owing to the irritation, is the physiological form of that which, psychologically considered, is a sensation; and, logically considered, is the occurrence of a case. The explosion through the efferent nerve is the physiological form of that which psychologically is a volition, and logically the inference of a result. When we pass from the lowest to the highest forms of innervation, the physiological equivalents escape our observation; but psychologically, we still have, first, habit,—which in its highest form is understanding, and which corresponds to the major premise of Barbara; we have, second, feeling, or present consciousness, corresponding to the minor premise of Barbara; and we have, third, volition, corresponding to the conclusion of the same mode of syllogism. Although these analogies, like all very broad generalizations, may seem very fanciful at first sight, yet the more the reader reflects upon them the more profoundly true I am confident they will appear. . . .
>
> Deduction proceeds from Rule and Case to Result; it is the formula of Volition. Induction proceeds from Case and Result to Rule; it is the formula of the formation of a habit or general conception,—a process which, psychologically as well as logically, depends on the repetition of instances or sensations. Hypothesis [which Peirce also calls "abduction" and "retroduction"] proceeds from Rule and Result to Case; it is the formula of the acquirement of secondary sensation,—a process by which a confused concatenation of predicates is brought into order under a synthesizing predicate.

Peirce at his estate, "Arisbe," near Milford, Pennsyvania, where he had hoped to establish a school of philosophy

We usually conceive Nature to be perpetually making deductions in Barbara.

For Peirce, logic is an evolutionary process of knowing. It is the process of consciousness within the universe, which has produced human intellect within its set of rules and habits. Out of the nothingness that existed before the creation of the universe the categories of the signs arose through a process of logic: "Thus the zero of bare possibility, by evolutionary logic, leapt into the *unit* of some quality. This was hypothetic inference. Its form was:

Something is possible,
Red is something;
Therefore, Red is possible."

In some logical manner the qualities of the cosmos defined the future nature of the cosmos in all its complexity. That logical manner employed chance as the abductive logic of the universe, law as the deductive form, and habit taking as the inductive, as Peirce explains in "A Guess at the Riddle." His logic suggests the evolutionary unity of inanimate cosmos, plant, animal, and human intellect—all are part of one semiotic system, and the execution of a habit in all places has the form of the deductive syllogism in Barbara.

The logic of habit-taking and its execution is also basic to Peirce's ethics. In "Evolutionary Love," the last of his series of articles in *The Monist* (January 1893), he writes: "Thus, habit plays a double part; it serves to establish the new features, and also to bring them into harmony with the general morphology and function of the animals and plants to which they belong." The logic is a process of normalization for order. In the same vein, Vincent Potter argues from Peirce's later writings that the meaning of any proposition is its "capacity for governing future action through the knower's exercise of self-control." John K. Sheriff, likewise, contends that the order of semiotic logic defines ethics, including self-control and self-sacrifice. For that reason, Peirce's classification system—which he never completed—lists the normative sciences of "esthetics, ethics, and logic" ahead of all other forms of study except mathematics and the categories. The normative function of the logical process defines human behavior, as well as the evolutionary functioning of the cosmos.

Peirce continues to play a major role in discussions of semiotics and its applications, particularly to language. Eco is only one of a plethora of scholars who use Peirce's semiotic theory in language and literary studies. Marcel Danesi examines Peirce's semiotic in relation to the history of language, James Jakób Liszka uses it to understand the symbolism in mythology, and Victorino Tejera and Floyd Merrell are among the many who apply it to literary criticism. Merrell has used Peirce's ideas more broadly than most to tie Prigogine's work and Peirce's cosmology to human understanding in literature. In theology, Peircean research groups have been established in Giessen and Marburg, Germany, and some are scattered throughout the United States. Orange and Michael L. Raposa published the first books on Peirce's views of the nature of God and the human condition, and others, such as Sheriff and Robert S. Corrington, are beginning to explore some of these ideas. Potter discusses some of the theological issues but mainly deals with ethics, which remains a fertile field for Peircean research.

Seminal work in mathematics has centered around Peirce's logic and his existential graphs, a special geometric nomenclature used in his logic; Don D. Roberts has made the definitive beginning study of the graphs. Carolyn Eisele's 1976 edition of Peirce's mathematical papers is perhaps the most significant work on Peirce undertaken by a single individual; if not for her, much of Peirce's mathematical writing would have been destroyed. Little has been done with Peirce in psychology, apart from limited work in cognitive science and even more-limited work in education by Eisele, Marjorie Siegel and Robert F. Carey, and George W. Stickel, although a growing number of scholars are becoming interested in those areas.

One could easily spend a lifetime studying Peirce and a second lifetime applying his ideas to one field or another. Peirce is, indeed, fertile ground for any scholar.

Letters:

Semiotic and Significs: The Correspondence between Charles S. Peirce and Victoria Lady Welby, edited by Charles S. Hardwick and James Cook (Bloomington: Indiana University Press, 1977).

Biography:

Joseph Brent, *Charles Sanders Peirce: A Life,* revised and enlarged edition (Bloomington: Indiana University Press, 1998).

References:

A. J. Ayer, *The Origins of Pragmatism: Studies in the Philosophy of Charles Sanders Peirce and William James* (London & Melbourne: Macmillan, 1968; San Francisco: Freeman, Cooper, 1968);

Justus Buchler, *Charles Peirce's Empiricism* (New York: Harcourt, Brace / London: Kegan Paul, Trench, Trübner, 1939);

Patricia Churchland, *Neurophilosophy: Toward a Unified Science of the Mind-Brain* (Cambridge, Mass.: MIT Press, 1986);

Robert S. Corrington, *An Introduction to C. S. Peirce: Philosopher, Semiotician, and Ecstatic Naturalist* (Lanham, Md.: Rowman & Littlefield, 1993);

Marcel Danesi, *Vico, Metaphor, and the Origin of Language* (Bloomington: Indiana University Press, 1993);

Paul Davies, *The Mind of God* (New York: Simon & Schuster, 1992);

John Deely, Brooke Williams, and Felicia Kruse, eds., *Frontiers in Semiotics* (Bloomington: Indiana University Press, 1986);

S. Morris Eames, *Pragmatic Naturalism: An Introduction* (Carbondale: Southern Illinois University Press, 1977);

Carolyn Eisele, ed., *A History of Science: Historical Perspectives on Peirce's Logic of Science,* 2 volumes (The Hague: Mouton, 1985);

Max H. Fisch, "Introductory Note," in *The Play of Musement,* by Thomas A. Sebeok (Bloomington: Indiana University Press, 1981);

Eugene Freeman, *The Categories of Charles Peirce* (Chicago: Open Court, 1934);

Michael Cabot Haley, *The Semeiosis of Poetic Metaphor* (Bloomington: Indiana University Press, 1988);

William James, *Pragmatism: A New Name for Some Old Ways of Thinking; The Meaning of Truth, a Sequel to Pragmatism* (Cambridge, Mass.: Harvard University Press, 1907);

Leon Lederman and Dick Teresi, *The God Particle: If the Universe Is the Answer, What Is the Question?* (Boston: Houghton Mifflin, 1993);

David Lindley, *The End of Physics: The Myth of a Unified Theory* (New York: Basic Books, 1993);

James Jakób Liszka, *The Semiotic of Myth: A Critical Study of the Symbol* (Bloomington: Indiana University Press, 1989);

Bonnie E. Litowitz and Phillip S. Epstein, *Semiotic Perspectives on Clinical Theory and Practice: Medicine, Neuropsychiatry, and Psychoanalysis* (New York: De Gruyter, 1991);

Floyd Merrell, *Semiosis in the Postmodern Age* (West Lafayette, Ind.: Purdue University Press, 1995);

Merrell, *Signs Becoming Signs: Our Perfusive, Pervasive Universe* (Bloomington: Indiana University Press, 1991);

Merrell, *Signs Grow: Semiosis and Life Processes* (Toronto: University of Toronto Press, 1996);

Edward C. Moore, ed., *Charles S. Peirce and the Philosophy of Science: Papers from the Harvard Sesquicentennial Congress* (Tuscaloosa: University of Alabama Press, 1993);

Moore and Richard S. Robin, eds., *Studies in the Philosophy of Charles Sanders Peirce: Second Series* (Amherst: University of Massachusetts Press, 1964);

Grégoire Nicolis and Ilya Prigogine, *Exploring Complexity* (New York: Freeman, 1989);

Donna Orange, *Peirce's Conception of God: A Developmental Study* (Lubbock, Tex.: Institute for Studies in Pragmaticism, 1984);

Vincent Potter, *Charles S. Pierce: On Norms and Ideals* (New York: Fordham University Press, 1997);

Potter, *Peirce's Philosophical Perspectives,* edited by Vincent Colapietro (New York: Fordham University Press, 1996);

Ilya Prigogine and Isabelle Stengers, *Order out of Chaos* (Toronto: Bantam, 1984);

Michael L. Raposa, *Peirce's Philosophy of Religion* (Bloomington: Indiana University Press, 1989);

Don D. Roberts, *The Existential Graphs of Charles S. Peirce* (The Hague: Mouton, 1973);

Richard S. Robin, *Annotated Catalogue of the Papers of Charles S. Peirce* (Amherst: University of Massachusetts, 1967);

Gary Sanders, "Peirce's Sixty-six Signs?" *Transactions of the Charles S. Peirce Society,* 6 (Winter 1970): 3–16;

Thomas A. Sebeok and Jean Umiker-Sebeok, *"You Know My Method": A Juxtaposition of Charles S. Peirce and Sherlock Holmes* (Bloomington, Ind.: Gaslight Publications, 1980);

John K. Sheriff, *Charles Peirce's Guess at the Riddle* (Bloomington: Indiana University Press, 1994);

Marjorie Siegel and Robert F. Carey, *Critical Thinking: A Semiotic Perspective* (Bloomington, Ind.: ERIC Clearinghouse on Reading and Communication Skills, 1989);

George Smoot, *Wrinkles in Time* (New York: Morrow, 1993);

George W. Stickel, "Physiological Basis for the Pragmatic Process of Learning," in *Proceedings of the Midwest Philosophy of Education Society, 1993–1994,* edited by Stickel and David B. Owen (Ames, Iowa: Midwest Philosophy of Education Society, 1995), pp. 195–223;

Stickel, "Presidential Address: Philosophy of Education for the Year 2000 A.D. Chaos Theory and the Philosophy of Charles Peirce," in *Proceedings of the Midwest Philosophy of Education Society, 1991–1992,* edited by Owen (Ames, Iowa: Midwest Philosophy of Education Society, 1993), pp. 3–34;

Victorino Tejera, *Literature, Criticism, and the Theory of Signs* (Philadelphia: Benjamins, 1995);

Richard Tursman, *Peirce's Theory of Scientific Discovery: A System of Logic Conceived as Semiotic* (Bloomington: Indiana University Press, 1987);

Barbara von Eckardt, *What Is Cognitive Science?* (Cambridge, Mass.: MIT Press, 1993);

Paul Weiss and Arthur Burks, "Peirce's Sixty-six Signs," *Journal of Philosophy,* 42 (1945): 383–388;

Philip P. Wiener and Frederic H. Young, eds., *Studies in the Philosophy of Charles Sanders Peirce* (Cambridge, Mass.: Harvard University Press, 1952).

Papers:

Charles Sanders Peirce's papers are in the Houghton Library of Harvard University, with copies at the Peirce Center, Indiana University–Purdue University, Indianapolis, and at Texas Technical University.

Stephen C. Pepper

(29 April 1891 – 1 May 1972)

Lewis E. Hahn
Southern Illinois University at Carbondale

BOOKS: *Modern Color,* by Pepper and Carl Gordon Cutler (Cambridge, Mass.: Harvard University Press / London: Humphrey Milford, Oxford University Press, 1923);

Aesthetic Quality: A Contextualistic Theory of Beauty (New York: Scribners, 1937);

Knowledge and Society: A Philosophical Approach to Modern Civilization, by Pepper, George Plimpton Adams, William Ray Dennes, Jacob Loewenberg, Donald Sage Mackay, Paul Marhenke, and Edward William Strong, as "The University of California Associates" (New York & London: Appleton-Century, 1938);

Selected Writings, by Pepper and other members of the philosophy department of the University of California at Berkeley (New York & London: Appleton-Century, 1940);

World Hypotheses: A Study in Evidence (Berkeley & Los Angeles: University of California Press, 1942; London: Cambridge University Press, 1942);

The Basis of Criticism in the Arts (Cambridge, Mass.: Harvard University Press, 1945);

A Digest of Purposive Values (Berkeley & Los Angeles: University of California Press, 1947; London: Cambridge University Press, 1947);

Principles of Art Appreciation (New York: Harcourt, Brace, 1949);

The Work of Art (Bloomington: Indiana University Press, 1955);

The Sources of Value (Berkeley & Los Angeles: University of California Press, 1958; London: University of California Press, 1958);

Ethics (New York: Appleton-Century-Crofts, 1960);

Concept and Quality: A World Hypothesis (La Salle, Ill.: Open Court, 1967).

OTHER: "Some Questions on Dewey's Esthetics," in *The Philosophy of John Dewey,* edited by Paul Arthur Schilpp, The Library of Living Philosophers, volume 1 (Evanston, Ill. & Chicago: Northwestern University Press, 1939), pp. 371–389;

"Santayana's Theory of Value," in *The Philosophy of George Santayana,* edited by Schilpp, The Library of Living Philosophers, volume 2 (Evanston, Ill. & Chicago: Northwestern University Press, 1940), pp. 217–239;

"Observations on Value from an Analysis of a Simple Appetition," and other comments, in *Value: A Cooperative Inquiry,* edited by Ray Lepley (New York: Columbia University Press, 1949), pp. 245–260, 377–380, 440–450, 454–455;

"A Brief History of the General Theory of Value," in *A History of Philosophical Systems,* edited by Vergilius Ferm (New York: Philosophical Library, 1950), pp. 493–503;

Nathaniel Lawrence, *Whitehead's Philosophical Development: A Critical History of the Background of "Process and Reality,"* foreword by Pepper (Berkeley: University of California Press, 1956);

"Types of Objectivity in Works of Art," in *Proceedings of the Third International Congress on Aesthetics / Atti del III Congresso Internazionale di Estetica* (Turin: Edizioni della Rivista di estetica, Istituto di estetica dell'Università di Torino, 1957), pp. 155–158;

"Evaluation and Discourse" and "Other Comments," in *The Language of Value,* edited by Lepley (New York: Columbia University Press, 1957), pp. 77–93, 283–286;

Andrew Paul Ushenko, *The Field Theory of Meaning,* preface by Pepper (Ann Arbor: University of Michigan Press, 1958);

"A Neural-Identity Theory of Mind," in *Dimensions of Mind: A Symposium,* edited by Sidney Hook (New York: Collier, 1960), pp. 45–61;

"The Art Department," in *Art from Ingres to Pollock: Painting and Sculpture since Neo-Classicism. An Exhibition Inaugurating Alfred L. Kroeber Hall and the Galleries of the Art Department of the University of California* (Berkeley: University of California Press, 1960), pp. 3–12;

"Wieman's Contextual Metaphysics," in *The Empirical Theology of Henry Nelson Wieman,* edited by Robert W. Bretall (New York: Macmillan, 1963), pp. 142–155;

"On Knowledge of Values," in *Mind, Matter, and Method: Essays in Philosophy and Science in Honor of Herbert Feigl,* edited by Paul K. Feyerabend and Grover Maxwell (Minneapolis: University of Minnesota Press, 1966), pp. 328–342;

Antonia Cua, *Reason and Virtue,* foreword by Pepper (Athens: Ohio University Press, 1966);

"Can a Philosophy Make One Philosophical?" in *Essays in Self-Destruction,* edited by Edwin S. Schneidman (New York: Science House, 1967), pp. 169–185;

"Lewis' Theory of Value," in *The Philosophy of C. I. Lewis,* edited by Schilpp, The Library of Living Philosophers, volume 13 (La Salle, Ill.: Open Court, 1968), pp. 489–502;

"The Justification of Aesthetic Judgments," in *Problems of Literary Evaluation,* edited by Joseph Strelka (University Park & London: Pennsylvania State University Press, 1969), pp. 140–152;

"The Search for Comprehension, or World Hypotheses," "The Ordinary Language Movement," and "Existentialism," in *The Nature of Philosophical Inquiry,* edited by Joseph Bobik (Notre Dame, Ind.: University of Notre Dame Press, 1970), pp. 151–167, 169–188, 189–211;

"Metaphor in Philosophy," in *Dictionary of the History of Ideas: Studies of Selected Pivotal Ideas,* volume 3, edited by Philip P. Wiener (New York: Scribners, 1973), pp. 196–201;

"Aesthetics," by Pepper and Thomas Munro, in *Encyclopædia Britannica,* volume 1 (Chicago: Macropaedia, 1974), pp. 149–163;

"Ideals in Retrospect," in *Mid-Twentieth Century American Philosophy: Personal Statements,* edited by Peter A. Bertocci (New York: Humanities Press, 1974), pp. 166–178.

SELECTED PERIODICAL PUBLICATIONS–
UNCOLLECTED: "The Nature of Scientific Matter," *Journal of Philosophy, Psychology and Scientific Methods,* 14 (30 August 1917): 483–491;

"What Is Introspection?" *American Journal of Psychology,* 29 (April 1918): 208–213;

"Changes of Appreciation for Color Combinations," *Psychological Review,* 26 (September 1919): 289–296;

"The Law of Habituation," *Psychological Review,* 28 (January 1921): 63–71;

"The Place of the Critic," *University of California Chronicle,* 23 (April 1921): 105–118;

"A Suggestion Regarding Esthetics," *Journal of Philosophy,* 19 (2 March 1922): 113–118;

"The Boundaries of Society," *International Journal of Ethics,* 22 (July 1922): 420–444;

"Misconceptions Regarding Behaviorism," *Journal of Philosophy,* 20 (26 April 1923): 242–244;

"Art and Utility," *Journal of Philosophy,* 20 (5 July 1923): 373–378;

"The Equivocation of Value," *University of California Publications in Philosophy,* 5 (1923): 107–132;

"Standard Value," *University of California Publications in Philosophy,* 7 (1925): 89–110;

"Description of Aesthetic Experience," *Proceedings of the Sixth International Congress of Philosophy* (1926): 423–427;

"Transcendence," *University of California Publications in Philosophy,* 8 (1926): 51–69;

"Emergence," *Journal of Philosophy,* 23 (29 April 1926): 241–245;

"Le But de l'Esthetique," *Hommes Revue de Philosophie et l'Esthetique,* 1 (April 1927): 111–116;

"The Professional Philosopher," *University of California Chronicle,* 29 (April 1927): 183–195;

"The Argument from Similarity," *Philosophical Review,* 36 (November 1927): 572–581;

"The Fiction of Attribution," *University of California Publications in Philosophy,* 9 (1927): 91–132;

"Philosophy and Metaphor," *Journal of Philosophy,* 25 (1 March 1928): 130–132;

"That a Theory of Universals Must Be Supported by Argument," *Philosophical Review,* 37 (May 1928): 261–264;

"Truth by Continuity," *University of California Publications in Philosophy*, 10 (1928): 27–59;

"Categories," *University of California Publications in Philosophy*, 13 (1930): 73–98;

"Middle-Sized Facts," *University of California Publications in Philosophy*, 14 (March 1932): 3–28;

"How to Look for Causality–an Example of Philosophic Method," *University of California Publications in Philosophy*, 15 (May 1932): 179–203;

"The Conceptual Framework of Tolman's Purposive Behaviorism," *Psychological Review*, 41 (March 1934): 108–133;

"A Contextualistic Theory of Possibility," *University of California Publications in Philosophy*, 17 (1934): 177–197;

"The Root-Metaphor Theory of Metaphysics," *Journal of Philosophy*, 32 (4 July 1935): 365–374;

"Aesthetics for the Layman," *San Francisco Art Association Bulletin*, 2 (November 1935): 2–3;

"The Order of Time," *University of California Publications in Philosophy*, 18 (1935): 3–20;

"The Quest for Ignorance or the Reasonable Limits of Skepticism," *Philosophical Review*, 45 (March 1936): 126–143;

"On the Cognitive Value of World Hypotheses," *Journal of Philosophy*, 33 (8 October 1936): 575–577;

"A Criticism of a Positivistic Theory of Mind," *University of California Publications in Philosophy*, 19 (1936): 211–232;

"The Individuality of a Work of Art," *University of California Publications in Philosophy*, 20 (1937): 81–98;

"A Convergence Theory of Similarity," *Philosophical Review*, 46 (November 1937): 496–608;

"The Arts without Artists," *American Scholar*, 7 (Autumn 1938): 403–408;

"What Is Good Taste?" *College of the Pacific Publications in Philosophy*, 2 (1938): 78–93;

"Art among the Liberal Arts," *Department of Art Education Bulletin*, 5 (1939): 122–127;

"Definition," *University of California Publications in Philosophy*, 21 (1939): 99–122;

"How to Fit Universities for Artists," *American Scholar*, 9 (Spring 1940): 192–200;

"Universities Discover Art," *Parnassus*, 12 (October 1940): 14–16;

"The Conditions of Social Control," *University of California Publications in Philosophy*, 23 (1942): 29–47;

"Metaphysical Method," *Philosophical Review*, 52 (May 1943): 252–269;

"The Esthetic Object," *Journal of Philosophy*, 40 (2 September 1943): 477–482;

"Reply to Professor Hoekstra," *Journal of Philosophy*, 42 (15 February 1945): 101–108;

"The Descriptive Definition," *Journal of Philosophy*, 43 (17 January 1946): 29–36;

"Art in the American College and University," *College Art Journal*, 5 (March 1946): 194–200;

"The Outlook for Aesthetics," *Kenyon Review*, 8 (Spring 1946): 179–187;

"Emotional Distance in Art," *Journal of Aesthetics and Art Criticism*, 4 (June 1946): 235–239;

"Art as a Vital Function," *Kenyon Review*, 8 (Autumn 1946): 668–672;

"The Artist in Our Society," *Agnes Scott Alumnae Quarterly*, 25 (Spring 1947): 3–5;

"What Are Categories For?" *Journal of Philosophy*, 44 (25 September 1947): 546–556;

"Values and Value Judgments," *Journal of Philosophy*, 46 (7 July 1948): 429–434;

"Aiken's 'Criteria for an Adequate Aesthetics': A Symposium," by Pepper, George Boas, C. J. Ducasse, and Katherine Gilbert, *Journal of Aesthetics and Art Criticism*, 7 (December 1948): 148–158;

"The Art of Delight and the Art of Relief," *Philosophy and Phenomenological Research*, 9 (March 1949): 480–485;

"Creative Training," *College Art Journal*, 9 (Spring 1950): 273–278;

"The Problem of Teacher Training in Art," *College Art Journal*, 9 (Spring 1950): 284–289;

"The Issue over the Facts," *University of California Publications in Philosophy*, 25 (1950): 121–139;

"Further Consideration of the Aesthetic Work of Art," *Journal of Philosophy*, 49 (10 April 1952): 274–279;

"A Balanced Art Department," *College Art Journal*, 11 (Spring 1952): 166–171;

"On Professor Jarrett's Questions about the Aesthetic Object," *Journal of Philosophy*, 49 (25 September 1952): 633–641;

"Is Non-objective Art Superficial?" *Journal of Aesthetics and Art Criticism*, 11 (March 1953): 255–261;

"The Concept of Fusion in Dewey's Aesthetic Theory," *Journal of Aesthetics and Art Criticism*, 12 (December 1953): 169–176;

"The Ethics of Engineers," *Journal of Industrial Engineering*, 5 (September 1954): 14–16;

"Natural Norms in Ethics," *Journal of Philosophy*, 53 (5 January 1956): 9–15;

"Discriminations in a Kandinsky Abstraction," *Horizon*, 1 (Spring–Summer 1956): 4–8;

"Looking at a Painting by El Greco," *Idea and Experiment*, 1 (March 1957): 4–7;

"Berkeley's Uses of the Test of Certainty," *University of California Publications in Philosophy*, 29 (1957): 89–105;

"The Criterion of Relevancy in Aesthetics: A Discussion. 1. The Alleged Circularity of the Relevancy

Criterion in Art Criticism," *Journal of Aesthetics and Art Criticism,* 16 (December 1957): 202–207;

"The Criterion of Relevancy in Aesthetics: A Discussion. 3. A Reply to Karl Potter's Criticism," *Journal of Aesthetics and Art Criticism,* 16 (December 1957): 214–216;

"Art and Experience," *Review of Metaphysics,* 12 (December 1958): 294–299;

"Sanctions versus Reasons for Value Judgments," *Ethics,* 70 (January 1960): 109–117;

"Liberal Education for an Adjustable Society," *School and Society,* 89 (11 March 1961): 102;

"The Philosophy of Julius Seelye Bixler," *Colby Library Quarterly,* series 5, no. 11 (September 1961): 287–295;

"Whitehead's 'Actual Occasion,'" *Tulane Studies in Philosophy,* 10 (1961): 71–88;

"Universality and Uniqueness in Art," *The Arts and Philosophy,* no. 3 (Spring 1962): 11–14;

"Evaluative Definitions and Their Sanctions," *Journal of Aesthetics and Art Criticism,* 21 (Winter 1962): 201–208;

"Honors Programs in the Arts," *Newsletter of the Inter-University Committee on the Superior Student,* 5 (May–June 1963): 10–12;

"A Proposal for a World Hypothesis," *Monist,* 47 (Winter 1963): 267–286;

"Controlled Experimentation in Criticism," *Journal of Aesthetics and Art Criticism,* 23 (Fall 1964): 153–158;

"On the Relation of Philosophy to Art," *Revue internationale de philosophie,* 18, nos. 68–69 (1964): 183–192;

"The Work of Art Described from a Double Dispositional Base," *Journal of Aesthetics and Art Criticism,* 23 (Summer 1965): 421–427;

"An Essay on the Essay: An Aesthetic Appreciation," *New Scholasticism,* 41 (Summer 1967): 295–311;

"On the Uses of Symbolism in Sculpture and Painting," *Philosophy East and West,* 19 (July 1969): 266–278;

"Survival Value," *Journal of Value Inquiry,* 3 (Fall 1969): 180–186; republished in *Zygon,* 4 (September 1969): 4–11;

"Autobiography of an Aesthetics," *Journal of Aesthetics and Art Criticism,* 28 (Spring 1970): 275–286;

"Feibleman's Aesthetic Theory," *Studium Generale,* 24, no. 6/7 (July 1971): 660–672;

"A Dynamic View of Perception," *Philosophy and Phenomenological Research,* 32 (September 1971): 42–46;

"On 'The Case for Systems Philosophy,'" *Metaphilosophy,* 3 (April 1972): 151–153;

"Systems Philosophy as a World Hypothesis," *Philosophy and Phenomenological Research,* 32 (June 1972): 548–553.

Stephen C. Pepper was one of the most original philosophers of the twentieth century. A leader in aesthetics and art appreciation and a forceful proponent of empiricism in ethics and value theory, he provided an empirical account of metaphysics that drew on the arts, as well as the sciences. For him metaphysics was central to philosophy, and he thought of metaphysical theories—or, as he preferred to call them, "world hypotheses"—as ways of marshaling the evidence in support of the major treatments of the subject matters of such fields as ethics, aesthetics, and general value theory. He was dubious of claims to certainty or infallibility and was convinced that the evidence did not point to any one aesthetics or theory of criticism as the correct one. Rather, he maintained that at least five relatively adequate aesthetic views were supported by a like number of world hypotheses of roughly equal adequacy, each hypothesis stemming from a fruitful "root metaphor." In addition to developing a new conception of metaphysics, he originated a world hypothesis of his own and made major contributions to various traditional views; he made similar contributions in ethics, aesthetics, theory of criticism, and the general theory of value.

Stephen Coburn Pepper was born in Newark, New Jersey, on 29 April 1891 to Charles Hovey and Frances Coburn Pepper. The Coburns owned vast timberlands in Maine, and Pepper's great-uncle Abner was governor of the state. His father was a well-known painter, and his grandfather, George Dana Boardman Pepper, was a Northern Baptist minister and president of Colby College, to which Abner Coburn left a substantial part of his fortune.

Pepper spent much of his first eight years in Paris, before his family settled in Concord, Massachusetts, so that he could attend school in the United States. But travel continued to form part of his education. Shortly before his twelfth birthday, as he says in the journal he began at that time and kept, off and on, for almost seventy years, the family traveled to Japan and on around the world, visiting temples, art centers, museums, art galleries, and places his father wanted to paint. He and his father devised a game in which each picked out the pictures he liked best in a room; then they compared notes, and each would say why he chose the pictures he did. Pepper later recorded in his journal that the game "was a wonderful education" for a future aesthetician, and he did not recall that his father ever embarrassed him for his choices: "Father had a wide tolerance and he let me like what I liked, and he showed me how much he liked what he liked and all the things he saw to like, and these trips through galleries were as if we were two boys on a fishing trip. I would simply get tired sooner than father or mother and sometimes would have to tag along for quite awhile or dangle my feet from the settee till they got through."

After the world trip, Pepper's parents hired tutors to enable him to catch up with his schoolwork. He then attended public schools in Concord. Pepper's only sibling, a sister, Eunice, was born on 28 January 1906; the difference in their ages was so great, he later said, that it was almost as if each of them was an only child. He finished his precollege work at Browne and Nichols School in Cambridge before enrolling at Harvard University, where he received his A.B. in 1913. A course with G. H. Palmer had convinced him that he wanted a career in philosophy rather than in law or poetry, despite Palmer's comments about the difficulty of finding a job in the field. As Pepper saw it, with the death of William James in 1909, the departure of George Santayana in 1911, and Josiah Royce's stroke, which left him voluble but less sharp, the heroic era of the Harvard philosophy department had just passed. The main weight of the graduate program was carried by Ralph Barton Perry, William E. Hocking, James H. Woods, and R. F. Alfred Hoernlé. The brightest students, including Pepper, Raphael Demos, R. M. Eaton, and Victor Lenzen, flocked to Perry's seminars in theory of knowledge and theory of value and insisted on logical and factual analysis. If a philosopher's statements would not submit to this mode of analysis, Pepper and his fellow graduate students regarded him as incompetent or insincere; John Dewey, with what Pepper called "his slithery and ambiguous terms," was their model of incompetence. The objective idealists Hocking and Hoernlé also had their reservations about Dewey. Pepper later admitted that at this stage he was so committed to mechanistic analysis that he was blind to what Bosanquetian idealists such as Hoernlé were trying to show him.

Pepper received his A.M. in philosophy from Harvard in 1914. On 14 February 1914 he married Ellen Hoar, the daughter of Congressman Sherman Hoar, who had died while attempting to improve sanitary conditions in army camps during the Spanish-American War. They had three children: Sherman Hoar, who died at sixteen in an accident; Elizabeth Hoar; and Frances Coburn.

Pepper completed a dissertation under Perry titled "A Behavioristic Theory of Value" in 1916. The theory is rather naive, but it is important in showing his thoroughgoing commitment to a naturalistic view at this early stage. His first scholarly article, "The Nature of Scientific Matter," which appeared in the 30 August 1917 issue of *The Journal of Philosophy, Psychology and Scien-*

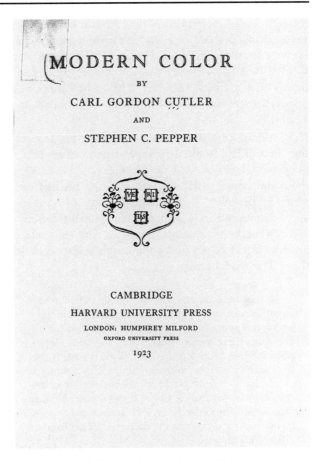

[MODERN COLOR

BY

CARL GORDON CUTLER

AND

STEPHEN C. PEPPER

CAMBRIDGE
HARVARD UNIVERSITY PRESS
LONDON: HUMPHREY MILFORD
OXFORD UNIVERSITY PRESS
1923

Title page for Pepper's first book, for which he did most of the writing but in which most of the ideas were those of the artist Cutler (Clemson University Library)

tific Methods, is a condensation of a portion of the dissertation in which he sketches the then-novel view that refined scientific data are primarily visual and that other qualitative data are reducible to them. This notion became a commonplace a decade or so later in discussions of pointer readings.

Pepper's support of World War I was based on his naturalistic theory of value. Initially, he accepted a cultural or even national relativism on the ground that no objective moral sanctions exist beyond those enforced by the group of which one is a member; but after becoming persuaded of the feasibility of President Woodrow Wilson's ideal of a world government capable of enforcing universal democracy, he decided that such a government could claim sanctioning power over national groups and might well bring into existence a universal human morality.

In 1916–1917 Pepper had an instructorship at Wellesley College. He then spent several months assisting Perry with a civilian war project in Washington, D.C., before enlisting in the army. After the war, philosophy jobs were scarce, as Palmer had predicted, but through Jacob Loewenberg, whom he had met at Harvard, Pepper learned of a teaching assistantship at the University of California in Berkeley. Working under George P. Adams, Pepper was the philosophy department's first graduate assistant. The assistantship was followed by a one-year instructorship in aesthetics for 1920–1921.

Almost immediately after completing his dissertation, Pepper had begun work on an empiricist aesthetics titled "The Laws of Art." He spent most of his time on the manuscript in 1918–1919 and during his first two years in Berkeley. In this factual study of aesthetic appreciation and its objects Pepper, with his commitment to mechanistic naturalism, deals with the materials and forms of art and with people's responses to them. The work begins:

> Just as there are physical, biological, and economic laws there are aesthetic laws. The organization of these laws into a system is the science of aesthetics. What distinguishes these laws from other laws and makes it possible to bring them together in a single system is that they deal with a specific subject matter. This consists in the things we like or dislike for themselves—or technically primary values. . . . Other things we like because they are means to things we like themselves. . . . Aesthetics may be defined as the science of things liked or disliked for themselves.

The first part of the work deals with "elementary likings and simple combinations of these composed of the qualitative aesthetic materials of sound, color, line, mass, meaning, and temporal and spatial rhythm." The second part treats syntheses of these elements into the larger organizations or groupings that constitute the arts of architecture, sculpture, painting, music, literature, dancing, and drama; it also includes a chapter on the appreciation of nature.

In 1922 Pepper submitted the manuscript to Yale University Press; it was rejected, and Pepper did not send it to any other publishers. But it provided the content for the highly successful introductory yearlong course on comparative aesthetics that he offered throughout his years at Berkeley.

In 1919 Pepper collaborated with the artist Carl Gordon Cutler on *Modern Color,* which became his first published book when it appeared in 1923; Pepper did not really regard it as his own work, since, although he did the writing, most of the ideas are Cutler's. In Paris during the academic year 1922–1923 Pepper wrote "The Cultivation of Taste," a much shorter manuscript than "The Laws of Art," in which he applies the general principles of that work to the special problem of enlarging one's taste. He sent it to Macmillan in 1924, and it, too, was rejected.

Introductory classes at the University of California consisted of three hundred or more students, depending on the size of the room, and at that time the university did not have adequate audio equipment. Pepper practiced speaking so that he could be heard clearly without amplification. He worked hard on both the content and the mechanics of his lectures; his material was fresh, well organized, and clearly delivered, and his own conviction of its importance, along with his obvious enjoyment of what he was doing, came through to the students. A large man, slightly more than six feet tall, attired in tweeds, friendly and genial, he was an impressive figure in front of a classroom and was even more effective in a graduate seminar, where issues could be explored at greater depth. His infectious chuckle had a pleasant effect even on students who might not have found the idea as funny as he did. His counsel was sought after, and he was an active and influential participant in faculty meetings. For some years he thought that he was more effective at communicating his ideas orally than in writing.

Adams and other colleagues at Berkeley helped to modify the dogmatic analytic orientation Pepper had brought with him from Harvard. As Adams's assistant, he was in direct contact with a leading philosopher whose approach included borrowings from Dewey and Plato. Adams's sympathetic treatment of Dewey gave Pepper second thoughts about his own position, but what really awakened him from his dogmatic slumber was a lengthy discussion with the pragmatist George Herbert Mead. On Adams's recommendation Mead had invited Pepper to teach courses on aesthetics and another on philosophy of nature in the 1924 summer session at the University of Chicago. The evening before Mead departed for the summer, the two philosophers talked in Mead's office until midnight. To Pepper's surprise, pragmatism, at least in the hands of Mead, turned out not to be a weak position supported by lax reasoning. Its categories were quite different from those of Pepper's atomic mechanism or naturalism, but, operating within them, Mead was able to supply a highly plausible interpretation of any experienced facts Pepper brought up and had ready answers for his arguments. For the first time in his life Pepper saw what the pragmatic position really was, and it came as a revelation. As he reflected on the discussion in the following days, he became convinced that what he had taken to be simple facts were facts as viewed through "atomistic spectacles" and that the pragmatic account was as well based as his own atomic naturalism.

The evening with Mead helped various other things fall into place for Pepper. In November 1923 he and his friend, the Berkeley psychologist Edward C. Tolman, had had extensive discussions in Giessen, Ger-

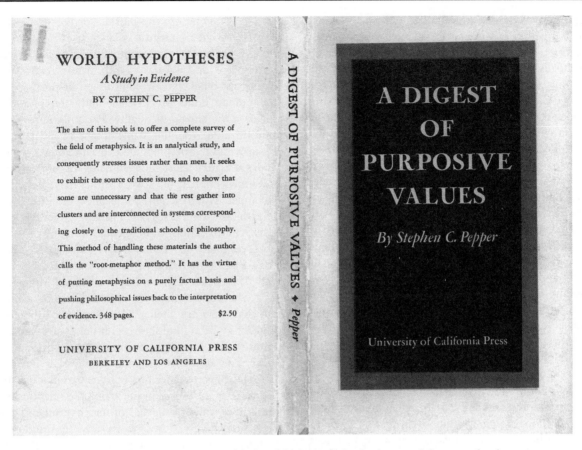

WORLD HYPOTHESES

A Study in Evidence

BY STEPHEN C. PEPPER

The aim of this book is to offer a complete survey of the field of metaphysics. It is an analytical study, and consequently stresses issues rather than men. It seeks to exhibit the source of these issues, and to show that some are unnecessary and that the rest gather into clusters and are interconnected in systems corresponding closely to the traditional schools of philosophy. This method of handling these materials the author calls the "root-metaphor method." It has the virtue of putting metaphysics on a purely factual basis and pushing philosophical issues back to the interpretation of evidence. 348 pages. $2.50

UNIVERSITY OF CALIFORNIA PRESS

BERKELEY AND LOS ANGELES

A DIGEST OF PURPOSIVE VALUES ✦ Pepper

A DIGEST OF PURPOSIVE VALUES

By Stephen C. Pepper

University of California Press

Dust jacket for Pepper's 1947 brief version of the theory of value that he expounded at greater length
in The Sources of Value *in 1958 (Bruccoli Clark Layman Archives)*

many, with the Gestalt psychologist Kurt Koffka. In keeping with his method of analysis Pepper had opposed Koffka's thesis that complex patterns, or Gestalts, exist that are ultimate and irreducible and not analyzable without residue into elements. His evening with Mead helped him to see that Koffka's way of viewing things disclosed important features of experience.

Thus, by making Pepper see that what he had taken to be one of the weakest of worldviews was actually one of the strongest, Mead led Pepper to rethink his position. If even pragmatism—or contextualism, as he called it—proved to be relatively adequate, another look at the views of Plato, Aristotle, Georg Wilhelm Friedrich Hegel, Hoernlé, and Palmer was warranted. As a result of the spiritual awakening occasioned by the evening with Mead, Pepper became so interested in the implications of contextualism that he engaged in several contextuatistic studies. He presented the results of some of these studies at the annual meetings of the University of California Philosophical Union. William Pepperell Montague, who was at Berkeley as Mills Lecturer from Columbia University, called Pepper's 1928 presentation "Truth by Continuity" the finest philoso-

phy paper he had ever heard. In this piece Pepper criticizes the account of the experience of similarity given by Platonic immanent realists and maintains that judgments of similarity are not judgments about hypothetical eternal qualities inhering in hypothetical points of space-time but are rather, as the pragmatists claim, judgments about convergent processes in experience. If two or more patterns converge on an identical response, they are similar; truth is a matter of continuities of such patterns as human organisms, measuring rods, clocks, and scales.

In January 1929 Dartmouth College offered Pepper a full professorship; he seriously considered it but decided to remain at the University of California. His promotion to full professor at Berkeley came in 1930.

In 1928 Pepper had begun writing a monograph, "The Philosophy of Criticism." When Dewey's *Art as Experience* appeared in 1934, Pepper read it to see how his own chapter on contextualistic aesthetics in "The Philosophy of Criticism" compared with this systematic work by the leading contextualist. To his surprise, Dewey's development of the view only partially corresponded to his. As he considered the differences, he became convinced that what he had written was more in accord with a consistently developed contextualistic aesthetics than Dewey's. He expanded the chapter on contextualistic aesthetics in "The Philosophy of Criticism" into *Aesthetic Quality: A Contextualistic Theory of Beauty* (1937), in which he shows, without engaging in polemics with advocates of alternative views, what he thinks a consistent pragmatist or contextualist should say. Pepper defines the aesthetic field for the contextualist as that of events with enhanced quality: "quality is the life of art, organization the body." By *quality* Pepper means immediately intuited experience, the "feel" of things–something on the order of Dewey's "had quality." Each event has a distinctive character, which is experienced as a totality; but distinctions can be made in it, each of which corresponds to a strand with its quality; and each event also has its relational structure or texture of strands. So one may say either that the quality of the texture is diffused into the strands or that the details are so fused into the perception of the whole that only subsequent analysis shows their number and diversity. Pepper explains quality through a detailed discussion of a Japanese print by Hiroshige.

It is commonly held that practical activity, conflict, analysis, and regularity are the chief hindrances to the realization of quality, but according to Pepper, "what kills beauty in big doses, is its greatest stimulant in moderation"; one of his most original contributions in *Aesthetic Quality* is his detailed documentation of this thesis. For him, novelty and conflict are the two chief means of enhancing quality. The artist uses novelty to help the viewer appreciate the uniqueness of events and to freshen his or her experience of them, but to intensify quality most effectively the artist must both set up conflicts and control them. The problem is not to resolve conflicts in some overall harmony but to hold them before the viewer so that their quality may be savored. Blocking the viewer's drives generates emotion, which strips away habit and reveals the qualities of things. Emotion, for Pepper, "is the very essence of quality"–indeed, it is "the very quality of the event itself when this event is voluminous, intense, and highly fused." It is also a means for enlarging the spread of quality.

Analysis and regularity, two alleged enemies of the aesthetic, have a special relationship to organization: "regularity is by and large the method of organization, and analysis is simply rendering explicit the elements of the method." Organization contributes to the increase of quality by extending its spread and depth. Without organization one does not have massive beauty. In his principal discussion of the topic Pepper treats three modes of organization on the basis of whether the elements of it are intrinsic to the work of art, are drawn from the outside, or are part one and part the other: intrinsic elements are pattern and design; extrinsic elements are "funded social interests," "schemes," and "scales"; and intrinsic-extrinsic elements are types. Pattern and design help to overcome the human limits of attention and interest and thus increase the spread of quality. Pattern combats confusion through grouping, while design attacks monotony by providing variety. Funded social interests, schemes, and scales that exist independently of, and are never fully incorporated in, a work of art may, nonetheless, be tapped by it to acquire for itself the organizing values of fashions, manners, laws, forms of government, customs, mores, and fundamental human drives. He observes that a novel such as *Vanity Fair* (1848) assumes the social organization of England at the time of William Makepeace Thackeray. Although this organization as a whole is not depicted in the novel, the actions of the characters are intelligible in terms of their relationship to, say, the English army. If the reader knows, for instance, that George Osborne is an officer in the army, the organization obtained for the novel is not simply that of the events described or suggested in it but that of the place of an officer in the army, the relationships of the army to other branches of the government, and so on. Accordingly, the reader readily understands Osborne's being in Belgium when Napoleon's army is advancing and sees his death as something that happens in a soldier's line of duty. In this way the organization of the army functions extrinsically to organize the book. Although schemes, which are systematic summaries of discriminations, and scales, which are selections of elements out of a scheme according to some rule, are abstract and relational, they function extrinsically in much the same way as do funded social interests.

Types, Pepper's third principal mode of organization, are extrinsic in that they exist independently of any particular work of art but intrinsic in that they appear fully, or almost fully, in the work. Types are groups of related strands that appear fully or almost fully in individual objects and are repeatable in other individual objects. The organizing power of types "is more evident than that of any other mode of organization"; they bring into art the value of recognition, a value that has been appreciated since at least the time of Plato and Aristotle. So types provide both an effective means of enhancing quality and a ready and secure organization. As might be expected from its definition of the aesthetic field, the contextualistic theory of criticism holds that the primary aesthetic judgment is, "This is a texture vivid in quality"; and the more vivid the quality and the richer and more extensive its spread, the greater its aesthetic value.

Aesthetic Quality was praised more enthusiastically and universally by reviewers than were any of Pepper's other books. Pepper was especially pleased by Irwin Edman's review in *The Journal of Philosophy* (Summer 1938) because, next to Dewey, he considered Edman the greatest contextualistic aesthetician of the time. Edman called the book "one of the most illuminating and engaging contributions to esthetics that has appeared in many years" and declared that "Professor Pepper is at his best in his explanation of what quality is, and how it is enhanced and apprehended. . . . The book is engaging and persuasive, because it avoids merely invidious polemics, frankly states the point of view from which it is written: that of a modified pragmatism, called by Professor Pepper 'contextualism.'" He added that the book "is convincing because with sensitiveness and scrupulousness it indicates and clarifies the organizations and schemes, psychological and technical, which contribute both to the enhancement and spread of esthetic quality." Each chapter "is an admirable study either of the fact of 'quality,' or the contexts in which quality varies, and the schemes on which it depends."

By 1938 Pepper had finished the manuscript for "The Philosophy of Criticism," which had grown to more than 550 pages. The work marks a break from his earlier exclusive reliance on dogmatic analytic mechanism and presents two of his most original contributions to philosophy: his conception of the root metaphor as a source of categories for a worldview and the idea that sound criticism is based on criteria derived from a relatively adequate world hypothesis. Its plan, as he sketches it in an unpublished autobiography based on his journals, "consists of giving the world hypothesis that serves as the broad empirical support of each major type of aesthetic criticism, following that with a description of the aesthetic theory that comes out of the world theory, and following the aesthetic theory with the study of the critic of recognized prestige who employed critical criteria based on the aesthetic theory." Pepper sent the manuscript to Charles Scribner's Sons, which had published *Aesthetic Quality*. The firm rejected it because the editors thought that it fell between two subject matters, metaphysics and aesthetics, and was not marketable as either of them and, hence, not marketable at all. Pepper accepted the judgment as final and did not try elsewhere; but he later noted in his unpublished autobiography that he should not have given up so easily, because this work, though "dated" by the time of his later reflection on it, was "the most elegantly planned book" he ever wrote, "unique in its design, and important for its well supported doctrine."

Pepper spelled out his reservations about Dewey's account in *Art as Experience* in his essay "Some

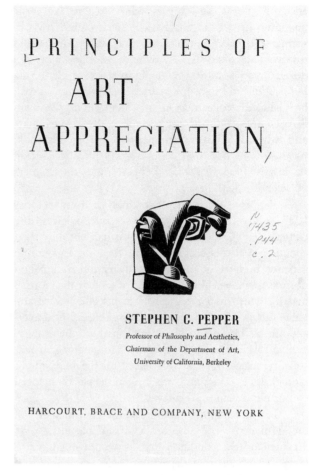

PRINCIPLES OF

ART

APPRECIATION

STEPHEN C. PEPPER

Professor of Philosophy and Aesthetics,
Chairman of the Department of Art,
University of California, Berkeley

HARCOURT, BRACE AND COMPANY, NEW YORK

Title page for Pepper's 1949 book, based on his lectures for his introductory aesthetics course (Thomas Cooper Library, University of South Carolina)

Questions on Dewey's Esthetics" in the opening volume of the Library of Living Philosophers series, *The Philosophy of John Dewey* (1939). He reports that he was excited to find that all of the features he had considered important were also emphasized by Dewey, together with others along the same line that he had not previously thought of; but he was surprised to find Dewey making some statements along organic idealistic lines that he himself had deliberately excluded. He argues that the pragmatic aesthetics is inconsistent in key respects with an organistic aesthetics and that to attempt to combine the two in one work minimizes the distinctive insights of the two views and adulterates and confuses their basic thrusts.

As Pepper summed up his publication record in his unpublished autobiography, by the time he was forty-seven he had written, as sole author, five books, two of them of major proportions, and only one, and that "a rather small one, had been published." He compared his success ratio in publication with the experience of salmon and turtles who have to lay large quantities of eggs to ensure one or two surviving offspring. He had written more than fifty articles and reviews, co-edited with Adams and Loewenberg a dozen or so volumes of the University of California Publications in Philosophy series, and co-authored with his California colleagues Adams, Loewenberg, William Ray Dennes, Donald Sage Mackay, Paul Marhenke, and Edward William Strong a widely used textbook, *Knowledge and Society: A Philosophical Approach to Modern Civilization* (1938), for which Pepper drafted the chapters on scientific method.

Pepper underwent psychoanalysis from October 1937 to July 1941 for some serious psychological difficulties. He believed that the analysis had not only therapeutic but also educational value for him: it gave him a better understanding of personality integration and normal mental health; and the concept of the normal person, which had a basic role in his later ethics and value theory, seemed to him to be not a statistical average but, as he says in his unpublished autobiography, "a natural norm of fully integrated functioning of personality structure" that was based on the individual's biological capacities and was "much deeper than social conformity to cultural patterns."

In 1938 Pepper was offered the chairmanship of the University of California art department. He accepted on the condition that he would not have to leave the philosophy department. He was convinced that Harvard and many other top universities had overemphasized scholarly and scientific values and neglected or disparaged aesthetic ones; he wanted to correct this situation, and Berkeley seemed to him ideally suited to carry out this mission. As he notes in his unpublished autobiography, the University of California "was burgeoning with greatness and was not yet hardened with tradition. New ideas could get rooted in spite of the expected obstacles, and once started, the growing reputation of the University could give them national recognition and support." He had the active support of the highly respected philosophy department, and other faculty members, such as music department chairman Albert Elkus, were eager to press for the same ends. In 1939 the path to change was made easier when Pepper was appointed assistant dean of letters and science, giving him supervision of all of the arts and some of the social sciences. By the end of his term as chairman a harmonious, solid, and vital department had been established; practicing artists had achieved academic recognition; and the department had grown in academic esteem.

While he was undergoing psychoanalysis, Pepper learned of a Harvard analyst's claim that philosophers, unlike engineers or physicists, tended to lose interest in their specialty under analysis. Believing that his "root metaphor" concept had important philosophical implications, he wanted to develop some of them for publication before he lost interest in the subject. Expanding the sections on metaphysics from his "Philosophy of Criticism" manuscript, he worked feverishly every hour he could spare in 1939 and 1940 to produce *World Hypotheses: A Study in Evidence* (1942). The fear that motivated him to write the book turned out to be unfounded: he retained a lively interest in philosophy to the end of his life.

In *World Hypotheses* Pepper maintains that metaphysical theories—or world hypotheses, as he calls them—can be studied and described, just as scientists study the objects of their specialties. World hypotheses are general accounts of what exists and how one comes to know it. They seek knowledge of any and all facts or experiences, whereas scientific hypotheses have restricted ranges of application. A world hypothesis is an integrated explanatory or interpretive account of the order and meaning of the full range of things, events, or happenings and their values or significance.

According to Pepper, most proponents of metaphysical theories have denied that their views were hypothetical, claiming that they were certain and indubitable. Pepper devotes the first part of *World Hypotheses* to arguing against such claims, maintaining that neither logic nor the history of past claims supports them and pointing out that they block investigation instead of encouraging a search for evidence. Like Charles Sanders Peirce, he holds that theoretical certainty is neither necessary nor desirable; claims to such certainty are fairly sure to be forms of dogmatism, which he defines as belief in excess of what the evidence warrants. One should steer a course between dogmatism and utter skepticism or disbelief, for both of these extremes go beyond the available evidence. He distinguishes two main kinds of evidence: "criticized" or "refined evidence" is critical knowledge that is definite, consistent, reasoned, and responsible but at times thin and abstract; "uncriticized" evidence is what Plato called "opinion"—the domain of common sense, "middle-sized facts," or "dubitanda." Knowledge, Pepper says, begins with this sort of precritical evidence rather than with some alleged certainty. Although no proponent of a refined theory is completely happy with common sense, because of its many shortcomings, each theory must use common sense to check its own findings.

But common sense calls for corroboration, which, Pepper says, takes two main forms: multiplicative corroboration is largely a matter of checking one person's observations against another's; structural corroboration consists in checking facts against facts and is predominantly the method of hypothesis. Pepper calls the products of multiplicative corroboration "data" and those of structural corroboration "danda." He illustrates the two kinds of corroboration by the example of how one may determine whether a chair is strong enough to support a person's weight. One can try sitting in it and ask some of one's friends to do likewise; if all agree that the chair is strong enough, its strength has been confirmed by multiplicative corroboration. Alternatively, one can investigate the way the chair is constructed, the materials of which it is made, and its present condition and judge that it is strong enough; this procedure is structural corroboration. The two main kinds of refined data are empirical and logical; nearly ideal exemplifications of the two are pointer readings and correlations among pointer readings for empirical data and such logical or mathematical rules as those of substitution, adjunction, and inference for logical data. The best illustrations of danda are the products of world hypotheses, for hypotheses of unrestricted scope provide the most extended corroboration of facts by facts. Empirical and logical data are elements of invariant evidence, but danda vary with the hypothesis; and in a world hypothesis, fact and interpretation tend to merge in a dandum. Accordingly, the strength of data comes mainly from their invariancy, and the persuasiveness of danda is based on the mass of evidence converging on the same point of fact.

The logical positivists were the most extreme opponents of metaphysics, calling it nonsensical. As Pepper interprets their position, their attack on metaphysics is based on the belief that knowledge ideally consists only of refined data and that structural corroboration is misguided or unnecessary. Pepper argues, however, that their opposition to metaphysics falls into either dogmatism or inconsistency. The undogmatic positivists must show that both common sense and danda can be interpreted in terms of data, and to do so they need a structural theory of their own. In other words, to maintain refined data as the sole norm of evidence, they must assemble their data in such a way as to drive out the claims of danda from various structural worldviews. But multiplicative corroboration alone is not sufficient for this purpose.

As Pepper sees it, the process of structural corroboration sets up a drive for hypotheses of unlimited scope and maximum precision, for "in terms of the corroboration of fact with fact one can never be quite assured that a hypothesis is precisely adequate to a fact under consideration unless he believes that no fact would fail to corroborate it." Thus, increasing the precision of a world hypothesis goes hand in hand with increasing its scope. By "being precisely adequate" Pepper means having the hypothesis exactly fit, conform to, apply to, describe, or refer to the facts under consideration.

THE SOURCES OF

VALUE

Stephen C. Pepper

UNIVERSITY OF CALIFORNIA PRESS
Berkeley and Los Angeles
1958

Title page for Pepper's magnum opus in the theory of value, in which he deals with "the problem of how to make well-grounded decisions in human affairs" (Thomas Cooper Library, University of South Carolina)

Pepper's "root metaphor" theory of the origin and development of world hypotheses is one of his most original contributions to philosophy. In formulating both world hypotheses and more restricted hypotheses, he says, one looks back over one's past experience for some analogous situation that might be applicable to the present problem. In the case of the world hypothesis, one is puzzled about the nature of the universe as a whole and casts about, as Pepper puts it in his later article "Metaphor in Philosophy" (1973), "for some pregnant experience that appears to be a good sample of the nature of things." This sample is one's basic analogy or root metaphor. One then analyzes the sample, discriminates its structural features, and generalizes them into a world hypothesis. Thus, for Pepper, as for Alfred North Whitehead, speculative philosophy begins with a restricted area of commonsense experience and checks to see whether its structure can be generalized to apply to the interpretation of other areas.

Pepper holds that there are only as many major world hypotheses as there are fruitful root metaphors. This number, he thinks, is probably ten or under, and the number of relatively adequate world hypotheses might well be even fewer. In *World Hypotheses* he describes at some length four that he regards as roughly equal in adequacy: the "formism" of Plato and Aristotle, from the root metaphor of similarity of form; the "mechanism" of Democritus, Epicurus, Lucretius, René Descartes, John Locke, and Isaac Newton, from the root metaphor of the machine; the "organicism" or absolute idealism of Friedrich Wilhelm Joseph von Schelling, Hegel, F. H. Bradley, Bernard Bosanquet, Royce, and Brand Blanshard, from the root metaphor of the organism; and the "contextualism," or pragmatism, of Peirce, James, Henri Bergson, Dewey, and Mead, from the root metaphor of the historical event.

The adequacy of a world hypothesis can be evaluated, first, in terms of scope and precision. To be a world hypothesis at all a view must claim unlimited scope, but this claim "is more a matter of intent and accepted responsibility than a matter of actual test." One can, however, check on a view's ability to deal with traditional philosophical problems and on how extensively it uses the label *unreal:* if most items of common sense are ruled out as unreal by the view, questions arise as to its scope. The criterion of precision includes consistency, coherence, variety, and fruitfulness. A second test of the adequacy of a world hypothesis is whether it keeps its basic analogy in view. A hypothesis that loses touch with its root metaphor in common sense tends to resort to empty abstractions and to become diffuse and imprecise. Trying to combine two or more root metaphors is confusing and, far from providing the best fruits of the component metaphors, is likely to prevent them from developing their distinctive potentialities. The time to try eclecticism, as Pepper sees it, is after each major view has been given a full opportunity to make its distinctive contribution. Pepper admits that nearly all of the great philosophers were eclectic to some degree; but their greatness, he argues, is derived from their creativity rather than their eclecticism, which actually hindered the realization of the cognitive possibilities of their new ideas. The third and most assured way of judging the adequacy of world hypotheses is to turn to the relatively adequate world hypotheses themselves. Each of them, according to Pepper, has its own theory of truth, through which it evaluates its own adequacy and points to its own shortcomings. Each relatively adequate world hypothesis will also have an account of other worldviews. In interpreting other worldviews it adapts their insights for its own use. No world hypothesis, however, can rule out another equally adequate view as unworthy of consideration; nor can one demonstrate the adequacy of one's own worldview by citing the shortcomings of other views, for even the best have shortcomings.

The book established Pepper as one of the most important living American philosophers. E. A. Burtt, reviewing it in *The Philosophical Review* (November 1943), called the work "a very constructive and hopeful departure in metaphysical discussion" in which the author "states conflicting ontological systems in such a way as to present each in the most favorable light possible, instead of gloating over the weaknesses of all but his own pet system." Burtt concluded: "If the times are ready for speculative work in such a mood as this, here is a prolegomenon to any future metaphysics." Charles Hartshorne, on the other hand, writing in a special issue of *Paunch* (1980) devoted to Pepper's thought, considers Pepper a better aesthetician than metaphysician and holds that Pepper's "basic monolithic empiricism kept him from appreciating the a priori or logical aspect of philosophical questions." Hartshorne claims that metaphors are rhetorical devices, whereas philosophical issues are primarily logical and are better "stated in considerable measure literally."

Pepper was on a leave of absence in New York from January to September 1942. He taught two courses, on metaphysics and aesthetics, in the Columbia University summer session and presented a paper, "Metaphysical Method," to the Philosophy Club, a group of philosophers from the northeastern states. Montague called the paper, in which Pepper developed some material along the lines of *World Hypotheses,* one of the most original presentations he had ever heard. Pepper also gave a lecture at Columbia titled "Ethical Ideals and Practical Policy"; it was developed from a manuscript he had written in 1941 for a short book, "Social Equilibrium," which he had brought to New York to show to a publisher. The theoretical material in the manuscript came from his lecture notes for his introductory philosophy course, while the historical content was hastily gathered from limited secondary sources. He intended the book as a popular presentation of the ideal of an "adjustable society" as a way of adapting American individualism to the necessities of centralization and security for such emergencies as World War II. The lecture was well received, but the proposed book did not find a publisher. Pepper was, however, later able to use some of the theoretical ideas in *The Sources of Value* (1958) and *Ethics* (1960).

In 1944 Pepper gave six lectures on aesthetics at Harvard; they were published, along with a supplementary essay on the work of art, as *The Basis of Criticism in the Arts* (1945). The book is an expansion, with many alterations and omissions, of the aesthetics sections of the unpublished "Philosophy of Criticism," taking up in turn mechanistic, contextualistic, organicistic, and form-istic criticism and applying each of them to sonnets by William Shakespeare and Gerard Manley Hopkins. The work proved to be one of the most profitable of all Pepper's books, although none of his royalties ever exceeded a few hundred dollars a year.

On 27 June 1945 the long-hoped-for offer from Harvard finally came; but by this time Pepper's roots in California were too deep, and the Berkeley philosophy department seemed to him better than the one at Harvard. His decision was made easier by the fact that his friend Tolman, who provided stimulus for various points in his work on value theory, had recently declined an offer of a professorship in psychology from Harvard. Pepper did serve for some years as a consultant to Harvard on philosophy personnel and programs. The Harvard offer was followed by inquiries from various other major departments in the eastern part of the country, all of which Pepper declined.

On his return from New York to Berkeley in 1942 Pepper had gone back to the subject of his doctoral dissertation, the general theory of value; he wanted to provide as comprehensive, solid, and psychologically detailed a work for the middle of the twentieth century as Perry's General Theory of Value (1926) had been for its early decades. The work ultimately became The Sources of Value. In 1945, however, anticipating that the project would take some years to complete, and needing a text for an advanced course on value theory he was teaching, he decided to publish an outline of his current ideas on values. In addition to its usefulness as a teaching aid, such a condensed account would enable him to get helpful criticism for the longer project; it would also establish his priority in the field in case someone else might publish a study with similar ideas before he could complete the more comprehensive work. But, as he noted in his unpublished autobiography, he need not have worried about the matter of priority: his analysis was so contrary to prevailing trends that his problem in the end was to get his colleagues to see the significance of his approach. He called the condensed version A Digest of Purposive Values, and it appeared in 1947.

In this work Pepper undertakes to provide a basis in observable fact for ethics and the other value fields. Purposes, he says, are important sources of value; accordingly, he analyzes purposive acts, especially appetitions and aversions; describes conative, affective, and achievement values and traces their relationships to each other and to the entire field of value; and sketches the principles of evaluation of values. Toward the end of the book he notes that over the individual drives and values is another basic source of values, a social survival factor based on evolutionary forces. The evolu-

tionary process is a natural tendency to which the drives must conform if a given system of them is to survive and propagate itself. Conditions of survival determine successful and unsuccessful forms in the struggle for life, and staying alive takes priority over achieving particular goals. The survival factor pushes for the social solidarity and efficiency of a functional society and restricts individual freedom. Drawing on his unpublished "Social Equilibrium," Pepper emphasizes the ideal of an "adjusted" or "adjustable society" as a means of reconciling individual claims with group survival. For his factual basis Pepper leans heavily on Tolman's Purposive Behavior in Animals and Men (1932), sometimes viewing Tolman's approach as mechanistic and at other times as contextualistic; this shifting interpretation created some confusion among Pepper's collaborators on Value: A Cooperative Inquiry (1949), edited by Ray Lepley. Pepper's main contribution to that volume, "Observations on Value from an Analysis of a Simple Appetition," grew out of his investigations for A Digest of Purposive Values.

Invited by Harcourt, Brace and Company to write a book on the visual arts, Pepper expanded his lectures for his introductory aesthetics course into Principles of Art Appreciation (1949). The work treats aesthetics from a mechanistic point of view, which Pepper thought was the simplest way of introducing the subject to American students. Aesthetic experience consists in consummatory pleasures and deals with things that are liked for themselves, and everyone knows what pleasures are and what it is to like something for itself. Besides, as Pepper says in "Autobiography of an Aesthetics" (1970), this hedonistic approach "brings art right down into everyday experience, on speaking terms with the delights of food, picnics, witty conversation, circuses, and sports"; once the student gets a feel for the fun of the arts, "we can safely enter into the appreciation of the richer, deeper things" without the risks of sentimentality or pretentiousness. He discusses, in detail and with apt illustrations, the general organizing principles of design, pattern, type, and emotion applicable to all the arts and applies these principles to the visual arts, showing the pleasures to be found in them. The text was widely used.

Pepper's journals for 1949 and 1950 include lengthy accounts of the University of California Board of Regents' attempt to institute an anticommunist loyalty oath. Pepper and Tolman were leaders in opposing the measure, and Pepper's colleague Loewenberg refused to sign the oath. The courts finally reinstated the nonsigners and awarded them back pay.

Pepper declined the offer of a position at the University of Illinois at Urbana-Champaign but accepted a visiting professorship there for the spring of 1949. He became chairman of the philosophy department the following year.

In July 1953 Pepper gave a series of lectures at Indiana University; they were published in 1955, along with some lectures he delivered in the spring of 1954 at the University of California, as *The Work of Art*. Pepper regarded this book as a sequel to the essay on the work of art in *The Basis of Criticism in the Arts*. He thought that the topic had been largely neglected in the history of aesthetics, and his book is an important step toward remedying this situation. He distinguishes three components in the work of art: the physical object; the immediately perceived object; and the object of criticism, which is the system of relevant perceptions of a normal observer. The third component is the proper object of aesthetic experience. Pepper maintains against the emotivists, who regarded aesthetic evaluations as mere expressions of feeling with no truth value, that it is an object about which true or false statements can be made.

Pepper retired from the University of California in the spring of 1958. In the fall he held visiting appointments at Hamline University and Macalester College in St. Paul, Minnesota, and engaged in some valuable discussions with Herbert Feigl of the University of Minnesota.

Also in 1958 Pepper's magnum opus in value theory, *The Sources of Value,* finally appeared. Pepper opens the work by saying that the problem that runs through the field of values is "*the problem of how to make well-grounded decisions in human affairs*"; the chief virtue of his book, he claims, "lies in its being a comprehensive hypothesis of the main lines of relationship among the facts bearing on human decisions." Pulling together ideas from ethics, logic, theory of knowledge, psychology, biology, aesthetics, economics, political science, anthropology, and sociology, he presents a comprehensive hypothesis to deal with traditional problems of value theory and to aid in making well-informed decisions in practical affairs. He emphasizes that the hypothesis is verifiable and corrigible and says that "Since this study makes no pretense at being a definitive theory, the process of thinking which led to each successive stage may be more helpful to other students of the subject than the actual conclusions reached. The chapters ahead may be truly considered as a report of one man's exploration and survey of this field as he penetrated deeper and deeper into its factual relationships." Following the evidence where it led, he continues, he found himself examining the subject matter in "a range extending all the way from simple likings and purposes to personality structure, cultural pattern, religion, and natural selection."

The Paul Carus Lectures · Series 13

Concept

and

Quality

Stephen C. Pepper

OPEN COURT · ESTABLISHED 1887

Dust jacket for the 1967 published version of Pepper's 1961 Paul Carus Lectures, in which he develops a fifth world hypothesis that he calls "selectivism" (Bruccoli Clark Layman Archives)

gave several public lectures, and on his birthday he delivered an honors address, "Towards an Adjustable Society." While in the Midwest he also spoke at the University of Michigan, Northwestern University, and Washington University in St. Louis. At the end of the semester he returned to Michigan for intensive discussions with Charles Stevenson so that the two naturalistic empiricists could try to narrow their differences; he reported that it was one of the most philosophically profitable days he ever spent. He also visited Lepley at Bradley University; he found Peoria a beautiful little city, which, he admitted in his unpublished autobiography, was "something to say of a name that is a by-word of all that is middle western worst." In the spring of 1950 Colby College awarded him his first honorary degree, and in 1950–1951 he and his wife spent a semisabbatical mainly in touring Europe. He completed his term as chairman of the art department in 1952 and

Using descriptive definitions, as opposed to arbitrary stipulations, Pepper arrives at the concept of "selective systems"; he considers this concept a prime instance of an empirical discovery made by philosophical reflection. In addition to being the guiding concept linking different levels of value, a "selective system operates to eliminate errors and accumulate correct results in terms of criteria embodied in the system." That is, it affords a dynamic natural norm. Pepper's approach is naturalistic, liberal, and broadly utilitarian. In concentrating on basic animal drives, he develops a view of human beings that is closer to Thomas Hobbes's than to Jean-Jacques Rousseau's more elevated conception, and one may ask whether he has taken adequate account of the socializing and acculturating factors in evolutionary developments.

In spite of the fact that it was a naturalistic treatment of value and, thus, contrary to the prevailing antinaturalistic trend in the United States and England, certain of the merits of the book were generally recognized. Bertram Morris said in *The Journal of Philosophy* (9 April 1959) that though the work "contains an overwhelming amount of material, scientific and philosophical, it is so adeptly organized as to invite the reader to savor the analyses with something like the enjoyment the author must take in setting them forth." W. H. Werkmeister calls it "the most comprehensive and the most detailed interpretation of value based upon the conception of purposive action. . . . It is an interpretation that has no rivals either in orientation or in type of analysis." The reviews ran from such high praise to condemnation of Pepper for allegedly confusing philosophy and psychology. Pepper himself thought that many of the best critiques came out in the psychological journals. To his distress, however, the volume was indexed by the Library of Congress as a psychology book. Therefore, in the spring of 1959, while he was visiting professor at Colby College in Waterville, Maine, he wrote a brief statement of its ethical applications that he titled *Ethics* so that it would be catalogued and shelved with philosophy books. It was published in 1960.

In 1960 Pepper and his wife spent a few months in Japan, which he had first visited with his parents in 1903, the year he began writing his journal. Shortly after they arrived, they had to return to the United States for his mother's funeral. Pepper received an honorary LL.D. at the June 1960 Berkeley commencement.

In the spring of 1961, while on a visiting appointment at Tulane University, Pepper was given his third honorary degree. He was also invited to give the Paul Carus Lectures for that year. The Carus lectureship is the American Philosophical Association's most prestigious scholarly award; it calls for the presentation of three lectures at an annual meeting of the association—in Pepper's case, at the September 1961 meetings of the Pacific Division at the University of British Columbia—and for the lectures to be published by the Open Court firm. Pepper was the thirteenth Carus lecturer; Dewey had been the first, followed by Arthur O. Lovejoy, Mead, Montague, E. B. McGilvary, Morris R. Cohen, C. I. Lewis, Loewenberg, C. J. Ducasse, George Boas, Blanshard, and Arthur Murphy. Pepper's Carus Lectures were published in 1967 as *Concept and Quality: A World Hypothesis.*

In *World Hypotheses* Pepper had outlined four relatively adequate worldviews; in *Concept and Quality* he develops at length a fifth, "selectivism," based on the root metaphor of the purposive act as a selective system. It holds that felt qualities are located in the brain; thus, in this one area "we are in immediate acquaintance with the qualitative object to which a scientific object is referring." In other words, he says, "the qualitative experience is the one actuality, and . . . the neural pattern is a set of physical symbols for the qualitative actual occurrence." Whereas in *World Hypotheses* he charged Whitehead with a bad form of eclecticism, in *Concept and Quality* he sees that Whitehead's "actual occasions" may be a form of the selectivistic metaphor.

Concept and Quality is a comprehensive synthesis of much of Pepper's previous thought and writing, with some important additions. The reviews were, in the main, quite favorable. Douglas N. Morgan wrote in *The Journal of Aesthetics and Art Criticism* (Winter 1969), "To few men is it given to witness the full fruition of a lifetime's dedication to philosophy and to our understanding of the fine arts: Stephen C. Pepper is such a man." To few generations, Morgan continued, "is it given to share the healthy enthusiasm and insight and sympathetic human fulfillment of a distinguished man and mind," but because of Pepper, "ours is such a generation."

Pepper remained active almost to the end of his life. He was consulted on topics from bridge design and academic planning to suicide prevention. He helped plan the University of California campuses at Santa Barbara, San Diego, and Santa Cruz. He also continued to lecture and to hold visiting professorships at such leading institutions as Williams College in 1964 and Carleton College in 1967. In May 1969 he lectured at Southern Illinois University in Carbondale on "Felt Qualities and Knowledge" and "Felt Qualities and Perception" and conducted graduate seminars. He was so impressed with the university that he decided to leave his papers to the Special Collections department of its Delyte W. Morris Library. One of the last pieces he wrote was part of the entry "Aesthetics" for the fifteenth edition of *The New Encyclopædia Britannica* (1974);

it was published just as he wrote it, without editing. Pepper died of cancer on 1 May 1972; his wife had died a few years earlier.

Bibliographies:

Elmer H. Duncan, "Stephen C. Pepper: A Bibliography," *Journal of Aesthetics and Art Criticism,* 28 (Spring 1970): 287–293;

Duncan, "Stephen C. Pepper: Additions to a Bibliography," *Paunch,* nos. 53–54 (1980): 73–80.

References:

Henry David Aiken, "The Basis of Criticism in the Arts," *Philosophical Review,* 57 (January 1948): 77–82;

Joan Boyle, "Comment on Duncan's Paper: Further Reflection on the Intellectual Biography of Stephen C. Pepper," *Journal of Mind and Behavior,* 3 (Autumn 1982): 381–383;

Antonio Cua, David B. Downing, Arthur Efron, Peter H. Hare, Bill J. Harrell, Earl R. MacCormac, Gordon Patterson, Andrew J. Reck, and Joan Walls, "Root Metaphor: An Interdisciplinary Conference," *Journal of Mind and Behavior,* 3 (Summer 1982): 191–322;

Elmer H. Duncan, "Toward Root Metaphor: Pepper's Writings in the *University of California Publications in Philosophy,*" *Journal of Mind and Behavior,* 3 (Autumn 1982): 375–380;

Abraham Edel, "Science and Value: Some Reflections on Pepper's *The Sources of Value,*" *Review of Metaphysics,* 14 (September 1960): 134–158;

Arthur Efron and John Herold, eds., "Root Metaphor: The Live Thought of Stephen C. Pepper," special issue of *Paunch,* nos. 53–54 (1980);

Lewis E. Hahn, *A Contextualistic Theory of Perception,* University of California Publications in Philosophy, volume 22 (Berkeley: University of California Press, 1942);

Everett W. Hall, "Of What Use Is Metaphysics?" *Journal of Philosophy,* 33 (23 April 1936): 236–245;

Rollo Handy, "Pepper's View of Value as Selective System," in his *Value Theory and the Behavioral Sciences* (Springfield, Ill.: Charles C. Thomas, 1969), pp. 120–144;

Raymond Hoekstra, "Pepper's *World Hypotheses,*" *Journal of Philosophy,* 42 (15 February 1945): 85–101;

Iredell Jenkins, "The Present Status of the Value Problem," *Review of Metaphysics,* 4 (September 1950): 85–110;

Joseph Margolis, "Professor Pepper on Value Theory," *Ethics,* 69 (January 1959): 134–139;

Karl H. Potter, "The Criterion of Relevancy in Aesthetics: A Discussion. 2. A Reply to Mr. Pepper," *Journal of Aesthetics and Art Criticism,* 16 (December 1957): 207–214;

James H. Quina Jr., "World Hypotheses: A Basis for a Structural Curriculum," *Educational Theory,* 21 (Summer 1971): 311–319;

Andrew J. Reck, "Pepper's Theory," in his *Speculative Philosophy: A Study of Its Nature, Types, and Uses* (Albuquerque: University of New Mexico Press, 1972), pp. 46–48;

Reck, "Stephen C. Pepper: Philosophy of Values," in his *The New American Philosophers: An Exploration of Thought since World War II* (Baton Rouge: Louisiana State University Press, 1968), pp. 44–80;

W. H. Werkmeister, "Stephen Pepper and the Sources of Value," in his *Historical Spectrum of Value Theories,* volume 2: *The Anglo-American Group* (Lincoln, Neb.: Johnsen, 1973), pp. 275–306.

Papers:

Stephen C. Pepper's papers constitute Special Collection 106 of Southern Illinois University's Delyte W. Morris Library in Carbondale. The collection includes published and unpublished manuscripts, lecture notes, correspondence, photographs, and drawings.

Josiah Royce

(20 November 1855 – 14 September 1916)

T. L. S. Sprigge
University of Edinburgh

BOOKS: *Primer of Logical Analysis: For the Use of Composition Students* (San Francisco: Bancroft, 1881);

The Religious Aspect of Philosophy: A Critique of the Bases of Conduct and of Faith (Boston & New York: Houghton, Mifflin, 1885);

California, from the Conquest in 1846 to the Second Vigilance Committee in San Francisco: A Study of American Character (Boston & New York: Houghton, Mifflin, 1886);

The Feud of Oakfield Creek: A Novel of California Life (Boston & New York: Houghton, Mifflin, 1887);

The Spirit of Modern Philosophy: An Essay in the Form of Lectures (Boston & New York: Houghton, Mifflin, 1892);

The Conception of God: An Address before the Philosophical Union by Josiah Royce, with Comments Thereon by Sidney Edward Mezes, Joseph Le Conte and George Holmes Howison, and Sidney Edward Mezes, Philosophical Union of the University of California, Bulletin no. 15 (Berkeley: Executive Council of the Union, 1895); republished as *The Conception of God: A Philosophical Discussion Concerning the Nature of the Divine Idea as a Demonstrable Reality* (New York: Macmillan / London: Macmillan, 1897);

Studies of Good and Evil: A Series of Essays upon the Problems of Philosophy and of Life (New York: Appleton, 1898);

The World and the Individual, First Series: The Four Historical Conceptions of Being (New York & London: Macmillan, 1899);

The Conception of Immortality (Boston & New York: Houghton, Mifflin, 1900; London: Longmans, Green, 1900);

The World and the Individual, Second Series: Nature, Man, and the Moral Order (New York & London: Macmillan, 1901);

Outlines of Psychology: An Elementary Treatise with Some Practical Applications (New York & London: Macmillan, 1903);

First Reader, by Royce, Charles H. Allen, and John Swett, revised by Annie Klingensmith (Indianapolis: Indiana School Book Co., 1903);

Josiah Royce

Herbert Spencer: An Estimate and Review. Together with a Chapter of Personal Reminiscences by James Collier (New York: Fox, Duffield, 1904);

Race Questions, Provincialism, and Other American Problems (New York: Macmillan, 1908);

The Philosophy of Loyalty (New York: Macmillan, 1908);

William James and Other Essays on the Philosophy of Life (New York: Macmillan, 1911);

The Sources of Religious Insight: Lectures Delivered before Lake Forest College on the Foundation of the Late William Bross,

The Bross Library, volume 6 (New York: Scribners, 1912; Edinburgh: Clark, 1912);

Logik, by Royce, Arnold Ruge, Wilhelm Windelband, Louis Couturat, Benedetto Croce, Federigo Enriques, and Nicolaj Losskij (Tübingen: Mohr, 1912); translated by Ethel Meyer as *Logic* (London: Macmillan, 1913);

The Problem of Christianity: Lectures Delivered at the Lowell Institute in Boston, and at Manchester College, Oxford, 2 volumes (New York: Macmillan, 1913)—comprises volume 1, *The Christian Doctrine of Life;* and volume 2, *The Real World and the Christian Ideas;*

War and Insurance: An Address Delivered before the Philosophical Union of the University of California at Its Twenty-fifth Anniversary at Berkeley, California, August 27, 1914 (New York: Macmillan, 1914);

The Hope of the Great Community (New York: Macmillan, 1916);

The Duties of Americans in the Present War: Address Delivered at Tremont Temple, Sunday, January 30, 1916 (Boston: Citizens' League for America and the Allies, 1916);

Lectures on Modern Idealism, edited by Jacob Loewenberg (New Haven: Yale University Press / London: Humphrey Milford, Oxford University Press, 1919);

Fugitive Essays, edited by Loewenberg (Cambridge, Mass.: Harvard University Press, 1920);

The Social Philosophy of Josiah Royce, edited by Stuart Gerry Brown (Syracuse, N.Y.: Syracuse University Press, 1950);

Royce's Logical Essays: Collected Logical Essays of Josiah Royce, edited by Daniel S. Robinson (Dubuque, Iowa: William C. Brown, 1951);

The Religious Philosophy of Josiah Royce, edited by Brown (Syracuse, N.Y.: Syracuse University Press, 1952);

Josiah Royce's Seminar, 1913–1914: As Recorded in the Notebooks of Harry T. Costello, edited by Grover Smith (New Brunswick, N.J.: Rutgers University Press, 1963);

The Basic Writings of Josiah Royce, 2 volumes, edited by John J. McDermott (Chicago & London: University of Chicago Press, 1969);

The Philosophy of Josiah Royce, edited by John K. Roth (New York: Crowell, 1971);

Selected Writings, edited by John E. Smith and William Kluback (New York: Paulist Press, 1988);

Metaphysics, edited by William Ernest Hocking, Richard Hocking, and Frank Oppenheim (Albany: State University of New York Press, 1998).

OTHER: Anna Boynton Thompson, *The Unity of Fichte's Doctrine of Knowledge,* introduction by Royce, Radcliffe College Monographs, no. 7 (Boston: Ginn, 1895);

Dialogues of Plato, translated by Benjamin Jowett, introduction by Royce (New York: Appleton, 1898);

Eugen Kuehnemann, *Schiller,* 2 volumes, translated by Katharine Royce, introduction by Josiah Royce (Boston & London: Ginn, 1912);

Federigo Enriques, *Problems of Science,* translated by Katharine Royce, introductory note by Josiah Royce (Chicago & London: Open Court, 1914).

SELECTED PERIODICAL PUBLICATIONS—UNCOLLECTED: "Kant's Relation to Modern Philosophical Progress," *Journal of Speculative Philosophy,* 15 (1881): 360–381;

"'Mind-Stuff' and Reality," *Mind,* 6 (1881): 365–377;

"Dr. Abbot's 'Way out of Agnosticism,'" *International Journal of Ethics,* 1 (1890–1891): 98–113;

"A New Study of Psychology," *International Journal of Ethics,* 2 (1891–1892): 106–111;

"Mental Defect and Disorder from the Teacher's Point of View," *Educational Review,* 6 (1893): 209, 322–331, 449–463;

"The External World and the Social Consciousness," *Philosophical Review,* 3 (1894): 513–545;

"The Imitative Functions and Their Place in Human Nature," *Century,* new series 26 (1894): 137–145;

"Preliminary Report on Imitation," *Psychological Review,* 2 (1895): 217–235;

Ethics Review of Ralph Waldo Trine, *In Tune with the Infinite: Or Fulness of Peace, Power and Plenty, International Journal of Psychology,* 1 (1898–1899): 124–126.

Josiah Royce is the chief American exponent of absolute idealism—or, indeed, of any type of idealism. He was a younger colleague of William James at Harvard; each of these great thinkers profoundly influenced the other, both positively and negatively, and is apt to be misunderstood if this mutual influence is not realized. Royce's work covers all fields of philosophy, but he is most important for his metaphysical system, his ethical theory, and his philosophical interpretation of Christianity. He was also the main figure who introduced the use of modern mathematics and logic as philosophical tools into American philosophy. His metaphysical system is developed quite independently of any standard religious affiliation, but its notable features include his unique proof of the existence of God, or the Absolute; his treatment of the problem of evil; and his theory of time, including the relationship of God to temporal events. His early ethical theory brilliantly solves the problem of the relation between knowledge and will as the basis of ethics. His later ethics is based on the conception that the prime need for human beings is to have an object of devoted loyalty; this conception is basic to his account of what is of permanent value in Christianity.

Royce was born in Grass Valley, California, on 20 November 1855 to Josiah and Sarah Eleanor Bayliss Royce. He had three older sisters. His parents had been brought to America as children when their own parents emigrated from England. His father's family had settled in Ontario, Canada; later, the elder Josiah Royce had moved to Rochester, New York, where he met his wife. They had come to California in a covered wagon in April 1849, during the Gold Rush. After some false starts they had settled in Grass Valley. Royce's lifelong interest in what constitutes a community owes much to his puzzlement as to the sense in which Grass Valley was said to be a "new town," when, to his childhood eyes, it looked decidedly old. Royce's father worked mainly as a traveling salesman, while his mother, who had a better education than her husband, started her own school for girls and boys. Both parents were highly religious–the father somewhat eccentrically, his mother more soberly. His mother's intelligent piety had a lasting influence on Royce, and his mature philosophical prose contains many deliberate echoes of biblical texts.

In 1866 the family moved to San Francisco, where Royce's parents opened a fruit store. Royce attended Lincoln Grammar School and Lowell High School. In 1872 he was among the first students admitted to the University of California, which at that time consisted only of the Berkeley campus. The teacher who most influenced him was Joseph Le Conte, a geologist with a philosophical bent.

Royce had shown outstanding intelligence from his earliest years, especially in mathematics and languages. His success at the university led to a loan from some San Francisco businessmen, which enabled him to spend the 1875–1876 school year in Germany. On the way to catch his ship in New York he stopped off in Boston, where he met James through a letter of introduction from Daniel Coit Gilman, the president of the University of California. In Germany he studied at the universities of Heidelberg and Leipzig and with the psychologist Wilhelm Wundt at Göttingen.

On his return to the United States, Royce took up a two-year fellowship at the recently founded Johns Hopkins University offered by Gilman, who had become the first president of that institution. He lectured on Arthur Schopenhauer and German Romantic poetry and earned one of the first four Ph.D. degrees awarded at Johns Hopkins with a dissertation titled "On the Interdependence of the Principles of Knowledge." Royce made some close friends in Baltimore, including a businessman, George Buchanan Cole, to whom he later dedicated *The Religious Aspect of Philosophy: A Critique of the Bases of Conduct and of Faith* (1885), and the orientalist Charles Lamman, with whom he continued the study of Sanskrit

Royce at age five (Harvard University Archives)

he had begun in Germany. Royce took serious account of Indian philosophy in his own philosophizing.

When his fellowship expired, Royce returned reluctantly to California, which, compared with Boston, Baltimore, and Germany, seemed to him an intellectual backwater. Since nothing else turned up, he accepted a position as assistant professor of English language and literature at his alma mater.

In 1880 Royce married Katharine Head. They had three sons: Christopher, born in 1882; Stephen, born in 1886; and Edward, born in 1889. Christopher became mentally ill in early adulthood, while Stephen and Edward became, respectively, a mining engineer and a musician. The marriage seems to have been a happy one, though Katharine Royce is said to have spoken of philosophy in general as "drivel."

Royce's teaching at the University of California was the basis for his first published work, *Primer of Logical Analysis: For the Use of Composition Students* (1881), which received a favorable mention in the British philosophical journal *Mind*. That same year he published in *Mind* his first philosophical piece, "'Mind-stuff' and Reality," in which he attacked the notion of "mind-stuff" advocated by the British philosopher W. K. Clifford.

Royce was able to teach some philosophy at the University of California but was confined mainly to literature. Feeling intellectually isolated, he wrote to James to

*Royce as a student at the University of California,
where he was a member of the University Cadets
(Collection of Nancy A. Hacker)*

untarist epistemology, according to which the mind postulates afresh at each moment the beliefs it finds most helpful. Lying behind all of these beliefs is an implicit postulation of a "Universal Thought," correspondence or noncorrespondence with which constitutes truth and falsehood, respectively.

Royce's first significant book, *The Religious Aspect of Philosophy,* was based on a series of public lectures he delivered at Harvard. The problem for ethics, Royce says, is whether moral thinking is an activity of the will, in which case ethics is purely subjective, or of the intellect, in which case ethics may be motivationally inert. Royce's solution is that while the intellect reveals that other people have volitions, this knowledge, unless it is merely verbal, is bound, other things being equal, to produce some concern for their welfare. For the adequate idea of a desire is itself a desire that, even if less strongly, seeks its fulfillment like any other desire. People are selfish because their ideas of the desires of others are inadequate. But the more they become aware of the mass of other minds, each with its own longings, the closer they move to the moral insight that they should aim at behavior that tends to harmonize the wills of different persons.

Royce goes on to argue that the existence of a Universal or Absolute Thought is no mere postulate but an objective truth that alone explains how the human mind can be in error, for error can only occur if the mind can home in on things external to itself other than by its concept of them, and such homing in requires that the finite mind and the objects about which it thinks belong together in a universal mind or thought in which they are united in a manner that is lost at the finite level. George Santayana remarked that it was typical of Royce to find the proof of "something sublime, like the existence of God," in "something sad and troublesome" like "the existence of error." Similarly, Royce sets out to show that the worst horrors of human life, taken in their full context, exhibit the fundamental goodness of things: first, a person who has repressed his or her powerful evil passions is more of a credit to the universe than one who has never felt them, and, second, evil provides the opportunity for heroic resistance. Evil is not goodness in disguise, nor a means to goodness, nor is it somehow good sub specie aeternitatis; it is and remains vile. But it has to exist if a good that outweighs it—the good of its conquest—is to exist.

Royce's next book, *California, from the Conquest in 1846 to the Second Vigilance Committee in San Francisco: A Study of American Character* (1886), was written at the invitation of the publisher, Houghton, Mifflin and Company, which was producing a series of histories of the states. The offer came about because the intended author had died, and Houghton, Mifflin editor Howard E. Scudder turned to Royce, with whom he was already in correspondence

inquire about the possibility of a job for him in the East. James arranged for Royce to substitute for him, each of them receiving half of James's salary, during James's absence in the academic year 1882–1883. Royce was appointed to a tenured post in 1885; he remained at Harvard for the rest of his life, becoming part of what is known as the "golden age of American philosophy" that was centered at Harvard. Royce and James became close friends, and their philosophies, though largely opposed on fundamentals, are to a considerable extent the result of their friendly sparring over almost thirty years.

In the East, Royce and others were aware of a certain uncouthness about him, stemming from the poverty of his California background, in comparison with the urbanity of the Boston and Cambridge gentility. His striking red hair, combined with the excited way in which he expatiated on his ideas to all and sundry, seems almost to have alarmed some of the genteel world in which he then moved. James's wife disliked him at first, perhaps for this reason.

In his dissertation and in three published articles in 1881 and 1882 Royce had advocated a kind of vol-

about *The Religious Aspect of Philosophy*. Royce later said in a letter to a friend, "A study of the political life of a growing state is, I find, of great use to a man like me, whose airy studies take him often so far from concrete fact." The book, in which Royce interprets the facts in the light of his own vision of how communities can be born out of strife, led to one of three great quarrels of his life. His research uncovered the fact that General John Charles Frémont, celebrated as the hero who had won California for the United States in the war with Mexico, had ignored government instructions to allow the territory to be absorbed by peaceful negotiation. The public dispute over the matter lasted for many years.

Royce's history of California was followed by his only novel, *The Feud of Oakfield Creek: A Novel of California Life* (1887). The work contrasts a man whose ethical beliefs actually inspire his actions with another who merely pays lip service to such beliefs.

In 1888 Royce, who had been working to excess, suffered a mental breakdown. Taking a year's leave of absence from Harvard, he traveled to Australia to recuperate. Thereafter, when overwhelmed by stress, Royce took sea voyages of various lengths.

Royce's next book, *The Spirit of Modern Philosophy: An Essay in the Form of Lectures* (1892), was based on public lectures he delivered to the intelligentsia of Cambridge. In part 1 Royce examines the philosophies of Baruch Spinoza, Immanuel Kant, Johann Gottlieb Fichte, Georg Wilhelm Friedrich Hegel, and Schopenhauer; in part 2 he presents his own metaphysical views. The most important aspect of the latter is his distinction between the world of description and the world of acquaintance. The first is the world as described by science and common sense; the second is the world of immediate experience that constitutes a person's inner emotional and sensory life. The first concerns the abstract structure of things; the second concerns their inner conscious life, if they have one. Ordinary human communication uses the concepts of the world of description, while the concepts of the world of acquaintance are private. Royce next shows that all things have an inner life and, thus, inhabit worlds of acquaintance; these worlds, however, are not altogether private, since all finite minds are united in the Absolute through which they permeate each other to some extent in social relationships. Unlike Clifford's "mind-stuff" theory, Royce's "panpsychism" does not regard mind as a latecomer in a cosmos that evolved through the aggregation of mental particles.

The second great public quarrel of Royce's life began with a book review. In his absence in 1888 some of his courses had been taught by a liberal religious thinker named Francis Ellingwood Abbot. Abbot published the lectures as *The Way out of Agnosticism: or, The Philosophy of Free Religion* (1890). Royce, who had unfa-

vorably reviewed an earlier work by Abbot, wrote in *The International Journal of Ethics* that the book was bad and derivative and warned readers not to take it seriously as a piece of contemporary philosophy. Abbot demanded an apology and asked Harvard to censure Royce for incivility. In the dispute that ensued, Charles Sanders Peirce took Abbot's side and James took Royce's. Little came of Abbot's efforts, and he committed suicide ten years later believing that he was a great thinker whose contribution was lost because of prejudice against his lack of an academic appointment.

Royce's next major work, *The Conception of God* (1895), originated as a lecture given at a large public meeting in Berkeley with replies from his old mentor Le Conte; a young California philosopher, Sidney Edward Mezes; and the "personal idealist" George Holmes Howison, a professor of philosophy at the University of California, who had invited Royce. His account of God, or the Absolute, is much the same as in his previous works, though the proof of God's existence as the all-knower is now inferred from human ignorance rather than from error. Royce also rectifies any suggestion that God, though initially defined as the all-knower, is not equally a feeling and willing being. Le Conte did not take Royce on directly but defended his own more inductive type of theism, while Howison objected to Royce's monism. The most challenging reply was that of Mezes, who said that whether or not Royce had proved the existence of his Absolute, such a being was not God in any sense relevant to religion. Unlike other idealists of the period, such as F. H. Bradley and Bernard Bosanquet, Royce always identified the Absolute with God.

In 1898 Royce published *Studies of Good and Evil: A Series of Essays upon the Problems of Philosophy and of Life*. All but two of the pieces had previously been published in journals. All are concerned with the problem of evil, a main theme in most of Royce's work.

In January and February 1899 Royce delivered his first series of Gifford Lectures at the University of Aberdeen in Scotland; he delivered the second series in January 1900. The lectures were published in two volumes under the general title *The World and the Individual,* the first series as *The Four Historical Conceptions of Being* (1899), the second as *Nature, Man, and the Moral Order* (1901). In the preface to the first volume Royce suggests that philosophers should ask what it is for something to be, that is, what one is saying of things when one says that they exist or that they are. For Royce, this question is equivalent to the question what makes an idea an idea of something real or existent rather than an idea of a fiction or fantasy. He lists three answers to the question that he considers inadequate and then formulates his own. The first answer is that of realism. The realist claims that if an idea of something as existing is true, it is true because the thing exists in a manner independent of the idea of it. Thus, the reason mermaids do not exist is that they do not pertain to the world independently of human or other ideas about them. In contrast, dolphins are real because they have a being that they would have without anyone having the idea of them. Royce argues that the concept of independence as deployed by the realist is incoherent. Nothing can be independent of anything else in the manner required, for any two things will either have properties in common or they will not. The second alternative is not a genuine option, since everything has something in common with everything else. It follows that they are not independent, for if the one thing were abolished, that property would be abolished along with it, in which case the other could not have it. Thus, complete independence is impossible and, Royce argues, so are less-extreme forms of independence.

The second answer is that of mysticism, according to which the real is what is immediately present to an experiencing subject; it is that which, when encountered, extinguishes all thought–it is just *there*. The great historical expression of this conception, Royce says, is found in the Hindu Upanishads. This doctrine has much to be said for it, Royce thinks, but in the end it fails because it destroys the contrast between an idea and its object just as the first conception exaggerates the difference.

The third conception of being, that of critical rationalism, Royce associates especially with Kant. It holds that the real is that of which the existence can be verified by certain standard procedures. Royce sees much in favor of this position, also; but its major defect is that things that turn out to be real on this procedure are identified only by the universals under which they fall, so that it is impossible to arrive at anything that is, in principle, unique as a genuine particular must be. This notion is, he says, an accurate description of one's access to the people and things around one: they can never be identified in a way that guarantees that one is homing in on the same unique object each time, rather than something answering to the same universals. But one certainly wants the objects of one's emotions to be unique, and only the fourth conception of being can account for this kind of reality.

The fourth conception is that of absolute idealism. Any idea, according to Royce, has an internal and an external meaning. The distinction turns on his belief that every idea has a purposive or volitional aspect. When one hums a familiar tune, it consists at each moment of some brief snatch of the tune; but this snatch is pregnant with the rest of the tune, and it contains the purpose of moving on to the completion of the tune. This present purpose is the internal meaning of the tune, while the complete tune is its external meaning. The same is true of ideas: the internal meaning of an idea is the fact that it points purposively to something, while its external mean-

ing–what it refers to–is that something in which its purpose is completed. Thus, real things are those that complete the purpose of one's idea of them. One may be consciously confused as to what the purpose is, and this confusion constitutes error. But for the Absolute the true purpose of every idea is fulfilled. This account does not rule out the notion of correspondence between an idea and its object, but the manner in which a true idea corresponds to its object is chosen more or less consciously by the idea itself; the idea is intrinsically purposive.

Royce sometimes called himself an "absolute pragmatist." His contention that every idea is purposive and never a mere passive reflection of reality allied him with pragmatism, while he was an absolutist inasmuch as he thought that absolute truth exists; such truth is the confrontation of an idea with the reality that fulfills its purpose, and that confrontation is only complete at the level of the Absolute. Royce infers, once again, that ideas and their objects must belong to a larger experience that includes them both as its components, for a fulfilled purpose must be mentally continuous with the purpose as initially unfulfilled. Thus, Royce here has a new proof for the existence of the Absolute.

To show how fundamental these four conceptions of being are, Royce discusses the way in which each of them tends to be associated with a different social attitude. Realism is the philosophy of conservatism and social order, because it encourages the view that things are what they are and are not malleable to one's choices; therefore, the status quo is not to be challenged. In contrast, the partisans of critical rationalism tend to be politically liberal. The mystical conception of being, Royce says, is a liberator from any sort of desiccated dogma. (This characterization contrasts somewhat with his criticism of it elsewhere as tending toward social escapism.) Royce does not specify what political orientation is associated with the fourth conception of being; perhaps it would be some form of ethical or idealist socialism, to which Royce himself seems to have inclined.

On this basis Royce elaborates, in the second series of Gifford Lectures, a vision of the world at large. As in *The Spirit of Modern Philosophy,* he distinguishes the world of description and the world of acquaintance; the first is the world as described externally by science and its commonsense grounding, the second the world as felt from within. Royce elaborates on this division by distinguishing the kinds of series in which things are arranged in each world. The series pertaining to the world of description are dense in the mathematical sense, so that between any two terms an infinite number of intervening terms exist, while the world of acquaintance is well ordered, like the natural numbers. The crucial conception for the world of description is "betweenness," for science proceeds by finding mediat-

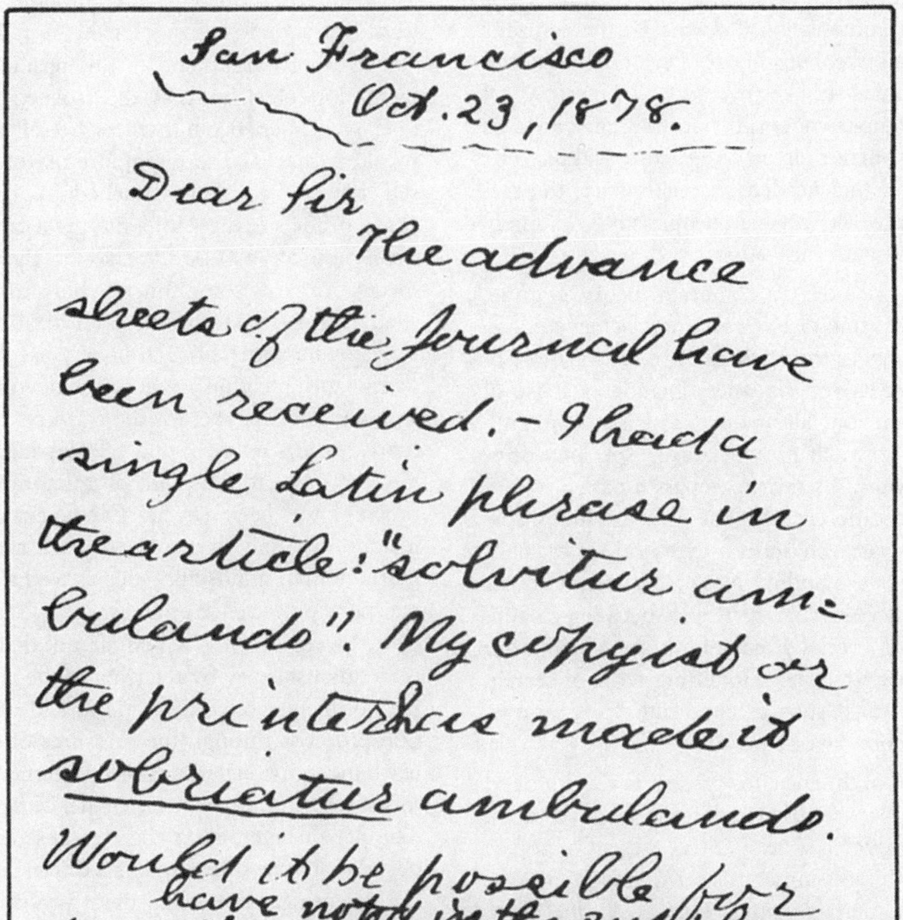

San Francisco
Oct. 23, 1878.

Dear Sir

The advance
sheets of the Journal have
been received. — I had a
single Latin phrase in
the article: "solvitur ambulando". My copyist or
the printer has made it
sobriatur ambulando.
Would it be possible for
have noted in the supplement
you to ~~~~~~~~~~~~~~~
of the Journal ~~~~~ this error
Otherwise the nonsense
seems too glaring. But the
matter is of little consequence.
— I should like to purchase
30 copies of this number of the
Journal, and have them forwarded by Exp. C.O.D.
Excuse haste — Yours, J. Royce

Postcard from Royce to William Torrey Harris, the editor of The Journal of Speculative Philosophy, *in regard to Royce's article "The Ethical Studies of Schiller" (University of Southern California)*

ing factors between each phenomenon it identifies. For the world of acquaintance it is "nextness"; the denizens of this world can be real neighbors of each other (as can the natural numbers–unlike the rational numbers). Of course, these are not two worlds but the same world as described from outside or as lived from within. The first conception is that needed for technology; the second is that of the world in which people have genuinely personal relations with each other.

The work includes an elaborate theory of time, which is, perhaps, one of Royce's finest achievements. Everything belongs to the unchanging consciousness of the Absolute, but its consciousness includes a sense of temporality spread out all at once, just as, in an infinitely feebler way, each of a person's "specious presents" contains within its short compass a past, present, and future. The difference is that the Absolute's specious present is not a phase in a temporal series: it is, rather, a *Nunc Stans* (Standing Now). A contrast seems to exist within the Absolute, however, between its unitary experience of a series of what for human beings are moments of time and its more totalizing sense of certain such series as a unity, such as constitute, for example, the history of a country or a person.

The notion of the specious present is also invoked to explain the apparent absence of mind from so much of the physical universe. The specious present of apparently inanimate things is much more extended than that of human beings, perhaps longer than a century; thus, their lives are so much slower than those of humans that communication with them is impossible.

Royce uses these ideas to argue for human immortality. All purposes are fulfilled in the real world of the Absolute, but only sub specie aeternitatis. *Sub specie temporis* (under the aspect of time), people must live on "for ever" because each person has or serves purposes that are never adequately fulfilled in his or her lifetime. One's true self is an ideal to which, temporally speaking, one never quite lives up, and it requires, therefore, an endless asymptotic approach. The fulfillment of this purpose is the Absolute's unified vision of this endless series.

In 1906 Royce gave a series of lectures on Kant, Friedrich Joseph Wilhelm von Schelling, and Hegel at Johns Hopkins University that was published posthumously in 1919 as *Lectures on Modern Idealism*. The volume is still useful as an introduction to these philosophers.

The Philosophy of Loyalty (1908), first given as lectures at the Lowell Institute in Boston, initiates a somewhat new phase in Royce's thought. Royce claims that the individual human being is inevitably wretched unless his or her life is inspired by loyalty to some great cause. Royce derives from this contention a foundational ethical principle that he calls "loyalty to loyalty." He presents it both as

a solution to the philosophical question of the basis of ethics and as a guide to living for the morally perplexed.

Royce's argument for this position starts with the psychological claim that the isolated individual, who does not experience himself or herself as belonging to a whole greater, and more important, than himself or herself, is wretched. This wretchedness can only be overcome if one's loyalty to some great cause becomes the main motivation of one's behavior. By a "cause," Royce means primarily some concrete but suprapersonal object, such as a nation, rather than an ideal such as universal suffrage. Instances of such loyalty are the devotion of a patriot to his country when this devotion leads him to live, and perhaps die, for the country; the devotion of a martyr to his religion; and the devotion of a captain to his ship, even to the point of going down with it when others have been saved. Other examples of loyalty include "a family, a church, or such a rational union of many human minds and wills as we have in mind when we speak of a science or an art."

Royce explains why a life not dedicated to a cause is so unsatisfactory by referring to the way in which people normally receive their moral education. This education proceeds through the pressures of social life, which teach the individual to conform to certain mores so as not to get into trouble with his or her elders and associates. The person internalizes these mores by that innate tendency to imitate others that is a universal characteristic of human beings. But while these pressures influence the person to a degree of social conformity, they also intensify his or her own self-will, which encourages the person to rebel against these constraints. The result is a constant tension between what individuals personally want and what they have been taught that they ought to do.

The person can only escape this miserable condition if his or her moral sense and self-centered emotions can be brought together. This bringing together can only happen if individuals develop a passionate love for something greater than themselves that becomes the chief motivation of their behavior and determines what they think they ought to do. This condition is what Royce means by a life lived in loyalty to a cause. Such loyalty resolves the sense of isolation that troubles those whose goals are primarily selfish, for the loyal person will then live in harmony with all others who share the same loyalty.

But, Royce realizes, much of the loyalty in the world is to evil causes. The members of a crime syndicate, for example, may be passionately loyal to their organization. But, Royce asks, what makes some causes good and some causes evil? He answers that since loyalty is what redeems human life, a person who grasps this fact will wish all human beings to have a cause to which they are similarly loyal. It is not desirable, however, for all people to be loyal to the same cause. The captain wishes other captains to be loyal to their ships as he is to his; he does not want them all to be loyal to the same ship. This realization should inspire in everyone an overriding loyalty to loyalty, a commitment to live so that loyalty spreads among humankind, with each group loyal to its own cause. An evil cause is one that can only prosper if the objects of the loyalty of others are imperiled or destroyed. Royce advises his readers to choose their own personal causes "for the sake of the spread of universal loyalty."

Royce notes that some have argued for the desirability of war on the ground that it provides the occasion for the supreme loyalty of those who are prepared to give their lives for their country. But he disagrees, for in war one wishes the object of the other side's loyalty to come to grief. And since loyalty is the supreme good, whatever hinders others from the chance to have their own object of loyalty is a supreme evil. Royce's argument here seems weak; it is doubtful that a war normally destroys the loyalty of the losing side, and Royce himself contends that the defeat of a cause can intensify loyalty to it and give a fuller view of what that cause was. Thus, the death of Jesus, apparently a defeat, promoted the development of the religion of which his death became the central symbol.

Any individual's overall loyalty will be a complex unity of a variety of more-specific loyalties. But what if these loyalties come into conflict with each other? Then, Royce says, the individual must choose the loyalty that best serves the purpose of making him or her a loyal person in a manner that does not threaten the loyalty of others. If the individual cannot reason out which loyalty this is, he or she must simply decide on one of them. Thereafter, loyalty to loyalty requires that, unless some new light is thrown on the matter by increasing knowledge, the individual must stick loyally to that decision, even in the absence of certainty that it is the right decision.

Royce adumbrates some metaphysical implications of the uniquely redeeming nature of loyalty. Loyalty "links various human lives into the unity of one life." But unless such a linkage is a reality, loyalty rests on an illusion. Thus, loyalty can only be ultimately justified by a monistic metaphysics for which human unity is a basic fact. If the unity is real, it must somehow exist as something that is somewhere experienced as a whole. In being loyal to something suprapersonal, such as a nation or even humanity as a whole, one must implicitly believe that this thing is as much, or even more, a real unit than one is oneself. This belief requires that the thing have its own suprapersonal self-consciousness. And this self-consciousness will be a distinct component within the Absolute Experience, just as is each individual human consciousness.

Royce and his wife, Katharine Head Royce, in the early 1880s (Collection of Nancy A. Hacker)

The supreme value of loyalty is peculiarly fitted, too, to show the necessary role of evil in the world. For, Royce asks,

what would be the universe without loyalty, and what would loyalty be without trial? And when we remember that, from this point of view, our own griefs are the griefs of the very world consciousness itself, in so far as this world-life is expressed in our lives, it may well occur to us that the life of loyalty with all its griefs and burdens and cares may be the very foundation of the attainment of that spiritual triumph which we must conceive as realized by the world spirit.

Also in 1908 Royce published *Race Questions, Provincialism, and Other American Problems*. He is extremely skeptical of the idea that some races are superior to others in innate mental endowment, and he argues that the solution to the race problem in the South is to escape from irrational prejudices and bring black people into the administration of law and other civic functions.

In 1911 Royce gave a series of lectures at Lake Forest College, a small coeducational Christian college north of Chicago. They were published in 1912 as *The Sources of Religious Insight*. Among the themes he discusses is the social nature of religious experience, as opposed to James's tendency to think of it as an essentially solitary phenomenon.

Royce in 1902 (Robbins Library of Philosophy, Harvard University)

The work that some commentators regard as Royce's finest, *The Problem of Christianity*, appeared in 1913. It had been given in part as a series of lectures at the Lowell Institute and then, in complete form, as a Hibbert Foundation lecture series at Manchester College of the University of Oxford. The notion of the Absolute as the superconsciousness of which all human minds are components figures rather slightly in *The Problem of Christianity*. Whether Royce had changed his mind on this doctrine or simply thought that he had said enough about it is unclear. Certainly, one motive for downplaying it was to answer the challenge of pragmatists such as Dewey and "new realists" such as E. B. Holt and Ralph Barton Perry that his idealism was too remote from everyday reality and the problems of modern life. Royce

dismisses indignantly any idea that his philosophy is an abstract system with no clear connection to practical questions as to how people should live. In this book, more than ever, his view of religion–in particular, Christianity–is based as much on empirical data as on abstract reasoning. He also stresses that commitment to a religion is never a mere inference from experience but as much or more an act of will.

James had similarly claimed that his *The Varieties of Religious Experience* (1902) was empirically based; Royce says that, great as that work was, it suffered from James's insistence that true religious experience was something that occurred in its fullest form only to individuals in solitude and independently of religious institutions. Such institutions provide, according to James, only a second-rate form of religion, a shadow of that which had inspired their founders. But Royce contends that the true religious experience is social and occurs only when an individual is a member of a "beloved community."

Royce begins his examination of Christianity by asking whether it has some essential message for humanity that is valid today and in the future, even if the detailed Christian story has to be rejected. He disclaims any concern with the life and personality of Jesus as quite outside his competence and, in fact, as of little religious significance. He contends that the attempt of some to see true Christianity only in the teachings of Jesus and to regard St. Paul, in particular, as diverting Christianity from this true essence is on the wrong track. In fact, without their development by Paul, Jesus' teachings lack adequate content. Christianity does, indeed, have an abiding message, which can be separated from its traditional myths and dogmas. It is to be found not in the teachings of Jesus but much more in Paul's epistles–though here, again, the essential message is independent of acceptance of Paul's Christology. In fact, Royce says, the true founder of Christianity is neither Jesus nor Paul but the early Christian community under Paul's leadership.

For Jesus the two great commandments were love of God and love of one's neighbor, and both God and the neighbor are individual persons. For Paul, however, a third individual existed, a superpersonal one: the Christian community, conceived by Paul as the body of Christ, whom it was salvation to love. The lasting legacy of Christianity, as Royce sees it, is not what, without Paul, one might take to be Jesus' simple message of loving one's neighbor as a mere individual. Rather, it comes from Paul's conception of how individual Christians were related to the Christian community, and only via that community to each other. Jesus, for Paul, was the personalized symbol of the unity of the Christian community. The essential message to be retained from Paul is that individuals are lost unless they experience themselves, and live, as members of a beloved community, loyalty to which is the main guiding inspiration of their lives: "The detached individual is essentially a lost being." Christianity, thus understood, is the religion of loyalty. As such, it is superior to other religions that have never similarly presented loyalty as the fundamental principle by which people should guide their lives.

In relating Christianity to the philosophy of loyalty, Royce says that loyalty is "*the practically devoted love of an individual for a community.*" This statement represents a slight shift in his conception of loyalty: *The Philosophy of Loyalty* left a certain ambiguity as to whether communities of the loyal were united by their devotion to a common cause, such as the abolition of slavery, or by their devotion to the community itself. In *The Problem of Christianity* the latter notion is dominant.

Royce sets out to expound and evaluate the message of Christianity from a purely psychological point of view, without introducing questions of its truth. The great psychological truth that is the core of Christian belief and practice is that an isolated human being is a wretched creature. Only when individuals live lives of loyalty to a beloved community can they avoid a general sense of purposelessness. Paul's epistles show that he was guiding the early Christians toward becoming just such an ideal beloved community. He expressed its peculiar unity by speaking of the individuals as members of a common body, "the body of Christ." Christians have subsequently conceived themselves as members of such a body whenever their faith has been a truly living one. Eventually, humanity as a whole will be this community, though loyalty to it will be mediated by loyalty to more-immediate groupings.

The ideas that as an isolated individual one is lost and that one can only be saved as a member of a beloved community constitute what Royce regards as the first two great ideas of Christianity: Original Sin and Redemption. The third great Christian idea is the doctrine of the Atonement, to which Royce gives a similarly novel twist. The idea that Christ died on the cross so that he, rather than the rest of humanity, should suffer the punishment that their sins deserve has made many Christian thinkers uneasy. Apart from the questionable notion of vicarious punishment, it does not allow the irrevocability of the past its due significance. Royce offers his own interpretation of the doctrine of Atonement by considering the case of a person who has betrayed the ideals by which he had committed himself to live. Such a sin can never be annulled as a blemish on the universe. But the sin can be atoned for vicariously by a nobler spirit than the sinner if its occurrence is made the basis for the development of a greater good that could not have been reached without the sin. This atonement does not wipe out the sin, but it does enable the sinner to be reconciled with the commu-

nity that he or she has betrayed by the sin. This reconciling is what Christ is deemed to have done by leading human beings to a higher form of life than they could ever have reached except as repentant sinners, and it is how humanity as a whole should seek to redeem its dreadful history. With this concept of atonement Royce further enriches his notion of the way in which evil is a necessary feature of a supremely good world.

Royce distinguishes three types of groups to which individuals can belong. The least unitary is the aggregate, such as people who happen to be shopping at the same store at the same time. Somewhat more unified is the crowd, which is a group of people engaged in a shared activity in which each person is aware of the part he or she is playing. Its existence is short-term, and no shared memory, expectation, or long-range purpose unites it. Finally, there is the true community, which "has a past and will have a future. Its more or less conscious history, real or ideal, is a part of its very essence. A community requires for its existence a history and is greatly aided in its consciousness by a memory." All finite human thought occurs in a momentary "now," but it is aware, at least implicitly, that it is carrying on a purpose originated in earlier momentary states of consciousness, and it also contains the willing of some future state of consciousness. This awareness of a past that it regards as its own and of a future that it wills or anticipates as its own, constitutes it as a phase in the life of a self. Similarly, a community exists when a multiplicity of human selves share much of the same past and the same future. This past and future consist mainly of events that occurred or will occur before or after the deaths of these selves: they include events involving the ancestors of the present selves, which each member of the community adopts as belonging to his or own past (Royce uses as an illustration the Maori who speaks of himself as having come over in the canoe in which his ancestors are believed to have arrived in New Zealand), and hoped-for events that each member of the community adopts as belonging to his or her own future. The adoption of a common past and future by finite selves that constitutes the existence of a community is similar to the adoption of an individual past and future that gives each individual self its personal identity. The past shared by members of a community may, to a greater or lesser extent, be mythical; likewise, the expected future, such as the New Jerusalem, may never come. But there must be *some* real past in common for a community to exist.

One might ask what makes two individuals different persons if they genuinely belong to the same community. Royce answers that at any one moment the two consciousnesses are, as far as the individuals themselves are concerned, quite distinct. But one's consciousness as it is at any one moment is not a self. It only becomes the consciousness of a self because it interprets itself as a phase in the life of a continuing individual. Equally, it interprets itself as belonging to a community with a conceived past and a likely future. Another aspect of the matter is that each person embodies a distinctive purpose, that is, a distinct component in the more complex purpose of the community.

As communities of memory and hope develop, the members become ever more closely linked by a shared love of the community's present activities. Thus is born the beloved community. The members of the Christian community share in memory the Crucifixion and Resurrection of Christ, in virtue of which they feel themselves saved; they also share the hope of the general resurrection and the eventual Kingdom of God to which they believe they will all belong.

A highly complex society such as the modern United States, Royce says, may be so little grasped as a whole by its members that it risks being less of a beloved community than less advanced nations, such as Japan, can still be. This danger of modern society can only be remedied if there are occasions of common celebration of the community's shared past and expected future that can unite all of its members in the love of it. Then, each can experience the present time of the community as his or her own present, ignorant though he or she must remain of most of its detailed activities.

Human life, then, exists on two levels, that of the community and that of individual persons. Each is as real as the other. Royce accordingly insists that a community is normally an agent in its own right; its actions are not just the sum of those of the individuals who compose it. Thus, "for our purposes," says Royce,

> the community is a being that attempts to accomplish something in time and through the deeds of its members. These deeds belong to the life which each member regards as, in ideal, his own. It is in this way that both the real and the ideal Church are intended by the members to be communities in our sense. An analogous truth holds for such other communities as we shall need to consider. The concept of the community is thus, for our purposes, a practical conception. It involves the idea of deeds done, and ends sought or attained. Hence I shall define it in terms of members who themselves not only live in time, but conceive their own ideally extended personalities in terms of a time-process. In so far as these personalities possess a life that is for each of them his own, while it is, in some of its events, common to them all, they form a community.

Nothing important is lost, for our conception of the community, by this formal restriction, whereby common objects belong to a community only when these objects are bound up with the deeds of the community.

Royce insists that the existence of a beloved community does not depend on any mystical blending of its members in an unindividuated mush. The selves in a community continue to exist as separate beings with distinct consciousnesses. Still, the community's members may well harbor the wish for a complete grasp of the community's life, and Royce is more than ready to hold that such a comprehension may actually occur. But this phenomenon is not what makes a community a community; instead, it is an occasional result of the community's existence:

> The distinctiveness of the selves we have illustrated at length in our previous discussion. We need not here dwell upon the matter further, except to say expressly, that a community does *not* become one, in the sense of my definition, by virtue of any reduction or melting of the selves into a single merely present self, or into a mass of passive experience. That mystical phenomena may indeed form part of the life of a community, just as they may also form part of the life of an individual human being, I fully recognize.
>
> About such mystical or quasi-mystical phenomena, occurring in their own community, the Corinthians consulted Paul.

And Paul insisted that this phenomenon did not need to happen and that on the whole it was better that it did not happen. Royce, it seems, is anxious that his account of communities should not depend on a notion of suprapersonal forms of consciousness, so that it might interest more-naturalistic thinkers who dismiss any such idea, while yet finding room for them as realities in which he himself believes.

Royce thinks that the love of each individual for his or her community cannot be explained by a purely naturalistic psychology. Thus, in some sense, such love "comes from above." And this fact can only be explained if the universe itself is a genuine community. The account of the nature of the universe that best suits the essential message of Christianity as delivered primarily by Paul, rather than by Jesus, is one that regards it as essentially social:

> The Christian view of life is dominated by the ideal of the Universal Community. Such is the thesis defended in the first part of this series of lectures. The real world itself is, in its wholeness, a Community. This was the metaphysical result in which our study of the world of Interpretation culminates.

To give more precision to this view of the universe, Royce presents a brief account of Peirce's theory of signs, by which he was much influenced in developing it. Suppose, he says, an Egyptologist manages to translate an ancient Egyptian inscription. Then there is

Royce with his Harvard University colleague William James at James's summer home in Chocurua, New Hampshire, in 1903 (Harvard University Archives)

a three-term relation that, according to Peirce, cannot be reduced to a two-term one. The terms are, first, the Egyptian text, referred to as the sign; second, the translation, that is, the English text; third, the English reader to whom the text is interpreted. Peirce's theory asserts that all communication has this triadic structure. It also claims that the process of interpretation is, in principle, endless, since the interpretation, which in this case is the English text, will itself need to be interpreted.

Royce claims that the universe is entirely composed of such triads of interpretation. Every event is a sign that a second event interprets to a third event. The most obvious illustration is the ideas that follow one another in one's mind. Whenever anything that could be called an idea occurs in the mind, it has to be interpreted by a second idea, which explicates it so that it will be understood by a third idea. It is only because ideas are a series of interpretations that any knowledge of the past or future is possible. A being whose mind did not consist of a series of signs would have no sense of anything other than the present moment:

Our memories are signs of the past; our expectations are signs of the future. Past and future are real in so far as these signs have their real interpretation. Our metaphysical thesis generalizes the rules which constantly guide our daily interpretations of life. All contrasts of ideas, all varieties of experience, all the problems which finite experience possesses, are signs. The real world contains (so our thesis asserts) the interpreter of these signs, and the very being of the world consists in the truth of the interpretation which, in the whole realm of experience, these signs obtain.

All proper communities are, then, communities of interpretation. The communities that really matter are those in which large numbers of members are bound together by a complex system of triadic relations. In such communities each member has a will to interpret other members to each other. But, of course, no interpretation is perfect; one person can never explain a second person to a third in any fully adequate way. But in all such communities there is a more or less explicit aspiration for some complete understanding of all by

Royce with three other members of the Harvard philosophy department–Hugo Münsterberg, George Herbert Palmer, and James–circa 1908 (photograph by Winifred Rieber; Collection of Dorothy Rieber Joralemon)

all. And this understanding is that far-off divine event toward which all are struggling.

Royce gives the impression that this account of a community replaces his old idea that individuals' access to a world beyond themselves requires that they belong with everything else in a single absolute consciousness. Yet, he hastens to assure his reader that the metaphysical views advocated in *The Problem of Christianity* are compatible with, and by no means a recantation of, his earlier metaphysical views. It is simply that here he is concentrating on that feature of the world that makes it a world of interpretation. He still holds that the whole community of interpretation is all included in the one Divine Thought, which, indeed, is itself the ultimate interpreter of everything (including itself).

Royce identifies three basic attitudes of the will with which people may face the universe, and he considers which one is the most appropriate if the doctrine of signs he has advanced is true. The first attitude is a will to live, to assert oneself as an individual. People who have this attitude will recognize that other persons are self-affirming in just the same ways as they themselves are. Insofar as it helps their own self-affirmation to cooperate with these others, they will do so. But if a conflict of wills arises, they will take the most selfish option and look out only for their own personal advantage. The second attitude is passive resignation: the individual may look askance on this world of willing beings and deny the will to live in the way Schopenhauer understood the saintly to do.

(Royce notes that this attitude is a Buddhist one and that Schopenhauer was wrong to associate it with Christianity.) The third attitude is that of the loyal individual. The life of such a person is dictated by loyalty to a cause; thereby the loyal person escapes the misery that characterizes the first two attitudes. This attitude is that of Christianity. On their own, individuals are lost; they can only be "saved" by being devotedly loyal members of a community:

> Practically I cannot be saved alone: theoretically speaking, I cannot find or even define the truth in terms of my individual experience, without taking account of my relation to the community of those who know. This community, then, is real whatever is real. And in that community my life is interpreted. When viewed as if I were alone, I, the individual, am not only doomed to failure, but I am lost in folly. The "workings" of my ideas are events whose significance I cannot even remotely estimate in terms of their momentary existence, or in terms of my individual success. My life means nothing, either theoretically or practically, unless I am a member of a community. I win no success worth having, unless it is also the success of the community to which I, essentially and by virtue of my relation to the whole universe, belong. My deeds are not done at all, unless they are indeed done for all time, and are irrevocable.

The purpose of religion is to bind people together in a loving community, and the early Christian church, under the guidance of St. Paul, is the best instance of such a community that has yet existed. Now, Royce says, taking inspiration from that early community, while abandoning most of its credal basis, people must pursue whatever means they find are the most helpful to bind humanity in general into a loving community.

Royce was always interested in logic and published several technical articles in the field. In the last decade of his life he made an intense study of developments in logic and mathematics by such figures as Peirce, J. W. R. Dedekind, Georg Cantor, and Bertrand Russell and tried to use them in his own metaphysics. This interest, and his consequent rejection of the Hegelian idea that the infinity of the mathematician is a "bad infinite" that has no place in philosophical thought, most divided him from the other absolute idealists of his time, especially his great British contemporary Bradley. Bradley argued for the unreality of most of the objects of ordinary thought by saying that to conceive any of them is to be entangled in an infinite regress. Bradley also denied that absolute idealism could ever satisfactorily explain how finite centers of experience are related to the Absolute; they are somehow included within it, but more-specific accounts must make use of concepts that are themselves finally incoherent.

Against this position, Royce argues in an appendix to the first volume of *The World and the Individual* that the unity of the Absolute can be grasped in a manner that does allow for the inclusion of infinite series within it, because a unitary individual can quite well include an infinity of distinct components within itself. He gives the example of a completely detailed map that is laid out on the ground in the mapped area: it must include a picture of the map itself and, thereby, an infinite series of ever smaller but otherwise identical maps. Thus, the map is a unitary whole, though it has an infinity of components. So it is with the Absolute.

In "The Relation of the Principles of Logic to the Foundations of Geometry," published in *Transactions of the American Mathematical Society* (1914), Royce elaborates a logical system of his own, System Σ, that, he thinks, shows how the Absolute can be conceptualized both as unitary and as infinitely complex. Building on the work of Alfred Kempe, he sets out System Σ as an uninterpreted formal system that can be given either a geometrical or mathematical interpretation. The article is a highly technical work that, as Royce himself said, was probably beyond the comprehension of most of those who were primarily interested in his metaphysics, ethics, and religious thought. Its philosophical novelty lies mainly in the path it wends between a Platonic and a pragmatic view of the concepts of logic, which Royce holds to be expressions of necessary truths about any will that is committed to acting "in an orderly fashion."

Royce introduced the study of modern mathematical logic into the United States. Among those to whom he taught logic at Harvard was C. I. Lewis. Thus, even if Royce's logic has not been paid much attention, it was a significant step in the history of American philosophy.

In *War and Insurance,* the text of an address delivered before the Philosophical Union of the University of California on 27 August 1914, Royce applies his notion of social harmony as requiring triadic, rather than merely dyadic, relations, to the then looming issue of war. War between nations, he argues, occurs because merely dyadic relations exist between them, with no mediating organization. Such a mediating organization could be provided by an international insurance company through which nations would protect themselves against the ravages of war. As many nations as possible would be encouraged to become clients. The insurance would cover damage suffered in war, provided that it had not been a result of the nation's own aggression. Just as domestic insurance binds the citizens of a country together by encouraging all to be concerned with the troubles of each, and thereby promotes loyalty to the social whole, in the same way international insurance against war will promote harmonious relations among nations.

Royce was intensely depressed when his beloved Germany, as he saw it, betrayed civilization in its prosecution of World War I–in particular, by the sinking of the British ocean liner *Lusitania* by a submarine on 7 May 1915, resulting in the loss of the lives of 1,198 noncombatants. This position led to extreme ill feeling (his last big quarrel) with his German colleague, the psychologist Hugo Münsterburg, who vigorously proclaimed the justice of Germany's actions. Royce's friends believed that his death on 14 September 1916 was hastened by depression caused by his feeling that Germany had become the enemy of humanity.

How far Josiah Royce can have been said to have lived his philosophy of loyalty is hard to say. He did not belong to any religious community, and he seems not to have been passionately loyal either to California or to the United States. If challenged, he probably would have described his greatest loyalties as being to his family and circle of close friends and, at a more general level, to the community of searchers for philosophical truth. He described himself as tending to a nonconformity that worked against the commitment to the community through which alone, he held, one can be saved. Royce was beloved as a teacher, colleague, and friend, but he showed some lack of sympathy for others in his scathing attack on Abbot. He was certainly a major thinker, and philosophers today would do well to take more account of him.

Letters:

The Letters of Josiah Royce, edited by John Clendenning (Chicago: University of Chicago Press, 1970).

Biography:

John Clendenning, *The Life and Thought of Josiah Royce* (Nashville: Vanderbilt University Press, 1999).

References:

James Harry Cotton, *Royce on the Human Self* (Cambridge, Mass.: Harvard University Press, 1954);

George Dykhuizen, "The Conception of God in the Philosophy of Josiah Royce: A Critical Exposition of Its Epistemological and Metaphysical Development," dissertation, University of Chicago, 1934;

Peter Fuss, *The Moral Philosophy of Josiah Royce* (Cambridge, Mass.: Harvard University Press, 1965);

Robert V. Hine, *Josiah Royce: From Grass Valley to Harvard* (Norman: University of Oklahoma Press, 1992);

Karl Theodore Humbach, *Das Verhältnis von Einzelperson und Gemeinschaft nach Josiah Royce: Eine Untersuchung zum Zentralproblem der Sozialphilosophie* (Heidelberg: Winter, 1962);

Edward A. Jarvis, *The Conception of God in the Later Royce* (The Hague: Nijhoff, 1975);

Bruce Kuklick, *Josiah Royce: An Intellectual Biography* (Indianapolis: Hackett, 1985);

Mary Briody Mahowald, *An Idealistic Pragmatism: The Development of the Pragmatic Element in the Philosophy of Josiah Royce* (The Hague: Nijhoff, 1972);

Gabriel Marcel, *La métaphysique de Royce* (Paris: Aubier, Editions Montaigne, 1918); translated by Virginia Ringer and Gordon Ringer as *Royce's Metaphysics* (Chicago: Regnery, 1956);

Frank M. Oppenheim, *Royce's Mature Ethics* (Notre Dame, Ind.: University of Notre Dame Press, 1993);

Oppenheim, *Royce's Mature Philosophy of Religion* (Notre Dame, Ind.: University of Notre Dame Press, 1987);

Oppenheim, *Royce's Voyage Down Under: A Journey of the Mind* (Lexington: University Press of Kentucky, 1980);

Daniel Sommer Robinson, *Royce and Hocking, American Idealists: An Introduction to Their Philosophy, with Selected Letters* (Boston: Christopher Publishing House, 1968);

George Santayana, *Character and Opinion in the United States, with Reminiscences of William James and Josiah Royce and Academic Life in America* (New York: Scribners, 1924);

Tribhuwan N. Sharan, *The Religious Philosophy of Josiah Royce* (New Delhi: Oriental Publishers and Distributors, 1976);

Bhagwan B. Singh, *The Self and the World in the Philosophy of Josiah Royce* (Springfield, Ill.: C. C. Thomas, 1973);

John E. Skinner, *The Logocentric Predicament: An Essay on the Problem of Error in the Philosophy of Josiah Royce* (Philadelphia: University of Pennsylvania Press, 1965);

John Edwin Smith, *Royce's Social Infinite: The Community of Interpretation* (New York: Liberal Arts Press, 1950).

Papers:

Josiah Royce's dissertation, "On the Interdependence of the Principles of Knowledge: An Investigation of Elementary Knowledge, in Two Chapters, with an Introduction on the Principal Ideas and Problems in Which the Discussion Takes Its Rise," dated 2 April 1878, exists in a handwritten original in the Johns Hopkins University Library and in a typewritten copy in the Harvard University Archives.

George Santayana

(16 December 1863 – 26 September 1952)

Charles Padrón
Stephen F. Austin University

See also the Santayana entries in *DLB 54, American Poets, 1880–1945, Third Series; DLB 71, American Literary Critics and Scholars, 1880–1900; DLB 246, Twentieth-Century American Cultural Theorists;* and *DLB Documentary Series 13, The House of Scribner, 1846–1904.*

BOOKS: *Lines on Leaving the Bedford St. Schoolhouse* (Boston: Privately printed, 1880);

Sonnets and Other Verses (Cambridge, Mass. & Chicago: Stone & Kimball, 1894; revised and enlarged edition, New York: Stone & Kimball, 1896);

The Sense of Beauty: Being the Outlines of Aesthetic Theory (New York: Scribners, 1896; London: A. & C. Black, 1896);

Platonism in the Italian Poets (Buffalo, N.Y.: Pauls' Press, 1896);

Lucifer: A Theological Tragedy (Chicago & New York: Stone, 1899); revised as *Lucifer; or, The Heavenly Truce: A Theological Tragedy* (Cambridge, Mass.: Dunster House, 1924);

Interpretations of Poetry and Religion (New York: Scribners, 1900; London: A. & C. Black, 1900);

A Hermit of Carmel and Other Poems (New York: Scribners, 1901; London: Johnson, 1902);

The Life of Reason; or, The Phases of Human Progress, 5 volumes (New York: Scribners, 1905–1906; London: Constable, 1905–1906);

Three Philosophical Poets: Lucretius, Dante, and Goethe (Cambridge, Mass.: Harvard University Press, 1910; London: Oxford University Press, 1910);

Winds of Doctrine: Studies in Contemporary Opinion (New York: Scribners, 1913);

Egotism in German Philosophy (London: Dent / New York: Scribners, 1916); republished as *The German Mind: A Philosophical Diagnosis* (New York: Crowell, 1968);

Essays in Critical Realism: A Co-operative Study of the Problem of Knowledge, by Santayana, Durant Drake, Arthur O. Lovejoy, James Bissett Pratt, Arthur Kenyon Rogers, Roy Wood Sellars, and Charles Augus-

tus Strong (London: Macmillan, 1920)–includes "Three Proofs of Realism," by Santayana, pp. 163–184;

Character and Opinion in the United States: With Reminiscences of William James and Josiah Royce and Academic Life in America (London: Constable, 1920; New York: Scribners, 1920);

Little Essays: Drawn from the Writings of George Santayana, edited by Santayana and Logan Pearsall Smith (New York: Scribners, 1920);

Soliloquies in England, and Later Soliloquies (London: Constable, 1922; New York: Scribners, 1922);

Poems: Selected by the Author and Revised (London: Constable, 1922; New York: Scribners, 1923);

Scepticism and Animal Faith: Introduction to a System of Philosophy (London: Constable, 1923; New York: Scribners, 1923);

The Unknowable: The Herbert Spencer Lecture Delivered at Oxford, 24 October, 1923 (Oxford: Clarendon Press, 1923);

Dialogues in Limbo (London: Constable, 1925; New York: Scribners, 1926; enlarged edition, New York: Scribners, 1948); enlarged as *Dialogues in Limbo: With Three New Dialogues* (Ann Arbor: University of Michigan Press, 1957);

Platonism and the Spiritual Life (London: Constable, 1927; New York: Scribners, 1927);

The Realm of Essence: Book First of Realms of Being (New York: Scribners, 1927; London: Constable, 1928);

The Realm of Matter: Book Second of Realms of Being (New York: Scribners, 1930; London: Constable, 1930);

The Genteel Tradition at Bay (New York: Scribners, 1931; London: Adelphi, 1931);

Some Turns of Thought in Modern Philosophy: Five Essays (New York: Scribners, 1933; Cambridge: Cambridge University Press, 1933);

The Last Puritan: A Memoir in the Form of a Novel (London: Constable, 1935; New York: Scribners, 1936);

Obiter Scripta: Lectures, Essays and Reviews, edited by Justus Buchler and Benjamin Schwartz (New York: Scribners, 1936; London: Constable, 1936);

The Realm of Truth: Book Third of Realms of Being (London: Constable, 1937; New York: Scribners, 1938);

The Realm of Spirit: Book Fourth of Realms of Being (London: Constable, 1940; New York: Scribners, 1940);

Persons and Places: The Background of My Life (New York: Scribners, 1944; London: Constable, 1944);

Persons and Places: The Middle Span (New York: Scribners, 1945; London: Constable, 1947);

The Idea of Christ in the Gospels; or, God in Man: A Critical Essay (New York: Scribners, 1946);

Dominations and Powers: Reflections on Liberty, Society, and Government (New York: Scribners, 1951; London: Constable, 1951);

Persons and Places: My Host the World (New York: Scribners, 1953; London: Cressest, 1953);

The Poet's Testament: Poems and Two Plays, edited by John Hall Wheelock and Daniel Cory (New York: Scribners, 1953);

Essays in Literary Criticism of George Santayana, edited by Irving Singer (New York: Scribners, 1956);

The Idler and His Works, and Other Essays, edited by Cory (New York: Braziller, 1957);

George Santayana's America: Essays on Literature and Culture, edited by James Ballowe (Urbana: University of Illinois Press, 1967);

Animal Faith and Spiritual Life: Previously Unpublished and Uncollected Writings by George Santayana with Critical Essays on His Thought, edited by John Lachs (New York: Appleton-Century-Crofts, 1967);

The Genteel Tradition: Nine Essays, edited by Douglas L. Wilson (Cambridge, Mass.: Harvard University Press, 1967);

The Birth of Reason and Other Essays, edited by Cory (New York: Columbia University Press, 1968);

Santayana on America: Essays, Notes, and Letters on American Life, Literature, and Philosophy, edited by Richard Colton Lyon (New York: Harcourt, Brace & World, 1968);

Physical Order and Moral Liberty: Previously Unpublished Essays of George Santayana, edited by Lachs and Shirley Lachs (Nashville: Vanderbilt University Press, 1969);

Lotze's System of Philosophy, edited by Paul Grimley Kuntz (Bloomington: Indiana University Press, 1971);

The Complete Poems of George Santayana: A Critical Edition, edited by William G. Holzberger (Lewisburg, Pa.: Bucknell University Press, 1979).

Collections: *The Works of George Santayana,* Triton Edition, 15 volumes (New York: Scribners, 1936–1940);

Atoms of Thought: An Anthology of Thoughts from George Santayana, edited by Ira D. Cardiff (New York: Philosophical Library, 1950);

Irwin Edman, ed., *The Philosophy of Santayana* (New York: Modern Library, 1953);

The Works of George Santayana, Critical Edition, 5 volumes published (Cambridge, Mass.: MIT Press, 1986–   ).

OTHER: "Ultimate Religion," in *Setimana Spizozana: Acta Conventus Oecumenici in Memoriam Benedicti de Spinoza Diei Natalis Trecentesimi Hagae Comitis Habiti: Curis Societatis Spinozanae Edita* (The Hague: Martinus Nijoff, 1933), pp. 105–115;

"A General Confession" and "Apologia Pro Mente Sua," in *The Philosophy of George Santayana,* edited by Paul Arthur Schilpp, The Library of Living Philosophers, volume 2 (Evanston, Ill.: Northwestern University Press, 1940), pp. 1–30, 497–560.

Santayana (standing, third from left) as a member of the Harvard Lampoon *staff during his undergraduate years (Harvard University Archives)*

George Santayana occupies a unique position in the history of Western philosophy, American philosophy, and American belles lettres. Born in Madrid to a Spanish father and a Scottish mother, Santayana spans, in his life and intellectual career, the nineteenth and twentieth centuries, the European and North American continents, intellectual disciplines, institutional and national loyalties. He was part of the "golden age of American philosophy" at Harvard University in the late nineteenth and early twentieth centuries. He eschewed technical philosophical terminology and logical symbolism and wrote in a poetic, clear prose intended to be understood by the intelligent layperson. Many people who are unfamiliar with philosophy and have never even read any of Santayana's works have heard his often-quoted remarks, both from *Reason in Common Sense* (1905): "Those who cannot remember the past are condemned to repeat it" and "Fanaticism consists in redoubling your efforts when you have forgotten your aim."

Jorge Ruiz de Santayana y Borrais was born in Madrid on 16 December 1863. His father, Augustín Ruiz de Santayana, had studied law at the University of Valladolid; he was also a widely read man who translated four of Seneca's tragedies into Spanish, as well as an accomplished painter. He entered Spain's colonial service and in 1845 was sent to Batang in the

Philippines, where he replaced the recently deceased governor of the island, José Borrás y Bofarull, and met Josefina Borrás, the former governor's daughter. He encountered her again in 1856 on a ship on which she was traveling from Manila to Boston. She was accompanied by her husband, the Boston businessman George Sturgis, whom she had married in Manila in 1849, and their children, Susana, Josefina, and Roberto. Sturgis died in 1857, leaving his widow in difficult financial circumstances. With aid from her husband's brother, Josefina and the children moved back to Madrid in 1861; she married Augustín there the following year. The family moved to Ávila between 1864 and 1866.

Josefina had promised her first husband that his children would be educated in Boston. Roberto was sent there in 1867, and in 1869 Josefina left with her two daughters. Augustín and Santayana remained in Ávila until 1872, when they, too, moved to Boston. Augustín returned to Spain after a few months, leaving Santayana with his mother at 302 Beacon Street; he lived there until 1881, when his mother moved to the Boston suburb of Roxbury. In spite of the embarrassment of being placed in a kindergarten class as an eight-year-old, Santayana rapidly acquired a command of English, while preserving his fluency in Spanish. He received a well-rounded, classical education at the Bos-

neglect of his progress in German. Learning that his fellowship had been renewed, he wrote on 3 July 1888 to his favorite teacher at Harvard, William James, that two years at the University of Berlin

> have convinced me that the German school, although it is well to have some acquaintance with it, is not one to which I can attach myself. After the first impression of novelty and freedom, I have become oppressed by the scholasticism of the thing and by the absurd pretension to be scientific. In fact, my whole experience, since I left college and even before, has been a series of disenchantments. First I lost my faith in the kind of philosophy that Prof. Palmer and Royce are interested in; and then, when I came to Germany, I also lost my faith in psycho-physics, and all other attempts to discover something very momentous.

Santayana circa 1889, the year he received his Ph.D. at Harvard (Photography Collection, Harry Ransom Humanities Research Center, University of Texas at Austin)

ton Latin School from 1874 to 1882 and entered Harvard University in the fall of 1882. He excelled academically from the start but felt somewhat estranged from the wealthy and socially elite student body. His biographer John McCormick comments: "Throughout Santayana's undergraduate years, and indeed all of his years of American residence, the conflict between Massachusetts and Castile, between Harvard and Roxbury in one hemisphere and Ávila in another, continued." He was, however, quite active in campus associations and formed lifelong friendships with some of his classmates. He was a member of the Art Club; the Hasty Pudding Club; Phi Beta Kappa; the Institute of 1770; the Chess Club; the Everett Athenaeum; the Philosophical Club, of which he was elected president; the Shakespeare Club; the O. K. Society; *The Harvard Lampoon;* and *The Harvard Monthly.*

Santayana graduated summa cum laude in 1886. He had received a Walker Fellowship for graduate study in Germany, and he sailed to Europe in the summer. After visiting France and spending a month with his father in Ávila, he enrolled at the University of Berlin in October. He was undisciplined about attending lectures or producing written work, and he spent most of his time with English-speaking individuals, to the

Santayana left Berlin in June 1888 and returned to Harvard and to his mother's house in Roxbury in September. Though his relationship with James was closer, he selected Josiah Royce as his dissertation supervisor. Rejecting Santayana's proposal that he write on Arthur Schopenhauer, Royce suggested a dissertation on Rudolf Hermann Lotze, a German metaphysician and process philosopher who had fallen into relative obscurity. With misgivings, Santayana agreed. He turned in a handwritten manuscript of 322 pages before the 1889 spring commencement; it was accepted, and Santayana became the third student in the history of the Harvard philosophy department to receive the Ph.D. (The dissertation was published in 1971.) The department offered him an instructorship, and he accepted. Once they were colleagues, Santayana and James's friendship blossomed.

From 1890 to 1897 Santayana lived in number 7, Stoughton Hall, on the Harvard campus. He wrote of these relatively carefree years: "My life and pleasures were still those of a student; I lived on intimate terms with a knot of undergraduates; I went to 'parties,' chiefly dinner parties in Boston."

The year 1893 marked a watershed in Santayana's life. Four unrelated events shook his world: the deaths of Warwick Potter, "his last real friend," and his father in Spain; his estrangement from his half sister Susana, with whom he had shared one of his warmest relationships, when she married and moved back to Spain; and his disillusionment with Catholicism.

Santayana's first published book was a volume not of philosophy but of poetry: *Sonnets and Other Verses* (1894). He continued to write poems and verse dramas for several years: the plays *The Marriage of Venus* and *Philosophers at Court* were composed between 1897 and 1901 but not published until 1953, when they appeared posthumously in *The Poet's Testament: Poems and Two*

Santayana when he was teaching philosophy at Harvard

Plays. He published the five-act verse drama *Lucifer: A Theological Tragedy* in 1899 and *A Hermit of Carmel and Other Poems* in 1901. Many critics have argued that Santayana's melodious, luxuriant prose style was essentially poetry in the form of prose.

Santayana's second book was his first sustained philosophical treatise. *The Sense of Beauty: Being the Outlines of Aesthetic Theory* (1896) is based on his lectures in the aesthetics course he taught at Harvard from 1892 to 1895. An analysis of the aesthetic sense in human beings, the book is divided into four parts: "The Nature of Beauty," "The Materials of Beauty," "Form," and "Expression." Santayana defines beauty as "pleasure objectified," or "pleasure regarded as the quality of a thing." From Santayana's vantage point, those rare individuals who give spectators or readers glimpses into the "permanent and universal do a greater service to mankind and deserve higher honour than the discoverers of historical truth." Reflecting on this work in *The Middle Span* (1945), the second volume of his autobiography, *Persons and Places* (1944–1953), Santayana wrote:

Very well: although I didn't have, and haven't now, a clear notion of what "aesthetics" may be, I undertook to give a course in that subject. It would help to define my status. I gave it for one or two years and then I wrote out the substance of it in a little book: *The Sense of Beauty.* . . . I sent it to Scribner, it was printed and did not prove a financial loss to the publisher, although it had neither a large sale nor a warm reception from the critics. However, it was a book, a *fact;* and it established pleasant relations between me and Scribner which have lasted for fifty years.

Santayana's appointment as assistant professor in 1898 dampened his close contacts with students. He moved off campus to his mother's house in Longwood. His own words capture the change: "My relations with undergraduates and with Boston society, although renewed, were renewed on a new basis. I no longer played the familiar companion or the young man about town. I was simply an elderly mentor or an occasional guest." Among the students who passed through Santayana's classes during his years at Harvard were the

Santayana's half sister, Susana Sturgis, in 1892 (Photography Collection, Harry Ransom Humanities Research Center, University of Texas at Austin)

future journalist and author Walter Lippmann, the future Harvard president James B. Conant, the future United States Supreme Court justice Felix Frankfurter, the future historian Samuel Eliot Morrison, the future philosopher Harry Austryn Wolfson, and the future poets Conrad Aiken, T. S. Eliot, Wallace Stevens, and Robert Frost.

Interpretations of Poetry and Religion (1900) consists of ten essays written over a period of years. According to Santayana, religion, as an expression of a way of life in touch with an ideal, is a manifestation of the poetical; conversely, the highest levels of aesthetic experience attained via poetry are analogous to a religious state of mind. Santayana links the religious and the poetical to the human longing for an ideal.

In 1902 Santayana was made a full professor at Harvard. In February of that year he published in *The International Quarterly* "The Search for the True Plato," and in September he published in the same journal the dialogue "The Two Idealisms." The dialogue became a highly effective form of philosophical expression for Santayana, culminating in his *Dialogues in Limbo* (1925). In May 1904 he published the essay "What is Æsthetics?" in *The Philosophical Review*.

The five-volume *The Life of Reason; or, The Phases of Human Progress* (1905–1906) is Santayana's first large-scale, systematic philosophical work. "Thought," Santayana says, "is a form of life, and should be conceived on the analogy of nutrition, generation, art. . . . Existence reveals reality when the flux discloses something permanent that dominates it. The brain, though mobile, is subject to habit; its formations, while they lapse instantly, return again and again." Santayana traces the activity of reason in common sense, society, religion, art, and science.

In February 1910 Santayana gave six lectures at Columbia University on Lucretius, Dante, and Johann Wolfgang von Goethe; he repeated them in April at the University of Wisconsin. They were based on a course he had been teaching at Harvard and were published that year as *Three Philosophical Poets,* the first volume in the Harvard Studies in Comparative Literature series. He treats Lucretius, Dante, and Goethe as exemplars, respectively, of the worldviews of naturalism, supernaturalism, and romanticism.

On 23 January 1912 Santayana sailed for Europe. Within two weeks, his mother died. On 6 June he sent Abbot Lawrence Lowell, the president of Harvard, his letter of resignation, in which he said: "The death of my mother, which occurred shortly after I left America, has made a great change in my personal situation, leaving me without a home in Boston and with most of my close friends and relations living in Europe. It seems clearly to mark the moment when I should carry out the plan I have always had of giving up teaching, returning to live in Europe, and devoting myself to literary work." A $10,000 inheritance from his mother, along with royalties from his books, made it possible for him to carry out this plan for the rest of his life. He never returned to the United States. In 1913 he published *Winds of Doctrine: Studies in Contemporary Opinion,* a collection of six essays: "The Intellectual Temper of the Age"; "Modernism and Christianity"; "The Philosophy of M. Henri Bergson"; "The Philosophy of Mr. Bertrand Russell"; "Shelley: or The Poetic Value of Revolutionary Principles"; and "The Genteel Tradition in American Philosophy," which had originally been delivered as a lecture to the Philosophical Union at the University of California at Berkeley on 25 August 1911 and which became one of his best-known works.

In *Egotism in German Philosophy* (1916), his only book-length work between 1911 and 1920, Santayana engages in philosophical polemics for perhaps the only time in his life. Two years into World War I, European civilization was in the throes of a conflict that seemed meaningless and barbaric, and Santayana was preoccupied with the sources in post-Kantian German philosophy of the principal aggressor's behavior and aims:

On the Three Philosophical Poets.

Falling untempered from the ethereal blue,
The light of truth might scorch the eyes, and blind.
Therefore these giant oaks their branches twined
And betwixt earth and heaven the lattice drew
Of their green labyrinth. Rare stars shone through,
Low, large, and mild. The infinite, confined,
Suffered the measure of the pensive mind,
And what the heart contrived it counted true.
Scant is that covert now in the merciless glare,
Stripped all those leafy arches, riven that dome,
Unhappy laggard, he whose nest was there.
Some yet untrodden forest be my home,
Where patient time and woven light and air
And streams a mansion for the soul prepare.

Manuscript for a sonnet by Santayana (from The Works of George Santayana, *volume 6, 1936)*

Santayana in 1907 (Photography Collection, Harry Ransom Humanities Research Center, University of Texas at Austin)

Egotism—subjectivity in thought and wilfulness in morals—which is the soul of German philosophy, is by no means a gratuitous thing. It is a genuine expression of the pathetic situation in which any animal finds itself upon earth, and any intelligence in the universe. . . . The perversity of the Germans, the childishness and sophistry of their position, lies only in glorifying what is an inevitable impediment, and in marking time on an earthly station from which the spirit of man—at least in spirit—is called to fly.

In 1920 Santayana published *Character and Opinion in the United States: With Reminiscences of William James and Josiah Royce and Academic Life in America;* most of the chapters in the book had been delivered as lectures to British audiences. In 1922 *Soliloquies in England, and Later Soliloquies* appeared. Composed between 1914 and 1921, these lyrical expressions of rhapsodic prose ("The human at best is a sort of song; the music of it runs away with the words, and even the words, which pass for the names of things, are but poor wild symbols for their unfathomed objects"), as Santayana designated them, are an instance of his emancipation from academic constraints in his writing.

Scepticism and Animal Faith (1923) is an introduction to and partial summary of the ontological system San-

tayana went on to elaborate in the four volumes of *The Realms of Being* (1927–1940). He says in the preface:

Here is one more system of philosophy. If the reader is tempted to smile, I can assure him that I smile with him, and that my system—to which this volume is a critical introduction—differs widely in spirit and pretensions from what usually goes by that name. In the first place, *my system is not mine, nor new.* I am merely attempting to express for the reader the principles to which he appeals when he smiles. . . . I think that common sense, in a rough dogged way, is technically sounder than the special schools of philosophy, each of which squints and overlooks half the facts and half the difficulties in its eagerness to find in some detail the key to the whole. I am animated by distrust of all high guesses, and by sympathy with the old prejudices and workaday opinions of mankind: they are ill expressed, but they are well grounded. What novelty my version of things may possess is meant simply to obviate occasions for sophistry by giving to everyday beliefs a more accurate and circumspect form. . . .

My system, accordingly, is *no system of the universe.* The Realms of Being of which I speak are not parts of a cosmos, nor one great cosmos together: they are only kinds or categories of things which I find conspicuously different and worth distinguishing, at least in my own thoughts. . . .

Moreover, my system, save in the mocking literary sense of the word, is *not metaphysical.* . . . Metaphysics, in the proper sense of the word, is dialectical physics, or an attempt to determine matters of fact by means of logical or moral or rhetorical constructions. It arises by a confusion of those Realms of Being which it is my special care to distinguish. It is neither physical speculation nor pure logic nor honest literature, but (as in the treatise of Aristotle first called by that name) a hybrid of the three, materialising ideal entities, turning harmonies into forces, and dissolving natural things into terms of discourse. . . . Now in natural philosophy I am a decided materialist—apparently the only one living; and I am well aware that idealists are fond of calling materialism, too, metaphysics, in rather an angry tone, so as to cast discredit upon it by assimilating it to their own systems. But my materialism, for all that, is not metaphysical. I do not profess to know what matter is in itself. . . . I wait for the men of science to tell me what matter is, in so far as they can discover it. . . . But whatever matter may be, I call it matter boldly, as I call my acquaintances Smith and Jones without knowing their secrets: whatever it may be, it must possess the aspects and undergo the motions of the gross objects that fill the world: and if belief in the existence of hidden parts and movements in nature be metaphysics, then the kitchen-maid is a metaphysician whenever she peels a potato.

My system, finally, though, of course, formed under the fire of contemporary discussions, is *no phase of any current movement.* . . . I think only the Indians and the Greek naturalists, together with Spinoza, have been right on the chief issue, the relation of man and of his spirit to the universe.

In twenty-seven chapters Santayana shows that if absolute certainty is demanded for knowledge, then all that can be known is the ideas one is having at the present moment; the existence of the external world and even of the self as a continuing entity is thrown into doubt, resulting in total skepticism. But such a belief is psychologically untenable; an irresistible impulse, or "animal faith," compels one to believe that such things exist.

The Realms of Being is one of the most original philosophical creations of the twentieth century. In its four volumes Santayana describes what he considers the four major modes or categories of being: *The Realm of Essence* (1927), *The Realm of Matter* (1930), *The Realm of Truth* (1937), and *The Realm of Spirit* (1940). Essences are infinite in number and universal in character; each essence is distinct from every other ("Every essence is perfectly individual"); they may be instantiated in matter or conceived by a consciousness, but they need not be; they are immutable; and they have no causal efficacy in the natural world. Matter is spatial, temporal, and changeable; it is independent of consciousness and ultimately unknowable. Matter is the encircling context of an individual's natural life. Truth is the part of the realm of essence that happens to be instantiated in existence; no truth is necessary. The realm of truth represents what could be, is already, or never will be known of all conceivable "significant facts in the realm of nature." It is like a map that is constantly being redrawn, with new islands and continents being charted but only at the cost of having sailed past other ones that just as easily could have been the charted ones. Truth per se never changes; what changes is the degree to which human beings understand it. Spirit "is only that inner light of actuality or attention which floods all life as men actually live it on earth. It is roughly the same thing as feeling or thought; it might be called consciousness; it might be identified with the *pensée* or *cogitatio* of Descartes and Spinoza." It is distinct both from its physical basis, which Santayana calls the "psyche," and from any particular content, in Santayana's thought. The psyche is an embodied "trope," which "defines a life, and marks its course from birth to death in some human creature." Tropes are essences, and since the psyche is a trope, it, too, is an essence. But it is an actualized essence, one that exists, or has existed. The psyche is what is unique to the individual. The "spirit lives in the quick interplay of each sensitive individual and the world, and often it is at its height when, after keen experience the brain digests the event at lei-

Santayana in the convent-clinic of the Blue Sisters of the Little Company of Mary in Rome, where he spent the last eleven years of his life (George Santayana Papers, Rare Book and Manuscript Library, Columbia University)

sure, and the body is sexually quiescent, or reduced by old age to a mere husk." The psyche is the source of the spirit; yet, at the same time, the spirit bestows consciousness on the psyche. This interaction produces individual preferences, tastes, and values: "Thus the spiritual function of the psyche is added to her generative and practical functions, creating a fresh and unprecedented realm of being, the realm of spirit with its original æsthetic spectrum and moral range and values incommensurable with anything but themselves. . . . All the themes and passions of spirit, however spiritual and immaterial themselves, celebrate the vicissitudes of a natural psyche, like a pure poet celebrating the adventures of lovers and kings."

For Santayana the 1930s were years of growing personal isolation. His half sister Susana had died in February 1918; his brother-in-law Celedonio died in May 1930; and his sister Josefina in October 1930. In an often quoted anecdote Santayana, when asked by a friend why he did not consider marriage, replied: "I don't know whether to get married or buy a dog." He visited Spain, the country whose citizenship he maintained throughout his life, for the last

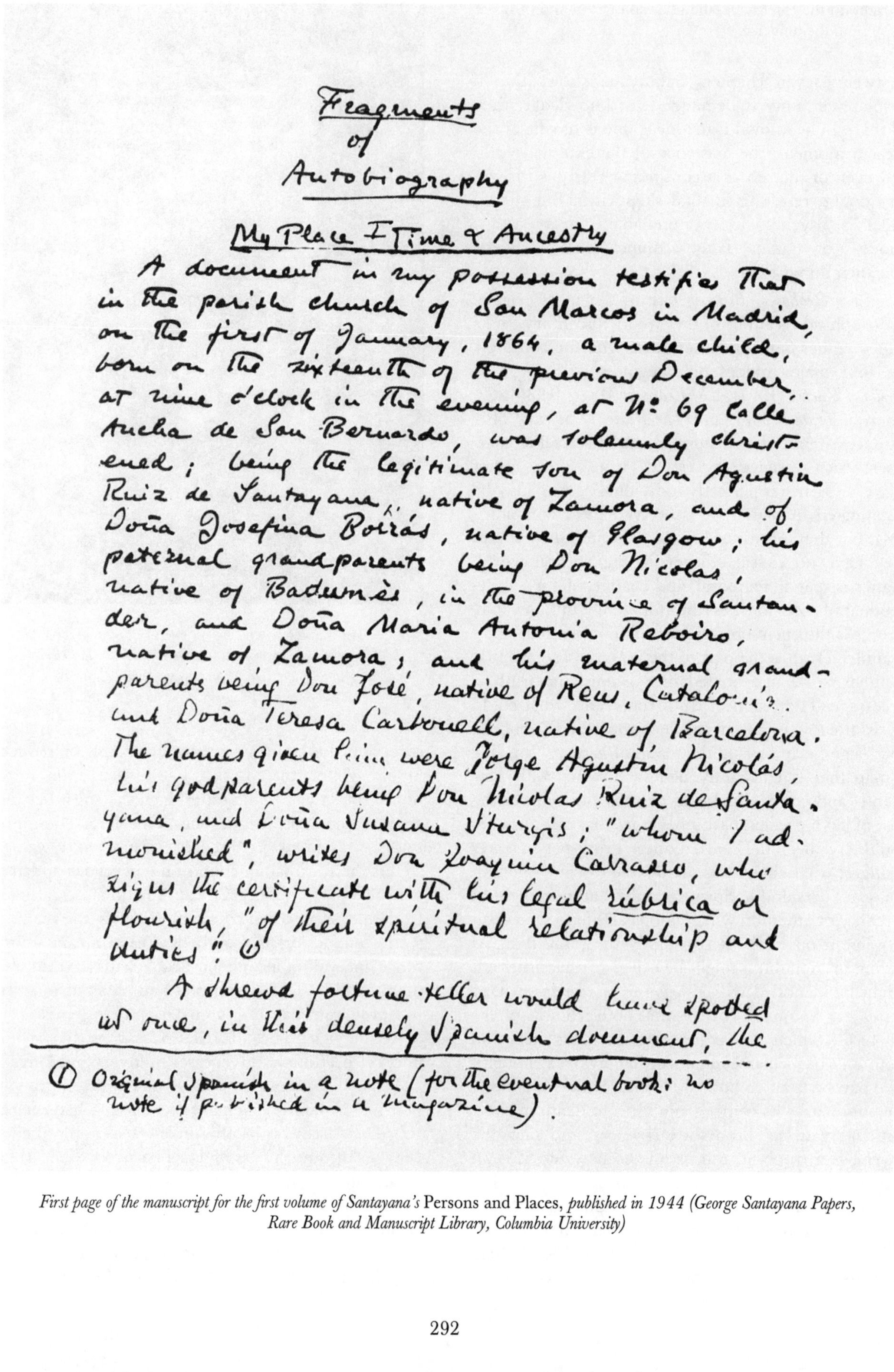

<u>Fragments</u>
of
Auto<u>biography</u>

<u>My Place I Time & Ancestry</u>

A document in my possession testifies that in the parish church of San Marcos in Madrid, on the first of January, 1864, a male child, born on the sixteenth of the previous December, at nine o'clock in the evening, at Nº 69 Calle Ancha de San Bernardo, was solemnly christ-ened; being the legitimate son of Don Agustín Ruiz de Santayana, native of Zamora, and of Doña Josefina Borrás, native of Glasgow; his paternal grandparents being Don Nicolás, native of Badumès, in the province of Santan-der, and Doña Maria Antonia Reboiro, native of Zamora; and his maternal grand-parents being Don José, native of Reus, Catalonia, and Doña Teresa Carbonell, native of Barcelona. The names given him were Jorge Agustín Nicolás, his godparents being Don Nicolas Ruiz de Santa-yana, and Doña Susana Sturgis; "whom I ad-monished", writes Don Joaquin Carrasco, who signs the certificate with his legal rúbrica or flourish, "of their spiritual relationship and duties". ①

A shrewd fortune-teller would have spotted us once, in this densely Spanish document, the

---

① Original Spanish in a note (for the eventual book: no note if published in a magazine).

First page of the manuscript for the first volume of Santayana's Persons and Places, *published in 1944 (George Santayana Papers, Rare Book and Manuscript Library, Columbia University)*

time in May 1930. Rome became his adopted home, a place, he says in the final volume of his autobiography (1953), "where the climate, the scene, and the human ways of my neighbours might not impede but if possible inspire me in my projected work and where I might bring my life to a peaceful end." Santayana says that he "desired solitude and independence; not in the English form of quiet home-life in the country, but rather after the fashion of ancient philosophers, often in exile, but always in sight of the market-place and theatre." He published *The Genteel Tradition at Bay* in 1931.

Santayana delivered two lectures in 1932: "Ultimate Religion" before the Spinoza Society in The Hague and "Locke and the Frontiers of Common Sense" before the Royal Society of Literature in London. The London lecture marked his last visit to England. A collection of five essays, *Some Turns of Thought in Modern Philosophy,* appeared in 1933.

Santayana completed his only novel, *The Last Puritan,* on 31 August 1934; it was published in 1935 and became a best-seller. The novel is the tragic narrative of Oliver Alden, a Harvard philosophy student who dies in World War I. Irving Singer says in his *George Santayana, Literary Philosopher* (2000), "Within the great variety of his achievements as an author and a thinker, Santayana's ability to combine philosophy and literary awareness is paramount in *The Last Puritan. . . .* In their unity they reflect his reality as he experienced it."

The German blitzkrieg into Poland began on 1 September 1939. "We live," Santayana wrote to his personal assistant Daniel Cory on 28 September, "in old-fashioned tragic times. . . . At my age the death of friends makes little impression; we are socially all dead long since, for every important purpose; but closing a life is (as Heidegger teaches) rounding it out, giving it wholeness."

For the last eleven years of his life Santayana lived at Via Santo Stefano Rotondo 6, in Rome, in the convent-clinic of the all-Irish order of nuns, the Blue Sisters of the Little Company of Mary. The first volume of his autobiography, *Persons and Places,* was completed in 1941 and published in 1944. *The Middle Span* and *My Host the World* were finished in 1944; *The Middle Span* appeared in 1945, but *My Host the World* was published posthumously, at Santayana's request, in 1953.

In a letter of 1 November 1944 to David Page, Santayana wrote: "I have finished all but one of the books I had hoped to write, and have interlarded another on an unexpected subject: *The Idea of Christ in the Gospels, or, God in Man.* This does not mean any change in my naturalism, but only a critical medita-

tion on religion, as it might have turned to Brahmanism or Buddhism." Santayana explains what moved him to write the work: "Being in a religious house, without many books of my own, I read the Sister's select library; many novels, and all Jane Austen, and a lot by Benson about the English Reformation: but besides I reread the whole Bible, most of the *Summa* of Thomas Aquinas, and most of Newman. This set me going, and you will see the consequence." *The Idea of Christ in the Gospels, or, God in Man: A Critical Essay* appeared in 1946. In the book Santayana critically dissects the "dramatic presentation of the person of Christ," Christ as a "symbol for the high moral and ontological mysteries," and Christ as God-in-man. Christ is the epitome of supernatural self-transcendence; but self-transcendence per se, or "spontaneous intent fixed upon an unseen object, is no vice peculiar to religious faith but is the very breath of intelligence in memory, expectation, perception, and natural science." In other words, one engages in self-transcendence in any instance when one is completely mentally engrossed. The concept of "God-in-man" is tragic: it is a petrified and hypostatized concept that has had the human excised from its humanity and, as a consequence, has lost its vitality.

On 6 April 1918, about seven months before the armistice that ended World War I, Santayana had written to Mrs. Frederick Winslow of Boston from England, where he had spent the entirety of the war years:

> Meantime besides my big book I am preparing another little one on the war, or rather on the psychological questions, how governments and religions manage to dominate mankind, in spite or (as I shall show) because of their irrationality. I am thinking of calling it "Dominations and Powers." In view of it I have been reading all sorts of things to fill the *lacunae* in my knowledge of which I am made aware as I write.

Dominations and Powers: Reflections on Liberty, Society, and Government finally appeared in 1951; it was the last book published in his lifetime. It is a politically conservative work in which he attacks liberalism and democracy for destroying human diversity and argues for aristocracy and hierarchy.

Visitors from around the globe visited George Santayana in his final years. The poets Wallace Stevens and Robert Lowell wrote poems in tribute to him. He composed lucid, reflective letters up until two months prior to his last day, ceasing only when his eyesight failed. He died on 26 September 1952.

Letters:

The Letters of George Santayana, edited by Daniel Cory (New York: Scribners, 1955);

Santayana: The Later Years, a Portrait with Letters, edited by Cory (New York: Braziller, 1963);

Cristina Molina Petit, "Lo Español en Santayana Correspondencia Familiar durante su Estancia en Roma," *Crisis,* 17 (1970): 67–81;

The Letters of George Santayana, 2 volumes, edited by William G. Holzberger (Cambridge, Mass.: MIT Press, 2001, 2002).

Bibliographies:

Shohig Terzian, "Bibliography of the Writings of George Santayana (to October 1940)," in *The Philosophy of George Santayana,* edited by Paul Arthur Schilpp, The Library of Living Philosophers, volume 2 (Evanston, Ill.: Northwestern University Press, 1940), pp. 607–668;

Ceferino Santos, "Bibliografía general de Jorge Santayana," *Miscelánea Comillas,* 44 (1965): 155–310;

John Jones and Herman J. Saatkamp Jr., eds., *George Santayana: A Bibliographical Checklist, 1880–1980* (Bowling Green, Ohio: Philosophy Documentation Center, 1982).

Biographies:

George W. Howgate, *George Santayana* (Philadelphia: University of Pennsylvania Press, 1938);

Luis Farre, "Vida y Pensamiento de Jorge Santayana," *Verdad y Vida* (Quito), 42 (1953): 129–170, 305–344;

Richard Butler, *The Life and World of George Santayana* (Chicago: Regnery, 1960);

Gamo J. M. Alonso, *Un Español en el Mundo: Santayana, Poesia y Poetica* (Madrid: Ediciones Cultura Hispanica, 1966);

Willard E. Arnett, *George Santayana* (New York: Washington Square Press, 1968);

John McCormick, *George Santayana: A Biography* (New York: Knopf, 1987);

José Luis Abellán, *George Santayana: 1863–1952* (Madrid: Ediciones del Orto, 1996).

References:

Willard E. Arnett, *Santayana and the Sense of Beauty* (Bloomington: Indiana University Press, 1955);

Jerome Ashmore, *Santayana, Art, and Aesthetics* (Cleveland: Western Reserve University Press, 1966);

George Boas, "The Legacy of Santayana," *Revue internationale de Philosophie,* no. 63 (1963): 37–49;

Stuart Gerry Brown, "Lucretius and Santayana: A Study in Classical Materialism," *New Mexico Quarterly Review,* 15 (Spring 1945): 5–17;

Justus Buchler, "One Santayana or Two?" *Journal of Philosophy,* 51 (21 January 1954): 52–67;

Richard Butler, *The Mind of Santayana* (Chicago: Regnery, 1955);

Paul Conkin, *Puritans and Pragmatists* (Bloomington: Indiana University Press, 1976);

Robert Dawidoff, *The Genteel Tradition and the Sacred Rage: High Culture vs. Democracy in Adams, James, and Santayana* (Chapel Hill: University of North Carolina Press, 1992);

Jacques Duron, *La Pensée de George Santayana: Santayana en Amérique* (Paris: Librairie Nizet, 1950);

Charles Hartshorne, "Santayana's Defiant Eclecticism," *Journal of Philosophy,* 6 (2 January 1964): pp. 35–44;

Michael Hodges and John Lachs, *Thinking in the Ruins: Wittgenstein and Santayana on Contingency* (Nashville, Tenn.: Vanderbilt University Press, 2000);

Ignacio Izuzquiza, *George Santayana o la ironía de la materia* (Barcelona: Editorial Anthopos, 1989);

H. M. Kallen, "The Laughing Philosopher," *Journal of Philosophy,* 1 (2 January 1964): 19–35;

Angus Kerr-Lawson, "Santayana's Epiphenominalism," *Transactions of the Charles S. Peirce Society,* 22 (Fall 1986): 417–432;

Kerr-Lawson, "Toward One Santayana," *Transactions of the Charles S. Peirce Society,* 27 (Winter 1991): 1–25;

H. T. Kirby-Smith, *A Philosophical Novelist: George Santayana and* The Last Puritan (Carbondale: Southern Illinois University Press, 1997);

Bruce Kuklick, *The Rise of American Philosophy: Cambridge, Massachusetts, 1860–1930* (New Haven: Yale University Press, 1977), pp. 351–369;

John Lachs, *George Santayana* (Boston: Twayne, 1988);

Lachs, *Mind and Philosophers* (Nashville: Vanderbilt University Press, 1987), pp. 67–88, 89–119, 120–140, 141–156, 157–169;

Lachs, "The Proofs of Realism," *Monist,* 51 (April 1967): 284–304;

Lachs, *The Relevance of Philosophy to Life* (Nashville: Vanderbilt University Press, 1995), pp. 50–61;

Corliss Lamont, ed., *Dialogues on Santayana* (New York: Horizon, 1959);

Henry Samuel Levinson, "Pragmatism and the Spiritual Life," *Raritan,* 10 (Fall 1990): 70–86;

Levinson, *Santayana, Pragmatism, and the Spiritual Life* (Chapel Hill: University of North Carolina Press, 1992);

Jonathan Lieberson, "The Sense of Santayana," *New York Review of Books* (31 March 1988): 49–55;

Bruno Lind, *Vagabond Scholar: A Venture into the Privacy of George Santayana* (New York: Bridgehead, 1962);

John M. Michelson, "Santayana on Scepticism and the Analysis of Experience," *Transactions of the Charles S. Peirce Society,* 8 (Winter 1972): 26–47;

Milton Karl Munitz, *The Moral Philosophy of Santayana* (New York: Humanities Press, 1958);

Kai Nielson, "The Moral Philosophy of George Santayana," *Darshana,* 2 (1962): 38–64;

Frederick A. Olafson, "George Santayana and the Idea of Philosophy," in *American Philosophy from Edwards to Quine,* edited by Robert W. Shahan and Kenneth R. Merrill (Norman: University of Oklahoma Press, 1977), pp. 148–175;

Overheard in Seville: Bulletin of the Santayana Society, 1 (1983–   );

Christopher Perricone Jr., "Distraction and Santayana's Idea of Progress," *Transactions of the Charles S. Peirce Society,* 19 (Spring 1983): 167–181;

Joel Porte, "Santayana's Masquerade," *Raritan,* 7 (Fall 1987): 129–142;

John Herman Randall Jr., "The Latent Idealism of a Materialist," *Journal of Philosophy,* 28 (19 November 1931): 645–660;

Andrew J. Reck, "Realism in Santayana's *Life of Reason,*" *Monist,* 51 (April 1967): 238–266;

Philip Blair Rice, "George Santayana: The Philosopher as Poet," *Kenyon Review,* no. 2 (1940): 460–475;

Richard Rorty, *Consequences of Pragmatism* (Minneapolis: University of Minnesota Press, 1982), pp. 60–71;

Paul Arthur Schilpp, ed., *The Philosophy of George Santayana,* The Library of Living Philosophers, volume 2 (Evanston, Ill.: Northwestern University Press, 1940);

Herbert W. Schneider, "Crises in Santayana's Life and Mind," *Southern Journal of Philosophy,* 10 (Summer 1972): 109–113;

Beth Singer, *The Rational Society: A Critical Study of Santayana's Social Thought* (Cleveland: Case Western Reserve University Press, 1970);

Irving Singer, *George Santayana, Literary Philosopher* (New Haven: Yale University Press, 2000);

Singer, *Santayana's Aesthetics: A Critical Introduction* (Cambridge, Mass.: Harvard University Press, 1957);

Singer, "The World of George Santayana," *Hudson Review,* 7 (Autumn 1954): 356–372;

T. L. S. Sprigge, *Santayana: An Examination of His Philosophy* (London: Routledge & Kegan Paul, 1974);

Anthony Woodward, *Living in the Eternal: A Study of George Santayana* (Nashville: Vanderbilt University Press, 1989).

Papers:

The largest collections of George Santayana's manuscripts and letters are in the Houghton Library at Harvard University; the Special Collections Department of Paley Library at Temple University; the Harry Ransom Humanities Research Center at the University of Texas at Austin; the Rare Books and Special Collections Department of the Princeton University Library; the Special Collections Department of Alderman Library at the University of Virginia; and the Rare Book and Manuscript Library of Butler Library at Columbia University. The Special Collections Department of Lauringer Library at Georgetown University has manuscripts, letters, and 120 heavily annotated books from Santayana's library. The Special Collections Department of the library of the University of Waterloo, Ontario, has 348 books, also heavily annotated by Santayana; a catalogue of these books compiled by the head of the Special Collections Department, Susan Bellingham, is available from the library.

William Graham Sumner

(30 October 1840 – 12 April 1910)

Robert C. Bannister
Swarthmore College

BOOKS: *A History of American Currency, with Chapters on the English Bank Restriction and Austrian Paper Money: To Which Is Appended "The Bullion Report"* (New York: Holt, 1874);

Lectures on the History of Protection in the United States: Delivered before the International Free-Trade Alliance (New York: Putnam, 1877);

Protection and Revenue in 1877: A Lecture Delivered before "The New York Free Trade Club," April 18, 1878 (New York: Putnam, 1878);

Andrew Jackson as a Public Man: What He Was, What Chances He Had, and What He Did with Them (Boston & New York: Houghton, Mifflin, 1882); revised and enlarged as *Andrew Jackson* (Boston & New York: Houghton, Mifflin, 1899);

What Social Classes Owe to Each Other (New York: Harper, 1883);

Problems in Political Economy (New York: Holt, 1884);

Protectionism: The -Ism Which Teaches That Waste Makes Wealth (New York: Holt, 1885);

Collected Essays in Political and Social Science (New York: Holt, 1885);

Alexander Hamilton (New York: Dodd, Mead, 1890);

The Financier and the Finances of the American Revolution, 2 volumes (New York: Dodd, Mead, 1891);

Robert Morris (New York: Dodd, Mead, 1892);

A History of Banking in the United States (New York: Journal of Commerce and Commercial Bulletin, 1896);

The Conquest of the United States by Spain: A Lecture before the Phi Beta Kappa Society of Yale University, January 16, 1899 (Boston: Estes, 1899);

Folkways: A Study of the Sociological Importance of Usages, Manners, Customs, Mores, and Morals (Boston: Ginn, 1906);

War, and Other Essays, edited by Albert Galloway Keller (New Haven: Yale University Press, 1911);

Earth-Hunger, and Other Essays, edited by Keller (New Haven: Yale University Press, 1913);

The Challenge of Facts, and Other Essays, edited by Keller (New Haven: Yale University Press, 1914);

William Graham Sumner

The Forgotten Man, and Other Essays, edited by Keller (New Haven: Yale University Press, 1918);

The Science of Society, 4 volumes, by Sumner, Keller, and Maurice R. Davie (New Haven: Yale University Press, 1927; London: Humphrey Milford, Oxford University Press, 1927);

Essays of William Graham Sumner, 2 volumes, edited by Keller and Davie (New Haven: Yale University Press, 1934);

The Forgotten Man's Almanac: Rations of Common Sense from William Graham Sumner, edited by Keller (New Haven: Yale University Press; London, Humphrey Milford, Oxford University Press, 1943);

On Liberty, Society, and Politics: The Essential Essays of William Graham Sumner, edited by Robert C. Bannister (Indianapolis: Liberty Fund, 1992).

Collections: *Selected Essays of William Graham Sumner,* edited by Albert Galloway Keller and Maurice R. Davie (New Haven: Yale University Press, 1924);

Sumner Today: Selected Essays of William Graham Sumner, with Comments by American Leaders, edited by Davie (New Haven: Yale University Press / London: Humphrey Milford, Oxford University Press, 1940);

Social Darwinism: Selected Essays, edited by Stow Persons (Englewood Cliffs, N.J.: Prentice-Hall, 1963);

The Conquest of the United States by Spain, and Other Essays, edited by Murray Polner (Chicago: Regnery, 1965).

TRANSLATION: Karl Christian Wilhelm Felix Bähr, *The Books of the Kings,* edited and translated by Sumner and Edwin Harwood (New York: Scribner, Armstrong, 1872).

SELECTED PERIODICAL PUBLICATIONS—
UNCOLLECTED: "The Crisis of the Protestant Episcopal Church," *Nation,* 13 (5 October 1871): 22–23;

"The Causes of the Farmer's Discontent," *Nation,* 16 (5 June 1873): 381–382;

"Professor Walker on Bi-Metallism," *Nation,* 26 (7 February 1878): 94–96;

"Socialism," *Scribner's Monthly,* 16 (October 1878): 887–893;

"Protective Taxes and Wages," *North American Review,* 136 (March 1883): 270–276;

"Evils of the Tariff System," *North American Review,* 139 (September 1884): 293–299;

"The Indians in 1887," *Forum,* 3 (May 1887): 254–262;

"Suicidal Fanaticism in Russia," *Popular Science Monthly,* 60 (March 1902): 442–447;

"Modern Marriage," *Yale Review,* 13 (January 1924): 249–275.

The economist, philosopher, and sociologist William Graham Sumner was a leading defender of individualism, private property, and laissez-faire capitalism in the late nineteenth and early twentieth centuries; he was also one of the most popular professors ever to teach at Yale University. His best-known work is his 1906 study *Folkways: A Study of the Sociological Importance of Usages, Manners, Customs, Mores, and Morals,* the only part of a projected masterwork on "the science of society" that he was able to publish during his lifetime. He is also known as the major American "social Darwinist" of the Gilded Age. Social Darwinism is the application of the biological concepts of natural selection and sur-

vival of the fittest, central to Charles Darwin's theory of evolution, to human society. The term implies a belief that social progress depends on healthy competition, and that the elimination of inferior members of society is inevitable—ideas that were seized on by some thinkers of the late nineteenth and early twentieth centuries to justify classism and colonialism.

Sumner was born in Paterson, New Jersey, on 30 October 1840 to Thomas Sumner, a mechanic, and Sarah Graham Sumner. He had two younger siblings, Joseph Graham and Esther Elizabeth. Both parents had emigrated from England. A champion of free trade and temperance, Thomas Sumner passed on to his oldest son an ethic of hard work and a skeptical attitude toward social "causes." The family moved twice during Sumner's childhood, first to New Haven, Connecticut, and then to Hartford, where he attended public school. His mother died in 1848; a few months later his father married Eliza Van Alstein, an austere and parsimonious woman who was detested by the Sumner brothers.

In 1859 Sumner entered Yale University, where he followed a mandatory curriculum of classics, science, and philosophy. His extracurricular activities included eating clubs, the Brothers in Unity debating society, and the secret Skull and Bones society. After Sumner graduated in 1863 a fellow member of Skull and Bones, William C. Whitney, the son of a cotton-mill owner, arranged for funds for Sumner to buy a Civil War draft substitute and to spend two years studying theology at the Universities of Geneva, Göttingen, and Oxford. At Oxford, Sumner read the Anglican theologian Richard Hooker's *Of the Lawes of Ecclesiasticall Politie* (1593–1662), which he liked both for its critique of a literal interpretation of the Bible and for its conservative political philosophy.

In 1866 Sumner became a tutor in classics at Yale. In December of the following year he was ordained a deacon in the Episcopal Church. He left the university in 1869 to serve as editor of a new Episcopalian journal, *The Living Church,* and as assistant pastor of a parish in New York City. In 1870 he became minister of the Church of the Redeemer in Morristown, New Jersey. At that time Episcopalians were divided into a High Church faction that stressed dogma and tradition; a Low Church faction that emphasized evangelical conversion; and a moderate Broad Church faction that was more open to reason and science than the other two. Sumner aligned himself and his journal with the Broad Church position.

Sumner's sermons dealt with two issues that continued to concern him throughout his career as a philosopher and sociologist. The first was the "warfare" of science and religion, where, as in the High Church–Low Church controversy, he sought a middle ground.

In "Rationalism," a sermon delivered in 1871 and never published, he told his congregation that he found "no great fault" in the writings of the evolutionists Charles Darwin, Thomas Henry Huxley, and Herbert Spencer: "They may be right or wrong in their speculations and theories," but they were "honest, sincere, and industrious" in their "method." The other issue, which stemmed from the High Church–Low Church debate, was the conflict between tradition and progress. "The traditions of centuries have a true *moral* authority," he told his Morristown parishioners on 6 January 1872 in a sermon published as "Traditions and Progress" in *On Liberty, Society, and Politics: The Essential Essays of William Graham Sumner* (1992). "We must begin with the world as we find it, that is, as it is handed down to us from the past." At the same time, the "true use of tradition" must be distinguished from "traditionalism," which he defined as the blind acceptance of "old errors" and "worn-out falsehoods."

On 17 April 1871 Sumner married Jeannie Elliott, the daughter of a New York City merchant, whom he had met at a party at Yale in the early 1860s. They had three sons: Henry Elliott, who was born in 1872 but died at four months; Eliot, born in 1873; and Graham, born in 1875.

In September 1873 Sumner left the ministry and took a newly created chair in political economy at Yale. That fall he was elected to the New Haven Board of Aldermen; he held the office for four years. He was also made an honorary member of the New Haven Chamber of Commerce. He joined the new American Social Science Association and was a member of its finance committee. In his first book, *A History of American Currency, with Chapters on the English Bank Restriction and Austrian Paper Money: To Which Is Appended "The Bullion Report"* (1874), he argued for a sound currency. Sumner's prose in this book and in his other early works is, as Donald C. Bellomy observes in his 1980 dissertation, "The Moulding of an Iconoclast: William Graham Sumner, 1840–1885," "frequently stilted, often latinate, more than a little long-winded"; Henry Holt, the publisher of *A History of American Currency*, remarked that the book never failed to put him to sleep. In November 1877 Sumner served on an electoral commission to investigate vote fraud in New Orleans during the Rutherford B. Hayes–Samuel Tilden presidential election the previous year, and in 1878 he testified before a congressional committee on labor unrest.

Sumner's experience as an alderman and his observation of vote fraud in the 1876 election left him disillusioned with politics. "I found out that I was more likely to do more harm than good in politics than almost any other kind of man," he wrote in 1903 an "Autobiographical Sketch" first published in *Earth-Hunger, and Other Essays* (1913), "because I did not know the rules of the game and did not want to learn them." Sumner finally gave up on politics altogether, even refusing to vote in the 1880 presidential race. Throughout the following decade he argued for the separation of politics and economics and for civil service reform aimed at reducing government corruption.

In *Lectures on the History of Protection in the United States: Delivered before the International Free-Trade Alliance* (1877), Sumner points out that tariffs benefit some Americans at the expense of others and leave consumers unaware of the real cause of the higher prices they are forced to pay. In 1878 he argued for a strict gold standard, instead of the use of both gold and silver to back the currency, in an article for *The Nation* titled "Professor Walker on Bi-Metallism."

The stage for Sumner's reputation as a social Darwinist began to be set with "Socialism," an 1878 article for *Scribner's Monthly* in which he defends the English economist Thomas Robert Malthus's doctrine that—as Sumner summarizes it—"Human beings tend to multiply beyond the power of a limited area of land to support life, under a given stage of the arts, and a given standard of living." Citing Harriet Martineau's depiction of the struggle of the individual against the wilderness in *Illustrations of Political Economy* (1832–1834), a favorite book from his youth, Sumner argues that the struggle for existence is inescapable. Socialists, he says, err in blaming rules of the "competition of life" in society, such as private property, for hardships that should be attributed to this "struggle for existence." In a review of Henry George's *Progress and Poverty* (1879) in *The New York Times* (6 June 1880) he says that George "wasted his effort" in critiquing Malthus, for "the 'Malthusian doctrine' is swallowed up in a great biological law." In several unpublished speeches and an essay, "Sociology," which appeared in his *Collected Essays in Political and Social Science* (1885), he made a statement that launched his reputation as a social Darwinist. "The law of the survival of the fittest was not made by man and cannot be abrogated by man. We can only, by interfering with it, produce the survival of the unfittest." Furthermore, a conflict with Yale president Noah Porter over Sumner's use of Spencer's *The Study of Sociology* (1873) in a senior social-science class associated Sumner with England's leading social Darwinist. Sumner wrote an open letter to the Yale Corporation and the faculty in 1881 challenging Porter's right to interfere with his selection of textbooks and threatening to resign. Sumner ultimately agreed not to assign the book.

Sumner's social Darwinism was confirmed for many by the publication of *What Social Classes Owe to Each Other* (1883), even though the book is devoid of evolutionist rhetoric. Sumner attacks humanitarian schemes in chapters with sermon-like titles such as "That It Is Not Wicked To Be Rich; Nay, Even, That It Is Not Wicked to Be Richer than One's Neighbor," arguing that those with money should not be compelled to support those without. Socialist legislation means that "A and B decide what C shall do for D," with the burden inevitably falling on "C," the "forgotten man" who works hard and pays the tax bill. The answer to the question posed in the title appears to be that social classes owe nothing to one another.

The charge that Sumner misused the theory of evolution to justify a dog-eat-dog social order was first leveled in print in *The New York Times* on 7 and 9 March 1883, first in a letter from Isaac Rice, a member of the Nineteenth Century Club, where Sumner in a recent speech in which Sumner had used the language of "fitness" and "unfitness," and then in an unsigned editorial titled "The Selfish Sciences." Sumner denied holding to a strict social Darwinian view in several articles, including "The Survival of the Fittest," published in two issues of *The Index* in 1884, in which he claimed that his use of the language of biology was intended merely as an analogy. Although he celebrated individual effort and laissez-faire economics, Sumner was highly critical of materialism and "plutocracy," a term he defined in a series of articles for *The Independent* in 1887 as "a political form in which the controlling force is wealth." In more general terms, he explains, plutocracy refers to the "increasing thirst for luxury" and the acquisitiveness that accompanies rises in large-scale industry. His arguments found allies both in the middle class, which naturally feared monopolies, and in members of the upper class who held vulgar wealth in disdain. Furthermore, despite his use of *The Study of Sociology,* he disliked the metaphysical nature of most of Spencer's work; his disagreement with Porter was not about the merits of Darwinism, social or otherwise, but about the nature of scientific method—Baconian induction versus Spencerian deduction—and academic freedom.

Nevertheless, despite the efforts of some modern scholars, such as Robert C. Bannister and Donald K. Pickens, the "social Darwinist" label has stuck to Sumner. In *The Goose-Step: A Study of American Education* (1923) Upton Sinclair branded Sumner "prime minister of . . . plutocratic education" who takes "ghoulish delight" in "glorifying commercialism." Richard Hofstadter's *Social Darwinism in American Thought, 1860–1915* (1944) includes a chapter titled "William Graham Sumner: Social Darwinist." A widely used collection of Sumner's writings edited by Stow Persons in 1963 bears the title *Social Darwinism.*

In 1890 Sumner had a nervous breakdown brought on by a work schedule that had produced 2 books and 60 articles in three years. Forty-two friends

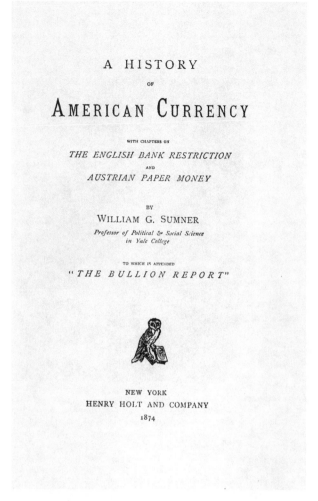

A HISTORY

OF

AMERICAN CURRENCY

WITH CHAPTERS ON

THE ENGLISH BANK RESTRICTION

AND

AUSTRIAN PAPER MONEY

BY

WILLIAM G. SUMNER

Professor of Political & Social Science in Yale College

TO WHICH IS APPENDED

"THE BULLION REPORT"

NEW YORK

HENRY HOLT AND COMPANY

1874

Title page for Sumner's first book, about which the publisher remarked that reading it never failed to put him to sleep (Thomas Cooper Library, University of South Carolina)

and supporters, including Whitney, Holt, and Chauncey Depew, provided him with most of the money he needed to take an extended retreat in Europe beginning in December. Sumner returned to Yale in the fall of 1892, but his subsequent output never rivaled his early productivity: between 1876 and 1890 he had published 9 books and 108 articles; in the six years following his breakdown he wrote 3 books and 16 articles. Afterward he averaged 2 articles a year and, with the exception of *Folkways,* was forced to leave unfinished his plan for a large-scale work on "the science of society."

Since the late 1880s Sumter had been moving closer to the inductionism that characterizes *Folkways.* In "The Absurd Effort to Make Over the World" (1894), collected in *War, and Other Essays* (1911) and frequently republished, he answers social reformers with an "appeal to the facts"—historical facts, in particular—in place of logic or the "laws of nature." He writes that

FOLKWAYS

A STUDY OF THE SOCIOLOGICAL IMPOR-
TANCE OF USAGES, MANNERS, CUS-
TOMS, MORES, AND MORALS .

BY

WILLIAM GRAHAM SUMNER
PROFESSOR OF POLITICAL AND SOCIAL SCIENCE IN YALE UNIVERSITY

Thus it is clearly seen that use, rather than reason, has
power to introduce new things amongst us, and to do away
with old things. — *Castiglione, Il libro del Cortegiano, I, § 1*

That monster, custom, who all sense doth eat,
Of habits devil, is angel yet in this,
That to the use of actions fair and good
He likewise gives a frock or livery,
That aptly is put on. — *Hamlet, III, 4*

What custom wills, in all things should we do't.
Coriolanus, II, 3

GT
75
.S8
1906

GINN AND COMPANY
BOSTON · NEW YORK · CHICAGO · LONDON
ATLANTA · DALLAS · COLUMBUS · SAN FRANCISCO

WILLIAM GRAHAM SUMNER (1902)

Frontispiece and title page for Sumner's best-known work, in which he presents his theory about the origin and development of the basic moral beliefs of societies (Thomas Cooper Library, University of South Carolina)

"the allegations of general mischief, social corruption, wrong, and evil in our society must be referred back to those who make them for particulars and specifications."

Sumner devoted much of his energy during the 1890s to the anti-imperialist cause. In 1896, in response to American support for Venezuela in a border dispute with British Guyana in 1895, along with mounting pressure for the United States to become involved in Hawaii and Cuba, he wrote "The Fallacy of Territorial Extension," which was collected in *War, and Other Essays*. After the Spanish-American War, on 16 January 1899, he delivered perhaps his best-known speech, *The Conquest of the United States by Spain,* to a largely hostile audience in College Street Hall in New Haven; it was published the same year. He warned that in annexing Cuba the United States was adopting the very values it criticized in its opponent. "My patriotism," he concluded, "is of the kind which is outraged by the notion that the United States never was a great nation until in a petty three months' campaign it knocked to pieces a poor, decrepit bankrupt old state like Spain." In "Purposes and Consequences," an essay written around 1900 and collected in *Earth-Hunger, and Other Essays* (1913), he argues that in 1898 American statesmen, while claiming to act in the name of liberty, had embarked on a policy that was certain to make it "exceedingly difficult, or impossible for us to exercise any liberty at all. . . . Since consequences are entirely independent of motives and purposes, ethics have no application to consequences."

In *Folkways* Sumner explains social behavior as a result of four basic instincts: hunger, love, vanity, and fear. These instincts are universal, he claims, and individuals in every society are driven by the desire to satisfy them. When trial and error reveal a particular method to be conducive to their satisfaction, the method tends to become customary for at least a significant part of a social group. Sumner refers to such methods as "folkways." When folkways that were at first experimental are reflected on, they may gain a moral sanction and become "mores." Notions of "good" and "bad" are outside the mores of a given society. The establishment of mores depends on the support of the most powerful factions in a society, so that "nothing but might has ever made right."

Folkways are not always beneficial to a society; irrationality, accidents, and "pseudo-knowledge" can contribute to their formation, and the result can be "positively harmful." Examples include "advertisers who exaggerate," "the ways of journalism," "electioneering devices," and "oratorical and dithyrambic extravagances in politics." Such phenomena are "not properly part of the mores," Sumner explains, but are "symptoms of them."

Some critics objected that Sumner, in his own judgment of mores as "good" or "bad," was appealing to an objective standard that, by his own argument, cannot exist outside of a given system of mores. Sumner's position was not, however, moral but scientific. The social scientist, he believed, must examine the mores historically and determine which had proved conducive and which harmful to societal survival. The scientific approach thus provides an escape from the logic of "might makes right," in that it distinguishes between a posterior analysis of mores and an anterior prescription of the way things should be. On the posterior view, "Nothing but might has ever made right, and . . . nothing but might makes right now." But on the anterior view, "If we are about to take some action and are debating the right of it, the might that can be brought to support the view of it has nothing to do with the right of it." By studying history the social scientist can indeed provide an anterior view and show the superiority of a set of values.

Restating the distinction he had made in his sermons between science as speculation and science as method, Sumner claims that science is both relative and absolute. As speculation or "-ism," science is no less subject to "fashion" than any other field of human activity; even "evolutionism," though "now accepted as a final fact," might one day be revealed to have been "only a fashion." Science as a simple investigation of facts, however, is not relative nor ephemeral.

Sumner says that the scientific outlook in this narrow sense is gradually entering into the mores of the elite that he refers to as the "classes." At times he seems to imply that social policy could be shaped by this scientific elite; but his historical, fact-based approach prevented him from accepting the optimism of his reform-minded contemporaries. Adopting a view similar to that of the French sociologist Emile Durkheim, Sumner observes that mores tend to take on a coercive power regardless of their instrumental value. Accordingly,

though Sumner admits that a certain degree of social change is possible, he is doubtful of the chances for premeditated, widespread reform. His position in *Folkways* thus mirrors that of "The Absurd Effort to Make Over the World," in which he says that "it is the greatest folly . . . to sit down with a slate and pencil to plan out a new social world."

Concepts such as "folkways," "mores," "in-group," and "out-group" soon became part of mainstream sociological literature. Nonetheless, fellow academics criticized Sumner's work for its cynical political implications and for its methodology. In a review in the *American Journal of Sociology* (November 1907) George Vincent of the University of Chicago complained that the ethnological data in *Folkways* "seem at times to overweigh the book by their sheer bulk and multiplicity." In an article titled "Objectivism in Sociology" in the *American Journal of Sociology* (November 1916) Charles A. Ellwood of the University of Missouri pointed out the affinity between Sumner and Durkheim in criticizing both for their objectivist approach to sociology.

Later generations of sociologists were more accepting of Sumner's analytical, fact-based method, but they tended to look toward Durkheim and his 1895 *Les Règles de la méthode sociologique* (translated as *The Rules of Sociological Method*, 1938) rather than *Folkways*. At least a partial explanation of Sumner's relative unpopularity lies in his failure to leave behind a "school" of followers. Yale was then primarily an undergraduate institution, and Sumner trained only six doctoral students; none of them went on to teach at universities of the first rank. Furthermore, his students often applied his work in ways Sumner never intended. Henry Pratt Fairchild, one of his doctoral students, was an avowed socialist best known for *The Melting-Pot Mistake* (1926) and polemical pieces arguing in favor of eugenics, birth control, and immigration restriction. Another student, Frederick E. Lumley, offered instruction in *Means of Social Control* (1925) to those who "find it necessary or desirable to take a hand in the work of control." Still others read *Folkways* as supporting a cultural relativism that held no one set of values to be any better than others. Sumner's only real disciple was Albert Galloway Keller, but his curmudgeonly personality prevented fruitful dialogue with other sociologists of his day.

Sumner's work was, nevertheless, influential to at least some sociologists looking for a more "objective," less reformist approach to their field. Robert E. Park of the University of Chicago said in 1932 that the "effect of his researches was to lay a foundation for more realistic, more objective, and more systematic studies in the field of human nature and society than had existed up to that time." Several leading sociological objectivists seconded this observation in doctoral theses written

Sumner in 1907

between the world wars. At Columbia University, F. Stuart Chapin and William F. Ogburn drew directly on *Folkways* in their studies of education and of child-labor legislation. To many later scholars, however, Sumner's writings seemed to have more affinity to anthropology or philosophical history than to sociology, and practitioners in those two fields took over the issues in which he was the most interested. Albion W. Small of the University of Chicago remarked in 1916 that he never thought of Sumner as a sociologist until the latter was elected president of the American Sociological Society in 1908.

The last decade of Sumner's life was for the most part unhappy. He was disturbed by the return to an older curriculum based less on science and to the new emphasis on publishing as opposed to teaching instituted by Arthur T. Hadley, who had become president of Yale in 1899. Sumner also struggled with health problems during the 1900s. He had never fully recovered from his breakdown of 1890, and in late 1907 he had a stroke that left his right arm paralyzed for several months.

In 1909 Sumner retired, and the university awarded him an honorary doctorate of laws. In December, despite his poor health, he traveled to New York to deliver the presidential address at the annual meeting of the American Sociological Society. There he suffered a final stroke, from which he never fully recovered. He died on 12 April 1910. He left behind voluminous notes and manuscripts relating to his unfinished "Science of Society," which Keller edited and published in 1927.

William Graham Sumner had many critics during his lifetime, but he was always known for his honesty and his willingness to address difficult issues directly. As the historian Bruce Curtis writes in his *William Graham Sumner* (1981), Sumner devoted his career to the study of "mysteries where there were no eternal verities" and to the upholding of the "moral absolutes of honesty, work, responsibility, and moral courage." After his death many of the problems Sumner had addressed, especially in economics and politics, lost their relevance, and Sumner's envisioning of sociology along narrowly inductive lines came to be viewed by many philosophers of science as naive and outdated; but his bold approach and his disdain for hypocrisy provide a perennial appeal to those interested in his life and works.

Bibliography:

Albert Galloway Keller and Maurice R. Davie, "Bibliography," in *Essays of William Graham Sumner,* volume 2 (New Haven: Yale University Press, 1934), pp. 479–507.

Biography:

Harris E. Starr, *William Graham Sumner* (New York: Holt, 1925).

References:

Dominick T. Armentano, "The Political Economy of William Graham Sumner: A Study in the History of Free-Enterprise Ideas," Ph.D. thesis, University of Connecticut, 1966;

Harry V. Ball, George E. Simpson, and Kiyoshi Ikeda, "Law and Social Change: Sumner Reconsidered," *American Journal of Sociology,* 67 (March 1962): 532–540;

Robert C. Bannister, *Sociology and Scientism: The American Quest for Objectivity, 1880–1940* (Chapel Hill: University of North Carolina Press, 1987), pp. 87–110;

Bannister, "William Graham Sumner's 'Social Darwinism' Reconsidered," *History of Political Economy,* 5 (1973): 89–109; revised as chapter 5 of his *Social Darwinism: Science and Myth in Anglo-American Thought* (Philadelphia: Temple University Press, 1979), pp. 97–113;

Donald C. Bellomy, "The Moulding of an Iconoclast: William Graham Sumner, 1840–1885," dissertation, Harvard University, 1980;

William L. Burton, "The Conservatism of William Graham Sumner," *Modern Age,* 4 (1959–1960): 45–51;

John Chamberlain, "William Graham Sumner and the Old Republic," *Modern Age,* 4 (1959–1960): 52–62;

Bruce Curtis, "Victorians Abed: William Graham Sumner on the Family, Women, and Sex," *American Studies* (Spring 1977): 101–122;

Curtis, *William Graham Sumner* (Boston: Twayne, 1981);

Curtis, "William Graham Sumner and the Problem of Progress," *New England Quarterly,* 51 (September 1978): 348–369;

Robert Garson and Richard Maidment, "Social Darwinism and the Liberal Tradition," *South Atlantic Quarterly,* 80 (1981): 61–76;

Richard Hofstadter, *Social Darwinism in American Thought, 1860–1915* (Philadelphia: University of Pennsylvania Press, 1944), pp. 37–51;

Albert Galloway Keller, *Reminiscences (Mainly Personal) of William Graham Sumner* (New Haven: Yale University Press, 1933);

Edwin M. Lemert, "The Folkways and Social Control," *American Sociological Review,* 7 (1942): 394–399;

Robert B. Notestein, "The Moral Rigorism of William Graham Sumner," *Journal of the History of Ideas,* 16 (1955): 389–400;

Notestein, "William Graham Sumner: An Essay in the Sociology of Knowledge," *American Journal of Economics,* 18 (1959): 397–413;

Robert E. Park, "The Social Methods of William Graham Sumner, and of William I. Thomas, and of Florien Znaniecki," in *Methods in Social Science: A Case Book Compiled under the Direction of the Committee on Scientific Method in the Social Science Research Council,* edited by Stuart Arthur Rice (Chicago: University of Chicago Press, 1931), pp. 154–175;

Park, "William Graham Sumner's Conception of Society," *Chinese Social and Political Science Review,* 17 (1933): 430–433;

Ellen F. Paul, "Liberalism, Unintended Orders, and Evolutionism," *Political Studies,* 36 (1988): 251–272;

Donald K. Pickens, "Scottish Common Sense Philosophy and *Folkways,*" *Journal of Thought,* 22 (1987): 39–44;

Pickens, "William Graham Sumner: Moralist as Social Scientist," *Social Science,* 43 (1968): 202–209;

Merwin A. Sheketoff, "William Graham Sumner: Social Christian, 1869–1872," dissertation, Harvard University, 1961;

Albion W. Small, "Fifty Years of Sociology in the United States," *American Journal of Sociology,* 21 (May 1916): 721–864;

Norman E. Smith, "William Graham Sumner as an Anti-Social Darwinist," *Pacific Sociological Review,* 22 (1979): 332–347;

Smith and Roscoe C. Hinkle, "Sumner versus Keller and the Social Evolutionism of Early American Sociology," *Sociological Inquiry,* 49 (1979): 41–48.

Papers:

The bulk of William Graham Sumner's letters, manuscripts, and published works are in the William Graham Sumner Papers in the Manuscripts and Archives division of the Sterling Memorial Library at Yale University.

Henry David Thoreau

(12 July 1817 – 6 May 1862)

Douglas R. Anderson
The Pennsylvania State University

See also the Thoreau entries in *DLB 1: The American Renaissance in New England; DLB 183: American Travel Writers, 1776–1864;* and *DLB 223: The American Renaissance in New England, Second Series.*

BOOKS: *A Week on the Concord and Merrimack Rivers* (Boston & Cambridge, Mass.: Munroe, 1849; London: Walter Scott, 1849);

Walden; or, Life in the Woods (Boston: Ticknor & Fields, 1854); republished as *Walden* (Boston: Ticknor & Fields, 1862; Edinburgh: David Douglas, 1884);

Excursions (Boston: Ticknor & Fields, 1863);

The Maine Woods (Boston: Ticknor & Fields, 1864);

Cape Cod (Boston: Ticknor & Fields, 1865; London: Sampson Low, Son & Marston, 1865);

A Yankee in Canada, with Anti-Slavery and Reform Papers (Boston: Ticknor & Fields, 1866);

Early Spring in Massachusetts, edited by Harrison Gray Otis Blake (Boston: Houghton, Mifflin, 1881);

Summer: From the Journal of Henry David Thoreau, edited by Blake (Boston: Houghton, Mifflin, 1884; London: Unwin, 1884);

The Writings of Henry David Thoreau, Riverside Edition, 11 volumes, edited by Blake, Franklin Benjamin Sanborn, and Horace Elisha Scudder (Boston & New York: Houghton, Mifflin, 1884–1894);

Winter: From the Journal of Henry David Thoreau, edited by Blake (Boston: Houghton, Mifflin, 1888);

Autumn: From the Journal of Henry David Thoreau, edited by Blake (Boston: Houghton, Mifflin, 1892);

Miscellanies (Boston & New York: Houghton, Mifflin, 1894);

Poems of Nature, edited by Sanborn and H. S. Salt (Boston: Houghton, Mifflin / London: John Lane, 1895);

The Service, edited by Sanborn (Boston: Charles E. Goodspeed, 1902);

The First and Last Journeys of Thoreau, 2 volumes, edited by Sanborn (Boston: Bibliophile Society, 1905);

Sir Walter Raleigh (Boston: Bibliophile Society, 1905);

Henry David Thoreau (ambrotype by E. S. Dunshee, 1861)

The Writings of Henry David Thoreau, Manuscript Edition, 20 volumes, edited by Bradford Torrey and Francis H. Allen (Boston & New York: Houghton, Mifflin, 1906);

The Moon (Boston & New York: Houghton Mifflin, 1927);

The Transmigration of the Seven Brahmas (New York: William Edwin Rudge, 1931);

Collected Poems of Henry Thoreau, edited by Carl Bode (Chicago: Packard, 1943; enlarged edition, Baltimore: Johns Hopkins University Press, 1964);

Consciousness in Concord: The Text of Thoreau's Hitherto "Lost Journal" (1840-1841), edited by Perry Miller (Boston: Houghton Mifflin, 1958);

Thoreau's Literary Notebooks in the Library of Congress, edited by Kenneth Walter Cameron (Hartford, Conn.: Transcendental Books, 1964);

Thoreau's Fact Book in the Harry Elkins Widener Collection in the Harvard College Library, 3 volumes, edited by Cameron (Hartford, Conn.: Transcendental Books, 1966-1987);

Huckleberries, edited by Leo Stoller (Iowa City: University of Iowa Press, 1970);

The Writings of Henry D. Thoreau, 12 volumes to date, edited by Walter Harding and others (Princeton: Princeton University Press, 1971-   );

The Indians of Thoreau: Selections from the Indian Notebooks, edited by Richard F. Fleck (Albuquerque, N.Mex.: Hummingbird Press, 1974);

Early Essays and Miscellanies, edited by Joseph J. Moldenhauer, Edwin Moser, and Alexander Kern (Princeton: Princeton University Press, 1975);

Natural History Essays, edited by Robert Sattelmeyer (Salt Lake City: Peregrine Smith, 1980);

The Journal of Henry David Thoreau, 2 volumes published, edited by John C. Broderick and others (Princeton: Princeton University Press, 1981-   );

Translations, edited by K. P. van Anglen (Princeton: Princeton University Press, 1986);

Faith in a Seed: The Dispersion of Seeds and Other Late Natural History Writings, edited by Bradley P. Dean (Washington, D.C.: Island Press, 1993);

Wild Fruits: Thoreau's Rediscovered Last Manuscript, edited by Dean (New York: Norton, 1999).

Edition: *The Variorum Walden*, edited by Walter Harding (New York: Twayne, 1962; revised edition, New York: Washington Square Press, 1963).

OTHER: "A Plea for Captain John Brown," in *Echoes of Harpers Ferry*, edited by James Redpath (Boston: Thayer & Eldridge, 1860), pp. 17-42.

SELECTED PERIODICAL PUBLICATIONS–UNCOLLECTED: "Aulus Persius Flaccus," *Dial*, 1 (1840): 117-121;

"Natural History of Massachusetts," *Dial*, 3 (1842): 19-40;

"Homer, Ossian, Chaucer," *Dial*, 4 (1843): 290-305;

"A Walk to Wachusett," *Boston Miscellany*, 3 (1843): 31-36;

"Dark Ages," *Dial*, 4 (1843): 527-529;

"A Winter Walk," *Dial*, 4 (1843): 211-226;

"The Landlord," *United States Magazine and Democratic Review*, 13 (1843): 427-430;

"Herald of Freedom," *Dial*, 4 (1844): 507-512;

"Thomas Carlyle and His Works," 2 installments, *Graham's Magazine*, 30 (1847): 145-152, 238-245;

"The Wilds of the Penobscot," *Sartrain's Union Magazine*, 3 (1848): 29-33;

"Life in the Wilderness," *Sartrain's Union Magazine*, 3 (1848): 73-79;

"Boating in the Lakes," *Sartrain's Union Magazine*, 3 (1848): 132-137;

"The Ascent of Ktaadn," *Sartrain's Union Magazine*, 3 (1848): 177-182;

"The Return Journey," *Sartrain's Union Magazine*, 3 (1848): 216-220;

"Resistance to Civil Government," *Aesthetic Papers* (1849): 189-211;

"The Iron Horse," *Sartrain's Union Magazine*, 11 (1852): 66-68;

"A Poet Buying a Farm," *Sartrain's Union Magazine*, 11 (1852): 127;

"An Excursion to Canada," 3 installments, *Putnam's Magazine*, 1 (1853): 54-59, 179-184, 321-329;

"Slavery in Massachusetts," *Liberator*, 24 (1854);

"The Shipwreck," *Putnam's Magazine*, 5 (1855): 632-637;

"Stage Coach Views," *Putnam's Magazine*, 5 (1855): 637-640;

"The Plains of Nanset," *Putnam's Magazine*, 6 (1855): 59-66;

"The Beach," *Putnam's Magazine*, 6 (1855): 157-164;

"Chesuncook," 3 installments, *Atlantic Monthly*, 2 (1858): 1-12, 224-233, 305-317;

"The Last Days of John Brown," *Liberator*, 30 (1860);

"The Succession of Forest Trees," *New York Weekly Tribune*, 1860;

"Walking," *Atlantic Monthly*, 9 (1862): 657-674;

"Autumnal Tints," *Atlantic Monthly*, 10 (1862): 385-402;

"Wild Apples," *Atlantic Monthly*, 10 (1862): 513-526;

"Life without Principle," *Atlantic Monthly*, 12 (1863): 484-495;

"Night and Moonlight," *Atlantic Monthly*, 12 (1863): 579-583;

"The Wellfleet Oysterman," *Atlantic Monthly*, 14 (1864): 470-478;

"The Highland Light," *Atlantic Monthly*, 14 (1864): 649-659.

Though not a professional philosopher, Henry David Thoreau is recognized as an important contributor to the American literary and philosophical movement known as New England Transcendentalism. His essays, books, and poems weave together two central themes over the course of his intellectual career: nature and the conduct of life. The continuing importance of these two themes is well illustrated by the fact that the last two essays Thoreau published during his lifetime were "The Last Days of John Brown" and "The Succession of Forest Trees" (both in 1860). In his moral and political work Thoreau aligned himself with the post-Socratic schools of Greek philosophy–in particular, the Cynics and Stoics–that used philosophy as a means of addressing ordinary human experience. His naturalistic writing integrated straightforward observation and cataloguing with Transcendentalist interpretations of nature and the wilderness. In many of his works Thoreau brought these interpretations of nature to bear on how people live or ought to live.

Thoreau's importance as a philosophical writer was little appreciated during his lifetime, but his two most noted works, *Walden; or, Life in the Woods* (1854) and "Civil Disobedience" (1849), gradually developed a following and by the latter half of the twentieth century had become classic texts in American thought. Not only have these texts been used widely to address issues in political philosophy, moral theory, and, more recently, environmentalism, but they have also been of central importance to those who see philosophy as an engagement with ordinary experience and not as an abstract deductive exercise. In this vein, Thoreau's work has been recognized as having foreshadowed central insights of later philosophical movements such as existentialism and pragmatism.

Toward the end of his life Thoreau's naturalistic interests took a more scientific turn; he pursued a close examination of local fauna and kept detailed records of his observations. Nevertheless, he kept one eye on the moral and political developments of his time, often expressing his positions with rhetorical fire as in his "A Plea for Captain John Brown" (1860). He achieved an elegant integration of his naturalism and his moral interests in several late essays that were published posthumously, among them "Walking" and "Wild Apples" (both in 1862).

David Henry Thoreau was born on 12 July 1817 in Concord, Massachusetts, to John and Cynthia Dunbar Thoreau. He had two older siblings, Helen and John, and a younger sister, Sophia. The family moved to Chelmsford in 1818, to Boston in 1821, and back to Concord in 1823. Thoreau had two educations in Concord. The first occurred through his explorations of the local environment, which were encouraged by his mother's interest in nature. The second was his preparation at Concord Academy for study at Harvard University. He entered Harvard in 1833 and graduated in 1837. The year he graduated he began the journal that was a primary source for his lectures and published work throughout his life. At this time, too, he inverted his names and began to refer to himself as Henry David.

Thoreau's working life began with a teaching job at Concord Center School that lasted only a few weeks because he was unwilling to use corporal punishment on his students. He and his brother, John, ran their own school from 1838 to 1841; their teaching techniques foreshadowed the pragmatic educational philosophy of John Dewey. During these years Thoreau developed a close relationship with Ralph Waldo Emerson, who served as his friend and mentor. Traces of Emerson's philosophical influence appear in all of Thoreau's writings, even after their friendship cooled.

In 1839 Thoreau met Ellen Sewall, the daughter of a Unitarian minister. At least partly on her father's advice, she rejected Thoreau's proposal of marriage. Thoreau's writing career was launched the following year when he began publishing essays and poems in Emerson and Margaret Fuller's new journal, *The Dial,* which became the home of much Transcendentalist writing. In July 1842 Thoreau published in *The Dial* "Natural History of Massachusetts," which established the basic direction and style of his naturalistic writings. The essay displays both his scientific interest and his Transcendentalist vision of the meanings to be found in human encounters with nature. In two essays published in 1843, "A Winter Walk" and "A Walk to Wachusett," Thoreau develops his naturalistic writing in the direction it later took in *Walden.* Although these early essays can be read as somewhat romantic literary descriptions, Thoreau has already begun to inject a philosophical edge into his writings. Walking becomes a metaphor for various other features of human existence. Also, nature's presence is not merely accepted passively; Thoreau focuses on its agency as an analogue and inspiration for human agency. Like other Transcendentalists, he was an idealist and believed divinity to be immanent in nature. This indwelling of the divine, he thought, allows nature to serve as a vehicle for human insight. Consequently, the central issue at stake in many of his early nature essays is the awakening of humans to their own powers and possibilities through encounters with nature.

Thoreau worked off and on at his father's pencil-making business, and in 1843 he served for a short time as tutor for Emerson's brother Edward's children on Staten Island, New York. Then, in 1845, he built a small cabin near Walden Pond on land that Ralph Waldo Emerson had purchased to preserve its beauty. During his two-year stay at the pond Thoreau completed the manuscript for *A Week on the Concord and Merrimack Rivers* (1849); it was based on a trip he had taken with his brother, John, in 1839 and was intended as a memorial to John, who had died of teta-nus in 1842. Thoreau also, of course, had the experiences that became the basis for *Walden,* and he began writing this work while he was still living at the pond. Also during his sojourn at Walden Pond, Thoreau spent a night in jail for not having paid his poll tax in protest of slavery. This episode laid the foundation for "Civil Disobedience."

After leaving Walden, Thoreau spent a year living in Emerson's home, helping with handiwork and the children while Emerson was lecturing in Europe. In January 1848 he gave a two-part lecture at the Concord Lyceum titled "The Relation of the Individual to the State." The lecture was published in revised form as "Resistance to Civil Government" in Elizabeth Peabody's *Aesthetic Papers* in May 1849. Later retitled "Civil Disobedience," it became his best-known and most influential essay.

In "Resistance to Civil Government" Thoreau works out his conception of the self-reliant individual's relationship to the state. The essay begins with an idealistic Transcendentalist hope for a government "which governs not at all." But it quickly takes a practical turn, asking what one can do—and what one ought to do—when the state acts in a systematically immoral way. Thoreau's immediate target is state-supported slavery in the United States. He chides his fellow citizens for directly and indirectly enabling slavery to continue in the Southern states, and he suggests that they find ways to act in resistance to the government on this score. He offers as one example of resistance the route that he and others had already taken of not paying taxes that might be used to sustain slavery. He also argues that economic support for slave states should be abandoned, even if it hurt commerce in the North. His suggestion that one can resist a government without resorting to violence gave the essay its notoriety; Mohandas Gandhi and Martin Luther King Jr. cited it as an influence on their own acts of resistance.

Thoreau's argument in "Civil Disobedience" is sometimes read as a libertarian tract, like Emerson's "Self-Reliance" (1841). From this point of view it is considered a defense of rugged individualism, if not anarchy. But such interpretations miss the central Transcendentalism of the piece. What both Thoreau and Emerson require is a careful turning to one's moral intuition, or conscience, as a guide when confronted by issues of major consequence. The aim is not to be left alone by the state to do as one pleases but to get the state, as well as oneself, to act in concert with human and divine conscience.

In the same year "Resistance to Civil Government" appeared, Thoreau published his first book, *A Week on the Concord and Merrimack Rivers.* Thoreau

Thoreau's older brother, John, with whom he took the 1839 trip that he describes in A Week on the Concord and Merrimack Rivers *(1849)*

attempts in the work to bring together his observations of nature with his commentary on human existence, but the book lacks the integrity of his best essays as the Transcendentalist commentary remains separate and abstracted from the sections of narrative description. The commercial failure of the book undoubtedly helped Thoreau in his preparation of *Walden.*

After the cool reception of *A Week on the Concord and Merrimack Rivers,* Thoreau traveled to Maine, Cape Cod, New Hampshire, and Canada. His excursions provided the material for future writing projects. He also continued to revise *Walden;* it appeared in 1854, the second and last book Thoreau published during his lifetime.

Walden is unquestionably Thoreau's major work. He condenses the two years he had actually spent in the cabin into a single year, and, beginning with summer,

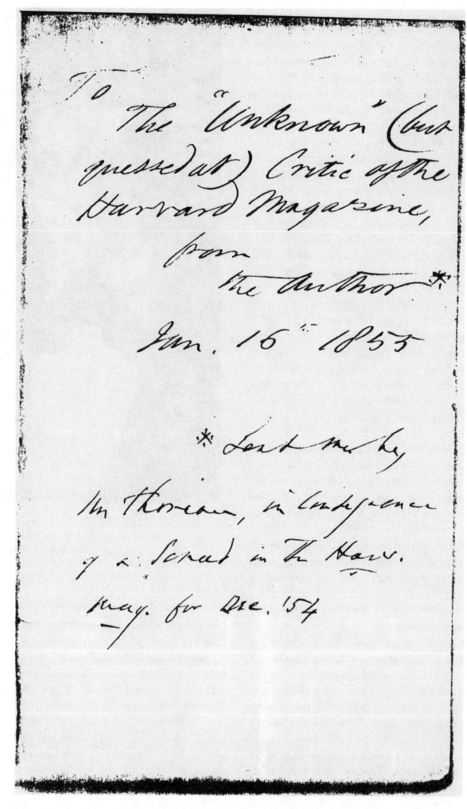

Inscription by Thoreau in a copy of A Week on the Concord and Merrimack Rivers *that he left in
Franklin Benjamin Sanborn's room at Harvard University (Rare Books
and Manuscript Library, University of Florida)*

takes the reader through the seasons at the pond. The central theme of the book is the cultivation of the self. Thoreau has in mind a specific audience: those who have become disenchanted with their everyday lives, "the mass of men who are discontented, and idly complaining of the hardness of their lot or of the times." His aim is not to have others imitate his move to Walden but to have them consider their own possibilities for improving their situations, for overcoming their "lives of quiet desperation." To this extent the book is like a Stoic treatise on life. It is, however, replete with irony, humor, and a philosophical and literary integrity that make it much more than a straightforward enchiridion.

To bring readers to their own awakenings, Thoreau first raises the question of a life's economy. He experiments with living "deliberately," paying attention to what he owns and what owns him, as well as to how he spends his time. An explicit antimaterialism underwrites much of the first two chapters. Thoreau does not dogmatically endorse an economic minimalism, however; the experiment in poverty is an attempt to find out what is important in a life—it is, in other words, a way of testing one's life. The post-Socratic theme is that simplifying one's life frees one to see more clearly. One will better perceive the world around one, will see what constrains one's life, and, most important, will be freer to explore one's inner self for divine insight. Because Thoreau sees himself as having been engaged in an experiment in living, leaving Walden is not a problem for or a contradiction of his philosophical outlook. When the experiment comes to an end, he looks forward without concern: "Only that day dawns to which we are awake. There is more day to dawn."

Thoreau seeks in *Walden* and many of his other writings to effect an awakening in a variety of ways. Nature plays a central role in most of these writings. On the one hand, it serves as a mirror and metaphor of human existence. It reflects the way one lives and provides exemplars of how one might live. In chapters such as "Brute Neighbors," "Sounds," and "Solitude" Thoreau asks his reader to attend to what is immediately present in nature: the actions of birds and chipmunks, the sounds of night and morning, silences both inner and outer. The effect is twofold: the reader learns from this attentiveness what he or she has not before perceived, and, more important, in the process Thoreau slows down the reader's world so that he or she might understand what it would be like to undertake his or her own experiment in attentiveness.

Nature also provides a metaphor for human growth. As many commentators have pointed out, the seasons of the text reveal the continuing possibilities for self-cultivation; one need not accept any routinized existence as final. Moreover, throughout the work Thoreau treats the reader to shifting focuses on morning, afternoon, and evening, revealing the possibilities of organic development even in short spans of existence. In attending to nature's inner energies for self-recovery, one begins to notice one's own possibilities for the same. This notion is good Transcendentalist doctrine: nature is a vehicle for and catalyst of self-reliance. It is a source of intuitions of "higher laws."

Finally, in a more practical vein, nature as wilderness provides an extreme against which one may measure one's own aliveness. Thoreau sees his time at Walden as a "border" life between the numbing overcivilization of the town and an untempered and unthoughtful existence in the wilderness. The border life, he suggests, is fruitful precisely because it allows one to grow, to participate in the recivilizing of one's own life. As in his earlier essays, he focuses on championing human agency and creativity. This theme of the wilderness becomes even more explicit in later essays.

In philosophical terms—terms that Thoreau did not himself use—Thoreau's Transcendentalism is fundamentally idealistic, with "higher laws" serving as the measure of human endeavors. But it is at the same time a philosophy of nature, though not a reductive naturalism. For Thoreau, Emerson's self-reliance needs nature's inspiration, example, and effects. To undertake the task of self-cultivation one must, as Thoreau sees it, work with and through nature. Thoreau's focus on nature brings him closer than most of his Transcendentalist colleagues to the later philosophy of pragmatism. His idealism is not the remote operation of mind in the world but the working of higher laws into one's own private thoughts and public practices. This position is his generic answer to lives of quiet desperation.

The return of the runaway Anthony Burns to slavery by the state of Massachusetts under the federal Fugitive Slave Law pushed Thoreau to take an even stronger stance than he had in "Civil Disobedience." He expanded his ideas from that essay into "Slavery in Massachusetts," which appeared in the abolitionist magazine *The Liberator* the same year *Walden* was published. His attack is now not merely on slavery in general but on his own state's complicity with an immoral law. Thoreau retains his Transcendentalist plea that one trust one's inner conscience to judge the state's actions, but he moves much closer to advocating the destruction of a state that engages in practices such as slavery. Though he does not openly propose violent action, he seems more amenable to it than he had in "Civil Disobedience."

"Slavery in Massachusetts" was followed by three essays on the radical abolitionist John Brown. Thoreau presented the first, "A Plea for Captain John Brown," in Concord on 30 October 1859, after Brown's raid on the

WALDEN;

OR,

LIFE IN THE WOODS.

By HENRY D. THOREAU,

AUTHOR OF "A WEEK ON THE CONCORD AND MERRIMACK RIVERS."

I do not propose to write an ode to dejection, but to brag as lustily as chanticleer in the
morning, standing on his roost, if only to wake my neighbors up. — Page 92.

BOSTON:

TICKNOR AND FIELDS.

M DCCC LIV.

Title page for Thoreau's philosophical account of his two-year residence—shortened to a single year in the book—in a cabin near a pond outside Concord, Massachusetts (courtesy of Special Collections, Thomas Cooper Library, University of South Carolina)

practical good. In this respect Thoreau again foreshadows pragmatic philosophy, especially the political and social involvement of Dewey. This feature of Thoreau's outlook needs to be emphasized, because many readers of *Walden* and Thoreau's nature essays are tempted to see him as a recluse.

Thoreau's nature study became more scientifically serious and less Transcendentalist in his later works. "The Succession of Forest Trees," which he delivered as a lecture to the Middlesex Agricultural Society on 20 September 1860 and published in *The New York Weekly Tribune,* marks this turn in Thoreau's career. Like many others, he had purchased and read Charles Darwin's *On the Origin of Species by Means of Natural Selection; or, The Preservation of Favoured Races in the Struggle for Life* when it was published in 1859. This book, together with other readings in forestry and natural history, provided the basis for the new studies. "The Succession of Forest Trees" still bears the mark of Thoreau's character; it is written with the usual irony and humor. Nevertheless, it deals seriously with seed dispersal and the growth of Northeastern forests. Its systematic philosophical import is to be found in Thoreau's continued emphasis on a cosmos of growth, cultivation, and change. Nature again establishes the basis by which human beings must gauge their own lives.

During much of the last third of his life Thoreau earned his living by helping in the family business and by working as a surveyor. His surveying provided ample opportunity to continue his studies of nature. But these years were marred by recurring bouts of tuberculosis, a disease common to the time and to Thoreau's family. In 1861 Thoreau suffered a difficult bout with the disease, and it was suggested that he travel as a treatment. He went west to Minnesota by boat and train. He returned home as sick as when he left.

By early 1862 Thoreau seemed to know that he was dying. He continued to work on his scientific studies, but with the help of his sister Sophia he also prepared several essays for publication in *The Atlantic Monthly.* They are among the best of his writings, and because they had been given as talks in the 1850s, they display a mature version of his Transcendentalism. They include "Life without Principle," "Walking," and "Wild Apples," all of which were published posthumously. In each, the self is treated as an agent in transition seeking ways to cultivate itself and learning to grow. There is no fixed Cartesian ego, only a questing "Walker, Errant," as he puts it in "Walking." The quest is itself motivated by a hope of discovering "higher laws" and of learning to live through them, of finding a practical wisdom. In "Life without Principle" Thoreau considers the Gold Rush and remarks that "a grain of

government arsenal at Harpers Ferry, Virginia (today West Virginia). It is primarily offered as a response to the negative press that Brown received for his efforts. The argument behind the defense of Brown is, however, clearly Transcendentalist. Thoreau lauds Brown as a man of principle, as one who resisted his government's institution of slavery as a matter of conscience; he represents what Thoreau called "a majority of one" in "Civil Disobedience." In "Martyrdom of John Brown" and "The Last Days of John Brown," written for separate memorial services for Brown held on 2 December 1859, the day Brown was hanged, Thoreau develops his portrayal of Brown as a self-reliant man of principle. These essays exemplify Thoreau's perennial claim that a philosopher is not merely a schoolteacher, a professor, a scholar, or a minister but an agent for

gold will gild a great surface, but not so much as a grain of wisdom."

In these late essays the themes of *Walden* return, but they are now expressed with the strength and poetic insight of a man facing death. Thoreau again focuses on how people might remain awake and alive when their daily "business" so often leads them toward sleep and living death–toward lives of quiet desperation. In each of the essays nature resides in the background as a measure of what humans do. Thoreau's Transcendentalist idealism is ever present, though seldom stated. The world is a world of truth and moral force; the individual's task is to awaken to that truth and bring it to bear on people's lives. This life of principle might be found in the moral energy of a John Brown, in the poetic insight of a Ralph Waldo Emerson, or in the living of a simple if unnoticed life. For Thoreau, any of these might be a philosophical life in his sense; philosophy, for him, is not a project of reclusive understanding and scholarship. His antimaterialism, his focus on nature's wildness, his emphasis on transition and the novelty of each day and season are all instrumental in bringing people to themselves and in finding ways to live sincere lives. As he states in "Life without Principle," there is no "such thing as wisdom not applied to life."

That Thoreau took his own philosophical journey seriously was exemplified several days before he died. An old friend, knowing that Thoreau was close to death, asked if he had any sense of what was to come. Thoreau's famous reply was, "One world at a time." He died on 6 May 1862.

Thoreau was a philosophical provocateur. He had a sense of philosophical system derived from the Transcendentalist movement and its various German and British influences. But he was neither an analytic philosopher nor an idealist system builder. He saw the practical import of the Transcendentalist movement and staked his claim there. He was a harbinger of the social, political, and poetical dimensions of American pragmatism, and his work did, indeed, become practically useful in the twentieth century. The influence of "Civil Disobedience" on Gandhi and King are the most notable instances, but they are not the only ones. Selective reading of *Walden* and of various of the nature essays has identified a dimension of Thoreau's thinking that helps underwrite environmentalism; for Thoreau the importance of wilderness was both metaphorical and actual. Moreover, in his responses to overreliance on technology and wealth as cures for the human condition, one sees hints of the ideas of Martin Heidegger and other existentialists. Thoreau's place in American philosophy is only now being given serious

Thoreau's younger sister, Sophia, who helped him prepare several essays for publication in The Atlantic Monthly *shortly before his death*

consideration; it seems likely that his influence will continue to flourish.

Bibliographies:

Francis H. Allen, *A Bibliography of Henry David Thoreau* (Boston: Houghton Mifflin, 1908);

William White, *A Henry David Thoreau Bibliography* (Boston: Faxon, 1939);

Thoreau Society Bulletin, edited by Walter Harding (1941–);

Philip E. Burnham and Carvel Collins, "Contributions toward a Bibliography of Thoreau, 1938–1945," *Bulletin of Bibliography,* 19 (September–December 1946): 16–19; (January–April 1947): 37–39;

Harding, *A Centennial Check-list of the Editions of Henry David Thoreau's Walden* (Charlottesville: University Press of Virginia, 1954);

Christopher A. Hildenbrand, *A Bibliography of Scholarship about Henry David Thoreau 1940–1967* (Hays, Kans.: Fort Hays State College, 1967);

A Bibliography of the Thoreau Society Bulletin Bibliographies 1941–1969 (Troy, N.Y.: Whitston, 1971);

Lewis Leary, "Henry David Thoreau," in *Eight American Authors: A Review of Research and Criticism,* edited by James Woodress (New York: Norton, 1971);

Annette M. Woodlief, "Walden: A Checklist of Literary Criticism through 1973," *Resources for American Literary Study,* 5 (Spring 1975): 15–58;

Jeanetta Boswell and Sarah Crouch, *Henry David Thoreau and the Critics* (Metuchen, N.J.: Scarecrow Press, 1981);

Raymond R. Borst, *Henry David Thoreau: A Descriptive Bibliography* (Pittsburgh: University of Pittsburgh Press, 1982);

Michael Meyer, "Henry David Thoreau," in *The Transcendentalists: A Review of Research and Criticism,* edited by Joel Myerson (New York: Modern Language Association, 1984), pp. 260–285;

Borst, *Henry David Thoreau: A Reference Guide, 1875–1899* (Boston: G. K. Hall, 1987);

Boswell, "Henry David Thoreau," in her *The American Renaissance and the Critics: The Best of a Century of Criticism* (Wakefield, N.H.: Longwood Academic, 1990), pp. 129–203;

Gary Scharnhorst, *Henry David Thoreau: An Annotated Bibliography of Comment and Criticism before 1900* (Hamden, Conn.: Garland, 1992).

Biographies:

Ralph Waldo Emerson, "Thoreau," *Atlantic Monthly,* 10 (August 1862): 239–249;

William Ellery Channing, *Thoreau: The Poet-Naturalist. With Memorial Verses* (Boston: Roberts, 1873); enlarged edition, edited by Franklin Benjamin Sanborn (Boston: Charles E. Goodspeed, 1902);

H. A. Page [A. H. Japp], *Thoreau: His Life and Aims* (Boston: J. R. Osgood, 1877);

Sanborn, *Henry D. Thoreau* (Boston: Houghton, Mifflin, 1882);

Henry S. Salt, *The Life of Henry David Thoreau* (London: Bentley, 1890);

Edward Emerson, *Henry Thoreau as Remembered by a Young Friend* (Boston: Houghton Mifflin, 1917);

Sanborn, *The Life of Henry David Thoreau* (Boston: Houghton Mifflin, 1917);

Léon Bazalgette, *Henry Thoreau, Sauvage* (Paris: Rieder, 1924); translated by Van Wyck Brooks as *Henry Thoreau: Bachelor of Nature* (New York: Harcourt, Brace, 1924);

Brooks Atkinson, *Henry Thoreau: The Cosmic Yankee* (New York: Knopf, 1927);

Henry Seidel Canby, *Thoreau* (New York: Houghton Mifflin, 1939);

Milton Meltzer and Walter Harding, *A Thoreau Profile* (New York: Crowell, 1962);

Harding, *The Days of Henry David Thoreau* (New York: Knopf, 1965);

Richard Lebeaux, *Young Man Thoreau* (Amherst: University of Massachusetts Press, 1977);

Lebeaux, *Thoreau's Seasons* (Amherst: University of Massachusetts Press, 1984);

Robert D. Richardson Jr., *Henry Thoreau: A Life of the Mind* (Berkeley: University of California Press, 1986);

Raymond R. Borst, *The Thoreau Log: A Documentary Life of Henry David Thoreau, 1817–1862* (New York: Macmillan, 1992).

References:

Stephen Adams and Donald Ross Jr., *Revising Mythologies: The Composition of Thoreau's Major Works* (Charlottesville: University Press of Virginia, 1988);

Charles R. Anderson, *The Magic Circle of Walden* (New York: Holt, Rinehart & Winston, 1968);

Thomas Blanding and Walter Harding, *A Thoreau Iconography* (Geneseo, N.Y.: Thoreau Society, 1980);

Gordon Boudreau, *The Roots of Walden and the Tree of Life* (Nashville, Tenn.: Vanderbilt University Press, 1990);

Richard Bridgman, *Dark Thoreau* (Lincoln: University of Nebraska Press, 1981);

Lawrence Buell, *The Environmental Imagination: Thoreau, Nature Writing, and the Formation of American Culture* (Cambridge, Mass.: Harvard University Press, 1995);

Buell, *Literary Transcendentalism: Style and Vision in the American Renaissance* (Ithaca, N.Y.: Cornell University Press, 1973);

Joan Burbick, *Thoreau's Alternative History: Changing Perspectives on Nature, Culture, and Language* (Philadelphia: University of Pennsylvania Press, 1987);

William Cain, ed., *The Oxford Guide to Henry David Thoreau* (Oxford: Oxford University Press, 2000);

Sharon Cameron, *Writing Nature: Henry Thoreau's Journal* (Chicago: University of Chicago Press, 1985);

Stanley Cavell, *The Senses of Walden* (San Francisco: North Point Press, 1981);

John Aldrich Christie, *Thoreau as World Traveler* (New York: Columbia University Press, 1965);

Reginald L. Cook, *Passage to Walden* (Boston: Houghton Mifflin, 1949);

Steven Fink, *Prophet in the Marketplace: Thoreau's Development as a Professional Writer* (Princeton: Princeton University Press, 1992);

Victor Carl Friesen, *The Spirit of the Huckleberry: Sensuousness in Henry Thoreau* (Edmonton: University of Alberta Press, 1984);

Frederick Garber, *Thoreau's Fable of Inscribing* (Princeton: Princeton University Press, 1991);

Garber, *Thoreau's Redemptive Imagination* (New York: New York University Press, 1977);

Michael T. Gilmore, "Walden and the 'Curse of Trade,'" in his *American Romanticism and the Marketplace* (Chicago: University of Chicago Press, 1985), pp. 35–51;

Wendell Glick, ed., *The Recognition of Henry David Thoreau* (Ann Arbor: University of Michigan, 1969);

Henry Golemba, *Thoreau's Wild Rhetoric* (New York: New York University Press, 1990);

Walter Harding, *Thoreau: A Century of Criticism* (Dallas: Southern Methodist University Press, 1954);

Harding, *Thoreau: Man of Concord* (New York: Holt, Rinehart & Winston, 1962);

Harding, *Thoreau as Seen by His Contemporaries* (New York: Dover, 1989);

Harding, *Thoreau's Library* (Charlottesville: University Press of Virginia, 1957);

Harding and Michael Meyer, *The New Thoreau Handbook* (New York: New York University Press, 1980);

William A. Herr, "A More Perfect State: Thoreau's Concept of Civil Government," *Massachusetts Review,* 16 (Summer 1975): 470–487;

John Hildebidle, *Thoreau: A Naturalist's Liberty* (Cambridge, Mass.: Harvard University Press, 1983);

Alan D. Hodder, "'Ex Oriente Lux': Thoreau's Ecstasies and the Hindu Texts," *Harvard Theological Review,* 86 (October 1993): 403–438;

William Howarth, *The Book of Concord: Thoreau's Life as a Writer* (New York: Viking, 1982);

Howarth, *The Literary Manuscripts of Henry David Thoreau* (Columbus: Ohio State University Press, 1974);

Linck C. Johnson, *Thoreau's Complex Weave: The Writing of* A Week on the Concord and Merrimack Rivers, *with the Text of the First Draft* (Charlottesville: University Press of Virginia, 1986);

Karl Kroeber, "Ecology and American Literature: Thoreau and Un-Thoreau," *American Literary History,* 9 (Summer 1997): 309–328;

Joseph Wood Krutch, *Henry David Thoreau* (New York: Sloane, 1949);

Leo Marx, *The Machine in the Garden: Technology and the Pastoral Ideal in America* (New York: Oxford University Press, 1964);

F. O. Matthiessen, "From Emerson to Thoreau," in his *American Renaissance: Art and Expression in the Age of Emerson and Whitman* (New York: Oxford University Press, 1941), pp. 3–175;

Robert Kuhn McGregor, *A Wider View of the Universe: Henry Thoreau's Study of Nature* (Urbana: University of Illinois Press, 1997);

James McIntosh, *Thoreau as Romantic Naturalist: His Shifting Stance toward Nature* (Ithaca, N.Y.: Cornell University Press, 1974);

Michael Meyer, *Several More Lives to Live: Thoreau's Political Reputation in America* (Westport, Conn.: Greenwood Press, 1977);

Walter Benn Michaels, "Walden's False Bottoms," *Glyph,* 1 (1977): 132–149;

Robert Milder, *Reimagining Thoreau* (Cambridge: Cambridge University Press, 1995);

Perry Miller, *Consciousness in Concord: The Text of Thoreau's Hitherto "Lost Journal" (1840–1841) Together with Notes and a Commentary* (Boston: Houghton Mifflin, 1958);

Mary Elkins Moller, *Thoreau and the Human Community* (Amherst: University of Massachusetts Press, 1980);

Joel Myerson, ed., *The Cambridge Companion to Henry David Thoreau* (Cambridge: Cambridge University Press, 1995);

Myerson, ed., *Critical Essays on Henry David Thoreau's Walden* (Boston: G. K. Hall, 1988);

Leonard N. Neufeldt, *The Economist: Henry Thoreau and Enterprise* (Oxford: Oxford University Press, 1989);

Sherman Paul, *The Shores of America: Thoreau's Inward Exploration* (Champaign: University of Illinois Press, 1958);

Paul, ed., *Thoreau: A Collection of Critical Essays* (Englewood Cliffs, N.J.: Prentice-Hall, 1962);

H. Daniel Peck, *Thoreau's Morning Work: Memory and Perception in A Week on the Concord and Merrimack Rivers, the Journal, and Walden* (New Haven: Yale University Press, 1990);

Henry Petroski, "H. D. Thoreau, Engineer," *American Heritage of Invention and Technology,* 5 (Fall 1989): 8–16;

Joel Porte, *Emerson and Thoreau: Transcendentalists in Conflict* (Middletown, Conn.: Wesleyan University Press, 1966);

Robert D. Richardson Jr., "Thoreau and Science," in *American Literature and Science,* edited by Robert J. Scholnick (Lexington: University Press of Kentucky, 1992), pp. 110–127;

William Rossi, "Poetry and Progress: Thoreau, Lyell, and the Geological Principles of A Week," *American Literature,* 66 (June 1994): 275–300;

George E. Ryan, "Shanties and Shiftlessness: The Immigrant Irish of Henry Thoreau," *Éire,* 13 (Fall 1978): 54–78;

Robert Sattelmeyer, "The Remaking of Walden," in *Writing the American Classics,* edited by James Barbour and Tom Quirk (Chapel Hill: University of North Carolina Press, 1990), pp. 53–78;

Sattelmeyer, *Thoreau's Reading: A Study in Intellectual History with Bibliographical Catalogue* (Princeton: Princeton University Press, 1988);

Robert F. Sayre, *New Essays on Walden* (Cambridge: Cambridge University Press, 1992);

Sayre, *Thoreau and the American Indians* (Princeton: Princeton University Press, 1977);

Gary Scharnhorst, *Henry David Thoreau: A Case Study in Canonization* (Columbia, S.C.: Camden House, 1993);

Don Scheese, *Nature Writing: The Pastoral Impulse in America* (Boston: Twayne, 1996);

Richard J. Schneider, *Henry David Thoreau* (Boston: Twayne, 1987);

Schneider, ed., *Approaches to Teaching Thoreau's Walden and Other Works* (New York: MLA, 1996);

Schneider, ed., *Thoreau's Sense of Place: Essays in American Environmental Writing* (Iowa City: University of Iowa Press, 2000);

Edmund A. Schofield and Robert C. Baron, *Thoreau's World and Ours: A Natural Legacy* (Golden, Colo.: North American Press, 1993);

Ethel L. Seybold, *Thoreau: The Quest and the Classics* (New Haven: Yale University Press, 1951);

J. Lyndon Shanley, *The Making of Walden, with the Text of the First Version* (Chicago: University of Chicago Press, 1957);

Lorrie Smith, "'Walking' from England to America: Re-viewing Thoreau's Romanticism," *New England Quarterly,* 58 (June 1985): 221–241;

Leo Stoller, *After Walden: Thoreau's Changing Views on Economic Man* (Stanford, Cal.: Stanford University Press, 1957);

Robert F. Stowell, *A Thoreau Gazetteer* (Princeton: Princeton University Press, 1970);

Bob Pepperman Taylor, *America's Bachelor Uncle: Thoreau and the American Polity* (Lawrence: University of Kansas Press, 1996);

Edward Wagenknecht, *Henry David Thoreau: What Manner of Man?* (Amherst: University of Massachusetts Press, 1981);

Laura Dassow Walls, *Seeing New Worlds: Henry David Thoreau and Nineteenth-Century Natural Science* (Madison: University of Wisconsin Press, 1995);

William J. Wolf, *Thoreau: Mystic, Prophet, Ecologist* (Philadelphia: Pilgrim Press, 1974).

Papers:

The largest collections of Henry David Thoreau's manuscripts and letters are in the Houghton Library at Harvard University; the Huntington Library in San Marino, California; the Henry A. and Albert W. Berg Collection at The New York Public Library; and The Pierpont Morgan Library in New York City. The rest are in smaller library and private collections.

Frederick J. E. Woodbridge

(26 March 1867 – 1 June 1940)

Angelo Juffras
William Paterson University

BOOKS: *Metaphysics* (New York: Columbia University Press, 1908);

The Purpose of History (New York: Columbia University Press, 1916);

The Realm of Mind: An Essay in Metaphysics (New York: Columbia University Press, 1926);

The Creative Intelligence and Modern Life, by Woodbridge, Francis John McConnell, Roscoe Pound, and others (Boulder, Colo.: University of Colorado, 1928)–includes "Philosophy and Modern Life," by Woodbridge;

The Son of Apollo: Themes of Plato (Boston & New York: Houghton Mifflin, 1929);

Spinoza, by Frederick J. E. Woodbridge; John Locke and His Essay, by Sterling P. Lamprecht: Tercentenary Lectures Delivered at Columbia University (New York, 1933);

Nature and Mind: Selected Essays of Frederick J. E. Woodbridge, Presented to Him on the Occasion of His Seventieth Birthday by Amherst College, The University of Minnesota, Columbia University. With a Bibliography of His Writings (New York: Columbia University Press, 1937);

An Essay on Nature (New York: Columbia University Press, 1940);

Aristotle's Vision of Nature, edited by John Herman Randall Jr., Charles H. Kahn, and Harold A. Larrabee (New York & London: Columbia University Press, 1965).

OTHER: *Studies in Philosophy and Psychology, by Former Students of Charles Edward Garman, in Commemoration of Twenty-five Years of Service as Teacher of Philosophy in Amherst College,* edited by Woodbridge, James H. Tufts, Edmund Burke Delabarre, Frank Chapman Sharp, and Arthur Henry Pierce (Boston & New York: Houghton, Mifflin, 1906)–includes "The Problem of Consciousness," by Woodbridge;

"Empiricism," in *A Cyclopaedia of Education,* volume 2, edited by Paul Monroe (New York: Macmillan, 1911), pp. 442–444;

"John Locke," in *A Cyclopaedia of Education,* volume 4, edited by Monroe (New York: Macmillan, 1912), pp. 58–59;

"David Hume," in *Encyclopedia of Religion and Ethics,* volume 6, edited by James Hastings, John A. Selbie, and others (New York, Scribners / Edinburgh: Clark, 1913), pp. 867–870;

"Berkeley's Realism," in *Studies in the History of Ideas,* volume 1, edited by the Department of Philosophy, Columbia University (New York: Columbia University Press, 1918), pp. 188–215;

"Some Implications of Locke's Procedure," in *Essays in Honor of John Dewey, on the Occasion of His Seventieth Birthday, October 20, 1929* (New York: Holt, 1929), pp. 414–425;

Thomas Hobbes, *Selections,* edited by Woodbridge (New York: Scribners, 1930);

"Locke's Essay," in *Studies in the History of Ideas,* volume 3, edited by the Department of Philosophy, Columbia University (New York: Columbia University Press, 1935), pp. 243–251.

SELECTED PERIODICAL PUBLICATIONS–
UNCOLLECTED: "The Place of Pleasure in a System of Ethics," *International Journal of Philosophy,* 7 (1896): 475–486;

"The Dominant Conception of the Earliest Greek Philosophy," *Philosophical Review,* 10 (1901): 359–374;

"Herbert Spencer," *Review of Reviews,* 29 (1904): 67–70;

"Jonathan Edwards," *Philosophical Review,* 12 (1904): 393–408;

"Consciousness and Meaning," *Psychological Review,* 15 (1908): 397–398;

"Faith and Pragmatism," *Chronicle,* 14 (1914): 319–323.

Frederick J. E. Woodbridge is notable for the influence his philosophy of naturalism and realism had on a subsequent generation of philosophers; his student John Herman Randall Jr. called him "the wisest man I ever knew." Through his teaching and the dissertation topics he set for his students, Woodbridge made the philosophy of Aristotle accessible to students and philosophers who otherwise would have shunned it. According to another of those students, Sterling P. Lamprecht, Woodbridge "was a leader, possibly *the* leader, in the movement in the United States in the twentieth century which made the history of philosophy one of the major philosophic disciplines." If not for the testimony of his many successful students, however, Woodbridge's influence would be virtually unknown, because he himself published little on Aristotle. He was content that his views be spread by his former students. Also, as a founder and editor of *The Journal of Philosophy,* he supplied a forum and encouragement for American philosophers.

Frederick James Eugene Woodbridge was born in Windsor, Ontario, on 26 March 1867 to James and Melissa Ella Bingham Woodbridge. The family moved to Kalamazoo, Michigan, in 1869. Wood-

bridge graduated from Amherst College in 1889 and attended Union Theological Seminary in New York City from 1889 to 1892. He then studied philosophy at the University of Berlin on a traveling fellowship from 1892 to 1894. At Berlin he came under the influence of Friedrich Adolf Trendelenberg's naturalistic interpretation of Aristotle and abandoned his plans for a career in the ministry. On his return to the United States, Woodbridge took a position at the University of Minnesota. On 25 June 1895, in Chicago, he married Helena Belle Adams of Cincinnati. He moved to Columbia University in 1902. In 1904 he and Wendell T. Bush founded *The Journal of Philosophy, Psychology, and Scientific Methods,* of which Woodbridge served as editor until his death; the title was shortened to *The Journal of Philosophy* in 1921. Woodbridge was dean of the Faculties of Political Science, Philosophy, and Pure Science at Columbia from 1912 to 1929, after which he returned to teaching. He was awarded honorary degrees of LL.D. and Litt.D. from several institutions and was Theodore Roosevelt Professor at the University of Berlin in 1931–1932. He retired from Columbia in 1937 and died on 1 June 1940. The Woodbridge Lectures at Columbia are named for him.

Prior to Woodbridge, Aristotle had generally been viewed as interpreted by St. Thomas Aquinas and later Thomists—an interpretation that made him unpalatable to secular philosophers. Since the seventeenth century, English-speaking philosophers had, for the most part, considered Aristotle to be as obsolete as fourth-century science and associated him with the much-disparaged medieval "philosophy of the schools." Hence, Aristotle's thought had little direct influence on most secular philosophers in the early twentieth century.

Were it not for Woodbridge, Aristotle would be a forbidding obstacle to those who read him in English. Modern Aristotelian scholarship begins with the Berlin Academy's reliable edition of Aristotle's works in Greek, published between 1831 and 1870. From this edition, translations were made into English. Despite the availability of this critical edition, in the second decade of the twentieth century—the period during which Woodbridge was teaching some of his brightest students—no modern English edition of Aristotle's *Physics, On the Heavens,* or *Meteorology* existed. Although the Oxford Classical Texts translation of Aristotle's works began appearing in 1908 and the Loeb Classical Library, with Greek and English on facing pages, in 1912, they did not supply easy access to Aristotle, because the translations were done by classicists who borrowed from the Latin vocabulary that Cicero had devised for introducing

Greek philosophy to Romans. For example, *substance,* a Latin-derived term used as a translation for the Greek *ousia,* was a source of confusion: *ousia* is a key concept in Aristotle's *Metaphysics,* but translated as *substance* it leads one to think of "that which stands under," which is not what Aristotle meant. *Substance* is more appropriate as a translation for the Greek *hypkeimenon,* which does mean "that which stands under." *Arete,* which means "habitual superlative performance," was translated into *virtue,* which carries the Christian connotations of faith, hope, and charity—none of which require skill in their manifestations. *Psyche,* which means "the whole body functioning" and, therefore, something that perishes with the death of the body, was translated into the Christian *soul,* with its connotations of immortality. It was—and still is—difficult to understand Aristotle's "four causes": for Cicero, a lawyer, "causes" were "cases" (*cause* and *case* are still used interchangeably in modern legal parlance); Aristotle's word is *aitia,* which means "explanation." In his teaching, Woodbridge recovered the Greek meanings of Aristotle's texts; he then used Greek terms, properly understood, to construct a modern naturalistic philosophy of his own. Werner Jaeger's *Aristoteles: Grundlegung einer Geschichte seiner Entwicklung* (1923; translated as *Aristotle: Fundamentals of the History of His Development,* 1934) supported Woodbridge's iconoclastic views and made it possible for him to advance his ideas with less opposition.

In 1930 Woodbridge gave a unified presentation of Aristotle in four lectures at Union College; the lectures were published posthumously in 1965 as *Aristotle's Vision of Nature.* Randall, who helped edit the lectures, says in the introduction that Woodbridge's book is important for the same reasons as Jaeger's: Aristotle's writings were composed as he changed and developed his ideas over a career of some forty years; Jaeger and Woodbridge show that it is no longer possible to take Aristotle as all of a piece, as an encyclopedia every line of which must be "reconciled" and made consistent with every other. For example, Aristotle's early fragmentary dialogue *Eudemus* asserts the immortality of the soul, while the *De Anima* (On the Soul) denies it. Also, Aristotle wrote separate treatises on logic at various times, but they were lumped together by later editors and called the *Organon.* Medieval interpreters regarded these treatises as a method of inquiry, but Woodbridge disagrees:

> Logic with Aristotle is . . . more of a study of language than it is a method of inquiry. This view has been forced on me by a study of him. It was not a

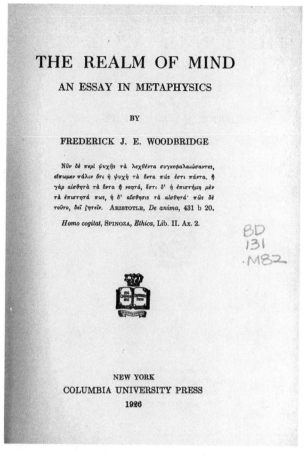

THE REALM OF MIND

AN ESSAY IN METAPHYSICS

BY

FREDERICK J. E. WOODBRIDGE

Νῦν δὲ περὶ ψυχῆς τὰ λεχθέντα συγκεφαλαιώσαντες, εἴπωμεν πάλιν ὅτι ἡ ψυχὴ τὰ ὄντα πώς ἐστι πάντα. ἢ γὰρ αἰσθητὰ τὰ ὄντα ἢ νοητά, ἔστι δ' ἡ ἐπιστήμη μὲν τὰ ἐπιστητά πως, ἡ δ' αἴσθησις τὰ αἰσθητά· πῶς δὲ τοῦτο, δεῖ ζητεῖν. ARISTOTLE, *De anima,* 431 b 20.

Homo cogitat, SPINOZA, *Ethica,* Lib. II. Ax. 2.

NEW YORK
COLUMBIA UNIVERSITY PRESS
1926

Title page for the book in which Woodbridge argues against the representational theory of perception (Thomas Cooper Library, University of South Carolina)

view I expected to find from that study. . . . Aristotle studied *nature* first—not logic—and then stated what was sayable about nature. . . . If a scientific method is a method of inquiry or investigation, I do not find Aristotle using his logic as such a method. When he inquires, he does so in a very simple and uncomplicated fashion. Sometimes I think he is almost incredibly naive. He observes, experiments, and then states the best he can the results he has found, just like the most ordinary of men. . . . He goes without preliminary to the subject-matter involved and follows where it leads him. . . . We go from identifications to observations of what has been identified. These observations are criticized until the appropriate or promising ones are sifted out and point to some statable result. Then the result is stated in what are called "categories." . . . The categories are what the investigation culminates in. They are the ends reached, and not the beginnings which constrain the inquiry. . . . When the categories become systematized, it becomes natural to begin any fresh inquiry with the question, "What categories are here appropriate?" Aristotle does this so repeatedly that it is

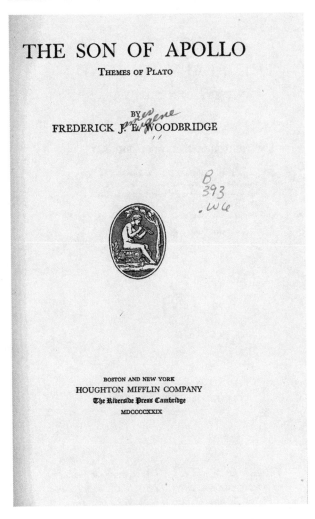

THE SON OF APOLLO

THEMES OF PLATO

BY

FREDERICK J. E. WOODBRIDGE

B
393
.W6

BOSTON AND NEW YORK
HOUGHTON MIFFLIN COMPANY
The Riverside Press Cambridge
MDCCCCXXIX

*Title page for the iconoclastic book in which Woodbridge
claims that Plato did not really believe in the
"Theory of Ideas" (Thomas Cooper Library,
University of South Carolina)*

natural to suppose that he goes from categories to things, and not from things to categories.

Woodbridge's *The Son of Apollo: Themes of Plato* (1929) was also iconoclastic. Because Plato's dialogue *Parmenides* refutes the so-called "Theory of Ideas," Woodbridge denies that Plato believed in such a theory and that Plato had a system of philosophy at all. That is, Plato was not a "Platonist."

Another influence on Woodbridge that he transmitted to his students was George Santayana's interpretation of Aristotle. According to Santayana, for Aristotle "everything ideal has a natural basis, and everything natural an ideal fulfillment." "Everything ideal has a natural basis" means that ideals without the possibility of attainment are pointless, and "everything natural has an ideal fulfillment" means that materials naturally encountered are capa-

ble, if not of perfection, then at least of improvement. Woodbridge adds in *Nature and Mind* (1937), "In that one sentence . . . I found an acceptable standard of criticism, for it seemed to me that ideals are significant as they round out and complete some natural function." Woodbridge was also influenced by Baruch Spinoza's metaphysics, in which "nature" encompasses all that exists.

Woodbridge's realistic and naturalic philosophy is based on his naturalistically interpreted Aristotelianism. Following Aristotle's method of working, he says in *An Essay on Nature* (1940), he has "not tried to write a theory of the universe, a theory of knowledge, or a theory of morals" but has tried "to analyze familiar and easily identifiable situations and follow the lead of the analysis." Consequently, as a result of his investigations, Woodbridge has written essays on various topics, most of them metaphysical. Lamprecht gives a succinct description of Woodbridge's metaphysics.

Where Aristotle spoke of matter and form, Woodbridge spoke of structure and behavior . . . to ultimate ideas to which the analysis of nature leads. . . . Woodbridge chose quite carefully to say that nature is structure, rather than say nature has structure. He thereby hoped to avoid the supposition of a *materia prima* which come to be structured or of a something I-know-not-what which lies behind the structures we empirically discover. Structure, he noted, is not a cause or agent. . . . And everywhere behavior, as our investigation of nature teaches us, is correlative with structure. Behavior cannot be reduced to structure any more than structure can be reduced to behavior. Furthermore, behavior can only be defined in terms of the end served. These ends do not operate; they are not efficient forces. . . . We discover a certain structure and may be able to ascertain how its parts are related to one another; but we do not feel content that we understand it until we also note how it behaves and what end it thereby effects.

In his often reprinted essay from *Nature and Mind,* "Natural Teleology," Woodbridge admits that many different natural processes are examples of teleology, inasmuch as they tended toward certain typical outcomes, but nevertheless, he denies that the universe tends toward some unitary outcome, denies that there is a cosmic eschatology. There is not "out there" someone or something that guides the universe toward some preordained end. Woodbridge calls his position "naive realism," although, in fact, it is quite sophisticated. He takes the world as he finds it in everyday encounters as primary, which leads to the principle of the Primacy of the Subject Matter.

That is, if inquiry should lead one to doubt the existence of the subject of the inquiry, then something is wrong with the inquiry: "I would make this the first step in metaphysics—the recognition that existence is primarily what it is and can neither be explained nor explained away. The most that can be done is to find out what it implies." In the essay "Confessions" in *Nature and Mind* Woodbridge contends that the "great error" committed by metaphysicians has been to mistake the implications of existence for its causes and to try to find "something more fundamental than existence, or prior to it, or in itself irrelevant to it. . . . Individual existences may be related to one another and compared, but the whole of existence can be related to nothing or compared with nothing."

The bête noir of Woodbridge's realism is British empiricism. The empiricists regarded judgment as a form of imagining in which the subject and predicate, each conceived as an idea, either went together (affirmation) or did not go together (denial). Thus, logic began to be conceived in mentalistic terms. Not only did knowledge consist of ideas in one's mind, set off against nature, but logical judgments—affirmations and denials—were taken to be about ideas in one's mind. The next step was to regard inferences also as a form of ideation in the mind. Subsequent treatments of logic by idealists have continued this process. Woodbridge, a self-professed naive realist writing at a time when idealism was the dominant philosophy, opposes this idealistic conception of logic and tries to undo it.

First, he argues against the unbridgeable chasm between mind and nature created by British empiricist epistemology. He argues against conceiving logic and thought in terms of irreconcilable and insoluble dualisms: "all psychological logicians, from Locke to our own day, have signally failed in dealing with the problem of knowledge. The attempt to construct knowledge out of mental states, the relations between ideas, and the relation of ideas to things, has been . . . decidedly without profit. . . . The lesson of these perplexing theories seems to be that logic, as logic, must be divorced from psychology."

In *The Realm of Mind: An Essay in Metaphysics* (1926) Woodbridge tries to establish three main points: first, that language, which everyone agrees conveys ideas, is a material exchange and, as such, is on a par metaphysically with every other material exchange; second, that ideas, although they are conveyed by material means, are not the material that conveys them but an effect wrought by the exchange and so not material at all; and third, that the ideas are acquired and clarified by experience—that is, by

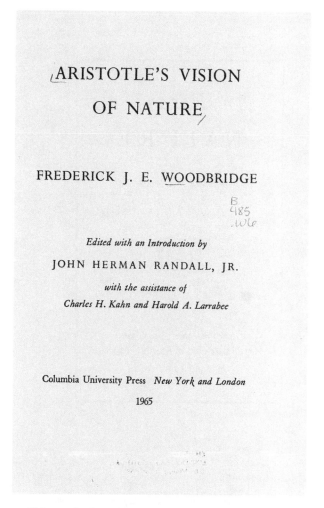

ARISTOTLE'S VISION
OF NATURE

FREDERICK J. E. WOODBRIDGE

Edited with an Introduction by
JOHN HERMAN RANDALL, JR.

with the assistance of
Charles H. Kahn and Harold A. Larrabee

Columbia University Press *New York and London*
1965

Title page for the posthumous edition of four lectures Woodbridge gave at Union College in 1930, in which he shows how Aristotle's ideas developed over a forty-year period (Thomas Cooper Library, University of South Carolina)

the contacts of bodies with the rest of the world: "To know a thing is to have an idea of it close to the conviction of the common man. He will hold an object in his hand, look at it, . . . and yet tell you he has not the dimmest idea of what it is. And you believe him. All presentative and representative theories of knowledge are damned by this experiment." An idea, Woodbridge concludes, "is never a copy, image, likeness, or representation of anything whatever." Ideas are acquired "through bodily operations. . . . They are a revelation of the world." Nor is the expression of an idea itself an idea: "I tell my neighbor in spoken words that matter is indestructible. The deaf mute tells the same truth in gestures. But what conceivable likeness is there between the truth conveyed and the means of conveying it? What it is for matter to be indestructible is like neither spoken word nor

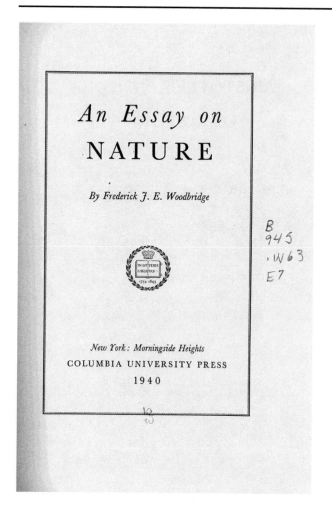

*Title page for Woodbridge's final book, published posthumously,
in which he dismayed some of his naturalistic followers by
seeming to admit the possibility of a supernatural realm
(Thomas Cooper Library, University of South Carolina)*

agile fingers. Neither, we may add, is it like anything that happens in the brain or in consciousness." An idea "is strictly *like* nothing at all." Ideas are "what can be translated from one mode of expression into another radically different mode without losing themselves or ceasing to be what they are."

Knowledge, then, is about the world, not about ideas. Woodbridge also thinks that logical and linguistic forms correspond in some way with the structure of reality, that true statements about objects and their relations have a structure that is isomorphic with the structure discovered in the world. In *Nature and Mind* he says that mathematics is "the crowning example" of order or structure "and with its many applications is powerful enough to prove that an order is not a human bias or an imposition on reluctant material. It is an implication of all existence, something to be set down as metaphysical; something which we creatures of a day never made—for if

we did, why do we rebel against it, cry over it?" Intelligible structure, not the mind, "is responsible for the intelligibility of the world." The structure of things limits what they can do, but "a genuinely productive activity . . . goes on within these limits." The structures "determine what is possible and the activity determines what comes into existence. The fact that the world is known and controlled by getting ideas through experience is a sign of the existence of this structure and activity."

In *The Realm of Mind* Woodbridge says that just as digestion "involves a chemical world, so our thinking involves a logical" or thinkable world. "And as by digesting we do not introduce chemistry into a world not already chemical, so by thinking we do not introduce logic into a world not already logical"; that is, discourse, or *logos,* could not be introduced into a world that was not already "discussible." Mental activity is part of the physical world; there is no separate mental world. But within the physical world "There are operations and activities of living beings which indicate a structure different from the mechanical, the chemical, or the biological." Hence, "we may have a means of distinguishing mental from vital processes. . . . We seem to be confronted with the fact that the operations of thought are subject to a structure which is not like that involved in the displacement of bodies, or in chemical combinations, or in life histories."

An Essay on Nature was finished before Woodbridge died in 1940 and was published posthumously the same year. It is really five essays; the first four are about "nature considered as a field of knowledge"; the final and longest essay, which considers nature "as the condition for the pursuit of happiness," dismayed many of his naturalistic followers. He says that "Ways and means of improving our knowledge of Nature constitute the only problem of knowledge I can find worthwhile," but "this does not warrant the conclusion that all the questions we put to nature can or would be answered if our knowledge were sufficiently improved. Knowledge is not adequate to answer them. We answer them in other ways. . . . The fact is that the pursuit of knowledge apart from the pursuit of happiness has no justification whatever and eventually becomes meaningless." Although Woodbridge is opposed to dualisms of all kinds, he says that "the dualism I have found important and arresting is that of the natural and supernatural." This dualism "arises, however, not in the pursuit of knowledge, but in the pursuit of happiness," because "Nature is insufficient of herself to provide security in the pursuit of happiness"; therefore, "if there is to be security it must be found elsewhere"—not in knowledge but in faith. "The thesis is then that the dualism of the natural and the supernatural is the dualism of knowledge and faith and that dualism arises, not because knowledge is pursued, but because happiness is pursued." The function of faith is not to provide knowledge about a "great beyond" but to supply security in the pursuit of happiness. Woodbridge notes that the German philosopher Arthur Schopenhauer is reputed to have said, "If you want comfort, go to the priest. I can only tell you the truth." Woodbridge does not say what Schopenhauer said. Instead, he says that since time immemorial, people have been seeking what knowledge cannot give them, the consolation of priests—that is, the security and consolation of faith. Given the fact that people do so—a thing is what it is and not something else—Woodbridge does not scorn it. Respecting the primacy of the subject matter, he acknowledges the function faith performs in the pursuit of happiness.

References:

Morris Raphael Cohen, *American Thought* (Glencoe, Ill.: Free Press, 1954), pp. 315–316;

Cohen, "Later Philosophy," in *Cambridge History of American Literature,* volume 3, edited by William Peterfield Trent, John Erskine, Stuart P. Sherman, and Carl Van Doren (New York: Putnam / Cambridge: Cambridge University Press, 1927), pp. 263–264;

Harry Todd Costello, "The Naturalism of Frederick Woodbridge," in *Naturalism and the Human Spirit,* edited by Yervant Krikorian (New York: Columbia University Press, 1944), pp. 295–318;

C. F. Delaney, *Mind and Nature: A Study of the Naturalistic Philosophies of Cohen, Woodbridge, and Sellars* (Notre Dame, Ind.: University of Notre Dame Press, 1969);

William Frank Jones, *Nature and Natural Science: The Philosophy of F. J. E. Woodbridge* (Buffalo, N.Y.: Prometheus, 1983);

Sterling P. Lamprecht, *Our Philosophical Traditions: A Brief History of Philosophy in Western Civilization* (New York: Appleton-Century-Crofts, 1955), pp. 486–497;

Hae Soon Pyun, *Nature, Intelligibility, and Metaphysics: Studies in the Philosophy of F. J. E. Woodbridge* (Amsterdam: Gruner, 1972);

John Herman Randall Jr., "Dean Woodbridge," *Columbia University Quarterly,* 32 (December 1940): 324–331;

Randall, "Introduction" and "The Department of Philosophy," in *A History of the Department of Philosophy* (New York: Columbia University Press, 1957), pp. 3–57, 102–145.

Papers:

"Papers 1884–1940," a manuscript collection of Frederick J. E. Woodbridge's unpublished correspondences, diaries, essays, lecture notes, and notes on reading, is in the Special Collections of the Columbia University Library.

Chauncey Wright

(1830 – 12 September 1875)

Anthony J. Graybosch
California State University, Chico

BOOKS: *Philosophical Discussions,* edited by Charles Eliot
    Norton (New York: Burt Franklin, 1877);
*The Philosophical Writings of Chauncey Wright: Representative
    Selections,* edited by Edward H. Madden (New
    York: Liberal Arts Press, 1958).
Edition: *Philosophical Discussions,* edited by Frank X.
    Ryan, volume 1 of *The Evolutionary Philosophy of
    Chauncey Wright* (Sterling, Va.: Thoemmes Press,
    2000).

OTHER: "Was the Act of Brutus in Killing Caesar Jus-
    tifiable?" in *Evolution and the Founders of Pragmatism,*
    by Philip P. Wiener (Cambridge, Mass.: Harvard
    University Press, 1949), pp. 218–220.

SELECTED PERIODICAL PUBLICATION–
UNCOLLECTED: "The Winds and the Weather,"
    Atlantic Monthly, 1 (1858): 272–279.

Chauncey Wright

Chauncey Wright was born in Northampton,
Massachusetts, in 1830–the exact date is unknown–to
Ansel Wright, a deputy sheriff and grocer, and Elizabeth Boleyn Wright. He was raised as a Unitarian but
became an agnostic. He attended Select High School in
Northampton, where, along with other students considered especially gifted, he was encouraged to do
advanced work. His interest in applied science and evolutionary biology was fostered by a science teacher who
could have been described as Deweyan in his approach
to education if John Dewey had been born fifty years
earlier. Wright was actively involved in doing scientific
work such as building a nature preserve and constructing astronomical tools.

A local philanthropist, Ann Lyman, encouraged
Wright's parents to send him to Harvard University.
Lyman provided financial support for Wright and
another Northampton student, James Bradley Thayer,
who became Wright's lifelong friend and collected his
letters for posthumous publication.

At Harvard, Wright studied mathematics with
Benjamin Peirce, the father of the philosopher

Charles Sanders Peirce. Wright read Ralph Waldo
Emerson's essays during his undergraduate years and
was most impressed by Emerson's critique in "The
Divinity School Address" of Christianity's exaggera-
tion of the person of the historical Jesus. Although
Wright was an agnostic, he agreed with Emerson's
insistence on the availability of direct revelation from
nature to all individuals.

Wright studied philosophy at Harvard with James Walker, for whom he wrote a paper arguing that human and animal intelligence differ in degree and not in kind. This paper foreshadows Wright's mature defense of Darwinism and the position he developed to explain self-consciousness as a biological phenomenon. Wright also wrote a paper on Julius Caesar and Marcus Junius Brutus that was sympathetic to Brutus.

After graduating in 1852, Wright was employed as a "computer" for the government-funded *American Ephemeris and Nautical Almanac;* Charles Sanders Peirce later worked for the same publication. Wright arranged his affairs so that he had a great deal of time for leisure and conversation: he routinely did his calculations for the almanac in just three months, remained unmarried, lived simply as a boarder, and did not travel. His early work shows the influence of Francis Bacon, Sir William Hamilton, and John Stuart Mill. He seems to have retained his agreement with Emerson's critique of institutionalized religion but was increasingly drawn away from metaphysical speculation and toward positivism. Still, in a 24 July 1866 letter to his friend Charles Eliot Norton he wrote, "I am not so much a positivist as to deny that mystical and poetical philosophies are valuable products of human genius; but then they must be works of real genius,–of a Plato, a Hegel, or an Emerson."

Wright was elected a fellow of the American Academy of Arts and Sciences in 1860 and served as its secretary from 1863 to 1870. He taught for a while at Louis Agassiz's School for Women in Cambridge, leaving because of Agassiz's unfavorable reaction to Charles Darwin's theory of evolution. Wright had been attracted to evolutionary thought before reading Darwin's *On the Origin of Species by Means of Natural Selection; or, The Preservation of Favoured Races in the Struggle for Life* (1859), and Wright's 1858 essay "The Winds and the Weather" is suggestive of natural selection.

Wright taught psychology at Harvard in 1870 and physics in 1874. He was not a success as a lecturer; his gift was for Socratic conversation. His intellectual life was centered in various "clubs," beginning with the Septem in 1856. Members of the Septem included Thayer, Ephraim Gurney, and the wife of James Russell Lowell's brother Charles. When the social network provided by the clubs disappeared from time to time, Wright would become depressed. But his conversational talent, gentleness, and good humor attracted friends such as Gurney and Norton, who sought Wright out for companionship and engaged in correspondence with him. Gurney revived the Septem in 1865–it had ceased meeting in 1861–and it met regularly until 1868. Some commentators suggest that Wright might have been an alcoholic by this time.

In articles in *The North American Review* Wright defended Darwin's views on evolution and natural selection and had criticized Herbert Spencer for failing to keep scientific and metaphysical speculation separate. Wright's work impressed Darwin, who arranged for his article "The Genesis of Species" (1871) to be reprinted as a pamphlet in England. Wright's most important essay, "The Evolution of Self Consciousness" (1873), was written in response to Darwin's request that he consider when phenomena could be said to be affected by the human will. Wright argues that self-consciousness does not require a new mental faculty but can be explained in terms of the application of awareness already found within animals. During the early 1870s Wright was also a member of the Metaphysical Club; other members included Charles Sanders Peirce, William James, Oliver Wendell Holmes Jr., Nicholas St. John Green, John Fiske, and Francis E. Abbot.

Wright inherited enough money when his father died in 1872 to give up his position at the *American Ephemeris and Nautical Almanac.* He traveled to England; the high point of his trip, and perhaps of his life, was his meeting with Darwin. Otherwise, however, Wright was not charmed by England or by travel.

Wright suffered a stroke at his desk on 11 September 1875 and died the next day. James wrote in *The Nation,* "Of the two motives to which philosophic systems owe their being, the craving for consistency or unity in thought, and the desire for a solid outward warrant for our emotional ends, his mind was dominated only by the former. Never in a human head was contemplation more separated from desire." Norton collected Wright's articles as *Philosophical Discussions* in 1877.

Wright characterized himself as a positivist. He was particularly critical of the use of science to support metaphysical or religious speculation. In his view, Spencer's mistake was to regard scientific laws simplistically as empirical generalizations. This mistake led Spencer to consider all speculative generalizations as equally scientific. In "The Philosophy of Herbert Spencer" (1865) Wright says:

> Mr. Spencer's law is founded on examples, of which only one class, the facts of embryology, are properly scientific. The others are still debated as to their real characters. Theories of society and of the character and origin of social progress, theories on the origins and the changes of organic forms, and theories on the origins and the causes of cosmical bodies and their arrangements, are all liable to the taint of teleological and cosmological conceptions,–to spring from the order which the mind imposes upon what it imperfectly observes, rather than from that which the objects, were they better known, would supply to the mind.

Wright's understanding of science was that theories play an important role in the prediction of observable events. Therefore, empirical evidence often attached to theories indirectly, through their use with other observations to make verified predictions. As Wright says in "The Philosophy of Herbert Spencer,"

> A fact is a proposition of which the verification by an appeal to the primary sources of our knowledge or to experience is direct and simple. A theory, on the other hand, if true, has all the characteristics of a fact, except that its verification is possible only by indirect, remote, and difficult means. . . . Modern science deals then no less with theories than with facts, but always as much as possible with the verification of theories,—if not to make them facts by simple verification through experiment and observation, at least to prove their truth by indirect verification.

Wright's focus on the role of theories in prediction and on the indirect nature of empirical evidence influenced the pragmatic accounts of science developed by Peirce and James.

Wright also insisted on the value-neutrality of science. He rejected teleological explanations of natural phenomena on the ground that it was impossible to determine scientifically what were ends and what were means. When events cannot be predicted, he said, one should assume that, as in the weather, a causal order is present but is too complex for human comprehension. In "Natural Theology as a Positive Science" (1865) Wright says,

> These discourses really aim, not so much to prove the existence of design in the universe, as to show the wisdom of certain designs which are assumed to be manifest. But for this purpose it is requisite to translate the facts of science, and conditions of particular effects, into the terms of the argument, and to show that these combinations are means, or exist for the sake of particular effects, for which, as ends, the universe itself must be shown to exist,—a task for which science is obviously incompetent.

Such an assessment might please one's religious or moral instincts but could not be supported by the phenomena; it was not scientific. Wright also applied his "weather" metaphor to the history of the universe, wondering if it might fluctuate between periods of order and disorder. A description formulated within an orderly period would then be a misrepresentation of the overall "weather" of the universe.

Wright assisted in the spread of Darwinism to the United States by criticizing the optimistic speculative evolutionism of Spencer and by defending Darwin against the objection of William Thomson, first Baron

Kelvin, that the scientific evidence placed the age of the solar system at about ten million years—much less than was required by Darwinism. In "Physical Theory of the Universe" (1864) Wright suggested that "cosmic weather" might account for variations in the use of energy that would be consistent with Darwinism and not with the nebular hypothesis on which Kelvin relied.

Wright's ethical theory is based on the existence of an order of ultimate values or ends that can be grasped by intuition. Yet, he held, the importance of these ends varies from individual to individual. Utilitarianism is the moral philosophy that allows humans to seek the ends that promote personal and social happiness. Natural selection is consistent with utilitarianism: it is the way nature works for the greatest good of the greatest number. But Wright saw little practical use for ethics and thought it arrogant and absurd to stake anything important on the truth of a philosophical theory. In a 13 August 1867 letter to Abbot he wrote, "Men conclude in matters affecting their own welfare so much better than they can justify rationally,—they are led by their instincts of reverence so surely to the safest known authority, that theory becomes in such matters an insignificant affair."

In metaphysics, Wright held that no scientific knowledge of ultimate reality is possible: "The highest generality, or universality, in the elements or connections of elements in phenomena, is the utmost reach both in the power and the desire of the scientific intellect," he says in "The Evolution of Self Consciousness." He allowed, however, that such a reality can be the object of faith or belief. The self and the objects of the scientific world are not metaphysical ultimates but constructions placed on phenomena. Ultimately, Wright came to believe that there was no reality behind phenomena.

Consciousness, Wright says, exists in higher animals, who distinguish the self from the nonself by the amount of control they can exert. Habits are evidence that animals have a rudimentary awareness of signs; if an organism could become conscious of its use of signs, it would have a rudimentary self-consciousness. Wright hypothesized that there could be, in animals with sufficient memory, recognition of the simultaneous presence of external signs and memory images. If such an organism also had linguistic ability, it would further clarify the difference in signs into a theory of self and nonself, leading to full self-consciousness. This view was the one that Darwin found so helpful.

Peirce and James spoke highly of Wright's ability in philosophical conversation at the Metaphysical Club. Unlike Socrates, however, Wright had no Plato to record his remarks; thus, one cannot be sure of the extent to which Wright influenced the development of the forms of pragmatism advocated by James and Peirce. Wright scholars seem to agree that Dewey, who had no personal contact with him, is the pragmatist closest to Wright.

Peirce and Wright certainly disagreed over the existence of chance in the universe: Peirce believed that real chance did exist, while Wright, a determinist, held that talk of "chance" or "probability" only reflects human ignorance of the actual causes at work. Yet, Peirce developed what he called "pragmaticism" as a theory of meaning and verification that emphasized the role of belief in empirical prediction, and he steadfastly refused to follow James's more speculative development of pragmatism to include forms of evidence that emerge from holding a belief to be true. Peirce's notion of philosophy was, then, closer to Wright's than to James's.

But Chauncey Wright might have had a greater impact on James. Both were "anomalous monists," holding that there is nothing behind experience and that self and world are constructed within experience. Also like Wright, James regarded intelligence as existing on a continuum from animals to humans. And James's "will to believe" is similar to Wright's position that such leaps of faith are natural but not scientifically justified. But James took a stronger position than Wright, arguing not only that one has a right to believe beyond the evidence when the option is genuine but also that anyone whose religious impulse has not been crippled by science will find such belief engaging.

Letters:

Letters of Chauncey Wright with an Account of His Life, edited by James Bradley Thayer (Cambridge: Wilson, 1878; republished, New York: Lenox Hill, 1971);

The Letters of Chauncey Wright, volume 2 of *The Evolutionary Philosophy of Chauncey Wright,* edited by Frank X. Ryan (Sterling, Va.: Thoemmes Press, 2000).

Bibliographies:

Edward H. Madden, *Chauncey Wright and the Foundations of Pragmatism* (Seattle: University of Washington Press, 1963), pp. 189–197;

Frank X. Ryan, "Bibliography of the Writings of Chauncey Wright," in *Philosophical Discussions,* vol-

ume 1 of *The Evolutionary Philosophy of Chauncey Wright,* edited by Ryan (Sterling, Va.: Thoemmes Press, 2000), pp. xix–xxi.

References:

Morris Raphael Cohen, "Later Philosophy," in *The Cambridge History of American Literature,* part 2, volume 3, edited by W. P. Trent and others (New York: Putnam, 1921), pp. 226–265;

William James, "Chauncey Wright," *Nation,* 21 (1875): 194;

Bruce Kuklick, *The Rise of American Philosophy* (New Haven: Yale University Press, 1977), pp. 63–79;

Edward H. Madden, *Chauncey Wright and the Foundations of Pragmatism* (Seattle: University of Washington Press, 1963);

Louis Menand, *The Metaphysical Club* (New York: Farrar, Straus & Giroux, 2001), pp. 201–232;

Menand, "The Socrates of Cambridge," *New York Review of Books,* 48 (26 April 2001): 52–55;

Frank X. Ryan, ed., *Influence and Legacy,* volume 3 of *The Evolutionary Philosophy of Chauncey Wright* (Sterling, Va.: Thoemmes Press, 2000);

James C. S. Wernham, "Did James Have an Ethic of Belief?" *Canadian Journal of Philosophy,* 6 (1976): 287–297;

Philip P. Wiener, "Chauncey Wright, Defender of Darwin and Precursor of Pragmatism," in his *Evolution and the Founders of Pragmatism* (Cambridge, Mass.: Harvard University Press, 1949), pp. 31–69.

Papers:

The Chauncey Wright Papers held by the American Philosophical Society include letters to Wright from Charles Sanders Peirce, Charles Eliot Norton, Francis Bowen, Susan Lesley, J. Peter Lesley, James Bradley Thayer, and William Sydney Thayer, as well as the manuscripts for Wright's "Was the Act of Brutus in Killing Caesar Justifiable?" and "Whether the Government of This Country Ought to Interfere in the Politics of Europe, to Aid or Countenance Those Who Are Struggling There for Liberty?" Wright's letters to Charles Eliot Norton, Grace Norton, and James Norton are in the Houghton Library of Harvard University.

Checklist of Further Readings

Anderson, Paul Russell, and Max Harold Fisch, eds. *Philosophy in America: From the Puritans to James*. New York: Appleton-Century, 1939.

Ayer, A. J. *Origins of Pragmatism: Studies in the Philosophy of Charles Sanders Peirce and William James*. San Francisco: Freeman, Cooper, 1968.

Blau, Joseph L. *Men and Movements in American Philosophy*. New York: Prentice-Hall, 1952.

Boller, Paul F. *American Thought in Transition: The Impact of Evolutionary Naturalism, 1865–1900*. Chicago: Rand McNally, 1969.

Caws, Peter, ed. *Two Centuries of Philosophy in America*. Totowa, N.J.: Rowman & Littlefield / New York: Oxford University Press, 1980.

Cohen, Morris Raphael. *American Thought: A Critical Sketch*. Glencoe, Ill.: Free Press, 1954.

Commager, Henry Steele. *The American Mind: An Interpretation of American Thought and Character since the 1880s*. New Haven: Yale University Press, 1950.

Conkin, Paul K. *Puritans and Pragmatists: Eight Eminent American Thinkers*. New York: Dodd, Mead, 1968.

Croce, Paul Jerome. *Science and Religion in the Era of William James*. Chapel Hill: University of North Carolina Press, 1995.

Dewey, John. "The Development of American Pragmatism," in his *Philosophy and Civilization*. New York: Putnam, 1931.

Diggins, John P. *The Promise of Pragmatism: Modernism and the Crisis of Knowledge and Authority*. Chicago: University of Chicago Press, 1994.

Festenstein, Matthew. *Pragmatism and Political Theory: From Dewey to Rorty*. Chicago: University of Chicago Press, 1997.

Fisch, Max Harold, ed. *Classic American Philosophers: Peirce, James, Royce, Santayana, Dewey, Whitehead*. Englewood Cliffs, N.J.: Prentice-Hall, 1951.

Flower, Elizabeth, and Murray G. Murphey. *A History of Philosophy in America*, 2 volumes. New York: Putnam, 1977; New York: Capricorn, 1977.

Frankel, Charles. *The Golden Age of American Philosophy*. New York: Braziller, 1960.

Goetzmann, William H. *The American Hegelians: An Intellectual Episode in the History of Western America*. New York: Knopf, 1973.

Goodman, Russell B. *American Philosophy and the Romantic Tradition*. Cambridge: Cambridge University Press, 1990.

Griffin, David Ray, and others. *Founders of Constructive Postmodern Philosophy: Peirce, James, Bergson, Whitehead, and Hartshorne*. Albany: State University of New York Press, 1993.

Gunn, Giles B. *Thinking across the American Grain: Ideology, Intellect, and the New Pragmatism.* Chicago: University of Chicago Press, 1992.

Hartshorne, Charles. *Creativity in American Philosophy.* Albany: State University of New York Press, 1984.

Hook, Sidney, ed. *American Philosophers at Work: The Philosophic Scene in the United States.* New York: Criterion, 1956.

Hook and Horace M. Kallen, eds. *American Philosophy Today and Tomorrow.* Salem, N.H.: Ayer, 1968; New York: Furman, 1935.

Kennedy, Gail, ed. *Pragmatism and American Culture.* Boston: Heath, 1950.

Kennedy and Milton R. Konvitz. *The American Pragmatists.* Cleveland: Meridian, 1960.

Kloppenberg, James T. *Uncertain Victory: Social Democracy and Progressivism in European and American Thought, 1870–1920.* New York: Oxford University Press, 1986.

Kuklick, Bruce. *A History of Philosophy in America, 1720–2000.* Oxford: Clarendon Press, 2001; New York: Oxford University Press, 2001.

Kuklick. *The Rise of American Philosophy: Cambridge, Massachusetts, 1860–1930.* New Haven: Yale University Press, 1977.

Kurtz, Paul, ed. *The American Philosophers,* 2 volumes. New York: Macmillan, 1966—comprises volume 1, *American Thought before 1900: A Sourcebook from Puritanism to Darwinism;* and volume 2, *American Philosophy in the Twentieth Century: A Sourcebook from Pragmatism to Philosophical Analysis.*

Lovejoy, Arthur O. *The Thirteen Pragmatisms, and Other Essays.* Baltimore: Johns Hopkins University Press, 1963.

Mackay, D. S. "Pragmatism," in *A History of Philosophical Systems,* edited by Vergilius Ferm. New York: Philosophical Library, 1950, pp. 387–404.

MacKinnon, Barbara, ed. *American Philosophy: An Historical Anthology.* Albany: State University of New York Press, 1985.

Marcell, David W. *Progress and Pragmatism: James, Dewey, Beard, and the American Idea of Progress.* Westport, Conn.: Greenwood Press, 1974.

Mayer, Frederick. *A History of American Thought.* Dubuque, Iowa: W. C. Brown, 1950.

McDermott, John J. *Streams of Experience: Reflections on the History and Philosophy of American Culture.* Amherst: University of Massachusetts Press, 1986.

Menand, Louis, ed. *Pragmatism: A Reader.* New York: Vintage, 1997.

Moore, Addison Webster. *Pragmatism and Its Critics.* Chicago: University of Chicago Press, 1910.

Moore, Edward C. *American Pragmatism: Peirce, James and Dewey.* New York: Columbia University Press, 1961.

Morris, Charles. *The Pragmatic Movement in American Philosophy.* New York: Braziller, 1970.

Mounce, H. O. *The Two Pragmatisms: From Peirce to Rorty.* New York: Routledge, 1997.

Muelder, Walter G., Laurence Sears, and Anne V. Schlabach, eds. *The Development of American Philosophy.* Boston: Houghton Mifflin, 1960.

Mulvaney, Robert J., and Philip M. Zeltner, eds. *Pragmatism: Its Sources and Prospects.* Columbia: University of South Carolina Press, 1981.

Murphy, John P. *Pragmatism: From Peirce to Davidson*. Boulder, Colo.: Westview Press, 1990.

Murray, D. L. *Pragmatism*. New York: Dodge, 1910.

Myers, Gerald E., ed. *The Spirit of American Philosophy*. New York: Capricorn, 1971.

Passmore, John Arthur. *A Hundred Years of Philosophy*. London: Duckworth, 1957.

Perry, Ralph Barton. *Characteristically American*. New York: Knopf, 1949.

Pratt, James Bissett. *What Is Pragmatism?* New York: Macmillan, 1909.

Reck, Andrew J. *Recent American Philosophy: From Puritanism to Pragmatism*. New York: Pantheon, 1964.

Rescher, Nicholas. "American Philosophy Today," *Review of Metaphysics*, 46 (1993): 717–745.

Riley, Woodbridge I. *American Thought: From Puritanism to Pragmatism and Beyond*. New York: Holt, 1923.

Rorty, Amélie, ed. *Pragmatic Philosophy*. Garden City, N.Y.: Anchor, 1966.

Rorty, Richard. *Consequences of Pragmatism: Essays 1972–1980*. Minneapolis: University of Minnesota Press, 1982.

Rosenthal, Sandra B. *Speculative Pragmatism*. Amherst: University of Massachusetts Press, 1986.

Rucker, Darnell. *The Chicago Pragmatists*. Minneapolis: University of Minnesota Press, 1969.

Santayana, George. *Character and Opinion in the United States*. New York: Scribners, 1920.

Scheffler, Israel. *Four Pragmatists: A Critical Introduction to Peirce, James, Mead, and Dewey*. New York: Humanities Press, 1974.

Schneider, Herbert W. *A History of American Philosophy*. New York: Columbia University Press, 1963.

Shahan, Robert W., and Kenneth R. Merrill, eds. *American Philosophy from Edwards to Quine*. Norman: University of Oklahoma Press, 1977.

Singer, Marcus, ed. *American Philosophy*. Cambridge: Cambridge University Press, 1985.

Smith, John E. "The Course of American Philosophy," *Review of Metaphysics*, 11 (1957): 279–303.

Smith. *The Spirit of American Philosophy*. New York: Oxford University Press, 1963.

Stuhr, John J., ed. *Pragmatism and Classical American Philosophy: Essential Readings and Interpretive Essays*. New York: Oxford University Press, 2000.

Thayer, H. S. *Meaning and Action: A Critical History of Pragmatism*. Indianapolis: Bobbs-Merrill, 1968.

Thayer, ed. *Pragmatism, the Classic Writings: Charles Sanders Peirce, William James, Clarence Irving Lewis, John Dewey, George Herbert Mead*. Indianapolis: Hackett, 1982.

Townsend, Harvey Gates. *Philosophical Ideas in the United States*. New York: American Book Co., 1934.

Van Wesep, H. B. *Seven Sages: The Story of American Philosophy*. New York: Longmans, Green, 1960.

Weinstein, Michael A. *The Wilderness and the City: American Classical Philosophy as a Moral Quest*. Amherst: University of Massachusetts Press, 1982.

Werkmeister, W. H. *A History of Philosophical Ideas in America*. Westport, Conn.: Greenwood Press, 1981.

West, Cornel. *The American Evasion of Philosophy: A Genealogy of Pragmatism*. Madison: University of Wisconsin Press, 1989.

White, Morton. *Pragmatism and the American Mind: Essays and Reviews in Philosophy and Intellectual History*. New York: Oxford University Press, 1973.

White. *Science and Sentiment in America: Philosophical Thought from Jonathan Edwards to John Dewey*. New York: Oxford University Press, 1972.

White. *Social Thought in America: The Revolt against Formalism*. London & New York: Oxford University Press, 1976.

White, ed. *Documents in the History of American Philosophy: From Jonathan Edwards to John Dewey*. New York: Oxford University Press, 1972.

Whittemore, Robert C. *Makers of the American Mind: Three Centuries of American Thought and Thinkers*. New York: Morrow, 1964.

Wiener, Philip P. *Evolution and the Founders of Pragmatism*. Cambridge, Mass.: Harvard University Press, 1949.

Contributors

Gary Alexander	*Illinois Board of Higher Education*
Thomas M. Alexander	*Southern Illinois University at Carbondale*
Douglas R. Anderson	*The Pennsylvania State University*
Randall E. Auxier	*Southern Illinois University at Carbondale*
Robert C. Bannister	*Swarthmore College*
George Cronk	*Bergen Community College*
Donald Dryden	*Duke University*
Richard W. Field	*Northwest Missouri State University*
Anthony J. Graybosch	*California State University, Chico*
Lewis E. Hahn	*Southern Illinois University at Carbondale*
Kevin J. Hayes	*University of Central Oklahoma*
John Howie	*Southern Illinois University at Carbondale*
Richard A. Hutch	*University of Queensland*
Angelo Juffras	*William Paterson University*
Murray G. Murphey	*University of Pennsylvania*
Charles Padrón	*Stephen F. Austin University*
Alan Richardson	*University of British Columbia*
Dorothy G. Rogers	*Montclair State University*
Sharon Scherwitz	*University of Wisconsin—La Crosse*
T. L. S. Sprigge	*University of Edinburgh*
George W. Stickel	*Kennesaw, Georgia*
Donald Wayne Viney	*Pittsburg State University*

Cumulative Index

Dictionary of Literary Biography, Volumes 1-270
Dictionary of Literary Biography Yearbook, 1980-2001
Dictionary of Literary Biography Documentary Series, Volumes 1-19
Concise Dictionary of American Literary Biography, Volumes 1-7
Concise Dictionary of British Literary Biography, Volumes 1-8
Concise Dictionary of World Literary Biography, Volumes 1-4

Cumulative Index

DLB before number: *Dictionary of Literary Biography,* Volumes 1-270
Y before number: *Dictionary of Literary Biography Yearbook,* 1980-2001
DS before number: *Dictionary of Literary Biography Documentary Series,* Volumes 1-19
CDALB before number: *Concise Dictionary of American Literary Biography,* Volumes 1-7
CDBLB before number: *Concise Dictionary of British Literary Biography,* Volumes 1-8
CDWLB before number: *Concise Dictionary of World Literary Biography,* Volumes 1-4

M

N

Q

W

The Cult of Biography
Excerpts from the Second Folio Debate:
"Biographies are generally a disease of
English Literature" Y-86